W9-CAO-209

WITHDRAWN

Ezra Pound
to his Parents

Ezra Pound to his Parents

Letters 1895–1929

Edited by
MARY DE RACHEWILTZ, A. DAVID MOODY
AND JOANNA MOODY

OXFORD
UNIVERSITY PRESS

OXFORD
UNIVERSITY PRESS

Great Clarendon Street, Oxford, OX2 6DP,
United Kingdom

Oxford University Press is a department of the University of Oxford.
It furthers the University's objective of excellence in research, scholarship,
and education by publishing worldwide. Oxford is a registered trade mark of
Oxford University Press in the UK and in certain other countries

Published in the United States of America by Oxford University Press
198 Madison Avenue, New York, NY 10016, United States of America

British Library Cataloguing in Publication Data
Data available

ISBN 978–0–19–958439–0

'Being family to a wild poet aint no bed of roses
but you stand the strain just fine.'
(EP to HLP, 9 January 1909)

'My Dear Son . . .
Growl and grumble some more'
(HLP to EP, 4 February 1919)

Contents

List of Plates

List of Facsimiles

Text facsimiles of letters numbered 135, 150 (note), 359, 509, 549, 613, 627, 776, 836.

ISABEL AND HOMER
A Double Memoir[1]

MARY DE RACHEWILTZ

> What one learns in the home one learns in a way one does not
> learn in school.   (EP, 1960 Interview)

On 9 April 1865 Lee surrendered; on 14 April President Lincoln was assassinated.
On 23 and 24 May soldiers of Grant and Sherman marched down Pennsylvania
Avenue, and then returned to their homes—as would their son's sons from the
Great World War. This we read in the printed address delivered on 'Lincoln
Night' on 12 February 1921, inscribed to Mr Homer Pound by T. Eliott
Patterson, a cherished memento. The Civil War had left its mark on both the
Weston and the Pound sides of the family. The photograph of 'Honest Old
Abe', who in 1863 had established 'Thanksgiving' as a National holiday, was kept
in the Pound family album. The tone of Lincoln's speeches, the background,
and the interest in Mazzini were transmitted from father to son and left traces
in the poet's mind. 'Poll-ticking' in the family must have been heated indeed if a
child throws his little rocking chair across the room because the wrong man has
been elected President. The Jenkintown *Times Chronicle* for 7 November 1896
published E. L. Pound, aged 11 years:

> A Political Fact.
> There was a young man from the West,
> He did what he could for what he thought best;
> But election came round,
> He found himself drowned,
> And the papers will tell you the rest.

Homer's line followed the events of the times, while Isabel's was upholding the
saga of the Pilgrims, reinforced by Henry Wadsworth Longfellow's *The Court-
ship of Miles Standish* of which more than 10,000 copies were sold in London the
day it was published. The connection to the grandson of the former Plymouth
schoolmaster, Peleg Wadsworth whose forebears had early settled in Duxbury,

---

[1] Parts of this Memoir were first printed as 'Pound as Son: Letters Home', *Yale Review* 75.3 (1986)
321–30.

was to be kept up—his success a model to follow. In the 1880s the bones of the forefathers were still being dug up in New England, while the Quakers sought new frontiers.

Tenderest of greenhorns, HLP was called in Hailey, according to Waller B. Wiggington *(Rendezvous*, Winter 1969); *una pasta d'uomo* [soft as dough / a sweet bun] by the people in Rapallo. In Wyncote, despite headlines in the local paper: 'No more Italians . . .', he had quietly defied the stupid suburban prejudices and raised money for the poor, welcomed immigrants to the Calvary Presbyterian Church where he taught Sunday School and was active as administrator. Both in Hailey and in Wyncote the local papers reported on his activities, well researched by Noel Stock *(Ezra Pound's Pennsylvania)* and Emily Wallace. In 1955, W. C. Williams wrote a vivid description of Homer in 1904 and 1905:

. . . he had the usual slight stoop to his shoulders affected by all old school gentlemen. . . . kindly, cultured voice, not without a good laugh close to the surface. . . When he spoke to me he reminded me of my own father, a touch of the old world though his accent was pure Philadelphia.

And W. B. Yeats, speaking of Pound's father and mother:

I don't think I ever met so charming a couple . . . There is one thing that puzzles me—how these people so intelligent and perfectly honest could admire the artistic horrors which Quinn was showing them

In Gais in my Tyrol they spoke with respect of a kind and humane *Mensch*. Standing in the cramped stable, with his son to translate, he told the small farmer—the horse in his stall to the left, the two cows and the heifer to the right and the pig sty in the opposite corner—of how his grandfather had clipped the horns of ten (in time it grew to a thousand) cows on their Wisconsin farm and they gave no more milk. So the small Tyrolean farmer could laugh with his neighbours at the stupid Americans, establishing somehow a link to Wisconsin cattle-owners through the generous grandfather who gave the farmer's wife a beautiful golden brooch and a gold chain with three coral cameos to keep for the child. And to my mother he gave a rare gold coin, set in a medallion with a lock of blond hair, all trinkets lost through World War Two.

My own memories: swinging on his foot; sitting on his knees while he drew a funny face on his breakfast egg in his hotel room in Bolzano; showing me how to 'shadow-play' with my hands on the wall. Listening to a language I could not understand. Scant snippets of childhood memories. His own candid reminiscing he set down after his retirement in Rapallo at his son's bidding, in *Small Boy. The Wisconsin Childhood of Homer L. Pound*. It was only after reading about the smell of fresh pine, the floating on a raft down the Mississippi and his encounters with lumbermen, that I realized how close our worlds were. And: *All ages are contemporaneous*.

The daguerrotypes, the silver, as well as a fair number of books—J. R. Lowell's *The Biglow Papers* (1885), among them—that had belonged to Mary

Weston, come from Isabel. Homer, apart from Congressional Directories, seems to have valued two items: his mother's edition of the Robert Burns poems with the annotation: 'This little book was given to me by my father when I was 8 years old, in the year 1844. It is the only one he ever gave me besides my school Books'. In 1958, Pound annotated in the back: 'Angevine mother of Homer L. Pound'. Celebrating Burns Night may have been a Loomis family tradition, along with Lincoln Day on 12 February. The other book Homer kept was O. S. Fowler's first edition of *The Practical Frenologist*. Whether in 1875 he met Fowler or merely used his text to measure his talents— or lack of—is open to speculation, but in 1932, prodded perhaps by Ezra, the numbers scribbled on the fly leaf show that he figured out he was 17 at the time. At that same age J. Q. Adams was also in a quandary. In Canto XXXIV, though in a different context, we find ' . . . phrenology and animal magnetism . . . '.

The *Diary of John Quincy Adams* must have provided much conversation between father and son in Rapallo in the early '30s while the *XI New Cantos* were being written. In Canto 99, with Pound's mind on filiality: 'prolong the animal spirits', seems to answer some of his own questions. Homer had brought with him the *documenta* making history. From his appointment to the General Land Office in 1882, to his Pension Certificate as Assistant Assayer in the Philadelphia Mint in 1928, together with the impressive 1914 Joint Resolution passed by the Wisconsin legislature relating to the death of Honorable Thaddeus Coleman Pound, not to mention scrap books with articles on and by T.C.P. and his speech in Congress that found entry in Canto 22.

When Wharton Barker in 1914 and others later on asked him to write his father's biography, he politely declined, saying his pen was not up to the task. In *Small Boy* he dropped hints about records to be found in the City Court House, 'Pound versus Pound' (p. 38) and he calls his father 'padre' when at age 12 sent to school, after his parents' divorce, but he leaves the plot for a Pirandello to unravel. He himself was too honest and compassionate and did not want to speak of the 'darker sides'. Even Weyerhaeuser, the 'Lumber King', mentioned negatively in Canto XXII as 'Warenhauser', was to him plain 'Fred' and not a dishonest man.

Homer only wrote of things he knew first hand and understood, like his report of the 1902 visits to foreign Mints and the hearty welcome he received as an emissary from the Philadelphia Mint. He would describe the coining presses, the automatic planes for adjusting planks working very accurately, the changing of designs, etc.:

On Friday, July 25, 1902, I visited the Mint at Rome, or as it is called della R.Zecca. Mr. Benton of Rome introduced me to Ing. Israel Sacerdote, Direttore della Zecca, and acted as interpreter. The Mint is situated back of the Vatican . . .

Paris, August 21st. Place de la Monnaies . . . Like Italy, the Government changes the design of the franc often . . . no granulations are taken. Wood and coal are used as fuel, and I saw no evidence of any new machinery.

'Isabel and Homer: A Double Memoir'

On the 3d day of September 1902, I visited the Royal Mint of London, England, and presented letter of Superintendent of Philadelphia Mint to the Deputy Master. . . . [And there follows the detailed description of the melting, furnaces, machines, coining, and the firm conviction that] we have the best institution for the coinage of monies in the world and the United States Mint of Philadelphia is held in high esteem by the bankers of Europe. . . . after having exchanged and used the coin of Spain, Italy, Switzerland, Germany, France and England, am still of the opinion that our coin is superior, both in design and workmanship.

Nowhere, he said, had he seen assay balances equal to the ones used by himself.

His interest in coins and coining never died down. As early as 1898 he learnt about the extraction of gold from seawater and corresponded with the President of The Electrolytic Marine Salts Co, in Boston, after having experimented and taken notes on 'panning' during his stay in Hailey. He wrote an article for the *Times Chronicle* on where gold can be found. Throughout his life he recorded and preserved what lay in his field and pursued little known topics, such as 'The trial of the monies in the Pix' as reported in the 1643 *Journal of the House of Lords*.

There is a small envelope in the case containing the 1928 coins of the Irish Free State, with his note dated 'Rapallo Italy Dec.3–1929': 'This set of Irish coin was presented to me by Mr & Mrs William Butler Yeats. Mr Yeats was chairman of the Committee that authorized these coins minted = Homer L. Pound'. With it there is also a letter from the Deputy Master & Comptroller of the Royal Mint, London, 4 December 1929, informing him that the Mint Report for 1927, with a Plate illustrating the New Irish Free state coinage, was exhausted, but the one for 1928 will be ready shortly. It must have been a happy beginning of his retirement, seeing his profession recognized and moving into the Rapallo apartment which he and Isabel took over from the Irish Senator, along with furniture cat and canaries. He probably remembered attending the Yeats Lecture in Philadelphia in 1914, and the letter from this famous poet, approving of his son's engagement to the 'very clever, very charming, very beautiful' daughter of an old friend of his.

By 1929, life in Wyncote had become a problem, and the worst economic depression in American history was already being felt. Homer had wondered whether 'Dictator Mussolini' would allow them to live in Italy after his retirement, and he wanted to know what his son thought of the Italian leader. 'Mama thinks he is needed to put, or keep Italy in order.' Pound encouraged his parents to join him, and Mr and Mrs Homer L. Pound were booked as passengers on the S. S. Minnekahda, leaving New York for London on 1 June 1929. The retirement annuity of 999 and 96/100 dollars was raised to $1200 in July 1930. Despite the Depression, the years ahead promised serenity.

In Rapallo, Homer was immediately taken into the confidence of his son and there followed trips to Gais to visit me and to Venice, while Isabel was left behind and tried to concentrate on learning survival Italian. The aborted draft of a letter to an imaginary friend—*Mio Caro Amico*—betrays a slight resentment at husband and son having gone to Lake Garda and the Dolomites and leaving her alone.

Maddening as it must have been to be told by his mother what to do and wear—even as late as 1939, before his trip to America, Isabel presented him with a list of whom to see, what bus to take in Washington, etc.—it was comforting to have an ally in Homer. In his youth, the 'bondage of the blood' the 'pigsty of the family' had to be broken in order to follow his inner voices. When he was fired from his teaching job, his first reaction was 'don't tell mother', but by the time he was 'recalled' he had made up his own mind and decided to go his own way. In his father he had complete confidence: 'If a man commit murder/ Should his father protect him? . . . He should hide him'. (Canto 13) Yet within Confucian authority, there are subtle distinctions between sincerity and veracity, degrees of loyalty and affection. The needle on Homer's scale weighing gold and a man's signature constantly trembling, as Ixion, the sensitive antenna of the race who carried the burden of writing 'the epic of the capitalist era'— David Moody's definition of the Cantos.

1942 found the old man stranded with a broken hip in the Rapallo Hospital and his son 'read him a few pages of Aristotle . . . to take his mind off it. Also to keep my own work in progress' as he told his listeners—if any—folks back in America. The vintage of the Civil War, 'Grapes of wrath', was flowing into World War Two and into Ezra's 'work in progress'. Hard to tell what was foremost on Homer's mind as he lay dying. From the correspondence we learn how strong the pressures of World War One had been: 'Yes—what about this war matter? We are wondering if Ezra Pound—will now be a little more charitable to his Native Land—and help all he can over there. Lovingly Dad.'

Homer never doubted the talents of his son and the importance of the P O E M. A letter opened by the Censor, written off the cuff, 10 June 1917, and addressed to 5 Holland Place Chambers:

My dear Son. Guess we better let W[oodrow]W[ilson]—out of our correspondence— WW and Mc—.Dad has to work under the regime—Will send the books as soon as I find them—Found one copy Ovid—last evening—will send you list soon.

Well this morning came the P O E M.

It took my attention—on the train—and I was in town almost before I knew it—It was a cool clear morning—I walked along the street with my head up—and felt the stimulus of the spirit—that breathed out from the MSS. I have been very busy all day— but at odd times have taken a fly—at the Poem. You wish a first impression—Well—

In reading it I can feel its sweep—and it is as I imagine like one going up in an Airship—The Mechanician has honored me with a seat—and we are soon up in the pure azure—

Time and space are nothing—We sweep the whole world—and just as we lose on ourselves—he drops me out—and here I am just pegging away—and it will be some time before the next Mss—comes—

I thank you for the compliment. My opinion does not seem of much value—but I am glad that in that little room—in London a son of mine can lose himself in such matters—but but—may I be permitted to suggest that as the poem is not for the Yahoos—for after the first word it soars away above the <u>crowd</u> so use a different word than 'hang'. It seems to me '<u>Listen</u>—all—would be a better word—ask D—if I am not right—

Has your proof been corrected—Look on page 17—'it <u>happened</u>—and now to think—you have it so—

I may be wrong—

Page 16 Prosperine—page 22 Proserpine—which is right—

I will read the poem more carefully when I get home this evening—of course there are many words and names that I do not understand as you well know—but nevertheless it gives one a desire to see the places—I wish, some day we can go over them together—

Lovingly Dad

Homer L Pound [signed in ink].

Perhaps the son would have done well after all to tone down the invectives instead of increasing them. Yet he remained the 'Mechanician' in Homer's eyes who kept running errands for him and followed also his political lead. Homer wrote letters to Senators, encouraged Social Credit, and, once settled in Rapallo, collected 'Durrant's Press Cuttings', indexed the reviews and articles pasted into a copybook which Isabel had started to use for her Italian exercises, thus complementing the scrapbooks containing articles by and on T. C. Pound, all this serving as background for Cantos, and lending his native speech to 'Ezra Pound Speaking'. He was spared the outcome of his son's misplaced American Patriotism.

What Homer would have liked mentioned in the Cantos was 'Uncle Joel's Panacea', and Pound may have remembered it at the very end, in canto CXIV. He is recorded among the 'good guys in the family' for having read Locke. A copy of his book had turned up in an antiquarian bookshop in Texas: Uncle Joel's 'Locke' found in Texas—associated with H. L. P's mention of Del Mar on Assay Commission. It's very much the Loomis-Pound side of the family that wins the day.

I wonder if the 'old man' who spoke of his 'forgettery' when he couldn't promptly recall a name, yet vividly remembered his dreams and delighted in telling them, considered the strange destiny of landing under the hill where Marconi, with his experiments, usurped the glory of Mahlon Loomis, the original inventor of world-famed wireless telegraphy. In *Radio's 100 Men of Science* by O. E. Dunlap (1944), we have a detailed biography of this 'Pioneer in aereal telegraphy'. On 21 May 1872, the US Congress listened to a long speech on the principle 'causing electrical vibrations . . . convertible into human language . . . disturbance to the remotest shores' and *almost* passed the Bill requesting $50,000 to develop his invention, but the idea was dismissed as 'absurd'. Loomis was ahead of his time; he died, it is said, heartbroken. The case was widely covered in the Press and in 1925 Mary Texanna Loomis dedicated her *Radio Theory and Operating* to Dr Mahlon Loomis. There is an ironic echo in Canto 38, of the Pope showing 'curiosity / as to how His Excellency had chased those / electric shakes through the atmosphere'. Whether Homer knew about the Loomis Radio College in Washington is not certain.

I know of no Loomis correspondence after the 1912 letter from Elisha Loomis, compiler of *The Loomis Family in America*, published in 1906. Homer's letters from folk back home were from his sister's family in Philadelphia, the Foot cousins, and the Busha and Patterson cousins in Big Timber, Montana. At least since the 1905 Loomis Convention it was taken for granted in the family that:

We of the Tribe of Joseph—son of John Loomis of Braintree in the County of Essex, burnt at Canterbury in 1566, for heresy: that is for being a protestant . . . in 1632 passengers on the 'Lion' . . . in 1636 went to Hartford with Rev. Thomas Hooker. . . . America need never despair as long as there are Loomises to burn.

Whether Homer paid the $1 to become a member of the Loomis Family Association is not recorded, but he had two copies of the 1906 Brochure and kept the genealogical charts up to date. Pound made ample use of the contents, and given that 'the muses are daughters of memory' one can sense a groping for roots in *Thrones*, Canto 96 in particular.

Isabel Weston Pound, the poet's mother, and her mother, Mary Weston, still remain somewhat elusive figures. If granddaughters knew how much I regret not having sufficiently questioned or listened to Isabel, the only grandparent I have known as an adult, they might find a way to draw old ladies from their caves or off their shelves (in E. M. Forster's words). They might even be patient enough to crouch at the foot of their pedestals and pick up threads.

Fortunately Isabel was an imaginative talker, but she recalled places rather than people and never spoke of either her parents or her son, only of Homer.

During World War One, she had tried to enlist. She wanted to become an aviator, but was assigned to skinning tomatoes. Thus ended her only attempt at a career.

The earliest letter we have is one Isabel wrote to her mother from Hailey, Idaho, on 22 May 1885, and it footnotes what seemed 'lore' in *Indiscretions*. It's a four-page letter confirming that there were lands, silver mines, and railroads to attend to, revealing an unbounded enthusiasm for the Camas Prairie with its streams and gulches. 'At one eminence we had a picture before us like Bierstadt's Rocky Mountains, peak after peak . . . Looking down the gully, . . . I could but think of the old patriarchs looking over into The Land of Canaan'.

Oddly enough, there is not a word about a baby to be born in October.

Isabel's wedding reception had been held on 26 November 1884 in the house of her uncle, Ezra Brown Weston, at 24 East 47th Street, New York, with the Rev. J. Clement French performing the marriage ceremony. We have only a few scraps of evidence: newspaper clippings, the invitation, the raw silk wedding dress, an ivory and lace fan, and a few bits of exquisite Tiffany silver. Isabel 'liked pretty things' and had a natural inclination for rhymed verse and polysyllables.

She also possessed nonchalance. On 1 June 1929, when she and Homer left for Europe to join their son in Rapallo: 'she got up from the table and walked out of the house without even clearing the breakfast plates'. This is the only viva-voce recollection of her I have, from one of her contemporaries, Esther Heacock, a Wyncote neighbour whom I visited in 1963.

The house on Fernbrook Avenue and its staggering list of contents was put up for auction. All clutter was left behind, including a small painting of herself which she either disliked (though it's 'pretty') or discarded because her son had not asked her to bring it along with the other family portraits. The present owner of the house kindly salvaged the picture, which now serves as the frontispiece to *Indiscretions* (in *Pavannes and Divagations*, 1958).

It was William Carlos Williams, prompted by Norman Holmes Pearson in 1955, who left us a detailed description of Ezra Pound's mother. She had liked him and trusted him as a friend. In her late thirties, with her hair done up in a careless but attractive manner, she struck the young medical student as shy and aristocratic, somewhat mysterious, as though about to take wing. He played the fiddle and she accompanied him on the piano after dinner. She also played for the song sessions at the young people's parties, and her chocolate cake was famous, though she was an indifferent housekeeper, as Williams recalls. She clearly was never interested in menial work:

She seemed to be rather surprised at the presence of her own son in the house which must, I think, have affected him to make him in his own eyes much of a changeling . . . She was to me a charming somewhat aloof figure, mother of a son who was absolutely not to be understood, a genius to whom she had given birth by inscrutable laws.

And how well did the son understand his mother? Their relationship was very intense, and hence sometimes strained. 'Pa' remained 'Dad' to the end, but 'Ma' became 'Mother,' and the tone was always somewhat formal. She impressed upon Ezra—'Ray', as she used to call him—her sense of decorum and her values. Even as a boy he realized she was under some kind of stress, but she was determined to keep up appearances. There was of course a lot of superficial banter, and at the age of 3 he seems to have committed some obscure misdeed (probably when he called his grandmother, Mary Weston, a 'steer'), whereupon his mother told him he was no longer a gentleman. Yet she continued to dress him in velvet, à la Lord Fauntleroy (the heavy lace collar and cuffs still exist), and oddly enough, Pound wore velvet dinner jackets all his life, though it raised eyebrows. He once did call his mother a 'proud presbyterian peacock' when she sent him a rather unfortunate photograph of herself dressed up for some occasion, looking majestic, severe, wearing an enormous clump of black feathers on her hat and a feathery black stole, totally unbecoming and in sharp contrast with pink and dimply Aunt Frank (Frances Weston), smiling in ivory lace and pearls. Both felt the need to reform each other. In a letter from Venice in 1908 he apologizes for not having recognized her right to hold ideas differing from his own and for his 'lack of intelligent sympathy' with her aims and views.

She would have liked him to compete with the Ivy League Pounds and Longfellows, had he not so quickly wrecked his academic career at Wabash. In Europe the obvious thing to be was an American ambassador. From London in 1909, under pressure to find a real job and make a living, he confessed to her: 'I never voluntarily do anything but write lyrics and talk to my friends.' So she suggested he write an 'Epic to the West'. Ezra reacted with a four-page tirade: 'What has the West done to deserve. it?' And did she not know that an epic needed a beautiful tradition, a mythical or historical hero and a damn long time for the story to lose its garish details and become encrusted with beautiful lies? Yet a most fruitful seed had taken root, and he hoped his scrawl would amuse her and begged her not to take it too seriously. Secretly he kept trying to live up to her expectations, showing off social engagements she would approve: 'Weekend with Lady Low in Dorset—not far from Pound, Poundsbury and Blandford.' Playing along with his mother's ambition, he sought lectures, teaching jobs, employment in the Foreign Service. He even considered making money. In 1910 he returned to New York ostensibly for this purpose, but in fact could not escape being a poet. He spent most of his time working on Guido Cavalcanti's sonnets. Having waited eight months, hoping in vain for some suitable position, a scholarship from the University of Pennsylvania, or recognition, he returned to Europe and wrote to his mother: 'I regret your lack of reconciliation.—You never seem to consider my necessity to live.—However, what's the use of arguing. I have my work to do and must choose my own way of getting it done.'

Pound also chose to marry into a family his mother would accept. Isabel had tried to salvage her son's engagement to H. D. years earlier. Now she complied readily with his wishes when he asked her to invite Dorothy Shakespear to their home in Wyncote. On 22 February 1914, he wrote her: 'I dare say I am going to be married. The family has ordered the invitations & stuff for the curtains etc. In which case I shall not come to America & if you want to inspect us you will have to come over here.' When he sent the 'curious announcements of the prenuptial reception', he discouraged his parents from attending the April ceremony, yet a few weeks later he suggested that his mother come to London in May and enclosed her fare.

To his fiancée, who was speculating about her future mother-in-law's hand-writing, he gave a swift appraisal on 25 March 1914:

Mother's handwriting??? New York, born 14th St. & second ave. when it was the thing to be born there, porched house, 23rd. st. also at proper time. Uncle's estate on Hudson, reckless rider. Married wild H.L.P. & went to a mining town, returned east to domesticity—traditions, irony, no knowledge of french literature in the original, admiration for the brothers De Goncourt. Early painting lessons, penchant for the pretty—horror of all realism in art. Belief in the pleasant. Would like, or would have liked—to see me in the Diplomatic Corps—'Ambassadour to the Ct. of St. James.' Believes that I should be well clothed. Prude if god ever permitted one to exist.

If by 'prude' the son meant that his mother was a woman of extreme propriety in conduct and in speech, he was correct. Homer would admit knowing of the darker side of some family member, but preferred to speak well of them and to say that he himself was not able to measure up to expectations. Isabel, knowingly or not, cut people dead, refused to acknowledge the existence of those who failed to meet social requirements, and ignored messages which threatened convention. But she was extremely loyal to her family and faced disasters with dignity and style. Nor did she pass judgment. She made statements and acted upon them: 'talking as though things were as she would have wished them but as they were not', according to Father Desmond Chute, an English friend of the family in Rapallo.

Homer and Isabel went to London together to meet their daughter-in-law and her family. Isabel's Wadsworthian background did not draw the kind of favourable response she had expected, yet after Homer's return to Philadelphia she stayed on for a while to live near her son. 'It has seemed very natural to have you here and quite odd now without you', he wrote to her when she was on her way home, un-resigned to her son's exile but aware that he 'had his work to do'.

Questioned by psychiatrists in 1946, Ezra Pound said that the death of his maternal grandmother when he was 15 was the first real sorrow he could remember. In *The Cantos* and elsewhere he celebrates his grandfather Thaddeus C. Pound, whose economic theories resembled his own. His maternal grandfather, Harding (Haddy) Weston, is treated lightly in *Indiscretions*.

I do not know when or how Isabel came in contact with her father. He had enlisted in the Civil War when she was barely 2 years old. When she identified for posterity some of the numerous daguerrotypes she inherited from her mother, her father as a young man gets a mere 'Harding Weston. Son of Grandfather James Weston.' In 1922 she had received a letter from the chaplain of the National Military Home in Dayton, Ohio, informing her that he was writing at her father's request. He said that the old man attended chapel and Bible class regularly but was in the hospital ward and would soon transfer to Hampton Home in Virginia. Isabel sent this letter on to her son and wrote on the back: 'This letter may give you a truer idea of your grandfather's condition and of US methods of dealing with disabled volunteer soldiers. Grants Forum has been the place where H. W. has aired his notions these many years.' The rest of the letter deals with news of her club, political elections, young professors at the University of Pennsylvania who admired Pound, and the autumn weather: 'We live in a golden glow, no frost nor dead leaves.' For more information about Isabel's father we must turn to the Harding Weston records in the National Archives: 'I am now upward of 80 years old and cannot make ends meet.' In 1915 he declared that he had not seen his wife for over thirty years, but he evidently knew that his daughter was married and living in Philadelphia. He may not have known that his wife, Mary Parker, had died in, and was buried with, her people in Hopkinton, Massachusetts—to keep up her ties, through her mother, with the Wadsworths.

Harding Weston started in 1905 to put in claims for his services as second lieutenant in the New York Volunteer Cavalry from 1861 to 1862. He had 'answered the first call by President Lincoln', but there is no evidence of wounds or medals. He gave as his profession 'newspaper and advertising man', which throws some light on Isabel's cryptic statement, 'he has aired his notions'. In 1922 he was finally granted $72 per month and became a pensioner in the National Military Home.

It was Homer who wrote to Ezra of the visit he and Isabel paid to his grandfather at Soldier's Home, Old Point Comfort: 'It is a great relief to your mother to have made the visit. For the past three years we have been talking about it. . . . He was somewhat interested in your photograph and reads without the aid of glasses.' At the bottom of the photo shown him, Homer had copied: 'Make strong old dreams / lest this old [our] world lose heart', and the old man had commented: 'That's fine.' The following year, on 10 February 1926, a telegram from Governor Thomson announced: 'Harding Weston died last night. Funeral ten o'clock Monday.' And it is again Homer who informs his son:

You will see by the enclosed that Harding Weston is no more. We will not go down to the funeral. Too long a trip and Mama not feeling equal to it. When we were there last July she left word as to just what to do and he will be buried in the Soldiers' Cemetery there among hundreds of others. And that ends that, now will come the settling up of his effects of which there is little left.

I have found no comment in Pound's letters to his parents either on the visit or the death. His life was hectic just then. Homer was alarmed; Isabel was suffering a 'nervous spell'. At her club an acquaintance whose son had just returned from Paris congratulated her for being a grandmother, but neither Ezra nor Dorothy had informed her that they were expecting a baby. Although those must have been hard times for Isabel, one has but scanty evidence of her emotions. She invited her son to take her into his confidence with her customary restraint: she wrote to him that several families in Wyncote had adopted children. The hint misfired completely. After that the surface shows no further ripples. Homer and Isabel celebrated their forty-second wedding anniversary somewhat sedately.

It is hard to imagine that Homer, when he had been up to Gais with Ezra to see his granddaughter, would have kept it secret from Isabel. He might have passed on the injunction: don't tell him that I told you. And Isabel was expert in ignoring what she did not approve of, trained by her own mother to 'ignore' her father. More likely, though, Homer would have feared one of her 'states' and, out of kindness, decided not to upset her.

When the complexity of Ezra's and Dorothy's *ménage* was finally revealed to her, she was sententious: 'one disloyalty leads to another', apparently ignoring the fact that her son's loyalty to his wife had allowed her daughter-in-law to present her with the photographs of a grandson. She refused the 'strange child' Ezra had tried to smuggle in, because 'one can not transfer affection'. In this mother and son were identical: once an idea had taken root in the mind it remained there—indestructible. The picture of the perfect wife must remain: a beautiful lady with dowry and culture who bears a son and always stands by her husband. Only a divine mind, alias Athena, decides between right and wrong. In good families one tries to avoid arguments, so it is put in writing:

July 31 / 39   Villa Raggio [Rapallo]

Dear Son
The situation is to me amazing – one disloyalty provokes another is understandible but why continue the deception so many years one cannot transfer affections –
Why be rude to your Mother, when we meet in Rapallo or elsewhere
y - v- t
Mother

It took Homer a few days longer to react:

Aug. 3 [1939]   [Rapallo]

My Dear Son.
A clap of Thunder out of a clear sky could not have been more startling than yours and D's letters. For over 10 years we have been here. D. has been giving us Omar's photos o k and it is hard to realize the truth. Why did you suggest our remaining? As matters have developed there is no pleasure in our continuing here.
We shall arrange to - depart -
Your Old
Dad

These two letters are among the few preserved in Pound's private files—what provoked them has been destroyed.

In November 1940 Homer requested that certain dividends be deposited in his Jenkintown Bank, which might indicate that cash was needed and available for the trip home. They were all packed and ready to return to America. But did not. What prevented Homer was perhaps not only Isabel's pride but his son's need that he should stay with him. After that date all business seems to have been conducted in Isabel's hand. Homer fell and broke his hip. War was declared between Italy and the US. Pound 'aired his notions'. Isabel nursed her husband valiantly until his death in Rapallo in 1942. As far as I know, no extant documents indicate that she responded to the circular of April 1942 from the Swiss Legation, offering help to return to America via Lisbon.

She found herself classed as an enemy of both the United States and Italy. She applied for her pension through the Swiss Embassy and was informed that her son was able to provide for her and that the 'U.S. will respond in time'. Her funds were cut off. She reacted by asking Ezra to secure Mexican black corn seed from the Agricultural Office in Rome. She also asked for 'lima beans and the large, deep yellow coloured rich-flavoured squash or pumpkin to be sown in April or May' on her terrace.

At the war's end she immediately got in contact with officials and old friends to arrange for her return to America. She wanted not to invoke clemency for Ezra but to remind the American authorities of the services rendered to the country by her family in the past, and to put the case before Congress. She again requested access to her frozen assets in order to pay for her own passage. Did they not think it unseemly that the widow of the first Register of the US Land Office, appointed by President Arthur in 1883 and with forty years' service in Philadelphia Mint, should have to depend on public charity. Her question remained unanswered, but she terminated the lease and tried to sell the furniture in Villa Raggio, in order to travel light, just as she had done on leaving Wyncote in 1929.

On 22 November 1945, her son wrote to her:

My dear mother,
    Wonderful plane trip, including Bermuda - escort most considerate. Only blot was being tired by night djeep ride before start. Note from H. L. Mencken. Mapels have called- informal chess club amiable & play badly enough to stand my poor playing. Fried chicken or rather poulade a la Virginia & chocolate ice cream to-day, Thanksgiving— wish you could have shared it–but the society is exclusive. Mr Peabody's anecdotes of Panama Canal zone etc.–in fact conversation level rather above that of politer tea circles. The papers seem to express the views I held some years ago with more acrimony than I ever did.

And he continues, informing her about the composer George Antheil publishing his autobiography and Salvador Dali having a picture show, well knowing that she liked to keep up with cultural events and that she would be pleased to know that two of the most respectable ladies in Georgetown, Ida and Lee Mapel, had called on him. Were it not for the signature, 'your obstreperous offspring', and the heading of the letter—'District of Colombia Jail Washington D.C. cell B 1/216'—one would hardly guess there was anything wrong. One giveaway is the crescendo in affection from the usual 'Dear Mother' to 'My dear' in that letter, and finally to 'Dearest' in the following letter written on 10 December from Gallinger Hospital:

'Isabel and Homer: A Double Memoir'

Dearest Mother,

You might like this hospital better than Rapallo, at least the steam heat and morning coffee. One of my guardian angels is reading Ron[ald] Duncan's 'Journal of a Husbandman' with deep interest.

Best wishes for as good a Xmas as possible. By mistake some coffee was sent to me instead of to you, but I hope you'll get some.

Love to D[orothy]

EP

and a bright new year

While waiting for transport to the US, Isabel had settled into Dorothy's study in Via Marsala, and in May had drafted a letter to her son: 'No sea bathing, no music. If you can have books from Congressional Library try Grayson . . . ' still advising him what to read! But the letter was never finished because she fell and broke her hip, ending like Homer, in the Rapallo Hospital. Dorothy left for America without her, but Isabel, refusing to give up, made arrangements for her own departure. Pound suggested I invite her to stay with me, but she gracefully declined: 'Dear Mary, were I as able as formerly I should be most happy to abide with you in your old Schloss with balcony and gorgeous view now I should add to your responsibilities. It is too early in season even to motor there later it would be a glorious tour but I hope to have passage on next boat for US.'

Some of her old friends around Philadelphia were looking for a home where she might stay, but no one encouraged her to go to Washington to be near Ezra. Finally, in 1947, she followed his suggestion to stay with me in the Tyrol, and Olga Rudge, who had tried to help her get passage to the States, brought her to Gais, so that her path did lead back to the mountains once more.

At the same time, her son was being held in an institution not far from where her father had spent the last years of his life. Did they both see the same flaws in the pattern? She never complained, though she must have felt lonesome and uncomfortable (her hip and arm never healed). I don't think she had a religious conception of things. She had her own mind and sense of irony to support her, as well as the conviction that 'Man is an artist, his life is his work', as she wrote to me before consenting to live with me. And she continued to be the artist in the Tyrol, which reminded her of Idaho, she said. No longer on horseback, but erect in her wheelchair. It had been a daring last adventure, but just as the climate in Idaho had been too rough, so were the cold and the altitude in the Pusterthal.

When she died, Pound took great pains about her memorial. He asked me to have the local sculptor, Heinrich Bacher, do a bas-relief of her as a young Madonna with her great-grandson as model for the Child. 'Isabel objected to being portrayed in old age', he wrote. He made accurate descriptions and sketches of the arms that were to serve as ornaments: 'Chevron part per pale 3 wolves heads and three crosslets (with barrel ends) With a crest: dragon with dart through its mouth—old Fordie [Ford Madox Ford] said Warwick killed one at Wormleighton where the Stirpe [family] is supposed to come from. And Homer Loomis Pound's birthplace and dates also.' How well Grandma Weston must have taught him his family history if in 1948 he could still remember such details. Unfortunately, Bacher's wooden tablet did not measure up to what Pound had in mind, but the inseparable, devoted parents remain evergreen in the mind together, like the 'Pines of Isé' growing together in Italy:

Chippewa Falls, Wisconsin 1858–Rapallo 1942
New York 1860–Gais 1948

Relatively few of Isabel's letters seem to have survived, but they span a long period, from 1885 to 1947, and give testimony of two indomitable spirits. In 1959 Pound returned to Gais to visit his mother's grave and told me, 'I have appreciated her too late and not enough.' Remains the hidden tenderness in Canto 99:

Odysseus' old ma missed his conversation.

A Note on This Edition

Over the years in which this edition has been in preparation, different people have made significant contributions. When D. D. Paige and his wife selected *Letters of Ezra Pound 1907–1941* (New York, 1950), they made copies also of the letters Pound had written to his parents which they found in the apartment of Via Marsala. The carbon copies were acquired by Yale and for many years served as the main source for biographies. When later compared with the originals deposited in the Beinecke Rare Book & Manuscript Library, dating turned out to be approximate. By 1955 the lease on the Rapallo apartment had expired and its contents came to Brunnenburg. One of the trunks contained bundles of brown envelopes with the letters to the parents, sorted by year and dated in what seemed to me Homer's hand. More letters turned up later among the papers salvaged at Sant Ambrogio.

In the early Sixties I started to order the family correspondence. One of the most amusing items I found among photo albums and daguerreotypes was an inch wide roll of ticker-tape that turned out to be a formal letter to grandmother Mary Weston: 'My dear M.W. Hearing that you would like a nice long letter. . . . I have now measured the length of this epistle . . . . It is needless to state I will not write you letters any longer. The exact length is 27 ft 10 ¼ inches long. With love from Mama and myself I remain your loving grandson E. L. Pound'. Written in pencil, with words his mother might have used: 'Did she have an altercation with Neptune?. .Do you want me to engage your passage to Europe'—he gives and asks for news.

So I thought it might be a good and new idea to bring out 'Pound's Letters to Four Generations', starting with one to his grandmother, and ending with those he wrote to his granddaughter even before she had a name: 'Chere Mlle x'. Yet, just as we did not follow his advice in naming her ('Banzai— Benedictions. I had a hunch i.e. general intuito, that it wd. be a femina. family names Angevine & Selina from Homer's side'), so did my project flounder despite the good will on the part of the Director of the Beinecke Library, Professor Louis Martz, who had a typescript of the letters to the parents and name index prepared for publication as early as 1980. Barbara Paulson and Ruth M. Hall spent time with me in Brunnenburg to help with research, dating, and retyping. But the project had been restricted to the 'Letters to the Parents' and eventually only to a selection of approximately 300 out of the 850 letters of the years 1895 to 1929.

When my job in the Beinecke Library was terminated, I enlisted the help of Professor Stefano Maria Casella, assisted by Marianna Cherchi and

Massimiliano Zampieri. Despite an excellent beginning, the project ran aground.

After reading Professor David Moody's manuscript for the first volume of his Pound Biography, I realized that he knew the material better than anyone else and would be able not only to prepare a definitive manuscript but also to find a suitable publisher.

Hence it is to David and Joanna Moody I am most indebted. My dream of the 'Four Generations', reaching from a ticker-tape through Radio Speeches into the future, must wait for another Era:

In Heaven have I to make?

Mary de Rachewiltz
Brunnenburg
June 2009

Editorial Note

All of the letters which Ezra Pound wrote to his parents up to March 1929, and which they kept, are printed here, and printed in their entirety. There is reason to conclude that not all his letters home are preserved in the collection now among the Ezra Pound Papers, Yale Collection of American Literature, in the Beinecke Rare Book and Manuscript Library of Yale University, but any of significance that are missing must be presumed lost.

As the dutiful only child of devoted parents, Ezra wrote home regularly, sometimes as often as every day, when he was away at college or abroad in Europe. He would address either his mother or his father, relating always to them as distinct individuals. After 1929, the year in which Isabel and Homer left Wyncote to live near him in Rapallo, Italy, the correspondence naturally became infrequent and ceased to be the invaluable record of his activities that it had been.

Our aim in editing the letters has been to present them in a form that would be as faithful to his idiosyncratic style and to the workings of his mind as is possible in a conventionally printed book, while putting no unnecessary impediment in the way of the general reader.

Pound's spelling departed liberally from the conventionally correct. Perhaps he was not well-schooled as a child. But his teachers may have had to contend with a verbally gifted child for whom words were primarily aural and oral, and who wrote the language as it sounded rather than as it looked on the page. As an adult he would do that consciously and deliberately. Add in his playful way with words, for punning or ironic effect, and it becomes impossible to tell error apart from invention. To correct or attempt to regularize the spelling of the letters would mute their 'sound of sense'—Robert Frost's key phrase—and would erase much of their special character and liveliness. We have not done that. Our care has been instead to preserve faithfully nearly all Pound's 'spelling mistakes'. Where the mistake is an obvious 'typo', however, such as *hte* for *the*, or *hiw* for *his*, we have silently corrected—the reader should not be irritated by the merely accidental. In the same spirit, where Pound typed 'U,S,A,' or 'a, m,', we have silently printed 'U.S.A.' and 'a. m.'.

Punctuation in correct English should mark the grammatical relations within a sentence; but Pound's mind did not work after the fashion of conventional grammar, and his punctuation in these letters does not obey its rules. It is rare to find a sentence begun by a capital letter, with clauses marked off by commas or by semi-colons, and closed with a full stop. Often it seems that he knew only one punctuation mark, the full point or stop, and that he used it not as a grammatical marking but rather as a rest, when hesitating or pausing for thought or for breath. With that, it was his idiosyncrasy when typing to hit the space bar two or even three times both before and after any punctuation mark. We have not regularized his punctuation, but we have edited it in some respects. In general capital letters have been neither added nor lowered. However, extra spaces around punctuation marks have been reduced to conventional practice, except where a full point within a continuous statement is clearly not a full stop but the marker for a pause or a break of some sort.

A regularly printed version of Pound's letters, such as this must be, cannot reproduce the original layout of his handwritten or typed pages, and this is a loss, as the reader can see by comparing the facsimiles with the printed transcription. Pound no more constructed formal paragraphs than he constructed formally correct sentences. He wrote rather—especially when typing—as if he were laying out on the page one thought or subject at a time while freely leaving spaces to mark them off from each other, and while indenting or not *ad lib*. His style reflects his mind which, as he told his mother in a letter dated 23 Feb, [1910], 'works by a sort of fusion, and sudden crystallization'. He found 'the dray work of prose . . . very exhausting', he wrote; indeed—here descending from the animal—'One should have a vegetable sort of mind for prose'. We have preserved Pound's 'crystallizations' as separate paragraphs. At the same time, as a printing economy, we have standardized indentations and the spacing between paragraphs, and have (with a few exceptions) omitted the vertical and horizontal slashes occasionally inserted by Pound to mark off paragraphs. His underlinings for emphasis have been reproduced as underlinings, not shifted into italics.

His afterthought insertions and corrections have been incorporated into the text within angled brackets, except for his very minor adjustments which have been silently incorporated. Minor deletions have been silently excluded. The very few editorial insertions are enclosed in square brackets.

The layout of headings, openings, and closures has been standardized. The numbering of the letters is of course editorial.

ALS = autograph letter signed;   **AL** = autograph letter not signed
TLS = typed letter signed;   **TL** = typed letter not signed
ACS = autograph card signed;   **AC** = autograph card not signed
TCS = typed card signed;   **TC** = typed card not signed

Where letter-headed stationery is used this is briefly described. Where Pound gives his address this is given; otherwise the place from which he is writing is indicated in editorial square brackets.

The letters are dated according to the best information available. Pound's own dating, whether it comes at the head of a letter or elsewhere in it, is the most authoritative and is here printed at the head of the letter without brackets. Dates in round brackets were added to the letters by one or other of his parents. These may represent a post-mark, or the date on which the letter was received by them; or in some instances it may represent their best guess when sorting the letters in 1925.[1] Failing a date of Pound's own we have accepted the parental dates, except where there is clear evidence of error. Dates and elements of dates in square brackets are editorial.

The editorial notes and commentary supplied in italics between letters are designed to provide only essential explanatory information. Information contained in the letters themselves is not duplicated. Persons mentioned in the letters are generally identified in the Glossary of Names. There is a list of abbreviations frequently used by Pound. One abbreviation, 'u.a.d.e.', has us still guessing.

On a personal note, it has been a privilege and a pleasure to edit these letters with Mary de Rachewiltz, whose conversation and generous hospitality has both lightened and enlightened our work.

ADM, JSM.

---

[1] Homer Pound mentioned in a letter to Ezra dated Jan. 11 [1925], 'For several days we have been sorting letters, yours and D's, from 1907 to date.'

Acknowledgements

Our grateful thanks are due to Massimo Bacigalupo, Archie Henderson, Charles Lock, and Elizabeth Pound for responding helpfully to requests for information; to Michael E. de Rachewiltz for supplying expert copies of some of the family photographs; and to Paul Shields of York University's Photographic Unit for skilled photographic work.

We are indebted to the Beinecke Rare Book and Manuscript Library, Yale University, for conserving and making available the letters of Ezra, Isabel, and Homer Pound, and Dorothy Shakespear Pound, and for supplying scans for the facsimiles. Peggy Fox and Declan Spring of New Directions Corporation have been unfailingly helpful.

Chronology

1632   William Wadsworth, a Puritan refugee and ancestor of Mary Parker Weston, EP's grandmother, sails from England to Boston on the *Lion*.

1635   Edmund Weston, another Puritan refugee ancestor, sails from England to Duxbury, Mass.

c.1650   John Pound, a Quaker, sails from England to New England; dies in New Jersey 1690.

1802   Elijah Pound III (1802–91), EP's great-grandfather, born.

1832   Thaddeus Coleman Pound (1832–1914), EP's grandfather, born in Elk, Penn.

1847   Elijah Pound and family move to farm at Catfish Prairie, Rock County, Territory of Wisconsin; move on to Chippewa Falls, Wisconsin in 1856.

1855   Thaddeus marries Susan Angevine Loomis (1835–1924) of Oneida County, New York State.

1858   Homer Loomis Pound, EP's father (1858–1942), born.
Mary Parker, daughter of Hiram Parker and Mary Wadsworth, and EP's grandmother, marries Harding Weston (1835–1927).

1860   Isabel Weston (1860–1948), EP's mother, born.

1864–9   T. C. Pound State Assemblyman and Speaker, Wisconsin.

1870–1   T. C. Pound Lieutenant-Governor of Wisconsin.

1876–82   T. C. Pound US Congressman for north-western district of Wisconsin.

1883   Homer Pound opens Government Land Office, Hailey, Territory of Idaho.

1884   Homer Pound marries Isabel Weston.

1885   Ezra Loomis Weston Pound born 30 Oct., in Hailey.

1887   Homer Pound and family remove from Hailey to New York City, in the winter of 1886–7, and stay there for some time with Isabel's Uncle Ezra Weston and Aunt Frank.

1889   Homer Pound appointed Assistant Assayer in Philadelphia Mint—family lives first in West Philadelphia, then moves after about two years to 417 Walnut St., Jenkintown, and in July 1893 buys 166 Fernbrook Avenue, Wyncote.

1892–7   Ezra's first schools: in 1892 Miss Elliott's school in Jenkintown; in 1893 the Misses Heacock's Chelten Hills school in Wyncote; in 1894 Florence Ridpath's private school, which in 1895 became Wyncote Public School.

1898   Enrols in Cheltenham Military Academy.
        European tour with Aunt Frank.
1900   Did not graduate from the Academy—may have attended a high
        school to prepare for university.
1901   EP enrols in College of Liberal Arts, University of Pennsylvania.
        Meets Hilda Doolittle.
1902   Second European tour with Aunt Frank.
        Meets William Carlos Williams.
1903   Transfers to Hamilton College, Class of '05.
        Meets Viola Baxter.
1904   Meets Katherine Ruth Heyman.
1905   Graduates Bachelor of Philosophy from Hamilton.
        Enters Graduate School of Arts and Sciences, University of
        Pennsylvania.
1906   Obtains MA; awarded Harrison Foundation Fellowship in Romanics
        for research towards PhD—spends May and June researching in
        libraries in Madrid, Paris, and London.
1907   Abandons PhD.
        Meets Mary Moore of Trenton, NJ.
        Appointed Instructor in French and Spanish and Chair of Department
        of Romance Languages, Wabash College, Crawfordsville, Ind.
1908   In Feb. resigns from Wabash College.
        Travels via Gibraltar and Venice to London. In Venice publishes *A
        Lume Spento*; in London publishes *A Quinzaine for This Yule*.
1909   In Jan. and Feb. gives short course of lectures at Regent Street
        Polytechnic.
        Elkin Mathews publishes *Personae* and *Exultations*.
        Begins to meet writers and people in literary society, among them
        Ernest Rhys, May Sinclair, T. E. Hulme, Ford Madox Hueffer, Olivia
        Shakespear and her daughter Dorothy, W. B. Yeats.
        In Sept. finds a room at 10 Church Walk, Kensington.
        In Oct. begins delivering course of 21 weekly lectures at Regent
        Street, Polytechnic—to be published as *the Spirit of Romance* in 1910.
1910   Leaves for Paris and Italy in March. In Paris, meets Margaret Cravens.
        Goes on to Sirmione on Lake Garda.
        Returns to London in June.
        Sails on 18 June for US, spends six weeks with parents at Swarthmore,
        then rooms in New York.
        Provença published in Boston.
1911   *Canzoni* published.
        Leaves US in Feb.
        March–May in Paris.
        June–July at Sirmione.
        July–Aug. with Hueffer in Germany.

	Back in London by end of Aug.
	In Oct. meets Alfred Orage and begins to write for his *New Age*.
1912	*Sonnets and Ballate of Guido Cavalcanti*, and *Ripostes*, published by Swift.
	May to mid-July walking tour in Southern France.
	Returned to Paris 8–27 June, following Margaret Cravens' suicide.
	Back in London beginning of Aug.
	Becomes Foreign Correspondent for Harriet Monroe's *Poetry* (Chicago)—until 1919.
1912–13	The moment of *Imagisme*—*Des Imagistes* first published Feb. 1914.
1913	In April via Paris to Sirmione.
	Meets Henri Gaudier-Brzeska in summer; also gets to know Wyndham Lewis.
	Begins association with Dora Marsden's *The New Freewoman: An Individualist Review*, later *The Egoist*.
	Receives Ernest Fenollosa's notebooks of Japanese *Noh* and Chinese poetry.
	'Contemporania' and 'Lustra' series in *Poetry* in Nov.
	Canzoni of Arnaut Daniel completed, but publication falls through.
	With Yeats at Stone Cottage Nov.–Jan. 1914.
1914	Feb.–April Gaudier sculpting 'hieratic head' of EP.
	20 April, EP and Dorothy Shakespear marry—they move into 5 Holland Place, Chambers, Kensington.
	BLAST no.1, Wyndham Lewis's *Review of the Great English Vortex*, dated 'June 20th 1914'.
	July, Archduke Franz Ferdinand of Austria-Hungary assassinated in Sarajevo.
	On 1 Aug. Germany declares war on Russia; on 3 Aug. invades Belgium and declares war on France; on 4 Aug. the British Empire declares war on Germany.
	Sept., T. S. Eliot introduced to EP, who sets about getting his poems published, in *Poetry*, *Others*, *BLAST*, and in EP's own *Catholic Anthology 1914–1915*.
1915	Jan.–Feb., EP and DP with Yeats at Stone Cottage.
	April, *Cathay* published.
	June, Gaudier-Brzeska killed—EP puts together *Gaudier-Brzeska: A Memoir* (1916).
	EP drafting early versions of cantos.
1916	End Dec. 1915 into Feb. 1916, EP and DP with Yeats at Stone Cottage.
	Sept., *Lustra* published.
1917	Jan., '*Noh*', or *Accomplishment* published.
	April, United States enters war.
	May, becomes Foreign Editor of Margaret Anderson's *Little Review*—till 1919.

June, July, Aug., 'Three Cantos' in *Little Review*.

28 Sept., T. E. Hulme killed.

Oct., The October Revolution in Russia—Lenin's Bolsheviks seize power.

Nov., EP becomes *New Age*'s music critic, as 'William Aetheling', also its art critic, as 'B. H. Dias'.

Dec., due to EP, Joyce's *Ulysses* begins to appear in instalments in *Little Review*.

1918   Composes *Homage to Sextus Propertius* (1919).

Pavannes and Divisions (essays) published in New York.

11 Nov., Armistice ends fighting.

1919   April–Sept., EP and DP in Southern France.

28 June, Peace Treaty with Germany signed at Versailles.

Oct., *Fourth Canto*, and *Quia Pauper Amavi* published—latter includes 'Three Cantos' and *Homage to Sextus Propertius*.

Meets Major C. H. Douglas in *New Age* office—beginning of active concern for economic justice.

Begins setting words of Villon to music.

1920   April, *Instigations* collects EP's important contributions to *Little Review* and *Egoist*, and adds 'The Chinese Written Character as a Medium for Poetry, by Ernest Fenollosa'.

June, *Hugh Selwyn Mauberley* published; also *Umbra: The Early Poems of Ezra Pound / All that he now wishes to keep in circulation*.

Becomes foreign agent for *The Dial*.

May–July, EP and DP in Europe: Paris—Sirmione—back to Paris.

First meeting with Joyce in Sirmione in June.

End of Dec., Pounds leave London for Paris.

1921   EP becomes acquainted with Cocteau, Picabia, Gertrude Stein, Brancusi, Hemingway, and George Antheil.

EP works on opera *Le Testament de Villon*.

Poems 1918–21, including Cantos IV–VII published by Boni and Liveright.

1922   3 Jan., T. S. Eliot in Paris with *The Waste Land* 'in semi-existence'. EP edits the manuscript and transforms 'a jumble of good and bad passages into a poem'.

Begins 'Bel Esprit' scheme with Natalie Barney to raise a fund for Eliot and other writers.

Meets William Bird who will start the Three Mountain Press which will publish several of EP's works.

Quinn purchases manuscript of *The Waste Land*, which *The Dial* will publish in November.

EP's translation of Remy de Gourmont's *Natural History of Love* published by Boni and Liveright.

1923   In Italy, EP and Hemingway take a walking tour.

In Paris, meets the violinist Olga Rudge in Natalie Barney's salon. Researches and writes the Malatesta Cantos, which become Cantos VIII–XI.

Meets Harriet Monroe for first time in Paris. Bride Scratton, whom EP first met in 1910, divorces her husband, naming EP as co-respondent.

Transatlantic Review, edited by Ford with assistance by Basil Bunting, appears in Paris. EP promotes and aids the journal.

Indiscretions published by Three Mountains Press.

1924   June, William Carlos Williams in Paris.

EP tours Italy looking for permanent home.

Sept., EP and Dorothy leave Paris for Italy, first to Rapallo then Sicily. *Antheil and the Treatise on Harmony* published by Three Mountains Press.

1925   Jan., EP and Dorothy settle in Rapallo.

Deluxe edition of *A Draft of XVI Cantos* published by Three Mountains Press.

9 July, birth of daughter Mary in the Italian Tyrol, child of EP and Olga Rudge. Child to be fostered and brought up there in local farming family.

1926   June, *Le Testament de Villon* performed in Paris.

10 Sept., birth of Omar Pound in Paris, son of Dorothy. Child to be fostered in Norland Nurseries and brought up in England.

Dec., *Personae, The Collected Poems of Ezra Pound* published in New York by Boni and Liveright.

1927   EP begins to edit and publish his little magazine, *Exile* (four issues).

1928   EP wins the 1927 *Dial* award for poetry.

Translation of the Confucian *Ta Hio or The Great Learning* published by the University of Washington Bookstore.

Sept., *A Draft of The Cantos 17–27* published by John Rodker in London.

1929   1 June, EP's parents sail from New York for London, then go on to Rapallo, where they decide to settle.

America 1895–1908

1. ALS

Oct. 1, 1895

Wyncote

Dear Ma,

I went to a ball game on saturday, between our school and Heacocks, the score was thirty-five to thirty-seven our favor, it was a hard fight in which wee were victorise.

They put on a colorerd man for first base and then to pitcher but he soon was knoct out as he gave two ma[n]y men baces on balls, as it didn't do any good they chucked him off, the umpire cheated untill pa came and then he quit he was accusde of being bubyed into it by the heacocks who it is sed paid him but he denies it.

Wee spent a pleasant sunday. Monday I went after wlnuts and picked for Dayton and Fousty as I could not cary home all I picked up and soo I now have a flour bag bull.

To day I went for chestnuts but got not enough to speak of (I went with Tom and Pud) then went up to Puds where we met Joe and then wee played pussy untill I had to go hom. Wee are well and happy, give my love to aunt Frank and Cousin Sady. As nobody has looked over this pleas excuse mistakes.

Love from all
your loving son,
E.L. Pound

In 1893 Ezra had been a pupil at the Misses Heacock's Chelten Hills School in Wyncote, the suburb of Philadelphia where his family lived. In 1894 he moved on to Florence Ridpath's private school, which, in October 1895, had just become Wyncote Public School. His mother was evidently visiting with her Aunt Frank, Frances Weston, who kept a boarding house with her husband Ezra Weston at 24 East 47th Street, New York.

+≻═≺+

2. ALS

4 / 28 / '96'

New York

Dear Pa

yours recieved this morning.

Ma went to humanity with Miss [*torn*] last night. And is busy scribleing thread on the scurt of the dress she made the waist of the other day.

We hope to come home the first of next week but tont know the day.

Ma Weston wont come home with us. Ma says to douse the palm if you havnt watered it.

b. all well and hope you b.

With love
E.L.P.

Pa's X. Ra

+======+

3. ALS

Nov 15 '96

Wyncote

Dear Ma

You are greatly missed at Oak Lodge, and still more so when neither you nor Pa are here.

Yester-day. We went to the city and saw The Minstrels which we enjoyed greatly; the description would fill ten sheets of paper and so I will not send it. The chief topics were McKinley Bombarded, Bycycle Crazy and Our Public Safty. We went to Wanamakers and had some cream (more than we could eat).

You know you promised to buy me some stamps, so I sent the list by Pa, did he give it to you? If he didn't you will find it in the upper outside pocket of his over-coat.

Pleas excuse this writing as I sprained my little finger, playing football - not when unde a lot of fellows but when I tried to catch the ball which struck the finger with considerable force.

We are well and hope you are.

With best wishis from M.W. and my self.
I remain your loving son
and for the present
your X Ra.

P.S. The stamps on the list which are marked (-) are the ones I have not.

Oak Lodge *was the house next door to the Pound's in Wyncote.* **Wanamakers** *was a department store in Philadelphia.*

+≻—≺+

4. ALS

June 7 / 97

24 / E. 47

Dear Pa

I recieved your letter Saaturday and meant to answer yesterday.

I got my printer this morning and will send you a men you menu in my next letter.

When you come over on the fifteenth bring all thee wheels
Aunt Frank is going to have mine cleaned for me.
This is a day I havent much to say
Except wee are well, and

hope you are the same
I remain your loving Ra
And ma your loving,
Dame.

+≻—≺+

5. ALS

6 February 1898

Wyncote

Dear Ma,

I have not written becaus I expected you home <u>Monday at the longest</u> or before. But as you stay until Thursday I thought I would write.

The coasting has been fine until yesterday when the rain spoiled it. Tom and I, on his sled, started in our drive-way and went down past Cases and up the rode to Chelten Hills.

The slaying has also been fine and I have had a good time hooking them. I went with Mr. Bean up past Glenside and back.

I got a fine 'flevable' yesterday (just too late for the coasting) (retail price $4.00 down at Suppless for $2.70 just a size smaller than Toms.

I have finished my 'exams' and think I passed well, certainly, better than last month.

3

In arithmetic I got 75 $^{3/7}$ for exam (I went over them all twice and thought I proved them. But my daily average will pull it up to nearly 90. I have not seen my other papers yet. I had a full holiday Saturday as we had no 'exams'!

We are all well and hope your are. I am glad you dont need 'pepto' (or knead bread) and are having a good time.

With love to all from all

I remain

'X ray'

P.S. nobody knows I am writing this and I have a bad pen, so please excuse writing and spelling.

E. L. Pound

'mural decorations'

xxxxxxxxxxxxxxxxxxxxxxxxxxxx

xxxxxxxxxxxxxxxxxxx

as you like the date at the end

Sunday Feb. 6th [1898]

In September 1897 Ezra had enrolled in Cheltenham Military Academy, located in Ogontz, Pa., a mile from his home. He continued there, at times as a boarder, until the spring of 1901. **Mr Bean** *ran the local livery stable. A* **flexible** *was a sled which could be steered.*

---

6. ALS

June Fri. 10, 1898

C[heltenham]. M[ilitary]. A[cademy].

Dear Ma

I am serving detention today, as I had too much 'Strawberry Vegetable' last night, I rode over with the Browns and was to have come home on the eight o'clock train, but missed it and had to wait till ten.

There were races and jumping matches there, I came second in the high jump, Skinny Dayton beat me, Mr. Brown treated me to a $.10 ice cream and some cake I had eight lemonades and some crackers, later I got the Mucilage bottle, after playing around and having a good time, Dayton and I went down to the drugstore, we bot some candy and Dayton treated me to soda.

I got to bed about ten and woke up late this morning so I did not get my History done.

This is the last day of regular lessons.

Tomorrow we have the first period exam and some lessons.

As I have no lessons in the first period I think the third form will have the Spelling exam, for the medal.

Monday we have exams in English and Arithmetic.

Tuesday we have History, and Latin.

In the evening we have the declamation contest, which I hope to win.

I have been over my piece with Dr Rice several times.

Meadow-Brook goes well, I have been over to the Nealys several times, they have a one hores boling alley (but it is lots of fun) also a tennis court overgrown with weeds, and a net which is used for a jumping bar and is very easy to crawl through, a William goat which is guaranteed to go where he wants to, the other day when he could not turn around he would jump the shafts. They also have a pond the size of a dish pan, but nevertheless we have packs of fun.

We are all well and hope you are

Love to all and from all

and

I remain

your affectionate son

E.L. Pound

Man (who is in sleig with his best girl, turning on boy who has been stealing a ride) 'You naughty boy, did you overhear any of our conversation'.

Boy, 'No sir, couldn't hear nothing but smacks,'

————

'Horse, to groom who is grooming his hind feet, 'Remember the Maine',

'We want cheep Postage'
E .L.Pound
&
Others

Four more days until vacation
Then we leave this —— plantation,
No more Latin, no more Greek
No more smoking on the sneak,
No more lessons, no more books
No more teachers sour looks
No more spelling no more grammar
Nor more of the profeshiun crammer

E.L. Pound's Lettetter Grade <u>ooo</u>
detention 30 minutes for careless writing
C.M.A.
C.M.A.
Raj! Raj! Raj!

Raj. Chelten, Raj Ham,
Raj Raj Cheltenham
Hooraj, Hooraj,
C.M.A.

I have maths to do
D—— this Blane detention,
I shall try to pass away the time
with a [?]
'Plutarch fine
'Dont like it too long [?]

Any old thing
D—— the, ——, ——,
——, ——, ——, ——, ——,
——, ——, ——, ——, ——,
——, ——, ——, ——, ——,
——, ——, ——, detention

Mucilage, a brand of glue. Meadowbrook, a nearby town—Homer Pound stayed there that summer. The US battleship 'Maine' blew up in Havana harbour in mysterious circumstances on 15 February 1898, and the event was made the occasion for the US intervention in Cuba's struggle for independence from Spain: 'Remember the Maine, to hell with Spain', became a slogan of the time.

In the summer of 1898, Aunt Frank took Ezra and his mother with her on her European tour, sailing from New York on June 18 and returning in mid-September. The battle of Santiago in June–July 1898 ended the Spanish-American war.

+⊨=⊨+

7. ALS [*letterhead*] Grand Hotel de Saxe, Bruxelles

July 5, 1898

Dear Pa

We are now in Bruxells as you see by the heading.

Yesterday morning we left London, after going around and seeing the sights. The first day we went through the Tower and St Pauls. When we were going through the place we met the chief warden and had a very pleasant talk with him, about the different battles he had been through. He wore 5 medals, one for gallant service and good conduct (or for not being caught at pranks, as he said). Another for gallant service at Lucknow. Another for being at Chartoon (or some other famous Indian battle, and 2 others. He has a son in the regiment which fought at Iahlga hights. (He was a Scotch-man.

6

We went to Kennelworth Castle (or the ruins of it. And also to Warwick which is still the home of the Earl of Warwick, the guid kept our party, after the others had left and showed us the dining room, where no visitors are allowed. The croud were shown only a certain suit of rooms which are open to visitors, except when occupied by one of the royal family as they were by the Prince of Wales, the week before.

We then went down to Stratford and saw Shakers birth-place, tomb and memorial.

The day before we took a drive through London & saw the Albert.

I selebrated the 4th (yesterday) by being overcome by the English Chanel. and depositing both breakfast and lunch in its depth.

In the evening we took a drive throu Brusseles.

Please excuse my bad writing as I am in a great hurry and am using a bad pen.

With love from all
I remain
your loving
X Ra.

Vive L'Amerique
Hurrah, Santiago has fallen.

+▷══◁+

8. ALS

Jan. 18th [1899]

C[heltenham]. M[ilitary]. A[cademy].

Dear Mama

Quite a few things have happened since I last wrote Wednesday Reed & I went over home & got the foils & the chess men, we fenced that afternoon & in the evening went in to the city to show off our grand act as a 'Picked corps of cadets from C. M. A.'. we did ourselves proud & have been excused from all drill since & will be for sometime to come, as Major is now breaking in the 'Pups'. Reed & I have used up our spare time in contending on the chess board since then. I also have a challenge from the Major for tomorrow night & one from Mr. Doolittle.

I am going over to dance tonight & expect a good time. Things are going a little better here as I only got two demerits last week!

I recited 'The bivouac of the Dead' this afternoon & got a pretty fair mark (I think). I have tried to write a composition & have here inclosed the first coppy, I thought perhaps you would like to see it.

(Do NOT publish it.) nor read it to anyone (I here quote Pa's last letter) 'mind now'

Tell Pa that I received the cash he sent & was duely thankful, I have since have found my purse.

As my cheverons were off for the crack drill they have since disapered.

My time is now nearly up. I must go & take the guard squad which by a miracle (or some oversight of the Majors – the same thing) I am not on. Tell Pa I met 'Bob' Scellenger at Company I's blow out, however met none of the officials who were at C.M.A. last year.

With love to you all

Good Bye.

E.L. Pound

P.S. This will be the last letter I write as one written later would not reach you before Monday

E.L. Pound

'**The Bivouac of the Dead**', *a 96-line poem written in 1847 by Theodore O'Hara to honour his fellow soldiers from Kentucky who fell in the Mexican-American War; its opening stanza appeared on many memorials to Confederate soldiers killed in the American Civil War, and on memorials in Arlington National Cemetery.*

Ezra did not complete his fourth year at Cheltenham Military Academy, apparently transferring instead to a nearby high school. In September 1901, not yet 16, he enrolled in the College of Liberal Arts, University of Pennsylvania, with the intention, as he later expressed it, 'of studying comparative values in literature (poetry)'. The following year he 'enrolled as special student to avoid irrelevant subjects', with the result that by the end of that year he had about exhausted his options. He applied then to be admitted to Hamilton College in upper New York State. Dr Melancthon Woolsey Stryker was President of the college.

⊹⊱—⊰⊹

9. ALS

June 11. (1903)

Hamilton [College]

Dear Dad.

I came up here on the Empire State Express. Albany. Utica. about 54 miles per. hr. on average.

Saw Dr. Stryker this P.M. & arranged my course. I shall graduate with '05' O.K.

Am delighted with about everything.

The college is set way up in the hills & there is a fine view down the valley to Utica & beyond. There seems to be dandy crowd of fellows here. I am staying with Clark.

I don't know as there is much more to write I have only been here a few hours & I think I have done my full work qualifying for my degree in two years.

Left everything in New York O.K.

Enjoy yourself. get out to Willow Grove & enjoyourself, etc. This fountain pen seems to be a little short of ink. so

good night

Son

+>==<+

10. TLS

July 22, 1903

New York

Lieber Vater.

Noddings egzitemendz didding. Odervise dings vas az dey vas. I send this epistle that thou mayst have cognizence of the aforesaid fact.

We are all able to imbibe nurrishment . I am writing this by bum gass light. Dont forget to send over my bathing suit. und quiq. did it. This wassing chewsday you having left moon days there is not much to write.

Next day.

Received your letter this A .M. Have been making over my summer ward-robe all day. I just teell you I am the warm article when I get into my unkle Jimmes hand me downs.

Every body well. Remember us to the Elys.

so long, with love

Son.

unkle Jimme, *probably Dr James Beyea, whom Aunt Frank would marry in 1906.*

+>==<+

11. ALS

Sunday A.M. (8 September 1903)

Georgetown.

Dear Dad.

I received your letter & one from mother. Am enjoying myself. Rex & I went over to camp meeting thursday night. that is to say Rex found two people with horses & bugays that were able to be persuaded they wanted to go.

I drove with Robt. Houston. He is collector of customs for Delaware & has been west & is a very interesting man to meet. We had a dandy drive about fourty miles there & back. The camp was a little too high joint & fussed up to be the real thing. We are going to a black one some time this week. I think that Idea about my going to N.Y. a very decent one. May be home Thursday or Friday. I have been playing tennis & bumming & walking etc. nothing startling. I shall hear 'The Boss' hold forth later in the day.

Dont know of anything more by way of news.

You better send me a scad if you want me to get home I am short on carefare. It cant be helped.

With this cheering thought I leave thee.

Farewell etc
My signature
Ezra Pound

Your Bum imitation of the style
[*squiggles here*]
What you want in a signature is originality & character.
Make it $2. I am already short more than 1.

+≡≡≡+

12. ALS

[*beginning of letter missing*]

[mid-September 1903]

[Hamilton College]

that is such as 16th assistant secretary to the ministers office boy at Berlin, or door keeper to his highmuckyness at St. James. I suppose I am young enough to start in law & get $30 a year by the time I am 90. I suppose 1000 a year is a pretty good starter for an infant anyhow even if you do have to go to Figi to get it. Ergo I suppose that if I could get a job as consular pupil or cleark it would be a good thing. 1000 is certainly more than I could make at law for several years after I had finished a 3 year law course & more than I would get in a Wall St. office for a few years after quitting college. & besides I think the consular service would be more enjoyable than Wall St. there goes chapel bell so I stop till later.

Heard good strong sermon from Dr. Stryker on Transfiguration on the Mount. & on the subject of raptures generaly & against trying to stay enraptured when you ought to be getting buzzy. ate Dinner. Got bed with good matress for $6. so you needen't send up cot unless convenient I can use it very well as a divan if you want to send it. I will also need a wash bowl pitcher etc.

Also rugs & any carpet you can spare.

I expect to be tolerably settled by wednesday. Please send stuff as soon as you can. to Clinton N.Y. or to Utica if quicker & I will go down there for it.

I am very sorry to have to write for the xtra $40, the $56 for board was unforseen. Hope it will be O.K. somehow.

Are the churches with you. I will walk down to Clinton with this & mail it.

Give my love to mother.

So long for now

With love

Son.

P.S. Dont forget football stockings & shin guards, lamps, german dictionary. Excuse blots but the blotting paper is worn out. Don't be afraid to send several blankets.

Good Bye -

Ezra Pound.

<hr>

13. ALS

Monday night (20 September 1903)

Hamilton [College]

Dear Dad,

You have heard that I am pledged to KE. & also some of the particulars. If you know anything of Frats you know that KE, AL & ΨY stand in a class alone & that I don't believe I could have made a better choice. you will first ask about expense it stands thus. if I stayed up here in (South) I should have to buy a stove, big enough to heat two rooms, & as I am on the ground floor & should need carpets to keep down the dampness, & I also do not get benefit of other fellows heat as do fellows on second & third floor.

Thus you have about

stove	15	
carpt	10	anyway
coal	5	
————		
30		

which I should need almost immediately. as it is I pay

25	initiation fee
6	room
6	dues
————	
39	

about which there is no hurry, which makes my frat entrance only about nine dollars.

Also next term I will eat at KE house at less cost than at 'Commons' & wont have to pay up in advance. This may seem as if I was trying to defend going into KE as merely paying for the exchange from stoves (which you have to tend yourself) & kerosene & Steam heat & electric light.

As for assotiation and so on a fellow here must join a fraternity or be out in the cold. I don't know as I can explicitly name advantages but you ought to be able to understand. If you don't, I don't know what you can do about it.

Talk frats with someone who has been in one. I have been for about twenty four hours & am noticing a difference already.

I don't walk up the campus alone anymore. This may be as expressive as anything.

I will get my mail tomorrow I suppose. I have five classes today so I haven't had time to go for it. In future of course it will be sent to the house.

Besides the fellows I mentioned we have Schwartz, back from the Phillipines, & Drummond a Sophomore who walks on crutches & apparently has all his life, both fine fellows whom you feel have something in & to them. A senior Wood whom I should like you to meet, several more whom I shall describe as I get to know them better.

Hallman knew of you in C.E. About the first thing he asked me when he found out where I was from, was whether I was connected with Mr Pound who was etc & so on in the C.E.

(Hallman from Ambler, whom I mentioned before). Hope Mr. Eckfeldt can give you a good account of him, but I won't try to predict what your highly esteemed chief will say about anyone. Probably 'Ugh.'.

I haven't done much to day except go to classes. Will probably move to KE Friday as it is becoming colder & I might as well be settled as soon as possible

Shall need a little more cash for books.

I promis Spousi	1.50.
Wards Eng. Poets	1.25
Pope's 'Battle of the Books'	.20
Life of St Paul	1.25
Gosse Eng. Lit.	1.25

I have about 1.50 to pay laundry bills etc. to Oct 15. Will do my best to come out even at Xmas. of course no other term, this year or next will be so expensive. I can't quite see how & it's too late for me to puzzle it out to night.

Don't see as I can get on much more cheeply than I am doing. It will all come out right somehow. Dont worry (all very easy for me to say when you are doing the paying, I know).

Good night

Lovingly

Son

Tell mother I have found my shin-guards so she needn't hunt for them any longer. I haven't used them yet however.

In spite of the optimism of this letter Ezra did not join KE and remained one of only three in the class of '05 who did not belong to a fraternity. It has been suggested that a letter from Penn's KE effectively blackballed him. In his first year he was in Hungerford

Hall, known as 'Old South', a building then 100 years old which provided large draughty two-room suites with large fire-places, very expensive to heat. 'C.E.' = Christian Endeavour, a religious organization of which his parents were active members. 'I promis Spousi', presumably I Promessi Sposi *(1827) by Alessandro Manzoni. Ezra would have learnt in due course that* The Battle of the Books *is a prose satire by Jonathan Swift.*

No letters survive for the rest of this fall trimester, and none for the following winter trimester.

He frequently refers to Hamilton professors in shortened forms:

Hermann C. G. Brandt, Professor of German—'Schnitz', also 'Schmity'. Pound
Frederick M. Davenport, taught Law and Political Science—'Davy Dav'
Edward Fitch, Edward North Professor of Greek—'Little Greek'
Rev. Joseph Darling Ibbotson—'Bib'
Albro David Morrill, Professor of Biology—'Bugs'
Rev. Oren Root, Professor of Mathematics and Registrar—'Square Root'
Arthur Percy Saunders, Professor of Chemistry—'Stink'
Samuel J. Saunders, Professor of Physics and Instructor in Astronomy —'Pill'
Dr William Pierce Shepard, Professor of Romance Languages and Literature—'Bill'
Rev. William Harder Squires, Professor of Psychology, Logic, and Pedagogics
Dr Melancthon Woolsey Stryker, President of the college, known as 'Prex'
Dr Frank Hoyt Wood, Professor of American History

Pound sometimes refers to his German studies as 'Dutch' (for 'Deutsch').

---

14. ALS

[BUZZARD ROOST Hamilton College]

Apr 29. (1904)

Dear Dad.

Glad to get your letter this morning.

I want you to please see Vice Provost Smith & find out if I can get credit at Penn. for work done up here, without taking exams there, that is. Will certificate of work here be accepted there? Please try to see Dr. Smith pretty soon. I think it will be better for you to see him than for me to write to Dean Penniman.

I guess I'd better come back where I belong. I could keep my nose in a book as long as I was frozen in but now it's decent out I can't seem to get any work done and as the work was the single advantage up here, the discomforts & inconveniences & things in general don't seem to balance. I get more tired of the place every day & if it is as bad as it is now it will be worse next year. Fudge. I want to get back where I know somebody & where I have beds made, etc. etc.

13

In short I guess my optimism about the joint here and its advantages is about played out.

I supposed I could have decent quarters next year but all the rooms in the new dormitories are for two or three men, and as all the fraternity men room with their own men, and as all the fellows fit to room with are in the frats. I can't get a room without paying double. i.e. $180.00 and they aren't worth more than $60.

I think also that by the end of this term I will have gotten far enough along in french to get just as much out of the French course at Penn. also can probably take my Spanish there about as well. & be respectably comfortable. As I wrote some months ago, there are only three of us & we might as well get acquainted while we have the chance.

I suppose I'll be away from home quite enough after next year. And also it seems an awful waste to pay carfare up here & board & room rent when I might stay at home & have everything better for less.

I have thought about this & written before. This is the third time & the third time goes. Of course at the end of a term, as you are leaving the place it seems very decent, & when you are away from it it is very nice. But I guess I belong at old Penn.

These reasons are pretty well mixed up. But I wish you'd go see Dr. Smith. You needn't tell mother I'm feeling this way about things as she has enough to worry about. So have you for that matter. Anyway I guess it runs in the family to keep cheerful.

Good Bye

Son

Love to you and mother.

My work here will be equivalent to 16 2/3 units at Penn. but I suppose particulars will be arranged at Deans office later. All you need to do is to get Dr. Smith to have my certificate received. O.K.

E.P.

Guess everything is for the best. Will know enough to stay where I belong in future.

+=+=+

15. ALS

May 3 [1904]

BR. [Hamilton College].

Dear Mother,

Got your unexpected letter this morning .Take a freshman instead of a dog when I walk.

Essay on early poetry of W^{m}. Morris.

Nothing doing .
Weather remarkable for its decency
u.a.d.e.
French Notre Dame.
Dago. Now purgatory, instead of hell, being lighter & more fitted for spring reading.
Remember me to Cousin Sadi.

Much love to Dad & yourself.

Son.

Down In Clinton to get socks, garters, etc. otherwise nothing doing.
Wednesday May 3.

+≻══≺+

16. AL

SUNDAY MAY 8th [1904]

BUZZARDS ROOST [Hamilton College]

Dear MOTHER.
Got vicious Wednesday evening & went into Utica & saw 'In Old Kentucky'. Sandusky Doolittle still says the lines that Dad's been quoting for the last eighty years. Show quite enjoyable.

Prex going away Friday evening. I had quite a pleasant visit with Mrs. Stryker. Also saw Dr. Wood later. Square Root preach a mighty good sermon this A.M.

We play Syracuse university in chess tomorrow.

+≻══≺+

17. ALS

Tuesday May 10 [1904]

[Hamilton College]

Dear Dad
Considering that I refrained from drawing on May 1, also the high price of corn, the increase of crime & the overcrowded condition of the state's prisons, also the wealthy & the increase due to the Russo-Japan war, I would not refuse 10 or 15 sample leaves from the flourishing tall green bay tree provided of course that they were thrust upon me with due formality, tact & persuasion. I even would refrain from returning them if they arrived anterior to the fifteenth of the month.

Next. enclosed please find one (1) unfinished letter to mother written Sunday.

15

Also. Syracuse squashed us in chess. considering the relative size of the joints it is not surprising (2100–200).

Of course it would have been very nice to win only we didn't.

So long
Ezra Pound

P.S. The books were THAIS

CRIME of SILVESTRE BONNARD IN ENGLISH.

Thanks for ordering them, hope they come soonly quick

EP

---

18. ALS

[? late May 1904]

[BR Hamilton College]

Dear Mother,

Yours received.

Got rash Saturday & spent one scad on a hoss an wagin fer to go aout drivin in. P.S. I didn't went alone also. etc.

She is pretty nice also, her face looks more like a face than a coal scuttle.

Also went to Utica & spent $.50 or $.60 on a square meal.

Chapel here yesterday A.M. Communion P.M. Went into Utica to Grace Church in evening but they had changed time of service. Met Dick Elsea & we went around to another joint. A cuss from General assembly got up & talked some words. (rather as Lower only with Irish accent) gave us fourteen names of great men in a string, each time as if it were something new & surprising.

P.S. We found our hats & I don't know exactly what his last point was.

This is my bussy day & its over. Got more mediaeval philosophy in one Canto of Dante's Paradise than I ever expect to get again. Bill spent most of the time elucidating. he told me if I wanted any more I could go to Thomas Aquinas & the other mediaeval latin writers

I said 'No thanks this is enough' so we go on to Canto X. Also beat two men at tennis, one only weighs 250 lbs. - the only trouble with him is that you can't get the balls around him.

It's now 9.30 & nothing more wonderful has happened.

Good night
Love to you & dad.

P.S. I want Dick to stay over night & perhaps a day or so when I come down. so fix it or keep it quit.

P.S. he won't eat so very much even if he has been on the job here.

---

19. ACS

Monday [14 June 1904]

BR.[Hamilton College]

Dear Mother,

Chapel yesterday. Prex used up all English hendecasylables & all he knew of four foreign languages 25 minutes complicated hot air: nothing said.

As usual this my full day. Dago Xam this week . rest of Xams next. Get to N.Y. week from Saturday. Sold stove, fellows will take Chair & Table in fall & sell bed for me. Nothing doing

Good night
Love from
Son

+≡+

20. ALS

June 21 (1904)

Hall Commons [Hamilton College]

Dear Dad,

Dago Xam off last week. French yesterday . Two more tomorrow. Three more days of—

Pleeze rush the coin & make it $20.

I don't want to walk to N.Y. if I can help it.

(ex)Kuss brevity

Communication from Penn O.K. will take those terms if I cant get better

Guess I'd better quit & git to bed.

Prex & Square Root both tomorrow & what I dont know is selling at 7.22 ½

Good night
Your Pore overwurked
son
Ezry.

+≡+

21. AL [*letterhead*] Port Jefferson Hotel

8. A.M. Thursday, July 28 (1904)

[Port Jefferson, New York]

Dear Mother.

Mrs Skidmore being suddenly called away to Philadelphia (relative sick or something) also my time being up, I transfered myself & belongings, as you see. Place, $7 per. clean, grub OK. I guess, eatable & plenty, mine host, large & anxious to please, seine Frau likewise, am satisfied just at present anyhow . Superficial polish is lacking but unnecessary. Have been boating, rowing, playing tennis, driving, etc. Margaret left Tuesday & Louise & I, accompanied her across the sound to Bridgeport, 'decent sail on a steam boat'.

Thank you for the socks.

I shall stay here a week or two more, I guess.

Hope you are comfortable & enjoying life. Realy not very much to write. Am enjoying life in the usual manner of people 'off the job'.

Am ready for my remittance on the first, although not broke.

Love to you & Dad.

I reckon thats all.

Good Bye.

In the summer of 1904 Pound's parents had let their house in Wyncote and were renting a house in Philadelphia in order to be near their work in the Italian Settlement. Ezra spent part of the summer in Port Jefferson, where the Skidmores, a Wyncote family, had a summer residence; and part with Aunt Frank in New York City. The Doctor mentioned in relation to Aunt Frank would have been Dr James Louis Beyea whom Aunt Frank married in 1906—sometimes referred to as Uncle James.

22. ALS [*letterhead*] Port Jefferson Hotel

Sat. Jul. 30 (1904)

[Port Jefferson, New York]

Dear Mother,

Things going on about the same. Bathe, walk, visit around in evenings, sail or row.

There is nothing particular to write about anything in particular, usual health treatment, nether novel nor exciting, calm peaceful laziness

Love to you & dad, & remember the flag is still there & refrain from telegrams to people who have other things to do, s.v.p. your last arrived sometime after my letter started, Mrs. Skidmore got back from Phila. a little later.

Good Bye,

Son.

'Scuse me for livin'

 Also delay not to remit.

Yes thank you.

23. ALS [*letterhead*] Port Jefferson Hotel

Tuesday 9. A. M. [2 August? 1904]

[Port Jefferson, New York]

Dear Mother,

Received your letter at breakfast. I may come home Saturday & if so will want no more clothes. If I decide to stay longer will write for some.

My quarters are clean, about a ¼ mile to Skidmores & little way from sound.

Thank you for coin. will write dad. shall pay board to day up till next Saturday, & thereby get a pull with the house & the excess coin out of my system.

I am just living along enjoyably

& as I shall probably live to be eighty odd I have no time to indulge in such diversions & getting run over, drowned, drawn & quartered & all that. Went to church sunday , Episcopal, tennis with Louise yesterday A.M. took a tub bath for sake of cleanliness rather than a swim. Spent evening at Skidmores with Louise Miss Chamber & a friend of hers. Have slept & am awake.

Also have payed $8.50 for ten days board.

Guess thats all. (i.e. untill Sat.)

Be good to yourself, & enjoy life the best way you know how, & don't worry about me. I am not rich enough to have anybody steal me for my beauty.

So long
With love
Son.

Have written Dad.

+≥=≤+

24. ALS [*letterhead*] Port Jefferson Hotel

Friday, Aug 5 (1904)

[Port Jefferson, New York]

Dear Mother,

I recon I'll hang on here a week or so longer.

Seems to be healthy. You don't mind do you I seem to be useful.

Doings nothing out of the ordinary. Sail picnic Wednesday, tennis & swim yesterday. Dance tonight. - interesting sociological study in certain fazes of present day americanism.

Old small seaport, with superficial summerality buttered over it. Don't think there is anything for you to come down for. Hotel wouldn't suit you, & you can't crawl over the schooners in dry dock & don't care much more for still salt bathing than I do. Am reading Richard II in off time.

Guess that's about all.

Much love to you & dad.

Good Bye

Son.

+=—=+

25. ALS [*letterhead*] Port Jefferson Hotel

Wednesday [10?] (August 1904)

[Port Jefferson, New York]

Dear Mother,

Rain,

no excitement, no, I don't want any more clothes. Nothing happened since I last wrote.

Mailed a letter to you from Mrs Skidmore yesterday. she is fussed because you might think something or other about her not writing before. You know she was called away just after your telegram or note or something, & wrote after she came back a week or more ago, Yes. yes, well it was mislayed & she gave it to me to mail yesterday with a few million excuses.

It's all right, isn't it. Yes, thats all.

Begoodtoyourself.

Love to you & dad.

Son.

+=—=+

26. ALS [*letterhead*] Port Jefferson Hotel

Tuesday [16 August?] (1904)

[Port Jefferson, New York]

Dear Mother,

Received your note at breakfast. Glad to hear dad is coming over to keep you company.

Living enjoyably, sailed on Skidmore's Yacht for first time saturday. The Doctor having been in & out on cruises & having boat fixed up at other times. Also sailed yesterday. Life quite decent.

Think it best for me to return to Hamilton this fall, as I find the discomforts forgotten in a month or so & only the benefits & pleasant memories only remaining. Also Root is [?] to disregard. & at the end of senior year there I shall be able to speak French German & Spanish fairly well & have my reading knowledge of Italian in reserve.

Also I shall know something. If I go to Penn. I would have no foreign language in useful shape. Also if I studied & did the social & fenced & did nineteen other things, Chess, Houston Club etc. I doubt very much if I would be much pleasure to you all at home, & It would cost more at home & I'd need clothes & so on & so on ala Sophomore year only worse probably. And Hamilton will be better next year & I will not be an outsider. I realy think it best and I don't want to chuck up something worth while for a little pleasure & comfort the doing what you don't like is more beneficial than the plush lined epicureanism of an effete society.

I think I'll be more a man at the end of it.

Cheer up.

Son.

---

27. ALS

(Sept. 5 1904)

New York.

Dear Dad,

If mother & you can see no more in my $5 than a pin, why its extravagant & if you cant see any more than that I'm sorry and will try to explain a few things to <u>you</u> when I get home.

And try to understand that the V has not gone for 'nothing but a pin!

Everything here O.K. nothing doing.

Thank you for check.

Son.

---

28. ALS

Friday [5–9] (September 1904)

24 E 47. [New York]

Dear Mother.

Everything here O.K. I am reading & doing odd jobs for the joint & occasionaly hearing Miss Heyman play. It's a comfort to find a person with brains & sense. once & a while. dont know as there is anything to tell. Aunt Frank has been very nice & agreeable . & I have been a model child. Hope you and dad are enjoying life.

Heard Morgan twice & McKay once last sunday. all good.

Said so long to Camp. after the ceremony. He's a wonder only I didn't tell him so.

Things very peaceful comfortable & generaly salubrious & agreeable.

Guess that's all.

Much love to you & dad
Son.

Camp., *Campbell Morgan, a renowned preacher.*

+≻══≺+

29. ALS

[12–15] (September 1904)

24 E 47 [New York]

Dear Dad,

I have been having a very decent sort of a time. Have met some very nice friends of Miss Heyman etc. etc. We took a trolley wander the other day. Went to see the Hermitage & struck Gardimont & the sound. then came over through the hills & woods to Tarrytown bummed around in an old curiosity shop there for a while & from there to Hastings where we took dinner with some real white folks & came back to town. went out once red devil riding with more friends of Miss Heyman & in general am enjoying life. Tell mother that last sunday I went to church with Aunt Frank & this Sunday she went with the Doctor & I went to the cathedral after finding several other places closed or uninviting & also that the service was good.

Guess thats all Hope you & other will manage to keep as joyful as you seem to be

Good Bye.
With much love to you & mother.
Son.

Miss Heyman also desires to be remembered to you both.

EP

+≻══≺+

30. ACS

[22 September 1904]

[Utica, New York]

Utica OK

It is cold, send coin for coal & stove, otherwise everything OK.

Left 24 E 47. OK & joyfully, am now sitting on fence rail waiting for trolly.
Here it comes
Good Bye
Son

+≔≕+

31. ALS

Monday [26] (September 1904)

[Hamilton College]

Dear Dad,

Check received, thank you very much.

Coal in, stove up, nothing underway as yet.

Will write more as I have time. Much love to you & mother.

With double french, anglo-saxon, spanish, analytics & three hours of Prex's hot air I expect to come home a corpse.
Good Bye,
Son, .

+≔≕+

32. AL

Wednesday [28 September 1904]

Hamilton [College]

Dear Mother.

This being the first evening I have had time to breathe I went down & saw Dr. Wood for a while. Talked his trip abroad for a while & then went down & talked books etc with Bib.

Find Anglo-Saxon very fascinating. Also French of Descartes & Pascal. Eng. Lit. Comedy before Shakespeare. & Junior French. Tragedy, Corneille's 'Cid' just now.

Analytical geom is the first respectable mathematics I have interviewed for some time.

& I suppose Prex. hot air about Parliamentary Law is harmless. Spanish of course not far enough along to be of interest yet.

Altogether I expect to have about time enough to take ½ breath to every 75 hours & 1/3 sneeze to every 150 weeks. However the work is very fascinating, & if I can get it done in any respectable manner it will be very nice.

Only I expect to come home on ice
or have a new think tank put in or the old one enlarged, or something.

Guess I'll get into the swing pretty soon
Tell dad that commons is between $50. & 52.

Room	6
Contingent	8
Tuition	25
Books	8 +

          ——   Paid, Books, Carpet, Coal
       91   & Stove out of 20. received.

make check 90.I guess Oct. first will be time enough for him to send it. I haven't any idea what day of the month it is. If it has to be in before I'll let you know

Cheer up & enjoy life, both of you will try to end up strain as soon as possible.

etc.

Please don't part my name in the middle.

it's EWL or Ezra W.L. or the whole thing or Ezra Weston Pound but not E. Weston Loomis Pound.

Also I did not forget razor & whisk broom, cause I have one of each with me.

& Dick met me.

& I don't know what kind of carpet it is, 'cept it's cheap & all that was left.

& I got it in Clinton.

& the stove's mos' as big 'ez 'er room.

Also about the faculty. I have seen two tonight only I can't put all their conversatzione on paper. Also Bill Shep. has invited me down & consider'n it's Bill & he don't do that sort of thing much, why I'm going.

& as I don't seem to have any blotting paper that blots, I think I'll get some.

Much love to you & Dad.

Guess that's all for now.

Good night.

━┥

33. ALS

[29 September – 6 October 1904]

Hamilton [College]

Dear Mother.

Passed Trig. exam yesterday.

Read John Lyly's 'Alexander & Campaspe' for Bib. also some of the 'Lais' of Marie de France.

Read 'Lear' a day or two ago, & have out of the library now. Henley 'London Voluntaries.' 'In Hospital.' etc. 'A History of Italian Lit.' & Flaubert's 'Salammbo' in French.

We finish Corneille's 'Cid' tomorrow. Having Pascal's 'Penses' in Sr. Fr.

Anglo-Saxon. is for the literature. and if you will pay expressage I'll send you a list of a few of the things in Ang-Sax worth reading. besides. Beowulph. Ormulum, Brut. King Alfred's writings (Lord knows how many) Cynewulf, et alii ad. inf.

Just now it is Alfred's account of the voyages of Ohthan & Wulfstan.

Guess that's about all just now. Thank dad for the $90. can pull along without the rest till. convenient.

Good night.

Bee good to yourselves as you are to me & you'll get on OK.

Will go to bed now if I don't get interested in something.

With Love,
Son.

+≻═━═≺+

34. ALS

Friday [7] (October 1904)

[Hamilton College]

Dear Mother,

I have a chance to go into the New Dorms. have found a freshman who is respectable for a room mate.

It will foot up to about twelve dollars more a term. (Room I am now in & coal & oil & $12. per term) Beds made, room swept, place to bathe with out walking way over to gymnaseum.

Suppose it would be healthier. & surely more comfortable. cant even get people to carry in coal this year.

Lots of other things, I'd rather put coin in . but think it would be quite sane to get out of present quarters.

Let me know what you think, if I go over Dad'll have to send up $35, after middle of month.

if it's inconvenient I can stay where I am.

Everything O.K.

Much love to you & dad. Hope you won't starve.

Sons in college are a darned bum investment don't you think.

Good Bye.
Son.

*The **New Dorms** were the newly opened Carnegie. Pound was in Room 10, with Oswald Prentiss Backus, Jr., a **freshman**—EP frequently refers to Backus as 'the skeleton'.*

+≻═━═≺+

35. ALS

Thursday [13] (October 1904)

[Hamilton College]

Dear Dad.

I have to pay for the room now. & thirty is necessary. & I said thirty five because there's football subscription & shoe soles. & I can't sell stove now. What was left of coal. paid remainder of book store account. So 35 now would fit best if possible. but will squeeze on 30. if . you give the word.

Mails seem off the handle somewhere, nothing anywhere on time.

I'll come home to vote if you say so.

Called on Bill Shep last evening.

Reading, Garnetts 'Hist. Of Ital. Lit.'

Racines 'Andromaque' in Jr. Fr.

other stuff as usual.

seems strange to feel steadily bathed & clean at this end of the line the effete luxuries of steam heat & bath tub & warm water bother me. Also freshman, he means well, but – Oh, not bad, for a freshman. 6 ft 2 in. weight 129.

so fasiun. [*sketch to indicate very tall and thin*] Name Backus

ancient god of booze oh how changed art thou in thy form.

Haven't time for kindergarten or I might make a man of it.

Much love to you & mother.

Will try to write to Grandfather.

Good Night

Son.

⊶══⊷

36. ALS

Friday evening. [14 October 1904]

[Hamilton College]

Dear Mother.

No wonders.

Have found a white mans history of Italian literature & am enjoying it.

Racine's 'Andromaque,' brings in some familiar characters of Iphigenia. Orestes, Pylades etc. only on another job.

George Peeles 'Old Wives Tale'. ante Shakesperian, interesting historicaly, but hardly to be read for itself.

did it this evening.

Spanish going smoothely

manage to get a blood in Anylit. ocasionaly. it's the first sane 'math' I have found for some time, am not expecting to continue it beyond required time, however.

Just at present I would rather have books than steam heat & a bath tub but I suppose the latter are healthier.

I also suppose it would be sensible for me to go to bed.

Much love to you & dad.

Son

Suppose you are sticking pins into the club, & dad saving dagoes. don't be afraid to write when you feel like it.

EP.

Wrote to Grandfather last evening.
Also.
Don't you want to send me a couple of bed sheats?

Son.

+>=—=<+

37. ALS

[15–20 October] (1904)

H[amilton College]

Dear Mother.

Please continue to adress my letters - especialy when they contain cash - to Clinton Mass. it insures quicker delivery.

Wattel? the civic club. Havent yet heard anything from Mrs W.

Backus mother in today. She's all to the good.

rooms so	S	[*sketch showing layout of*
E Window	Bed Bath closet	*study with fireplace, bedroom,*
	Study fire place.	*bath & closet*]

Suppose A. F. wanted something besides patent medicine samples. Poor Doc. Mebbe 'e means well too!

Me? Oh I haven't time to see. Plugging at Sordello & Dago Lit. also got Taines 'Lectures on Art' & some of Stevenson's essays today. also a full course [?], Eng Lit over as diversion occupies a little time. <u>Oh yes, I got the check</u> . don't forget that I say so here & write later as to why I don't acknowledge it.

Dont be alarmed by the picture of the freshman . he aint so worse. & as for comfuts I havent time to notice them.

I know this scratch is a wreck but please excuse it.

Much love to you & dad & write as often as you can please.

Ezra Pound

Yes I exercise a little, walk yesterday for 1½ hrs.
Am O.K. as to body.

EzraP.

+>=—=<+

38. ALS

Friday. [21 October 1904)

Hamilton [College]

Dear Dad,

Box arrived this afternoon, thanks orfully, everything right side up etc.
Have been re-hashing my 'hot-air' to hand in tomorrow, everything O.K.
Am still in Taine & Garnett, no excitement.
Am gradually getting the 'fresh' trained.
Realy nothing to write.

Goodbye.
Much love to you & mother.
Edables right on the spot.
Tell mother 'the' sheet came from New York.
Son.

⊢⇒—◄⊣

39. ALS

Sunday. Oct 30 (1904)

H[amilton College]

Dear Dad,

Blew myself to 'Il Trovatore' last evening. pretty good bunch, on stage. quite enjoyable.

$1 for standing room & I pinched a seat about 8th row orchestra.

Suppose I'm the first cuss that ever took in grand opry in boots. didn't think of going till after supper & had to hustle. The son of the manager sat in front of me, 'aet' 8 yrs. his views on grand opry between the acts were uplifting.

His opinion of the show 'Pretty good half bad'. I enquired about the other two performances, the one in the after-noon had been the same only a little different. And the one the night before (Lohengren, I found out later from Dr. Wood) well, he'd been sellin things up stairs, but I'd orter be glad I didn't went. you know them people in short skirts (Gypsy camp 2nd act). Well just the same only women in tights in a row & men behind 'em just singing most every act.

He sighed for a 'Travotore' in 4 acts, 'cause there aint no killin in it.' People dying of their own accord seemed a little too tame to suit him.

Kid looked like a fish.

Have been having a pretty good birth-day

Penn-Harvard victory gave me a chance to celebrate without anyone catching on to the fact it was a birth-day.

Am at peace with the world.

Man whose eye I bunged up last spring has been up here all evening.

Don't know that there is much more to write. Be good to yourself.

Much love to you & mother & be careful of the civets. Which branch of your work do they give you a chance to graft in.

Well Good-night. many happy returns of the day. Saw Dr. Wood after Opera last night & had a pleasant spiel.

Grub still holding out. almonds & cake especialy good.

Good Night.

Son.

civets, *for the civic club of which his parents were members.*

+>====<+

40. ALS

Nov. 2 (1904)

H[amilton College]

Dear Dad,

Consignment of coin is arriv. thank you. Had very pleasant letter from Grandfather this a.m.

Sofa pillow from Miss Weber.

Pleasant call on Bib. last evening.

Penn-Harvard game . rather satisfactory? Well now just maybe perhaps.

On halloween the freshmen placed most of Prex's live stock in different class rooms, & moved his pig stye, or chicken coop or something up on his front porch.

I witnessed several slimers enticing a boy into the Hall of Science. otherwise no excitement.

Well good night.

Much love to you & mother

Son.

+>====<+

41. ALS

Friday 8. P.M. [4 November] (1904)

H[amilton College]

Dear Dad,

Glad to get your letter this a.m. What ward are <u>you</u> driving in,

What's the dago note worth per hundred?

Room-mate improves on acquaintance.

29

Who's? Eddie got?

Why don't I get my expenses paid to come home & vote? Democratic parade in Clinton, magnificent, oh yes.

Saw the republican father of the Demycart wat wuz riden a hoss at the head, saw the ole man, I say a rubberin outer his stoar winder lookin zif if he'd like ter chaw nails.

Bill Squires is runnin fer congress & 'Pill''s was a carryin a lamp & I jes tell yew, oh it wuz grait.

the republicans is goin ter blow in Uitiky ter night

Me. Oh I've got through Sordello. & am plugging Taine 'Philosophy of Art.' etc. also have some work required by college to fill in with. Yes.

Guess this is about all.

A lot of love to you & mother.

Good night.

Kid.

1904 was an election year. Rev. William Harder Squires ran for Congress as a Democrat, unsuccessfully, the district being overwhelmingly Republican. He was supported by his colleague Professor Samuel J. Saunders.

⊹—⊢—≣⊹

42. ALS

[5–7 November] (1904)

[Hamilton College]

Dear Ma.

Pleeze don't let dad bewty up the country so much I wont be able to find my way home. Will the sivic stic pay my way home to vote? does it use red or green paint to decorate the burg. Dont let the governor git to doin the divert stunt with the spots so as he enlightenes his proboscosis. its tew early fer him tew begin to be a fly one.

Wots 'e git . for being a civet.

Who'se the Kyrle Belew you be spoutin with about your infermation gang?

Yes. I got my old furniture & am lettin the slimer do the rest. Ballad book is up here.

Taines lectures on Art. are the real thing. Read 'em to your current picken bunch if they have time to imbibe a bit of horse sense.

Do have dad be careful of the civets.

Getting back to XVI French. French lectures on Fr. Drama. everything else as usual. Why do you skin the Wa Way Back press out of so much stuff. Why dont you cash in & draw chips . the joint is just as near broke as you are. don't take the last free piece of paper off their backs. they may need it fer fuel this winter.

I got a bid to Eddies Weddin, guess I'll go if he'll send me a pass too.

Now dew be careful & don't get your feet wet . & cheer up. Guess that's about all.

Hope you & dad are enjoying life.

Much love to both of you

Son

+>——=+

43. ALS

Sunday (14 November 1904)

Hamilton [College]

Dear Mother.

Things going on about the same

Bill Squires preached this A.M. . the cuss that beat him out for Congress will adress the YMCA this P.M. - 'all in the family'. nothing unusual or surprising.

Am invited to Backus join for Thanksgiving so I suppose I'll get a square meal.

Much love to you & dad.

Son.

+>——=+

44. ALS

Wednesday [16 November 1904]

[Hamilton College]

Dear Mother.

Monday & Tuesday full. today time to breathe.

Account of Caedmon in Ang-Sax. Begin Cyrano, in Jr. Fr.

Also 'Satyres Menepen' on the League, scrap of it in Sr. Fr. .

Christian Evidences with Prex four hours more a week from now on.

Have finished 'Death's Jest Book' & Gosse's introduct. to beddoes.

flattered my vanity on his 'B. a dish for a few literary epicures' & those who enjoy will be able to pick out his excellencies without my saying more'.

Have worked around to Morris today not feeling like Paracelsus or Henry IV. Grub fairly decent for a while. As I said invited to Backus joint for Thanksgiving.

In reply to your letter. if my invitations multiply every time I get new clothes I'll never buy any. I dont want that kind.

31

I am short on cuts because I used nearly all I had by getting off the job a moment or two & leaving these 'here' parts. I bought a hatchet & a tack-hammer & a knife in clinton.

Spanish not particularly exciting.

Am going over to Organ-Violin spiel in the chapel. Clark Organist & Prof. Saunders 'Stink', spiel there Wed. 5 P.M.

Cheer up both of yey.

Much love from your wayward wandering, ill mannered loutish etcerish.

Kid.

P.S. You aren't to blame for my defects you know

I got 'em all in that nasty college

So keep happy & don't worry about my feet.

E.P.

*From the Hamilton Handbook: 'Each student has a privilege of absence from 12 per cent of the assigned exercises in each department. . .', and a limited number of '**cuts**' was permitted from the daily morning chapel. Students kept careful track of cuts in their handbooks.*

⊹══⊹

45. ALS

Thursday [17] (November 1904)

H[amilton College]

Dear Mother.

I could very easily & beneficialy invest about $90.00 in clothes but dont need to, & have more underware than I can wear out for ages. I did not laike Water Babies.

Backus is from Rome. I got all the stuff from 24 E 47

I dont know what use manners abrupt or otherwise would be up in this wilderness.

Absolute isolation from all 'humanity' does not tend to increase punctiliousness.

Don't be alarmed, there are a few white folks even up here.

Nice disagreable sort of letter isn't it? Glad you & dad seem to be enjoying life.

I dont suppose anyone can live in books steadily & not get grouched occasionaly. Have seen & heard nothing out-side this cramped narrow lopsided hole except last Saturday .

I'm not grumbling only it gets monotonous.

Next morning.
Guess I'm feeling better or am more wide awake. cheer up.
Much love to you & Dad.
E.P.

+≔≕+

46. ALS [*letterhead*] Ithaca Hotel

Sunday [20 November] 1904

[Ithaca, New York]

Dear Dad.

As you see I hev broke out. I'd been bottled on that desolate mountain top about as long as I could stand it, so I'm taking a little vacation. Break it gently to mother. she wanted me to get shoes instead of enjoying life. I think you'll understand the situation better, you left on the front of an engine once yourself, guess it runs in the family.

My telegram not arriving promptly I found it incumbent upon me to spend yesterday P.M. in the library looking up Celtic Philology & translations of the Vedas

spent a pleasant evening & am going to chapel in a few minutes.

I suppose I'll need about 20. in the middle of the month to get straightened out on, bust a bond, you'll have to do it before the year's out & I don't want you & mother to starve just to keep me in foolish enjoyment. Incidentaly I have had the first two meals (last night & this morning) that haven't been a blasphemy against digestion since I left home.

I suppose I'm real devlish but I'm not a — bit sorry & I'm not going to hatch up any mock repentences. I'd only been out of Clinton once (Opera) & hadn't done anything in Clinton except get mail & buy hardware. & I needed some sort of a variety & I'm taking it. – you wouldn't pay my way home to vote – I have thought of going to a cheaper hotel for tomorrow & saving $1, but don't know as I will.

Anyhow I'm enjoying myself now & you will please enjoy life also.

I shall probably be back in Hamilton when you get this as I am not long on either cuts or coin.

Rejoice with them that do rejoice & don't think of the morning after.
With much love to you & mother.
Your wayward son
Ezry.

Pound wrote of his father in Indiscretions, *'He had left one school on the cow-catcher of an engine; he was placed in the military school at Shattuck, Minnesota, and ultimately assigned to West Point. Appointments to this institution are not easily obtainable. . . .*

[H]is family placed him on the train, and he, speculating on the advantages of the nation's finest and most efficient military and mathematical education, "got off halfway" and returned to his natal state.'

---

47. ALS

[25 November 1904]

H[amilton College]

Dear Mother,

Had a very pleasant time with the Backi. yesterday, they're white folks & they sure did treat me right.

Have replied to Mrs. Weber. Hope you folks fed well. Your letter here when I got back at 1 P.M. today.

Hope this gets to you in time to wish you many happy returns of the day. If it dont I wished 'em before anyhow.

Time to rub up Spinach for Unkle Bill.

> Good Bye.
> Son.

[Verso]

Dear Dad,

Many happy returns of the day. Suppose it's time I sent you a letter or that you wrote to me. anyhow let us have peace. Enjoy yourself. as I have just remarked to mother 'it's time for me to get on the job'.

> EP

Remembrances to Grandmother & the Foots.

24 November 1904 was Thanksgiving. The Backus family lived in Rome, NY. Homer's and Isabel's wedding anniversary was on 26 November.

---

48. ALS

[26 November – 1 December 1904]

Hamilton. [College]

Dear Dad,

Certainly I can peg out till the fifteenth but it will take 35 or 40 then. I had to borrow the 60 cents car far for Thanksgiving & have had to get postage stamps on credit since having attempted to pay for books, paper etc. on Mon 18. & I have my laundry & football subscription & some class dues which I don't intend to pay. Was thinking of staying up here over Xmas but they have extended the vacation so that wouldnt pay.

I can go on borrowing postage stamps till the 15th but as I say it will take 35 or 40 then. & I'll need it on the mark. cheer up.

It would be more convenient to have $5 or 10 now but never mind. I'll draw 20. on a bond now if that will suit you better. Of course I know its wicked to borrow but if my credit wasn't good I couldnt send this charming billet, till the 15th.

Love to you & mother.

Good Bye.

E Pound

Cheer up it's the last year.

+≻═≺+

49. ALS

Friday [2 December 1904]

H[amilton College]

Dear Mother.

Had a rather enjoyable time in Ithaca. hear VanDyke sunday & Dr. Cuth, who was a personal friend of Browning's lecture monday both good spielers. Have been rather busy since I got back.

no particularly exciting news from the hill. You see why I haven't been out supporting democratic candidates for congress.

Hope the new guests are white.

Dont know just where I am at, three freshmen have been gassing here for a couple of hours.

Guess that's all.

everything O.K. Only I have enough stuff to fill my time from now till never.

Good night.

Much love to you & Dad.

son.

+≻═≺+

50. ALS

Sunday (9.15 a.m) [4 December 1904]

Hamilton [College]

Dear Daddy.

You asked a while ago about der vedge Σ.K. well I guess der grizis is past and ve air loogin upways. Committee of 8 discussed by-laws here last

35

evening & celebrated on cider & popcorn , as has been done a couple of times   previous.

So I guess she's sliding . & the hardest part of the job over. Sorry to hear Homer is sick. I dont suppose it would fit to get the Kid out into the country?.

Glad the dagoes are getting filled, otherwise::

Exams getting near. Have been reading Shakespeare, & Michael Field's 'Callerhoë', & an old '12th night mess up,' 'Narcissus'

Cyrano, still interesting. & as the Anglo Saxon is Aelfrics homilies & as the old boy sticks pretty closely to his vulgate it's comparatively easy for the day or so. Thanksgiving a comfortable bust in the routine.

Evening.

Love to you & mother.
Time for bath
Good Night.
E.P.

Homer, Homer Foote, Ezra's cousin.

⊹═══⊹

51. ALS

Thursday [8 December 1904]

H[amilton College]

Dear Mother

Two reviews & an exam tomorrow. & two weeks more on the job here. Will be home on the 24th. I don't know as there's anything of special interest.

Had a five oclock lunch with Dr. Hennessy in Utica yesterday.

Next morning

Exam in Parlamentary law gone O.K. Math reveiw decently done. time to get to Saxon.

Good Bye
Much love to you & dad.
Son.

⊹═══⊹

52. ALS

Sunday [11 December 1904]

[Hamilton College]

Dear Dad,

No news except that I'm going to make up some greek this vacation & take it next couple of terms for my A.B.

Exams on the program will get home the twenty fourth.

There's realy nothing to write. Same old round. Prex. preached this morning. Thank heaven Xmas is coming.

More than enough to do. A bit of time to read now & then.

Much love to you & mother.

Ezra Pound.

Pound had been admitted to the Latin-Scientific Course 'for such as offer German and French in substitution for Greek', and would consequently graduate Ph.B. (not A.B.) His attempt to get up his Greek did not lead to his passing any exams in Greek.

+⊱━⊰+

53. ALS

Monday [12 December 1904]

[Hamilton College]

Dear Mother.

Ang. Sax. exams tomorrow a.m. .

No great amount of time to read or to hunt for amusement. Spent an hour or more on greek this morning.

I've got quite a little to do on that job before Jan. 10 if I want it to be any use.

I'm a bit tired of half-baked languages though & I think I will enjoy the classic dialectum after I get respectably into it.

I suppose five languages will about fill my time next term also.

The skeleton may learn fencing sometime, I tried him yesterday for the first time & he shows readiness & fitness to learn.

I dont know that there's much to say except that I'll be glad to get home.

Suppose I ought to get on the job but guess I'll go to bed.

Much love to you & Dad –

Good night

Son.

P.S. You ask about weather - the snow for several weeks, or a month, about 15°. for an average I guess. havent time to bother with it.

Ang. Sax done O.K.

<hr>

54. ALS

(17 December 1904)

[Hamilton College]

Dear Father,

Your letter came this morning. Passed Ang. Sax Xam & have been plugging greek since. Knowing my preparation in said classic tongue you can appreciate the sprightliness of the job.

Guess it will keep me pretty busy from now till Jan 10

Friday.

Senior french done. on last ¼ of greek sentences. but still have enough reading & grammar to do to keep busy during vacation.

Sat. a.m.

Your check arrived . thank you very much.

Have handed in my Greek sentences, & have a breathing space before Spanish exam.

Much love to you & mother.
Good Bye
Son.

<hr>

55. ALS

Sunday night. [? 18 December 1904]

[Hamilton College]

Dear Mother,

Prex. gave a rather good review of Isiaha this morning.

Somebody talked in YMCA. about Law as a life work & I found a very decent article in the Fortnightly Review on Fiona Macleod

Also I have a nasty Spanish exam tomorrow.

I don't like the beastly language any better than I liked the people. it seems to have been made for the sole purpose of saying vile things easily. Sort of a loose lipped filthiness inseparable from it. And fools compare it with the Italian.

Guess I'd better go to bed & get spruced up for the conflict.
Much love to you & Dad.
Good Night.
Son.

Good Morning.
Nice Morning.
  EP.

+≻══≺+

56. ACS

[9 January 1905]

[New York]

Grand Central 8.20
  & the earth still revolves on its own axis once in 24 hrs.
  A. F. Looking much better.
  Everything O.K.
  Guess I'll go for the train

E. P.

+≻══≺+

57. AL

[10–11] (January 1905)

[Hamilton College]

Dear Mother:
  Passed Analyt. The faculty of mathematics in consultation could not fathom my method but the key problem demanded & equation & I wrote it.
  despite the formulae etc. supposed to be necessary thereto. & which I didn't know.
  Your letter here tonight. My reception in N.Y. not noticible in any way. A. F. looking much better & behaved very decently.
  I called in the evening & returned by 9.55.
  Things here comfortable.
  Please send my knife, & nail tools if you find them.
  Also if dad will send $10 the rest can wait till the 15th.
  Have been reading a few moments in Taine. The more I get of the man the more I respect him.

Guess we'll be able to work the at home scheme next winter
More in time.
Everything cheerful.
Good Bye

The mathematicians were apparently unimpressed by Pound's intuitive method: his transcript recorded a mark of zero for the examination in Analytic Geometry, and a failing grade E for the course.

58. ALS

[15–18 January? 1905]

Hamilton [College]

Dear Dad,

Comiserat supplies on hand. thank you very much.

No news here except that I am going to be transferred to some more advanced work in german, which will probably be more interesting.

Hope you are feeling considerably better by this time. Am preparing to go fuss around the library a bit — The janitor just in to discuss art & dancing & whiskey as a remedy for colds. - no I haven't the cold -

Everything O.K.
Much love to you & mother
Ezry
Remember me to Miss Whitechurch & Mrs Lovell

59. ALS

Thursday [19 January?] (1905)

Hamilton [College]

Dear Mother,

I've evidently got a very interesting course that will keep me ocupied about 25 hours per day.

Have been reading a bit more Taine. & if I can continue mechanicaly for the next three months. I ought to shovel in a quite sizable amount of 'booklarnin'. I find I'm requiring more exactness of myself which I suppose is good – (& the first sign of scholasticism?) –

Course. Saxon, German (Goethe's 'Egmont') French - Jr. (Molière 'Les Femmes Savantes' Sr. Fr. – Old French Poetry.) Spanish 'Galdos' Dona Perfecta.

(you may tell Miss Whitechurch & Mrs Lovell. I'm reading about 'a perfect lady.' even if the name sounds like a cheap cigar).

Eng. Lit. on the side.

– Tradegy in general.

Also Bibliography. Literary & Dramatic study of Book of Job – & Debate.

Breathing done seventeen seconds per diem at 8.23 11/35 A.M.

Don't be alarmned at the color of this paper: it realy isn't my fault.

Next A.M. going to breakfast.

Much love to you & dad.

E.P.

+≒≒+

60. ALS

Friday [27 January?] (1905)

Hamilton [College]

Dear Mother,

Chronicle of diddings.

Mon. Tue. Wed. on the job hard.

Wed. P.M. Señor Don Caballero BILL SHEP. gave a scrumbunctuous lecture on Mediaeval Poetry.

Yesterday I took a sort of day of rest. 2 hrs. on German & Saxon in A.M. 2 hrs. Bibliography P.M.

Evening went down to Clinton to see underclassmen put a Melodrama on the bum. The village cops rather bummed the Aufbummnsetzung, & the thing was only moderately exciting. merely a little howling etc.Today Sax. Fr. & Sp.

Want my glasses now I've started with them please send some extra & hustle the repairs - I suppose you got them O.K.)

Sr. French is going to be about my nicest job this term.

Your clippings interesting.

Remember me a las Doñas Perfectas.

Hope Pas ears are getting better.

Also as you've had a birthday many happy returns.

Molière's 'Femmes Savantes' very amusing.

German a bit difficult to take hold of again. Spanish going better.

Wish you could have heard Bill's lecture. You would have revised your opinion of your 'Smoke dried Skeleton'.

Enjoy yourself.

Much love to you & dad.

E. P.

I think next winter at home will be very nice.

In a letter dated 17 March 1917, EP wrote to James Joyce: 'I put on glasses at age of five or six, at about twenty I found . . . that an inharmonic astigmatism was supposedly driving toward blindness (probably very remote) and also twisting my spine.' His optician, Dr Gould, having discovered the required correction, 'I suddenly felt "a weight lifted", and have had practically no bother since.' (Pound/Joyce 100–101)

+‖‖+

61. ALS

[28 January – 1 February?] (1905)

[Hamilton College]

Dear Mother,

Temperature hasn't been below 20 below. & we haven't had anything terrible in snow line.

Bibliography is attracting my special attention just now.

It seems, or at least Paleographical end of it seems to be the collection of interesting things that history & literature over-look.

Were you aware that in VI century scholars used to come from all Europe to Ireland to study greek. – that is merely one item I've stumbled over. I got Putnam's 'Books and their Makers during the Middle Ages' two bully volumns, & may get a few more things if I can retain the σπονδην long enough.

Does Pa enjoy so much decoration on the exterior of <u>private</u> correspondence.

He can't get any money out of me with his advertisements. Although they are very nice.

It's very good to get letters from home though even if they are inartistiferous externaly

There is prospect of a gathering of three or four sane people to read & kuss & discuss various topicae literarum.

We began today by disecting Emerson's 'Self Reliance'. It happened to be a freshman 'rhet' assignment. So I butted in & helped 'em tear it out.

Joseph(us) Davis. Reminds me a bit of Jack Huntington. Huntington is out this year getting 'is 'ealth bolstered up. Guess we'll get quite a bit of fun out of the stuff & it will be good practise.

Next morning,

Have had a bewildering lecture on french philology & dutch to [?]

Good bye
with love
Ez

σπονδην, libation or drink-offering, but was Pound punning upon 'spondulics'.

+‖‖+

62. ALS

[2 or 3] (Feb. 1905)

Hamilton [College]

Dear Mother,

Have just been reading a mediaval account of the legendary pilgrimage of Charlemagne & of his first sight of & ride on a musical merry-go-round.

Thus is the study of philology & the search for the latin root made aggréablé. Bill gave a very inspiring lecture in Chapel Wednesday P.M.

The old French & Saxon are the chief matters of interest just now. Things chawin' along. My schedule is so arranged that I can bhone about 14 hrs. per. d without using any imagination as to where or what to do it on. Of course I'm not doing this, but I seem to be doing enough to keep my head above water. Oh yes, it's plenty cold up here, it frivolettes along from 20 below to 10 above pretty regularly. may be hotter or colder. I haven't had time to fool with thermometers.

Also madam you needn't begin to crow just because I happen to hear a little emmerson.

He and all that bunch of moralists.

what have they done? Why. all that is in their writings that's good is from the bible & the rest is rot.

They have diluted holy writ. They have twisted it awry. They have it is true weakened it sufficiently for the slack minded & given vogue to the dilutation. The chief benefit of reading them is this. You can't trust a word they say & the exhileration produced by this watchfulness for sophistries is the only benefit. The joy I get from the mediaevalians is this. You current eventers think you'r <u>so</u> modern & so gol darn smarter than anybody else that is a comfort to go back to some quiet old cuss of the dark, so called silent centuries, & find written down the sum & substance of what's worth while in your present day frothiness.

I'm not yelling anti-progress, but it's good to know what is really new

Only if you want to boast your progress stick to chemestry & biology etc. things that change per decade.

But for love of right mercy & justice. don't try to show off modern literature & brain quality

Oh yes. 'E'merson to make one think! (merely to detect his limitations)

But find me a phenomenon of any importance in the lives of men & nations that you can not mesure with the rod of Dante's 'Alegory'.

Symbolize the development, (the evolution if you will) of individuals & nations; the striving upwards, of humanity.

symbolize it so that your symbol shall be true for the ages.

Do it in emerson, do it with chemistry, do it with the new discoveries in agriculture. Pope, the superficial - in stamping into coin the gold of old thought made some remark about mans most fitting study being man, and untill you can show me men of today who shall excell certain men sometime dead, I shall continue to study Dante & the Hebrew prophets.

[But excuse me they had no watch cocks & electric motors and wilson & gibbs sewing machines. ergo, I should drop them & learn what is going on in the world. *This paragraph much struck over in pencil*]

Good night. I might become too sarcastic.

Much love to you & dad.

Lovingly

Son.

Remember me to Miss. W & Mrs. L.

Also in continuing I beg you not to think I praise Messire Dante Alleghieri merely because he wrote a book most people are too lazy to read & nearly all the rest to understand.

Ecce homo.

He fought in battles where he probably encountered much more personal Danger than Mr. Rooseveldt in Cuba. He also held chief office in his city & that for clean politics & good government.

Also he was a preacher. who will rank with Campbell Morgan in extent of his influence & some centuries before Luther he dared put a pope in hell & a pagan without its gates & prophecy the fall of the temporal & evil powers of Rome.

He was incidentally a poet a lover & a scholar & several other trifles served to round out his character although it is not recorded that he was President of a U. S. steel trust or the inventor of pin wheels. excuse me for not putting it more mildly. Of course if you don't want Dante, you can use a Bible. It's even better.

E.

---

63. ALS

[5 February?] (1905)

Hamilton [College]

Dear Mother,

Eveything going nicely, no special news. Football supper last night. Whole college in Commons, speeches etc. Prex, Square, Davy, etc.

Prex preaching today. Communion this afternoon.

Lit. Club at Bib's Friday evening. read part of Midsummer Night's dream together, ate & smoked.

Love to you & father & grandmother when she shows up.

Good night.

Son.

64. ALS

Thursday [9 February?] (1905)

[Hamilton College]

Dear Mother,

Plenty to do. Bill gave very enjoyable lecture yesterday. Am still sawing 'Books & their Makers'. Marivaux & Spanish, enjoyable also. Blew up Prex on subject of 'commons' & hope for improvement.

Call the Kaat daam or daamkins or Hickoryhellbenders, or Hiltydiltydevilty-damkins if you want a nice appropriate name. Also remember me to Mss. W. & Mrs. Lovell.

Have not seen any spots on the sun. Have a bid to eat in Rome tomorrow but it's too far to go for a meal.

Don't know much more that has happened. Everything calm.

Good Bye
Love to you & dad
Son.

+≻══≺+

65. ALS

Saturday (13 February 1904)

[Hamilton College]

Dear Mother,

Wheels still revolving. found your various bunches of stamps O.K. thank you quitely.

Next week is Prom. week. shan't . attend.

Θ.Δ.X. has invited me to their own dance Wednesday & I shall go to that. Nothing writable except book-titles. We begin Beowulf . pretty soon.

Am reading Anatole France 'Manequin d'Osier' for diversion. & shall today finish 'Vol. 1 Books & Makers'.

Work interesting, & about the only interruption is the necessary & healthy rough housing of O. P. Backus. He has provided boxing gloves as a substitute for general mix up & we have a text on Jiu Jitsu.

Have gathered a very decent gang of freshmen who have begun to meet here decently & in order on Tuesday evenings.

Guess that's all.

Remember me to Miss. W. & Mrs. L.

Much love to you & dad.
E.P.

+≻══≺+

66. ALS

Sunday, Feb. 12 (1905)

[Hamilton College]

Dear Dad,

Prex preached finely this A.M. on doing things <u>now</u>.

Since chapel I have visited around a bit & read about Japanese missions till the author began to try narrowly & bigotedly to detract from the Jesuit work there.

This fuss about catholic form & ritual makes me tired.

Do you go to a child in the infant class & preach infinite God? No. You tell it Bible stories & show it pictures.

The catholic church came when all men were as children, & gave them chance & made them worship wonderfully, by music, by cathedral building, by copying books, hour by hour, & year by year, when others were fighting.

And the men who now try to tear down its structure are little better than the rabble who broke the stained glass of the cathedrals a few centuries ago.

Admitted they have processions on Sunday in the slums.

Compare this part of the Roman church to the corresponding part of your own. – your colored exhorters - – or even churches that are supposed to possess culture. <u>and</u> <u>are</u> <u>you</u> <u>much</u> better off. I'm not arguing for modern catholicism by why in heavens name can't even the yellow journalism of our church give credit where it is due in the past.

Scuse this out burst.

only I guess there isn't much more to write.

Next week is Prom week, have bids to two of the dances as I believe I wrote.

Much love to you & mother
remember me to Mrs. L. & Mss. Whitechurch.
Son.

Monday.

This didn't get off this A.M. but things have gone on as usual. No new developments.

Good night.

Do you want to look up systems of shorthand and get me a simple 'begin-book' on the simplest method! Never mind if you haven't time.

E.

+≻·≺+

67. ALS

[16 February?] (1905)

H[amilton College]

Dear Mother,

Surprised that you let Dad have the next morning feeling after the Assay Commission.

Hope the rest did him good, but I don't approve.

Please don't worry about clothes.

I blew Prex in the library.

Saw Mrs. Prex at ΘΔΧ dance Wednesday & she behaved real well. Shall call amicably sometime in the future.

Today is 'off' to let the college in general recover from the prom. As I didn't attend I'm living easy. Have a bully stack of books on hand & am feeling joyous. will answer more in detail when I haven't the suspicion that the mail is going before I get through.

Love to you & dad.

Remember me to Miss W. & Mrs. Lovell.

Good Bye

Son

Thank dad for paper.

68. ALS

[22 February] (1905)

Hamilton [College]

Dear Mother,

Being as haow it's Washingtons Birthday. The monotony busts a bit. Heard the best Washington Spiel ever this a.m. & from an Englishman, a Dr. Cadmon.

he air a winner.

Have begun Beowulf & been reading Deutscher Gedichter & resting this day.

As soon as I enter a biled shurt I shall start for Senor Guillemus Pastor, alias Bill Shep. for to pay the same a call & return a book of french translations of O. F. & Provencal romances of XIII cent.

Don't worry about my pants. I don't know where the skeleton gets its raiment but I don't want any from the place wheresoever.

Much love to you & dad.

Thursday a.m.

Charming evening with Bill. have gathered stuff to start my studies in Provencal & extended work in Old French & learned what books I must gather from the four corners of earth.

I suppose 'Peire Cardinals' will be the particular troubadour that I shall study for the next couple of years.

Also stoped in to see Dr. Wood. & had very pleasant call.

Must go to the German translating so good bye.

If dad can find a copy. of Beowulf. Edited by A. J. Wyatt Published. by. Cambridge Press please send it right away. if necessary to order it don't get it. understand.

if there is a copy on hand get it. but no use if it has to be ordered.

No other edition wanted.

Good Bye
Son.

⊹⊱━⊰⊹

69. TLS

28 February 1905

Hamilton College

Dear Dad

Killing time before Dutch with Georege Day's type writer / Dont know that there is any thing in particular that I think of just now only I might as weel write to you as do anything else. Every thing moving smoothly. To go back to the begining of things Saturday. Got diligent and did Mondays stuff also some extra Old French. Sunday. Square Root gave a bully Spiel. Mentioned the fact that the people who hitch to stars need to see that the traces are in good condition. Also several other things of more exalted sentiment. He is a fine old Seer of the inside of things.

Monday as usual and today does not seem to be about to bring forth any new thing of great wonder. .

Time for Dutch. Good bye. Much love to you and Mother. Remember me to Mrs. Lovell and Miss Whitechurch.

Goodbye
Kid.

Feb. 28. 1905

⊹⊱━⊰⊹

70. ALS

(5 March 1905)

Hamilton [College]

Dear Mother.

Yesterday was quite a day. Two decent classes & two of tomorrows jobs done in A.M.

P.M. about two hundred pages of French on Raimon de Miraval troubadour of Provence.

Evening. Called on Bill he was pleased with what I had been about during week & is willing to give me some Dante which is not catalogued next term. as this is not usual I called on Little Greek who has charge of schedules in general & he brought forth his wife that I might be well received & seemed well disposed to the Dante arrangement.

Going on my homeward way at 10 P.M. I noticed Bib's lights ablaze & knowing that he is still mostly college boy despite his family & professorship I dropped in & we smoked & ate & talked for an hour or two longer. All three calls were very pleasant. Today we have been hearing wonders about medical missions

The Skeleton has just returned from his vine & icicle tree with eatables & it's time to go to bed.

Good night.

Much love to you & dad

Remember me to Mrs. Lovell & Miss Whitechurch. Also. considering my hasty announcement of my last gang feed I hereby give warning that on or about Apr. 5 I desire to have certain of my friends fed at dad's expense.

Guess that's all

Good night

Son.

---

71. ALS

[6–10 March?] (1905)

Hamilton [College]

Dear Mother,

Am amusing myself with grip or rheumatism or a sore throat or all of them together, so your coin arrived no too soon for extras.

Who wants anymore than $20 per. I got $6 on Feb 1. & 15 in the middle & supposed I had my march 1st due.

Dad never said anything about the last check lasting till the middle of this month. I supposed if I stayed up on this barren crest & didn't spend my stuff I could have it for books.

I shouldn't object to a hair cut either if I can get out & down to Clinton before all the V goes on imported grub. I am quite comfortably fixed. the skeleton brings in the grub & I warm it or cook it on Walt Jones chafing pan.

Got to crawl out tomorrow as my cuts are about gone. As to my extravagance this term I have been off the hill four times, twice on faculty calls,

twice to theatre	1.25
(car fare to Utica	25
	———
	1.50

Under conditions of commons grub I do not consider $1 per week for extras at Madam Kelly's as terribly wild. especialy, when one considers that no self respecting man can expect men to bring their own tobacco to his apartments merely that he may have the appearance of being host in his own room. Wherefor. I claim that 5. per month to 'hold up your end' isn't mad. Now $5 per & Laundry & Books & by the way I need $15 or 20. of Philological stuff sometime between now & commencement, aside from course books etc. Also I must order a gown very soon.

Guess I'll stretch out the folds of my back & daub up my epiglottis with vaseline.

Cheer up I ain't going to croak.

Love to you & dad

Good Bye

Remember me to Mrs. Lovell & Miss Whitechurch

E.P.

Thank you muchly for the coin.

EP.

⊣⊨⊨⊩

72. AL

Monday [7 March 1905]

[Hamilton College]

Am on the job & feeling very good. Yours here. Only when I get used to using female physicians there'll be, oh Mother. I suppose you get excited when you hear I got a pain but - specimens of your advise would get me in the gook house if carried out.

1. 'Drink plenty'
2. Get a she doctor (from utica with 5 in clinton that wear pants)
3. Eat ten tons of drugs. etc ad inf

Anyhow I've got over it.

Will forward your Burn-o-quirote by freight.

Have a fill on the house.

This wont get mailed if I dont quit now so I end.
Cheer up am rejoicing in health.

Love to you & dad.
remember me to Mrs L & Miss W.
Everything O.K.

＋═══＋

73. ALS

Sunday (14 March 1905)

[Hamilton College]

Dear Mother,

Nothing in particular to write. Am feeling considerably better. shall go out tomorrow. I suppose I needed a rest. havent read much or done anything else.

I get home Apr. 5 at about 11.30 A.M. & want the feed that afternoon at four thirty as other vacations end then instead of beginning.

I get about nine days off. Crowd about same size as last time.

if you can rope in her ladyship Miss Harriet Quick you may do so but for St Satan's sake don't try to get a substitute if you cant, for I have no confidence whatsoever in your choice of women.

Man here that will mail this so I quit.

Good bye
Love to you & dad
Remember me to Miss Whitechurch & Mrs Lovell.
E.P.

＋═══＋

74. ALS

[13 March 1905]

H.[amilton] C.[ollege]

Dear Mother,

Your letter received. I feel more comfortable thanks awfully. I suppose I'd better adress a letter to father, pretty soon. Only it's all the same.

Things here pleasant for March.

guess I will transport this down hill & get it off this evening.

Have been to four houses today which rather fills the time, ergo no excitement since last night.

Love to you & dad. remember me to Mrs Lovell & Miss Whitechurch.

Good Bye.
With lots of love for you & dad.
E.P.

got note from Dr. Child saying he was glad I was to be at Penn. next year & asking if he could be of any assistance to me in any way.

<hr />

75. ALS

March 15 (1905)

Hamilton [College]

Dear Dad,

Dont know that there is much to write. am merely on the job. Chanson de Roland as extra just now.

Everything running smoothly. Have been measured for gown. Gown & cap. will come to about seven scaddi (6.70 exact) I believe.

As I said, nothing special. The gang met here last evening (Tuesday) peacibly & enjoyably. Shall probably go to senior club tomorrow.

Remember me to everybody.
Much love to you & mother.
Good night.
Son.

<hr />

76. ALS

[c.20 March 1905]

H.[amilton] C.[ollege]

Dear Mother,

There aint no details. I just get up & go to classes & eat etc. I got a Clinton doc. same as bifore & I now owe him 3 scaddi. I have paid 5 scaddi of laundry bill . have gown & cap coming. have paid for having my grub sent over while sick.

have had a hair-cut so the first thing I need to do when I get home is to see a tailor. By the way there is a ghost of a chance that I may escape Fri. Mar 31. so please get dad to ship my return coin in season. I shall bring a trunk.

You scorned my suggestions about the cat. What kind of soap does the dog use. has he fleas will he squeak.

So Doc. aren't going to get his fare paid how cute, evidently I'm not the only pebble that won't get chucked across the pond. Well I can make enough to pay my way which is more than the Doc. can do.

I don't expect to eat at 4.30. that's the time the show begins well eat about ¼ to 6 same as last time.

One week more & then exams.

'Davy Dav' preached this A.M. & talked some idealized horse sense which is rare.

My extra work with Bill next term will be in Provencal 'The Troubadours of Dante'.

Remember me to Miss W. & Mrs. L.

Love to you and Dad
Good night
Son.

P.S. You can get Mai Reed for the 5th if you like. Only send a civilized invitation if you do. Don't get the coachman to ask her mother.

---

77. ALS

[27 March 1905]

H.[amilton] C.[ollege]

Dear Dad,

Exams in Spanish & Bibliography off today. Ang. Saxon tomorrow.

$15 will do for expenses but need $6.50 more for cap & gown which I got today.

Have exams next four days straight & may be able to leave Friday but it is a bit unlikely. Please send coin so I can leave then if things fit.

15. will leave me a very narrow margin & if you have one or two loose you might drop 'em in. Can hole out though but it will be vara close.

Had a shock sunday. 'Schmidts.' der potentate met me in the middle of a mud puddle & informed me his wife desired my presence at dinner.

Had no idea I so stood in with the dutchman. Had a charming time, good eating and some old books of interest. Visited with 'Bugs' for an hour or so in the evening & ended up with Dr. Wood. Guess that's all the bulletin this evening.

Love to you & mother
Luck to your dago fund.
Son.

Monday evening

---

78. ALS

[28 March 1905]

H.[amilton] C.[ollege]

Dear Dad,

Am supposed to be bhoning for Dutch Xam. Thank you much for coin. Won't be home till wednesday. Leave here Tuesday apr. 4. Had charming evening with the dean. only he won't let me out friday. Prex wants to be remembered to you.

Spring weather. Ought to get on the job.

Love to you & mother.

E.P.

79. AL

[29 March 1905]

[Hamilton College]

Dear Mother,

4 xams did. Old French tomorrow. There wont be any feed party as I can't get a quorum.

I won't be able to leave here till Tuesday, u.a.d.e.

Love to you & dad.

Remember me to Mrs. L. & Miss Whitechurch.

Ought to get on the job.

Good Bye

Wed. evening.

80. ALS

[12 April 1905]

H[amilton College]

Dear Mother,

Passed Job xam yesterday. Have seen Prex. Bill Squires & Bill Shep. . Made arrangements to get cream in mornings & take 6 or 7 meals per week at commons. which will I think prove satisfactory as I don't have to pay my commons bill in advance. Dad can hold back $30 of the check he was to send Apr. 15 & send it $15 May 1 & $15 June 1. if that will be more convenient for him.

I have no cuts this term. but it don't worry me as there were only a few of them I could have used to advantage.

Guess I'll turn in more tomorrow.

Love to you & dad.

Remember me to Las doñas Perfectas.

E.P.

Everything O.K.

*Pound had received an 'E' for **Job** the previous term, and was required to re-sit the exam.*

+⊱━━⊰+

81. AL

[13 April 1905]

H[amilton] C.[ollege]

Dear Dad,

Have run a successful bluff at several recitations today. & held my kindergarten session.

Otherwise nothing startling since I wrote last evening. Played a bit of tennis. Applied to the dept. of chemistry for credit for two hours experimental work. due to fact I am getting two meals a day for myself. 'Stink' said the subject came under Advanced Psycology so no action has been taken

Hope you have pleasant trip to N.Y.

+⊱━━⊰+

82. ALS

[14–15?] (April 1905)

H[amilton College]

Dear Mother,

Things moving pleasantly.

My course as you know is pleasant.

Old Spanish. The Cid

Old French. Chansons de Geste

Old Provencal. The Troubadours

Old English. Chaucer.

Jean Paul Richter's German

& the Physics Prof. as much fun to watch as Keller, or any slight of hand wonder.

You can mail me 1/4 lb. Ackers best pulvarized Java coffee, if you please.

Snow this afternoon but spring is coming about July 1.

Guess I'll bathe & go to bed.

Love to you & dad.

Good night.

E.P.

━━━━

83. ALS

Sunday 16 April (1905)

H[amilton College]

Dear Dad,

Yours received, thank you ($90).

Getting under way smoothely & am going to take things a bit easier. 'Square' Root preached this A.M. on not being weary in well doing.

don't know that there is much to report.

Weather cold with snow flurry.

Love to you & mother. Will write to Chippewa some time soon.

Remember me to Mss. W. & Mrs. L.

Also give my regards to the dog.

Guess that's all. & will now go in quest of a postage stamp.

E.P.

Sunday.

Apr. 16

━━━━

84. ALS

Tuesday [18] (April 1905)

H[amilton College]

Dear Mother,

Your letter here. have had my kindergarten this evening, after which Dick Elsey & I put in some grub at commons, sandwitches & coffee to wit.

I get my lunch at Madam Kellys. Toast. Coffee, apple Pie without tacks & garden hose and such like trifles of fascabulistria.

You can get seats at the mask & wig for less than $4. so cheer up. you've got the advance sale reports or something off.

Also Ive enough collors here to ware for some time but I earnestly desire my diamond tiara gold shoe buckles & my jeweled gallouses.

56

Next day.

Paid tuition today. The ten dollar graduation fee has to be paid now so I should like an extra X as soon as.

'Pop' Weber is going to New York & wants to see the stock exchange. Can you send to your relatives the enclosed envelope & have them enclose permits & remail it to him. He will be there from saturday till Wednesday so please hurry.

Coffee arrived this evening thanks.

The last of this letter ought to be to Dad as he is chiefly concerned.

Anyhow I want him to have sent to Leon Jenks, Hamilton College, Clinton N.Y. such publications of mint or treasury dept. as contain information on chemistry or Assaying, s.v.p.

Guess that's all for tonight.

Much love to you & Dad.

Remember me to Mrs. L. & Miss W.

Son

Weather fine. Have been getting circulated around the country & bit.

Also paid Doctor for last term ($3.)

Mask and Wig was a University of Pennsylvania musical and dramatic society. Joseph John Weber (1877–1946), and Leon Jenks (1876–1940) both graduated with the class of '05, the latter as Bachelor of Science.

+≻—≺+

85. ALS

[19 April] (1905)

H.[amilton College]

Yes'm, the glasses is com.

There don't seem much sense in scrawling trifles with history making itself on the other side of the world.

Bill Shep. course of Lectures on Mediaeval things, goes on in Chapel wednesday afternoons. Todays less interesting to me personaly because there was less new to me in it. But the one last week was a beauty. The work in old French absorbing. & Moliere 'tres amusante'

German stupid. Spanish improving, Saxon as usual. Bib gave some decent points on Hamlet yesterday. only he gives one ore instead of metal usualy. .

Did you notice the name W^m. C. Williams in that mask & wig list. .? Myra have anything to say?

Much love to you & father. Remember me to Mrs. Lovell & Miss Whitechurch.

57

Got to get to bhoning Deutch. Ach sphidgch.

Good night
Son.

How be you all. What's my daddy doin'?

Also Benissimo Salutes a Signores Perazini & Sanhtis

> *The events making history **on the other side of the world** were probably the failed Russian revolution of 1905, and the war between Russia and Japan—the capture of Mukden in March had completed the defeat of the Russian forces in Manchuria.*

86. ALS

[24?] (April 1905)

HAMILTON [College]

Dear Mother,

Got your letter this a.m. Hope you had a pleasant Easter.

Heard Prex. a.m. Called on Bill Shep in P.m. & went to Grace Church in Utica in the Evening. music excellent. Merely by way of parenthesis I want to say that the extra $10 I had to fork out for Graduation fee has left me very short. & while I could stand siege for a week. you would add to my menu by sending two or three plunks at once. for he that hath not rocks the same shall not eat in the desert places. My menu today was pleasant but my larder will be low eer the first day of ye coming month of May so please remit.

but to return. I spent a pleasant afternoon with Bill.

We worked from Trout Fishing to Old French & back by way of some most excelent parodies, one on our friend Mr. Browning's Ring & the Book, which would I believe please Miss Whitechurch.

But to the point. I have added eggs to my bill of fare. & have forty thousand three million & three things to do before to morrow. Wherefor

With love to you & Dad.
E .P.
Remember me to Miss W. & Mrs. L.
E.P.

Oh yes. Called on Bib & Dr. Wood Friday, they are living together so it is quite convenient.

Also spent an evening with Dr. Hennesy in Utica. I don't know as you will recognize the name without the feminine ending on Dr. But as I said I have things for tomorrow.

Good night
E.P.

87. AC

[3] (May 1905)

H.[amilton] C.[ollege]

Dear Dad,

Yours received scaddi quindecem plunks fifteen thank you.

Things moving along as usual. One more month & most of my work is over. June being rather a formality than anything else.

The Cid. is extremely interesting & other stuff going well.

Got posted above 9.3 in Physics review so even that is moving well.

Much love to you & mother
There goes chapel bell.
Good Bye.

Wed. A.M.

By the way you may be interested in this translation of the Bilengual Alba or Dawn Song. It is in mediaeval latin with Provencal refrain.

Oldest Provencal written. MSS of 10th century & song probably older.

I give 3 versions of refrain as spelling of time was unfixed & meaning is ergo not absolutely determinable. The first is I think best & closest.

'Belangal Alba' was printed in the Hamilton Literary Magazine *in May 1905, and reprinted as 'Alba Belingalis' in* Personae (1909).

88. ACS

May 4. [1905]

H.[amilton] C.[ollege]

Dear Mother,

Being out of stamps I send this tonight. Have written Dr. R.E.T. stating my training in 8 languages besides my own & if he wont resign in my favor he may get me a position as bellboy. Bought a pair of low brown heavy shoes, about 10 ft long, this P.M. & played a bit of tennis.

Will answer your letter & fathers sometime. Will look up Wadsworths on return if have time.

Good night.
E.P.

Dr R. E. Thompson was President of Central High School, Philadelphia—Pound was evidently applying for a teaching post.

89. ALS

Sat. [6 May 1905]

H.[amilton] C.[ollege]

Dear Father,

Received coin last evening thank you very much.

Everything going very nicely.

Made my dinner call at 'Schmity' Brandts last evening. I am managing to keep my work in the A.M. & get out on the tennis courts in the afternoons. weather now fine.

Hope you enjoyed N.Y.

am now ready to drop in on Bill Shep. after which I may see if any one is at home a few houses further on.

Guess that's about all now.

Love to you & mother

E.P.

Remember me to Miss W. & Mrs. L.

Will write more tomorrow.

E.P.

+>=—=<+

90. ALS [*letterhead*] Hamilton College, Clinton, N. Y.

Sunday [7 May 1905]

[Hamilton College]

Dear Mother.

I have just finished my first draught of Giraut de Bornehls Tenzon.

'S-ie-us. quier conselh, bell ami Alamanda'.

It contains sixty eight lines & only five rime sounds. & has been a stumbling block to several.

Of course the translation isnt over yet. but ive got my rime scheme & a translation to fit it . . that is to say its done only it isnt.

Prex preached a philological sermon this a.m. Good Y.M.C.A. this P.m.

pleasant call on Bill Shep . last evening.

Monday.

On the job again.

Good Bye

Son.

Love to you & Dad.

+>=—=<+

91. ALS [*letterhead*] Hamilton College, Clinton, N. Y.

Saturday P.M. [13] (May 1905)

[Hamilton College]

Dear Mother,

Bill lectured on 'Tristram' yesterday. otherwise nothing out of the ordinary.
Sunday.

Prex preached A.M. Good speaker at Y.M.C.A.

Am enjoying life. Guess that's all. Things nearly over. Three weeks of regular work & then a bunch of exams. & physics continuing a bit longer.

Guess I'll quit & go to bed.

Lovingly
Son.

Love to you & dad.

Remember me to Mrs. Lovell & Miss Whitechurch.

Good night.

E.P.

Dick & I been spending evening together. Ice cream at commons as diversion allthough the heat is by no means oppressive.

⊹⊱══⊰⊹

92. ALS

[14] (May 1905)

H.[amilton] C.[ollege]

Dear Dad,

I have no receipt from Embick. (answering ? in letter of May 1).

Have had a couple of track meets here during week. which has relieved me of a couple of spanish recitations.

Two weeks more of full pressure.

The french exam comes two weeks from Wednesday & I ought to do some hitting only probably won't. Am managing to keep out doors a bit which is probably better for me.

Remember me to Miss. W. & Mrs. L.

Much love to you & mother.

Hope your Italian mortgage money is coming well.

Monday A.M.
Chapel bell going.
Your letter in.

Good Bye
Son.

The **Italian mortgage money** *was for the building of the First Italian Presbyterian Church which Homer was helping found in Philadelphia city. (Further mentions in letters* ***99, 100,*** *and* ***185.***)

╬══╣╬

93. ALS
[15] (May 1905)

H.[amilton] C.[ollege]

Dear Mother.

Yours received. Also a very pleasant letter from Dr. Thompson. Job already promised but he will keep me in mind – warm interest in future etc.

Sure I'll take job in C.M.A. Latin or English dept. (or Fr. & German if necessary.)

have mislaid Furner's address so dad can put him on. I could hold down Latin at Cheltenham with less trouble than any other job I could get.

Fudge with tutoring. will try kindergarten if you like better. exception. Anybody desiring a tutor for traveling can have me at special rates.

There realy isn't any thing up here to make it of use to come up for commencement.

Guess I'll retire to me downy lectulum.

Love to you & dad.
Good night.
E.P.

lectulum: *accusative of 'lectulus' (Latin), meaning 'a little bed'.*

╬══╣╬

94. ALS
[16] (May 1905)

H.[amilton] C.[ollege]

Dear Dad,

I don't know how your memorandum works.

On original plan there was

	15.00	allowence for May
Board	16.00	since I didn't pay advance
Grad Fee	10.00	which I paid out of other funds
	───	
	41.00	

62

of this I received 5. Apr. 27
15. May 3
10. ʻ 19
—
30

How do you think I can eat & buy shoes & pay base ball & class dues & get books –($5 worth I should have payed for with money I advanced for 'grad' fee).

Also I've got to have another pair of pants unless I want to wear my best suit to bum round campus in & tennis shoes.

The figures I gave you were as close as possible & made no allowance for anything. - I am trying to keep inside but I can't go any less, especialy without warning.

Love to you & mother.

E.P.

& please get the other $11 off pretty soon.

+>━•━◄+

95. ALS

[17] (May 1905)

H.[amilton] C.[ollege]

Dear Mother,

First exam 1 week off. time not superabundant.

guess I was too vicious in my letter to dad but he has gotten twisted somewhere & Ive had to borrow the price of my dinner for three days the check not arriving till this A.M.

I've got to begin stuffing for French exam which covers two whole years work, not merely the last term . & comes a week from wednesday.

Weather wet & damp, no tennis . nothing but the job.

Went to Bill's last evening but he was finishing up some proof so I retired & played a bit of chess with the Watsons. I need some of that variety of exercise in worst sort of way . to untangle the kinks in the philological part of my nut.

Believe I told you I had nice letter from Dr. Thompson.

Got to go to dutch.

Good Bye.

Son.

Watsons *was a drug store with chess tables in the rear, in Clinton, about a mile from Hamilton.*

+>━•━◄+

96. ALS

Saturday [20] (May 1905)

H.[amilton] C.[ollege]

Dear Mother,

Things as usual.

Walt Jones took me to a dance in Utica yesterday & had more fun than since I left home. Jo Davis is going to feed me tomorrow.

Week more of grind & then I'll have a bit of leisure.

Guess that's all.

Love to you & dad.

Remember me to Mrs L & to Miss Whitechurch and the people at Tioga.

Goodbye.

Son.

*Walt Jones, class of '08, was in Pound's Tuesday evening freshmen group; **Jo Davis** was Jones's roommate. **Tioga** was the district of Philadelphia where Susan Angevine Loomis, his paternal grandmother, lived, and also his Foote cousins. **David Foote** is mentioned in Pound's 27 May letter.*

97. ALS

[21 May 1905]

H[amilton] C[ollege]

Dear Mother,

Got notice from Furner & have replied. concerning C.M.A.

Had a very pleasant evening at dance Friday & spent the night with Jones. Yesterday I had dinner & supper with the Davises in Utica & came back this A.M. Took Stephen Philips 'Herod' on car in & out.

Guess I'll manage to rake up a new enthusiasm didn't know Steve was so there with the goods. Took Stevenson's 'Wrong Box' as mental cocktail Saturday to relieve serious workings of me massive intelek.

Am very broke having foolishly paid for three dollars worth of books & delivered several scaddi to Madam who getteth me lunches & occasional breakfasts, etc as before specified.

(My Utica trips were economies as I got thereby 5 meals for $.65 counting church collection in expenses. I have a quarter for tomorrow dinner & the same for Wednesday whereafter I beg, sell or borrow or extend my credit system.

Dad has got twisted somewhere. He has three sets of memorandi and is correct according to one.

There is my board money which was to come $15 on May 1 & 15 on June 1. & there was the first memorandum I gave him & he will have to add & get the sum if he expects me to exist. scuse me for kicking but I am far from home & facing starvation & am going to stop being a dead loss to the family before long.

don't want anybody to starve on my account or get excited or anything. only -

Cheer up.

And you needn't quit writing even if you are broke. Guess I'll quit this. Will be home before such a great while.

Love to you and dad.

Good night.

E.P.

+≻═≺+

98. ALS

[27] (May 1905)

H.[amilton] C.[ollege]

Dear Dad,

It's Saturday evening & I am going to quit work till Monday, they can give their bloomin French exam prize to who ever they feel like.

Bib & Dr. Wood. gave the senior class a very pleasant reception Thursday night. Mrs. Ibbotson asked after mother & if she were coming up for commencement.

Your letter asks about money.

The memorandum as you have it is as I gave it to you at home. I suppose. please remember that I did not pay my board bill in advance as figured on. ergo there is $4 per wk. to be added to my allowence. wherefor instead of $15 & $10 you may send me $20 & $20. You remember you were to send me at the first of the term money for tuiton. room & <u>commons</u> & I am not in commons. & the $48 for commons didn't come then. but was to be sent in sections to pay my eating expenses wherever I might eat – – – is it clear. hope so. Thanks.

Wrote to Furner in answer to his notice C.M.A. no news as yet.

Congratulate David on his age. next time you see him, better late than never.

Tell mother I'm wearing me new pants.

Tell mother I am going to loaf from now on till commencement & take some of my next winter work in the summer school & then loaf till C.M.A. or wherever I go opens so that during the winter I won't be taking a whole course at Penn and teaching too. and as for my physical condition as long as I can run a half in my clothes with the galooks that are supposed to be trained & play five or six sets of tennis in real sun & since I am taking now 50% more work than the regular seniors, I am able to take nutrition & am not entirely a corpse. so she & Furner needn't compare notes on my going into a decline. Also I am graduating the youngest in my class & with the rep. of being the best read man therein & am not going to kill myself cramming for prize exams. he dicho. After this bombast I subside into calm.

I am not an authority on Bartram Gardens or Country fairs for libraries, but I presume they are O.K.

Oh by the way. is there a fellow in Phila. by the name of Weaver. There's a rumor that he has Hearst & Depew. beaten for 1908 at Washington by the iz. Where is Jimmy Miles during the tornado. I hear everything getting cussed but Unkle James. has he wormed out of the presidency of councils into the peace of the sheriff's job? or what?

But as I was about to soliloquize. Mathew S. Quay being no longer on the quarter deck the ship of state is wiggling a bit ain't she? -

To change the subject. I have written to Wyncote church for my letter. Thought it would be a good thing to be enrolled in the college church here before I left.

That's about all I think of now.

Love to you & mother
Good night.
Son.

---

99. ALS

[31] (May 1905)

H.[amilton] C.[ollege]

Dear Mother,

The battle is over & if my name don't end in - ovitch or -umfztzkjj I may get a ten cent honor.

I went boldly into action & am now finished. & await the press reports which will not come for several weeks.

from the above you may deduce that I have taken ze French exam and am now breathing after the conflict. if I am licked it is because somebody else knew more than I did not because I didn't do me damndest. 6 hours scribbling at '440 to the dot' is almost a day's work.

Glasses arrived early this A.M.

Glad to know you are festivising in Johnie's front yard When do I leave Clinton? June 29.

Jones is one of my kindergarten & V.P. of club.

dance in private hall. Davis. room-mate of Jones, spent last Saturday night in my own boudoir since you inquire.

Spent yesterday training for today's exam.

P.M. drive with Miss Baxter, that family being about the whitest I have discovered in these desolate regions. Guess I have wiggled a pen about enough for one day.

Good night.

Love to you & dad.

Son.

Remember me to Miss W. and Mrs. L.

Tell dad his dago coin seems to be coming slow but shure.

E.P.

+≻═≺+

100. ALS

[1] (June 1905)

H.[amilton] C.[ollege]

Dear Dad,

Your letter here thank you. Its so comfortable to have it in on the dot. I have been resting today that is I went to physics, played tennis three hours, & have just finished my spanish exam.

that is its all done, but still needs some revision. – no I dont take it in a classroom, it's outside work.

Sorry but it will be inconvenient for me to help you lay the corner stone. Glad to hear mother is having some frivolity.

Guess that's all that has happened since last evening.

With love

Son.

+≻═≺+

101. ALS

[5–6] (June 1905)

H.[amilton] C.[ollege]

Dear Dad,

Glad you've gotten some sort of a job any how. Will try to write a respectable letter sometime soon.

Glad your Italian fund is filling. will write when I am not so tired . dance other evening & tennis today & it's getting late .

Exams all done & gone except physics.

Love to you & mother .

E.P.

+≻═≺+

102. ALS

[12–13] (June 1905)

H.[amilton] C.[ollege]

Dear Mother.

I don't know just where to begin.

Saturday, driving with Miss Baxter & supper at her house. (Baxter not being the name of the people I knew last year).

Sunday, went to Rome & fed on the house of Backus. To day after Physics I went to Clinton & played chess with a celebrity the Watsons had garnered in for my amusement I managed to hold up 3 to his 5 games. & returned to commons for supper.

Friday before all this I played tennis till I was about dead. Wednesday night before that was the K.P. oration contest & freshmen dance. & I guess that's as far into the archives of the past as I can penetrate. there realy isn't much by way of writableness. Oh yes. Parlor paper. Guess I won't give any long distance advice, especialy as it can wait till my return in the role of le petit veal enbonpoint.

Also there's 6.50 class tax that I hadn't reconed in my expenses. I don't just know why but everybody has to soak up. commencement fol de rol etc.

Tuesday A.M.
Going to Physics review & then will mail this.

Love to you & Dad.

E.P.

+>===<+

103. ALS

[14 June 1905]

H[amilton] C[ollege]

Dear Mother.

Wednesday & a day of rest.

What do you & dad think about my taking a couple of courses at U. of P. summer school. July 5 – Aug 15.

I have thought it over rather carefully & as I have before me three weeks of rest I think I will be about ready for some light work. say Greek. French elocution & advanced Eng. comp.

perhaps some of it will count on my M.A. work. Things calm here. The Baxter family still make things a bit more pleasant for me than would otherwise be possible.

Guess that's about all.

Love to you & dad.

Ezra P.

+≻═≺+

104. ALS

Friday [16 June 1905]

H.[amilton] C.[ollege]

Dear Mother,

Weather realy warm at last.

Tennis yesterday A.M. with sun comfortably around 90.

Read some of T.L. Peacock in P.M. which same will return to library soon. I shall be wildly dissipated this evening & go to a strawberry vestibule in Utica.

Otherwise I am endeavoring strenuously to rest. Suppose my means of sustinence are underway (or under weigh as you prefer).

Am gradualy getting my household stored in trunk. if it weighs over 600 lbs. shall get reckless & have it crated.

Guess that's about all.

Love to you & dad.

Remember me to Mrs. L. & Miss Whitechurch

E.P.

P.S. Tell Dad 'mi conducho es arrivato. XXVII Scaddi. 27.00 Rcd. Thanks.

EP.

+≻═≺+

105. ALS

Sat. A.M. [17 June 1905]

H.[amilton] C.[ollege]

Dear Dad,

Coin in last evening. Thank you. If I squeeze a bit out of the French prize Xam guess I can hole out. Pleasantly warm here raining just now. Nothing exciting has taken place since last evening.

Strawberry vegitation enjoyable.

My shoulders feeling pleasant where the tennis tan has leaked over the accustomed boundries.

69

Well. I go to Clinton to get the shoes I left there to be half-soled. & this note goeth likewise with me also yet. Yes. Yes.

Good Bye

.Kid.

+⇒—=+

106. AL

[19–21] (June 1905)

H.[amilton] C.[ollege]

Dear Mother,

Yours received. Sell that tutor idea with a discount unless you can find some dam fool millionaire on the travel. I've been doing nothing long enough & shall work this summer. If I can get any sort of a job.

Shall get home July 1.

will stay to Senior ball commencement evening if I get enough out of french exam coin.- results announced saturday.

Spent Sunday at Baxters. & have been reading Scott & Stevenson & using plunge since then.

Guess that's about all.

Love to you & dad

Strange - I thought it had been raining rather hard, too.

+⇒—=+

107. ALS

June 22 (1905)

H.[amilton] C.[ollege]

Dear Dad,

Your fatherly advice at hand. all exams passed & over with except Physics which comes Saturday a.m. As to coin to get home on.

Have about enough to live on for a week ergo. About 15. for travel $3. bills unpaid . + 2. extr.= 20 . and for convenience you may ship it as soon as may be. Monday at latest, i.e. monday night.

Called at Baxters last evening & am resting for Physics exam.

Must quit & get this mailed.

Love to you & mother.

E.P.

+⇒—=+

108. ALS

Friday [23] (June 1905)

H.[amilton] C.[ollege]

Dear Mother,

Today have had several rough=houses, played a bit of chess with a freshmans kid brother, prepaired some 100 odd pages of physics eaten some Campbells soup, etc.

Heard from W^m C WIlliams last evening. he fell on my neck over several pages. Guess the gang treated him square. or he seems to think so anyhow. He wanted to be remembered to you & Dad. He & Van Cleve were coming out to call . but Van got sick & went home so it was aufgebusted.

Remember me to Mrs. L. & Miss. Whitechurch. .

Love to you & dad.
Will arrive home shortly. Guess that's all.
Good Bye
Lovingly Son.

---

109. ALS

[28] (June 1905)

H.[amilton] C.[ollege]

Dear Dad.

Conducho arrivatio scaddi 20. Thank you.

Beat out Eddie Root in French & came in 2nd. for 20. Eiserman getting 1st. Commencement formalities tomorrow & then the chapter is ended.

Two letters from mother & some mild idea about my being vice consul to sibolulia. - all right. I'd just as soon go if there's anything in it. Thank the ladies perfectas. when I know more of it I will say more. Guess I'll get this into the mail. will be home too soon to make details worth while.

Love to you & mother.
E.P.

In October 1905, 'Mr Ezra Weston Pound' was registered as a regular candidate for the degree of Doctor of Philosophy in the Graduate School (Department of Philosophy) of the University of Pennsylvania. No letters are preserved from the Fall and Spring semesters of 1905–6, when he was living at home with his parents while working for the MA in Romance Languages. Six of his seven courses were in Provençal, Old French, Italian, and Spanish, and were taught by Dr Hugo A. Rennert, a Spanish specialist; the seventh was a 'Latin Pro-Seminary' on Catullus and Martial with Dr Walton Brooks McDaniel. Rennert encouraged Pound to go on to do research towards a PhD, and secured for him a Harrison Foundation Fellowship worth $500 and tuition fees. His doctoral *thesis, to be prepared under Dr Rennert's direction, was to be a study of the 'gracioso' in the plays of Lope de Vega. With the instalments of his Fellowship in prospect Pound set off, as soon as he had fulfilled the requirements for the MA, to commence his research in the libraries of Madrid, Paris, and London. He sailed from New York on the 'König Albert' on 28 April and landed in Gibraltar on 7 May.*

+⟫━⟪+

110. ALS [*letterhead*] Dampfer 'König Albert', Norddeutscher Lloyd, Bremen
Sat. A.M. [28 April 1906]

[crossing the Atlantic]

Dear Mother,
 Safe on board, have seen Althouse but am not yet introduced to party. Those I have seen look quite respectable. Introduction by letter to some friends of Miss Kittie Davis.
 All well at the Weston. State room satisfactory boat seems good. Havent got my feet wet as yet.
 Guess that' s all.
 Be good to yourself & dad.
 Love to you. both .and remember me to Mrs Lovell & Miss Whitechurch.
Lovingly,
Ezra
Bunch of unassorted mail. have already found two letters.
Thank Dad for telegram.
EP
3 french gunboats in N.Y. harbour.
Got bully letter from Gen Woodruff to his 'Excellency' etc. Bill Collier.

The Weston at 28 East 47th Street was where Aunt Frank ran her boarding house.

+⟫━⟪+

111. ALS [*letterhead*] Dampfer 'König Albert', Norddeutscher Lloyd, Bremen
[2 and 7 May 1906]

[crossing the Atlantic]

Dear Mother.
 4th day out. boat steady as a clock, everything good but the pens.
 Captain's dance last night.- extreme work, due to scarcity of males.
 Senorita Martinez daughter of Chile's minister (who is on board with family.) Certain other people who are pleasant but whose names convey nothing.

San Francisco survivor from Caruso. Co. with whom I talk a mixture of Ital. Span. & French. Brightest man on board a Dominican Monk from Ottawa. Canada. – Makes our average preacher Rev. D D. etc. look like a bean hill. Broad & sound. Raymond Rouleau of the freres precheurs in co. a funny kindly little German 'welt' priest and a bishop. whom they say is a very good man & who seems to think that his being bishop excuses him from trying to impress people., With M. Rouleau I talk French & english on Dante middle ages, things in general. & u.a.d.e. think he is about the best thing on the ship.

Miss Harding, Middletown N.Y. also refrains from boring me. in which she is accompanied by Miss Stanley. – Beside which the passenger list is as usual. – good. not wonderful: weather a dream so far. & boat a wonder of steadiness. guess this suffices for now.
Wed. May 2. before dinner.

Arrive. Gib. This P.M.
all ink stands busy.
Gen. Gill of Baltimore is I think the only other important passenger on board. whom I have not mentioned. The sea has been a mill pond all the way and I have eaten two month's rations in the last week. Another dance. Captain's dinner & I think no other excitements. been reading Kipling's 'From sea to sea' & in general resting & feeding myself.

Had fine view of Azores. acc. guide book and colored like the best water-color in our parlour.

Realy nothing unusual except the calmness of the sea.

I shall stop at Hotel Bristol this evening. start tomorrow for Madrid. making my stop off or stops off where I find it convenient. Love to you & dad. & remember me to all the people who I might write to and don't.

I have enjoyed the passage

Kipling 'Imagine a shipload of people to whom time is no objcct with no desires but three meals a day & no emotions save those caused by a casual cockroach.' – for this voyage. deduct the cock roach, as the boat is clean.

With this word painting I end.

Love to you & dad.

Ezra Pound.

Hotel Bristol O.K.
Benamore going on to Madrid & will see me fixed.

Ezra.

112. ALS [*letterhead*] Fonda Simón, Grán Capitán, 7.

Mayo 8, de 1906

Córdoba

Dear Mother.

To Cordova without earthquakes. met an Andaluzian gentleman Texas broke, who was traveling with his nephew but gave me the greater part of his atention. He goes on to Madrid to night but will leave some adresses at Cooks for me in case Benamore's prove unsatisfactory.

I strolled about Cordova this P.M. with the lordly and indiferent mien which my common sense told me was the only escape from the 'muchachos'. it lasted till one squelched 'humoresco' began to bawl at a blocks distance. 'Alý. Senor de Cordoba Senor de Cordoba'.

I thought I might have overdone the part so I turned a corner & softened my sternness to an expression of benevolence. Wherat the 'populacho' took offence that I wore a black rain coat instead of a pink umbrella as is the custom in hither spain among the effete.

a gentleman with a rawhide whip, kindly decended from his cart and stoped their crys for 'perrito' & 'cigarillo' with the aforesaid whip, for which I thank him. after this I returned to my hotel where I patiently await an 8 o'clock dinner. Dont be alarmed at the math on this sheet, its merely computations for the trip to 'Alcazar'. by which I escape an all night ride. starting early tomorrow morning. Dined in Gib. last night with some steamer people so am pulling away slowly.

For tonight. With love to you & father

Ezra Pound

Pound wrote a more dramatic account of his adventure in a letter to Viola Baxter on 9 May:

I left Cordoba at such an early hour because the citizens of that part of the ancient city which lies most remote from civilization took offense at my keeping dry in [a] black rain coat instead of a pink umbrella & showed their displeasure by throwing ancient vegetables & fragments of the pavement at me.

It was caused in this fashion– I desired to see the town by myself – & not with the aid of a guide who would talk only about things I knew & be profoundly ignorant of everything I didnt.

I knew the only safeguard against the 'muchachos' was absolute regard for my own affairs wherefor I assumed said hauteur castellaño. It worked till one humorist, who had got a turn down, began to bawl at a safe blocks distance 'Senor de Cordoba' (Lord of Cordoba), 'ahi Senor de Cordoba.' Thinking I had perhaps overdone the part I turned the corner & went to the other extreme, i.e. gave a 'cigarillo' to a kid that wanted it. Whereat there were 5000 – – – – other 'muchachos' desiring smokes and perritos (so called because the people being indifferently educated in zoology mistake the little lion (of Leon) on their 5 centime (1 ct. U.S.) pieces for a bow-wow.

– I replied that I was not giving cigarettes to all Cordoba & to their 'cinco centavos!!' I made answer 'cinco diabolos! Vaya al diabolo.' – Whereat the street map of Cordova ((the houses put up wherever an old Moorish wall hadnt fallen down)) . . . became indistinct & I failed to find my route to the "Fonda Simon!

Whereat the before mentioned bouquets began to come my way. A ladylike mule driver stung by my sarcasms on Castillian courtesy kindly removed most of my following with his rawhide, for which I thank him – some of the 'militaire' formed in behind & I arrived without damage in the civilized part of the town.

＋＞—━＝＜＋

113. ALS [*letterhead*] Madrid Postal, Escritorio Publico
[10 May 1906]

Madrid

Dear Mother

Am charmingly fixed here in Madrid. - Senora Carmona - is the name of the boss. and tax 7 pesetas per day. that makes. $9.80 a week and is more than I expected to pay. but place seems charming and if you had spent the hour and ¼ as I did in inspecting the hotels of Madrid you would have grabbed the hospitality of aforesaid pension with avidity.

Senora C. speaks a beautiful Castillian which is also good. An american professor whose name I also forget spent 9 months there which sounds well.

Have started Cook's to get me return passage if possible on the Patricia - Holland American from Boulongue. July 8. Think I can hold out till then at present rates.

Will write more when I get time. Started out for a stroll before lunch and this is the result.

Love to you & dad.
EP

＋＞—━＝＜＋

114. ALS

May 13. (1906)

Madrid

Dear Dad,

Your note arrived too late to be of use for adresses. Am very well fixed. Library convenient, have found the 'Francessilla,' play I thought I might have to go to England for.

Dont know which is worse this ink or pencil.

Have been in library & galery & walked around town a bit. Finished & mailed my job for Mr. Chester.

My Spanish seems to work pretty well.

Next morning.

Rain as usual. I think I described my trip up in last note. Cordoba. Alcazar. Madrid country wonderful in color. poppies & all that sort of rot.

Dale? yes his bunch were the people who invited me to eat at their table in Gib. He comes here in a couple of weeks.

As my work 'volvers' to day I shall fuss up & present my classic mug at the embassy.

Suppose the tea fight will be over by the time this reaches you.

There will not be much variety in my letters until the kings wedding.

All the plays now 'on' are new & worthless. There will however be an 'Auto Sacramental' at the wedding jamifycation & will try to squeeze some copy out of it.

I go now to the library.

Good Bye.

Love to you & mother.

E. P.

*The **job for Mr. Chester** was possibly the article he was drafting a few days earlier, but if so it was not used. The **wedding** he hoped 'to squeeze some copy out of' was the marriage on 31 May 1906, of King Alfonso XIII to Eugenie Victoria of Battenburg—it so happened that there was an attempted assassination of the bridal couple on the day.*

+══+

115. ALS

May 18. (1906)

Madrid

Dear Mother,

Things continue pleasant. Half hour with his nibbs Mr. Collier yesterday. being fiesta the biblioteca was geshut. They have fiesta every day or so I have to spend some of my time reading some of Lope's plays I have bought . not in the edition you are familiar with however -

People here at S^{ra}. Carmona's pleasant. Crowd from Canada that pass very well.

Prado here O.K. Velasquez an a1 object and some other stuff that is interesting.

Shall do Lope's treatment of the Romeo & Juliet story this a.m.

Collier behaved nicely. A course of study is not an eventful thing to letterize about.

A gent in pink satin pants was trying to swallow a crowbar in front of the house yesterday but I didn't remain to see if he succeded.

Realy this is about enough before breakfast.

Love to you and dad.

Ezra.

+≽==≼+

116. ALS

May 20 (1906)

Madrid

Dear Mother,

His nibbs the embassador returned my call Friday. with Mrs. Collier. I was out but met them at the street corner & was invited to but in at the embassy again.

Note from Dale this a.m. he hits Madrid in about a week.

Very pleasant people here at the pension.

At Mr. Collier's recommendation I took the best available girl out. to the Romero de San Isidro. this P.M. and watched the noble spinach peasant celebrate his patron St. with danse & bell ringing & paper flowers.

The city is not uninteresting as I get to know it better.

Finished Lopes 'Castelvines y Monteses' his treatment of the Romeo & Juliet story . and have squeezed several thesis pages out of that & the Francesilla.

One of the other U.P. fellows has shown up in Madrid & is staying with a sister of my landlady. He is deutch and I don't know whether to disturb his repose or not.

Haven' t had time to look up Perazzini's friends yet.

Everybody treats me like a white man and when I get through at the library I am ready to rest & be entertained.

Have applied for return passage on July 8 but havent yet received reply - this is not public. as the U.P. is to be allowed to continue in ignorance of the fact that I am not staying here till the end of August.

Next morning.
Nothing more.

Love to you & Dad.
E .P.

+≈≈+

117. ALS

May 23 (1906)

Madrid

Dear Father,

The exchange on Spanish money being far I have been unable to stretch my coin over the intervening gulf. - I have a line on a return ticket to Paris at ½ rate which will bring me there a week earlier than I expected & broke. if you can ship 50. so as to reach there by June 15. you will save me from bluffing the town on a bright smile & an empty pocket. Of course 25. then & the other 25 later will amount to the same thing.

I do not regret going at that time as I think I can finish necessary work in the library here. & the two-weeks of Sorbonne lectures will be of value more than equal to what I loose here. besides it will let me find out how & where to live cheaply in Paris.

The living in Madrid is not cheap. especially now. This place & another under same head are the only things of the kind in Madrid & from what I hear of life in Spanish families I am content to have omitted trying it.

The library is open for such a short time that I can get more work done most anywhere else. .

I have however done ½ of what is necessary & can finish easily if they dont close it entirely during wedding week.

Address Cook. 1 Place de l'Opera (there are 2 Cook offices in Paris).

Will write again this evening or tomorrow. Must go to library now.

Love to you & mother.
Ezry.

+≈≈+

118. ALS

May 24 (1906)

Madrid

Dear Mother:-

As usual it is 'fiesta' so I shall do my work here at the house.

As I explained to father I have

78

(Day later)
got a cheap ticket to Paris & get there June 15. for two weeks Sorbonne lectures.

It would not be well to send anything by Spanish mail now anyway.

I was interrupted yesterday by arrival of the Dales. They had gotten rooms somewhere else & not speaking Spanish were in being swindled & made miserable generaly.

They are now here myself & an 'abogado Espanol' i.e lawer (court pleading not necessary) having assisted in the shift.

Mr. Dale took me to the best show I have yet seen - not saying much, as they play nothing but skits & run three a night.

The Dales are a relief as the last infusion here is a bore in four sections. Spent yesterday P.M. improving my Spanish on the Senora's relatives.

Speaking of fiestas the spaniard needs one or two a week to prevent his working, were it necessary. They never have two in sucession . because a couple of days are necessary in which to rest up for the next fiesta. .

I had been starting an article on the Auto sacramental for Mr. Chester but I believe they are not going to have it now. so I shall quit & give him a historical sketch of it next winter if he happens to want it. I now go to a book shop to get a list of plays in a certain edition of Lope's, which job it would take about two hours. 6 men & no end of red tape at the Biblioteca to get done.

I trust my last letter to dad is not still in the P.O. here. It requested 50 to Cook 1 place de l''Opera, Paris. best by International Mercantile Marine. Checks.= If he wants anymore instruction on that form of note, see Althouse.

Good Bye.
Love to you and dad.
Son.

✛══✚══✚✛

119. ALS

[31 May 1906]

Madrid

I have been watching what has happened. you can get it in papers & from stuff I have sent on to Mr. Chester in a half baked condition. The illustrations are the best yet seen. Double letter from you & dad May 18 & 20 received.

Shall finish sort of a bibliography of Lope's inedited mss. this week & get out of the heat. This a.m. Mr. Dale & I called on Jose Echegaray the leading Sp. dramatist of today. Dale played him like a trout. He has got everybody stiffed when it comes to the interview line.

Mr. D. is going to Paris & has turned over his press tickets to me. Military review tomorrow & ?? afterwards.

Went to Toledo friday. scrawled for Mr. Chester yesterday P.M. Harry Smith writes from Munich but I shall not be able to meet him. My view of Wedding procession as I, I think wrote, was from the Ministerìo de gobernación, where I got the approach both ways i. e. route [*sketch*] good perspective.

Leonard Williams author of 'Land of the Dons' to my left & some german correspondent to right.

an acquaintance saw the bomb thrown . about 8 minutes after the king passed me. - guess I didnt write this either - in general am taking all thats going.

More later

Ezra.

---

120. ALS

[1 June 1906]

[Madrid]

Dear Dad,

Do wot you please with verses. I think it was the Cosmopolitan that discretely refrained from accepting them.

They <u>are</u> slightly impolite. Be sure you get finished copy not drafts.

I might this a.m. impersonate the press of N.Y. & San Francisco at the military review but it's too Hot so I'll hie me to a library.

Besides I wouldn't give the cab fare for all the arms of Spain.

Good Bye.

Ezry.

---

121. ALS

June 5 (1906)

Madrid

Dear Dad.

I have just finished a report on over sixty unpublished or little known mss. of Lope's plays in the Biblioteca National & feel learned as hell.

If it were not for the Rev. Padre José Maria de Elizondo of the Capuchins I might still be paddling round the INCUNABULAE in an aimless sort of way & getting only 2nd rate stuff. He has ordered the University library to open up to me. so I shall take a fly at that tomorrow.

The palace library is still closed. shall see Collier if they don't send me an invitation to call by tomorrow.

Did I tell you of the remark of the academy librarian when I asked for works on Lope 'Ugh, why do you come here? Your own professor has made the best there is.'

Hurah. real rain 1ˢᵗ I've seen of course there were sprinkles two weeks ago. but this is real sahibs rain.

This with a real bath I went forth & bought yesterday make me feel as though I might once more be guilty of an act of christian charity.

E.P.

⫟⊨══▬◁⊦

122. ALS [*letterhead*] Crédit Lyonnais, Madrid, Service des Accrédités

June 8. (1906)

Hell [Madrid]

Getting ready to leave it. This credit L takes ½ hr. to give me $10 in french coin. Do you wonder I trade with Cook. Unfortunately Cook has no french boodle. I have wasted already 40 minutes from my last day in the library.

it will have taken 6 visits to the palace 8 days & the embassy to get back to palace library. Oh the giddy speed of the place.

Damn.

I go to Paris to night. 1ˢᵗ stop Burgos. second Paris. Will see if I can get more done to the square inch there. This place fit only to loaf in & not well fit for that

P.M.

Got my permit for King's library this P.M. but the librarian had to change his shirt for a reception. so I was alowed to sit around for a quarter of an hour & then told the books wouldn't be shown me.

The señora comforts me with the fact that Shepperd of Columbia stayed here 4 summers & never got in at all. Thank heaven I'm off for a civilized country. Smith wants me to come to Munich but he'll have to wait a year or so.

Love to you & mother
Ezry

Beautiful Blotter.

⫟⊨══▬◁⊦

123. ALS

June 13 (1906)

Paris

Dear Mother.

Charming trip up from Madrid. Burgos. St. Sebastian, Bordeux, Tour, Blois (& Chambois) Orleans, Paris. All on about $5 more than the real car fare.

Will try to literate them for Mr Chester. but as I do not expect he can make any use of them, you can get the mss from him.

They will be good ads for some touring agency if they're too bum to print. As Symons & Rud Kip are the only people alive who can write readable travel articles it will be no disgrace to botch it.

I trust my financial note reached father in due season. Am here of course a few days earlier. The pension is good & I presume they will feed me for several weeks without wanting any coin. Have about $6 left & enough clothing to be respectable if I wear all my whole things at once.

Don't be alarmed I can subsist for a month yet. if there has been any hitch in the movements of the board of trade.

Shall look up Dondo. examine Sorbonne method & the 'Lope' collection in the librarys here. my time is realy very short for it however the climate is more energizing.

60 & more mss. examined in Madrid not so bad.

Have my thesis so I can roll it out in a month's more home work. provided I can get hold of Grillpartzer & Farinelli here.

If the U of P. wants me to look up those authorities more fully they'll have to send me to Munich with better pay.

it is pleasant to come to a country where the bath is not a curiosity. I have just ordered one & shall take it shortly.

Love to you & father.

Ezra

*Pound's **article for Mr Chester**, 'Burgos, a Dream City of Old Castile', appeared in Book News Monthly in October. The Austrian dramatist Franz **Grillparzer** (1791–1872), Hugo Rennert had written, 're-established the repute of Lope throughout the continent of Europe' (The Life of Lope de Vega (1562–1635), Glasgow, 1904).*

⊹≈⊹

124. ALS

June 15. (1906)

Paris

Dear Dad.

Order Arrives. O.K. have found Dondo he is teaching in Modern School here. If I can get a pleasant Job. I may stay a bit longer. 3 weeks is very short for the national-Sorbonne librarys & perfect french accent.

Smith wants me to come to Munich but dont see how I can manage it. especialy as I expect to return there in a year or so.

Am doing Burgos with an Arthur Symons-Kipling effect but dont suppose Mr C. will be able to use it. Have some good cards for illustrations will ship it in a few days or a week. Wish I could hear how my other stuff went. It wasn't what he asked for but it was all there was.

it is very amussing to read your 'have you met Dale. – do you see Dale. Considering he was taking me everywhere, etc. theatres. interview . with 'Echegaray' etc.

Have a card from him now reminding me that I am to call when I get to N. Y.

Dondo is waiting for me to go to lunch.

Good Bye Love to all will answer. details in Mother's letter later.

Ezra

⊹╼━╾⊹

125. ALS

June 25 (1906)

[Paris]

Dear Dad,

I do not find very much in the Paris libraries. Have however gotten some things in old book shops that are more than worth coming here for.

The consul general wants 10.50 fr. for an affidavit to let me use the National library here. After my kind treatment at Madrid I do not feel like encouraging such nonsense. Besides there is practicaly nothing there I want. Will add $3 & go to London for British Museum & perhaps the Lord Holland library.

By the way you might get me courtesy of the port when I come back. (Patricia. Dover July 8.) I have nothing dutiable, but it saves fuss. You might even drop over to N.Y.if you are in the humor.

If there is anything utterly damnable in this world its an ink well 9/10 empty, so that you cant get a pen load of ink.

Good Bye
Ezra.

As I am coming home in two weeks there does not seem much use in long epistles.

There is only one civilized country in the world.

Love to you & mother
KID.

Under the title 'Interesting French Publications', Pound reviewed in September's Book News Monthly *two books he had picked up in **the old bookshops***, Origine et esth-étique de la tragédie *and* Le secret des troubadours, *both by M. Péladan. He also bought Ghero's great collection of Renaissance Latin poets.*

⊹╼━╾⊹

126. AL

June 26 [1906]

Paris.

Dear Mother,

It is a good thing for me to write when the spirit moveth. Paper is a thing of minor consideration.

Spent the day in the Louvre. met some people I knew on the K. Alb. & am peacefully back chez Mm. Bret awaiting dinner.

A few more americans here & Paris would sound like a civilized town. Glad Dad lived through the shirt tail parade 'sans peur et sans reproche'.

Yesterday as several times before I took tea with the Misses Mapel who have seen fit to be very decent to me both here & in Madrid.

In spite of your general objection to my way of doing nearly everything nearly everybody seems to treat me very decently.

Nice kind charatible world dont it?

As I have remarked before I am home

[*pages missing*]

+>=—>=<+

127. ALS

[2 July 1906]

8 Duchess St. | Portland Place. | Lunnon.

Arrived saturday

Heard Cambell yesterday.

Dale wanted me at Warwic pagent today . but hadn't had time to be sure of meeting him so went to Museum & have just enough there to keep me comfortably busy.

Charming trip up. Amiens fairly interesting. Abbeville which post cards will show you. one of quaintest towns in france & unamericanised.

Le portel. fishing villiage for night. Boulogne, castle & ramparts . & smooth chanel crossing.

Got some old editions of Martial that will be the equivalent of about a 3 hours course next winter have my ticket from here to Dover & home so am sure of arriving. also have $1 american so can get my trunk sent across N.Y.

have also enough sinews of war to pay expenses.

Brit. museum authorities pleasant dont think I shall try for Ld Holland collection as I have probably seen its equivalent & time is not over long.

It is a joy to get near a good cigarette once more if one smokes. they are awfully handicapped in traveling.

Met the Harding crowd in Paris & suppose they are now in London but have not time to look them up.

maybe I'll find it but will see them on steamer so it don't matter.

Don't suppose there'll be any fuss at port but u.a.d.e you might come over if it don't bother you.

Much love to you & mother.

Remember me to Miss Whitechurch & Mrs Lovell.

They will approve of my being in London. It is a joy to get to a white country

well. yes. yes. .

Good Bye

Kid

House here very good

+>=+=<+

128. ALS

[5 July 1906]

London

Dear Mother

Museum here has proved very important not only for major work but for minor.

Have chewed a small hunk from its knowledge plant daily.

Tate galary this a.m. & my first real appreciation of Turner.

Am going to museum now for another swat.

It is the best place to feel like an ant I have yet discovered.

Overwhelming ignorance is the only comfort left one.

Have been turning leaves of Lope's autograph mss. etc. ad inf.

met part of Miss Harding's friends at Tate this a.m. I do not think I shall have time to meet Dale.

Love to you and Dad. This is about the last I guess the last letter I write as its only 3 days till sailing time.

British Museum.

Waiting for books & utterly without anything writable in my head.

This is undoubtedly the best place for study I have found & shall make it my first stop when I come back to Europe for any further work.

Smith sent me a list of the fellows from Munich. since Smith and I are abroad I do not so much regret the fellowship . tea. I have Smith to thank for <u>one</u> comrade in the goodly (?) fellowship that share the profits.

My Lope's have arrived so good bye.

Love to you & Dad.

Son

85

Pound sailed for New York from Boulogne on 8 July 1906. According to the doctoral degree requirements he now needed to add a further dozen credits to the dozen earned for the MA. In the Fall he did six courses with Rennert, all in the Romance literatures—Old Provençal, Old French, Early Italian Poets, Dante, Old Spanish, Spanish Drama—and a further course in French Phonetics for which he received no credit. In the Spring he signed up for five courses in the English Department, fell out with the professors, and refused to submit himself to examination by them. His Harrison Fellowship was not renewed, and he abandoned the doctorate, determined to continue his literary work in his own fashion. In the summer of 1907 he was drafting articles in the hope that Carlos Tracy Chester would accept them for Book News Monthly. *In the following letter he mentions various topics: his 1906 passage through Abbeville; Latin poetry of the Renaissance (Augurellus); Jacques August DeThou's* Historia sui temporis (1604–20), *and the English historian Thomas Babington Macaulay; Rembrandt and Fra Angelico. Only two articles (about the Renaissance Latin poets) would appear in* Book News Monthly, *in January and February 1908. Pound was also applying for teaching posts—he mentions Franklin and Marshall College in Lancaster, Pennsylvania, and Wabash College in Crawfordsville, Indiana. The latter was seeking an Instructor in French and Spanish to be Chairman and sole member of its newly formed Department of Romance Languages, and Pound was to be interviewed by its new President, Dr George Lewes MacKintosh, at the beginning of August.*

⊹═══╪

129. TLS

[July? 1907]

[Wyncote]

Dear Mother:

Bob Lamberton came out yesterday so we ate your bloomin shrimps. Also the olives have been attacked. Yesterday I finished my abbeville Spiel. which goes to C. T. C. to day. Incidentaly I have been getting some other stuff done but your interest is confined to what sells. I presume.

Grandmother and I get along quite well. We do not butt into each other's affairs and on investigating the matter this morning I found she was not bothered by my taciturnity. 'Said' she was more or less unsociable herself but that she believed in letting people be as happy as they could without interference, that I was thinking about other things etc. that it was all right.

Confusus, oh hell how does the old chink spell his name?

Katharine brought home a trunk load of books half of which i have promptly borrowed, so I don't have to chase into Phila to the library for some time. Have as said finished abbeville, and started a Latin article on Augurellus. DeThou and McCauley is the next one to be finished I guess.

From your reports of Howard and Sadie, i guess the whole damn tribe is on the war path. 'How wonderful is art!!'

Have done two rather good things one for Rembrandt and the other for Fra Angelico . . they need eight or ten reproductions of the old masters (six or seven Rembrandt's, a Raphael, a Leonardo and Angelico's Annunciations), to make them fully comprehensible to any one who does not know the old painters, and I suppose they will be difficult to use on this account. . However it is some satisfaction to do a decent thing once and a while . even if it don't buy pork and gasoline.

To day is realy glorious, but why talk about the weather.

I don't know that there's any thing else. Franklin and Marshall is up the flue and Wabash has not written yet.

Guess that's all.

Remember me to Aunt F and cousin Sady and anybody else promiscuous.

E.P.

None of the articles mentioned here were published. However **Augurellus** *does get a mention at the end of 'Poeti Latini', the last chapter of* The Spirit of Romance. **Franklin and Marshall**, *a College in Lancaster, Pennsylvania.*

+≻━≺+

130. ALS

[c.5] (August 1907)

Wyncote

Dear Mother,

Wabash nailed & everything most delightful. whole d—d dept. French, Spanish & Italian to run as I bang please.

½ hr. with Dr. MacKintosh & twas did.

& Blessed of most blessed jokes on you dear. I did it without those essentials of all life. a coat. a collar. a neck-tie. also my shoes were not shined.

After 21 yrs. blessed be the howly naime of St Andy Carnegie I can retire to Venice on half pay & live & loaf as I please. Probably full prof.ship in 2 yrs.

I couldn't have hit a neater job if I had made it myself (barring pay for lst 2 yrs. which is a very small matter)

Lovingly -
Ezra

The **Carnegie** *Foundation for the advancement of teaching was endowed in 1905. Pound's 'great solace' at Wabash would be its Carnegie Library.*

+≻━≺+

131. ALS

[12–14 September 1907]

[on the way to Wabash College]

Indiana at large, a week or two late.

Expecting to arrive sometime. but will come back by other route or not at all. Buffalo to Gallion, makes Bobadilla seem like St Regis.

How'effer I still live altho the Babalonian research implements will be needed to restore me to recognizable form. gee. talk about 'Rure' this here tew states Ohiey & Injannyea - just reeks with that 'deliberate motion acquired by those who have much to do with nature in her more open phazes'. 1 stone house, (i.e. part stone) for last nine hours (most), corn, corn, corn. an terbakky.

'Aaandersun!! Aaanndursun!!'

Aaanndursun is at least on the time table. which most of the Tobacco plants we have stopped at, aint . . and we are only 1 ½ hrs behind time. how cute!

also you can mail me my cuff-buttons.

And to think we pity the 'pore ignorunt furriner!' Gawsh, I wont be near so caustic about Yourupeen decadence the next time I see it.

Sincerely yours

E.P.

⊹⊱══⊰⊹

132. ALS [*letterhead*] The Crawford, Crawfordsville, Ind

Monday [16?] (September 1907)

Crawfordsville

Dear Mother,

Dr. King has been driving me all around this P.M. for rooms. I guess I will make out pretty well.

& am staying here so I wont have trouble, about shifting things . . from one house to another.

I am pretty tired now. But everyone seems kindly disposed & town is not so worse.

E.P.

Saw Pres. McKintosh for a few moments. shall retire & rest up for tomorrow.

Think I have found a congenial person in the prof. of greek.

His house is being papered & he & his wife are living in a tent but I am invited for tomorrow night.

Of course I shall not go . . .

But then . . .

E.P.

Love to you & Dad.

*Dr Robert Augustus **King** was Professor of German at Wabash (1891–1918). The **Professor of Greek** (1900–16) was Daniel Dickey Hains. After first putting up at the **Crawford Hotel**, Pound rented the north wing, with a private entrance, of **Milligan Place**, a 19ᵗʰ century house at Milligan Terrace and Meadow Avenue. The house was owned by Joseph Milligan, and his brother-in-law, Chalmers E. Fullenwider, a local real estate agent, also lived there.*

$+\!\!\geq\!\!=\!\!\prec\!\!+$

133. **ALS** [*letterhead*] The Crawford, Crawfordsville, Ind

[17–18? September] (1907)

[Milligan Place, Crawfordsville]

Dear Mother,

Delightfully settled in most delightful place in town.

Gothic windows, trees, private door, milk & cream off place.

(Hotel here when I want to eat immoraly).

Fullenwider. 3 minutes from class room.

Find out what it will cost ship some strips of carpet & my rug. by express.

Have bought a Davenport that opens out into a bed.

also a book case.

carpet alone is lacking.

people very nice. no frills, but I think we will congeen.

If you go to town I might have another of the rugs. also look up freight rates.

But I don't think I'll have any stuff sent.

Just carpet.

there are the old strips & the Bokarra.

Have found more nice people.

The Kings drove around here for me last night to say that Fullenwider pere had decided in my favor & that the gates were made open.

Huge parlor at my disposal when the family aren't having company.

Family, old people & son of about 28, & I like them.

Good Bye

E.P.

$+\!\!\geq\!\!=\!\!\prec\!\!+$

134. TLS

Thursday [19? September 1907]

Milligan Place [Crawfordsville]

Dear Dad:-

One French class of 57 so big that I had to annex the back of the chapel. 30 in Spanish and about fifteen for other French . . One Rodyheaver also new here on Faculty, being the brother of mothers gay song bird. I believe he was at the house one evening. News paper here prints his name Rollenheaven.

There is a southish atmosphere here that I rather like. I think you would call the folks white .

I want some carpet strips and my little rug (and another if there is one to spare) also some pillows and if package is to be sent. 1 lb. Ackers best Java pulverized .

The people here present me with tomatos and peaches and the like and the town has restaurants altho I think I can do quite well for myself. I have found a good baker who will deliver at my door etc . .

The son of our minister to Belgium is coming here this evening to get some special assignments and in general the class of students is above what I had expected.

Several of the faculty seem quite white, quite realy. Of course it is possible to buy pillows and carpet here.

Also there are quite many things for me to do.

Good Bye.

Love to you and mother

E.P.

+≻——≺+

135. ALS

[22–27 September 1907]

[Crawfordsville]

Dear Dad,

- Rug & pillows received. sometime . you will find my last winters over coat, the one that was brown dyed black & you will steal it without mothers knowing . & send it & the brass student lamp. everything going finely . . Pink tea for faculty at Danny Hains, in a few moments so I shall put on a collar & sally forth.

Love to you & mother.

E.P.

+≻——≺+

90

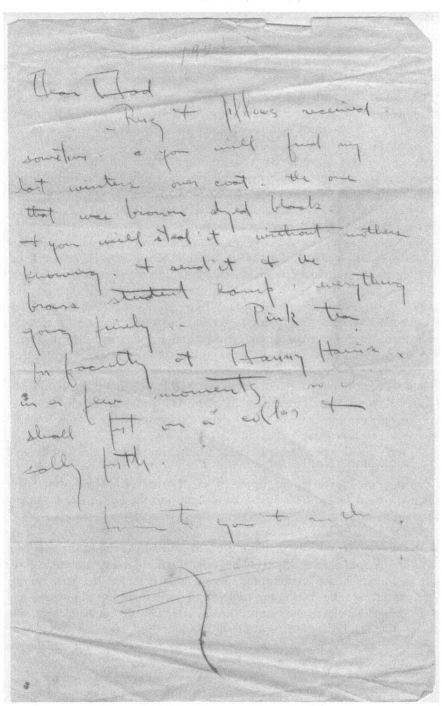

135. ALS, EP to HLP from Crawfordsville, [22–27? September 1907].

136. TLS

Monday [30 September 1907]

Milligan Place [Crawfordsville]

Dear Mother:-

I have just dined 4 boiled potatoes, getting stuck there I save the fifth for a salad., cream, nuts rye bread, coffee, apricots a la patent process. Realy you need not worry about my getting fed. Even the kunnel begins to cease to fear my sudden demise.

As for 'George' [Lorimer] and your rumors of war. I am not sure that sub-editorial jobs are either permanent nor alluring. no vacation from June to Sept. . no being thru your set work by 11 A.M. no pension.

Not that there is any serious liklihood of a prominent but vulgar weekly needing my thoroughly competent assistance.

MacKintosh complimented me on apparently succeeding at my present vocation. It seems that rumors of war reached him to the effect that I was running my various classes to the satisfaction of the patients.

Besides Mr. Chester said I was 'trained for something better' than editorial work . . Of course a job with some flash to it . with a chance to show off my gol-darsted brilliancy. A job with $2000 padding and I would turn aside to consider it. But realy ye knaow ones freedom after 11 a-m, and the prospect of a salary sometime in the future, to say nothing of the summer months. c'est quelque chose.

Besides hack writing does not allure me. And I am about as likely to make something worthwhile in my spare time here as I would be anywhere???? may be. The only real advantage in a job such as you visionify about is that it would bring one in touch with people.

???? can't one find people when one gets loose from here in the summers .??? que sais je??

What's the use in fussing about it till the sucker nibbles at the bait anyhow . Next fall? yes I would take an edit. job then after I had had my vacation.

And be sorry for it???

To things present. I have my floor covered with a Crex rug light green with 'wall of troy border' in dark green. I hemmed me this day a green burlap cover for this little table and a curtain for some ugly little shelves the Mrs. giv me, very convenient little shelves, not to speak disrespectfully, but not ornamental when littered with teeth-and hair-brushes. When I get a decent cover for the big dining table that holds everything. I shall be about fixed. Hopeing the green of the davenport will fade into the Crex and Burlap shades before forever. The red linen cover of the big table does not help.

The open stove is a wonder . cook, wood fire, coal fire, ornament, use, heat. fire in no time . and will I suppose after a few more attempts burn all night. it keeps red ashes already.

I suppose my special seniors will be here shortly.

Love to you and Dad.

E.P.

oh yes, what did it cost to get the pillows here? tell me that & I will know what is - what is not worth having sent.

Mosher wlll do my part of the Quick wedding. Give her the picture if you like, but she would know it to be second hand & I doubt if it is easily replaceable. however that is as you will. You can have it to give or to keep.

E.P.

+>===<+

137. TLS

Oct 3. (1907)

[Crawfordsville]

Dear Dad,

Your letter welcome this A.M. . Shall be most happy to get coats.

As they pay by the quarter in this collabaloobus I am not anxious to invest in any seal-skin boleros or silk bychamers.

My credit seems to be quite good however. Get the brass lamp in with the coats. brass student lamp that I had at Hamilton ye knaow.

Mother will be glad to know that I have purchased bed room slippers, more blankets, heavy under ware . potatoes, more than I shall ever eat (for 25¢). That she can keep her patent medicine advertisements.

Dinner with the Kings sunday.

As far as 'the right track' is concerned there seems to be plenty to be done here. Of course if you can find as good a job for me somewhere in the effete east I would be very likely to abandong me 'igh callin' and skidoo to paats more plush lined than Hoosicr.

Believe I am to be interviewed this evening for the college monthly.

And as far as people are concerned the prevalent color around here seems to be 'white'

The Danny Hainses are especialy decent, and, oh in general things are much better than could have been expected. what is the Oct. Book News doing for its country??

Rodyheaver seems to be the sort that gets to Y.M.C.A. meetings but not to the foot ball games. By the way we play Michigan at Indiannopollis before so very long.

Love to you and mother.

Thats about all I happen to think of now.

EP

+>===<+

138. ALS

Saturday [5?] (October 1907)

[Crawfordsville]

Dear Mother,

Everything O.K. Find the Thomases (dean & wife) quite charming on closer acquaintance.

Also Whittam & one of the instructors in English congenial. Called on Cragwalls also but place overrun with crescent family. very destructive of conversation . altho I like Mr. & Mrs. C. when at large.

Some of my students employed in restaurant here look after me when I attend & get me white meat & extra pieces of things. Have just had visit from a couple more who feel need of boosting. Some find it inconvenient that I am so familiar with all available methods of bluff & that I insist on work, all the work & no substitute for work except intellegence - which is rare -

Got some packing boxes & green burlap . instead of a $45 buffet last week & they increase my convenience.

Love to you & dad & remembrances to Aunt Frank & cousin Sady.

Lovingly
Son

139. ALS

Saturday [12 October? 1907]

[Crawfordsville]

Dear Mother,

One Stephens, asst. in English, new here, is proving a very sane & joyous companion. we eat ensemble a good part of the time & consider a combination bungalo, with fuller & more civilized arrangements.

Tea party at Σ.K. house last night. nobody seems to take very violent aversion to me.

Both Milford (Eng. Lit.) & Cragwall (Math) seem agreable & intellegent.

I am trying in what spare time i get to do some writing (not letters) so dont expect much in my scrawls.

E.P.

Thanks for $V. did I acknowledge?

140. ALS

Monday [14 October 1907]

Cv. [Crawfordsville]

Dear Mother,

Various probable incidental expenses deter Bungalo. Present arrangement of lunching together in my room & dining au restaurant seems quite convenient & also he has to be near his chief for a good deal of his work, so well situated bungalo is hard to find. perhaps we wont.

You might drag Hilda into that Musical Club affair dont think it would cause any violent calamities. She is working at one of the conservatoriums or natalo-riums or piany schools or wot'el

Her uncle demonstrates that there is a slight tendency toward the musical in the family.

Pleasant evening at the Thomases yesterday and met the Editor of the local paper, one McKane.

One Emanuel (a stewdent in whom there seems to lurk a germ of the humanities but whom the rest of the faculty have not been allured by.) is going to take me to the studio of one Vance (who has studied in Paris & who seems human & paints with some finish.) this evening. Ergo I hie me to get tomor-row's hot-air cooked up for serving in freshman, senior doses respectively.

Love to you & dad
E.P.

+⟫══╾═⟪+

141. ALS

[16–17? October 1907]

[Crawfordsville]

Dear Dad,

Of course everything is O.K. if I die I'll telegraph.

Hope you have fun on your Carolina bat.

Am shifting to a place with bath, gass & furnace heat.

Large reception by the Dean. $4.00 for pumps. Otherwise no cataclasms. probably will get around to writing a letter sometime.

Dinner with the Rolands yesterday. (Hohnsburg family . Knew cousin in C.M.A.)

Au rvoir
love to you & mother & remembrance to Aunt Frank.
E.P.

+⟫══╾═⟪+

142. **TLS**

Sunday. [20 October 1907]

[Crawfordsville]

Dear Mother,

Indianapolis yesterday for Michigan game and a touch of civilization. Game quite worth while only one touch down against us in the first half and even in the second half good resistance.

Things here comfortable, bath, gass etc. and a few more decent people, in fact I have quite as large a circle of acquaintance as I have time for.

You know that I am more interested in makeing things than in writing about unimportant details and that when I get anything worth while written you will get it in print. Deans reception a week or so ago. biled shirts etc. but what in heaven is the use of filling up paper with that sort of rot. I dont yet understand the spasms father got into over my not writing.

I presume Dad will manage to find that rubber strip that I need for type-writer. I also wanted the brass lamp instead of all the family old clothes but don't send it now.

Love to you & Dad.

E.P.

+———+

143. **ALS**

[c.20 November 1907]

[Crawfordsville]

Dear Mother,

Thanks for the pyjamas, of course I didn't want 'em - needless to state etc. wherefor you are to be doubly commended for doing yer dooty.

You needn't bother about the Xmas fair cause I guess I'll be driftin home about then.

Things drift on.

I am going to move again on Monday.

Vance proves human & paints pretty well, especialy mural stuff.

Stephens gone home for Thanksgiving.

Snow today.

Guess that's all

E.P.

In October Pound had moved from Milligan Place to a rooming house 'with bath, gass &
furnace heat'—a place to which came 'all the travelling show folk'. His moving again is
likely to have been in consequence of two of his students having found him sharing his

dinner in his room with a variety actress from across the hall—an English 'lady male impersonator' who was broke, hungry, and down on her luck in Crawfordsville. Assured by Mary S. Young, an eminently respectable young widow who had befriended him in his previous lodgings, that Pound had spent the best part of the evening innocently with her, President MacKintosh cleared him of immorality, but may have advised him to find less risky lodgings. His move this time was to 412 South Grant Avenue, immediately across the street from the campus. Here a pair of spinster sisters, the Misses Ida and Belle Hall, let rooms to bachelor professors and took a close interest in the life of the college.

+>—+—<+

144. ALS

Monday [December 1907]

Cv. [Crawfordsville]

Dear Dad,

Merry Xmas to you & mother.

Don't know as there is anything more to be said.

Thanks for your donation, also tell mother I don't need the pyjamas till next winter having bot a supply here a while since.

Expect to give a few private lessons in Spanish & augment the till.

One Fred. Vance here, quite human, is making some drawing for 'Abbeville' which I have partly re-written. He has had about ten years abroad & is on the 'Reader' staff.

Otherwise no high wind.

Remember me at Tioga and merry Xmas.

Love to you & mother

E.P.

+>—+—<+

145. ALS

Tuesday (7 January 1908)

[Crawfordsville]

Dear Mother,

10.15 and tired with writing a lecture for tomorrow. Trip fairly well slept off.

You were rather nice about your pendent & saphire & things in general.

I was probably too weary or too stupid to show my appreciation.

You can send me the saphire if you wish or simply give it to Hilda some time when you & she are alone.

Love to you & dad.

I am going to retire about now.

EP.

*Pound and **Hilda** Doolittle had been engaged, unofficially, since 1905. Her father disapproved; Pound's parents were sympathetic.*

†⊨⸺⊨†

146. ALS

(9 January 1908)

[Crawfordsville]

Dear Mother -

   I dont know that there is any thing especial.

   Two lectures out of the way. I can't send 'em to Dad 'cause they're only notes & my improvizations & reading out of books.

   Things run smoothely. that is about all there is to be reported.

Love to you and Dad

EP

†⊨⸺⸺†

147. TLS

[mid-January? 1908]

[Crawfordsville]

Dear Dad:-

   Received proofs of my article but from looks of matter next it it seems that it is about to be shoved over among the book reviews and unsigned . . I should like to have you drop in to the office and investigate. The thing looks very, very well in type – a wonder for proof – but I shall not return the proofs untill you make sure that it is to be printed as a bone fide article and properly signed. Dont raise the roof, but quietly mention that I am about the only person in the country fitted to treat of this period of literature, etc. Also the order from the book store here will not come in unless it is to be signed i.e. the article on Flamininus.

   First find out if they intend to act in a decent fashion, My guess from the proof may be wrong. If they are snippy, See Chester and J.W.

   I can scarecely afford anonymity yet.

Be gentle dear.

EP

Book News Monthly published in February 1908, 'M. Antonius Flamininus and John Keats. A Kinship in Genius', and gave the author as 'Ezra Pound / Professor of Romance Languages in Wabash College'.

†⊨⸺⸺†

148. ALS

Jan. 30 (1908)

[Crawfordsville]

Dear Mother

Every thing going OK. This being day of prayer for colleges I am getting a chance to get various things done.

chiefly whanging the typewriter & moving . books over the fence. I move Saturday.

I am quite tired, but as I am about the only person that has escaped the grippe one can rejoice that it 'aint no wusser'. Your 'Packman' spiel quite interesting.

Love to you & Dad.

EP

'I move Saturday' was almost certainly an indication that everything was not going OK. A chorus girl from a stranded burlesque show had been found in his bed one morning by the Misses Hall after Pound had gone out to his eight o'clock class. They telephoned Dr MacKintosh and one or two of the College trustees, and Pound was invited to resign, and readily did so.

149. ALS [*letterhead*] Hotel de L'Europe, Anvers

[early February 1908]

[Crawfordsville]

Dear Dad.

Please send me 5 more copies of Book News for Feb.

I don't know that there is anything in particular to say. I am jamming out mss all the time I am not in class room.

suppose something will stick somewhere sometime.

if I keep on long enough.

Nothing, as said, nothing miraculous to write.

Love to you & mother

E.P.

150. **ALS** [*letterhead*] Department of Greek, Wabash College, Crawfordsville, Ind

[13?] (February 1908)

[Crawfordsville]

Dear Dad,

Have had a bust up. but come out with enough to take me to Europe. Home Saturday or Sunday. Don't let mother get excited.

Ez.

I guess something that one does not see. but something very big & white back of the destinies. has the turning & the leading of things & this thing. & I breath again.

Lovingly.

E.P.

In fact you need say nothing to mother till I come.

It had become known that Pound had found the young woman 'penniless and suffering from the cold' on a downtown street in the bitter night following snowstorms and blizzards, and had taken her in and given her his bed while he slept on the floor of his study, 'fully clothed . . . wrapped in his topcoat'. On 15 February, Mary Young put in writing for President MacKintosh her exoneration of Pound from the November scandal; and the President then wrote:

My dear Prof. Pound:

I desire to recall you, as Instructor of French and Spanish in Wabash College, believing after investigation that the rumors circulated regarding your character are without foundation.

G. L. MacKintosh

However, on the 17ᵗʰ he had occasion to write:

My dear Mr. Pound:

I have your letter of this inst. stating that you do not see fit to resume your work at Wabash. I trust you may have a pleasant Journey abroad, and that much success and happiness may come to you in the line of your profession. Believe me, you have my best wishes now and always.

Yours sincerely,
G. L. MacKintosh

President's Office,
Wabash College.

Crawfordsville, Ind., Feb. 15th 1908

My dear Prof. Pound:

I desire to recall you, as Instructor of French and Spanish in Wabash College, believing after investigation that the rumors circulated regarding your character are without foundation.

G. L. MacKintosh

150n[a] G. L. MacKintosh to EP, Wabash College, Feb. 15th 1908.

President's Office,
Wabash College.

Crawfordsville, Ind. Feb. 17th 1908

Mr. Ezra Pound,
Instructor in French & Spanish
Wabash College, Crawfordsville Ind.

My dear Mr. Pound: I have your letter of this inst. stating that you do not see fit to resume your work at Wabash. I trust you may have a pleasant journey abroad, and that much success and happiness may come to you in the line of your profession. Believe me, you have my best wishes now and alway.

yours sincerely
G. L. MacKintosh.

150n[b] G. L. MacKintosh to EP, Wabash College, Feb. 17th 1908.

151. ALS

[17 February 1908]

[Crawfordsville]

Dear Dad,
    Have been recalled but think I should rather go to ze sunny Italia.
    I'll be home in a few days.

E.P.

Have had more fun out of the fracasso than there is in a dog fight & hope I have taught 'em how to run a college.

E.P.

+≻═≺+

152. ALS [*letterhead*] Charles E. Lacey, 12 East Main Street, Crawfordsville, Ind.

The Book Store

[20? February 1908]

[Crawfordsville]

Dear Dad.
    Will have to postpone that Italian trip of mine, a bit.
    Thought I could get off right away.
    Wanted also to see Mrs. Benton. you needn't excite mother if you have not already read her my last note. Am having the time of my life & begin to take an interest in things here.
    I dont know whether I can get home within a week or not but would like to start before the steamer rates go up for the summer.

Lovingly
E.P.

Pound sailed from New York on 17 March 1908, on the Cunard Royal Mail Steamship 'Slavonia', and was in Gibraltar by the 23rd. He had an engagement through his travel agent to act as courier and 'gard-enfants' to a wealthy American family, the Dunlaps, during their tour of Tangier and Spain 6–18, April.

2

Gibraltar, Venice, London: 1908–11

153. ALS

March 23. (1908)

King Edwards Institute Gib.[raltar]

Dear Dad,

Am waiting for Cap. Hill acc. Dr. Baileys direction. he will probably drop in in an hour. or there about.

Trip over, most — rough part way & consequences. But delightful for last five days.

Don't know that there is anything in particular to note about it. without doing three days work of descriptions.

I am landed right side up with care.

Love to you & mother.

Will start my buissness arrangements tomorrow & then run up to Ronda to wait for Mr. Dunlap. Saw him in N.Y. as I think I wrote.

This is merely to say I have arriv.

E.P.

Delightful talk with Mr. Hill.
Will see the captain this evening.

E.P.

+⇒⇐+

154. ALS [*letterhead*] Althouse's Select Foreign Tours

716 Chestnut Street, Philadelphia

[c.1–2?] (April 1908)

London Hotel, Gib.

Dear Mother,

Your very welcome letter at hand with 'Terrone's' photo on the back of Schelling's 'book-puff'. I think I said in my last that the 1st part of the voyage was hell. during storm we got no ventilation in state rooms but I preempted the smoking room so that was O.K. Otherwise everything comfortable. My steward quite as good as any 1st class, and the people more interesting & in the main quite as well behaved as 1st class passengers. Syrian, hungarian, sicilian, greek (you see the Cunard goes all the way round Italy to Trieste & Fiume.

You may tell Mrs.Weber that she would be quite an ideal person for the sort of tour I want to take and that unless she can find some other intellegent person with a decent interest in rather faded pictures & out of the way corners, such as the council hall at San Gemignano where Dante was received in 1299 or the galleries in Perugia etc. ad inf. Dunlap is paying $15 per day in Spain. but I could reduce that quite a bit in Italy where our R.R. distances would be much shorter.

Never more than 3hrs. by rail at once. & preferably less. To avoid discomfort, land Genoa, thence Lucca, Pistoia, Florence (Pisa we have both seen, so put ? after Pisa). Siena, Perugia (Orvieto & Spoleto???) (Arezzo, Florence) or direct to Rimini, Faenza, Ravenna, Bologna, Reggio (Modena) Parma, Ferrara, Mantua, Padua, Venice, Verona. Nice & the Riviera up thru France via Carcassonne, Bordeaux, Tour etc. or at will. or Munich, Vienna, Prague, Budapesth. Sailing home, Cunard from Fiume or as first from Cherbourg. The part I write this for is the Italian itinerary. I see I have left out San Gemignano, after Siena.

Proposed October specialty, Sicily itin. Naples, Paestum, Amalfi, Ravello, Messina, Girgenti, Syracuse, Palermo ('La felice') Giardini. Taormina. This for October or November. or March. next year.

If begin in Oct. to lead down into Tunis, Algiers, Egypt etc. - P.S. Italian lakes left out at end of Ital. itinerary. They would come in at the end when it began to grow warm. I should realy be very glad if Mrs. Weber should decide to come. We ought to arrive as near May 1 as possible to catch the best part of the year. Will wait for her here at Gib if she cables what ship she comes by. Friedrich der Grosse. N.Y. leaving April 11th is I am afraid too early for her convenience. Königin Louise. Apr. 18. brings an althouse party. so she could be looked after in transit. arriving May 1st at Genoa. This is the most suited to the matter in hand. The König Albert is a better boat but does not arrive till May 15. leaving May 2. I shall take it kindly if you transmit madame on the 18th, she is quite good sport enough to take a chance & just such a sudden start, especialy as the other party would be on board. Dunlaps $15 rate includes everything premier classe. R.R. etc. I don't suppose she would want anything inferior although. as I said the best would come a bit cheaper in Italy on account of the shorter distances. You may tell her that her fear about my getting bored is pure bluff on her part.

The white star sailings are no improvement on the Lloyd. & more inconvenient. The Cunard Carpathia Apr. 9 too early? Slavonia Apr. 30. little improvement on the König Albert but does not go to Genoa. <u>No</u> improvement on Kgn. Louise. her real choice is between the Louise sailing Apr. 18. & the Albert May 2. - Cable me to meet the Louise at Gib.

yrs. Rsptfly. etc.
Ezra Pound
conductor

Italy should be the 2 months May & June. June in north, Venice etc. with possible but not recommended stop in the lakes until July. Scenery bores Mrs. W. almost as much as it does me. Je vous assure that she should arrive in Genoa on May day. pray let us argue no more about it. we will regard it as 'fait accompli'.

Adresse: London Hotel, Gibraltar.

Dunlap arrives April 6.

Gib is a delight of roses & wisteria at this time of year, & I presume the harbor here would be famous as Sorento if people had stopped here to look at it for a few days at a time instead of using Gib as a second Bobadilla junction effect. Have spilled a bit of ink since I came ashore, the roof is quite suited for my purposes. Love to you & dad. Cap. Hill & wife very pleasant. haven't yet found time for a second call but shall soon.

Guess that's all. Continue to stir up trade.

Good Bye for a day or so

E.P.

Althouse will arrange Mrs. W's. passage O.K.

London Hotel management a British Dowager so I am fully fed.

---

155. ALS [*letterhead*] London Hotel, Gibraltar

Apr. 4. (1908)

[Gibraltar]

Dear Dad,

Things moving serenely. Dunlap ought to get here day after tomorrow.

Gib is not a wildly exciting place but comfortable. the harbor gets more interesting as one knows it better. .

they are having 'Siege week' mock scrap etc. so we get canonading mostly at night

Realy very little to write, you know the place. Benamore has posted me at his club so I can have people to talk Spanish with when I feel like it.

Don't know of much more.

Love to you & mother

E.P.

Struck a neat edition of Italian gospels. You ought to use at mission will mail sample

---

156. ALS [*letterhead*] Grand Hotel, Madrid, Sevilla
[9–10? April 1908]

[Seville]

Dear Mother,

This Hotel is well enough known to you. also this town.

I have here four infants. so guess I shall rake out enough to subsist on for a week or so more. so you needn't worry about my feed for the present.

But glad to have you drum up any stray trade you see lying around loose. Shall be in italy by time you get this, unless I pay $5 & go on around the toe & up the Adriatic to Fiume or Trieste & from there to Venice.

I think I could gondole for a few weeks without any detriment to my health or very much to the exchequer.

By the way. Elson is about the most livest thing in Tangier. Had bully good gallop over hills to his home - next to the Perdicaris place, which we inspected.

Mr. Gomery, our minister (diplomatic) there is a cousin of the Scudders. which fact I remembered at the last moment. dropped into a bally reception, & had a pleasant five minutes with his blarsted excellency. who was trying very hard to escape the reception.

Rais Uli was bashful. & as no decent person will have any thing to do with him. my connections were of no use for a glaring yellow journal interview.

The head of the moorish customs spent about an hour sic-ing up the old thief. after which I got weary & declined to get up early next morning to see a person who does not seem very impressive at close range.

His 'encampment' before the british embassy is three small dirty tents.

Due to his bashfulness I had to content myself with a minister of war & a governor or two.

Cadiz a white sea town very attractive.

Guess that's all for the moment

Love to you & dad
E.P.

Pound had expected to have just one child to look after but was to be paid more because there were four. **Rais Ulli,** *Ahmed ibn-Muhammed Raisulu (1875–1925), was a Moroccan brigand who had kidnapped, in 1904, Ion Perdicaris, a wealthy Greek settled in Tangier, and had demanded from the Sultan of Morocco $70,000 and control of two of Morocco's wealthiest districts. President Theodore Roosevelt, under the impression that Perdicaris was a US citizen, had despatched the Marines to Morocco and made of the kidnapping an international incident, thus persuading the Sultan to meet the kidnapper's demands.*

157. TL

[11–17 April 1908]

[Spain]

Dear Mother:-

Things comfortable. Three of my infants are 'waiting' at about the best restaurant in town, which is quite near since I have moved. ergo I get a half chicken or at least a pretty near whole breast in a 2O¢ with coffee order. Otherwise no news. I have I think explained that the usual details of life are of nothing but existence and should in common decency be forgotten as soon as possible

Oh rot . . I am not a writer of letters except under certain conditions and I am not going to try.

When I have anything to say I shall say it and in the menetime unless I telegraph you can use your common sense and presume that I still live.

Thank you and dad for birthday gift. Will collect when I get home next June altho I am by no means sure that the proceeds will go for a claw hammer

Heard from Miss Nicolai, yesterday.

Guess that's all.

Love to you and Dad .

158. ACS

17 April, 1908

[Granada]

Job over tomorrow everything O.K.

E.P.

159. ACS

April 22, 1908

[Genoa]

Arrived O.K.

E.P.

160. ACS

April 24, 1908

[Verona]

Genoa-Pavia-Milan. This from Verona. enroute for Venice.
Mantua tomorrow.

+>——<+

161. ALS [*letterhead*] Hotel Victoria, Gênes

[25–27 April 1908]

[Vicenza]

Dear Mother:

If you do not rember Genoa as a quite charming place, we must have been veree badly conducted. Diverse galeries plus picturesqueness etc.

This is from Vicenza there being here an abundance of rain & two hours before the Padua train. if the rain continues I shall go on thru to Venice.

As indicated on postal I landed at Genoa. & have come up via Pavia - Milan, Verona. the milan-verona trip is interesting, via Brescia & the shores of Lago di Garda.

I got no mail from you on my return to Gib so suppose it is awaiting me in Venice (have requested Cook Florence to forward my letters there).

I believe I reported my Spanish personal conduction as being satisfactorily concluded.

Met Prof. Nitze on hotel omnibus in Granada . don't know that anything else has happened that need be recorded.

Got a bit of writing done in Gib. before I started thru Spain - & a little bit since.

Think I have written everything else before this.

Good bye.

E.P.

+>——<+

162. ACS

April 28, 1908

[Venice]

Venice arrived OK. & comfortably fixed.

E.P.

Tea at Dr. Robinsons yesterday.

109

Pound found a room over a bakery at Ponte San Vio 861, not far from the Grand Canal and on the way between the Accademia and Santa Maria della Salute.

⊹══⇥⊹

163. ACS

[early–mid-May 1908]

[Venice]

Things O.K. guess I can hold out on present stores till June 20th or 30th.
There is only one Venice.
The Robertsons (Scotch Church Pastor) delightful.
Some pleasant folks at Hotel Milan who feed & gondole me now & then.
Don Carlos next door but one & Eleanora Duse's wisteria vines quite near.
Academia & Franchesi palace also within sight of the trees I use to loaf under.
be good to yourselves.
E.P.

⊹══⇥⊹

164. ALS

May 26 (1908)

[Venice]

Dear Dad

Today or tomorrow will mail you a 'Rais Uli Myth' or 'Tangier in Dry Point'

Try first on 'Outlook' then if not accepted Everybodies, McClure, Cosmopolitan, Book News in order.

you might enclose a copy of the 'Thumb Box Tangier' in the June book news. if it is out by the time my mss. arrives.

Be careful in your typewritten copy because I probably wont be able to see the proof

if they want exactness you better send my mss. also.

This will make 3 enclosures (1) Book News article - (2) type writ copy & (3) mss.

Get pay from Booknews (for 'first' Tangier) & send it as soon as possible.

Will also send a short story for you to try on 'Black Cat', or any old thing.

By the way the Evangelical Institute – (Boy's manual training school) here is in real need of a little coin. Converse hasn't forked up this year & any stray hustling that can be done on that account would do no harm.

Will try to get some more stuff off as soon as convenient.

Keep the advertising of 'A Lume Spento' in full motion – advance orders to be desired & no vulgarity of publicity need be shunned.

The Tangier will take the place of the letters you have been trying to get out of me.

The story is a comfortable & gruesome pack of lies.

'The <u>Tangier</u>' is <u>not</u> to be <u>cut</u>, <u>mangled</u> & twisted into mildness because the editors don't like some of the lines. print it where it goes <u>as</u> <u>is</u> even at less pay. it is worth $50 . . but don't suppose you will manage to get that -

Love to you & mother -
E.P.

Everything here OK.

None of the articles and stories Pound wrote merely for money were accepted for publication. A Lume Spento ('With Tapers Quenched'), his first book of poems, was being printed at his own expense by a Venice printer, A. Antonini.

╪══╪

165. ALS

May something near the end. [1908]

Venice

Dear Mother.

I will either today or tomorrow mail you one or two short stories. 'La Duquesa's Necklace' you may copy & try first on Smart Set & afterwards, if rejected, where you like.

The second one 'Genoa' I think I shall call it. you may do with what you like.

In typing leave good triple space between the lines. it is much easier on the editorial eye & consequently on the temper. If I do not get the 'Genoa' copied. will send the 'Necklace' alone.

Your letter came yesterday. if you wish to be quite useful. you may send me some visiting cards – the plate is at Wright's – also about fifty sheets of the best armorial writing paper. – plain gold arms as usual. The package post is not expensive so you can send matched envelopes or not as you like.

I don't care to count too much on getting the Vermont or Idaho job you know . – & my applications will get in very late coming from this side.

Of course it was only a question of a year or so, before I should have attempted to establish my self in London. And as events have always shaped themselves to hurry me along a bit faster than I should have moved my self, it may be that I am not to wait.

Apropos of something to do. you know Venice is nothing but a rather small wet villiage where you can see most anybody if you hang round long enough.

A few days ago I met Wolf. Ferrari. the composer of 'Das Neues Leben', an opera composed on Dante's Vita Nuova – Frank Damrosh presented it in N. Y. last year & had written to the Ferraris that he would come any where to see them this summer. (I have seen the Maestro twice since & he has consumed my cigarettes, & I expect to see him again.)

Now it befalling that there is probably no one in the U. S. that knows the Vita Nuova more intimately than I do it seemeth good to me that I should 'do' Mr. Wolf Ferrari for 'Book News'. as the first of a series of celebrities concerning whom America is semi-ignorant. As Ferrari goes to Munich before long Damrosh will miss him. : Also as he is very intimate with Humperdinck, the 'Hansel & Gretel' composer, I presume there is a second sketch in the offing.

The people who fed me off & on at the hotel Milan were a certain Miss Wells, well along in the afternoon of life. & a 'plain Massachusetts person' Norton by name, whose papa happens to be Charles Elliot Norton. our foremost American Dante Scholar. & whose unkle has a gentle little job as President. of Harvard. As she wandered into about every book shop in Venice. asking gently for 'Il Lume Spento' & raising a row because they didn't have it, I presume she is good for getting the book. which has much of its source in old Provence & early Italy. before a couple of readers who will be intellegent enough to understand it.

Lauder, who is I presume synonimous with 'art in Scotland' was also at the 'Milan' during their stay, & did not seem to object to my appreciation of what he was doing.

By the way. if any one mentions a certain 'F. R. Whiteside' who happens in a quiet unostentious way to be making American art. — because he is content to do without the blare of the bassoon. & never content until his stuff is absolutely <u>right</u> –. if any one happens to mention this person. you may say that after his studio. a great many of the so called 'old masters', Murillo for instance, become impossible for their crudity. while not even Velasquez invalidates the undeniable <u>right</u> (truth, understanding, call it what you will.) of Mr. Whitesides color. or the intellegent charm of such of his work as is himself, & with which he is beginning, just beginning to be somewhat content . .

I have got a $10. contract to teach the Italian tongue so presume I am safe till the end of June. at which time. unless some advance orders for a certain book arrive prepaid I anticipate the desire for coin. which coin ought to arrive.

Book News,	$10 – $15
Wheatley. Crawfordsville.	$25
McKintosh.	$ 100

Of course Mr. Antonini. will come in for a fair proportion of the book money. but the ads must be kept going. & an american reprint must not be too far behind the Venice edition.

Send Dad to Book News to talk up that 'personalities' stunt. he can bluff better in person than I can on paper. – send him right away. – I think I have given the data. Me. the Dante student. Me the rising light. Mr. Ferrari. the composer of the opera on Dante's 'Vita Nuova' presented last winter in N. Y by F. Damrosh. Mr. F. whom Damrosh wants to see & probably can't – more to follow. The Book News. needs variation on continuous string of literary personalities.

Suppose I could do Marie Van Vorst. later. or Symons or E. W. Hornung. if they want literary stuff. But suggest the variety of music, paint, sculpture.

The short story series is intended to supercede my 'Town' articles. using the town atmosphere & description as stage setting & trailing across it a faint thread of incident. This does not show as strongly in the 'Necklace' & 'Genoa' as it is to in 'Verona' & the Venice story.

The 'Sulle Zattere' that I sent with the 'Tangier in Dry Point' is not one of the series. The incident in that Poesque yarn happend to one 'Sid' Skidmore. by the way. all but the romantic slip of paper & the post mortem animation which I added for the benefit of the 'genteel peruser'.

Love to you & dad,
E. P.

My dear mama, some of the things in the tales, diction etc. may not be exactly what you would have used. but most of it is carefully considered & used for purposes. perhaps more clearly seen, on the third reading than the first. I find in 'Genoa' the word 'spat' which I however do <u>not</u> want changed into expectorated. The editors will do enough messing. so even where you object. I ask a fairly exact copy.

---

166. ACS

May 31 [1908]

[Venice]

Have sent the photo for the Saints as mother requested. Weather here wonderful. No particular excitement. The comet painter. my friend Italico Brass has a whole room of pictures at the International exhibit here. & the show is rather good.

Lovingly
E.P.

---

167. ALS

[May or early June 1908]

[Venice]

Dear Dad.

In fireing up that press notice in the Hailey papers, you might have them suggest that there is a vague chance of the Univ. of Idaho securing my services if they run hard enough. Personaly I am not dazzled by the job. but it would do if nothing better turned up. Get me detatched to the London corps diplomatique for the winter if you realy want to please me. I enclose another notice . in case the package mailed a few days ago failed to reach you.

Hump up Kildare. also & start a run on Wanamakers book dept. for my last work.

What did the Inquirer PAY for <u>post cards</u>. . Tell Rogers that for $50 I'll do him a nice column on modern Tangier & Rais Ulian atmosphere . as it <u>is</u> and <u>was</u> not as one got the impression of its being from American reports.

Please forward enclosed slip to agency. address. me Poste Restante. Venice.

Write answers to any more vacancies over $1500 giving glowing account of my career. & saying $2000 is my figure.

Love to you & mother.

E.P.

Get preannouncement of my book into Book News.

+⊨═⊨+

168. ALS

June 18 (1908)

Venice

Benign & Reverend Parent.

Your opening question 'on what are you existing?' is one answerable in several & diverse ways according to point of view.

Upon this balmy eve, June 18th. in the year of our Lord 1908, I am in the sense physical existing on ham 25 centesimi, bread 10 c. plums 10, chocolate 25. making in all 14 american cents expenditure which is very extravagant. & the chocolate in the nature of superabundant luxury. As a check for my Book News article did not get sent on or about June 1st it is difficult to say on what I may be living when you receive this.

(if by the way you have not already received & sent one or two checks from Crawfordsville.)

After the slender supply of sheckles now by me empursed shall have disbursed itself there remains a building on the grande Canale 'Un Monte de Pieta' to wit an official & government Hock Shop. Thither will I repair, may hap, Oh Excellent Theophilus!, with a suit case an overcoat, a suit, a checked suit of clothes a bit too warm for the Venetian June, after that there would be certain other trifles, a tuxedo a bit out of fit. etc. After which were there need I could, I trust, starve like a gentleman. It's listed as part of the poetic training, you know. & one would accept it with that mordant american humor that is after all one of the very few possessions worth having.

I am by no means sure it would not be pleasanter to starve the body in Venice than to starve the soul in a backwoods hamlet.

Of course there is no particular need of either. You may, by the way if McKintosh have not yet sent his check. notify him of your suspicion that I could use it, a condition for which you consider him rather responsible & saying that the pitance with which I started for my beloved Italy being about 'gustato' you would take it kindly of him, to remit. (100$)

Also with one Brother Wheatly, Brick House, next Big 4, station, Crawfords-ville. Give greeting in the name of peace, & suggest that $25. now 3 months due on furniture. should be sent. The agreement was that they pay at end of 3 months – march. april. may. make it now overdue.

As to my short stories. I do not send them with my own approval nor do I ask yours. I write them in the first person of any character that comes into my head, & say anything I can think of that might make 'em sell.

At least you've got to try to make 'em sell if you expect me to eat. When I get to London I'll look after that myself.

Unless a rather big scheme I'm working at turns out well. or unless Vermont shows more anxiety than is yet apparent there is neither reason nor means for my coming to america.

I of course shall not leave here, where I am very cheaply & comfortably settled, untill I have the car fare or some definite prospect.

Again as to short stories. I am not a story writer & do them as a matter of necessity. I find the first person easiest to write in. I do not accept responsibility for any philosophy or views therein expressed.

If the expression of an opinion looks readable it goes. if you find them 'off' I regret it but accept & expect it. if you get disgusted, I also regret it but remember that the action of feeding is conventional & that mother approves convention. In some matters I agree with my kind mama. – In some matters I don't, that is also regrettable, but our view point is different.

Also please don't try to sell my book.

I came very near telling the first man who ordered a copy that he didn't realy want it & that he wouldn't be able to understand it & that I therefor didn't want to sell it to him. But a crescent bussiness sense or some regard for his feelings over came me. & I became silent.

The publisher gets a bit less than 1/3, this is between ourselves.

The edition is small. – both of these things I want kept to yourself. strictly . If I can kick up enough row of reviews, I'll make somebody reprint. on the strength of having sold the first edition very quickly – perhaps. I should from choice have printed about 50 copies to give away, but couldn't afford it. Ergo this vulgar desire for advertisment. As it is I want the copies of this first edition to go to the intelegent people who'll understand.

The book is to be a rarity and I value one copy placed in the Norton family. (or with your friend Ella Wheeler – who may be valuable in another way) much more than several copies sold to a Lower-Dutch contingent.

Guess that's enough ripping for one evening.
Love to you & mother.
E. P.

+=—=+

169. ALS

[June 18 1908]

Venice

Dear Dad.
May have been a bit caustic in my note of this early evening. Trust no damage done. Always regard the literary structure when you find the substance over raw. Thank you.

Your remark on the Tangier's article that some of the stuff could have been used by itself is quite correct. But dam it all. please understand. That the only way to get that same stuff accepted is to tie it up with packages of what is salable. I may not have demonstrated as yet that I understand the magazine world but I have learned a little of what they don't want which is something. if Aunt Frank wants to remit those orders prepaid there will be no objection raised. Also if I get the orders early I may be able to send the books over by someone & save postage or express – be sure of arrival. also edition is as I said a bit small & as I have several people barking I may have the pleasure of declining the orders that come late. It comes out as do the european books in thick paper cover (grey green) only. but is printed on hand-laid paper in good big type (9 point). Remember I want to get more orders for it than I can fill - It is a novelty for a book of poems to run out of print in a hurry. & will make good advertising for my second book. & no one need know the size of the edition but you & I & a very very few.

Dr. Robertson was very kind about playing post-boy with your letter & with the coin when it arrived, but as he is a man of sixty one can hardly have him making 2 Trips on every money order. Besides the poste restante or 861 Ponte San Vio is quite sure to reach me. Certified check on Cook & Sons or American Express orders are quicker than P. O. Orders which require about 2 weeks to get cashed. after the first slip comes.
Love to you & mother.
E. P.

+=—=+

170. ALS

[19–25 June 1908]

Ponte S. Vio 861[Venice]

Dear Mother.

Your letter is most kind. only you mustn't take my stuff so personaly. the 'necklace' is perfectly fictitious. I used certain incidents out of my own experience. as I should always do, because it is easier & because one knows them more correctly than one would know trumped up & more imaginary ones. if it is necessary for me to continue writing fiction I shall probably commit murder & arson in the first person. – I can't write comfortably in any other – I only know what I would do under certain circumstances. & I have to write from the inside –this is why novel writing bores me.

Of course the big men leave a volume or two well done. Rosetti, one vol. & some translations & a little prose Browning 2 vols. etc.

Harpers don't want my stuff, wont want it for 5 years. It is probably un saleable. because it is not the right kind of 'pour' for the other magazines. Am going to try some real true ghost stories for the 'Home Journal' next. Only it is so much harder for me to do the purely mechanical side. just the pen work than it is for me to make the things in my head.

Thanks for the order for 5 vols. I hope the check will get here soon.

Please don't get your sympathies fussed up over anything I write. of course it may be a tribute to the literary expression. but then. you may be a bit prejudiced in the favor of the writer. if I had a stenographer here. there are several things. I would get done before tomorrow.

'Back of the Franchesi' story, like 'Pavia' only more bloody.

'The Big Ship' spooks, like 'Sulle Zattery'.

'Gib' Gibralter, a la Tangier, only more 'intime'.

'Ghost Stories.' real psychic research rot.

'The Second Calerin', like 'Gib' only I'd need more time.

'Wolf-Ferrari'

'Some American musical work abroad'. To say nothing of straightening out that damn novel. –

Also a short story of the 'Professors Rose Garden' perhaps

––––––––––

Met Mascagni here at the Lido last evening. Damrosch gets a lot more out of an orchestra, but then - - - - -

Collecting autographs is vulgar & bourgeoisesque but buissiness sense increases in me. suppose sometime I can use Pietro's to embellish a pot-boiler & adorn a wail.

The June air here in Venice is quite wonderful & I am almost myself again. Expect I'll have to dynamite Antonini if I am to get that book done in time to see Wilson in Brussels. or get to London

Want to have a month up the Thames somewhere & meet Bill Yeats (& one or two other humans if convenient.)

I don't know that the world is being so darn hard on the picked chicken. I haven't starved yet. True. there is ever the possibility nay more the apparently inevitable opportunity to starve. but something or other always has turned up. I'm not keen on much more scholastic messings. but have written the registrar of 'Baliol' college Oxford for particulars. as to the Doctorate. Rhodes fellow-ships are gotten in U.S.A. on scholastic & athletic standing, of which I have neither. Guess I'll pull out some how or other. wouldn't object to a bit of hurry at the Indianna end of my finances. but suppose that in stall ment will have started before you get this.

$2.40 spent on 3 pairs of different gloves. plus my patent leather pumps and my one very swellegant tie admit me anywhere. And all italian dress suits fit so badly that mine, especialy as I do not make the mistake of wearing the wrong colored tie & weskit. is quite 'au fait'. Also my hight & my coifure help down here.

The 'Bart si mowitches' Russian Consul General to Berlin, on furlough, graced a very small afternoon tea here a week or so since also ornamented by yr. hmbl. svt.

'Long' our consul here spoke very beautifuly about old Mr. Byington, when I drifted in at the consulate the other day. 'Long' is a pits burg pennsylvanian. by the way. old Quay ring I should judge. diluted with a long stay in Italy.

Im going to honor you with an envelope of the stationary I'm using to keep up the family reputation untill the 'armorial bearings' arrive. The paper is stamped in the same sort of type only. thus. === < on what I should consider the wrong side only which I use in order to be 'au courant.' it is extravagant but seems to be effective. I wish the envelopes had a bit more goo on 'em.

The american reprint has got to be worked by kicking up such a hell of a row with genuine & faked reviews that Scribner or somebody can be brought to see the sense of making a reprint. I shall write a few myself & get some one to sign 'em. & Ella Wheeler will have to be drugged into another & Austin O'Malley, if possible. & I'll try 'Bib' Ibbotson for the north woods & Howland of the Indianapolis . something or other. thru Milford & George Emanuel, who'd hock his bloomin little soul for me, I think, for some yellow journalism in the back woods & the Chippewa Eagle. & then a collection of notices. & maybe something in the nature of opinions from the Nortons. & some London rumblings. and a wire perhaps or 'Spittin' Dawson' who is probably responsible for that notice you sent me about 'Johnie Powell' etc. etc – & the exhaustion of the first edition. - one has to live - it aint poetry. but it's chess of a sort. - Antonini's move just at present. these remarks are strictly en famille –

I am to figure always as the modest violet – I am, fame knocked unsought – most every body else having knocked there previous. as a matter of truth I don't care about a 'rep' but it's probably easier to make a living & be let in peace after you get one. 'Imogen Guiney' is another person for you to send announcement to. also dad to Owen Kildare. & you to Marie Van Vorst - she ought to be workable for a review. especialy if you are anxious about my sustinence. Dickey Green. also will be interested & Mr. Chester probably quite a good person with whom Dad could take council. Get Woodward talking also. Graham can talk quite pointedly. & for any length of time. he may start things at the University also, in a gentle – but firm & un ostentious manner.

Guess this is about enough scratching for one day.

Love to you & Dad.

EP.

---

171. ALS

June 26 [1908]

Venice

Reverend & benign parent:

Your $10 P. O. order arrives. I am not yet in actual want but I presume that by the time the P. O. pays the order I will be able to use the danaro' quite comfortably. thanking you kindly for the thought. Mother wrote of a further order for books. is that included in this $10. you do not mention it.

Have moved to more airy quarters. overlooking 3 canals. (one of them the big Giudecca.) a garden & a grassy corner of St. Trovaso.

My old ladies rented their rooms for a year so I was able to make the change comfortably. Saw Dr. Robertson this A.M. nothing startling on the Tapis. Havent heard from Antonini for 10 days but presume he'll get thru sometime.

Converse note evidently implies that he intends to chip in sometime for the home. Mr. A. will doubtless rejoice.

Love to you & mother

E.P.

Thanking you for the <u>advance</u> yass 'ir

> *Pound had moved to Calle dei Frate 942 on the Giudecca side of the island in the San Trovaso quarter. Miss Norton was one of the 'old ladies' who had invited Pound to stay in the apartment they had leased but were not using.*

---

172. ACS

[June 1908]

[Venice]

Dear Dad,

Nothing special to scrawl. I still eat. & suppose the Indiana sheckles will arrive before that privilege is denied me.

Love to you and mother.
E.P.

+≻══≺+

173. ALS [*letterhead*] Hotel Royal Danieli, Venise

7 July. [1908]

[Venice]

Dear Dad:

Glad I did n't write you before dinner yesterday the note might have caused perturbation. I being at that time quite disgusted 'with the stupidity of most everybody'. Mac. was told to send the stuff to <u>you</u> . not a check to me for you to change to P.O. order & send. Dr. Robertson may be able to use it if he don't he'll have to support me till it gets collected. I have seen 1st proofs for end of book & half of it is printed. so it may get done some time.

I am quite pleased with the printers work. & think it will look respectable externally at least. High festivities here for the fourth. from which I am about rested.

I don't know what to do about coming home. There is certainly no sense in coming till . I get a job. it being cheaper. much to live over here. I want to see Wilson in Brussels & some of the real people in London.

Wm B. Yeats more especialy.

Also why try to sell my very amateurish prose tales to the realy good magazines. Ten cent periodicals are my limit. for a while.

Believe the press is about awaiting my royal inspection at other end of town.

Love to you & mother. & for heavens sake send the Wheatley's & the Book News check in some sane manner.

Lovingly
Son.

+≻══≺+

174. ALS

[c.11 July 1908]

[Venice]

Sound trumpet. let zip the drum & swatt the big bassoon. It pays to advertise. ergo spread this precious seed. Haily shall read my biography. The Chippewa war eagle may summarize my gee-loorius career as about every copy sold means one more day's eat for your wandering child spare thou no pains. It is poetry & of course not a popular work but you needn't mention that fact. Let mother inflame the curiosity of her relatives & the Times Chronicle slop over on 'literature in Wyncote'. I will fire Indiana & Upper N. Y. my self.

As you dont know whats in the book you are expected for the present to say anything that will stir up advance orders. The Inquirer or Bulletin may note another University man in the Literary Field. Mr. E. P. Sometime Fellow in U. Penn. a promising magazine writer. etc.

Word reaches us that A. Antonini. etc. is about to publish. etc.

'With Tapers Quenched.'

You understand that what we want is <u>one</u> big hoorah of fore announce-ments. & <u>one</u> <u>more</u> big hoorah of reviews.

I give you & mother carte blanche to incite all our numerous family. (there ain't goin' to be no free list. I need the money) five lire id. est. 1 scad ($) the copy. Order in advance.

Besides what newspapers in the far west & Phila & the distant family con-nections send notice to

T. B. Mosher. Publisher. Portland. Me. (simply the card)

Edith Lewis McClure's Magazine.

Dr. Geo. Gould, 1722 Chestnut. St.

& Burt Hessler, Ishpenning. Mich.

E. W. Wilcox (also get me her adress as a review from her

would about keep me in 'orzo' id. est. barley soup for a month.)

G. C. Woodward. Reed & Pettit. 3^d & Chestnut.

W. G. McFarland. Oak Lane.

Mrs. Carson. Book News.

R. H. Titherington. Munseys

Evans. if you can find his adress.

In other words. knowing that your papa was in congress. I expect you to apply. You understand that what people think after they get book is a secondary matter. what I want <u>now</u> is advance orders. culled from general curiosity. the sale on pure & exalted literary merit will begin later.

Tax $1 (five lire.)

Besides it will give mother a nice new topic of conversation.

She is also to deliver Mrs. Weber into my hands for July if she can manage it.

By the way the american press in announcing this volumn of genuine wax work poetry can anticipate my return in the fall with a novel on Spain. & some short stories plucked by the way side.

I see no reason for keeping the press in the dark concerning my movements. nor for keeping the great american public in a state of nervous suspense.

Remember my scholarly career. my sojurn in Spain at the time of the wedding. Magazine work. Poems in the press. Novel & Stories coming.

Whang. – Boom – Boom – cast delicacy to the winds for I must eat.

Of course I figure as the modest retiring rose in all this.

Love to you & mother.

E. P.

---

175. ALS

[c.14 July 1908]

[Venice]

Dear Dad.

Your order for 10. copies arrived. thanks. dont approve of scrawling authors name over everything but will submit if you insist. it is a practise restricted chiefly to the lowest rungs of the ladder.

It is much better advertising not to do it. as everybody who has any license to have an autograph copy would have personal letters with aforesaid autograph.

The custom is boorish, but if you think it will make anyone happy all right. it savors of Elbert Hubbard & Lower nevertheless.

Also arrives a letter via Florence with various enclosures.

Might try a slip on the Coltons. as the book has already paid ¼ the publishers rake off I don't expect any $400 difficiency.

Came very nearly telling the first man that ordered a copy that he was too dumb to understand it. & that I did not wish him to have a copy. but my business sense intervened.

Dr. Robertson called with your letter & we had a pleasant hour. pictures of 10th & Kimball. were a bit of a surprise to his nibbs.

Enclosed slip. please return. Will mail another pack of lies in form of a short story later today. Hope it is mushy enough to sell. Could get that darn novel off my hands in about 2 weeks more if I had a stenographer.

Can't see any reason for my coming back to some God forsaken mud flat to teach skewl. You might stir up Furner 1420 Chestnut St. to sic out a job in New York City or <u>Phila</u>. $2000. However I am not anxious to spit my gizzard into the north atlantic so soon for the mere privilege of getting a little money.

Would like to force an american reprint of 'A Lume Spento' with, say, Scrib-ner.

That ass Eldridge writes as if your letter had shown a strong desire for me to get the job in Moscow Idaho for — sake don't do any thing to encourage such an attitude. - Guess my note will set him straight in his mind. Never under any circumstances send a photograph. I see on closer inspection that this Eldridge person is merely a dean.

Remember one or two facts.

1st· I can teach romance languages.

2nd· I can teach em to just as many people at once as can be packed into a class room.

3rd· I don't give a rip whether I ever teach romance language.

4th Let the mountain come to Mo'ammed.

5th· McKintosh came to Wyncote. & the next man can go to hell. or await my convenience.

6th· Such details as Ph. D. are of no weight at all against a bit of personality. the sort that gets the gang together & makes things move.

7th· That any professorial salary is only about 1/10 what it is worth to leave Venice & come into Mr. Murphy's back yard.

The agencies, & the publishers are dogs that have to be whipped into their place. and any body that tries any other method only gets shoved to the wall.

Have seen signatures like that of J. G. Eldrige before. I fear that should I be imprisoned in Moscow Mr. E's life would not be made any happier.

A full grown idea catching him a mid ships might do some serius damage.

Unfortunate error on his part prevents him from knowing who he is writing about so I presume he is to be forgave.

'A good position for you to take with Furner is that You wish me to come back to U. S. & that I don't want to. wherefor you want to have found a good enough job to bring me back.–

ze finesse.   chere papa   ze finesse.

Also you need'n't mention my age.

Boom that article in the Haily War-yap as I want to have a bit of fun with Moskow.

Love to you & mother.

E.P.

+≈=≈+

176. ALS [*letterhead*] Le Grand Hôtel, Venise

[c.18] (July 1908)

[Venice]

Dear Dad.

Mr Smith & Althouse party are stopping at Grand Hotel, & I have been sumptuously fed there.

123

Am going up to London about first of Aug. So send all mail cr. 8 Duchess St. Portland Place, London.

Also get, if you can courtesy of the port, for Miss. M. A. Derby. Sailing from Genoa July 23 or 4. North German Lloyd. (don't know name of boat) she may cart over some copies of A Lume Spento if it gets done. which it ought as I have seen last of it in print.

Dale is in Eng as I wrote. also will Smith & Althouse there.

I am using this gaudy ink because I dont care to buy more black & leave a surpluss of this behind me. neither do I care to pack the same among my neck ties. Venice is still as charming as when I arrived. but I suppose I'll get back here again before forever & I can probably find more congenial work in London. besides Venice is no winter resort.

Be good to yourself.

Love to you & mother.

E. P.

---

177. ALS

Monday July 20 [1908]

[Venice]

Dear Dad:

I am sending you 15 copies of A Lume Spento. They are <u>not</u> finished right and you needn't use 'em except on people who wont notice the difference

The damn fool printer has cut off a good half inch of margin & rough edge & made the thing look like a Sunday School hymn book. Luckily there are only 20 copies spoiled.

however I thought you were in a hurry to see what the book was & I wont keep you waiting any longer. Some people may find the smoothe edges pleasanter or they might do for binding. <u>Drat it all</u> however. -

Will try to send you the others by end of week.

Also you'd better get that Book News check, or Wheatley's $25. off to London 8, Duchess St. Portland Place as soon as possible.

Met the Mulfords. Pa. Ma. & Little Spencer yesterday morning. Sent their regards etc. to mother. The strain only lasted for about four minutes so I survive with nothing more than intense feeling of weariness on this the day after.

Dont hand those copies of my book around without explaining that they are 'sbagliato' i.e. not in proper shape. Better get off the subject as it <u>irritates</u> me after six weeks delay.

Suppose I'll get over it. I don't feel that it would do any grave damage to any one if I should get a job of some sort in London.

If Venice were not the most beautiful face on earth I should have the doleful dumps & have 'em bad. but its impossible with the sky & the sea wind here.

Give my love to mother.

As to ? ? ? what do I do.

Somedays I don't other days it's scribling of a most uncommercial variety.

You have my hearty sympathy for having possibility of genius in the family but I suppose it cant be helped

Cheer up & hope for the worst.

Yrs. with filial devotion.

Ez.

That aint intended for sarcasm either.

E. P.

+⊨⊨⊨+

178. ALS

[27–28 July 1908]

[Venice]

Dear Dad.

As I wrote. I am starting for London at the end of the week.

Smith seemed pretty certain he could get me some lecturing with the Poly-technique. – If he don't, guess you'll have to stand to the pumps till I land something. if those damn Wheatleys havent sent their $25 due me on furniture. I wish you'd write to 'Fred Vance' Crawfordsville & tell him I say its a hell of a note for me to be over here on the bloomin & those muckers 2 or 3 months late on their payment. . there ought to be something in London ($) when I arrive.

Better write to 'Danl Hains' in C. ville & not to Vance.

Tuesday

2 more letters from home. It is very pleasant to hear from home, you know. It is beginning to get hot here & I shall be glad to move northward when McIntosh check gets reported. The Robertsons had it deposited & I have drawn aginst it thru their kindness. $21 ballance due Mr. Antonini & $8 against it. so the venture has about paid for itself you see already and 70 copies left to sell. I cant get so awfully stung & it's good advertising.

Edition was 150 copies but keep it dark as when I state as I hope to before long 'First edition' exhausted' I wish to give the impression of a larger circula-tion. — eh, naturaly.

Smith as I said thought he could get me in touch with the polytechnique (& give me a tour. beginning May 1 '09 besides). If Wilson is in Bruxelles – about which I am not sure – I'll get him to fork over introduc. to Embassy in London.

125

But I put not my trust in princes nor them in authority. they're usualy too 'wise' by the time they get into authority. Mother has a way of asking 'if' I'd do or like certain places, positions, jobs, etc. Tell mother she may accept for me any situation paying over $1000 a year. if I in the mene time have killed the golden goose its easy enough to decline it.

With about ½ hr. to shave & get to an appointment I shall close because if I don't it i.e. the scrawl will lie round for a day or two more.

Love to Mother & Aunt Frank. remember me to cousin Sarah. etc.etc.

As ever . only more so.

EP

+≈=+

179. ALS [*letterhead*] Le Grand Hôtel, Venise

Aug 3 [1908]

[Venice]

Dear Dad:

Have not got started for London yet: shall go thru direct. have manouvered 3 half columns of news into Venetian papers & 'telegraphic' to N. Y. Herald Paris. I dont mean that I wrote it I arranged the events. The affair at the Countess Morosini's tomorrow night is also in its way the out come of my manouvers.

Have fallen upon a delightful family. H Dudley-Murphy. one of our real painters.

The Book takes with the gang here. Might work a subscription edition of my later stuff if I had more time here.

Love to you & mother

EP

Pound arranged two private concerts for Katherine Ruth Heyman in Venice, one at the **Countess Morosini's**—*referred to in canto III, along with other details from this stay in Venice—and the other in the hall of Liceo Benedetto Marcello, for invited guests only (as reported in the* Gazetta di Venezia *of 28 July 1908). His* **'telegraphic'** *to the Paris edition of the* New York Herald *appeared as a letter to the editor on 21 June 1908 under the heading 'The Event of the Coming Piano Season'. A translation by Marco Londinio of Pound's poem 'For Katherine Ruth Heyman (After one of her Venetian concerts)', was published with the title 'Nel Biancheggiar' in an article by Londinio, 'Celebrità contemporanee: Miss Katherine Heyman', in* La Bauta, *Venice, 9 August 1908.*

+≈=+

180. ALS [*letterhead*] Ezra Pound, 861 Ponte S. Vio, Venice

Aug 10 [1908]

[Venice]

My Dear Mother.

Starting for London Tomorrow.

One of my poems appeared (Translated by the 'Dirretore' himself) in La Bauta (The Venetian Colliers) saturday. Saw him Today & he wants more. gave him A Lume Spento. & read him some new stuff which i shall copy for him.

'But how you onnerstan' Venice!!' You onnerstan' it all'.

If I can make Venetian verse to suit the Venetians I suppose it ought to satisfy me. after a fashion.

I go with pleasant introductions in Paris which I shan't have time to use. & more to London.

Check finaly cashed you see.

Met Althouse this A.M. Miss Chamberlin or Mrs. – of 24. E. 47th in his party.

———

I go to London on divers chances. if Smith convinces the Polytechnique that I can lecture, I shall be spared the throes of ocean voyaging.

I will have this ready to mail in the morning.

A.M.

Was considering a subscription edition of my Venetian stuff but shall yap up the London publishers a bit first.

By the way - this packing up puts me in mind of it. - I wish you would have my veree big hencoop chair sent over to Frank Whitesides' studio. If he'll have it. Would rather have it waiting for me there where I will be glad to use it whensoever I come back. Than to consider it in its present very bourgeois surrounding, etc.

Love to you & dad.

EP

8 Duchess St.
Portland Place. London.

Here goes. will drop a postal from Paris en passant.

EP

Rememberances to Aunt Frank Cousin Sady & the rest.

Pound arrived in London in the second week of August 1908, and stayed, for as long as his credit held out, at Miss Withey's comfortable boarding house in Duchess Street, off Portland Place between Oxford Circus and Regent's Park in central London. He was

known to Miss Withey, having stayed there with Aunt Frank in 1906, and she took him in at the reduced rate of £1.1s.6p p.w., her advertised rates being 'from £2.2s to £3.13s.6p per week'.

<hr />

181. ALS [*letterhead*] St. Ermins Hotel, St. James' Park, S.W.

[c.17–20] (August 1908)

8 Duchess St. [London]

Dear Dad.

I've got a fool idea that I'm going to make good in this bloomin villiage. You'll have to stand to the guns for a month or so.

The remittance I suggested as a greeting for my arrival here has not arrived. & my assets are something under 1£ but my name is good here and so is the board. It is also time that I had a few weeks of regular living. I suppose it'll make a good six weeks to get realy under way. But Wheatley & Book News ought to pay most of it. If they don't? there remains the chance of selling something. a slender one but . . .

<hr />

As I wrote mother. Londonio. the 'dirretore' of La Bauta ('Colliers' of Venice) has already printed a translation of one of my verses. & has promised to print as much more as possible. Especialy the Venetian stuff. And as he is a man of some standing. with a couple of published works on higher musical criticism. I think a good deal of his praise & his 'But! how you 'onnerstan' Venice. you 'onnerstan' it all.'

It ought to help me with the publishers here. especialy if i have enough of his printed stuff to back it up.

The enclosed page of La Bauta may explain certain mysteries. I left the lady in Venice after arranging the two appearances mentioned in the article. Shall endeavor to 'manage' appearances here in season. You needn't worry about 'affinities'. If I succeede in my position of secretary manager. well & good. It has so far brought me into contact with a good many people whom I am glad to know. & who will be of use to know later. My sources of possible income are therefor. – Lecturing or Teaching at Polytechnique, Publishers & magazines. Commission on concerts & concert engagements. for the first pianiste of Europe. you can boom the same in the italian papers of Philadelphia. and among what so journalistic connections you have. I want a New York-S. Francisco tour for the winter after this. so all free advertising is of help.

The Paris Herald reported her after the first concert 'Complete mistress of her instrument, bringing out all its capabilities' 'Favorite in Berlin.' Italian press loud in her praise . . . as you can see from enclosed which you can get translated at the mission.

The 'casa Morosini' mentioned as the scene of her second success in Venice is where the German Emperor visits when in Venice. (The Countess Morosini's). Considering neither of us went to Venice with any introductions I dont feel that the management was so awfully rotten. – Luck plus hustle, I suppose. and then she is the finest woman pianist in Europe – which is of course a good deal of assistance.

You can as I say boom american art abroad. also note. The only american who has ever dared to introduce 4 american composers at one German (Berlin) piano concert. I shall get enthusiastic in a moment or so. – which is against my code. However just talk the few facts here enclosed to a few journalists. and send me copies of printed results. (can use 'em here perhaps) also remit notices (advance) & reviews (if any) of A Lume Spento. To use on publishers here.

Guess that's fairly explicit.

Also as for the coming home. as I have before said. I am just as likely to succede here as there. if I have a tour thru Spain for Althouse in May. I save $125. & two hells of sea by staying here. The delay on cashing McIntosh check has made coming home impossible any how, so argument wouldn't do any good.

Here's for the goin' on.
EP

+≻══≺+

182. ACS

(26 August 1908)

8 Duchess St. Portland Place [London]

Dear Dad.

Have established my credit with your 2£. down to 1s 5d. but in no danger of starvation.

I am glad you like the book. think my art is progressing.

a Mrs. Richardson is taking home a copy to have reviewed in Baltimore.

Elkin Mathews cant use anything before Xmas.

nothing definite at Polytechnique yet.

Send a copy of A Lume Spento to Scribner. saying there may be demand for reprint. also that my later Venetian stuff is being translated into Italian. & ask if they wish to inspect it. ask for careful reading of A. L. Spento, as it is not a surface thing. ? then as to using reprint of A. L. S. or including some of it in the second volumn. i.e. Stir 'em up any old way

do same to Mc clures with another copy.

Guess that's all the card'll hold.

EP

+≻══≺+

183. ALS

Aug. 27. [1908]

[London]

Dear Dad.

The arrival of Jesse James'es $1 makes me comfortable about buying a postage stamp.

I have seen Mitchell of the Polytechnique & think he'll do all he can. – after Sept. 20. – I saw him just as he was leaving for Baltic tour. Smith thinks I can have party for Spain about May 1ˢᵗ.

If I can hang on here in London I can get literary position that would take ten years at home. I have introductions etc. & unless there is some definite salaried position waiting for me. I see no sense in dying on two atlantic trips. Get me a paying job & I'll come very quickly. But if I've got to be an object of charity. I can be so here to much better advantage than any where else. I don't think I'll need more than one London season. – I'd have to have it sometime. & this looks as if it were it.

I have the two books to push. – A L Spento. and 'San Trovaso'. my Venetian work.

Told John Lane's manager yesterday that I was quite competent to sell an edition of blank paper. – that line of talk seems more effective than the 'great literary merit' stunt.

the Venetian stuff is as I should say painted on ivory where A. L. S. is on canvass. if I get the two underway. there is I think sufficient stuff that I did not bring with me. to make a third volumn.

There is enough as far as bulk goes to make a 4ᵗʰ & 5ᵗʰ - but I object to turning out mediocre material.

I think with that I'd get 'rep' enough to make people pay some attention to my prose by products.

If you'll poke anybody & everybody, from the Times Chronicle up into giving <u>REVIEWS</u> & send 'em to me as soon as given. It will be an excellent club to use on John Lane or any other publisher. – announce 'San Trovaso' indefinitely 'cause Lord knows when it'll get into print – but announce it.

Think I shall enclose a note for Mrs. Wilcox & let you forward it. It is quite certain that I can create quite as much stir at home from this side as if I were there. It is quite certain that if I come home I get no recognition here at all. Ergo unless, & untill you have a paying job to offer we will consider the north atlantic uncrossable. For a month or so unless somebody pays in what they owe me. I am the object of the paternal charity. – It's a bit rough on you but it costs no more than a steamer ticket. & it don't need to come all at once. As I have intimated my board here 1£ 1s. 6d. is more than I care to spend – but it is the one place in London where I am known, & have credit. also the $2 I might save by going somewhere else wouldn't half pay for the discomfort. 'they are taking me here for a good deal less than the regular rate – also I don't dare trust to pick up meals etc for much longer. you see its ten or eleven months since I have indulged in the regular routine diet. however these details are not of particular interest.

Dale seems to have disapeared. had his colleague Melzer. nailed in Venice however. – Have an invitation to come over to Paris & watch the Wright bros. fly. if I could get the man who invites me to back me up as he is doing to the giddy aeronauts. It would help some. Don't know whether the flights of the immagination would so appeal.

Confound it there seems to be such a lot that I might get done if I can manage to hang on, that it seems worth while to 'plunge' a little.

Thats all
EP

I think you can perhaps do better than this enclosure for Mrs Wilcox. Get a review out of her in the N. Y. Journal. (or any where else) say I need 'em darn bad. I would rather have you use your own note than mine but suit yourself. Mine'll do I suppose.

+≡≡+

184. ALS

[c.1–3 September 1908]

8 Duchess St Portland Place -W- [London]

Dear Dad:

I think I begin to see daylight if you can keep on the safety valve a few weeks longer. Have a vague idea I am going to be a success. Don't mention it.

As for clothes which you so kindly mention. I presume I do need a few. a suit would I suppose be in the long run just as economical as getting a light colored vest & a few frills. but if you haven't $20 handy I can push a long for quite a while on a hat, vest & a couple of new neck ties. you might mail my blue winter underware. 2 sets. and one of the <u>old</u> dress-suit chest protectors. not your own. if you can't get at the old ones. dont bother.

? Did you ever get a yarn of mine (of which you may have disapproved) called 'Pavia'.

? Did you start Danl. Hains after the Wheatly $25.

I continue to meet people who seem alive.

By the way. mother keeps writing about Whitelaw Reids. has she any direct introduction to them. Thru Woodford or any one. I think I could use 'em if I had a new suit of clothes. no hurry.

Also will you send a copy of A L Spento to Leonardo Terrone. better send him note first cr. Fencing Club. U. of Penn. & get his adress.

I don't know that there's much more. There's no use writing about things till they happen.

Love to you & mother.

EP

Also remember me at Tioga.
I believe I thanked you for 2nd 2£. Recd. so far in London 4£

+>==<+

185. AL

[c.8–9 September 1908]

[London]

Dear Dad.

2nd epistle arrives, £6 & 11.

The book now having paid expenses. I get out of it clear profit on all copies that may henceforth be sold.

Congratulations on your corner stone. - guess its a darn sight more important than my printing 15 versiculi

as for a permanent job on the U. S. Side. I'd be by no means backward in taking one in the civilized part of our great & glorious.

The rooral deestricts <u>are</u> too rich for my quiet urban blood.

If you would only attack some person of influence in a dark & cavernous alley & wring from him a promise of my employment I might be able to come back before I frighten the trembling world into recognition of my gee-lorious services. If you can't I'll have to bide my time.

If I could get enough into my head to take my Doctorate at the Sorbonne it would not be a bad thing - I would seem to have wasted time but I havent realy been up to steady study, much before now. & my mucking round the latin in the Museum here will use up about all the scholastic energy I'm likely to have before March.

The last lecture is Feb. 22. I think. and unless there is a very good reason. I'll sail the day after.

The 'corner stone' was for the First Italian Presbyterian Church (later referred to as 'F.I.P.C.').

+>==<+

186. ALS

[c.mid-September 1908]

[London]

Dear Dad:

I suppose Mr Elkin Mathews must be seriously considering a reprint from A. L. S. or he wouldn't be having me compile introductory matter for the same.

At least he says he wants to & he understands that the financial end of the game is entirely 'up to him'.

Have been lunching with a friend of Whistlers (who is going to take my 'Histrion' to Forbes Robertson, some time next week. a person 'palmèe' by the French Academy for prose. a poet who wants to 'push' my stuff in Oxford.

a hostess who had collected us.

In the language of Huck Finn. 'This here water aint so <u>darn</u> cold'

But let us have no undue excitement.

The English 'Daily Record' from Dresden . comes to hand with a reprint of 'Nel Biancheggiar'

EP
Adios. love to the mother.

⊹≻══≺⊹

187. ALS

[before 15 September 1908]

[London]

Dear Mother.

Have just disposed of 2 copies of A. L. Spento so feel I can dissipate a postage stamp. I begin to feel that somehow or other its London for the winter. if you are going to bring Hilda over I recommend Venice for next season. one can do the palatial there at a more convenable figure. You make remarks on wardrobe I am not sure I ought to branch out in that line until I am making my board. However if you wish & have the velvet. 3£ will give me an elegant tea gown & 1£ for umbrella & furbelows. The galosh & parasol are demanded by this milieu.

Did I tell you that I found the How arms described in detail in the opening of Longfellow's Way Side Inn. you probably knew it but you had never told me.

Will you mail the enclosed review to Dr. Gould. after you read it, please.

Give Mr. Hurlburt. my congratulations. (for what they are worth).

Have seen Miss Norton several times lately & met several new people who wont do me any harm strategicly.

People begin to get back to town & I presume I wont find much trouble in keeping my time filled. after Sept. 15.

Sunday

There seem to be several chances of something to do. 'San Trovaso' goes to J. M. Dent for examination tomorrow.

Also I note a teaching vacancy. & another stray job that I shall investigate.

If. – speaking mildly – I can get the 2 books moving. & etceteras the winter will not be exactly wasted. Keep joyful – you dont seen to be in much difficulty about it – remember me to Aunt F. Cousin Sady, etc.

Guess that's all.

With love

EP

There were distant family connections both to Henry Wadsworth **Longfellow,** *and to the* **Hows** *who once owned the Wayside Inn at Sudbury, Massachusetts, celebrated by Longfellow in his 'Tales of a Wayside Inn' (1863). See further letters 362 and 751.*

This is the description of the Howe arms in Longfellow's Tales of a Wayside Inn:

> But first the Landlord will I trace;
> Grave in his aspect and attire;
> A man of ancient pedigree,
> A Justice of the Peace was he,
> Known in all Sudbury as 'The Squire.'
> Proud was he of his name and race,
> Of old Sir William and Sir Hugh,
> And in the parlor, full in view,
> His coat-of-arms, well framed and glazed,
> Upon the wall in colors blazed;
> He beareth gules upon his shield,
> A chevron argent in the field,
> With three wolf's heads, and for the crest
> A Wyvern part-per-pale addressed
> Upon a helmet barred; below
> The scroll reads, 'By the name of Howe.'

William Hurlbut's *play* The Fighting Hope *was first produced in September 1908 at the Belasco Theater, Washington, DC, with Blanche Bates in the leading role.*

188. ALS

[c.23 September 1908]

[London]

Reverend Parent.

It looks as if the Polytechnique meant business. And Dent & Co. get polite concerning S. Trovaso. nothing is settled yet but as the Poly is discussing terms I think something will happen. If I can give the course in 2 or 3 places I will be quite comfortable. the thing will begin this month if it goes.

I have written Hilda what notes I want sent me. tell her <u>not</u> to send the Fioretti of St Francis as I bot a 2nd hand copy this P.M.

I am afraid (unless the Poly. pays more than I think it will.) that I shall have to continue drawing on the home exchequor for a couple of months. to get refitted. Think I got a rather good piece of cloth this evening. 2£ for suit suppose I'll make 'em think I intend to pay for it . when they get it made. If they dont they can put it in cold storage for a month.

With a room at 6s per wk. & getting my own breakfasts coffe. & buns. (3^d.) I think I'll get into line before so very long. Now that the American postage has come down to 2 cents.

I am finding enough books in the British Museum to keep me amused. It is refreshing to get at 'em again after the first real vacation from books I've had for six years.

Also tell Hilda not to send the 'Childrens Crusade' if inconvenient. I think I can borrow a copy. . to send however. the copy of 'The Half Hour' the little green pamphlet Evans & I started.

I don't know that there's much else to put in. If I get permanently into the Polytechnique. It'll mean that I get 3 or 4 months a year in London. If I get into the Poly. at all. I guess I'll stick. Combine that with a 'conducted party' & a couple of months in Italy with U.S.A. every other year. and I should feel I was geographicaly correct. as it were fitted into them there parts of the earth where I belong.

Of course this is all pipe dream. I won't know for sure about the Poly for several days. our friend Smith will deserve a good lot of thanking if the deal hitches. the course would end by March. & I ought to get enough in hand by then to run home for Easter. & start back with a party. in May.

Here's smiling.

Love to you & mother.

EP

189. ALS

27 September 1908

[London]

Reverend Parent:

4£. Thank Gawd it has came. Thanks to my friends & G. L. Lawrence (Loan Agt) I have survived. the week.

I think when I get home, whenever t'ell that is, I will know a h-l-l-l-l of a lot of things wot I didn't us't'er.

I may be easier to live with. In the langwidge of the immortal Mr. Kipling "I wish that myself could talk to my self

As I knew 'im a year go.
I could tell 'im a lot that
    would 'elp 'im a lot
'Bout a lot that 'e didn't know."

As for the future: Mr Churton Collins has been obliging enough to die. I may substitute my course for his at the Polytechnique. Mitchell, brings it before the Governors tomorrow. also he has had my synopsis typed to send to 14 other Polytechniques. If the deal don't go thru, guess I'll come home by that one horse line from Liverpool to Phila.

As Mr Smith put me next to the Polytechnique. you might drop down & thank him.

Guess Wheatley is a bad egg.

I move back to a respectable part of London tomorrow. 7s. a week for room & eat where I like. guess I'll be able to run it at that. the Duchess St. was over high but a good investment as I am invited to eat there when I like & met some pleasant & perhaps useful people there.

Am after a couple of translating jobs for the week coming.

(this is Sunday Sept. 27). Hope you & mother continue as happy as you seem. things will I presume settle for me in a week or so.

Guess I'll turn in, & be ready for the war-path tomorrow.

Thanks again for the £.

EP

Pound's money having run out he had raised ten shillings from a pawnbroker, borrowed another ten shillings from the singer Elizabeth Granger Kerr who had befriended him, and had moved briefly to a cheap Islington lodging house, with an out of order bath and no hot water, and with 'unthinkable and unimaginable' food and odours. He was now about to move back to central London, not far from Duchess Street, having found an affordable clean room in Mrs Joy's boarding house, 48 Langham Street.

190. ALS [*letterhead*] 861 Ponte S. Vio, Venice

[29 September–10 October? 1908]

[48 Langham St. London]

Dead Dad.

You must have messed up things with Scribner. I have no intention of paying for an American edition. After E. W. Wilcox & a few others get the thing reviewed. somebody may take it. with some improvements. – a few of the weaker things cut out & some later stuff in serted. But under no circumstances think of subsedizing an American edtn. Mosher seems to be in a reasonable state of mind & he is by far the best person to have print the first Am. Edit. However there is nothing for you to do there immediately.

The Polytec. is having my syllabus typewritten to send around to varius places. – Perhaps I can even give a few lectures there this season. – in consideration of course for next year. etc.

I also seem in train to get at some of the magazine people.

Expenses.	two piece suit. 2£.	half paid.
	hat	10s/6.
	socks	5s/6

as long as you can send 3 & 4£ orders. (preferably 4 of course. you needn't worry about the extras. I've got to get a vest some new neck ties hand kerchiefs etc. you better send the two suits of winter underware its new. & the difference between $4 & the postage on it is worth saving. just now. that sort of thing is expensive here.

I think this is the town for me to get settled in. only wish there weren't so much drain on your exchequor in the process. However I suppose it would be just as long & much if I were in Phila. – I always seem to spend $1 a day there above my feed & sleepin' anyhow. However I'll crawl out some time. so keep on smiling. Order 4£. cashed today. (Oct. 1. assignment.).

To answer some of your questions.

Threnos. means Death.

Tintagoel. is the name of a castle in Wales or Cornwall I think. Legendary in Tristam & Iseult story.

Villonaud. is a compound on name Villon. for one Francois Villon. a french poet of the XIII century, or the XII or XIV. I'm no good at dates. If you remember seeing Southern in 'if I were King' at the Broad St Theatre. you'll remember one modern attempt to bring him to life & light.

Stevenson (Robt. Louis) essay on Villon. & his 'Lodging for the Night' or 'Sire Maletots door' are much more historicaly accurate.

In the two Villonauds, I was trying & think succededed in expressing the Villon spirit.

you can get translations of most of his things.

Swinbourne has done the Epitaph in form of a ballad written when expecting to be hung. & Rosetti has made the best translation of the 'Ballad of Dead Ladies' on which the 'Villonaud for this Yule' is modled.

Villon copied it twice himself in a ballad of Dead Knights. & one for the Holy Apostles.

His prayer to the Virgin is held highly, & also some gruesome things of the lowest life of Paris.

You will recall the first act of McCarthy's play, perhaps.

Guess its dark enough to go forth & eat.

Love to you & mother, & keep on smiling,

E P

P. S. You may tell Miss Humphery that I was interested in her selection of titles. I am interested to find that nearly each one of the poems I put in has found some one to whom it appeals. I am not particularly interested in doing or writing ordinary things – I think also my rakeings from the Renaissance stuff here in the Museum will attract a bit of notice. later or sooner.

By the way Tyrone (Leonardo) is at 3907 Pine St., Fencing School. – you can send the book to him there if you have not already done so.

Guess that's all.

By the way you might send a notice of A L Spento to Mr. Zimmerman (cr. Ried & Fort. gents. furnishers. Reading Terminal)

Kildare has not yet written.

E P

'Threnos' and 'the two Villonauds' were included in A Lume Spento.

+≥——≤+

191. ALS

11 October 1908

[London]

Dear Dad.

The enclosed explains itself. As soon as I get that next winter engagement <u>fixed</u>, I will send you data & see what you can do with the university extention people. I suppose I'm luck to get it even for next year.

There may still be a chance at some of the 'branches' for this year, but I suppose it's unlikely. However as soon as I get a signed contract for next season (30 lectures in course). I think I can use it as capitol & get something or other. If on the strength of it you can sound the Univ. extention & get me something thru <u>Jan-April</u> - it would help. - of course there's no use sending over mss. etc as I directed Hilda.

I am doing work at the British Museum that ought to bring results . and I think if I can meet the right people . the results may not be so long delayed.

This oct. 11. I suppose your Oct 1. contribution to the sinooz of war will be arriving shortly.

Thanking you in advance etc.

I expect to hear Mr. G. B. Shaw this evening. cant find any notice of Campbell Morgan. There's a Campbell heir that seems better known.

Dont know of much more. have put out some new lines. and am trying to keep in motion.

Love to you & mother.
E. P.

+≻==≺+

192. ALS

19 October [1908]

48 Langham St. W. [London]

Dear Mother:

Suppose I'd better stay on & see things thru. Guess the 'Quinzaine for this Yule' will be out by Dec. 1. am just using a few of the newer things. 'Truslowe & Hanson' Pub. unless something unforseen arises.

Am lunching at the Savage Club with Mostyn Pigott on wednesday.

Had supper last evening with some friends of G. B. S. & think I may get into things before forever.

I think I mentioned to father that the Poly. would probably give me six lectures after Xmas. & wants the full course of 30 for next season. Also they want to print circulars for it immediately. Which when done you can bring to the notice of Pug Tompson. & the Univ. Extension. & perhaps get me some spouting nearer home. The U. S. is just as much in ignorance concerning Romance Literature a la E. P. as is London. & there is no reason why they shouldn't pay backsheesh in like manner. From say. End of February (3^{d} week) to April 30.

I want father to keep the fire burning under Smith & Althouse so that there will be no fluke on the spring tour thru Spain.

Thats all I happen to think of just now.

Love to you & Dad.
E. P.

Oct. 19

A Quinzaine for This Yule / Being selected from a Venetian sketch-book—'San Trovaso' *was 'Printed and Published by Pollock & Co.' in an edition of 100 copies in December 1908; a further 100 copies were printed for Elkin Mathews in late December. Pollocks printed the Polytechnic's syllabuses. The syllabus for Pound's first* **six lectures**, *issued in December 1908, described them as* A Short Introductory Course on The

139

Development of the Literature of Southern Europe ... by Ezra Pound, M.A. (Sometime Fellow in the University of Pennsylvania) author of 'A Lume Spento', 'A Quinzaine for this Yule', etc. *The lectures were to be given on Thursday afternoons at 5 o'clock, commencing on 21 January 1909 and running through to 25 February.*

+≻━≺+

193. ALS

[21 October 1908]

[London]

Dear Dad.

Underware arrived. one suit. OK. & 2 strange articles inches thick that I never bought or used.

? ? ? Where's the other suit of velvet.

————

to matters of more interest.

Will send you printed sylabus of my short course of some lecturing & typed outline of the longer course. Also I hope notice of the Xmas book.

Make my debut in the St James Gazette sometime soon & will probably get a review of A. L. S.

If with this & the mosher catalog. you & mother cant get me some lecturing in U.S.A. for March & April, I shall loose my respect for your diplomatic ability.

Had lunch at the Savage club with Mostyn Pigott today.

The enclosed note explains why I have not seen C. M.'s name on church services notices.

Have not yet got the terms I want on my second booklet.

Dont try to buy out Mosher as you did Scribner. I want to get home in March anyhow & have him do a second volumn.

I wonder how much mss. you are sending over to need such an awful lot of postage.

By the way if you can get me U.S. lectures in January I could cut the short Polytec series here. – The thing is to get the appointment.

That is between you & me.

I dont know that there is much more to write.

I suppose this will reach you about the time I am celebrating my 23d. Kalendem natalem. I wish you many pleasant returns of the day.

Love to you & mother
(& such others as you think prudent)
EP

'Histrion', a poem from A Lume Spento, *appeared in the* Evening Standard *and* **St. James's Gazette** *on 26 October 1908, and a brief review of the volume appeared in a supplement to the paper on 26 November. It may have been Pound himself who wrote: 'It is wild and haunting stuff, absolutely poetic, original, imaginative, passionate and spiritual. Those who do not consider it crazy may well consider it inspired. Coming after the trite and measured verses of most of our decorous poets, this poet seems like a minstrel of Provence at a suburban musical evening.'*

---

194. ALS

[c.26–27 October 1908]

[London]

Pater meus. et molto honrado.

Arrives $20. Tante gra_zie_ also epistle from your wife. my Lady Mother. I enclose my de-butt in the Synt Jymes Gazoot.

'Histrion' is (by way of glossary) derived from the same origin as histrionic. appartaining to an actor etc. Would have dedicated the lines to Mr. Forbes-Robertson, if I had thought soon enough.

As the St James has a bigger circulation than any 2 evening papers in London, & only prints about 4 poems a week it is a fairish good thing to get in touch with.

I go forth again to stir up sedition.

You might as well leave Mosher to me.

After I get his catalog with my blast in it I shall endeavor to devour, chew, masticate etc. a few of the pubs. in this our present villiage.

The climate here is hell. the liquid part of that same.

Comfort my lady Mother by saying I buy shoes (high) & rubbers tomorrow when I cash the M.O.

You might have the 'Histrion' copied in Chippewa. Idaho. Times Chronicle etc. if convenient.

Evening Bulletin ought to give me a whoop pretty soon.

just drum 'em up. especialy if you have reporters who are bored by presbitery meetings etc.

Stuff 'em full.

My present adress is 48 Langham St -W-

Guess thats all.

Love to you & mother

E. P.

As Thomas B. Mosher mainly reprinted already published works, he must have been considering reprinting A Lume Spento. *In* The Bibelot *of November 1908 Mosher* announced that his 'New Catalogue covering every title I have published, 1891–1908 inclusive, is now ready', but it listed nothing by Pound. (See letter 199.)

┽═┾═┽┾

195. ALS

[November 1908]

[London]

Well!

Looking more like a proud presbyterian peacock than ever. . A la directoire with feathers & aa' that. having opened a recent package I so discover you. It has by the way occurred to me of late that for some years past I have been so over busied contemplating abstractions & the marvelous working of my mental internal workings that I have not taken time to regard you as an individual with a certain right to think, hold ideas etc. for yourself.

& not necessisarily ideas in accord with my own. It seems to me that this action or rather lack of it on my part rather demands some sort of apology on my part which I here tender. It dawns upon me gently that perhaps the holding of a contrary opinion on your part is not a sin against the eternal order of things, and that however diversely we may regard life, society. etc. we may at least commence a polite acquaintance, or even broach some unexplosive intercourse. The necessity of reforming you does not any longer seem imperative. your opinions if egregiously incorrect & illogical may perhaps have some raison d'etre.

I suppose I might have granted these things before in a general way. but of late they have been borne in upon me more understandingly.

It seems to me that there have been times when no one has taken any particular trouble to consider what you wanted, & why you had a certain right or reason to want it.

Lack of intelligent sympathy (I presume it is called.) with your aims, views. etc.

I begin to perceive that there have been diverse & definite times when I might have displayed a little more horse sense to you ward without serious detriment to anything in particular.

Ebbene.

Manaña mejor.

A rividerci,

E. Pound

┽═┾═┽┾

196. ALS

Friday Nov 20 (1908)

[London]

Dear Mother,

Your note finds me too preocupied with externals to enter into discussion as to phases of genius.

I am beguiling myself with that neuralgic affectation of the peri - - nerve which is dignified by the cognomen of Shingles. it is about as dangerous as chicken pox & as uncomfortable as necessary.

Bill Sharps best friend is doseing me with Rhus tox & when all my vocabulary isn't used up on my sensations I'll write more.

E. P.

May say that Bill Sharps amicus is a licensed M.D.

- just as a word of comfort to you -

Proof of 'Quinzaine in this A.M.

Will get overcoat when I rise from this if youll direct me how to get credit.

Guess I can manage it.

Love to you & dad.

EP

197. AL

Saturday Nov 21 (1908)

[London]

Dear Mother

Dr Byres Moir brought the luster of his presence into mine abode this A. M. & said the worst was over. no harmful effects. to remain quiet til Monday

As for an overcoat I dont know how you expect me to get credit, but then.

Am being well looked after here.

To answer some ?? in your & fathers recent letters.

Am correcting proof for 'Quinzaine'. which will be out about Dec.1. This not being Italy it will not have to be printed in dabs in order to have the 'w's hold out.

2. I should not have cast my vote for Taft & certainly not for the vice-president. - (he may be different from his family, but even then). -

3. My luncheon at the Savage club was good - except the oysters. - as M. P. got 'em as a special delicacy. I did not tell him so - the truth is however that the english oyster tastes very much like decayed leather slightly flavored with zinc.

To answer dads question 'who is Mostyn Pigott'. M.P. is a sandy moustasched englishman, very pleasant to talk to, who thinks that he & somebody else killed the boom in poetry started ten years since by John Lane.

I have not gone to the mint. nor to John Pound. Leadenhall (and a number of other streets).

? about this & Doyle house This place is quite O.K. Doyle wasn't.

+>===<+

198. ALS

(24 November 1908)

[London]

My Dear Mother:

I have ariz from my couch of discomfort & again read your note of perturbation.

? Enlarged Ego. Kipling? Milton? etc. You seem to want descriptive instead of Dramatic poetry. thats all.

If you will read Browning's 'Men & Women'. his 'Dramatists Personae'. Some of Theocritus or Ovid's 'Heroides' you will find that they are done somewhat as my stuff. I mean. they procede from a centre outward. not from one point of the circumference to another.

Also if you will take Hamlet's soliloquy. or most any of the greater passages of Shaxpere you will find them written in the 1st person. – I don't care to bother with fitting every poem or passage I knock off with a whole play – even if I were able to.

As for Mr. Milton. – when I want to do a Comus I'll translate or adapt some of my renaissance latin stuff. –

Dante of course the most sympathetic of the crew.

without Plato. Shaxpere. Dante. for a major triad literature would be pretty well stove in:

As for Kipling, & conditions etc. His stories show India much better than his verse.

Show me one good poem & I'll show you 2 stories. Besides. he doesn't seriously write poetry except on very rare ocasions.

As for descriptive verse. unless one have realy something new to describe. we are overstocked with it. – miles of it.

Of course the trick is to make one's characters live. Theres the rub. when it comes to bewteeous nat'r. – I resign in favor of the painter.

In comparing my stuff with everybody in general. it may be just as fair to compare what I do before 23 with what they did before 23. one develops sometimes. you know.

I am by the way trying a historical stunt. on Portugal. trying to hit a happy mene between 'Sordello' which is fit meat only for cranks like myself who enjoy using their mental senses. and the Tales of a Wayside Inn which are mostly twaddle or verging on it.

(that is to say. they haven't much poetic magic about them.)

Early poetry is apt to be subjective, but I can't see that mine is so, an overwhelming part of the time.

Of course if one does not feel what one writes it is rather foolish to expect to make any one else feel it.

Guess that's enough for one spasm.

Love to you and dad.

E.P.

┼──────┼

199. ALS

[November 1908]

[London]

Dear Dad.

Your 4£. for overcoat. arrives grazie tanto – <u>a la madre</u>. Give her my most best salutations. Mosher has changed his mind but I dont mind much. – Had had all the fun of expecting his edition without the bother of correcting it.

If you can get 'Histrion' copied why cant you get A. L. S. reviewed? A. L. S. seems to have made a hit at Terrone's. several of the gang according to him. are interested.

Enough copies of the '15' are ordered to pay for ½ edition. & I know of some more wanted so presume it will go thru O K.

that is I presume a fair start as there has been hardly time for people to reply to cards.

By the way. the next 'ad' in the inquirer. can drop the 'Prof'.

Ezry. Pound. M. A. Author of A. L. S. – Lecturer on Romance Literature to the London Polytechnique – <u>sounds</u> more symposius. – I dont suppose my few introductory lectures will flood us with wealth. but they'll do for 'adv'.

By the way I think we'll have a paragraph on those lectures later on. when I send you the 'Poly' 'ads.'

Also one on the new book. Let 'em learn who the hell I am. – not that I am anybody in particular – but it will help me to get a modest & comfortable job if people think I am.

I am up & comfortable so there need be no worry over my day or two of retirement from active life.

Had a bully good letter from Terrone – hm. mentioned it on page 1. –

Guess. thats all.

Love to you & mother.

EP

┼──────┼

200. ALS

[November 1908]

[London]

My Dear Mother.

Arrives 4£. thank-you. can hardly get an overcoat therewith but shall continue rejoiceful.

As for your dearly beloved Mulfords, let me remark en passant that at the time of our Venetian encounter their own hopeful was in as dire need of a shave as I was. The old man not having had one for a decade is I presume out of the running

I dont know that my annals for the past week have been wildly exciting. I am meeting more people which may or may not be of advantage later on.

Who are your Boosy-Ogdens? that are to be honored by an introduction.

Am to lunch at the Ker-Seymers on Sunday & have tea with some of the Fiona McLeod crowd.

Think I may pack off to Whitby for the month between the time my book ought to be finished & the time my lectures commence. Have knocked off a few things. & begun a Masque of Portugal. which I may or may not finish. Otherwise there seems to be a lull in the excitement.

Love to you and dad.

E.P.

⊬═╾═╼╫

201. ALS

[27–28? November 1908]

48 Langham St. [London]

Dear Dad.

The 'Quinzaine' goes to press today. As the last copy was sold yesterday I cant send 6 to Mr. Chamberlin. Will send 2 or 3 out of the few copies I had reserved for my own use & suggest that he transfer the rest of his order to my next stunt which ought to be along in a couple of months.

of course if Mathews or Unwin want to buy the standing type there'll be a second edition of '15' quite soon but that is uncertain. You needn't write Chamberlin 'till I know.

Wad of clippings from mother arrives also today.

Had my thanksgiving dinner solus at Pagani's which has the best feed in London & where the waiters hang round me for the sake of a few words of Italian. the other week one rotund person seeing the effect of my 'palare' tried his. It was OK. for bout three lines & then he got stuck on 'testa di vitello' & the waiter explained gently in suavest french. It's the little things that help.

Saw Yeats at a matinee of his 'Deirdre' yesterday but as he was in one part of the house & I in another there was nothing more than seeing.

Till later

EP

❧──❧

202. ALS

[c.10–11 December 1908]

[London]

Dear Mother:

Am shipping on a faint flavor of Xmas that I got in Tangier.

For Dad, I am sending a less valuable but more long drawn out affair.

The Quinzaine I sent some days ago & hope they have reached you.

Elkin Mathews seemed to think favorably of a reprint a few days ago. but I have not his decision yet . so shall not count on it.

In answer to questions. I do ocasionaly read the london papers. especiary when they print what I have sent in.

The last poem in the Quinzaine was printed in the St James Gazette. two or three days ago.

Dad can get it reprinted if he likes in the Inquirer. Noting that it is in my second book also.

Leave off the 'Prof' before my honoured cognomen. s.v.p.

'Nel Biancheggiar' is the pome.

Well. Merry Xmas to both of you. & heres hoping I'll be home for the next one.

E. P.

Pass my rememberances along the line. Tioga. N. Y. etc.

*The **last poem** in* A Quinzaine for This Yule *was 'Nel Biancheggiar'. In the* St. James's Gazette *of 8 December 1908 it had the title 'For Katherine Ruth Heyman (After One of Her Venetian Concerts)'.*

❧──❧

203. ALS

Dec. 14 [1908]

[London]

Dear Dad:

Your note arrives with a certain dull thud. I have been more or less engaged in refitting - mine armour & mine underware, that is not underware, but

147

supplies generaly which were a bit on the wane. - Also since my illness I have not tampered with any excess of economy. I think however after two more dabs of $20 you can cut down to $15 & I will see what can be done to diminish that same. it will depend on how many people come to the lectures & whether I get outside lectures etc.

I did get a sixpense & I am not going to Whitby.

I enclose sample of scotch grey. 1 suit. £5. I wish I had seen it before I bot the stuff I am now wearing. the thick one is my overcoat.

Well its midnight so I'll ring off.

My lectures will keep me here till the very end of Feb. so it will be March anyway before I get home. - and then there <u>may be</u> some conducting so dont let our lady mother be too disappointed if there is a bit of uncertainty in the date.

Good luck.

Love to you & mother,

E. P.

+≻══≺+

204. **AL** [*letterhead*] Yates Library, High-class Stationery, Printing Sample

[late December 1908]

48 Langham [Street, London]

My Dear Mother:

Have delayed sending more Quinzaine 'ads' because there wernt any more Quinzaines for sale. Elkin Mathiews is having a second edition printed now so will send the cards.

If orders come to me or to Pollock, however I get the whole thing so you needn't send any explanations with cards.

I found one of our friend 'Storks' little books for sale at Mathews this p.m. so it is to be seen that I am not the only Amurkhan 'butting in'.

Dont know that there is anything more of particular note, except my rare economy in using stationers samples. which is highly commendable.

Love to you & Dad

Hope Aunt Frank comes out sunny side up. Give her my regards.

Aunt Frank, now Mrs Frances A. Beyea, had opened 'a new modern fireproof apartment hotel', The New Weston, on Madison Avenue and 49th Street in the summer of 1906, but lacked the necessary capital for such an ambitious move up from her boarding house and was in financial difficulties. The mortgagors would foreclose early in 1909.

+≻══≺+

205. AL

Dec. 23 [1908]

[London]

Dear Dad.

Your '15' ought to have reached you before Xmas as they were sent much before your letter which I received today. I am rather glad you disliked it at first & liked it better the second time.

It is, naturaly, different from A. L S it is perhaps better in some ways. one can not say as much in 20 pages as in 70. compare it with 20 pages of the other book,

It laks, on the surface, the virility. & vitality of A. L. S. but it lacks several faults of A. L. S. also.

The workmanship is perhaps finer. The Sandalphon is in some ways the biggest thing I have done.

Also the 15 is not, can not be built into a whole as is A. L. S. in A. L. S. the poems are fitted together. arranged, theoreticaly at least, so that one mood leads to the next. The '15' is seperate poems without sequence . . but singly I think you will find the poems stand as well or better than those in A. L. S. altho I can readily see how one or 2 of the A. L. S. verses are much nearer to <u>you</u> personaly than the 15.

<u>Good</u> art ought to grow on one, however, & the things with lasting charm are not always the things that please at the first flash.

Sent you some polytec ads today – thought you might like to know who the — I am.

Have invitations to 2 Xmas dinners so suppose I'll get fed somehow on that respectful day.

As for the other songs you are sending. – perhaps I can make out of them a book that will suit you better. – they need an awful lot of finishing tho before they'll do to print.

Well Happy new year to you & mother. Thanks for your mission greeting.

Recd. £4. <u>with thanks</u>

a couple of little packages sent from here last week may have arrived in Phila.?

206. ALS [*letterhead*] Yates Library, Printing Stationery, Sample

3 January 1909

48 Langham St. [London]

Dear Dad:

They tell me my lectures are already being advertised in the London papers. Otherwise: Library work progressing also 'The Portal' my next opus is coming on, should like it to appear in April or May.

I don't know whether the Poly will have some tourist work for me between Feb. 28. & Althouse possible party or not.

By the way if you have any copies of A Lume Spento left. hang on to 'em and mail me two. (I sent you 40 at first I think??) not quite that either, I guess,

I think I told you the 2nd edtn of the –15– was out. – mailed you one? suppose I'll hear tomorrow whether the 1st ones reached you in time – as they should have done.

Luck to you and mother for the new year.

E.P.

Jan. 3. 09.

'The Portal' became 'The Dawn', a prose and verse sequence apparently modelled on Dante's La Vita Nuova. In May, Pound would decide against publishing it.

+≻━≺+

207. ALS

Jan. 7 [1909]

48 Langham St. [London]

Dear Mother:

Your tea party cavalier Griffeth Gribbell is a person whom I do not recognize on the street. I can not remember that during our long & ardent friendship we have ever, either one of us, either given or received salutations or even mutual signs of recognition. - Are you quite sure it wasn't Banker with whom you conversed. -

If the 'Babschen' alias Miss Minerva Derby comes to Philadelphia you can be polite to her, if you like. As for E. W. Wilcox. - she has declaired once before the world that on one ocasion she was seen in respectable company.

I guess dad can live it down.

She evidently wanted to be kind.

When however my verses appear arranged thus.

composite.

Two stanzas + end of one poem + mid-riff of same second poem. . I confess the effect is wierd even to me. I presume she tried to give me more space & that her article was 'cut' to fit space. but the effect is a joy. & I confess I was never so glad of my contempt for the opinion of the swinish multitude as when I saw myself as presented in my 1st kindly intended review. - Her apology for writing it at all, as expressed in the 1st ¼ column will have to be accepted, as I was fool enough to ask her to do it. - from the practical side it's 'publicity' for which I should be glad if I made patent medicine instead of poetry.

I hope dad didn't patronize the journal too extensively.

As it is impossible to suppose that even Ella could survive continued reading of her own 'stuff'. she is I presume in blissful ignorance of what realy <u>appeared</u>.

As for Keith. I still have glasses. - did Dad ever pay him for my last pair? $1.75 ? I think.

As for the '15' you need not be afraid of it. it lacks the more obvious vigor & virility of A. L. S. but the workmanship is finer & more finished. & a great many people prefer it.

While intended primaraly for people who have already read the 1st book. It does no harm. if it goes alone.

The 'Sandalphon' is quite sufficient in itself. & in many ways the biggest thing I have done.

The book is not my work as you know me. but just as Mr. Cobb. picked the 'Amphora' for its 'finish'. Bill Williams takes 'Nel Biancheggiar' as my best.

there are people who like a thing done right. - a perfect bit of ivory - (or cloisonè to take a comparison less congenial to me personaly).

personaly I prefer 'Rodin's' style of thing - most of the time. but.

As it is pleasant to have a house built by ones own hands so with books. -

Now a house isn't all roof, or door, or foundation, & the furniture differs for different rooms.

In a mans complete work. there should be something for every mood, & mental need.

cf. Shaxpeare.,

It is only the minor poet who fills merely one or two kinds of need.

Dont be disturbed by the size of the book.

I have at hand 232 pages of a young oxfordian whom I am to meet. 'Griffyth Fairfax'. I see no reason why he shouldnt be Tennyson or Swinburne to the coming generation.

1st reading delights. - for 30 - 40 pages. - then indifference.

then comes boredom.

then enui, then one is done. & utterly indifferent as to whether one sees more of his stuff or not.

Page 9

There are two kinds of artist

1. Waterhouse who painted perhaps the most beautiful pictures that have ever been made in england.

but you go from them & see no more than you did before. - the answer is in the picture.

2 Whistler & Turner. - to whom it is theoreticaly necessary to be 'educated up'.

when you first see their pictures you say 'wot 'T-'ell'. but when you leave the pictures you see beauty in mists, shadows, a hundred places where you never dreamed of seeing it before.

The answer to their work is in nature.

The artist is the maker of an ornament or a key as he chooses.

So. Long.

E. P.

The review of A Lume Spento *which Pound had asked his father to solicit from* **Ella Wheeler Wilcox** *appeared in the New York* American Journal Examiner *of 14 December 1908, under the heading, 'A New Singer of Songs. The Greeting of a Poetess of Established Fame to a New Comer Among the Bards'. The review gave as one poem the two stanzas at the end of the volume, 'For man is a skinfull of wine', + the last thirteen lines of 'La Fraisne', + the long middle stanza of 'La Fraisne'.*

---

208. AL

[January 1909]

[London]

Dear Mother.

By the way, as P. S. to yesterdays note - if my room is big enough for a person. 5 ft 4 in. long. you might invite the Babschen. (alias Miss Derby. 504 N. Meadow St. Richmond Va) to use it for a week. if she comes up alone. if she comes up with a friend or so of course you cant.

After study abroad she finds, I guess. Richmond about as entertining as I did Indiana. what ever you can do for her. please write - as soon as possible & tell her you'll be glad to see her. whether for afternoon tea, or for a week - as suits you.

Am enclosing circulars. - If you can get 'em before Pug Thompson. - Century Bureau 1420 Chestnut St –

Penn charter. - any anything else convenient. & try for summer work also. . should think it might help.

Remember for business purposes. 'I have a good job. You and dad want me in America.'

---

209. ALS

Jan. 9 [1909]

[London]

Dear Dad:

Your bully good letter drifts in this evening.

Being family to a wild poet aint no bed of roses but you stand the strain just fine.

Goin up to the Adams Automobiles house tomorrow to meet a innocuous one from Oxford. - Beautiful work he does but no guts. (the Term guts is a technical one in all art).

Great gee gosh it begins to look as if some of these west end swells was goin to turn out to hear me. spiel.

- orful thought -

Ran into one Pifer in Museum Wednesday. from Wabash. - over here on Rhodes fellowship - invited me down to Oxford for week end when the weather gets fit.

Says they have nobody on my job at Wabash. & not much $. so guess I was lucky to get out. - fellows found out chair was vacant & all registerd for romance langs.

Have rec'd 3 copies of Ella's 'Aa' so suppose it has been seen by one or two people.

If you haven't forwarded my letter to her dont do it. - not important either way

Have you sent her the '15'

Glad the church is coming on.

————

Monday. A. M.

Pleasant yesterday.

Fairfax a 'ginger bread rabbit' but pleasant to meet.

at dinner met also a long thing that talked very interestingly about Mexico- 'all right but he's a Larzelere.' (Elliot by legal cognomen. but he runs in the Larzelere class.)

however it amuses one. & all save capitolists are safe. I guess.

So Long

Love to you & mother

EP

153

210. ALS

[January 1909]

48 Langham St. W - [London]

Dear Mother:

Tea at the Fowlers . reading my new stuff for Mathews book. -

Friend of William Morris wants me to lecture in Birmingham & is going to stir up something there if he can.

'Personae' as I plan it

Introduction

16 from A. L. S.

12 New things. - Two or three quite long -

Am taking it to E. M in the morning so will close & finish copying the introduction.

Love to you & dad,

E P

+>====<+

211. ALS

Jan. 19 [1909]

48 Langham St. [London]

Well mother mine:

We appear to be working out of the amateur class: Mathews is using the 'Personae' in his best series. - real live book with ornamentation & whiskers i.e. binding. - March. 1. set for selling time.

Some of the new poems are rather longer than anything I have before attempted.

Now is the acceptable time for you to send me the names of several book shops. in New York & Phila. & I will have Mathews attack them.

The Polytechnic is giving me a very pleasant hall to spout in. That celebration begins day after tomorrow.

If I am worth my salt I'll get Lecture V squeezed into a magazine article. some time before 1912.

Am at work on 'the Portal'. otherwise no thunderbolts.

Love to you & dad

EP

Jan 21.

55 people at first lecture . all survived. Shaxpeare comedies drew 19 so I presume I am fairly well in line.

You can have Mrs Beatty send my name, adress, & qualities to Mrs Cloman just as soon as you like. I am not sure whether or not I have met her. She either was to be and wasn't at a certain tea party. I think wasn't. But I should prefer an invitation to tea. via Idaho.

Letter from Chippewa this A.M.

I enclose not from the friend of Wm Morris. of whom I spoke in my last note. in connection with Birmingham.

Just why he happens to be so much attending to my affairs I dont know, but I am quite willing that he should continue.

Next week 2 lunches and a dinner, on deck - Manning to be on deck. I like his 'Vigil of Brunhild' quite much.

Fairfax as I think wrote wants to shove my stuff in Oxford.

Glad the F.I.P.C. is on the rise.

love to you & dad.
EP

+>━━>━=<+

212. ALS

Jan. 25 [1909]

[London]

Dear Dad.

Recd. 4£. Thanks awfully was expecting but 3.

As Mathews edition of 'Personae' wont be out till March 1. I suppose I shall not be leaving for a week or two after that date.

Also there may be some polytec. touring jobs.

What about Althouse.

Also. Scheme:

When I get the announcements of the book. - I want you to take one of them . & a lecture 'ad' to a certain A. J. P. McClure - with whom you are I believe acquainted. After so doing. I want you two to see if there is any way in which I can give said lectures at the Princeton summer school.

You might mention that Mathews is giving me the same terms as he does Maurice Hewlett I suppose that's a fair start.

Mr King seems to be stirring up divers corners of the United Kingdom . he forwards me to day a letter from Prof. Dowden of Dublin. whom he seems to have succeded in interesting.

But as for plans definite I dont see that it has been possible to make any. The current seems to have turned in my direction.

My royalty begins after the expense of the edition has been made - I want american copies ordered thru the trade but there's nothing for you to do till I send the announcements

I think I wrote that the 'Personae' is a reprint of the best of A. L. S. and about 35 pages of new stuff. also introduction & notes.

Well it behoves me now to be up & out of this.
Love to you & mother
E.P.

+⊨⊨⊨+

213. ALS

Sunday [31 January 1909]

48 Langham St. [London]

Dear Mother:
the week has been fairly full and I have got very little letter writing into it.
Sunday. dinner at the Adams.
Monday. Lunch Mrs Fowlers & afternoon with her doing a review of 'Manning's 'Brunhild'.
Tuesday. To Lady Russells to see Miss Schletter do a parlour play. lunch following, the chief star being the wonderful, old countess of Guerbel, better known as 'Jenny Ward', Lady Russell also invited me to come to dinner & to the play when 'Miss Ward' does Coriolanus. and Miss Schletter told her to have me there when the Forbes-Robertson's come as F-R, wished to meet me.
I have some doubts of his real anxiety to see me, but the 'Histrion' seems to have interested him.
Wednesday. Manning down to London, for lunch at Mrs Fowlers, Fairfax down from Oxford & 3 pages of regrets from Sargent.
Manning realy writes.
Thursday lecture in smothering fog. corporals guard including Sir Edward Sullivan who hadn't been able to be in to tea on monday & Henry Waller. (opera staged in Berlin by special order of the Kaiser).
Thursday. lunch with Miss Lowther at the house of a lady with wonderful saphires. (also the daughter & governess had been out to my spiel on the Troubadours'.
Tea with Manning and a certain Mrs Shakespeare who is undoubtedly the most charming woman in London
Saturday. Lunch with Manning & Mrs Fowler. at the Barkers who may want some private lecturing.
Mr. Barker remarked after lunch in a most satisfactory tone that I was the last man he would take for a poet. (I tell you this for your especial comfort).
Then to Portland Hotel to hear Waller's new ballet music before he takes it over to berlin.
Dinner. at the Birds, Mine host knew the Cour de Laine & seems to have been everywhere., magnificent Hogarth's etc, left with Sir Edward after an enjoyable evening, & he is going to send me his translations from Dante.

Sunday. & I have just come from a lecture by Gertrude Kingston. (sunday league lecture) & also one of the Lady Russell lunch party.

I think thats about all since my last.

Oh yes. Mathews, as I flatly refused to dedicate the 'Personae' to George Wyndham. (Ld. Rector Edinburgh University, & lately chief sec. for Ireland) has gone after that 'fastidious darling of fortune' to have him write me a preface. but I cant say I am awfly interested in the result.

Manning is sending my stuff to Henry Newbolt & introducing me to Lawrence Binyon.

Otherwise there is no excitement that I remember at the moment.

Love to you & dad

E. P.

The second 'Thursday' an error for 'Friday'?

+—+—+

214. ALS

Sat. 10 P.M. Feb. 6 [1909]

[London]

Dear Mother:

Have just finished a 'Latinists' article for the 'Fortnightly'. dont know that they'll want it but the editor thinks he is 'pretty sure to like it'.

Pleasant tea with Mathews on Thursday. he wants to introduce me to Selwyn Immage Binyon & one or two others before I leave town.

Note from Manning yesterday about nothing in particular. otherwise no excitement.

Found my editor a very delightful ex-jesuit as I may have written. I dont know whether the 'Personae' will get a preface or not. there are enough hypothecated prefatii in the air. I have writ one at Mathews request. Thorp (editor) wants to write one. Mathews wanted Wyndham to write one. I want Hewlett to write one. Mathews is by now wants Hewlett, but he has already asked Wyndham. ergo ? ?

However, I shall have Tea with Mrs Fowler tomorrow & let the management manage the preface.

Love to you & dad.

EP

The Fortnightly Review *did not publish the* **'Latinists'** *article.* **Personae** *appeared without a preface.*

+—+—+

215. ALS

[9–10 February 1909]

[London]

Dear Dad:

No trouble at all to stretch the lectures over a years course. Would much prefer it to emasculating a years course into a few lectures as I am now doing. - 4£ rcd. Thank. <u>you.</u>

Have had delightful couple of hours with Lawrence Binyon. the Wordsworth - Mathew Arnold of Today & we lunch together on Friday.

Wednesday A.M.
Mathews has just sent in 5 books of Arthur Lewis whom he is bringing to my lecture tomorrow.

I guess he'll get me introduced to about all the men who happen to be in London between now & march 3rd

Adios,
EP

Arthur Lewis was a young English poet published by Elkin Mathews.

216. ALS

Feb 11 [1909]

[London]

Dear Dad:

Your last epistle was quite comfortably epistlatory. For the first time in some time I've the leisure to realy consider an answer. - I've been interested in the whoop of the Italian work but probably haven't written so.

Your Dads letter is gone. when one travels in a pair of suit cases. one keeps nothing which one can do with<u>out.</u>

Today another rotten day for lecture. - The fog two weeks ago at the starting time of most of the 'Poly' lectures has up-set the rest also so I dont stand badly with the management.

I had a delightful lunch with Elkin Mathews before the lecture; & he is introducing me at the Poets Club dinner on the 23^{d}.

Sturge Moore & Hillaire Belloc. are the other attractions. –

To morrow it is Binyon; he seems to be one of the best loved men in London. a sort of pervading slow charm in him & in his work. - get his 'A Supper' if you find it handy. it is different from most of his work. or rather it is a sort of finish to one side of his work. as you get it in 'London Visions'.

I dont exactly see how I can get out of this by March 3ᵈ. but will try to start by then.

Had the luck to find the proofs of Hewlet's new book yesterday & enjoyed them much.

Mathews has turned his shelves over to me to browse in & I find the contemporary people seem to be making as good stuff as the theoretical giants of the past.

Glad to hear Aunt Frank has $ to go south, from the way mother wrote one would have expected to find the good lady selling matches on the street.

My chief advertising agent (in the social line) has gone to Africa so there is a bit of a let up in the giddy whirl.

Ah yes. Mr Cobb. ? does Mr Cobb at the age of 180 years expect to find the rising generation a thing that will not ocasionaly startle him?

item of information. the new book is 'Personae' it is not a reprint of A. L. S. - although a part of A. L. S. happens to be reprinted in it. - Say 'How' to Messrs. Eckgfeldt. & Flinn'. also to 'Nat' & Billy Emery.

Remember me also to Dicky Green.

I wrote you did I not that the stretching of the lectures over a year would be quite agreeable. –

Temple College. ('University' by courtesy & bluff. - hush man hush) for the winter. & Princeton Summer school if it can be worked. - only dont go off half cocked at it. - I'll try to give you the proper ammunition before long.

Love to you & mother.

EP

—————

217. ALS

[mid-February 1909]

[London]

Dear Dad:

From what I have just heard at the Polytechnic there is no. $50 steamer on March 3. so I will have to stay till the 10ᵗʰ. Sorry but it might have been necessary for the book anyhow -

I'll need $20 or $25 more. rotten luck for you.

However I think every day I stay helps the sale of 'Personae' I seem to be getting much closer to people.

Have been seeing a fair bit of Binyon. - we lunch together again tomorrow.

Have just got back from an afternoon with some friends of Yeats.

The '15' seems to be getting into the right hands. Commendations in todays mail from Henry Newbolt & Dowden.

If you have'n't the $20 or 25. just write to say so . & I'll manage something somehow . or wait till its convenient.

Love to you & mother,

As the American mail seems delayed this week there is nothing to answer.

EP

+⊢⊶⊣+

218. ALS

[21 February 1909]

[London]

Dear Dad -

Wot have been doing?

hm. Wednesday is too long ago to remember.

Thursday I read 'The Dawn' at the Shakespears. after lunch. - Then lectured. Then the Adams automobiles took me to dinner & a show.

Friday. They (the Schusters) gave me Ellen Terry to look after at the lunch party. and then I went to see Selwyn Image who does stained glass. & has writ a book of poems. & was one of the gang with Dowson - Jonson - Symons - Yeats. etc. - talks of 'when 'old Verlaine' came over etc. Then tea at the Shakespears. (they are quite quite the nicest people in London.)

Saturday. Mr. John Todhunter. (done various books etc. knew Browning & Morris etc.

Today. - had accepted lunch so couldnt go to the Binyons. - Ernest Rhys's to tea. & Miss May Sinclair carted me thence to the Lyceum club for dinner. - (also someone else who has done some very decent illustrations for Yeats)

From which place I have just returned.

Tuesday coming. Dinner at the Poets Club

several loose ends.

Invitations to Rhys' tea club & an evening there.

I think the Shakespears & Selwyn Image. are about the most worth while out of the lot I have come across.

I dont know that there is much more to say. Everybody seems to treat me rather decently and I dont mind at all.

Love to you & mother-

E. P.

+⊢⊶⊣+

219. ALS

[22 February 1909]

[London]

Dear Dad.

The 10£. arrive. Thank you very much. It will do till April 1 & perhaps Althouse can find something in Spain by that Time.

Mathews has some delay with the printers so I dont know how much longer the job will keep me here. The 'Dawn' is finished & it would be a good thing if I could float that also.

I have by this evenings mail a long appreciation of the '15' from May Sinclair. & a delayed appreciation of 'A. L. S.' yesterday from Josephine Preston Peabody. - Hewlett I meet at the poets club tomorrow.

When I do come home when ever that is. it will be on the cheap line Liverpool to Phila.

Of course every week I stay here is a help in a way. But even a celebrity must eat. I am <u>not</u> yet a celebrity. But it is indisputable that several very well known people are interested in what I am doing.

I suppose worrying won't do any good. I have tried it at times but it seems of no particular assistance.

I don't know that I am any more anxious to consume your income than you are that I should consume it. BUTT.

However keep on grinning.

Guess that's all.

EP

Perhaps a few quotations from Miss Sinclair will relieve the situation. and show that I am not an utter superfluity in all walks of life even if I have no <u>market value</u>.

In writing on the '15' she says that some of the poems are perfect. The 'Litany' the most poignant - and that some of the prose should be 'set up in sight of every writer in prose or verse'. (which is going Some - especialy as there was no particular reason why she should have given up her own mornings writing to reading mine, & that there was no necessity of her writing to me about it in any case. she also says that the voice is 'distinctly new' & that it 'has things to say'.

I regret that I am not for your sake a captain of industry, but I suppose it is better to be succeding at something than at nothing at all.

Good luck

E. P.

+⊨—+—⊨+

220. ALS

Monday [1 March 1909]

[London]

Dear Dad:

Ernest Rhys took the trouble to find me in the museum today to see if my book were out. - which means a review when it does come out.

Am going down to Mathew's country place on saturday, to eat & read 'the Dawn.' . – (Fairfax up for sunday noon - & supper at the Rhys'es)

The town seems to want to treat me white. To secure the american copy right on 'Personae' simultaneous publication in U. S. & eng. is necessary as this can't be done. we are going to copyright just enough of the book to prevent any one printing it in U. S. without our leave.

That is to say <u>you</u> are to have the lines that follow printed. . just 10 or 20 copies. cheapest paper. – any old thing. & file them at the congressional library. or patent office or whatever. is right.

on a day I shall name. when I am sure of it.

The thing has to be 'published' i.e. filed. in Eng. & U. S. on the <u>same day</u> if the law is to be valid.

The stuff that follows is to be printed.

It seems that our friend Mosher & others have the habit of printing my friends things & paying them nothing . . . The little device here following. enables one to make it inconvenient for them when they try. –

Just print it in a strip. & file 3 or 4 copies in Washington. & sell me the rest. – but be careful about the date. you'd better have the printing set up at once.

[?]

E.P.

+⊱⊰+

221. ALS

<u>Mar. 8</u> [1909]

[London]

Dear Dad.

Have just recd your sick in bed with la grippe letter. I feel like a thief & a robber. However the book is n't out. Maurice Hewlett is still ill, but there is a meeting planned when he recovers. & Yeats is coming over from Ireland soon & I dont think such chances of acquaintance should be lost except for absolute necessity. they are worth too much, in too many ways. this being in the gang & being known by the right people ought to mean a lot better introduction of 'Personae'. reviewing etc.

May Sinclairs belief in my work ought also to be valuable. & Ernest Rhys is having me down to a meeting of his 'Rhymers Club' I think sometime this week. You will see from the enclosure that Manning is making an awful effort to get out of the dilletante class. - to say the least. - His book ought to give mother conversation enough for a decade.

As for $. I ought to need no more till April 15. if that s any comfort. . I dont seem to be built as a 'provider'. however as there is nothing in sight in U. S. before the Temple University lectures. and as there are sight here certain advantages - which may indirectly in some dim but not unimaginable future help me to earn at least a fraction of my food.

as a matter of fact I think I am earning my food more or less by the pure charm of my lyric personality. - at least the dinner last evening wasn't bad. - but the d— thing cost me 26 cents to get to. no b'gosh 36. there & back, of course it was a $2. dinner, but the nucleus, the bally nucleous. one has to have.

I think I did write you that Yeats expected to be here Friday & couldnt or didnt get here. & that Mrs Shakespear has him nailed to meet me when he does come.

she has done a half dozen novels & a couple of plays herself by way of diversion.

I think the jack pot is worth a few more rounds any how.

Love & luck to you & mother.

EP

The enclosure would have been Pound's review of Manning's Brunhild, *which would appear in April's* Book News Monthly.

+≡+≡+

222. ALS

15 March [1909]

[London]

Dear Mother:

The first proofs have come & gone corrected. & my publisher & I are still on speaking terms but if my publisher says to the man who was supposed to be editing my immortal pearls, what my publisher said to me about the man who was supposed to be editing. etc. ehem.

Hewlett is away ill, so there will be no protective preface. - I am quite as well pleased.

Fairfax was up from Oxford yesterday, en route for south France. I let him feed me & correct proof & went over his latest efusion. - a 'Michael Angelo' - which is quite splendid. Quite, quite the real thing & much stronger than anything he has done.

Went from there out to the Rhyses for supper. It is very pleasant to have people who have been more or less flooded with literature all their lives believe that you know your job.

If father has not had those excerpts printed yet. let him wait till I write again as it may not be necessary. I am working on the Troubadours, at the Museum, fairly steadily but I dont know whether anything much will come of it. I have found some interesting stuff, . but then —

Binyon has sent me a ticket for his lectures on Oriental & European Art. The first one was intensely interesting.

I think I sent you a notice of Fred's book. – a few more wont hurt. - a stupendous work enlightened by a certain humoresque quality.

I seem to fit better here in London than any where else, if I can only guess wots the answer to the problem of sustinence. Perhaps if I go into retirement for a year at Temple 'University' I'll be able to work out a system. I have two weeks & two days wherein to concoct something. Not that there is any reason to concoct anything this month rather than last month or the month before.

However. This goes to the post <u>now</u> immediately.

Compendium of fool philosophy can wait.

Love to you & dad, & enjoy yourself.
EP

+≍+

223. ALS

[c.24 March 1909]

[London]

Dear Dad,

I enclose clipping from Publishers Circular.

Dont bother with that printing & copyright. I am sorry to have bothered you with it. but hope you haven't spent very much on preliminaries. . The thing wont hold, if we import the Eng edtn. etc. - <u>all</u> <u>off</u>.

Have just come from hearing Binyon lecture, & meeting Sturge Moore.

To morrow I dine with one Konody an art critic. Friday. The Shakespears & Miss Sinclair.

Letters in from you & mother this a.m. - good to hear from you now & then.

? The '<u>Dawn</u>'. is a sequence of prose & verse . . The poems being from the last lot I had you send over to me. The Fortnightly returned my article but requested me to let them know when I had another. I want to see if the reviews of my book wont be good enough to <u>help</u>. before I make any applications for much of any thing. My clothes have not yet arrived at a condition to exclude me from any place I have attempted to enter. I'm not doing society, ye knaow.

I am engaged in that gentler pursuit. meeting the few people I want to know.

Swinburn happens to be stone deaf with a temper a bit the worse for wear, so I haven't continued investigation in that direction.

As for the rest, I read their books to see if I want to meet them, & then it depends on whether they happen to be in London.

The society flare. which depends on $. & a variety of gorgeous raiment is a very different thing.

I have my Tux & two suits of clothes. which is precicely one suit of clothes more than I have any real need of. I shall never allow my self to be so encumbered with excessive possions, in the future. The only thing I object to is the cut of the english neck tie. but as my waistcoat happens to be cut ungodly high this dont matter.

From the days or two days delay in the recent mails I imagine the north Atlantic is particular blue hell about now.

My room is 12 x 7. & clean & warm also in the central part of London I shouldn't change if I had 20£ a month. I can as I said last week 'make out' till the middle of April, quite comfortably. I have not heard from Althouse.

Tell T. C. P. I hope he has shaken the grippe.

Considering what Binyon draws to his lectures. I should say mine were moderately successful. and were as good a start all things considered, as could have been expected. & they will help, have helped indirectly. It will depend on whom I meet & what the book does. whether it will seem best to give the 'longer course' in some shape or other, <u>here</u> next winter. - or to concentrate on Temple Univ.

You might take the lecture circulars & this notice of Mathews' to McClure. & see what he thinks about the chances for Princeton summer school. It can't do any harm. Also I am so <u>well</u> it is ridiculous to consider it.

Mother's questions. No my 'social doings' are not so darnd expensive. a slight increase in laundry bills & a certain allowance for tube fares & shoe polish. - boot blacks, to be exact. - Considering my next 3 days. include 3 dinners & 1 Tea mothers moralizing on the sustaining power of tea. is perhaps not over apt. besides I make it on this very table when I wish. - also

No literature is made by people in other professions. - except in the rarest of cases, when like Lamb the other profession was a mere mechanical drudgery from which he escaped into his life.

Burns plowed, Villon stole, & lived on his friends. Horace, lived on his friends Dante on his enemies. sometimes they starve or gain a precarious emolument, or when like Tennyson they have more d— sheckels than they can use, they add impertinence to platitude & get a royalty of 10,000£ per. anum., Watson gets a pension from the crown. Binyon gets paid for doing pretty much what I do in the museum. Yeats lives in Ireland. Heine had an uncle. Stevenson didn't. etc. enough of this.

————

Good luck. & it is very foolish not to be amused at nearly everything in the world.

EP

+≡≡≡+

224. ALS

<u>Easter</u> (April 1909)

[London]

Dear Mother:

I seem to have run short of everything in the paper line, except this fools cap. - News?

Sir Aubrey Dean Paul - dropped in this P.M. to ask me to lunch for tomorrow. He has some plan of introducing me to the Edgerton - Castles. but I dont know whether they are included in tomorrow. Tuesday Mathews has made an appointment for me with the head of Appletons. - also to ends unknown. - probably to none at all. -

Friday I had tea with Miss Sinclair & we dined together at Pagani's, her intellegence was a comfort after Thursday evening at the Sturge Moores where aesthetics unchastened with mental training had been somewhat wearing.

I dont know whether the opera is going to work any miracles or not.

I am working under bonds of strict secrecy. & making, constructing the show rather than merely making a libretto.

The musician has had several operas on in N. Y. & elsewhere. one set by special command of the German Emperor. & he has just got back from Berlin where Willie. has accepted a ballet. So you see I am not working with a rank amateur nor an unfed aspirant. Of course there's nothing certain in the job - but it seems worth trying. I expect to give him two acts almost in-tact by Wednesday. - of course there will be no return financial for a year at the very least -

However I believe in the play and am enjoying the building of it. As it is for music I dont have to bother with a lot of smart elic stuff which would be required in spoken drama, but can stick to the realy poetic matter, & work in simpler outline. I have almost convinced myself that opera could be a legitimate art. and the musician, O marvel, of marvels seems to have sane moments & to be able to think in other things besides musical notations. However dont permit yourself too great a luxiuriance of hopes unhatched.

Also this large, picture book entitled 'London Eng.' still amuses.

Luck to you & dad.

(I just mailed 'Personae' last week so I suppose you have it).

EP

'Appletons' were American publishers. 'Willie' in Berlin was Kaiser Wilhelm, 'the German Emperor'.

┼══════┼

225. ALS

Apr 15. [1909]

[London]

Dear Dad:

Have heard nothing from Althouse. But I saw the President of Appletons & he wants me to write a book. not a novel but a scholarly readable stunt. I think I shall go to Italy to do it as I can live there more comfortably & probably save enough in 3 months to buy myself clothing wherewith to be suitably appareled here in the fall. The certainty of the 'Poly' lectures here next winter seems better than the chance of nothing or something in U. S.

It may look like casting very much bread upon the waters. But perhaps the mine is worth developing. I suppose having found a publisher here for poetry & having made a small beginning at lecturing & having an american publisher sending around town for me in order to apologize for not being able to handle poetry & to see if there's anything of mine he can use, and to have certain people who ought to know believing in my stuff. is at least clever salting.

There may seem more whim than reason in my going to Italy, but I want the sun. also I have been here eight months - stagnation. it will be nine in May.

I have only been out of London once. - the spirit of motion moves me also my Italian is getting rusty. –

Besides I would go to Venice now with introductions to the Eden's who have those acres of garden on the Giudecca.

At least it seems so much the inevitable thing that I have just written to Venice. I want my simple pleasures. boiled potatos & beets in olive oil - cheap, warm & wholesome. & very much I want the sunlight which never is in England.

I hope incidentaly that you understood my last letter to mean that I could live until May 1. i.e. that I hoped your pious contribution would <u>arrive here</u>. not leave U. S. A. on that date. After that I'd like. $30 here on May 15. & then 15 in Venice on the 1st. June. then 15. June 15. & then the $20. as usual.

I wrote you a letter thanking you for the <u>V</u> thought - of the book. – didn't I?
To morrow is the publication day.
Love to. you & mother.
EP

+⟩══⟨+

226. ALS

[c.20 April 1909]

[London]

Dear Dad:

Have just received proofs of my 'Sestina Altaforte.' from the 'English Review'. so I presume they intend to use it.

The Review is probably the best magazine in the country. and if the page numbers I & II on the proof mean any thing, I am evidently going to have the place d'honneur in the June number.

I suppose the sestina is about the most blood curdling thing the good city has seen since dear Kit Marlowe's day but it seems to have effected an entrance.

The cute little thing is supposed to express the unadulterated lust for battle, & incidentaly Bertrand of Born in a peevish humor. I think it is fairly acurate.

I can hardly read it aloud because an acurate rendering would require a 54 inch chest.

Guess thats all the newest. Oh yes. your girl's letter. I think you'll find the literary expression of all that in the 'Fioretti of St. Francis of Assisi' you'll find the book among mine I think.

It seems to me that he covers the set of feelings in the letter you sent me.

It is interesting however to see it.

I hope you'll find your $14,000. could use a bit less. but then . ?

Hope to have some reviews of Personae to mail you in a few weeks.

Saw an 'ad' of it the other day wherein I am being presented as a somewhat riotous person.

Ah. well.

This to the post. I return your copy . of 'Lena' as you may find further use for it.

Tell mother my clothes will do till I get back from Italy. I don't know any one who knows De Morgan. & the Bensons live (all of them, I believe) out of London.

She ?s about the poets club. I thought I wrote that it was a bore. The only poet in it didn't show up. . They discussed every thing under heaven except poetry & at interminable length.

Be it said to G. B. Shaw's credit that he expressed his habitual ignorance more entertainingly than anyone else. Hillaire Belloc sang to illustrate his points

168

(most of which were unsound) Hewlett (who did not speak,) invited me to lunch to decide which one of us had been most bored. and then got sick, so it was called off. & he's been away for his health & I haven't seen him since.

Adios
EP

+>==+==<+

227. ALS

[c.27 April 1909]

[London]

Dear Dad:

This paper was supposed to be grey when bought. so pardon the sentimental color.

I am sending you first blood. the London Daily Telegraph. Apr. 23. The review is by W. L. Courtney editor of the Fortnightly Review.

For english conservatism in space that is worth. $6.25 per inch it is not so rotten. . You notice that Hewlett gets about ½ the space. – nothing personal in the comparison.

Have you time. to take it to the Book News. & to the Inquirer. etc.? The more the sell ier

I have this morning written a Ballad of Simon Zelotes. which is probably the strongest thing in english since 'Reading Gaol'. . and a thing that any one can understand.

It may come out in a day or two. if not I'll write it you. I guess I'll send it any how. get it printed any where & as often as you like. There is no copywright on it. I don't intend there shall be.

Remember also that however unconventional the language may be. it is very much that which the horny handed old Cananite might have used. – A man given to noticing what appeared & not fussing for subtlties.

Adios
EP

W. L. Courtney's *review was of the just published* Personae. *The* '**Ballad of Simon Zelotes**', *retitled* 'Ballad of the Goodly Fere', *was published in October in both* The English Review *and Pound's next collection,* Exultations. *It received much favourable notice, and was reprinted in the Philadelphia* Evening Bulletin *in December, and in the Alumni number of the* Hamilton Literary Magazine *in 1910.*

+>==+==<+

228. ALS

Apr. 30 [1909]

[London]

Dear Dad:

I shall not go to Venice. the London game seems to have too many chances in it to risk missing them by absence.

I believe there are some more reviews coming in due time. Also I want to strike a double blow with two volumns published simultaneously about September (or before)

If I can draw a big enough crowd to the 'Poly' lectures in the fall. there'll be a living in them.

? Would . Princeton summer school pay my passage over & back . and any thing over that would be worth as much as getting better known . ?

I had a note of appreciation from Laurence Binyon yesterday. . & he will review me when he gets back to town if he can find a place to do it.

Ernest Rhys is on the job. & the New Age Crowd were howling last evening that they wanted to 'feature' 'Personae': & that it hadn't been sent to them. The Bookman is holding off till June. in order to get more space.

The ½ col. In The Telegraph was by the editor of one of the best Reviews.

& the editor of another was . the one to advise me to stay here & not go to Italy.

That is a great number of unhatched eggs. – but I think I'll set.

I've got an appointment to go out into the country and am not dressed yet. So will write later.

Yeats has . at last arrived and I had about five hours of him yesterday. –

Until I get a bit more time.

EP

Thanks for the £5.

love to mother.

<hr>

229. ALS

[c.mid-May 1909]

[London]

Dear Dad:

Plans? etc. - I am going to migrate into that part of London known as Hammersmith where a friend will lend me a garden & a hammock. & where for several months it is to be presumed that there will be sunshine.

As to finance. - you must not send me more than $20 at a time. and I am going to try to draw not more than $250 altogether between now & a year from now. I have not had time to write this week and I must now get ready for some people who are Taking me out of Town in their motor. I enclose notes from Binyon & Yeats. both of whom seem inclined to be decent to me.

As Yeats is the greatest poet. of our time I thought you might like the autograph.

I suppose I needn't have been so excited over your sending Zelotes to the cosmopolitan, but Bierce is a person by whom it is more honour to be cursed than praised. You might send my letters cr. Elkin Mathews. Vigo .St. W. until I find where my new room is to be. - as for definite object of activity -

1. To get myself sufficiently well known so that my next seasons lectures will have sufficient attendance to pay all my expenses. for 5 months if possible.

2. To write as much good stuff - as I can.

Guess that's all.

now I must buy soap: & shave & git. -

Love to you & mother
EP

---

230. ALS

[after 27 May 1909]

[London]

Dear Dad:

Enclosing the not particularly well written review from the 'New Age'. poor stuff. but 'adv'. will get you the oxford 'Isis' sometime.

As you say the 'Trinity' job looks good, - if it hasn't been filled 3 months before the agency heard of it - Its too good a job not to have been looked for, however 'eres 'opin'.

No special furor during the last week I find one Victor Plarr. of the old Rhymers club. most congenial. He is in on Sunday supper-&-evenings. Yeats. Monday evenings, a set from the Irish. Lit - Soc. eats together on Wednesdays. - & a sort of new Rhymers gang on Thursdays.

I wish those of my American friends who realy want specimens of my immortal scrawls would begin to order the same thru Wanamaker or Brentano, because no firm is going to import English publications until there is some faint indication of a demand, of course Mathews wont begin to print the 'Dawn' until 'Personae' has paid for itself .

The review enclosed isn't so worse . have just reread it. of course Flint is more interested in his own not over expert style than in the book. but then - que voulez vous?

Manning's new book is out & is delightful. – otherwise no scandal.

A plus tard.

Love to you and mother

EP

*F. S. Flint's **review** of Personae was in the New Age of 27 May 1909. The 'sort of **new Rhymers gang**' which met on Thursdays was T. E. Hulme's group of young poets who had split off from the Poets' Club—for some names, see Pound's 2 August 1909 letter (no.239). In 1912 he would describe his 'Imagistes' as 'the descendants of the forgotten school of 1909'.*

+≻═━≺+

231. ALS

[June 1909]

10, Rowan Rd. | Hammersmith | London. W.

Dear Dad:

Please, what am I to eat if you send me $10 instead of $20. on June 1st.?

The Eng. Rev. does not badly for me 3½ pages. & 2 pages of my stuff. Will mail it when I get a chance and the other reviews as I get them.

Have seen Yeats, Binyon, & Huffer in the last two days.

Just now as it is 7.55 you must pardon me if I depart in search of food

Love to mother to whom I will write sometime in the dim future when there is food for correspondence.

Ezra P.

*The **English Review** of June 1909 contained a review of Personae by Edward Thomas, and Pound's 'Sestina: Altaforte'. Edward Thomas also reviewed Personae in the Daily Chronicle of 7 June 1909.*

+≻═━≺+

232. ALS

[3–4? June 1909]

[London]

Dear Dad.

Recd. £3. thank you. guess that'll be all right. if you send 4. on June 15. – Sorry you find me such a bum correspondent.

However. The chronicle & the review may have put in a good word for me.

The Bookman is as I said reviewing me in the next number, also photographing me, & lunching me at the savage club in order to extract details concerning my past career & dire intentions.

I am racked with arranging my next book - of poems. . I've got 30 odd, but it is the devil to get them arranged in any sort of order. – I want the Zelotes. & the Sestina. tone to predominate.

etc – no use talking till it is done.

However. I hope to justify my existance.

Love to you & mother.

E.P.

⊣≻⊸≺⊢

233. ALS

[7–10 June 1909]

[London]

Dear Dad.

Enc. chronicle for June 7- . Eng. Rev. mailed.

The Bookman wants me photographed at their expense for a July number.

Will you have the mss of my play 'Quevedo' fished out & sent to me. packet marked Q, I think.

'Il Vesuvio' arrives with 'Nel Bicancheggiar' in it.

Life comfortable –

Love to you & mother

EP

⊣≻⊸≺⊢

234. ALS

Friday . June 11 [1909]

[London]

Dear Mother:

Have been spending a delightful evening, went out to the Rhys'es & they took me on to dinner with a most charming person, friend of Swinburne, Sir Richard Burton, Leigh Hunt etc. - the sort of an audience where appreciation is worth while . –

Rhys expects to review me in the Bibliophile. & St.John Adcock is interviewing me for the Bookman on Monday.

Eng. Rev. sends £3. for the Sestina - so if. Dad. only sent $10 on June 15 it will be OK . if he sent $20. let him send $10 the next Time. i.e. July 1.

173

I am still pottering with my next collection of poems which I think I will try
on Murray - no use in over egging one basket

Guess thats all at the moment -

Love to you & dad,

E-P

+≥━━≺+

235. ALS

[? end of June 1909]

[London]

Dear Mothr.

Enclosed 1 tirade caused by phrase in your letter, quoting some one in
Montana.

l recpt. 4£ to Dad.

l note from the Observer

The tirade is to be read purely for 'style'.

EP

Epic to the West ? ? My Gawd ! !

What has the west done to deserve it - -

Whitman expressed America as Dante did mediaeval europe - & america is
too stupid to see it - (- of course the result is somewhat appalling , but then -)

Kindly consider what an epic needs for a foundation -

1. a beautiful tradition.
2. a unity in the outline of that tradition.
      vid. The Oddessy -
3. a Hero - mythical or historical -
4. a darn long time for the story to loose its garish detail & get encrusted
with a bunch of beautiful lies -

Dante in a way escapes these necessities - in reality he dips into a multitude
of traditions. - & unifies them by their connection with himself.

Poor Longfellow tried to hist up an amerikan epik.

Camoens. is the only man who ever did a nearly contemporary subject with
any degree of success & he had the line of Vasco de Gamas voyage for unity. &
the mythical history of Portugal for back ground -

———

Mrs. Columbia. has no mysterious & shadowy past to make her interesting.
& her present - oh. ye gods ! !

one needs figures. to move on the epic stage & they have to be men who are
more than men, with sight more than mansight, They have to be picturesque.

———

174

Bret Harte, Longfellow - (epic?) So I behold a vision - Rockfellow marches in purple robes thru a cloud of coal smoke, Morgan is clothed in samite, and the spirits of the 3ᵈ heaven foster their progress enthroned on trolley cars

'J'ai lutte contre les empererurs de l'acier, contre les paladins du fer, contre les princes de la porcherie. Ils ont voulu me briser les reins, mais je les ai solides' says Theethedore Rosenfeldt. - as quoted by the satirist on the 'Journal de Paris'

————

When business begets a religion of 'Chivalry in affairs of money', & when 3% per annum is metamorphosized into the clult of an ideal beauty. . & when america can produce any figure as suited to the epic as is Don Quixote.

and when the would be litterati cease from turning anything that might in 500 years develop into a tradition, into copy at $4 per. col. within four . hours of its occurrence.

Then there may begin to be the possibility of an american epic.

An epic in the real sense is the speech of a nation thru the mouth of one man

Whitman let america speak through him. - The result is interesting as ethnology.

————

Just at present I can see America producing a Jonah, or a Lamenting Jherimiah.

But the american who has any suspicion that he may write poetry. will walk very much alone, with his eyes on the beauty of the past of the old world, or on the glory of a spiritual kingdom, or on some earthly new Jerusalem, which might as well be upon Mr Shackletons antarctic ice fields as in Omaha for all the West has to do with it. - Canada, Australia, New Zeland, South Africa - set your hypothetical scene where you like.

Epic. of the West - it is as if I asked some one to write my biography. - it is more as if I had asked them to do it 12 yeas ago.

It is truly American - , a promoters scheme. it is stock & morgages on a projected line of R. R.

which last sentence is the only one in the language of my native land. - surely we parley Euphues.

As for 'fame' what the hell do I want for 'fame'. in the sense of notariety among people who know less about poetry than they do about pease & who wouldnt know an Idyl from an Idol or a poem from purple rhetoric.

I should like to make a bit of poetry, but if I should realy do something in that line america would never realy find it out. They'd hear a lecture about it . & swallow somebody elses opinion. & persist in their ignorance of the original.

Praise from Yeats, or appreciation from a circle that have listned to Swinburne reading his own verse. are if you come to consider it. rather preferable. to competing with Munyon, & Beechams Pills, for American celebrity. - Paderewski cost $80,000 before he landed in america. 'adv.'

glory like all else has become a 'product', one desiring it may buy as much as he cares for or can afford.

Intellegent understang still remains a pearl without price. but there are already a number of imitations, on the market . clever imitations to deceive almost the elect.

I hope the scrawl will amuse you. dont for heavens sake take it seriously.

Personae was noticed in the **Observer** *of 20 June 1909.*

---

236. ALS

[4 July 1909]

Weybridge

Dear Mother:

Until now I have, I believe, refrained from asking for your congratulations, but as London has finaly offered to me its ultimate laurel, & even the throats of the discrete have opened themselves in congratulation I feel that you also may be expected to join the throng. To be brief 'Punch' has taken cognizence of my existance.

To be sure it is not a full page, such as is accorded mssrs Shaw, or Asquith. . but two inches, in the most Punchian & most correct form.

But even that must be regarded as a beginning. & many are beginning to regard me 'seriously' who because they never read poetry, and are accustomed to mistrust the judgments of those who do, had not thought of doing so before.

Even from Paris I am felicitated.

This is I think July. 4. & I am week ending with the Howards,

Tuesday there is Violet Hunt's garden party, I don't know what else I have on . for the week.

I am beginning to get ocasional free. tickets to the opera & I think there is a 'comand' show on Friday.

Of course . my manners are still too damn good – horrible encumberance – but I am learning to forget them. .

Ah yes. Rhys's 'Masque of the Grail' is on Tomorrow, out of doors performance.

The Rhys'es croud has I think the wholesomest & perhaps most delightful atmosphere I have found in London

Ehm. – Bed-Time.

Guess . I'll ring off.

Love to you & dad.

EP

*This paragraph appeared in **Punch** of 23 June 1909 under the heading 'Publishers' Announcements. Mr. Welkin Mark's New Poet':*

> Mr. Welkin Mark (exactly opposite Long Jane's) begs to announce that he has secured for the English market the palpitating works of the new Montana (U.S.A.) poet, Mr. Ezekiel Ton, who is the most remarkable thing in poetry since Robert Browning. Mr. Ton, who has left America to reside for a while in London and impress his personality on English editors, publishers and readers, is by far the newest poet going, whatever other advertisements may say. He has succeeded, where all others have failed, in evolving a blend of the imagery of the unfettered West, the vocabulary of Wardour Street, and the sinister abandon of Borgiac Italy.

237. ALS

[end July 1909]

[London]

Dear Mother:

I am to give 21 be d – d. lectures at Polytec. & I wish I wuz ded.

Rhys thinks he is going to get me some commissions from Dent. . Short history of every thing from the beginning of creation until day after yesterday next, or some such.

Such advantages are a great incentive to get sufficiently famous immediately, so as to be able to escape the necessity.

I expect this afternoon to meet The French Professor of 'Toronto' (Univ. of). who is about to resign. – It would be better than 'Your baynier' spelled Urbania. Ill. – altho. d— cold.

Thank dad for 4£. recd. will write him direct also. Am dining tonight with some $. . U. S. also acomplished – why they want me I don't know.

My regards to Aunt Frank, Sarah. & who so ever.

Louisa in particular if she still exists.

Love to you & dad.

EP

238. ALS

July 30 [1909]

[London]

Dear Dad:

Mother has I suppose forwarded my note so you have by now my thanks for £4. r. and the news of my lectures. There are to be 21, & there is some talk of some sassiety spiels on the side but that is all 'in the air' as yet.

I shall want the following of my books sent me if you can find them.

If you can not. you might ask Hilda if Julia Wells has them. & get them returned.

1. Marie de France 'Lais' (paper covered old french text with german notes)
2. Poema del Cid. (spanish paper covered.)
3. Aucassin & Nicolette. Mosher. (25 cent book). Translated by Andrew Lang.
4. Mackails 'Latin Literature' red boards.
5. Chrestomathie du Moyen Age. by Gaston Paris. (Greenish boards. about 3 x 4 ½ inches chunky.)

Rhys had a scheme for getting me a comission from Dent to work the course up into a book . I don't know what it will come to.

Young Brown has n't showed up yet.

Mathews is off on vacation. Shall try to dynamite him into action as soon as he returns.

It's a long road, but I suppose I'm getting over it. quicker than most.

Fell upon certain Crawfords here. ex Washington of a generation gone. Pound? Pound. – uh. Thadeus C Pound. - name not unfamiliar. & a few bits of gossip. about Blaine. vs. Ingersoll. etc. .

By the way. you might send also a little french book.

6. Peladin 'Origin et Aesthetique de la Tragedie.'

Have you by the way ever discussed me & the diplomatic corps. with your reverend parent?

I am <u>not</u> a literary hack or a school master. , realy. and one can not write good poetry 24 hours a day.

Consular service be damned. . one might as well get into the patent office.

I think I'll drift home next spring or there abouts.

EP

Ingersoll had lent powerful support to **Blaine** *as a contender for the Republican nomination in the 1876 presidential election, but the two men fell out after 1881. Another bit of gossip might well have been that Blaine had kept Thaddeus C. Pound out of the cabinet, and the latter had in turn kept Blaine out of the presidency—'They cut each other's throats', is how EP put that to Kavka in 1946.*

+⇌+

239. ALS

Bank Holiday, Aug. 2. [1909]

[London]

Dear Dad:

Glad to get your letter this A.M. Sorry you are feeling the 'all alone' no Binyon. no Pound state of affairs. . Is Whiteside home? he is not bad company. In fact better than most here.

You ask for more detail - Well I have arranged 21 Polytec. lectures & am trying to keep acquainted with enough people to get them well 'personaly advertised.' I write pomes now & then. Have been working at Psaltary settings for some of them with Florence Farr. . youll find her in Yeats essay on 'Speaking to the Psaltary'. also it was at her theatre that the first Ibsen (in english). and. the G. B. Shaw plays were brought out. 'the Court Theatre discovered me at my own suggestion' writes G. B. S.

She also has done a few books on 'The Book of the Dead' (Egyptian).

The crowd I meet on Thursdays consists. of Storer.whose poems I'll send you in the dim future. Hulme who writes articles on Philosophy. Flint who writes poetry - so so. (did review of me in the New Age). Fitzgerald who journalisms & poetizes somewhat. - ocasionaly Tancred. (stock exchange). who does epigrams. of a Horatian-Herrickesque variety. & admires my sonnet. - Th' Amphora', above the rest of my works.

August is supposed to be the empty month here. - well Ive got to clothe my self & go to lunch with Mrs Foster. (ex-Fairfax of Virginia - being perhaps a better clue to the identy)

As for introducing you . 'why certainly . come right over & be welcomed with open arms. enclosed . checque to defray expenses.

£ 1000	4.11.44
Bank of England	
Pay to H. L. Pound. on order.	
£ 1000	
One thousand £.	E. Ton.

if you find it insufficient just let me know & I'll forward whatever loose change I happen to have on at the moment -

More - later,

EP

+⊨⊨⊨⊩+

240. ALS

4 August 1909

[London]

Dear Dad.

Along with your dolorous epistle there arives a note from Hilda with a photo of you looking quite joyous - - Dago Pic nic affair. - I trust you have returned to the mood of the photo - Here's hoping.

When you send the books I asked for . please send the little paper copy. of 'Aristotle's Poetics'. (Longinus 'on the Sublime' bound with it.).

Mathews talks about printers estimates so I presume he intends to bring out the 'Exultations'. shall feel sure when I sign the contract.

Supper with May Sinclair on Monday. The Crawfords (ex Washingtonians) yesterday. I go out to see Katharine Tynan Hinckson with the Meynells tomorrow.

I think there were divers other things to say but I have forgotten them. . Mothers penny photos. are very delightful.

Mais vous mon cher . papa. que voulez vous. ? Are you Trying to parody me, or were you just feeling savage - . The photo of you on picnic is however redeeming.

Do you see anything of Woodward?

Till later.

EP

Aug. 4

+⊨══⊨+

241. ALS

[August 1909]

[London]

Dear Dad.-

Things moving pleasantly. Hope to send you another publishers announcement before long.

Dining with the Mennels to morrow - (Francis Thompson's Mennels').

Violet Hunt's crowd seems to be interesting.

Manning in Town, & Mrs Shakespear back from Paris.

No news in especial. -

Love to you & mother

EP

+⊨══⊨+

242. ALS

[August 1909]

[London]

Dear Mother:

I don't know that my doings are much more than meeting people. –

Last Sunday it was the Meynells – (Alice & Wilfrid Meynell – Francis Thompson's friends). William Watson had been resurected from some pliocene strata and boomed 'The Purple East'. at us.

Monday Miss Tobin. (Translator of a good deal of Petrarch) took me out to the Alma-Tademas.

Wednesday. I met Señor Pegna of the Spanish Embasy. at Baerleins. (Baerlein of divers books). & talked Lope de Vega with him.

Last night Arthur Symons & I were guests in a small theatre. supper party. he is still at times . a bit dazed. but talked well a good deal of the time, and there is hope of a complete recovery. – he is very like some of the pictures of Coleridge.

To night I am due to dinner with Edmund Gosse. he is variously 'The Literary Arbiter' or (acc. The Rhyses 'An excellent foolometer'). That is to say that E. G. never gives voice to any critical opinion untill it is so apparent that nobody can deny it.

'Personae' is reported to have 'begun to sell' – 'to be going' and I guess the fall edition of my later stuff is pretty certain.

Love to you & Dad.

EP

<hr>

243. ALS

[before 17 August 1909]

[London]

Reverend Parent:

1. The whoop of the Chipperwaw Buzzard arrives. The editor seems to have been flabbergarsted. -

2. A person, presumably W. Brown called here last week & . left a verbal message with my land lady who promptly forgot all of it but a dinner invitation to a place she couldn't remember the name of.

I have not been able to hire a Scotland Yard 'tec. & the offense has not been repeated.

3. I am going down into Kent for a couple of days. visit-

4. my adress hence forth is to be.

10 Church Walk. Kens. W. London.

nearer town & with old Kensington church yard under my windows. also nearer most of my friends.

More later

EP

+⋟⋞+

244. ALS

[before 17 August 1909]

10 Church Walk | Kens. W. | London

Dear Dad:

Am luxuriating in a new sizable room with a bit of green church yard below. - A relic of an old parish near the middle of the city.

Have just returned from a couple of days, very delightful, in Kent.

Enc. - samples of the new 'ad' will forward more later with a list of people to whom I would like them sent.

Am sending a few to mother by this same mail.

Recd. £ 4 . much thanks.

Chippewa Whoop arrived as I think I wrote.

Good Luck,

EP

+⋟⋞+

245. ALS

[before 17 August 1909]

10 Church Walk | Kens. W | London

Dear Mother.

Am luxuriating in a more sizable room over the old Kensington Church yard. Have just got back from a couple of days with the Fowlers in Kent. delightful place to loaf in.

I enclose the 'ads' of 'Personae.' The Eau Clare wallop has not arrived but the yowl of the Chippewar Eagle has been heard.

Remember me to anybody you like.

The Tadema house is full of splendour & bad taste.

Symonds is dead. Symons is recovering from a variety of nervous breakdown which requires close attention from some one else. But he no longer thinks he is J. P. Morgans partenor etc. & confines himself to reminiscences of Whistler, Beardsley, Condor & Yeats & theories of art.

182

You realy mustn't worry about my food I have not been underfed for months 21 lectures October to March. syllabus to follow.

Luck to all

EP

+══════+

246. TLS

[August 1909]

[London]

Dear Dad.

I dont know that I have done anything noteworthy during the past 3 days. The weather still continues beautiful, which is most remarkable.

I send along some more ads.

You might send them on to

> Hessler.
> Dr C. G. Child – U. of Penn.
> Dr. C. Weygandt ." " "
> ~~Dr. Chamberlain~~
> Woodward . 327 Chestnut. St.
> W. G. Mc Farland Oak Lane.
> Whiteside
> Prof. Milford. Crawfordsville.
>   "   Danl. Hains   "
> Robt. Winter   "
> F. J. Doolittle Oak Lane.
> C. T. Chester   ?

Guess thats enough for once.

Realy thats hall. have merely eaten, slept, & conversed for the last three days.

Luck & good morning to you

EP

(10 Church)

+══════+

247. ALS

17 August [1909]

[London]

Dear Mother.

Take you into my confidance? Certainly. . come in as far as you like.

The wish for extermination was metaphorical & quite natural considering the prospect of a long job in which I had no interest.

183

You know I have never made any pretense of loving labour or believing in its dignity. I never voluntaraly do anything but write lyrics & talk to my friends. - if I were not tone deaf . I might compose & if I were not so demmed clumsy I might paint or sculp. as it is I participate in the other arts by proxy & stimulation.

Nothing else matters. Religion being as I have said . 'another one of those numerous failures resulting from an attempt to popularize art.' & the beauty of christianity , that it is essentialy artistic & irreligious . . The real application of christianity would destroy all governments & all churches & all institutions. & supercede them.

———

a quotation from Homer also fits.
'Let all unite to give praise to Ulysses
'For that he knew many men's manners & saw many cities
To return to my 'Beginnings of romance poetry'.

I happen to have gotten interested in it, before I have finished the first chappter. which is a blessing.

Of course its got to be more or less diabolicaly clever or there'll be no fun in doing it.

it will have to cauterize the germanists & surpass them in accuracy. or at least equal them. & yet seem careless. (all this is not for general quotation.)

I am sick of the rotten sloppiness of dilletante critics but I've got to pretend to be with them more or less. - at least.

I am tooth & claw against the encyclopedists.

Also Ive got to grow a prose style as concise as Stevenson's.

all of which may be entertaining & will certainly be troublesome. considering I now have absolutely no prose style at all.

or a d— bad one which is worse.

Dent thinks that if I can write poetry I can certainly write prose. & I shall not try to undeceive him.

Just now I have got interested in Apuleius. & having an interest in anything is a most salutary. & difficult thing.

I've been interested in something else today but I forget what. -

Cresctimbene's book on poetry in the vulgar tongues I guess.

& the influence of the new Testament on Apuleius. & of Apuleius on Shakespear. . or some such irrelevent detail.

The intellect is a very nice whirlagig toy. but how people take it seriously is more than I can understand.

I wish my typewriter could be fixed & shipped to me. They are expensive here & almost unrentable.

So far as is discernable my health is excellent.

Brown called & left only a verbal message which my landlady forgot. quite promptly ergo. I have not seen him.

The Appletons. merely said they'd be glad to see any book I did.

Dent begins definite negotiations. proposes definite royalties. & a time of publication. also he is about 5000 % better than 8 appletons.

Enough for this evening
EP

10 Church Walk. | Kens. W | London.
Aug 17

⊢══⊣

248. ALS

Aug 28 [1909]

[London]

Dear Dad.

I wish you'd mail over my tennis raquet. (wrap the face so as to keep it dry.). It ought not to be too large or heavy.

Also my 'Dante'. Moores. <u>edition</u>. (white. canvass. – hidden under brown paper cover.).

The 'Chrestomathie du moyen age' by 'Gaston Paris.' must be in my trunk as I had it in Crawfordsville.

also the 'Provenzalische Chrestomathie' large flat blue book. by 'Appel'.

Off to the museum. now.

Love to you & mother.
EP

⊢══⊣

249. ALS

[August 1909]

10 Church Walk | Kensington | London. W

Dear Dad:

If you can find the following books I'd like 'em forwarded.

Gedichte. = of <u>Heine</u> (small squarish black book

<u>Villon</u>. Poesies. (in blue slide. box-cover

'Ei desprecio adiedecido' a paper leaflet by <u>Lope de Vega</u> (not the bound vol. of his plays.)

I think they were all in the little trunk

There are some of Katharine Proctor Saint's books there also if she wants 'em.

Also if you find a <u>small</u> vol. of <u>Horace</u> you can send it, but I don't think you will find it.

And I could do with the <u>Dante</u> if it dont make the package too heavy.

That's all I think of at the moment.

love to you & mother.

. E.

Salutations to grandmother - also

*Pound had tutored **Katharine Proctor**, daughter of a successful Philadelphia business-man, at her home in Wyncote. She was now married to Lawrence Saint, an artist in stained glass.*

+⊨━⊨+

250. ALS

[August / September 1909]

10 Church Walk | Kens. W. [London]

Dear Dad

'Settentrion' is 'The Wain' That is the constelation of the 'Great Bear' or 'The Big Dipper'

My health is O.K.

Sold 3 poems to the English Rev on Saturday to come out in October number.

I think I shall keep the procedes as a birthday present to me from you & mother. & procure some raiment.

The things of Yeats that you want to read are.

'The Wind among the reeds'. 'Red Hanrahans song for Ireland'. & one or two of the short lyrics in some of the other collections.

Father Bensons 'Light Invisible' compares interestingly with Yeats mystical studdies.

Am using the Hunt's tennis court for diversion. & spas.modicaly screwing the 'Spirit of Romance' alias the 'history of the world' into shape for Mr. Dent.

Love to you & mother

EP

***Settentrion** is mentioned in Pound's 'Alba Belingalis', reprinted in* Personae.

+⊨━⊨+

251. ALS

[September 1909]

[London]

Dear Mother,

Just a line of good morning. I should have been up & at the Museum an hour ago.

I send along this delightful onslaught from the Nation. It is pleasant to be abused by one who knows nothing beyond the fact that he is annoyed. The 'adv' value is good & the reviewer has caused a good deal of amusement. - at himself -

I send on the proofs of the Eng.Rev. poems.

'Nils Lykke' for Dad's benefit. is the name of one of the characters in Ibsen's 'Lady Inger of Östret'.

Yesterday spent out of town.

Today I will get some tennis with Hueffer at Violet Hunts court if the rain holds <u>off</u>.

Love to you & Dad.
EP

*The **'onslaught from the Nation'** of 28 August 1909 was an unsigned review with the title 'Heresy and Some Poetry'—Pound's 'grave error' was his disregarding the established 'laws' and 'the high and nameless, but rigorous logic of poetry'. The **poems in proof** for October's* English Review *were 'Ballad of the Goodly Fere', 'Nils Lykke', and 'Un retrato' (reprinted as 'Portrait from "La mere inconnue"').*

+>==<+

252. ALS

[September 1909]

[London]

Dear Dad,

Just a good morning before I hasten hence to the multifarious affairs of the day.

Have managed to get my history of the world under weigh Thank heavens.

Love to you & mother
EP

+>==<+

253. ALS

[September 1909]

10 Church Walk | Kens. W. [London]

Dear Dad.

I am sweating over this fool book for Dent.

The prospect is very horrible. I think breaking stone would be preferable to compiling a literary history.

I may feel differently after lunch.

Can you get my own typewriter adjusted & shipped to me.

Also when you send my next $. please . send it payable at 'Kensington High St. Post Office'.

Thus saving me a long perigrination to the other end of Town.

Mrs. Shakespear has angelicaly offered to do emanuensis work on the book which means that she will insist more or less on my getting it done.

I am very glad . because otherwise I am not sure that I should ever have the stamina to finish it.

You may picture me in a state of interrupted torture from now until the dam thing is finished.

U.a.d.e. I may feel better after lunch.

I have been scribbling all the morning. I am sure no one was ever intended to write literary criticism in the morning.

Enough of this.

Tommy rot.

Good luck to you

EP

254. ALS

Sept. 9 [1909]

[London]

Dear Dad

'Ehultations' has gone to the printer. I wish something could be done to stir up the sale of 'Personae'. as Mathews is still in the hole on that venture. – however there is plenty of time for it to make good. I suppose he must see daylight or he wouldn't be running the second book.

I hope to get to the end of the Troubadours. (i.e. chap III) in 'The Spirit of Romance' sometime this week & to that end I must get me out of this & into the mausoleum.

I enclose another wad of 'ads' as mother wrote that you had run out of them.

I mailed her a tirade from the Nation & the proofs of the eng. Rev. poems which I suppose she has or will send on to you.

I think 'The Spirit of Romance' is realy going to be good. –
Remember me to the Tioga folks.

Love to you & mother
EP

+══+

255. ALS

[September 1909]

[London]

Dear Mother

First thought of doing the Glaucus myth on reading the lines from Dante quoted over it.

The poem is supposedly a lament of the girl left behind when Glaucus was turned into a sea-god by eating a <u>ceilam grass</u> –

or by alegory if one so choose to interpret it – had an extention of consciousness which enabled him to experience the feelings of a sea creature – a consciousness partly cosmic. The equation ought to hold good in any case where the mans further or subtler development of mind puts a barrier between him & a woman to whom he has become incomprehensible.

John Galsworthy in his 'Island of Pharisees' a rattling good novel which I have just finished reading. Does pretty much the same thing. objectively instead of subjectively.

The volumn which you had published at 10ᵗʰ & Washington Ave. is perhaps more satisfactory. The new binding is decidedly superior to the original tin covers.

Give my glad hand to Pirazzini and any one else you like.

Am trying to get to the end of the chap. on narrative poetry in S. of R.

so long.
EP

'*An Idyl for Glaucus*' *is in* Personae.

+══+

256. ALS

Monday. Sept. 13. [1909]

[London]

Dear Father.

Recd. £4. thank you very much

Just back from a weekend in Kent. – Manning & Fairfax down also.

189

Mother sends a copy of 'Life.' underlined.

1. certain commendations of matrimony. a state which I should find highly impractical at the moment.

2. a disparaging paragraph on expatriates, which seems to have been composed by someone convinced that the True flower of American civilization is the Swedish emigrant who goes to raise wheat in 'Saskatchawan & Manitoba'.

Dent proposes a royalty. as follows.

1st 1000   10%

2nd 1000   12½ %

3rd 1000   15%

4th 1000   20%

I suppose it'll come in sometime in 1910.

I get paid for the poems in October. 3–5£ I suppose.

I think it wise to use whatever it is on some new raiment.

Page must be an ass to have picked out that Browning thing but I suspend judgment until I see his splurge. – it all counts as 'adv' – personaly 'adv' can be dam'd only it means 'L.s.d.' & therefor must be encouraged.

I am sorry I can't as yet supply the family with anything but topics for mother's conversation but perhaps that's better than nothing at all.

Love to you both

EP

Curtis H. Page *reviewed* Personae *in September's* Book News Monthly.

+⸺⸺+

257. ALS

Sep. 14 [1909]

[London]

Dear Dad.

Surprised you didnt get my thanks for £6 sooner. - I wrote quite a long letter I think -

Book News arrives - pleasantly intended, but not much acuteness behind it. however one doesnt expect a man to waste his brains on a book review.

'Poor dear, yes, his hearts in the right place.' Novelist on Courtneys review of yours truly.

Thanks for the books, Dante, Aucassin, etc.

I thought my old letters fairly safe, but seal 'em up & put them in your safe if you think wise. I suppose it would be a better place.

Typewriters are so expensive here $5 a month would soon run to more than the freightage on my own. & besides I'm used to that queer keyboard. <u>Don't</u>

send it if it is <u>very</u> expensive. but I should like you to find out how much it would come to.

I enclose a few lecture prospecti & now I must be off.

EP

letters mailed Phila. Sep. 2 arrived Sept. 13.
Phila. Sep. 7. arv. Sep. 14.

+⫻===⫻+

258. ALS

19 / 9 / 9

[London]

Dear Mother,

I enclose the Polytechnic 'ads'. Am working on the narrative stuff now. i.e. about. Nov. 22. on the lecture schedule. & chap IV. for the book

We are having a run of decent weather for our Tennis.

The Page review is laudatory. as you say. The Milwaukee sentinal has not arrived. The Yukon stamp is duly pedagocical.

Of course your ideas on prose are quite erronius. I should never think of prose as anything but a stop-gap. a means of procuring food. Exactly on the same plane with market - gardening. if a thing is not sufficiently interesting to be put into poetry, & sufficiently important to make the poetical form worth while, it is hardly worth saying at all. I dont know that there's much more in the way of news.

Remember me to Aunt F.

Love to you & Dad
EP

+⫻===⫻+

259. ALS

24/9/9

[London]

Dear Dad.

Have gotten some reviewing to do for the Daily News.

Met. Scott-James & Edward Thomas at the Square Club dinner on Wednesday. (The fellows who have reviewed me to advantage as you may remember) I am sitting to a sculptor for my bloomin' head in the mornings.

The town begins to refill.

met Herbert Trench, poet, theatre-manager etc. at luncheon at Clariges. etc. more anon.

EP

Looks as if, several people were coming to the lectures.

Gallup records no review by Pound in 'the Daily News' in 1909.

+>==>=+

260. ALS

Oct. 2 [1909]

[London]

Dear Mother.

Shackleton was rather fine last night. Irish? well rayther!

'Exultations' is thru the first proofs. practicaly correct.

And I am working on the 'Tuscans' for lectures & the 'S o.R.'

You will see by the √ √ marks on the Mathews list that several of my friends are also indulging in the vagaries of Parnassus.

Please send the proofs of the Eng. Rev. to dad. The darn thing costs 62 cents. (2/6.) and I dont care to indulge in a dozen copies . as the verses are also in 'Exultations'. - Also send him the 'Nations' remarks.

Now must I get me on the job.

Love to you & dad,
EP

+>==>=+

261. ALS

[6 October? 1909]

[London]

Dear Dad,

Send the 'Zelotes' to Colliers . . if you like. offering 'American serial rights' & saying it appears in Oct. English Review. . which does not circulate in the U. S. as it takes the English rights on a good many articles copywright in the U. S. -

Scribners are the only other periodical fit to deal with.

EP

send. 'ad' slip. also

+>==>=+

262. ALS

7 October 1909

[London]

Dear Dad:

Excuse excitement of note yesterday but I was between lateness & a dinner appointment.

I of course <u>dont</u> want Bierce to touch any of my stuff. - Harpers, Scribners Century, Atlantic - yes - but the English. Review Here is better - after the thing gets printed here. it can be copied in the U. S. papers. -

Good heavens. Bierce's Touch can queer almost anything The man is a stark raving idiot, you know.

I suppose I'll go up to visit Manning in Lincolnshire some week between lectures, & probably this. month.

Love to you and mother & congratulations on New Church.

I go now in quest of food.

E P

7 -10 - 9

+<del>--</del>-+

263. AL

[10–11 October 1909]

[London]

Dear Dad.

I remit the pages of the Eng. Rev. will send the rest of it if you want it. but its hardly worth while.

Have today finished a speciman chapter of the S . R for Dent to take to America.

Your type-writer people wanted to do too much. - I only wanted the main back spring attended to but I shall be able to manage without the machine. quite comfortably I think. The 'Chrestomathie du Moyen age' ought to be in my trunk. unless it is with some books which I lent to Julia Wells. . Hilda might ask her for it.

+<del>--</del>-+

264. ALS

Oct. 11th [1909]

[London]

Dear Mother:

The first lecture will be pulled off this evening.

Have been down in Kent for week end. at Mrs Fowlers.

Left a speciman chapter of 'S. o R' with Dent this A.M.

Tomorrow I go up to Lincolnshire. to stay till the next lecture with Manning & Arthur Galton.

Galton is an old friend of Mathew Arnold, & has known about everyone since the flood.

Both Manning & Galton will be useful in discussing the opening chapter of the book, as they probably know their latin literature much better than I do.

Dent appologized for not having had time to read the Dawn. but repeated what he said last week i.e. that he thought he'd be perfectly safe in saying he'd publish anything I sent in. I suppose the Dawn will come out in the early spring. & the history about the same time or a bit later.

Exultations is set for the 25th of this month.

I guess that is about the sum of the news.

Love to you & Dad
EP

⊹⇒⇐⊹

265. ALS

12 October 1909

[London]

Dear Dad.

Have written to the Hon. T. C. & had the copies of <u>Personae</u> sent to him.

The lecture last night brought out about 20 people in the rain. But there are more coming. next week. I think. - at least a number of people who are supposed to be going to come were not there. - so there is hope. - people are not all back in town either. -

I want 40 . and to that end I shall start more violent operations. this day.

Now off to Lincolnshire.

<u>Congratulations</u>!!! on Church
EP

12 / 10 / 9

⊹⇒⇐⊹

266. ALS

[12–17 October 1909]

[Edenham]

Dear Mother.

I am spending a delightful week here in Edenham with a 14th century church out side the window, & a 11th century castle not far off.

Have been grinding out lectures & History most of the time.

Still on the 'Tuscan School' preceding Dante.

shall be glad to get the monumental work off my chest.

Prose is <u>not</u> my metier. - Thank heaven!

Have just finished reading a life of Abelard & started Macchiavelli's 'Prince'.

Also written an ode in Provencal form which is no trifle. Two letters this A.M. on the poems in the Eng Rev. Galton. likes the 'Zelotes'

Manning wrote this beautiful <u>Persephone</u> yesterday.

perhaps it will interest you.

————

Yea, she hath passed hereby & blessed the sheaves
And the great garths & stacks & quiet farms,
And all the tawny & the crimson leaves
Yea, she hath passed with poppies in her arms
Under the star of dusk, through stealing mist
And blessed the earth & gone, while no man wist.

With slow reluctant feet & weary eyes
And eyelids heavy with the coming sleep
& small breasts lifted up in stress of sighs
She passed as shadows pass amid the sheep.
While the earth dreamed & only I was ware.
Of that faint fragrance blown from her soft hair.

The land lay steeped in peace of silent dreams
There was no sound amid the sacred boughs
Nor any mournful music in her streams,
Only I saw the shadow on her brows
Only I knew her for the yearly slain
And wept & weep until she come again.
(Frederic Manning)

I go back Monday to lecture.

Love to you & dad,
EP

195

Manning's poem was published, at Pound's instigation, in The English Review *in December, with the title 'Koré'. Pound's 'Canzon: The Yearly Slain', the opening poem in his* Canzoni *(1911), was 'Written in reply to Manning's "Koré"'.*

---

267. ALS

[c.19 October 1909]

10 Church Walk | Kens. W. [London]

Dear Mother:

Attendance at lecture somewhat better.

2 or 3 Poems more gone in to Eng. Rev. - I dont know whether they'll go into Dec. or Jan. number.

Exultations ought to be along before very long. this week I suppose.

Tennis is off considering the weather:

Bill Williams is as I suppose you know, in Leipzig, studying.

The young man (you mention in your note) his chances for happiness, depend largely on his Temperament , & his income. Most men of course object to intellegence in a woman I personaly dont, but then I am, thank god, not marrying the lady in question. of course <u>she</u> may be in love with the young man, in which case his chances for happiness are absolutely nil.

However I am not realy in a position to decide the precarious question you submit to me. Let us hope they see enough of each other before they take the plunge.

Nothing in particular transpires. here.

I see the people I like, & my style is said to be improving (prose & verse.).

Love to you and dad.

my regards to Sarah, Aunt Frank & the Dr.

Yrs

E.P.

---

268. ALS

[c.20 October 1909]

[London]

Dear Dad.

Another lecture off my chest.

Have ordered a 5£ suit at the expense of the Eng. Rev.

The boss of the 'Express' says I'm to have a try as reviewing for them.

Have resurected a beautiful Canzon form from the Provençal which has never been used in English & think the poem is good enough to print -

Ow some ever you never know your luck.

I enclose some of my proof. - The Translation from 'Lope de Vega' may be of use for your Xmas cards.

I have managed the spanish rhythm as no other Translator of the song has done. - you can see from the 6 lines of spanish perhaps.

The Spanis g. pronounced k The ñ as ny . thus 'nin yo' a as ah.

More anon.

Love to you & mother

EP

*Gallup records no review by Pound in '*the "Express"*'. The '*proof*' would have been from* Exultations, *which included Pound's translation of Lope de Vega's 'Song of the Virgin Mother' from his play 'The Shepherds of Bethlehem'. The '6 lines of Spanish', to be found at the end of the poem in* Provença *(1910), were apparently in the proof though they were not printed in* Exultations. *Pound mentioned the song in his lectures—see* The Spirit of Romance *p. 210.*

⊹⤞⤜⊹

269. TLS [*letterhead*] The Portland Hotel

Oct. 24 [1909]

[London]

Dear Dad:

Recd. £4. Thanks. I am sure I have written acknowleging the 2 previous orders.

I have 2 (perhaps 3) more poems accepted by the Eng. Rev. but there's no pay before Dec. 11th. from them. The Nov. number having gone to press. I cant be sure they'll go in till Jan.

Have paid for my winter suit $25 out of the Sept. October. poems.

I will see what can be done with the Polytechnic about immediate relief, but I can't expect very much from them – yet at any rate.

Hueffer & Miss Hunt are trying to stir up the <u>very</u> <u>very</u> gilded to have me lecture privately. that may come to something. The reviewing isnt yet under way.

Cut off 1£ from your next remittance any how. & I hope to write that you can halve or dispense with the one after that. & let the Eng. Rev. do the 3rd. I cant promise it now, however.

The Simon Zelotes ballad seems to have moved things. letters complimentary from one of the cabinet & Cunningham-Grahame, & others. & about 150 subscriptions stopped by the horrified.

This P.M. I met Sir Percy Scot, (who would take their Gally fleet into action if it went. The one who changed Berisford's order "Paint Ship" into "Painting comes before gunnery" when the Kaiser was being entertained. – a quiet unobtrusive little person.

Love to you & mother. & more later.

EP.

There were three poems by Pound in the January **English Review**, *'Canzon: The Yearly Slain', 'Canzon: The Spear', and 'Canzon: To be Sung beneath a Window'. The first and the third were declared to be in the stanza-form of Arnaut Daniel, the second in that of Jaufre Rudel.*

╪═╪

270. ALS

[29 October 1909]

[London]

Dear Mother.

Thanks for your birthday wishes & apropos of your remarks on 'ballast', a number of things which contribute to my success so far, & will contribute more to it in future, are certainly traceable to that 'ballast' or cargo or what so you choose to call it.

I mean to <u>my</u> success as seperate from the success of my poems, which is in part due to my own.

Of course the term 'social sense' can not be applied to anything I possess, but the substitute which serves me very well in place of it. is presumably due to you.

Why this sudden & most unbecoming modesty in your letter, I dont quite make out. David plays the flute, & I have sold enough poems to buy a suit of clothing. whereat you most unnecessarialy begin to justify your existence.

Who, may we ask, has dared to question it.

There are certainly too many non-auto-supporting artists in the world, but what other class except paupers in the east end & clergy in Spain. are super-numarary.

Personaly I have never known a time when you weren't wanted in several places at once. Certainly 3 generations of impractical men need someone to hint ocasionaly that the practical isn't ipso facto damnable - ballast if you like - but why not rudder or something more theatrical. .

Ehem. It is to be presumed that you were writing unseriously, you have been known to speak or write in that manner. I believe.

———

I have been interrupted & lost the general drift, of this epistle perhaps you can find it

EP

David Foote, Pound's cousin.

+≻═━═≺+

271. ALS

Oct. 31 [1909]

[London]

Dear Dad.

My birthday has passed peacably. My lecture was better attended last week as I wrote to mother.

The Polytechnic has not yet sent me a statement of how we stand on season tickets but have promised to do so & will I suppose in the near future.

if a venerable person calling himself J. M. Dent turns up at the mint some fair morning treat him kindly as he is one of the biggest publishers in London. . I told him to call if he had time. Show him the machinery.

impress him with your importance & mine, & extend any hospitality you can. He may arrive before this note as he has had a 10 days start.

I dont know that there's any thing else to mention.

Hope the Governor recovers before long, & both ways at once.

Love to you & mother
EP

I enclose the new 'ads'

+≻═━═≺+

272. ALS

4 / 11 / 9

[London]

Dear Mother

Dent to the best of my knowledge is only hunting an american publisher for the spirit of Romance.

I have not the Ogdens address.

As for apparel I am imbibing cod liver oil & wearing a life belt like the rest of the inhabitants my overcoat is very heavy & you have no need to worry on that account. The Zelotes suit of clothes is a success.

199

As for food my new landlady does me quite well for lunch when I'm in. She, remarkable for a british female, can cook.

As for dinners. I have had invitations all the week. this being Thursday I go to the Dents. to night.

this sort of things leaves me enough to dine on, nutritively, on such evenings as I dine alone.

Salutations to everyone

Love to you & dad,

EP

*Pound's **landlady** at 10 Church Walk was Mrs Langley, 'a yeoman's daughter from the north'. She and her husband managed a grocer's shop on nearby Kensington Church Street, and kept a couple of hens in their yard for fresh eggs.*

+≻═≺+

273. ALS

[9 November 1909]

[London]

Reverend Parent:

I'm dam'd if I know what you mean when you say I haven't acknowleged your 3 last remittances. Ive done nothing but begin letters to you with '£4 received . with 'thanks' for about six weeks.

4£ = $19.48.

Another 4£ came last night thank you. very much.

Planh = Lament. Book mailed yesterday.

Sestina . . a particular verse form

Laudantes decem. Etc. 10 In praise of the beauty of Joan Temple

Nel Biancheggiar = In the white light or whitening of the dawn.

Nils Lykke. name of a character in Ibsens 'Lady Inger of Öströt'.

5th lecture given yesterday audiences female with exceptions.

Hows T. C. P.

Your clipping on Watson about as uninteresting as he is, poem worse than even his usualy are. most of London hasn't heard anything about it. John Lane publisher is evidently doing well for William in the States

If you get my letters at all you have certainly got my receipts of 4£. 4£. 4£.

read over the letters. if you've kept 'em and see if somewhere in my scrawl you dont find a heiroglyphic of that sort.

There has been no startling event in my life for the week past.

Love to you & mother.

E. P.

*The **book 'mailed yesterday'** would have been* Exultations, *just published by Elkin Mathews. It contained the five poems commented upon. Pound's **fifth lecture** was given on November 8. **William Watson** (1858–1935) was a fairly prolific minor poet.*

+≻⊷≺+

274. ALS

10 / 11 / 9

[London]

Dear Dad -

Recd. $30. odd from Polytchnic this evening, so you can let up that amt. - that is. presuming. you have mailed $15 on Nov. 15 (before this arrives) send nothing. Dec. 1. & $10 .on Dec. 15. I doubt if I get any thing ($) from the Eng. Rev. before the middle. of Jan.

have sent another canzone to the Fortnightly. . Its edtr. gave Personae the first ½ col . notice. so theres a chance. -

Love to you & mother
E. P.

+≻⊷≺+

275. ALS

Sunday. Nov. 14 [1909]

[London]

Dear Dad

Letters from you & mother last night.

The editor of the 'Fortnightly Review' writes to say he 'will gladly accept' a canzone which 'I have been good enough to send'. & will try to bring it out at an early date . so there is prospect of another slight relief.

The fog is nothing short of murderous, I hope it will clear before tomorrow night.

I will answer mothers letter later.
EP

*'**Canzone:** Of Angels' was printed in* Fortnightly Review *in February 1912, having been already published in* Canzoni *(1911).*

+≻⊷≺+

276. ALS

[November 1909]

[London]

My Dear Mother.

This is my busy day . at least I thought I had succeded in doing absolutely nothing until I began to count up my notable achievements. I thought I was living up to L'isle St Adams' ideals but there are these sins against me.

1. I have cleansed my hairbrushes with amonia.
2. I have taken my dinner jacket to a tailor to have it refaced & generaly tidied.
3. I have purchased the enclosed.
4. I have writ 3 letters besides this.

Besides this I think I can conscientiously say that I have done nothing at all.

I did think of shaving but decided against it. Beauty lies in the eye of the beholder & I shall not go forth to get beheld . wherefor a dignified leisure is to be preferred to an opprobrius scraping of the jowl.

Congratulate Whiteside for me s.v.p.

The remaining 4 chapters of the S of R are all of them half done. which is some comfort.

I shall now go forth & eat. mightily in the hopes that it will stimulate me to further' effort . re. that confounded book.

Love to you & Dad,
E. P.

---

277. ALS

23 – II- 9

[London]

Dear Dad

Recd. 3£. sent Nov. 15.

Thanks. very much.

Will you please write to Judge Beaty & see if there is any reason why I shouldn't have the Rhodes Scholarship from Idaho.

a rumor reaches me from Oxford that it is vacant. I suppose Beaty will know any committe that there may be controlling it.

I am investigating here.

Dont, please say anything to <u>anybody</u> until we find out.

I could use £300 a year quite nicely.

EP.

am writing to mother by same mail.

278. ALS

23 – 11 – 9

[London]

Dear Mother.

One letter from you yesterday . dated . Nov. 11.
another today   „   „   16th.

Containing £3 arrive.

Thank you.

Mrs Marks (Josephine Preston Peabody) wrote that she she would send me the 'Piper' as soon as it was out. The acquaintance is by book & letter only.

Your first letter suggests Jim's poem on 'The Fly whose Mother has Told him.' Jim = J. Gryffith Fairfax.

A light weight overcoat is of use in England only in July. Dam the climate.

It is now noon

10 letters & no book done this day. ergo. i desist.

Love to you & Dad.

Of course i go on meeting people.

H. G. Wells.

One servian regicide - now covered with diplomatic honours,

& a number of people - not in who's who.

Thank heaven there are only 3 more lectures before the Xmas let up.

EP.

Mrs Marks' play **The Piper** *was awarded the Stratford-on-Avon prize worth $1500 in 1910.*

+>—<—>+

279. ALS

Dec. 5, [1909]

[London]

Dear Dad:

Thanks for your letter.

Am to be guest of Poets club on the 20th., address them on <u>Arnaut Daniel</u>, & listen to some of 'em spout my own productions.

Saw Wilde's 'The Importance of Being Ernest' last night, delightfully done.

Yeats is in town again & I shall see him at the Shakespear's on Wednesday.

I am sending the only kind of 'Photo' I have. Have already sent one to 'Literary Digest'.

Let Trumbull publish my Tangier letter if he thinks it so — remarkable.

You might mail me any of the stories I sent you from italy - I may be able to knock them into sellable shape - I dont think so . but should like to have 'em - (type written, if you've typed 'em - don't bother if you have n't.).

Do you want me to return the letters youve sent me of Trumbull etc.?

Please return the enclosed notice - as the Review costs 2/6 per copy. and I dont want to buy another.

I haven't seen any other interesting notices yet. The papers are reeking with politics & not much room for anything else just now.

I wish you'd make out a list of the 25 poems. which you'd select for an American edition.

I am laying pipe . to that end. - if you'll make me a list of your 25 poems. & if mother will make a similar list of her favorites. I'll be greatly obliged. - of course I probably wont be guided by any opinion but my own but I'd like to have others. make the selection out of all four books.

I am sending 2 copies of the 'Quinzaine' also.

Now will I arise to go forth.

Love to you & mother

EP

An Elliot and Fry studio **photograph** *of Pound illustrated an article on his poetry in the* Literary Digest *of 27 November 1909. There was an unsigned* **notice** *of* Exultations *in December's* English Review.

+=====+

280. ALS

Dec. 7 [1909]

10 Church Walk. | Kens. W. [London]

Dear Dad.

Have picked up a few sheckles on private teaching so you needn't send any $. till Jan. 1.

Send $20. then, please, unless I write to the contrary.

This week has been & seems likely to be full –

Sunday. Florence Farr, Tea. Konody critic who has led the not side of the . tea. 'not by Leonardo . wax-bust' - affair. & Victor Plarr's - for a supper.

Monday, Lunch- 'Blanco Posnet' at the stage society, tea with Yeats. & the Shakespears, dinner, Lecture, & to Yeat's rooms, till midnight. .

Today. private lessons, V. Hunts, tea, .

Tomorrow, lunch with Hueffer, & Yeats - Shakespear combination in the afternoon.

Thursday - Warlicks concert.

Friday, I meet the members of the Poets club who are to read my stuff at their next dinner,

Saturday , I go to see Mrs Wm Sharp. - (he was Fiona MacLeod, as you may know).

Thats all except a few details.

Now I will hie me to the feathers, with your kind permission.

Will answer mothers letter later - just received it.

Love to you & her.

E.P.

P.S. Shaw's 'Blanco Posnet' will amuse you. here with an Irish company trying to reproduce an Arkansas accent it is most diverting.

The New York Times *of 28 November 1909, carried a brief report on the **Leonardo wax bust** affair. A wax bust supposedly by Leonardo had been acquired for the Kaiser Friedrich Museum in Berlin. English experts were asserting that it was in fact the work of one Lucas, an English artist who stuffed the interiors of his wax busts with old clothes to save wax. Examination of the bust in question had just discovered within it about two square feet of rotting quilt not more than fifty years old.*

---

281. ALS

Friday 10 / 12 / 9

[London]

Dear Dad,

have raked in another £2 so you need send only $10. on Jan 1., or if inconvenient I can do without any thing till Jan 15th. - send nothing Jan 1. & $20 Jan 15th. if its easier. if by any chance you have sent anything on Dec 15th. before reciving my last letter.

Then send nothing Jan 1. & $10. Jan 15th.

I hope you & mother'll have a joyous Xmas.

This ought to reach you some time before so I wont make it a Xmas. letter. - I think I gave my weeks schedule in my last note so wont repeat. Yesterday the weather was hell. Today its like April. thank heaven.

I've still got my chapter on the Spanish stage to block out, hope to get at it next week.

More anon.

EP

282. ALS

11 – 12 - 9

[London]

Dear Mother:

The Literary Digest for Nov. 27th has not yet arrived.

I think its time K. P. got another idea, one a year is quite enough, for her, but this Blake-Mendlsohn. thing has been working overtime.

? my wardrobe. ? I have a new suit, as you should know. I have two remnants of suits in which I do not venture out. except in the immediate neighborhood for morning erands. - one I shall send as a Xmas present to a gipsy friend of Plarr's - the other I shall use for my rail road journey to Italy. on April 1st. or as near that date as possible.

My evening clothes still hang together.

I shall get some new ones next fall - the finance comittee permitting.

I have seen one of Judge Lindseys articles in Everybodies, I think, most thrilling.

The Poets club has elected me an honorary member in view of my coming address to them on the 20th. - you understand that the so called poets club is no more composed of poets than the Savage club is of people more savage than some others on this island.

I am started on my chapter on Spanish dramatic poetry.

Monday is the last lecture this term.

I must now forth or I'll miss connections

Love to you & dad & a merry Xmas.

E. P.

+ >—• <+

283. ALS

13 – 12 - 9

[London]

Dear Mother:

Manning forwards me this from the 'Spectator'.

There is a longer notice in 'The Tablet' but I have not yet got a copy - only read it in the library.

The 'Mercure de France' is reported laudatory.

'Lit. Digest arrives this A.M.

There have been several more or less violent attacks in the dailys but I have not yet made a tour of Fleet St. to purchase the back . numbers containing them.

I wrote only saturday so theres not much new.

Luck to you & dad

EP.

The most violent of the reviews of Exultations *was by Edward Thomas in the* Daily
Chronicle *of 23 November 1909.*

+⟞⟝+

284. ALS

Dec 15 [1909]

[London]

Dear Dad

The Bulletin 'ad' arrives.

What made him think I was more than 6 ft 2 inches in hight. ? Cause I aint. - cut off four inches & come within range.

I am to address the Poets Club at their December dinner on Monday. Dec. 20<u>th</u>.

Apropos you can speak to your Bulletin friend if you like. He can chance the event being pulled off according to schedule or wait until I write the results. - this you can make clear to him without implying that I suggested it.

Material for the press.

ehem!

vid. next page.

R. B. Cunningham Graham, in the 'Saturday Review' for Nov. 27 refers to me along with Henry James & George Moore among the 'best living writers'.

I address the Poets Club on 'Arnaut Daniel finest of the troubadours'.

n.b. The poets club is not necessarialy composed of poets any more than the Savage club is composed of people more savage than the normal inhabitants of London.

Among the guests, unless prevented. His blarsted excellency the Amurikan Ambassador. Sir H. Beerbohm Tree. & divers other literary & thesparian arc-lamps.

The most masterly of my poems will be delivered by the clubs expositors, including The Irish bard. Cambell - arrayed in the robes of his order.

Alarms & excursions.

———

Of course certain of these details may not come off.

but thats the program.

more anon,

E. P.

Your reporters name is Hallowell Irving - or some such 'Hallowell.' is O.K. I cant read the last so well.

+⟞⟝+

285. ALS

21 – 12 - 9

[London]

Dear Dad,

Poets club feed quite a success The ambassador didnt show up. - but then I had said at the first sending out of invitations that I had no desire to meet Mr Whitelaw Reed. & so his bid was sent rather late after I'd reconsidered him from the 'adv' stand-point.

However if your reporter hasn't already printed the affair.

Simply say - a number literary celebrities. - Cambell in his bardic robes read the Goodly Fere splendidly - I was lucky to have him.

more anon. I must out. & give a lesson.

Love
E. P.

<hr>

286. ALS

[December 1909]

[London]

Dear Dad

Thanks for the Xmas £.s.d. - I thought you'd have recived my letter saying dont send anything until Jan 15ᵗʰ.

However I can use the gift quite comfortably. in a general overhauling of my wardrobe.

Nothing has happened since I wrote last. Colourless notice in the observer. I am however past the point where the reviews make much difference.

Will have some Exultations mailed to you. – I am already late for my days job at the mausoleum.

Love to you & mother
E. P.

The brief notice in the Observer *of 26 December 1909 began: 'One is glad to welcome another tiny volume of most delicate verse from Mr. Ezra Pound, whose* Personae *had a charm of fancy and of finish that has carried it to a high degree of success. It is quite safe to say that few new poets have so quickly become known to literary London.'*

287. ALS

I - I — IO

[London]

Dear Mother.
    The sample of Percy MacKays . wont wash.
    man & amphibiAN, umbrageous green, primeaval, hawk.

———

How do you 'pierce' with a 'scan'.

———

Wont do, dear mother, rum diction.
Haven't read Hewletts 'Open Road' so can't discuss it.
As for wives? It ought to be illegal for an artist to marry, or nearly that. .
There may be some male organisms sufficiently pachidermatous to stand a team
of wives but they properly belong to some robuster age or more salubrious
climate.
    I can understand a series with intervals of recuperative length, but the simul-
taneous , no , no.
    If the artist must marry let him find someone more interested in art, or his
art, or the artist part of him, than in him. After which let them take tea together
three times a week, the ceremony may be undergone to prevent gossip, if
necessary.
    I haven't seen tributes to Gilder over here, but I never see anything. I doubt if
any american work is noticed here.
    I am glad to have the Outlook with the 'American Academy of Letters &
Arts'. of course an academy never has a beneficial effect on art. But it gives the
be dam'd canaille something to bow down to & thereby makes life easier for
the artist, especialy for the artist who is a bit of a hypocrite. However the
establishment of an academy shows an attempt at intellegence on the part of
the american public, all attempts to act intellegently should be commended.
    For the encouragement of work which 'shows ernest & persistent endeavor'
there is nothing like an academy. I should hate to have to read all the works of
the extant academicians, - a stodgy lot - but they compare very favorably with
other academicians.
    I suppose I'll join the dam thing when I'm asked. – adv. mighty force adv.
Have you read 'Bishop Bloughram's Apology' - My 'Browning' is some where
about, if you haven't.
    I saw Miss Sinclair sunday evening. & had tea with Rhys a week or so ago.
    Yeats left this morning for Dublin. He is the only living man whose work has
anything more than a most temporary interest. - possible exceptions on the
continent -. I shall survive as a curiosity.

The art of letters will come to an end before A. D. 2000. and there will be a sort of artistic dark ages till about A. D. 2700.

The last monument will be a bombastic, rhetorical epic wherethrough will move Marconi, Pierpont Morgan, Bleriot, Levavasour, Latham, Peary, Dr. Cook, etc. clothed in the heroic manner of greek imitation. Contending with mighty forces, as giants against god, with 'cubic resistance' & 'full pressure' & with 'geographical societies of Denmark'.

I shall write it myself if threatened with actual starvation.

A mixture of MacCawley - at his worst + cowley, & dryden. should take the public ear. with an occasional Kiplingesque dissonance & a flavour of cockney. pardon. 'flyver'

Enough of this. it is time to feed my face.

Love to you & Dad.

E P

I trust the tone of the letter will cause you no anxiety. my digestion is perfect.

E P

+≍≍+

288. ALS

12 - I - 10

[London]

Dear Dad:

I sent you some more 'notices', I mean publishers slips, yesterday.

Also wrote mother a long letter - mostly rot I guess.

The Eng Rev has been sold & the new management, writes that 'it looks forward with great pleasure to my valuable contributions'. A letter from the Edtr. of 'Everybodies' yesterday. He is a well meaning person. When he was here last summer he afforded me some amusement. My general attitude being that 'I had realy nothing against him personaly but that as an 'editor' - he was naturaly offensive to any self respecting artist,' – I say this not vaunting , but for your strictly private amusement. I shall get them subdued if given time.

I have replied & sent him a bad poem. If he prints it obediently I'll send him a good one.

There should be some £. s. d. coming in, in a week or so.

I don't know what % the old Eng. Rev. Co. is paying up. but whatever there is ought to be in soon.

By the way, do you happen to know the exact time of day I was born? or something near it. ?

I mailed you the Jan Rev. several days ago.

The Oxford sinecure would have been comfortable but cramping. it does not grieve me to see Crooks get it. it'll educate him - I shouldn't realy have liked it, but of course the £. s. d would have made it impossible to conscientiously refuse.

Thanks for the Calenders. They are very neat.

The Poets. club.? The dinner was very like the first dinner of the club I attended, only instead of G. B. S & Hillaire Belloc jawing the gang, Your precocious son efused & listend to his immortal works being rendered with different degrees of competency. Cambell - the 'dark man from the north' read the 'Goodly Fere' splendidly. I wish I had his voice.

The paper I read will be the second chapter 'Il miglior fabbro' in 'The Spirit of Romance'. after it there was a general discussion of Troubadour matters I answered ninety leven questions, etc .

It was Xmas week and there were about 70 members of the club on deck.

Love to you & mother.

& don't get lost in those peculiar american snow storms. –

E. P.

*Hueffer had run out of money and been forced to sell his **English Review** to Alfred Mond (1868–1930), a prominent industrialist, financier, and politician. Mond then fired him and put in Austin Harrison as editor. With his next letter Pound enclosed Harrison's note accepting 'Canzon: Of Incense' and 'Thersites on the Surviving Zeus', and they were printed in the April number of the review.*

+⇒⇐+

289. ALS

Jan. 13. [1910]

[London]

Dear Dad:

Considering that I mailed the within mentioned canzon & satire, on Jan. 12. I consider that this note shows most commendable promptness on the part of the new editor.

I wonder how long it will take us to teach american editors to behave in manner so befitting.

The Spanish Dic. & <u>mss.</u> arrive. Thanks. - also thanks for the pictures of the U. o P - & my old dormitory room. As I have just mailed you a letter there is little for me to narrate.

Love to you & mother

EP.

+⇒⇐+

290. ALS

20 January 1910

[London]

Dear Mother:

If my family is in such a wild state of desiring to see me I suppose I'd better apply for a fellowship at UoP or something of that sort. I request you & Dad, to say no more in public than that 'you'd like me to do something of that sort.'

There'se a faint chance that I might land a 'Fellowship in English'. but no need to publish the fact that I am applying.

I suppose no decent job is open 'till I take their rotten Ph. D. - Continued residence in America is of course most revolting to think of. But I might survive one winter, and it would be useful perhaps. One might get an american publisher & certain american outlets for one's stuff.

I teach Mrs. Fowler, Lady Antonia Maude, Mrs. Baker & Mrs Don.

mostly read over the <u>mss</u>. of the book. or translate from the Poema del Cid & other mediaeval stuff; for their dilectation.

Tell Dad not to send any £. s. d. on the first. I haven't received anything from the Review. but Hueffer has ordered them. to pay me. & there'll probably be something coming in from the lessons. .

I've got to give a lesson in a few moments. & the first half of the book goes to Dent this P.M. I want to look over it once again. ergo. in haste.

Love to you & Dad,

E P

20 – I – 10

+════+

291. ALS

21 - I – 10

[London]

Dear Mother:

Dad's letter contains multitudinous questions concerning my health. The winter has not been severe. I have been quite well and free from colds since November.

I delivered the 1st ½ of the Spirit of Romance to Dent yesterday. Then tead and dined at the Styans, with a friend of the Bensons and Sickert. - an artist of distinction, one of Whistler's pupils. I am to meet the Bensons some time in the indefinite future.

I can't see that there's anything American open except a possible fellowship at U of P. which I will apply for. - only don't publish the fact that I'm applying as there is scant likelyhood that my appointment will receive <u>unanimous</u> acclamations.

I might just as well be here as in Dakota. I suppose. What does R. A. Green say about openings in Princeton?

To your questions. ? The book as discipline? humph ! ! yes it does solidify the lecture material. Delivering 'notions' to an audience is an uninteresting performance but it does not bore me very much.

If you can get me a few one night stands. - Current event clubs at $100. per. night I don't mind lecturing in the U. S.

The Troubadours are the best popular material I have.

What you write about Wyncote trying to suppress another aspirant is as disgusting as it is american.

The charming attitude of the American denizen toward anything artistic which it has not been told to admire, by some third rate journalist, always delights me. Of course the childs play may need discouraging, but if so Wyncote wont know it. it's very likely quite good, in which case Wyncote will be equaly incapable of finding it out.

My glasses were discarded only for photographic purposes.

Et maintenant - I will get thru a few letters & get at my Villon chapter.

Love to you & Dad.

E. P.

24 . Jan. '10

I think you'd better have my oculist send me a pair of lenses. 1 right & 1. left. this shape.

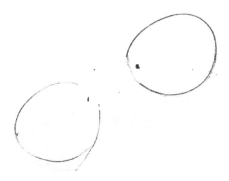

oculist is Kieth. 41. s. 18th st. I wonder if father ever paid my last bill there. $1.75. I think. my stock of spare lenses has run out so the pair had better be sent as soon as possible –

Love

EP.

The lenses are not oval but sort of triangular.

---

292. AL

[30 January 1910]

[London]

Dear Mother:

Have sent in my application for fellowship - will drift home sometime in the summer if I get it.

Are you joshing when you talk about coming over - It seems a bit luxurious - if practicable I should suggest your coming to north Italy for the unocupied part of the year & coming up to London when people are coming back to it.

I shant mind being in Phila. for one season if the fellowship game goes thru - of course - as I have written - you cant expect me to seriously consider America as a permanent place of abode.

Have you seen Kiplings 'Actions & Reactions' – I recommend it.

I dont know that the news is very various. - Lunch party on Friday with Cunningham Graham, Sidney Colvin etc. - Dance in P.M. - little dull.

Thursday. Dinner . with Konody The 'not by Leonardo' side of wax bust controversy.

The attitude of the new R. A's toward that august body is entertaining.

I think I wrote that the first half of the S. of R. had gone to the printer.

4 assorted dinners down for coming week.

---

293. ALS

Monday, Jan 31 [1910]

[London]

Dear Mother.

Your letter arrives. I'm glad to see <u>Clay</u> has got a decent job (Morgan. Yale Asryiology. etc).

Small, Maynard & co. of Boston are prepared to give 'extended consideration' to my stuff. - The opening of a scheme for U. S. A. edition.

The condition of my mind gives no alarm to my friends here . no experts have as yet pronounced against my sanity.

Mrs. Sharp is pleasant, kindly & a little dull. The Fiona McLeod & the Yeats set are not the same. (not by a dem sight. delicately ballanced temperaments do not remain perpetualy congenial.).

I sometimes wear evening clothes to my lecture - usualy when I have been dining out. I have no need of the black night shirt.

If Robt. Bacon looks anything like his photographs he doesn't interest me.

I enclose an unfinished letter written yesterday.

Love to you & Dad
E. P.

+==+=====+

294. ALS

[31 January 1910]

[London]

Dear Mother:

Thank you for your January present. (it's too late to label it new Year's). I will hie me to a hosiers & purchase many socks, Recd. $10 from Dad. – naturaly as they are both on one money order.

I hope father received my note telling him not to send anything on Feb. 1. . I don't think he need send anything before March 1st. (I can't say for certain. but I think £. s. d. are coming in.) Unless he hears to the contrary then. - Nothing to be sent until March 1st (4£).

<u>Mss</u> & dictionary. arrived, thank you. . Glad to hear Woodward has not plucked a lemon from the pear-tree of Love.

I have not been to the mint, or the tower. or the Russel Hotel.

When I go to church I usualy wish I hadn't. The carols I heard on Xmas were disgusting profanity and the trial of 'preached to death by wild curates' does not appeal.

The catholics are no better as they don't stick to their ritual but try to talk. I shall wait until I find myself in some southern climate . where they understand religion. The only worship of God I can at the moment remember having witnessed was in a little synogogue in Gibraltar & in San Pietro at Verona.

Most of the so called 'Christian' sects ought to be sued for breech of copyright.

There's an old fellow at 'All Souls' that has some of the right stuff in him. but les autres!

I lecture on the 'Paradiso' this evening. In the mene time I will polish off my chapter on Villon.

Love to you & dad.
EP

*For what Pound witnessed in the **synagogue in Gibraltar**, see canto 22. The 'old fellow at "All Souls"' may have been 'the very aged Snow' mentioned in canto 74: 'and the very aged Snow created considerable / hilarity quoting [Sappho's] φαίνε –τ-τ-τ-ττт-αί μοι / in reply to [Cavalcanti's] l'aer tremare'.*

---

295. ALS

Feb 5 [1910]

[London]

Dear Dad.

Yours. recived. I hope you got my letters in time to prevent your 'resuming'.

Please fire up again on March 1st unless you hear to the contrary. I dont think you will hear to the contrary. The election has held up everything for a month.

The lectures haven't caught hold since the Xmas vacation. & theres nothing doing in the book trade. Dent thinks May will be the earliest advisable time to bring out either of the books. My private class proves lucrative however.

The two new poems will presumably come out in March number . not Feb.

Spent Thursday night at Dent's. He's an interesting old scoundrel. He said he was sorry not to have seen you but he was doing the whole U. S. in about 3 weeks. & had only about 1 day in Phila.

It has been a full week & I must get to polishing up my chapter on Lope de Vega.

Love to you & mother
E. P.

---

296. ALS

Friday. Feb 11 [1910]

[London]

Dear Mother:

In case the U. P. should not feel sufficient need of me to overcome its natural repugnance. Please insert the following 'ad' in some reputable daily.

POET
Out of a Job.

Specalties: incicive speech, sarcasm, meditation, irony (at special rates), ze grande manair, (to order) will do to travel, or stand unhitched while being fed. Price 1£ per. hr. - special rates for steady consumers.

———

Now that ought to dew the job tidy like.

I've never seen the first display of the Ledger. It is however enlightening to know that I have been made 'members' of the poets club.

I believe the 'stained glass person' is one you mentioned about a year or so ago, is it not? I see Gilbert Doolittle has also taken the plunge.

These times be perilous.

The article on literary life in washington is rather depressing. However I shall not have to meet much of 'literary' america when I return.

Bliss Carmen is about the only one of the lot that wouldn't improve by drowning. However I don't feel called upon to superintend the operation.

I don't know that anything startling has occurred here. Classes, lectures, scholarly prose works, proofs of Canzoni. - regular routine. plus a certain amout of tea & conversation. Harmless variety of existance.

Pray heaven I never attempt any further work in prose, otherwise nothing purturbing.

There is a novel about to appear called 'The Simple Life'. I think you will enjoy it. I had the proofs of the beginning in private audition monday.

I am giving another reading from my own immortals at the Fowlers on Wednesday.

Ehem. The evening wears on. I hope Dad will blow himself to a new overcoat.

Peace be with you. .

What is your candid opinion of the Saint, the only description I have had is from a source perhaps not capable of unbiased judgement.

E P.

*The '**stained glass person**' was Laurence Saint, who had married Katherine Proctor. Pound's application for a fellowship at the **University of Pennsylvania** was unsuccessful. Dr Hugo Rennert, the supervisor of his abandoned doctoral research, had tried to secure one for him, but it was objected that Pound was not 'intending to continue a professor'. Ford Madox Hueffer's **The Simple Life Limited** was published in 1911.*

297. AL

15 February 1910

[London]

Dear Dad:

Arrives letter & glasses OK.

I shall probably send you nothing but post cards between this day Feb 15. & Feb 28. when my <u>mss</u> of the last half of the book goes to the publisher. Church walk is quite quite satisfactory. Mathew's is fairly respectful. we get on quite nicely.

Bill Williams is coming over from Leipzig the first week in March. I shall be quite glad to see him.

Love to you & mother. Keep your feet dry, dont get typhoid. be sure & wear flannel next to the skin

with love
your wayward child.

+≻═≺+

298. ALS

Feb. 19 [1910]

[London]

Dear Mother:

Thank gord the last chapter is off my chest. I've goth this week to copy out the Dante chapter and make such minor additions to the rest as I d ---- -eh. deem prudent.

Bill Williams is coming over on march 3 for a week. as I think I wrote.

Derwent Wood, sculptor, recently made R.A. is feeding me at the 'Chelsea Arts' (club) this evening. The club is putting on Hedda Gabler, for the evenings diversion.

Will you sometime when you've nothing better to do, send me information as to the exact hour of my birth. Judging purely from conjecture one would say it was 10.40 P.M. or there abouts. . but when exact information is procurable one does not need to depend upon conjecture. The foregoing sentence probably appears insane. There are however about half a million people, some of them intelligent, who still believe in the possibility of planetary influences. Chemistry is one hundred and fifty years old. & was born out the discredited clap trap of alchemy, to which - having become sane & systematic it is striving to return. Pardon me for talking like a tract.

When astrology is taken hold of systematicaly by modern science there will be some sort of discoveries.

In the mene time there is no reason why one should not indulge in private experiment & investigation. Ehem.

Josephine Preston Peabody has sent me her 'Piper' play. It begins prettily & with considerable charm - but ends in a mess - it is saturated with that lolly pop. & sugar candy philosophy which rots so much american art.

Mrs Wood wants me to translate some french & Italian songs for her concert program & as I only have till dinner time to do five songs. perhaps I'd better attend to it.

love to you & dad.

E P

Mrs Wood, who sang under her maiden name Miss Florence Schmidt, was to give a recital at the Bechstein Hall on 1ˢᵗ March, and wanted the translations for the printed programme. There were four poems by Verlaine, the first of them 'Clair de Lune'.

+‡====‡+

299. ALS

Feb 23 [1910]

[London]

Dear Dad:

Don't know that you can do anything at the U. of Penn.

I have <u>also</u> applied for a better job at 'Hobart College . Geneva. N. Y.')

What 'Post' was your clipping in. I suppose I'll see it sooner or later.

Title signifies. (p. 27. Exultations.) Nine (songs) in praise of Joan Temple

Have had a letter from Ames . who wishes me well but considers the fellow-ship will be likely to be retained by the present holder.

I hope mother is well, I am copying out my Dante chapter. The book is finished . - bar a few additions which I shall probably tie onto it.

Luck stay with you.

Love to you & mother

E. P.

+‡====‡+

300. ALS

Feb. 23 [1910]

[London]

Dear Mother:

We have just read over the final chapters at the Shakespear's. The book is done bar a bit of copying out and a few unweighty additions.

219

I have applied for a job at Hobart Cawlege, Geneva. N. Y. ($1300. paid the present prof.). I suppose there's a fair chance of getting it. The book ought to make that sort of thing easier.

I hope I never write another book in prose - or any prose again except perhaps the introductions to certain things which I intend to translate.

Notably some plays of Lope de Vega. Some troubadour things and the Poema del Cid, in something like the original meetre.

My last lecture is set for 'Bank Holliday' (Easter Monday) by an oversight. as it was a supplementary lecture, I shall be able to escape it altogether. & take my proofs to Verona for Easter. where I shall have sunlight and quiet for my final revision.

I shall sail in June, presumably, bar more than unreasonably delay the book will then be out. I may be able to leave 'El Desprecio Agradecido' translated, to be published after my departure, but I shall not wait to finish it.

My mind, such as I have, works by a sort of fusion, and sudden crystaliza-tion, and the effort to tie that kind of action to the dray work of prose is very exhausting. One should have a vegetable sort of mind for prose. I mean the thought formation should go on consecutively and gradualy. with order rather than epigrams.

Ehem it is 8 by the orologue I will sally forth and dine.

Love to you & dad. I hope you are finding interesting things to read. How are the Skidmore's. do you see any thing of them?

Concerning my reported insanity? I don't quite understand your question. No particular reports of my insanity have reached me. If such reports are gaining ground I can only reply with Voltaire. : 'He calls me rogue, thief, liar, parricide, assassin; I judge that in all points we do not exactly agree.'

A bientot –
loving Son

+‒•‒⊣+

301. ALS

Feb. 26 . [1910]

[London]

Dear Mother:

The last of the book has, thank heaven, gone to the printer. It is a great relief to get it out of the house. I breathe with lighter mind.

I believe you are having stirring times in the city of Brotherly Traction. with your black hussars, and trolly cars, and city 'cops' all in a row. I trust they are not taking your particular front yard as a scene of action. It is of course written in the stars that 1910 is a year of upheaval. China & Tibet seem to be obeying the comets with some precision.

I wrote I think. that Bill W^ms is coming from Leipzig next week, & Manning from Lincolnshire . the week after. Nothing remarkable has happened in the past day or so.

Love to you & dad -

make my salaams to whoever is worth while saluting.

EP

A strike by the trolley workers of the Philadelphia Rapid Transit Company had begun on 19 February, and the use of armed and mounted police against the striking workers was provoking city-wide riots. A general strike followed and lasted until the end of March. In its struggle for independence from China, Tibet had just decreed the expulsion of all Chinese from its territory—China would shortly assert sovereignty over Tibet.

---

302. ALS

March 1 [1910]

[London]

Dear Dad:

I'm afraid I'll have to ask you to remit £4. on the 15th also. as my income appears precarious. I don't know when the Fortnightly is going to use or pay for the canzone they accepted some months ago. Please remit to Poste Restante, <u>Verona</u>. Italia. I hope the sun & the quiet will make me forget that I've been grinding at that horrible prose since August.

I hope mother is of a calm mind with regard to my Italian amble. But it doesn't seem sane to return to U. S. A. before June. & I might as well have the intervening time where it will help my 'language' (presuming I'm to profess next winter). and my constitution. I am I believe fairly fagged. I feel O.K. this morning but I want a bit of reserve force before I try that hell wallow which the polite call the Atlantic. (Rev. 21. 1.[1]). I've got five or six appointments to keep in the course of this day. : Ergo excuse me while I shave & make ready. -

Love to you & mother

E. P.

---

[1] 'And I saw a new heaven and a new earth; for the first heaven and the first earth were passed away; and there was no more sea.'

303. ALS

[2 March 1910]

[London]

Dear Mother:

I send along Mrs Wood's concert program. The translations are not particularly valuable, having been scribbled off. The lot of them in one day . all but the first Verlaine, which I had done, more or less, some time ago. The concert was agreeable

one cant make poor poetry into good by translation, even if it were well done.

By a system of barter the tickets . one acquires by knowing one set of people, pay off dinner debts etc. - you wrote about 'giving pleasure' etc. – one relies rather on one's self & one's own work however than on chance perquisites.

Nothing in particular is taking place, except microscopical buisiness quibbles over . contracts etc. The Eng. Rev. has not used my poems this month. Mathews says I'm to have some sort of a dividend sometime soon. If they have another be dam'd 'General Election' it will interfere with. my next set of reviews. I trust Loyd George. will suffer due torments hereafter.

I hope Philadelphia is still on the map. despite the reports of devastation which reach us.

Considering my present Temper, you may congratulate my family that I'm to have some Italian sun before appearing in its (my family's) bosom. Poor Bill is coming just in time to get the backwash of the winters grind.

I hope the discipline will be good for him.

It is rumored that Yeats intends to say something decent about me in one of his lectures next week. but as he has never been known to do anything he intended to, I shall take some stock in the rumor . after it has been verified by fact.

The gods avail you.
Love to you & dad.
EP

+≍+

304. ALS

Feb.6 [6 March 1910]

[London]

Dear Mother. .

Bill has arrived & I am attempting to broaden his mind by showing him the wonders of our dusky & marvelous city. As you know the list of the specified sights I need hardly enclose a catalogue

Monday. A. M.

No American mail. so there's nothing to answer. I'm off to the museum to write my Leopardi & Metastasio lecture. for next week. Shall turn Bill loose on the parthinan marbles.

Till later –Love to you & dad.

Weather here is sunny, for a wonder.

EP

We dine with the Shakespears & probably go on to Yeats at . home. to night.

EP's 'Feb.' is obviously a misdating for 'March'.

+═══+

305. ALS

March 9 [1910]

[London]

Dear Dad:

I'm sorry awfully sorry mother's laid up. I hope by the time this arrives she'll be cheered up a bit.

Thanks for the £4. I'm correcting proof . & I've got to go out in about ½ hr.

Bill has been shipped off to look at the tower.

Will write later today, or tomorrow

Love to you & mother

E. P.

+═══+

306. ALS

12 March 1910

[London]

Dear Dad:

Bill has left for Paris after a weeks festivity.

The 'Fortnightly' sends proofs of a canzone, so there'll be something from them soon. (£. s. d.).

I think maybe you'd better send the regular amt. to Poste Restante, Verona, again on the 1st of April. however . as there may be delays & checques are hard to cash in Italy. also I may shift my base there after 3 or 4 weeks., but it may please you to know that there are some assets at this end, even if they dont bring instant relief.

I'm on the wing at this moment, and as I have written in my last six letters, 'will continue 'later'.

Love to you & mother

E. P.

Manning comes down for a few days next week . & I go . a week from Tuesday.

EP

This is Saturday. March 12 1910.

⊹═══⊹

307. ALS

12 – 3 '10

[London]

Dear Mother:

Bill has gone & the planets resume their accustomed orbits. We had a spasm of endurable weather but the cold has returned.

I feel that Bill's mind has been duly benefited by his brief sojourn on these here island shores.

I suppose my canzone will appear in the 'Fortnightly' review, for either March 15 or April 1. - presumably the latter. The defunct Eng. Rev. company has paid up so my fare to Italy is more than covered.

We had a delightful dinner at the Fowlers last night before Bill's departure, and I took him to see Yeats on monday, & crammed him with Turner & other such during the rest of the time. I dont know whether or no he & his brother will get up into my corner of Italy or not.

Am dining to night with the Woods.

I shall sally forth now to return divers portions of private libraries which have been lent me.

Love to you & Dad,

EP

Many years later William Carlos Williams wrote in his Autobiography *(chapter 20): 'It was an instructive week for me. We shared a small second-floor room. It was an intense literary atmosphere, which though it was thrilling, every minute of it, was fatiguing in the extreme. . . . It seemed completely foreign to anything I desired. I was glad to get away.'*

⊹═══⊹

308. ALS

15. March [1910]

[London]

Dear Dad:

Arrive letters from you & mother and the 'Digest' ad.

Bill seemed to feel educated when he left. He goes to paris, then to his brother in Rome.

Your civil and civic war seems to be continuing full blast.

As to finances There are several assets but I cant tell when they'll pay so youd better stand to your guns if possible. I should rather be loose in Italy with $10+ than –$10.

I suppose you got my letter suggesting that you send £4 to Verona on the 15$\underline{th}$ (i.e. today). I guess youd better repeat operation on April 1. - If its not a strain.

I dont care whether it's Geneva. for next winter. but we hope it'll be something.

I enclose note for mother.

EP

+⊨⊨⊣+

309. AL

[15 March 1910]

[London]

Dear Mother:

In reply to several questions. of yours.

There's no particular need of my return to London, except that it is just as cheap as to sail from Italy, and I may have a translated play to dispose of. or something.

also I don't want to carry all my possessions into Italy.

also it would be well to appear here when the book comes out.

I don't know anything about Piper. I suppose he's in Oxford.

As for plans. I start for Verona one week from today. - one week from this moment, more or less, I start to cross the lovely channel. I breakfast in Paris, presumably with W. M. Rummel. . I proced via M^t. Cenis, & Turin to Milan & sleep that night at Bergamo. proceding thence to Verona at leisure.

Bill may come up to north Italy if he don't go to Spain

The Shakspears or the Konodys may be in. or pass through my town during april or may. Konody has done all that part of Italy. with a fine tooth comb, - alias 40 HP. - and the Shakespears usuly put up at the Edens - (of the Venetian Garden).

My wardrobe is I believe fitted for the journey. The italian climate & food are both cheap & agreeable.

<hr />

310. AL

Monday. March 22 [1910]

[London]

Dear Mother:

Letters from you & Dad this. A.M.

I start for Verona tomorrow. - Rummel is going to put me up over night in Paris, so the longeur of the journey will be pleasantly broken.

Had rather interesting day yesterday went over the new Weslyan building which Ricards is putting up opposite the abbey. He understands 'space' in building. I think he'll have one of the finest, if not the finest foyer in London.

Lunched with the distinguished novelist who is writing 'The Simple Life'. it may come out as a serial in Harpers, he took me on to Lady Low's for tea. which was quite endurable.

Evening. with Manning, at the Fowlers.

I don't know that there's any thing in particular to say about Manning, he is rather intellegent as you judge from his prose & from one or two of his poems. We disagree upon most matters are pretty well in accord in the belief that we are the genmeration or at least the only significant writers under thirty.

In which faith we write parodies of each other. . compose poems upon each others frailties & vanities, abuse each other in public with a virulence which terrifies the bystanders.

In fact our friendship is as firmly founded as could possibly be desired -

I now go to walk with Hueffer. . at 2.30 I go to the Stage Society. at 8.30 . I lecture. Tomorrow I lunch with Violet Hunt, tea with the Shakespears. and depart at 8.45.P.M. for Paris.

Love to you & dad.

The 'new Wesleyan building' in Parliament Square and opposite Westminster Abbey, formally opened in October 1912 as headquarters of Methodism in London, is now known as Westminster Central Hall. Its Great Hall seats 2000.

<hr />

311. ACS

[25 March ? 1910]

En route [to Italy]

Dear Dad

Rummel has kept me two days in Paris, & given me a charming time. Shall drive around Turin tomorrow A.M. and procede to Milan or Bergamo.

Spring is already loose in the french country. –

I write this on the train.

E.P.

+>==>==<+

312. ALS

[27 March ? 1910]

<u>Verona</u>

Dear Dad:

Arrived but not yet settled, ink precarious ,

Will write more fully , when I have breakfasted & found permanent quarters.

No, I dont think you'll have to pay for my passage home. & dont think you'll need to send any more remittances. The news may perhaps be comforting.

Spent night before last in Bergamo -

an hour in Brescia, yesterday. & have been hunting suitable lodgment here in Verona since then.

More anon

EP

The financial condition is decidedly comforting.

*Pound's **financial condition** had changed dramatically in Paris. Walter Rummel had introduced him to his close friend Margaret Lanier Cravens (1881–1912), an intensely idealistic student of the piano from Madison, Indiana, and she had spontaneously offered to place enough money at his disposal annually to free him to concentrate on his poetry, while insisting that he should tell no-one.*

+>==>==<+

313. ALS [*letterhead*] Hotel Eden, Sirmione am Gardasee

[March 1910]

Lago di Garda

Dear Mother.

Ecco mi. in a real hotel, 3 meals a day 'Tutto compreso' clean, full of sunlight. on 'Lago di Garda' which some ridiculous german who used to own the hotel calls 'Garda see'. Also it comes at the sane price of 7 lira. per day. which I can afford. –

I shall stay here and absorb sunlight for a month or two. Bar running up to Venice to dine with the Snivelys when they arrive there I expect the Shakespears will land on the lake somewhere, or in Verona in a months time.

I've forgotten just what I wrote from Verona. . I believe I told dad that he could 'hang up' on the remittances & that I'd probably not need any help to get across the beastly atlantic. I'll fill in the details when I get home.

I walked over here from Desenzano yesterday. ate a table d'hote which made me tremble for the financial consequences, fainted with relief when the bill was brought. 2 lira. 50 centimes. - thought the place looked predestined. 'combinato'ed for a month. have miles of Lago di Garda under my window. , what I take to be the dome & campanilli of Brescia in the hills beyond it. snow capped mountains to the north when I lean out of the window. & a Scalliger castle behind the hotel.

Desenzano - crouches in proper Whistlerian fashion on the opposite ledge of the lake - & in short - bar the 'luce electrica' & a few details, it's the same old Sirmio that Catullus raved over a few years back, or M. A. Flaminius more recently. To day I have fetched my luggage by boat from Desenzano, sunbathed for two hours, shaved & begun to cope with my correspondence.

Unless I go up to Venice, or Belluno with the Shakespears, I dont see why I shouldn't stay here until I return to England. The cooking is good & the place is clean, oh miraculously. also one cant buy any thing but postage stamps & penny bottles of ink within eight miles distance, so I don't see that I'm likely to be ruinously extravagant.

Ebben - a certain Miss Scarborough whom I met in Paris presented me with a collection of Spanish poets - of Lope's time - which seems more or less as a command of Providence to make 'certain additions' to Chap· VIII· of 'The Spirit of Romance'. to which labour I address me.

Love to you & dad.
- E P.

Hotel Eden
Sirmione. <u>Lago di Garda</u>

> *An inscription in the collection,* Castellanos Poesias Selectos *(Madrid, 1817), now in Yale University's Beinecke Rare Book Library, reads '**Elisabeth Scarborough** / 17 rue Eugène Delacroix / To Ezra Pound'—17 rue Eugène Delacroix was Margaret Cravens' Paris address in 1910. For the '"**certain additions**"' to* The Spirit of Romance *see the last page of 'The Quality of Lope de Vega' (before the 1929 addition).*

+⟩━⟨+

314. ALS [*letterhead*] Hotel Eden, Sirmione am Gardasee
[April 1910]

[Lake Garda]

Dear Dad:

For the teenth time you & mother & everybody have howled 'Why Verona?'

Verona is perhaps the most beautiful city in north Italy. The church of San Zeno is the ultimate perfection. ergo Verona. I might have written a book on Can Grande de la Scala. – it happens I'm going to write about Guido Cavalcanti in stead. Dante wrote a good deal of the Divina Commedia in Verona & the 'Paradiso' is dedicated to Can Grande. Why Verona? Why Italy? simply if one were not bound by necessity one would live in Italy most of the time & visit Spain now & then. & in Italy one would live in divers different places for several months. I began on Venice. – now its Lake Garda.

I happen to like Verona. & just now it happens to be more convenient & perhaps better for my health to be in the country.

All the apartments in the particular pink marble palace in Verona, in which I wish to reside, happen to be rented. I arrived a couple of weeks too late.

As for Roosevelt. my opinion hasn't varied much. I've got my American edition without having him write a review in the Outlook - The review would still be useful – if convenient I shall meet him. but I shouldn't experience any disappointment if I don't. He will have my immortal works thrust upon him. – he probably has had them thrust upon him by now. . We should probably take a violent dislike to each other. so perhaps he'd better derive his opinions from the printed page.

In answer to Mother's questions.

Desenzano. is 40 cents worth from Verona. & five miles from here.

I don't see that my 'sudden accession of wealth' need be regarded as either so d----d sudden or as wealth.

I've jawed all winter at the Polytec. I've been writing a book for six months, I've given lessons in advanced kindergarten aesthetics. My poesia begins to go in the magazines at about £5. a dip. Jan. Eng. Rev. paid in March. April. Eng. Rev. just. paid. Fortnightly proofs returned. Eng. Rev. 3 new poems received & presumably to appear. Sudden! hm. – well. we hope we're on the way.

There are, thank god, no americans here. The Shakespears arrive next week. I like the exceptions to the American people. the rank & file frankly do not delight me. The typicaly American attitude of mind makes me desire to administer the boot-point to the typical american posterior.

if you had a free income of $500 a year I should certainly advise you to take a plot of ground here on Lake Garda & save me the pain of crossing the Atlantic.

There is of course nothing more delightful than the American exceptions. , one meets them on both sides of the wet. But the residue are hybrids & half-baked. You need not repeat these remarks, & out of consideration for my American Publishers I shall not make them in public.

The Australian papers are publishing your sons Phiz. with comment.

I shall get back to London about the middle of June. I rather want to meet the Saint family. if they can be divorced from the Ellises. – Willie becomes more & more repugnant the more one considers him. of course I shan't wait forever. If Saint is half the artist some people think he is, it might be well for him to know one or two people. – of course I can't find out much about it.

Katharine is in no condition to judge. Hilda guarantees his possibilities

In vain do I endeavor to find out whether he wants to be a great artist. or whether he is begining to be one.

Ellis is enough to ruin any young man, I mean in the artistic sense. Ellis would depress more art out of a person of tender years than a term in the house of commons. Ellis, given a free hand would have him turned into a steward on the liner & into a draper on landing in London.

However let us turn our mind to pleasant subjects. Mother is quite right in supposing that Sirmione is the lost paradise. I've been about a bit & I guess I know heaven when I arrive. I shall take a good six weeks more of Italy. & I shall come back again just as soon as ever I get the chance. I wish somehow I could import you & mother, but the means are not yet at hand. – give us time reverend parent – give us time.

and we will try to deliver you, even if its only for a few months at a streatch from punching american bells in a -- -- – -- be dam'd time-clock of government manufacture.

Ellis is the sort of man who approves of time clocks. I wonder he dont keep one in his front hall. My God. if I do meet T. Roozenstein. we'll have one topic of conversation at least, out side the realms of poetry & the celtic sagas.

Oh well. you do get some Italy, & you've got a church to get it in. & after all its what we get done not what we go thru, or what we get paid for it, that realy matters.

Is there any vague chance of your getting transferred to one of the other assay offices. – Carolina – or N. Y. or anything? – Oh well enough of this.

Love, to you & mother –

E. P.

Remember me to the folks at Tioga.

*In the **Australian** Book Lover of 6 April 1910 there was an article on Pound by Griffyth Fairfax under the heading 'A New Experience'.*

315. ALS [*letterhead*] Hotel Eden, Sirmione am Gardasee

[April 1910]

[Lake Garda]

Reverend Parent:

Your last P.O. is made out to the Postmaster at ---- Italy.

Now ---- Italy is more or less spacious.

Fortunately I am not pressed for the money and if you can get it at your end quicker than I can here, do so . . If not try to find out where it has gone. I shall of course make what inquiries are possible here.

The order. is no. 37924

   Middle City Station.

sent . March 31.

Fortunately, as I have remarked it dont happen to matter whether the order is paid now or on the 4th of July.

I haven't sent you the proofs of the S. of R. because it would rather waste your time to read the first set. a number of mistakes . which alter the sense. – 'or' for 'as' and that sort of thing – The revise is begining to come in, & its practicaly O.K. so I think it'll be better to wait until that's ready or til part of it is ready. Besides I rather want the whole book here. & I have it only in first set of proofs. I'll start it your way in a week or so.

I dont know that there's much else to say. Williams has gone to Spain. The Snivelys will be in this part of Italy soon . – also the Shakespears.

Sirmione is only about 8 feet wide so there isn't much chance for events of world wide interest.

Love to you & mother.

E.P.

⊢═══⊣

316. ACS

[April 1910]

[Lake Garda]

Dear Dad.

Small, Maynard & Co. are going to publish an American edition of your sons immortal works. Viva la Boston. ! The ledger clipping arrives – naturaly they print a poem which I have withdrawn from circulation – however. – adv – I don't clearly remember your lame boy – hope he gets his job. Yeats did not mention any of the younger generation. . – as I predicted –

Tell mother Bank Holiday is sacred in England. nothing can take place. Tell mother . not much 'literature' sprouted in the Time of charlamagne. – people lied about him after his death. – hence the epics . – Hope you are well again.

E.P.

Small, Maynard *would publish in November 1910* Provença | Poems Selected from Personae, Exultations, and | Canzoniere. *The* **Philadelphia Ledger** *had reprinted* 'La Regina Avrillouse' *from* A Lume Spento.

╫═══╫

317. ACS
[April 1910]

[Lake Garda]

Dear Dad:
    Your second money order has been paid so you needn't worry over that matter. I think the Italian P.O. showed some intellegence in placing me in Italy 'at large'. Tell mother the 'Boston Publication' was arranged by letter & by sending 'em my works. I'll consider her 'photograph' when I get to Venice. The weather is a marvel & nothing has happened since my card yesterday.
                                E.P.

╫═══╫

318. ACS
[April 1910]

[Lake Garda]

    5000 Germans have this instant descended upon us. and as the 'piroscofo' is already half way across the lake I suppose they'll stay.
    There are realy only about 10 – but it causes great commotion in our quiet life here. The one German family which has been here, is most remarkable. – one can sit in the dining room with them without hearing them eat.
    I have returned more proofs to Dent. & presume that with the exception of proofs, the life here is perfectly hygenic.
                                E. P.

╫═══╫

319. ALS [*letterhead*] Hotel Eden, Sirmione am Gardasee
[April 1910]

Lago di Garda

Dear Dad:
    This time-clock business is a dam'd indignity. I hope having me off your hands financialy in some sort of way ballances matters.

232

I suppose its this N. Y. Custom house affair that has started the row?

About 4/5 of the book has been corrected & there seems to be a chance of my standing on my own $s. for some time.

I wonder if the U. S. edtn. will pay anything except 'la gloire'.

News comes from London that Yeats has been saying nice things about me. – not so valuable in private as they would have been on the platform but just as gratifying personaly. To the effect that 'There is no younger generation (of Poets). E. P. is a solitary volcano.' 'If he writes rhyme like an amateur he writes rhythm like a master.' – Well he hasn't seen the later work where we begin to consider whether we'll rhyme or not.

There was more but it comes indefinitely.

As this is private conversation it can not be used on reporters or publishers

Snively is coming over & I may return to the U. S. with him, if we can accomode our times of motion. I wish I could manage to have you & mother come here instead, but it'll take a melodrama or something of that sort to set me in that financial rating. I doubt if farming pays much here. I choose Italy because there is no sun fit to be called such in England. . You ask about the trip. . I spent two days with Rummel in Paris, stopped over trains in Turin, spent Easter in Brescia, routed around Verona two days looking for rooms, & not finding anything to suit me came here. – I chose Verona because the Church of San Zeno is the last word, the ultimate perfection. – only one can't sit in it all day or sleep in it. – so I'm here. San Fermo is also magical. – I've called it San Pietro – by mistake in Guillaume de Lorris belated – a Vision of Italy. San Fermo (Maggiore. it is realy.), is pretty much battered. but San Zeno is pure magic, inside & out – I think you have post cards of it from 1908 its toned brown - pink outside & the inside. is proportion lifted into a sort of divinity.

I shall spend some time in Verona before I go back to England, –

One sees the top of Brescia cathedrall in the hills the other side of the lake here.

Bergamo 'Città Alta' is an old walled town with the new city in the vally below it.

This Sirmio, as you may be able to see on a map - is a nose running out into Lago di Garda. so fashion

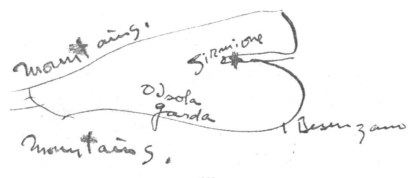

Sirmio itself. is about like this

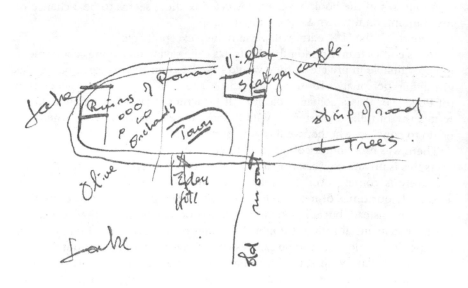

Love to you & mother.
E. P.

'Guillaume de Lorris Belated. A Vision of Italy', *was included in* Personae *(1909).*

+———+

320. ACS

8 May [1910]

[Lake Garda]

Dear Dad:

Dined . with the Snivelys in Venice on Friday & returned here yesterday. Venice seems rather like a machine shop after Sirmione. Have mailed the selected sections of an 'Eng Rev., Chesterton is an overgrown wind-bag. - Shaw's review of the book was diverting.

Sorry I cant take on Bennets mine just yet. I'm afraid Snively isn't sailing back early enough for me. Shall stay here another week then take a few days in Verona & Vicenza, a week or so in Venice & then start for England.

Mathews publishes 'The Dawn' together with a few Canzoni as his fall exposition of yrs. truly. Shall see that matter through while I am in London.

234

This means that I have 3 different books in divers states of publication at present. - you'd better send my mail to 'Poste Restante . Venice. until further notice.

Love to you & mother
E. P.

Sirmione.
May. 8.

+≒≓+

321. ALS

[June 1910]

[London]

Dear Mother

Dont forward any more mail - Shall be home by the end of the month -

London is very busy & not at all the sort of place one would leave if one were in search of diversion.

I hope to occupy myself with some profitable & commercial enterprise immediately on my arrival in the U. S. . I should like a few days on the Sound with Prof. Skidmore, but dont make any other social engagements for me. as I probably wont keep 'em.

I've had my rest in Italy. & the first heat of the battle is more or less over.

Called on your Coomans -Woodward contingent but they were out.

And as my days are as the weavers shuttle I dont know that I'll find time to call again.

Love to you & dad.
EP.

+≒≓+

322. ALS [*letterhead*] Royal Mail Steamship 'Slavonia'

[25 June 1910]

[New York]

Dear Dad.

Your letter & mothers received

Had pleasant trip over to New York

Guess there is nothing to add to what I said before leaving.

Scarf also arrived. This last moment before starting.

Is not a time for me to shine in correspondence

Love to you & mother.
E.P.

Pound told Margaret Cravens in a letter dated 30 June 1910 that he had crossed on the 'Lusitania'. He was about to join his parents who were renting a house at Swarthmore for the summer, and would be with them for about six weeks.

—●—

323. ALS

Monday [August 1910]

[New York]

Dear Dad.

How long are you going to stay at Swarthmore. ? there may be a slack week along toward the end of the month when I could run over.

Rummel departs for Boston this evening.

One Seumas O'Shiel bored us to death last evening. Farwell is under the weather. No news of any particular importance

Ezry.
Love to you & mother

If you want me to come mail me that 100 trip ticket a day or so before hand.

—●—

324. ALS

[August ? 1910]

164 Waverley Place [New York]

Dear Dad.

Had Bacon go over financial end of the game . he says its very straight conservative. – I guess it's the real . real . Sorry you have'nt a few shekels.

I have written to aunt Frank. & if your mint friends have anything loose, let 'em send it. – mentioning me. – yrs. tly. is drawing a comission on anything he can place.

Lindsey is a bit of a pedagogue. but Medbury is a man after my own heart. – I'm to have a shy at a job with the concern when it gets under weigh. = Shares. par. $10. now 5.50 – you cant have mine just yet.

You don't say whether or no you've xpessed my laundry. ???

Love to you & mother.
Ez.

Francis S. Bacon, 'Baldy Bacon', figures in Canto 12: 'Baldy's interest / Was in money business. / "No interest in any other kind uv bisnis," / Said Baldy'. He 'ran up to 40,000 bones on his own, / Once, but wanted to "eat up the whole'r Wall St." / And dropped it

236

*all three weeks later.' When Pound met up with him in Manhattan in 1910 he was
employed as a clerk in an insurance office, 'selling odd sorts of insurance'. It seems that
neither Homer nor Aunt Frank were persuaded to play in his game.*

+⇒⟸+

325. ALS

October 7 [1910]

[New York]

Dear Mother:

Dined with rather an intellegent crowd at Cosgrove's last night.

O'Shiel dragged me out to supper tonight.

I continue with Guido. Have seen Kennelly once or twice - good chap.

The Cones? are same as ever only a bit more so.

There's a studio with a shower bath attached, on Washington sq. which I
shall take on Nov. 1. if it dont get rented to some one else before then.

I dont need any more clothes immediately Thanks awfuly.

The 'science of poetry' hardly worth reviewing. I sent off some copy on it to
Book News. which they may print if they can read it.

Julia Well's is established here in N. Y. more or less comfortably. Looked a
friend of Mrs Fowlers pleasant but dull.

Cosgrove's crowd, as I indicated, seem alive

send me a few blotters. If you want me to use 'em, I'll probably go on
forgetting to buy 'em for the next six months.

Love to you & dad

Ezry

*Pound had moved to 270 Fourth Avenue (now Park Avenue South) by 2 November. His
review of* The Science of Poetry *and the Philosophy of Language by Hudson
Maxim was published in the December* Book News Monthly.

+⇒⟸+

326. ALS

Tuesday night [October 1910]

[New York]

Dear Mother.

Lunched with Farwell - two days ago, Expect to see Bynner tomorrow.

I go down to stay with Bill W^{ms} , from this Thursday to end of week. Next
Wed. I go down to have dinner & spend the night with Wm Wadsworth.

Have had pleasant half hour with Spooner's secretary. The senator being out
of town on a case.

Hilda arrived today & is safely stored with Julia Wells.
Dined with the Baxter's saturday.
The metropolitan gallery has finaly gotten some interesting pictures.
one of the finest Goya's I've ever seen.
When is Aunt Frank coming to Town - ?

Love to you & dad

Ezra.

John Coit **Spooner** *(1843–1919) had been US Senator from Wisconsin until 1907, and was now a Corporate lawyer in New York.*

+>=+

327. ACS

[4 November 1910]

[New York]

it still rains. . I go to Colonia tomorrow. Its too wet to move about so I have not called on Aunt Frank The expess Co. says it will deliver goods as soon as strikers permit. -
I have spent a day or so enriching my mind . preparatory to doing the introduction to Guido.
The S.S. Times. Sends $50. - which will serve for December. - I think the cover design will be well done. also

Love to you & dad

E. P.

The **Sunday School Times** *(Philadelphia) published Pound's 'Christmas Prologue' in December 1910.*

+>=+

328. ACS

[8 November 1910]

[New York]

Returned from Colonia. & saw Aunt Frank & Sarah for a few moments last evening. being *en passant* for a french evening . with the Del Mars. (friends of Mrs. Fowler).
guess thats about all . Am working on my introduction to G C.

Love to you & dad.

E.P.

+>=+

329. ALS

Friday, 12 midnight [November? 1910]

[New York]

My Dear 'exceptional' mother.
one buys coffee at Vantines. – rather bad coffee – to my opinion.
I have sent off the <u>mss</u> of two volumns during the past few weeks. – shall go down to Williams . to type some prose in a day or so. My desk is getting some what cleared up.
I've taken to Propertius. & have by way of variety, just finished a diverting but rather loosely written novel by Disraeli: 'Endymion', a good deal of wisdom & no ideals.
Yeat's new volumn is announced. I met his father on the Avenue this P.M. & know that at least one copy has reached this side.
Dined with Bacon, this evening.
Mrs Augustus W.- is very ill.
Called on Aunt F. & Sarah. Tuesday . . cant remember – when what else happened. – or what I have written to you
anyhow its about time to retire

Love to you and <u>dad</u>.
EP.

+>=<=<+

330. ALS

(21 November 1910)

[New York]

Dear Mother:
Don't know when I wrote last.
Tuesday. , Welsh dramatic edtr. Herald, took me out to see Blanche Bates. first night of Nobody s Widow.
Thursday, to Russian Symphony.
Welsh writes quite good poetry.
Dinner with Cousin Charles on Friday. . The feminine side of the family spends most of its time at Chatham.
Yesterday I had tea with him at the Barnard club & we proceded thence to the domicile of Augustus.
Met Dale at the Theatre. Tuesday.
The Guido has been sent off to Small Maynard & I am considering my next english edtn. of poems.
Powys. whose quotations you sent - is evidently an inaccurate ass or else its the reporter who quotes him.
Zeublin is correct. but its rather hard on the Am Democracy.

I have always said that Whitman was America. it's a two edged insult.
If Parkhurst would strangle his assistant his church would be endurable.
Glad Smith is provost.

———

My felicitations on a joyous anniversary to you & father.
accept the mud coloured book as a land mark. (article to follow).
Your loving son
Ezry.

Small, Maynard did not publish Pound's **Sonnets and Ballate of Guido Cavalcanti** *until April 1912, and though the Introduction was dated '15 November 1910' it was in fact 'finished up' in Paris the following year. The '***mud coloured book***' would have been* Provença *just published by Small, Maynard with a 'tan dust jacket printed in dark brown and green'. John Cowper* **Powys** *(1870–1963) was visiting Philadelphia in November 1910 on one of his popular lecture tours. Charles* **Zeublin** *(1866–1924), was a Chicago sociologist associated with Hull House and Northwestern University Settlement; a popular lecturer, often on controversial subjects, his critical analysis of business activities had led to his removal from his post as Professor of Sociology in the University of Chicago in 1908.*

+≕≕+

331. ALS

[November 1910]

[New York]

Dear Mother
  Delightful evening with the Chas. Wadsworth - Charles is evidently the decorative member of the family. Madame was most cordial. - Will is slightly bored by law & has agrararian ambitions.
  Dined with Aunt F. & Sarah. & met mrs Ransome. the night before.
  All of both gangs send their regards.

Monday.
Spent yesterday lunching & dining around with Miss Elizabeth & her friends. . . - one Welsh musical critic of the Heralad - I like very much. - clippings arrive this A.M.
  Stairway I wrote about, Burgos, not the one Morgan bought!.
Everything O.K.
Love
Ezry.

+≕≕+

332. ACS

[24 November 1910]

[New York]

Going down to Bills for Thanksgiving dinner. Don't think much has happened. Thanks for the clippings. . I'm at work on my new collection of poems for London. – expect to be moderately employed for a week or so.

Love to you & dad.

E. P.

There are no letters for December 1910 and January 1911. For part of December, Pound may have been with his parents in Philadelphia—they were renting at 1834 Mount Vernon Street, near to the Mint. By early January he had gone down with jaundice and was in hospital. His 'first full day up and about' was in early February.

╪══╪

333. ACS

[11 February 1911]

[New York]

About to take train for Bill's.
Who said I had the milk COLD?
Dined at Baxters, yesterday.

Will write,

EP.

╪══╪

334. ACS

[13 February 1911]

[New York]

Have been rusticating at 'Bill's'. wrote a card from N. Y. on Saturday – but think I forgot to mail it.

Salutations

EP

N.Y. Not finding my other card here. I conclude that I sent it. The 'Tracey' photos of E. P. are very fine.

Mathews ready to blaze away on my 'Canzoni' -

╪══╪

335. AC

[15 February 1911]

[New York]

I've got things here fairly settled. There's a rare chance of my coming over from Saturday till Tuesday. if you want me.

+⟞═⟝+

336. ALS [*letterhead*] Barnard Club, Carnegie Building

[February 1911]

[New York]

Dear Mother.
Read 'The New Art in Paris' in the February Forum:
There's an answer to a number of things.
That ought to prove my instince for where I can breathe. .
It's mostly news to me. but of the right sort.

EP

+⟞═⟝+

337. ALS

[February 1911]

[New York]

Dear Mother
Father will assure you that I lunched yesterday. Mrs Worthington kept me on to dinner, partly becasue I am an agreeable person partly because there was a painter, sculptor whose name I forget, who wanted to meet me.
Milk at my bedroom door this A. M.
I regret your lack of reconsiliation
You never seem to consider my necessity to live. If I muck around here thru' the summer, I wont at the end of it have done anything that I haven't done before . . However what's the use arguing . I have my work to do & must choose my own way of getting it done.
Flos collegit rerum , saith the good Augurellus.
I don't see that my stay on this side has much 'conserved' my finances.
I know of a Jowett, but think he is dead.

Love to you & father.
I am feeing quite fit, thank you,

Ezry.

+⟞═⟝+

338. ALS

(Feb. 1911)

[New York]

Dear Father

I'm sorry for the desolation in my wake. It has not been particularly easy for me to go.

I realize a number of things besides the fact that I am leaving considerably more comfort behind me than I shall find.

I am glad that you see a little reason in my performance.

Whatever I may seem to have done or left undone, my time is still a time of preparation, not a time of accomplishment.

Here there is nothing so new or . so different to build into the work.

My bodily health seems to be coming on all right enough, now that there's some prospect of a mental activity which isn't continualy dependent on introspection ,

The Poetry Society meeting last evening was more enjoyable than might have been expected.

I dined with the Wadsworths who asked after you & mother

Ezry

339. ACS

[21 February 1911]

[New York]

Arrived N. Y. OK. Trunk still here

EP.

340. ALS [*letterhead*] On board The Cunard R.M.S. 'Mauretania'

[22 February 1911]

[New York]

Dear Mother.

You perceive that I have gotten thus far. – After 'Carmen' last evening.

The trunk had not gone, but will., at least Welsh is looking after it.

I enclose key.

I think Miss Tracy will send you copies of the photographs.

It is still rather early in the morning

Hope you and father enjoy your tea this afternoon, & the rest of the season.

Love to you both.

Ezra

3

London: 1911–14

341. ALS [*letterhead*] On board The Cunard R.M.S. 'Mauretania'
Saturday [25 February 1911]

[at sea]

Dear Mother:

Trip so far, not too marine. Weather mostly quite bright, & not very cold.

The wind rocks us a bit but the motion is slow & not too disturbing.

Anyhow there's only the rest of today, tomorrow & part of Monday.

Heard 'Carmen' with welsh before embarking.

<u>Sunday</u>.
Thank gord we get in tomorrow. Nothing much more is likely to happen so I guess I'll post this.

Love to you & dad
E. P.

Monday
Past Queens town, & Fishguard only a few hours off & I'm still up and able to <u>write</u> .

<u>London at last.</u>

+>==—=<+

342. ALS
[2 March 1911]

[London]

Dear Mother.

I've had three splendid days here in London, and tho' I very much tired out , I look years younger than when I left New York. My mind feels more like a living entity than like a bottle of cold cream.

I'm off to Paris this A. M. as I am not fit for the eight hour conversation day. Have seen Yeats, Plarr. Hueffer May Sinclair, Lady Low. etc. all of whom are revivifying.

Love to you & dad.

Ezra.

+≈≈+

343. ALS

[3 March 1911]

[Paris]

Arrived Pairs:
life begins to look up

EP

Pound stayed in Paris for three months, at first in a pension at 3 rue de l'Odéon not far from the Jardin du Luxembourg, then with Walter Rummel in his apartment at 92 rue Raynouard, across the river from the Tour Eiffel. He spent a good deal of time with his musician friend, and with Margaret Cravens who had moved to 29 rue du Colisée within walking distance of Rummel's apartment. He finished off his book of translations of the poems of Guido Cavalcanti, began translating the poems of Arnaut Daniel, and worked intensively with Rummel on the relations of words and music in the songs of the troubadours. While he was in Paris Margaret Cravens commissioned separate portraits of Pound and of herself from an American painter, Eugene Paul Ullman.

+≈≈+

344. ALS

[March 1911]

[Paris]

Peace, comfort, rest, at last. I certainly showed unsuual intellegence, even for me in coming to Paris. A beautiful object answering to the name. of Romanelli came & read from Il Paradiso for us yesterday.

I'm very comfortable in a big pension by the Odeon, but shall go out to Walter's place in a week or so. - about as soon as I shall be fit for mental activity.

Hueffer wants me to come to Giesen for a few weeks later in the summer.

London was, as I think I wrote quite delightful but much too active for my present tastes.

I am here quite contented & my health will presumably improve in consequence -

Love to you & dad

.E.

+≡≡≡+

345. ALS

[March 1911]

[Paris]

Dear Dad.

Enclosed evidence that my health is improving.

I've been to more music & seen some more pictures.

And the envelope that mother is so excited about was brought from home as a book mark. -

Why dont you forward my mail?

I suppose my trunk arrived. I have a vague memory that some one wrote me that it had.

Be good to yourselves.

E.P.

+≡≡≡+

346. ACS

[12 March 1911]

[Paris]

Life moves quietly I suppose I'm improving. I go to Walter on Friday to continue there.

no disturbance except Arnold Bennet with whom I dine on Tuesday.

E.P.

+≡≡≡+

347. ACS

[March 1911]

[Paris]

    Encamped with W.M.R: attended enchanting concert some few nights ago. believe my health is still improving, weather beginning to imitate spring more closely.

Yours

E.P.

+≻—≺+

348. ACS

[March 1911]

[Paris]

Dear Dad.
    Yrs. recd. Times. review. etc. genealogy. etc –
    some photos that I did <u>not</u> want forwarded.
    another concert this evening. will send program later.
    Arnaut procedes.
    weather very cold but clear.
    liver quiet-

Love to you & mother

E.P.

W.M.R. sends regards
[*Rummel's hand*] Kindest regards from Walter Morse Rummel

    Provença *was reviewed in the* New York Times Review of Books *of 12 March 1911.*

+≻—≺+

349. ALS

March 26 [1911]

[Paris]

Dear Mother.
    Enclosed notes on my diversions.
    I am to inspect the studio of a brand new painter sometime this week.
    'Arnaut' procedes - I am getting more vigorous
    I dont know that theres much more.

247

I wander about the Bois & the Tuileries - & divert my mind with the french classics.

Love to you & dad.

E P.

⊦═══⊧

350. ALS

[April 1911]

[Paris]

Dear Dad:

Recd – envelope with various letters in it.

Yeats is over here & that affords diversion.

Am dining with Hewlett monday. & am about quite recovered I think walter. has gone to Berlin for a week. –

Am sitting for a portrait & am standing to scrawl this as my appointment for sitting – just due –

Love to you & mother.

EP.

⊦═══⊧

351. ALS

April 17. [1911]

[Paris]

Dear Mother:

Had pleasant day at St. Germain, yesterday, Spring is here completely.

Uhlmann has finished my portrait , its a good bit of paint , & a good likeness, will send you photo. of it later.

Hewlett ought to arrive this evening.

Yeats & Lady Gregory are doing a fairy book & I get chunks of it read over to me.

I have not yet received the proofs of Guido or of the new poems. but I suppose there's no necessity for haste.

Love to you & dad,

Ezra.

⊦═══⊧

352. ALS

[May 1911]

[Paris]

Dear Mother.

Dont be so elegiac about the house matter. . I may throw that Italian Villa & come home in June, if I can get thru' with the Arnaut stuff in the library here

The Cone's , Elizabeth & Grace, turned up yesterday.

The Mapels whom I knew in Spain in '06 discovered me by accident about a week since.

Have had Yeats out to Versailles on a ghost hunt this P. M. & dined with Lady Gregory afterward.

Lady Low is coming over sometime soon. I'm not sure but Paris is the easiest place to see 'London'.

Yes I read something of Kennith Graham's ages since. & I've met Evelyn Sharp.

Love to you & dad
EP.

353. ALS

[May 1911]

[Paris]

Dear Father.

Yrs. recd. - my faculties for composition are mostly directed toward Arnaut Daniel, I admit.

As to impressions: Paris you know. . It is pleasant now but not very warm & I think I'll go south.

Yeats I like very much. I've seen him a good deal, about daily, & he has just. gone back to London . As he was here for quiet, one got a good deal more from him than when, as before, he has been occupied with other affairs. He is as I have said often before, a very great man, & he improves on acquaintance.

Hewlett was very pleasant & has invited me to visit him at Settignano. (outside Florence.). he was very tired, after his channel trip, (when I saw him here.) a little dull, seemingly entangled in the 'county family' conventions, a great deal of his work is bad. but he has his moments.

Bennet is a popular novelist, an ex journalist from a manufacturing Town. , with a sense, of humour - more or less laboured. He does not interest me, but might have interested me more if I had been feeling more vigorous.

Yeats & I went down to Davrays, for tea last wednesday. Davray. is a sort of critic here or here abouts. The place was full of the same. Had a rather good talk with Leguis, one of the professors at the Sorbonne.

The crop of poets at present existing in Paris. seems a rather gutless lot, given over to description. The picture shows are various. The Salon Independent, has some very interesting pictures in it & two masterpieces by Dezire, Castellucho, & Le Doux, also have good things. . & Matisse one canvass is well painted. Freaks there are in abundance. The old salon has two or three good groups. - & the 'Artists Francais' nothing at all.

12 out of the 15 canzoni of A. D. are done after a fashion. so I may have some spare time before September after all.

Love to you & mother.
E P.

+⊨══⊣+

354. ALS

16 May 1911

[Paris]

Dear Mother:

I dont know what I said in my last note or when I wrote it.

I've seen a number of Cezanne pictures in a private galery.

have met Walter's brother who paints & plays the cello. & diverts me more or less

Walter goes to London in June & I guess. I'll go to Italy about then.

I believe my preface is getting on. & that Mathews has at length started operations.

Love to you & Dad
.EP.

May 16th.

*Pound was finishing up the **preface** or introduction to his Sonnets and Ballate of Guido Cavalcanti, with translation and introduction by Ezra Pound, to be published by Small, Maynard in April 1912. Elkin **Mathews** was to publish Canzoni in July 1911.*

+⊨══⊣+

355. ALS

[May 1911]

[Paris]

Dear Dad.

Dont bother too much about the U. o. P. I've got my 'eye' on something better. Shall know in Sept. - or may be before . . If that falls. thru' I shall go to Siena and write a book. I'm off for Italy in a week or ten days.

Hope your father's cataracts are disposed of.

Am correcting . proof of 'Canzoni' for Mathew's so suppose you'll have that to divert you before long.

I dont know where Ames - could have written. I certainly got no word. - you might drop a card to Miss Flynn, 270 Fourth Ave & see if there's any mail there.

Did you ever get my trunk?

Love to you & mother
EP.

---

356. ALS

[end of May 1911]

[Paris]

Dear Mother.

I start for Sirmione tomorrow-

address just .

Sirmione, Lago di Garda,

There's no sense in my coming home in June, now that the university has displayed its so fine discretion. The next job I'm likely to get is on this side. . & as I've had few expenses & several checks. my financial wind is pretty good.

Kennerly is 'delighted' to have another poem for the Forum. . I thought it was bad but now I know it.

I've got another prose book in my head to do after I finish Daniel. and a rather nice trip to take after I leave Sirmione. . Verona, Mantua. Ferrara, Ravenna, Rimini, Bologna, Pistoja, Lucca, Siena.

Bill Williams brother is in Rome. & I may winter there. Hueffer wants me in Giesen for some work but I dont know whether it's worth while.

I go over the Simplon - leaving here about 2 P.M & getting to Garda for lunch the day after. . off the Train at Desenzano about 9.

Physicaly I am in pretty good trim. have had trouble with the water but thats straightened out. you will by no have received the first of Mathews proofs. & I will send the rest soon. Small Maynard. announce that they are about to begin work on the Guido.

I expect to finish Arnaut in Sirmione, by July 1st which is two or 3 months sooner than I at first expected.

I heard 'St Sebastian' the new De Bussy opera. The music is very wonderful, & D'Anunzio's libretto quite the <u>worst</u> thing even he has perpetrated. I'll probably finish this in Italy . as I'm cook in this ranch & the chops are on the grill.

E. P.

'The Fault of It', a poem Pound never published again, appeared in **Forum** *in July.*

+≻—≺+

357. **ALS** [*letterhead*] Hotel Eden, Sirmione am Gardasee

[July 1911]

[Lake Garda]

My Dear Mother 'Out-of-a-Job'

Cheer up. , Give us time & we'll buy a family farm some where on the Veronese side of the lake, . .

The prose book was to have been about philosophy from Richard St.Victor to Pico della Mirandola, or more or less so, but I'm casting about for something more lucrative. – The manufacture of of false teeth or something of that sort.

I see Boris Sidis has written a book with guts, if one may judge from a review.

I may go up to see Hueffer after all, & from him over to London in the autumn.

Bill W^{ms}. Brother has been here for a few days & I expect to see more of him in Verona.

You have the proofs of Canzoni, by now. Small Maynard announce what type they are going to use, so perhaps they'll get to sending proofs fairly soon.

I shall now go forth & souse in the lago.

Salutations to your family. I forget the name of the Barrington house so send this via the mint.

Love to you & dad.
EP.

Boris Sidis (1867–1923) published Philistine and Genius *in 1911.*

+≻—≺+

358. **ALS** [*letterhead*] Hotel Pension Chiave d'Oro Verona

[July 1911]

[Verona]

Dear Mother

I've been Veronizing with Williams. & 'done' Mantua & Goito with him. and poked up the library here. & seen the gallery. I'm going back to Sirmio for a couple of weeks. then I shall look in at the Ambrosiana library in Milan, & go north to act as Hueffers secretary for a few weeks & thence to London = If you dont rent the house I might pull out in March or April of next year.

I'm packing for the afternoon train & have forgotten my descriptive passages - - I always do on some account or another.

I have refitted my wardrobe here to some advantage.

Walter is in London about to publish some of his music to my words. Bliss Carman is reported as about to incorporate some of me into the 'Oxford Book of American Verse.' Have been reading Lorenzo di Medici & Sismondi's 'Italian Republics'.

Love to you & dad.

EP

remember, to aunt Frank etc.

Three Songs of Ezra Pound for a Voice with Instrumental Accompaniment by Walter Morse Rummel *were published as separate items of sheet music by Augener, London, in September 1911. The songs were 'Madrigale' and 'Aria' from* Canzoni, *and 'Au bal masqué'. In January 1913, Rummel's setting of 'The Return' was added to the series. Pound was not in fact incorporated into* **Bliss Carman's** *anthology. His approaches to the publishing firm of* **Macmillan**, *mentioned in the following letters, bore no immediate fruit*

+≻═≺+

359. ALS [*letterhead*] Hotel Eden, Sirmione am Gardasee

[July 1911]

[Lake Garda]

Dear Dad.

Macmillan Co. are the people I want. - We rejoice that the bloomin' mountaing has came to Mo'ammet.

I have just written them at length. Offering four seperate contracts on as many 'opii'. Two done 1 begun & one in state of nebula.

I was going to write you a letter but I've forgotten what about.

Send me T. C. P.'s address I want drop him a card. - just a card – I've got nothing in particular to say.

I'll probably be able - to let you know in September whether or no I'll want to be in Wyncote for the spring & summer. - March to November 1912.

Let me see. I've been to Verona & Mantua with Bill William's brother. I go to Milan next week to see a mss of Arnaut which is supposed to have the music as well as the words of one or two of his canzoni. Thence to Giessen where I shall do a bit of work for Hueffer. Thence to London.

You will by now have recd 'Canzoni' & have seen that I'm beginning to get my stuff properly bound & printed.

I'm working on a book about the Renaissance. and I think in my mild way that it will give me a chance for a little straight hitting. 'Gord be merciful unto Israel in that day.'

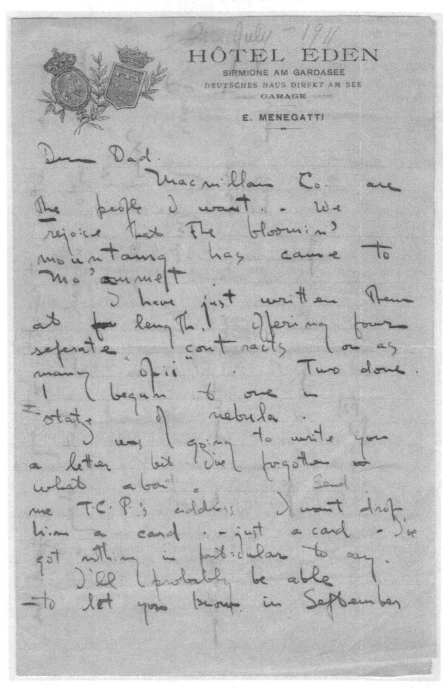

359. ALS, EP to HLP from Lake Garda, [July 1911], *first page*.

Next A.M.

Proofs of Guido pp. 2 - 45 have just come so we turn our attention upon them.

Love to you & mother

Ezry.

Address for August . . until Aug 20.
anything mailed before Aug. 15th

    c / o. F. M. Hueffer

        15 Friedrichs Strasse

            Giessen a / L

                Germany.

After that in care of

    Elkin Mathews

        Vigo St . London. W.

---

360. ALS [*letterhead*] Hotel Eden, Sirmione am Gardasee

Saturday July 22 [1911]

[Lake Garda]

Yaas 'm.

I'm living in 'Eden Hotel' as the paper indicates.

MacMillan as you are probably aware is at my feet. & I've just put thru' another much more delicate bit of diplomacy. The proofs of the Guido have begun to arrive. about 1/3 of the book has been corrected. Hilda is I believe spending the summer some where in Touraine.

What Kelly ? of Clinton. I am aware of the nature of Bennets 'Buried alive'- also of the nature of Bennet

I go to Milan Wednesday to see a <u>mss</u> of Arnaut that's supposed to have some music in it. - Jean Beck the best authority on provençal music, writes me naively that he is going to Illinois 'dont je vien d'etre nomme professeur' - poor devil, 'e dont know what he's in for.

Tell father that the poem he enclosed in your note is <u>very</u> bad technicaly, & just what one would expect from the 'Century' magazine. . It arent wot the fellow . says its the appallin' way 'e sez it.

If he wants to see the same thing properly done let him get 'A Moor Song' by Marion Cran. Walter has set it.- I guess I can get you a copy when I get to London if you dont find one before.

Last night was, by the way, one of the dates in history. The kings letter to Asquith plus what it means . . is a very great event. in so far as it shows the growing weight of opinion it should be a great encouragement to the Independents, Lafollete. etc. - -

Bill's brother has been mucking about Ferrara, Ravenna, etc finding it hot & disagreeable - he may get round here for another bath before I go.

my address for Aug. is

c/o. F. M. Hueffer

    15 Friedrichs Strasse

      Giessen a / L

        Germany.

Anything mailed after Aug.12

c/o. Elkin Mathews

    6^{b} Vigo St

      London. W .

Love to you & dad.

Ezry.

*In his **letter** to the Liberal Prime Minister, Herbert Asquith, the recently crowned King George V had agreed to create by Royal Prerogative as many as 250 new Liberal peers if that were necessary to overcome the opposition of the Conservative majority in the House of Lords to Asquith's Parliament Bill—a bill designed to limit the power of the Lords to delay legislation supported by a majority of the House of Commons. The effect of the bill was to assert the authority of the Commons over the Lords. In the event the Lords allowed the bill to pass into law in August and the Royal Prerogative was not exercised.*

361. ALS [*letterhead*] Hotel Belle Venise, Milan

July 27 [1911]

[Milan]

Dear Mother:

I'm delighted with Milan, contrary to me expectations & remembrance - Perhaps this too expensive hotel has something to do with it. I have had a delightful morning in the Ambrosiana, found a <u>mss</u> of Arnaut with musical notation which accords exactly with my theories of how his music should be written. - which same. is very consoling.

I can't think of much else, The cathedral you remember. The 'Brera' you may or may not I shall go over to it pretty soon & regard its Treasures.

I find by my mornings work that my eyes are vastly improved by my general condition.

Have been doing some new poems of my own as well as studifying & shall probably emit another volumn in the spring of 1912.

The Brera closes at 4. And as it is now 2.30. I guess I'd better be moving along. =

Love to you & dad & regards to the assembled company.

Ezra.

*The **Brera** Gallery is famed for its collection of North Italian painting. From Milan Pound went up to be with Hueffer at Giessen, a small German town north of Frankfurt-am-Main, stopping off on the way in Freiburg-im-Breisgau to show his copy of the Arnaut manuscript to Emil Levy, the great scholar of Provençal literature, as recorded in Canto 20.*

╫══──══╫

362. ALS [*letterhead*] 2^A, Granville Place, Portman Square, W.

[c.22 August 1911]

c/o. Mrs Worthington. London

Dear Mother:

Back here at last. I had very little time to myself while with Hueffer, not that there was much work done, but we disagree diametricaly on art, religion, politics & all therein implied; & besides he's being married this afternoon or else this A.M. & going to the dentists in the P.M, I cant remember which & he was in the state of anticipation - I was dragged about to a number of castles etc. which were interesting & about which I persistently refused to enthuse. – He gets to London in October. & Walters coming over for a week at that time. I shall be here with Mrs. Worthington for a while, any way she'll know where I am so you can send mail to this address.

I have this A. M. purchaced 1 hat. 2 pr. gloves, 1 tooth powdr. 1 soap. ordered some visiting cards. & bought 2 ties.

I came straight up from Giessen yesterday, stopping 2 hrs. in Cologne. & . 4 in Brussles. . = Brussles at 4 a.m. is more charming than I remembered it to be. I found St. Gudule's open & the great square with it's gilt gothic, town hall & the guild house. deserted & clean.

I think I wrote you from Milan. Where I also found the town hall. & a few churches I'd forgotten were quite worth stopping fore. - also a house turned into a museum . the 'Poldi-Pezzoli'.

You might get Hueffer's. 'Ancient Lights' - (I believe the american edtn. is called '<u>Memoirs of a young man</u>' or some such. and 'The Simple Life Limited' by Daniel Chaucer. - was the novel I spoke of.

Also your 'wyvern or dragon' or worm, on the coat of arms is also in the Warwick arms. and Wormleighton is the place where Sir Guy of Warwick killed the beast . & the How's took it for crest. presumably when they recived the baronetcy of Wormleighton, under the earls of Warwick or on union with that family. so you can pretend you're descended from one of the 7 champions of christendom if it'll give you any particular pleasure. -

I'll find out this P.M. who's in town & what's to be done at once. The more people who are away the more work I'm likely to get done. Tho' I'm not wildly anxious to get to the museum.

They're howling for me to come to lunch .
Love to you & dad & saltions to the assembled -

Yrs

Ezra.

*Pound had previously referred to the How **coat of arms** in letter 187.*

┼═══┼

363. ALS

Aug. 29. [1911]

[London]

Dear Mother:

Hueffer & I kept the peace, but it cant be said that either of us got much work done.

I have just come back from a week end with the Fowlers, I am afraid they are going to bore me - or rather - that they dont belong in my new & rearanged cosmos. Saw Fred Manning here last week & he wants me up at Edenham for a while, Lady Low invites me down to Dorset, & Walter comes over for the 1st. week in Oct. -

I ought to know pretty soon what arrangements I shall make for the winter. 'Everybody 's away' but I dont seem to find much enforced solitude.

You will be pleased to know that I have bought a hat, an umbrella, two pairs of gloves, 100 visiting cards & one or two other articles the precice nature of which I can not at this moment recall. . Yeats is coming over to America for a few weeks, his address is vague & in general 'care of the Irish Players' The players are well worth seeing and if you happen to go with father or any presentable member of the family you might send a card to him.

As for Germany, I don't approve of it tho' Giessen is a 'model town'.

I had as I think I wrote, a very pleasant afternoon with the lexicographer Levy (Lehvèè) in Freiburg. , looked at Cöln by starlight & Brussles in the pale dawn, also Hueffer dragged me about to Neuheim, which is a springs & baths hell, and to several castles in the vain hope of broadening my mind.

He & I are in Punch together, I'll scratch up a copy somewhere send it along.

Otherwise things are hung up & waiting for those Borstonese to get the Guido out of the shop.

Love to you & dad. & salutations to the rest,

yours lovingly

E. P.

c/o. Mrs. Worthington
2ª Granville Place. London. W.

*The paragraph in **Punch** of 16 August 1911 began: 'A new poet is about to swim into our ken in the person of Boaz Bobb, a son of the Arkansas soil, who has long been resident in London studying Icelandic literature for the purposes of a new saga of the Wild West. . . . '.*

+=====+

364. ALS
Monday. Sept 11th [1911]

Worth Mautravers. | Dorset

Dear Mother:

I can't remember when I wrote what to whom. I am down here for a few days with Lady Low, in sight of the channel. – a little west of Southampton. in a wild 'unEnglish' sort of country. not far from Pound, Poundsbury, & Blandford. – almost in sight of Corfe Castle. & some prehistoric barrows. Theres a charming Elizabethan manor about a mile off which rents for £35 per annum – which is encouraging.

Clinton Scollard called before I left London & I lunch with him on Wednesday. He seemed in the proper frame of mind & brought some small talk from Hamilton. – I took him to see Plarr & found that dignified official at the college of surgeons with his family, in the general confusion of summer repairs, experimenting with vacuum cleaners. Mrs. Worthington is at the chior festival at Worcester.

Ez
This has got to go now for the post
Love to you & Dad –
E P.

*Pound may have been thinking that the **Elizabethan manor** would be a suitable place for him to set up house with Dorothy when they married. Her reaction to his description of it was sceptical: 'I should greatly mistrust that £35 house! It probably has no drains (or few, which is worse) & no water supply—but sounds nice with its gate-posts. Or else its horribly haunted.'*

+=====+

365. ALS
15 September 1911

[London]

Reverend Parent:

I shall be stopping on here or here abouts until spring. I shall want my over coat. I suggest that you place same in <u>my</u> trunk. (black canvass object.) with my grey wooly dressing gown. my extra p^{rs} pyjamas & shirts. & my musical instrument & consign same to me at my present address. - Said musical instrument being I believe in cr. of the Baxters. 234 W. 104th St . N. Y. mother can stop for it on her 'way thru' said city.

Clinton Scollard has been here. & we have had two very pleasant mornings together.

I wrote you or mother that I had been staying in Dorset.

dined at Chorley Wood with Mathews . yesterday. Sunday I'm to inspect G. R. S. Mead. editor of the Quest.

I enclose the first notice of C. - the announcements. I've already sent you the Athanaeum. The Times. had a short notice sometime ago. I haven't collected the notices. but . they'll be quoted on the 'adv' slip . before long.

Rhys. has returned to town & things in general should begin to liven up in a week or two. I've seen Plarr, & Binyon. etc.

A number of favorable signs in the wind but nothing very definite to report.

Love to you and mother.

Ezry.

Fri. Sep. 15

⊶⊷

366. ALS

17 September 1911

[London]

Dear Mother.

I make you out a little before your aunt and a bit above 'grindle'. This in the photo sent.

I have already written to H. L. P. concerning the forwarding of my over coat.

if you haven't already left Barrington. I want you to collect my musical instrument from the Baxters. (234 W. 104th St N.Y.)

That is if I left it there.

Also I want him i.e. H. L. P. to put into the trunk the following books. Provencalishe Chrestomathie.= half of it is <u>torn out</u>. Large flat blue.

Anglo Saxon 'Grammar' or 'Reader redish brown.

Chaucer . — green. fat.

I wrote to dad yesterday or friday so there's not much new. I have spent the P.M with G. R. S. Mead. Edtr. of the 'Quest' who wants me to throw a lecture 'Troubadour Psycology' whatever the dooce that is . for his society which he can afterwards print.

Clinton Scollard has been here. & seems to think Hamilton needs my services. However he is <u>not</u> the board of trustees. & upper N. Y. has a rotten climate. or rather one that is only kept from that state by constant refrigeration.

260

Yesterday.

I raked out a couple of pictures in the Wallace gallery which I had forgotten. I dont know that there's much else - nor is there likely to be before Oct.

Love to you & dad,

Ezry

Sunday. Sept. 17th

*Pound lectured to the Quest Society early in 1912. His **lecture** was printed in* The Quest *in October 1912; and included in a new edition of* The Spirit of Romance *in 1932 as chapter V, 'Psychology and Troubadours'.*

+⊨══╪+

367. ALS

[28–30 September 1911]

[London]

Reverend Parent.

The portrait is by Ullman. - is now in Paris. - will probably be used to replace Miss Gioconda in the Louvre.

The note in Punch refers to Boaz Bobb.

Blandula. Tenula, Vagula. from Emperor Hadrians address to his soul. See Walter Pater's. 'Marius'

gentle, tender, wandering. only the 'ula' is a diminutive - which makes the adjectives all more or whimsical, . or ironical.

Und Drang. - full phrase 'Sturm und Drang' Storm & Stress.

Sept. 29

Went down into the country this P.M. and met the Bahi. = charming old man. - simple. - a little prolix but as he speaks only persian one cant tell how much one looses thru the interpreter. From what I gather there are 3,000,000 or more followers of this light in Persia. & it seems in all ways commendable.

I dont know that there's much news . have refound Hulm who does criticism of current philosophy. - and one or two other people begin to return to town A few more proofs to correct. The girl whom Hilda brought out to Swarthmore has done some verse which I've got put into the Forum for her. (to appear. Nov.).

I thought it very good. but dont know whether it was done by accident or whether she will go on . She seems to have absolutly no critical sense. No ability to know what part of what she does is good & what part nonsense.

I believe they and Walter descend upon us in a week or so.

Next morning.

There seems to be no further rush of ideas to my head. It was Punch for Aug. 16. - Literary Notes,

and I'm informed that I'm in this weeks number also.

Love to you & mother.

Ezry

*'**Blandula, tenulla, vagula**' is a short poem, and '**Und Drang**' a sequence of twelve poems, in* Canzoni. *The '**Bahi**' was the son of the founder of the Baha'i religion—the meeting is recalled in Canto 46. **The girl** Hilda Doolittle brought out to Swarthmore was Frances Gregg.*

+≻━⊶━≺+

368. ALS

Oct. 6 [1911]

[London]

Yes. I sent you that Athanaeum.

Walter is over here & we're taking a place together up till Xmas. probably - if not for longer.

Hilda & Mrs Greeg. & Frances are here. I don't know for how long. Four of F's poems will come out in the Nov. Forum.

There've been a number of tea-fights etc.

Mr. & Mr H. L. Pound are invited to my own especial tea fight on Friday the 13th Oct.

Mrs. Worthington has turned over the apartment to me. & it will be a very distinguished function.

Walter sends his regards to you & mother. & I give him this now as he is going out to post

Love

.E.

+≻━⊶━≺+

369. ALS

[October 1911]

[London]

Dear Dad,

Walter & I have taken on part of an infinitessimal house
address .

39 Addison Road <u>North</u>. London. <u>W</u>.

If the trunk has gone to Xprs. office . I can get it. O.K. if not send it to that address.

I guess I can get round the corner all right. Tho' I've enough on my mind to keep me fairly occupied.

If you haven't sent the trunk yet leave that empty picture frame in it.

That's all I can think of that I might want, beside the books I've mentioned

send all mail from now on to Ad. Rd. North. . note that its the road north. & its London <u>W</u>est. i.e. (W.).

I'm having a jamboree on Friday as I think I wrote.

E. P.

Love to you & mother

⊹⊱⊰⊹

370. ALS

[12 October 1911]

[London]

Reverend Parent:

If one Shakespear, H. H, should write unto thee see that thou answer him even after this wise, altering no jot nor tittle upon pain of my wrath.

H. H. Shakespear Esq.

Dear Mr. Shakespear:

Naturaly my son has not mentioned this matter to me, but if he wants anything he is very likely to get it. Any items he may have given you about his finances are presumably correct. He is no longer in bonds of necessity. My home is at his disposal . and I only wish he would make more use of it than he does.

He seemed rather preocupied when he was last with us but it might have been Guido Cavalcanti.

If there is anything else I can do for you in the matter please let me know

Believe me, yours very sincerly

Homer L. Pound.

(date . etc.).

Dearest Dad.

I think that will be about all. I realize I am a remarkable child but don't go to spreading the eagle. =

You might add in a <u>P.S.</u>

P.S. His work is rather remarkable

263

You can change the phrasing if you think its too much mine.

I get $1000. a year apart from what I make at royalties, poems sold to magazines, lectures, etc.

if another deal goes thru' theres $750 <u>more</u> per anum in it. and I've got a few other things in the offing that I am too busy to bother about.

If he asks any specific questions you can send him that information.

yrs in filial devotion
Ezry.

dont try to embroider on any of this

guess thats all.

+===+

371. ALS

Friday Oct 13 [1911]

[London]

Dear Dad:

Never mind the letter I wrote you last night . don't wait for Mr. Shakespear to write but send him at once the following. (on as imposing stationary as you like.).

H. H. Shakespear
  8 John St. Bedford Row
  London W. C.

Dear Mr Shakespear:

My son receives $1000 a year apart from what he gets directly from sale & royalties of his books.

Very sincerely yours
H. L. Pound.

= The statement.happens to be true, but you need not comment upon it to him. I have received orders to do my <u>own</u> work & not to worry about the immediate returns. But that is no body's business except my own. and the less said about it the better.

I am, as you may have surmized from my epistle of yesterday, attempting to marry the gentleman's daughter. I shall do so in any case but dont want to disturb the sepulchral calm of that english household more than need be.

She'll have about the same ammount of her own so we shall do very nicely. Especialy if this other affair comes off.

You may remember what a poor photograph of the lady looks like. I shall not indulge in further comment – apart from the evidence of my published works - which are very inadequate.

yrs. in filial piety.

Ezry.

P.S. I suppose in case of dire necessity you might go on my bond for such an amt.

Of course I shan't ask you too if I can help it.

I dont expect to require any such measures.

Pound and Dorothy Shakespear had been told by Olivia Shakespear at Sirmione in May 1910 that their marrying was out of the question so long as Ezra lacked a secure and sufficient income. In effect he had been ordered to keep his distance from Dorothy and not to communicate with her, and this he had done for over a year. In August of 1911, after they had begun writing to each other again, he had declared to her mother his firm intention of marrying Dorothy, and had been told again that it wouldn't do given his limited and uncertain earnings. In October Dorothy had sent a note to Pound to the effect that if they were to continue seeing each other he should speak to her father, Henry Hope Shakespear. Pound called the same day on Mr Shakespear at his office, but the solicitor was not persuaded that he had 'the means of supporting a Wife'. For the time being Dorothy and Ezra had to settle for taking tea together twice a week with Olivia Shakespear as chaperone.

+≻══≺+

372. ALS

[21 October 1911]

[London]

Dear Mother:

There are a number of things I might write if I were in the humour. I think I wrote that I've taken a place with Walter.

39 Addison Road North. London. W.

He will be here till Xmas. Yeats has not yet returned. Hilda is here with the Greggs. & I saw the Snivelys for a few minutes some time or other. My own time & energies are fairly well occupied elsewhere. Likewise there are a fairish number. of meals to be eaten hither & yon. Mrs. Hueffer. (as was. V. H.) ought to have returned yesterday so there's one more pleasant room open again etc. etc.

As nearly as I can make out I've done nothing useful for some weeks except correct a few proofs. & translate an old french song for W. R. - very dull song at that, only he wants to print it in both languages. I gave a quite large tea party last week and as nearly as I can make out I was about the only person whom it bored immeasurably.

I've met & enjoyed Mead. . who's done so much research on primitive mysticism - that I've written you at least four times - let me cease this addled communication.

EP.

Love to you & dad.

+⊱━⋅◆⋅━⊰+

373. ALS

[c.31 October 1911]

[London]

Dear Mother.

Thanks for overcoat (money order.). yr' last can not be regarded as encouraging, (also you should put street no. on yr. letters if you expect 'em to arrive.

If things are in the state you say . you'd better stop bothering about my overcoats.

I have survived another anniversary.

The trunk has arrived safely.

I will write some time or other.

Yours
E. P.

Love to you & father.

+⊱━⋅◆⋅━⊰+

374. ALS

[early November 1911]

[London]

Dear Dad:

I enclose the 'Punch' for Aug 16th.

Mothers letter without a street number, was more or less ambiguous however . I procede under full steam. And London is, as usual, more hospitable than the land of freedom.

Hueffer is over for few weeks. & the last few days have moved quite pleasantly.

There'll be a pome in the Smart Set sometime or other. (I'll let you know when) & I've translated some songs for Walters musical publisher.

Love to you & mother.

E.P.

Pound's first appearance in **Smart Set** *was 'Silet', (the opening poem in* Ripostes), *in May 1912. Walter Rummel's* **music publisher** *was Augener, London; and the* **songs** *were probably the ten in* Selection from Collection Yvette Guilbert / English Translations by Ezra Pound, *published by Augener in April 1912.*

━━━━

375. ALS

[before 6 November 1911]

[London]

Dear Dad:

Thanks for your letter.

The 'startling statement' wouldn't have been unexpected as he had asked me to write to you & I had told him I had done so.

Having known me almost since my arrival here. he wanted some sort of credentials, & some sort of assurance that my improved circumstances weren't purely hypothetical or temporary.

As the source is anonymous, & the donation voluntary I cant very well ask for a sealed document - nor explain it fully to H H S - & so asked you to back up the statement.

Try to take into account the English mind. - the respect for parental authority etc. which is supposed to prevail in these Islands - - & write if you haven't done so. that I act with your sanction & that my statement of my income as (1000) besides what I make is correct.

Guess we'll wait until July. anyhow:

I've got to move to 10 Church Walk. - & go to a luncheon during the next 75 minutes. so pardon brevity.

.E.

address 10 Church Walk
  Kensington W
(just off High St. Kens & in St Mary Abbots church yard.
[*sketch map*]

━━━━

376. ALS

[mid-November 1911]

[London]

Dear Dad:

There seems to be some liklihood that I shall be holding forth weekly in the 'New Age' (38 Cursitor St. - E. C.) on poetry etc. I wish you'd hunt out those prose articles I did last winter. - they're in the top of the little trunk - I may be able to to use parts of 'em. I am supposed to have a fairly free hand - rope to hang myself or something of that sort.

You may as well spread the news. - subscription to said sheet 8/8. . i.e. $2.15 per 6 months. Views 'advanced' & usualy unsound.

Any way they're going to print translations from Saxon, Tuscan & Provencal which is very enlightened of 'em. & will give me some sort of start in periodical work. . I suppose I'll be in next week or the week after so you'd better start your subscription with the 'Nov. 23' number.

Love to you & mother.

clippings & a letter from mother recd.

E. P.

---

377. ALS

[before 25 November 1911]

[London]

Reverend Parent:

I think you may set to rest the mind of madame.

Incidentaly I send on my salaams. & respects for the anniversary - I intended to do so last week.

I seem to be on the verge of a new publisher who has promised me much more advantageous terms. - tho' its not yet in writing -.

I am to write weekly for the New Age. - first instalment has been enthusiasticaly recd. .

The Daily News liked my sample review.

I'm applying for some lectures at Cambridge, tho' I dont much want 'em & the chances are uncertain.

But in any case I seem likely to earn my salt. & much more likely to earn it here than in the U. S.

It dont much look as if I should return to U. S. A. in the spring. Thanks for the offer of the house but dont hold on to it on my account.

Remind our mother that we have padded for several months & that we paid our hospital expenses last spring. & that we recently dropped $60. on a dentist without groaning.

If I did come home I think four of us would fit into the Wyncote place quite comfortably. But if things continue here with the wind in the present direction it may be just as enjoyable for you to look in on us here or hereabouts. I haven't a spare photograph of Dorothy, & she's off to the country for several days & may not have any when she gets back so you'll have to possess yr. soul in patience. Besides you saw a photo' of her once & approved of it.

I appreciate the 'house' & your offer of it very much but things always seem to get on faster on this side. I'm to have a shot at dramatic criticism in the New Age, whenever I like. & the editor promised to pass me on to other papers that can pay higher rates. At present he is taking just what I have in stock, mediaeval poetry. etc.

Had lunch with Manning yesterday, & dined at Hewlett's.

Etc. I ought to get on to an article now.

Love to you & mother - & don't be down 'earted .

Yr. beamish boy.

Ezry.

The **New Age** *was edited by Alfred Orage, who would pay Pound a guinea (£1 1s) for each weekly contribution. The first of a series of twelve articles under the heading 'I Gather the Limbs of Osiris' appeared in the issue for 30 November, and the last in the issue for 22 February 1912. An editorial note stated: 'Under this heading Mr. Pound will contribute expositions and translations in illustration of "The New Method" in scholarship".' The 'translations and expositions' were of the Anglo-Saxon 'Seafarer', and poems by Cavalcanti and Arnaut Daniel. Orage introduced Pound to the* New Age's *'new publisher', Charles Granville of Stephen Swift and Company, and Granville was about to offer Pound £100 a year for ten years in return for publishing all his new books.*

Pound's review (unsigned) of The Dialogues of Saint Gregory *appeared in the* **Daily News** *on 11 November. He was not appointed to lecture in* **Cambridge**. *The two* **poems** *mentioned in the next letter were 'Echos. I [&] II', printed in the January* North American Review, *and reprinted (with variants) in* Ripostes.

+≡≡+

378. ALS

[early December 1911]

10 Church Walk. W [London]

Dear Mother:

There'll probably be two poems of mine in the North American Review some time or other.

My course in peptomized culture is started in the 'New Age' & will doubtless irritate numerous worthy people.

Dorothy is lunching with me tomorrow. I dine with Lady Low on Wednesday - 'Authors Society' dinner on Friday.

Got $60. for the translations of the Yvette songs.

Walter goes back to Paris Thursday, but will be here again in the Spring. Hueffer back after sending $20,000 marconigram to 'Colliers' anent the new cardinal. Yeats off to Dublin.

If my new arrangement with Swift & Co. goes thru' it will mean another $500 per. year.

I find Mead rather interesting. & Hulme is giving rather good lectures on Bergson. - you'll find his stuff in the New Age – also.

Ask father to send me <u>govt</u>. reports on Immigration.

Love to you & him.

E

+⊨━━⊨+

379. ALS

[9? December 1911]

[London]

Dearest Mother:

I can't remember what's happened since I last wrote. My new publisher seems to be going to guarantee my continued existence.

Saw Hewlett last night & I'm having tea with him Wed. before Newbolt's lecture. Please get dad some Xmas ties & gloves with the enclosed. – you can't get a decent tie much under $1.^{50}. . & get 'em big enough

Mac Donald & Campbell, Broad & Chestnut are rather good.

Am just back from a very dull dinner of the 'Authors Society'. – art & 'litterchure' have little in common.

oh well. be good. & merry Xmas to you. .

. E .

+⊨━━⊨+

380. ALS

(9 December 1911)

[London]

Dear Dad,

Merry Xmas. please get mother some gloves, & a bunch of self respecting roses & what ever else she wants that the enclosed will cover.

E.

+⊨━━⊨+

381. ALS

14 December 1911

[London]

Reverend Parent:

As for H. H. S. I don't think you need bother to answer. £150 per. annum of the mentioned next 200£ are already in sight. and I caught $95. exclusive of this last month. Also I'm offered the use of a cottage on Lago Maggiore when I want it.

The status quo. is very pleasant and I see no reason to disturb it with argument.

I enclose a note from Rennert which explains itself.

It is now high time for me to go out to dinner.

I don't want to send New Ages I want it subscribed for, 38 Cursitor St. Chancery Lane. E. C. beginning Nov. 30.

There's a Poetry Review starting in Jan. – also. wherein I may corruscate.

Love to you & mother.

E. P.

*'H.H.S.', Mr. Shakespear, had written to Homer Pound that until Pound had a secured regular income 'in addition to a permanently secured £200 a year'—i.e. the money given to him anonymously by Margaret Cravens—he was obviously not in a position to marry. Dr Hugo **Rennert's** note, dated 8 December 1911, said that he had gladly written a letter of recommendation to Cambridge University on Pound's behalf.*

┼══╾═╼┼

382. ALS [*letterhead*] Old Rectory, Broad Chalke, Salisbury

Dec 24 [1911]

[Salisbury]

Dear Mother:

I'm down here with Hewlett, in whats left of a nunnery built in 1487. with a mill race and river at the foot of the garden. He at least has found his proper mediaeval setting. I believe we motor over to see Henry Newbolt, sometime or other, and get back to London by the same means a day or so later. The air invigorates and the bath is commodious, and the heat 'steam' and the air spring-like without.

I've revized one essay and written most of another - the finishing most.

Hewletts trilogy 'The Agonists' is certainly very fine in parts, and I think people may have to take him seriously as 'poet' as well as, as 'novelist' - not that they do take him very seriously as novelist - but I mean the poetry is as good as such as the 'little novels of Italy are, as prose.'.

I'm due to visit Manning, the other end of this week.

Hilda is to spend Tuesday with May Sinclair and she seems to get on very well with a number of people.

She resides, for some arcane and inexplicable reason, on the edge of Hampstead, back of beyond and not far from the Rhyses. Katharine has also sent her introductions to some of the sort of people one might expect. - but not quite as bad as one might expect. Discrimination is the thief of time.

The theory of my present visit here is that M. H. & I have each our table and inkpot and that we converse at meals and after dinner -

we 've wandered about a bit. and there's a post going in an hour or so so I close.

Love to you & dad.

E. P.

+≕≕+

383. ALS

<u>1912</u> HAPPY NEW YEAR.

[London]

Dear Dad.

If ever, or whenever S. M get the Guido printed they'll send most of the copies to you. & I want you to forward them as follows.
Mrs. Worthington
  'The Wyoming.
    55th St & Seventh Ave.
    New York.
Miss Gwendolen Baxter
  234 W 104th St. N. Y.
Miss Frances Gregg.
  5324 Greenway Ave.
    Philadelphia.
I think there are two other people whom I want them sent to but cant remember at the moment. - any how dont chew 'em all up. but keep 'em.

Mother's letter arrived about New Years. - I've ordered her 'New Age'

I shall be very busy for the next three months, and if I don't scribble down things the moment I think of 'em theyre gone.

I cant remember what else I had to say. Thanks to mother for her remembrance.

Love

. E .

P.S S & M's yearly catalogue. may amuse you.- I suppose they've sent it to you. if not you can get it & look up your family history.

+≕≕+

384. ALS

28 / 1 / 12

[London]

Dear Mother:

I suffer from a sort of aphasia of the pen, that is, the things I want to remember in order, are things for my lectures or for articles.

Yes this Mrs. Ullman is Eugene's wife.

Yeats lectured at the Shakspear's Thursday & one met divers people. The Ranee of Sarawak (Lady Brooke) amongst 'em.

I've been to the Colvins. (Sir. Sidney of the Stevenson Letters.) with Lady Low & to the Prothero's. (Quarterly Review.) under the same aegis.

And I've looked after Hilda to the extent of my abilities.

I'm taking Monro - (Poetry . Rev) to Yeats on Monday.

etc. etc.

New man at Princeton seems to have a glimmer of intellegence. - O. Bolger always was an ass.

etc.

Love to you & Dad.
.E P.

+≻≺+

385. ALS

21 February 1912

[London]

Dear Mother:

As to the questions in yr. last two letters .

I don't know.

    ditto.

    ditto.

Agitation vs 'Playboy' is political.

I am unlikely to call on Mrs. Woods until I meet her or am asked specialy.

? who the — is Mrs. Woods?

I'll send you prospectus of my lectures in a few days. I give them in Lord Glenconner's private gallery. I've already sent you adv. of 'The Quest'.

Met W. H. Hudson the other day at F. M. H.'s & was 'clean bowled.' : 'A Shepherds Life' is the only one of his books I've tried. He's between Borrow & DeFoe. & more readable.

Henry James & I glared at each other across the same carpet, about 2 weeks previous.

G. R. S. Mead is about as interesting - along his own line - as any one I meet.

I don't know anything about any one on the 'New Age' except T. E. H. (Hulme) who is a braw yorkshirman & very good sort.

Old Grinnel is back from Russia, & very enthusiastic, & disenclined to agree with Tolstoi & the general squalor & pessimism of the advertised russian litterati - He says its a going concern.

Frank Harris, is supposed to be a clever, but verminous object. I have not met him, & sha'n't, if I can help it

He is chiefly celebrated for Wilde's epigram.

Mr Harris. 'I have, by God, dined in every <u>good</u> house in London.'

O W. 'Yes, Frank, <u>once</u>.'

Personaly I believe him to be so vulgar that no one except H. G. Wells can ever give a successful immitation of him.

I'm going on to a lecture by Henry Newbolt, in a few minutes. He's done one good ballad a certain ammount of very mediocre work, & is personaly, very delightful. The good ballad is 'Drakes Drum' which you might get from the library.

Woodward's work on 'Coroners' is very diverting.

Flint, in return for being ressurrected has put me on to some very good contempory French stuff , - Remy de Gourmont , de Regnier, etc.

Manning & W R will both be here in March. I dine with Rhys tomorrow.

Love to you & dad.

.E. P

21 / 2 / 12

Synge's **The Playboy of the Western World** *was being performed in America by Yeats's Dublin Abbey Theatre Company, and a campaign protesting against it as an unpatriotic image of Ireland was being waged in the Irish-American press. The performance in Philadelphia on 18 January 1912, so outraged the local Irish patriots that the District Attorney had the police arrest the players for sacrilegious and immoral behaviour.*

Pound's three **lectures**, *'by the kind permission of Lord and Lady Glenconner', were on 'Mediaeval Poetry' and were to be delivered at 3.30 in the afternoons of 14th, 19th, and 21st March, to an audience limited to 50, tickets to be applied for to Lady Low. (Tickets 10/ 6, or £1 for the course of three lectures.) The topics were 'Tuscany, A.D. 1200: Guido Cavalcanti' (with Frederic Manning in the chair), 'Provence, A.D. 1190: Arnaut Daniel', and 'England, A.D. 790: Anglo-Saxon Verse' (with W. B. Yeats in the chair). Graham Cox* **Woodward** *had just published in Philadelphia* The Office and Duties of Coroners in Pennsylvania *(1912).*

✦

386. ALS

14 / 3 / 12

[London]

Dear Dad:

Walter's recital was great success.

Today I lunched at the Dilke's, party of four including Henry James who is quite delightful.

Have just got my first lecture off my chest & am ready to rest.

Have cleaned up $90 so far.

Have been very busy with one thing & another & can't stop at this moment to remember just what.

With love to you & mother

. E .

+>==+=={+

387. ALS

[March 1912]

10 Church Walk W [London]

Dear Mother:

I have delivered the <u>mss</u> of 'Ripostes' & have had pleasant tea with my publisher. & have met Henry James again & like him still more on further acquaintance. I suppose you'll find London in his books, now that he is in town he seems to follow a course not wholly sepearat from the strata. wherein I revolve.

Swift & Co. have taken over the 'Oxford & Cambridge' review so I suppose I'll have again some dignified locus wherein to appear. The English Review will print a poem in the June number, but I don't much care for their present management.

I heard the debate in the 'House' last Tuesday. - don't know whether or not I wrote.

Lady Glenconner is giving an evening at home on Saturday - which will I suppose open a new department of the menagerie. for our inspection.

Mead's lecture on 'Heirotheos' was very good. Tho' I personaly don't see why we shouldn't enjoy paradise when we get there instead of ratling the whole thing up & starting over again, however these be . hyper-coelestial heresies & Heirotheos is certainly more virile than the Pseudo-Dionysus.

before embarking on these affairs, I advise you to fortify your mind with the simplicities of Aristotle & Aquinas.

Saturday,
I may as well end this or it'll get lost in my papers.
Love to you & dad
E. P.

Ripostes *was to be published by Stephen Swift in October.*

<hr>

388. ALS

[after March 1912]

10 Church Walk W. [London]

Dear Dad:

Thanks for attending to the Barnard Club. & the blank checques. . Get mother some flowers with the $2 enc. over the .V .

My lectures are over & have done me very well. The 'mss' of 'Ripostes' has gone to publishers so thats off my chest. The coal strike will delay the 'Guido' still further.

I shall go South in <u>May</u> to avoid doing another scholarly work.

etc.

I must reread the 'De Vulgari Eloquentia' & get my 'Arnaut' ready for delivery.

Love to you & mother
E. P.

<hr>

389. ALS

[April 1912]

[London]

Dear Mother:

I dont know that there's any thing historical to report.

I have, thank heaven, seen the last of the Guido proofs.

Have been translating words of songs for Augners. the last lot from Yvette's collection & she says she may sing 'em in English herself.

I'm to go down into Sussex to visit an editor on Thursday. Yeats is back & burried in the wilds to finish a play. - whither I am to penetrate sometime or other. The place is alive again - I'm going to one of Meads lectures this p.m.

Violet (Hunt) Hueffers last book is very fine in parts. 'The Coach' about as good as Stevenson. - 'Tales of the Uneasy' is the name of the collection. and as its full of horrors you'd better leave it alone or else read it selectedly.

have you read F M H's 'Memoirs of a Young Man'. yet?
I go on to see the 'Russian Ballet' this evening
Love to you & dad.
E. P

*The '**Guido proofs**' were probably for the Stephen Swift edition of* The Sonnets and
Ballate of Guido Cavalcanti, *published in May 1912, the long awaited Small, Maynard
edition having come out in April.*

—————

390. ALS
[c.20 April 1912]

10 Church Walk .W. [London]

Dear Mother:
There seems to be a certain amount of whirl with nothing in particular to be
said about it.

Hulme goes down to Cambridge to qualify for a long neglected degree, &
I'm to visit him next Sunday & give a short informal discourse to a carefully
segregated audience. Mr Yeats' attic has a new carpet and new hangings, covers
etc, which act as a better background to his velvet smoking jacket.

Epstein has sculpted a very fine sun-god & done several other things
worthy of note. The sun-god might have been exkavited from Babylon & not
questioned as to authenticity. I'm not sure that the little jew hasn't more real
power than Rodin, tho' its bad to make comparisons & one never knows about
another art, what is remarkable & what only looks so.

Dorothy & her mother & I are going to see Pavlova dance, this evening, I've
been reading Anatole France & divers other works to get my french into
commission.

I suppose Mrs. Wilkinson (neè Gregg) will decend upon us for a day or so
next week

Mary Moore & Margaret Cravens seem to be enjoying each other's society
in Paris. M. M. also here for a week begining Saturday at some ungodly hour
A.M.

Please address all mail from now on c/o. W. M. Rummel. 92 rue Raynouard
Paris.

The D. Telegraph. devoted about a colum to W. R. last week. - mingling
intellegence with folly.

Let me desist. here comes my shaving water.
Love to you & dad.
. E .

Pound's 'informal discourse' was a paper read to an undergraduate literary society at King's College, Cambridge on 27 April.

＋━＝━＝━＋

391. ACS

April 30 [1912]

[London]

Off to Paris tomorrow, sorry you've been worried about mail. Health excellent. Hope mother is enlivened again. Will write at leisure in a day or so.

E .

＋━＝━＝━＋

392. ACS

[2 May 1912]

Paris

Arrived
<u>O.K.</u>
Air light, and sun going strong.
Country south of Boulogne, very beautiful. W.R. entangled in bussiness, but apparently healthy. I shall be here for 3 weeks inspecting the state of Art.

Yrs
. E .

＋━＝━＝━＋

393. ALS

[May 1912]

[Paris]

Dear Mother:

May is, as has been indicated. the time for Paris.

another week or so & I'm off to Poictiers & Angouleme. . Hewlett seems wearied by travel & will probably go direct to England from Greece. His 'Lai of Gaubertz' appears in this month's 'Fortnightly Review' - matter of which I sent him last year as you may remember.

Two poems of mine will be in the English Review for June.

I'm making a few small translations from Provençal for some tunes which Walter is resurrecting. The salon is even worse than might be expected.

Went to Davray's (Edtr. Mercure de France) on Wednesday, & the next person to come in was George Moore, He burbles in french rather better than in English.

As to certain questions in your letter. No. I dont believe you can gather my state of mind from my published works, Smart Set or otherwise. seeing they appear six or eight months after they are written. The relation of ones self to ones expression is various.

Theres one poem to appear in Ripostes which I have in vain tried to remember the cause of. I know about when I wrote it but I can't for the life of me tell what set it off.

For the present I have joined the Touring Club de France for the purpose of facilitating my passage thru' the Midi

I go back to London in October presumably .

Love to you & dad.
E. P.

Walter sends salutations.

╪══╪

394. ALS

[May 1912]

[Paris]

Dear Dad:

I enclose proofs of poems to appear in 'English Rev' for June.

I go south next week presumably via Poicters - Angouleme, Chalais.

but you'd better send mail c/o. Walter as I can't keep you posted in advance of where I'll be.

I suppose you've the 'Guido' by now as I hear a package of books has arrived from S.& M. in England.

Am reading Michalet 'Le Peuple' I think you might enjoy it. I presume it's translated - no not exactly new nor for current event club, still you might enjoy it, or his history which I have not yet attempted.

I've turned up several ancient tomes on the quais that I may be able to use in my work but haven't found much contemporary art that seems very valuable. – bar the regular line. Anatole France etc.

Love to you & mother:
E. P.

Salutations to Joe, & Virginia etc.

'The Return' and 'Apparuit' were published in the June **English Review**. *Pound was about to set out on a walking tour through parts of southern France associated with the Troubadours, with the intention of writing for Swift & Co. a book which would be at*

once about his travels and about the lives of the troubadours. He started on 26 May, and was in Limoges around 7 or 8 June. There he received a note from Rummel telling him that Margaret Cravens was dead, having shot herself cleanly through the heart, and he returned to Paris immediately. He resumed his walking tour around 27 June, concluding it three weeks later on 19 July. He then spent a week or so in Paris and returned to London about the end of the month.

395. ALS

[c.10 June 1912]

[Paris]

Dear Dad:

Those fools in Boston sent all my copies of 'Guido' to London after having assured me they would send 'em to you. Thank god I'm done with 'em, Small Maynard, I mean.

I'll write Dorothy to get the package & send you your copy.

I am back in Paris again, after finishing the first lap of my trip. - Aquitaine. that is, and I've got a fair sheaf of notes to show for it. I shall go back for the rest if I find I need or want it.

I have however covered the ground of the chief troubadours. The travel costs a bit more than it should.

You might send me copies of the various pages of 'adv' which you & mother have mentioned. - The gradual dawn of enlightenment in your far continent should be watched with intrest by the older civilizations.

Give my regards to Whiteside and any of the elect.

Hilda & a young chap named Aldington are both here in Paris. and Walter thinks he's going to marry a female musician here - Mary Moore was in London for a week before I left, & was to have come on here to add to the general festivity but she is sailing from Holland instead .

Good luck to you. Love to you & mother.

. E .

396. ALS

[c.21 June 1912]

92 r. Raynouard. [Paris]

Dear Mother:

W. R. is in London so I've this place to myself and am getting the first quarter of my book in order. I start rambling again this week I suppose - You'll get the detail when it's printed.

I've corrected the proof of 'Ripostes' so that will be with you in a month or so. I suppose you have, by now, & at last received the 'Guido'.

W. R. is going to marry a very charming pianist as soon as he can get enough birth certificates pass-ports, affidavits etc. to prove who he is and whether he is English, German or American. etc - as the french law seems very particular about marriage when the ceremony is indulged in.

Hilda's last Englishman is also very charming. Mary Moore has gone home via Holland. As for the Englishman, he has crossed the channel . and taken to drawing and velvet jacket, and they seem to share a talent for leisure. But they are probably too much alike for a 'life-interest'.

I believe she is to be with her family in Rome, this winter.

This first part of the book 'Gironde' I shall probably call it, hasn't been so much of a nuissance as I expected, and I've got one or two diverting notes from a <u>mss</u>. in the library here.

Hewletts 'lai' on the story I sent him from U. S. came out in the 'Fortnightly' for May this year and is rather better than most of his verse.

You might send me any american notices of 'Guido' that you come upon.

I shall now go up the road for a dish of tea.

Love to you & dad,
. E

Maurice **Hewlett's** *'Lai of Gobertz' was included in his collection* Helen Redeemed and other poems *(1913), with this note: 'I owe the substance of this lai to my friend Ezra Pound, who unearthed it . . . in some Provençal repertory'. Pound himself abbreviated the story in Canto 5.*

+≻━≺+

397. ACS

[1 July 1912]

[Rodez]

Gourdon, Cahors, Rodez.
From which last I send this.
Bang up cathedral & fairish good mountains.
yrs. t<u>ly</u> more or less weary with the days exploits.
Salutations.
E. P.

+≻━≺+

398. ALS [*letterhead*] Hôtel Terminus, Toulouse

6 July 1912

[Toulouse]

Dear Dad:

Sorry to hear that you're under the weather & hope that by the time you get this you'll be under weigh. again. The Wilson nomination ought to enliven things a little. I can't come home to vote - at least I dont quite see it in that light. but there ought to be something doing. You, of course will keep quiet and watch the fun. The french papers are rather amusing in their adjectives, 'l'austere ex-professor' etc. Bryan seems to have made a good grandstand performance. Will T. R. manage as neat an exit.? I've done 90 miles in the last four days 20 - 30 & two twentys. Rodez - Albi. here. I believe I'm fairly fit, but a bit weary this P.M.

I suppose I might come home some time or other. I might have managed it this summer if I'd known you were going to be really bored, but then I should n't be getting this dam book written, & I've got to go on writing books for the next decade if I'm to keep on drawing pay from Swift & Co.

I do hope you've got your Guido by now and that you find it diverting.

I suppose I'll start writing plays when I get back to London. There don't seem to be much else to do.

I don't see why I shouldn't come to the U. S. next summer, though, if you think it would enliven you.

I think I might arrange my work so as to permit it. . I've got to be in London this autumn however. And I'm getting thru' this present affair much more rapidly than might have been expected.

The next batch of road lies between Foix & Carcassonne. right up in the Pyrenees. . Rodez, also, was high enough to be quite cool.

Luck to you. & get over your heaviness.

Love to you & mother.

. E .

+====+

399. ALS

Aug. 5th. [1912]

[London]

Dear Dad:

Glad to get your letter. I suppose you aren't coming over. Perhaps . you might in the spring if I don't come to the U. S.

I don't know that there's much news.

Hueffer is in town so I get my tennis on their court.

I suppose the Ripostes will be out in September

I am working on my prose book & haven't been about to see people . etc. etc.

Said work in prose rather dampens my never violent desire to endite epistles.

Love to you & mother

. E .

W. R. is on the north coast of France.

We are bringing out some troubadour music some-time or other.

+≻═━═≺+

400. ALS

(August 1912)

10 Church Walk Kensington W. [London]

Dear Mother:

The Gironde is something over $3/4^{ths}$. done. I'm giving myself a course in modern literature and think it might amuse you to do the same. One is always hearing of Turgueneff & Flaubert. and thinking they'll be dull. and Russians are so disgustingly stupid that one can't mention 'em without a shudder. etc. any how I've taken the plunge.

I thought Turgueneff the only sane modern, after I'd read the 'Nichee des Gentilshommes', but Flaubert can give him points on how to write. T. is however the more charming mind, comprehension, or what ever you want to call it. And F. the absolute master of speech. James, and Anatole France are infants by comparison. . I don't know whether you've read much of either of them. I can't remember your having a crush on anything French except the De Goncourts. I'd take the things in french, if you can, Turgueneff was translated in part by Merimee, the english trans. by Constance Garnett is literal, I believe, but stupid. and much recommended. Turgueneff has lived and felt much more than Flaubert who seems to have 'understood' to have watched, etc.

eny how they'll probably amuse you more than the magazines.

Woodward's book on coronars, is not bad, by the way, though it's rather a sudden transition to mention it, and I shouldn't have done so, if I hadn't just caught sight of it on the shelf. I've got bak to south side of this house and so shall have more sun than I did last year, when the front rooms were taken before I got here.

I don't know that there's much news.

Love to you & dad

E. P.

+≻═━═≺+

401. ALS

(27 August 1912)

10 Church Walk. [London]

Dear Dad:

I can't exactly say its 'a promise' for next Spring, but I guess it will be all right. Provided Swift & Co. dont go bust, or there come a German invasion or something of that sort.

As W.B.Y. says of Moore's book . 'its a very amusing book, only it ought never to have been written'

I haven't bothered to read it. Have seen Moore once or twice at teas or dinners. He is regarded mostly as a joke, or 'a stupid old man' or what you like. No, I didn't get a copy of the 'Bookman' for April. – at least I don't remember any thing about it.

T.C.P. has <u>some</u> of my books hasn't he?

I don't feel like buying copies. especially now as I've taken in no 'extras' for some time and am not 'flush' and don't want to draw money from an account.

Letter from mother this A.M.

Tell her I don't know anything in particular about 'Story'. My walking tour will appear in volumn form, I can't put it down twice.

Nor yet Mrs Jananze. her I have not met ether.

I've got to run now. Luck to you.

What's the matter with Wilson? – of course I don't mind T.R. if he really means to smash the trusts, tarrif. express cos. etc.

Love

E. P.

*George **Moore's book** was* Ave, *a part of his autobiographical trilogy,* Hail and Farewell *(1911–14), in which he had written maliciously of Yeats and Lady Gregory.*

<hr>

402. ALS

(3 September 1912)

10 Church Walk W [London]

Dear Dad:

I suppose the time has run faster than I noticed. Any how the books seem to have arrived much sooner than I expected. Thank you.

I've writ six drastic articles on the U.S.A. & shall remit the 'New Age' as fast as they appear. - you might mention the same to Whiteside as he sometimes sees the paper, and may find them diverting. They begin with the 1ˢᵗ September number. I suppose it is 'Sept. 4' or something of that sort.

I've started my 'Tuesday' evenings and the first 2 have gone very well. Florence Farr came and read to us last week, from an unpublished english <u>mss</u> translated from the Bengali of Ramanath Tagor. . who is here now in London. & is a very great person indeed. Yeats is doing him an introduction and I'll send you notice when the book appears.

Marjorie Kennedy Fraser is coming tonight to sing us some Gaelic folk songs. - You may have come on her collection of Hebridean Songs. she has done valuable work in collecting them.

Some of Bill Williams verses are at last to be printed in the poetry Review.

And I've come on a young chap, by name Aldington, whose work interests me.

Mother will be glad to know that I attend Mrs. Wiggan's play <(Rebecca of Sunnybrook Farm.)> last night and strained my patriotism.

Also I am reading more James. if she hasn't read 'The American' 'Washington Square' & 'Portrait of a Lady' . they may divert her
  <u>etc,</u>

Love to you & mother
Ezry.

*The '**six drastic articles**' became a series of eleven, and ran under the heading 'Patria Mia' from 5 September to 14 November 1912. W. B. **Yeats' 'Introduction'** to Rabindranath Tagore's* Gitanjali—*Tagore's own prose versions of his Bengali 'religious songs'—is dated 'September 1912'. The book was published by the India Society in a limited edition later that year, and reprinted by Macmillan a dozen times in 1913, the year the Nobel Prize in Literature was awarded to Tagore. The October* **Poetry Review,** *devoted to 'Modern American Poetry', presented poems by Madison Cawein, Percy Mackaye, and William Carlos Williams, the last with an 'Introductory Note by Ezra Pound'.*

+⟩═⟨+

403. ALS

18 September [1912]

[London]

Dear Dad:
  Bookman arrives O.K. Thanks.
  Am having tennis with Hueffer each P.M.
  Reading Montaigne, and going on with the revision of 'Gironde'

Don't know that there's much else to be said.

This is simply a bulletin to state that I still live and breathe. – as per request .

Love to you & mother

E. P.

Sept. 18

Milton Bronner had reviewed Canzoni *in the April* **Bookman**.

+⊨━━≍+

404. ALS

25 September 1912

[London]

Dear Dad:

I suppose you'll receive or have rec'd a pile of circulars from 'Poetry' . a new magazine starting in Chicago. of which I'm Foreign Correspondent.

As per request. devote yr. self. to booming the same as my screw will depend on part on the circulation.

(address 1025 Fine Arts. Bld. Chi.)

if goods do not arrive.

2 poems, very small & unimportant by yrs. truly . in Oct. Number.

They will print all of my work that appears serialy in the U. S.

I return to my labours.

Love to you & mother.

. E .

25 <u>Sept</u>.

The first number of Harriet Monroe's Poetry (Chicago) *in October 1912 contained Pound's '***2 poems***', 'To Whistler, American' and 'Middle-Aged, a study in an emotion'.*

+⊨━━≍+

405. ALS

Oct 2 [1912]

10 Church Walk [London]

Dear Mother:

Cousin Clara also wrote that my 'brilliant mother' had been enlivening their sepulchral quiet or something of that sort.

The 'Patria Mia' is meeting with considerable success. Edtr. wants me to 'go on as long as I can keep it up' 'Best stuff on america since - - - etc' etc.

I shall be able to cut short the 'Gironde' and use the P. M. as second half . of 'Studies in Mediaevalism Past & Present'.

And the P.M. is glee where the other was very hard work so I am feeling more gay & irresponsible than I have for months.

I've slain the two edtrs. who tried to take advantage of my absence in the South. And my position as foreign rep. of 'Poetry' gives me the over-grip for the future.

I'm to meet Tagore . the great Bengal poet at dinner to-morrow. His stuff is really good. W. B. Y. is doing the introduction . so you'll be able to get details later

I'm invited to read in Vienna next Feb. but don't much think I shall go.

Am having Hilda to tea this P.M. she goes south in a week or so. I suppose you've written the Bentons?

I go out now for a morning constitutional & allow my landlady to clarify my apartment.

Love to you & dad.
. E .

406. ALS

10 October 1912

10 Church Walk Kensington .W . [London]

Dear Dad:

I am in my 'last ditch' and I want you, if you can, to stand to the guns. My patron is dead - has been for some months - Swift decamped & the firm is in liquidation. None of this bothers me much as I can by now look out for myself.

But Dorothy's family is making a row and the whole brunt of the thing seems to fall on her.

You being a human being would probably find it hard to understand the Englishness of things. I've been sick of the whole damn crew for some time. Anyhow there it is. we've 'broken the engagement' but that don't satisfy 'em. And there's the impass. I don't relish seeing her sold off in the society fashion.

You've invited me to bring friends home before now and I feel reasonably sure that you would put us up for a while if we bolted.

She won't take it at that unless. mother asks her.

I believe with what work I've now got behind me I would be able to find something to do in America. That isn't the point of this letter - Only I would be ready to stay there. & I wouldn't be in the state I was when you last saw me.

I know this is asking a good deal of you, and I make no bones of the fact that she has much less $. of her own than I thought when I wrote you thereanent a year ago.

287

And the affair is damn rorcky Still. – – – – –

I want you to cable a reply simply 'Come' or 'Dont'. mother must sign. And I want you & mother both to write her letters and enclose 'em in an envelope to me. It wont be any too easy for her to take such a full plunge into the dark - not after the way she has been brought up.

I know its 'impractical', I know the whole — string of thigs, I haven't been badgering about it for the last three years not to know more or less all that can be said both ways. I want you to stand to your guns - if there are any guns to stand to.

At least I've got my passage money.

Guess . that the board.

yours.

. E .

Oct. 10.

Charles Granville the manager of **Stephen Swift & Co.** *had run off to Tangier with a woman and the firm's cash. The liquidators agreed in December to honour Pound's contract to the extent of paying him £25 a quarter for one year and then a final payment of £65. Elkin Mathews took over the stock of Swift's* Cavalcanti *and* Ripostes.

407. ALS

[10 October 1912]

10 Church Walk [London]

Dear Mother:

I'm sending father a rather serious letter by the same post.

You'll probably take the matter more seriously than he does. And you'll see things that he won't see.

My finances have gone to smash, and Dorothy's family are bothering her beyond the bounds of endurance, and thats about the gist of it.

I want a roof - for a while at least. And she wont think of coming to the U. S. unless you ask her. I don't see any other way out of it.

You know what 'society' is and you know the sort of hardness and closeness that she has been fighting against for the last three years. You'll know more of it than I do. Anyhow. I think she has stood about as much of it as she <u>can</u> stand. And some things are worth while and some aren't .

If they'd only give me time to get things re-arranged here I might manage - but they don't seem disposed to.

You'll see by father's letter that I want you to cable me, permission to bring her home. And that I want both of you to write her letters, and enclose them in an envelope to me.

You can write me expostulations on a separate sheet - if you have any - but the matter is serious

And I want her to get a breath of something less sordid than the life she has seen about her.

We wont be any worse off than you were when you commenced - and on the whole I don't believe you've regretted much.

Anyhow. Theres the scenario.

Yours

E. P.

+⊨⊨+

408. ALS

Nov. 5. [1912]

[London]

Dear Dad:

Thanks for the ornament. Kalends natalis passed without disturbance.

'Swift' is busted. They caught the <u>mgr</u>. in Tangier with <u>some</u> of the goods. . They never published an edtn. of 'Provença'.

I enc. circular of last diversion. I'm on the executive committee along with Mortimer Mempes. & Yeats. etc. etc.

Craig is a great artist and very pleasing person.

I've got 5 poems from Yeats & 6 from Tagore. for 'Poetry' as you'll see . sooner or later. – also some from Aldington in next <u>no</u>. .

The Hirshes arrived a few days ago. etc. etc.

Love to you & mother

. E .

Meads lectures begin this P. M. and so on. Hueffer's mother in law is dead. & its rather a good thing. as she has been unconscious for about a year & a half.

Hilda is in Florence with her family. Mrs Wilkinson (née Gregg.) is with her husband in Chiswick & I see them now & again. not very often.

etc. etc.

Have done an article on Tagore, god knows when It'll be printed.

Pound was helping with an exhibition of **Edward Gordon Craig**'s *work at the United Arts Club. A short note by Pound accompanied* **Tagore's poems** *in the December* Poetry; *a much longer and more detailed article appeared in* Fortnightly Review *in March 1913. The poems by* **Aldington** *in the November* Poetry *were the first showing of Pound's Imagiste school of poets; they would be followed in January 1913 by poems by Hilda Doolittle over the signature 'H. D., Imagiste'.*

+⊨⊨+

409. ALS

(Nov. 29 1912)

[London]

oh well.

Cheer up. as I said on my card from 'the Albermarle'. The storm is over and judging from your last letter about our surviving ancestors, its a d–n good thing, I've been able to manage here.

I'm getting satisfactory terms out of Swift's liquidator, & meeting various edtr. of the commercial sort. etc.

N Age. wants me to have a shot at England. in the style of Patria Mia.

I send the last <u>adv</u>. there are 2 serious articles on my work in process. <u>etc</u>.

A few teas, and the old ring-around with wire-pulling concealed.

Life interesting at least

Lunch with Lady Low on Thursday. Meads lectures for this autumn, are interesting. Henri de Regnier is going to contribute to 'Poetry', and has written to me there anent. W B Y is in Ireland. . Craig diverting. Notice of Tagore will be in the Dec. 'Poetry' He has gone to the U. S. & is to return to Bengal via Japan. His son is taking some Post Grad work at Harvard.

Hilda seems to be enjoying. Italy, etc. etc,

Love to you & Dad,
E. P.

*Pound's '**shot at England**' ran for just four weeks—16 January to 4 February 1913— under the heading 'Through Alien Eyes'. One of the '**serious articles**' on his work was probably his new friend John Cournos's long 'interview', 'Native Poet Stirs London', in the* Philadelphia Record *of 5 January 1913; the other would have been F. S. Flint's March 1913 review of* Ripostes *in* Poetry and Drama, *the first half of which was (as Pound told Dorothy) largely dictated by Pound himself.*

+⟫━⟪+

410. ALS

[December 1912]

10 Church Walk [London]

Dear Mother:

Thanks for the wire. It was rather heroic of you under the circumstances detailed in your last note. Fortunately it won't be necessary to come now. and the air is cleared up and calm again.

I've just come in from a pleasant conflab with a possible publisher & a couple of teas. , etc.

Also I'm doing 'England' in the N. Age – more vigorously than I did the U. S. . I'm off to dine with Ford & V. M. H. in a minute or so.

The Times has bestowed 1½ col. of measured condemnation on the Guido - which is a valuable asset.

I <u>must</u> get on, to dinner.
Love to you & dad.
& Thanks again for the wire.
. E .

*The **valuable review** of Pound's* Cavalcanti *was in the* Times Literary Supplement *of 21 November 1912. The issue of 5 December carried Pound's response:*

> *Sir,– I have to thank your critic for his courteous review . . . but he seems to have misunderstood the aim of my work. I thought I had made it clear in my preface that my endeavour was not to display skill in versification but to present the vivid personality of Guido Cavalcanti. . . . Guido cared more for sense than for music, and I saw fit to emphasize this essential aspect of his work.*

---

411. ALS

<u>Dec. 3</u> [1912]

[London]

Dear Dad:

That's all. The situation has cleared. So I shan't be coming home.

Naturally I should have arrived duly and legally united. You needn't have been alarmed on that score.

Swift's liquidator has paid up. And the rest is a matter of having time to turn round in.

So we procede as heretofore. with due placidity and decorum.

I've been writing some new stuff in an utterly modern manner.

More broad sides in the N. Age. - England, this time. etc.

Etc. etc. F. M. H. doing some new & diverting novels.

Love to you & mother
. E .
Etc.

I'm going out to Mead's lecture . . and so on . as usual. This being Tuesday. And D. goes on painting chinese pictures.

412. ALS

[6 December 1912]

[London]

Dear Mother.

Thanks for your letter to Dorothy. I only saw it yesterday. & I'm sending you her answer along with this.

Thank dad for his also.

Yes. you were both very good about it.

Richard is here waiting for me to feed.

Have just been to tea with Miss Sinclair & a charming disciple of Tagore who is coming to dine with me next week and talk about Bengal.

More later

Lovingly

. E .

*In **her answer** Dorothy wrote that she felt 'not fitted to marry' Ezra until there was something for them to live on.*

+⊨=⊨+

413. ALS

12 December 1912

10 Church Walk [London]

Dear Dad:

Have received 'proof' of my article on 'Tagore' for the 'Fortnightly Review'. Heaven knows when the editor will ultimately print it.

Am correcting a book on Anglo-German amity, by a cheerful idiot who can afford to pay for such performances. That'll pay for a months board.

Richard has started for Italy. D. glad to get your letters. by way of introduction.

I'm going to lecture in Mrs Fowlers new chinese drawing room in January.

Am learning a bit about India from one K. M. Ghose a pupil of Tagore's. also struggling with the bengali alphabet which seems to have about 125 letters that all look exactly alike,

Ghose seems likely to take an intellegent interest in Dante which is more than can be said for most occidentals.

Walter says he's sent his troubadour stuff to the publisher & that I'll have proofs shortly.

I'd better shut this or I'll get plunged further into the anthology & forget it.

Love to you & mother.

. E .

12 / 12 / 12

Walter Rummel's **'troubadour stuff'** *was* Hesternae Rosae . . . Neuf Chansons de Troubadours des XIIième et XIIIième Siècles . . . Adaptation anglaise par Ezra Pound, *published by Augener in March 1913.*

+≻·≺+

414. ALS

Dec. 13- [1912]

[London]

Letter to hand –
Cash as follows, if you regard it as a mystery .

		incidentals .
Oct.	N.Age.	£ 2 -
	Eng. Rev	4 -
	Poetry	10 -
	S. Maynard	- 15
		£16 – 15
Nov.	N. Age.	£ 2 – 2 – 6
	Dent	– 9 –
	Poetry	2 - 2
		4 – 13 - 6
Dec.	N. Age	£ 5 – 5
corrections		10 - 10
	Anglo-German Amity	
	S. Maynard	4 - 5
		£20 - -

From. Swift. & Co.   £25.
   per quarter. for the past year. Last payment. end. of Nov –
Since Oct. 1. - £65 + . = $325

_____

I've lost my copy of the times. review.
<u>etc.</u>
   also I've got to get off to the museum.

E.P.

+≻·≺+

415. ALS

Xmas Eve. [1912]

Slowgh (more or less)

Dear Mother:

Am down here for a week with the Hueffers in a dingy old cottage that belonged to Milton. F M H. & I being the two people who couldn't be in the least impressed by the fact, makes it a bit more ironical.

I can't remember much of what has been going on.

Tea with your Mrs. Woods in the Temple on Sunday.

Yeats reading to me up till late sat evening. etc.

Richard gone to Italy

Dined with Hewlett sometime or other last week.

Have written about 20 new poems

3 days. later:

Impossible to get any writing done here. Atmosphere too literary. 3 'Kreators' all in one ancient cottage <u>is</u> a bit thick.

Xmas passed without calamity.

Have sloshed about a bit in the slush as the weather is pleasingly warm. Walked to the Thames yesterday.

Play chess & discuss style with F. M. H.

Am not convinced that rural life suits me, at least in winter.

Love to you & dad.

Greetings of the season to Aunt Frank.

. E .

Pound told Dorothy he was at 'Casa di Jiovanni Miltoni, Burnham Beeches (or some such—heaven knows what the P.O. address is)'. Burnham Beeches is near Farnham Common in Buckinghamshire, and a few miles to the north of Slough. However, John Milton's cottage was at Chalfont St, Giles, about four miles further on to the north-east of Farnham Common. Hueffer may have been playing games knowing Pound's disapproval of Milton. They walked to the Thames at Taplow. **Yeats** *was reading to Pound from his diaries.*

416. ALS

31 / 12 / 12

10 Church Walk [London]

Dear Mother:

Thanks for Xmas remembrance. - same to H. L. P.

Dinner with Plarr last night.

With Yeats this evening.

Have been banging type-writer all day, & runnig thru the weeks mail piled up here for me.

Hope Aunt. F is in order again. I'll remember her soap. one of these days.

Glad to be back in my own band box. If I don't get on with the correspondence I wont get out by tea time. - great calamity.

Have had a lot of modern french stuff sent me for Xmas. Shall probably lecture a little during Jan. etc.

Love to you & dad.

E. P.

Thank the Feet & grandmother for the Xmas reminder. Give them my salutations.

+>=—=<+

417. ALS

(January 1913)

[London]

Dear Dad:

Sorry about the Xmas. will try to do better next year. Am sending along Walter's latest which I suspect strongly of being wrong, so far as the relation to the poem goes. Haven't yet heard it played.

Will try to remember A. F.'s. soap. sometime soon.

A deal of dull mail this A.M.

Wrote yesterday or day before, didn't I.? at least I can't think of anything much that's new.

Note from Tagore who has retired to Urbana Ill. where, as he says, his friends 'out of their kindness of heart' leave him pretty much alone.

There is a charming tale of the last Durbar. anent R. T.

One Bengali here in London = was wailing to W. B. Y. 'How can one speak of patriotism of Bengal, when our greatest poet has written this ode to the King?', And Yeats taxing one of Rabindranath's students elicited this reponse. 'Ah: I will tell you about that poem. .

The national committee came to Mr. Tagore, and asked him to write something for the reception.

And as you know Mr. Tagore is very obliging.

And that afternoon he tried to write them a poem. and he could not.

And that evening the poet as usual retired to his meditation.

And in the morning he decended with a sheet of paper.

He said 'Here is a poem I have written. It is addressed to the deity. But you may give it to the national committee. Perhaps it will content them.'.

The joke which is worthy of Voltaire . is for private consumption only . as it might be construed politically if it were printed.

Well. I've got to get on to <u>affari.</u>

Yrs

. E .

Love to you & Mother.

╪═══╪

418. ALS

(11 January 1913)

10 Church Walk [London]

Dear Mother:

Enclosed announcement of my activities for week after next.

Ghose is coming in tomorrow A.M.

Feb. 2<u>nd</u> I go up to Oxford to converse with the Essay Society - whatever that may be. its 'Dons & Juniors' supposedly. and centres in St. Johns.

Next Tuesday I dine with a male orginization called the Phratry - whereto I was invited by a solemn & curious cleric. I expect it to be more 'English' than anything I've yet seen.

Have rec'd some french poems for 'Poetry' from Vildrac. one more from Yeats, expect 2 from Richard.

Am reading Flaubert's 'Education Sentimentale' thus late in life. As has been before remarked, the gentleman knew how to write. Also I've had various volumns showered on me for Xmas. Malarme, De Gourmont, etc.

Dr Gould has sent me his work on the 'Infinite Presence' which I have not yet aborded.

Love to you & dad.

Don't know that there's much else. Yeats is in town & in good forms. D comes back today from various country houses and a castle, etc. Mead has sent me a ticket for his lectures, as usual. I get rather the better of the exchange. Binyon is back wailing that the Fuller collection (chinese & Jap. art) in Detroit is better than anything they'll ever get here. He ought to know.

E.

*The **enclosed announcement** would have been of the three lectures he was to give 'By kind permission of Mrs Fowler' at her home, 26 Gilbert Street, Mayfair, at 3.30 on 21ˢᵗ, 23ʳᵈ, and 28ᵗʰ January. His topics were 'The Normal Opportunity of the Provençal Troubadour', 'Rabindranath Tagore', and 'Vers Libre and Systems of Metric, with reading from the Lecturer's own work'. Tickets 7/6, or £1 for the three lectures. In **Oxford** Pound was to talk about Cavalcanti.*

*Dr **Gould's** book,* The Infinite Presence *(1910), was 'a search for religion in biology'.*
***Binyon** had visited the Freer (not the 'Fuller'), collection.*

+⊨=≕+

419. ALS

(25 January 1913)

10 Church Walk [London]

Dear Mother:

Yes, naturally I'd like a secretaryship at the legation, or the London literary correspondentship for Gribbel's paper, or anything else with cash attached.

Incidentally I could manage either better than the present incumbents.

I think, in fact, the only time I have ever heard of the Am. Ambassador was from dear old Lady Lindsay, she was very 'old & grey & full of sleep' and she was very kindly and she got 'American' & 'poet' into her heard. and she went on ' Did you meet Browning?' (apparently the last poet whom she'd been used to setting about his P.s & Qs.) and then very drowsily 'You remember Mr. Lowell? he was your ambassador here.'

Also Violet did blow up the secretary of the legation because she thought they didn't look after me properly. - I don't imagine even the democrat will succeded in getting me in.

The Ledger might however manage some notes on letters etc. here & in Paris, if it once occurred to them. (cassion vaccum drill or some such instrument needed to cause it to 'occur.) that I not only know more about the matter, but am in a better position to get news than the ordinary imbecile.

─────────

I'd like to see a copy of Cournos interview in the Record. He seems intellegent, but couldn't tell how much of his article they would print. & expected them to cut out anything that was really good.

I've scraped about $100 out of the lectures. Small attendance, still its not everyone who can rant at two members of the National committee (Yeats & Hewlett) and three novelists.

My four vols. of poetry are to be collected into 2 and reissued. about March. - no new stuff, but it will be more convenient to have them bound up so and the set will cost $1.75 instead of $2.75. which should please the buyer.

'Poetry' the magazine, is very discouraging. still I can't expect complete illumination to descend on Chicago all at once.

Your Mrs. Woods is very quiet & well behaved and I like their place in the temple.

For god's sake don't mix the term 'Tea' english with 'Tea' american. 'Tea american' means in English 'crush' - which one <u>never</u> attends . – or almost never except for copy, to observe the animals or something of that sort.

Etc.

I am <u>very</u> much disgusted with the Jan. <u>poetry</u>. & with 40 other manifest-ations of American & English assininity. I suppose sometime I'll accept the fact that the human race is about as intellegent as the porcine, & resign myself and stop trying to make blind asses see fine gradations of colour. If they don't they don't I suppose & there's an end o' 't.

Why one is cursed with this missionary spirit, recurring, inextinguishable - stupid - I don't know.

I suppose even Whistler didn't arrive at his sane state of detachment until he was fifty.

Love to you & Dad.

Yours

E P

'Gribbel's paper' would seem to have been the Philadelphia Ledger, *which published Pound's 'Regina Avrillouse' in March 1910, but nothing else. The anecdote of* **'dear old Lady Lindsay'** *is recounted in 'Moeurs Contemporains VIII' (1918).* **'Violet'** *probably Violet Hunt. Elkin Mathews was about to* **re-issue** Personae *and* Exultations *as one volume, and* Canzoni *and* Ripostes *as another, using sheets of the first editions.*

+⟩═⟨+

420. ALS

4 / 2 / 13

[London]

Dear Mother.

Have had charming week end at Oxford. vid. enc.

I suppose if one got settled there one would be too damd comfortable ever to ever do anything worth while.

Thank God I've never been permitted to sink into the professorial state of energy.

Have sent A. Franks soap. one of the addresses wasn't correct. but I finally found it at the other.

etc.

Yeats in town. & intellegent.

etc.

Stuff for my next vol. of verse is accumulating with reasonable haste.

Love to you & dad

- E -

+⟩═⟨+

421. ALS

[c.February 1913]

10 Church Walk [London]

Dear Mother:

Have been smacking the typewriter stedily for the last ten days. 2 articles, 2 reviews, huge wad of a monstrous long poem. about 1200 lines done. and 1800 more coming.

Yeats in good form. I go to him on mondays usually.

Seats for the russian ballet a week from today.

I'm doing a new series of 5 articles in the N. A. which will be sent to H. L. P. when they appear. F. M. H. in Carcassonne, Richard in south italy somewhere. I think I'll go south as soon as its sure of being warm and return here for 'The Season'.

Mead is turned loose on the Upanishads.

Cournos is trying to work me into another interview.

Phila. artest named 'Demuth' came in last week. I'd met him in Bill William's rooms, years since - a pleasing person.

Also looked in on one Cippico. who has translated 'King Lear' & some of Keats into very good Italian.

Hewlett has another book of verse in print. Etc.

One John Helston has emerged from the labouring classes with a huge wad of poetry. some of which shows promise.

Romains (french) has a new book out he is interesting. etc.

I've corrected the proofs of Walters troubadour songs (at last.).

Love to you & dad,
E. P.

*The **new series** of in fact six articles for the* New Age *would have been 'America: Chances and Remedies', which ran from 1 May to 5 June 1913. The series was included in* Patria Mia *(1950).*

+⟩━⋅━⟨+

422. TLS

[28 February 1913]

10 Church Walk. [London]

Dear Mother:

Am sending on the 'Fortnightly' with my article on 'Tagore', please send it on to him within the week. I' don't want to buy another copy of the bloomin review.

Address. Rabindranath Tagore
    508 W. High St.
      Urbana Illinois.

He was giving some lectures at Harvard a few days ago, do try to see him if he comes to Phila . . . He has said nothing to me about any other trip except that to Boston. but then . . ..

I continue to receive various french periodicals, room stuffed with them.

Ghose is doing an article on me for some magazine in Calcutta.

I go to the Russian dancers tomorrow evening, the Debusy 'Apremidi d'un faune' etc.

Wrote a huge narrative poem last week, which the public will be SPARED. the new collection progresses.

Mathews is issuing me in two vols. instead of four. (my own poems)

A man named Seymour in Chicago is bringing out the 'Arnaut'.

Etc.

New series in N. Age hasn't begun to appear yet. It will be sent when it does. Spent last evening with a post impressionist named Etchells.

Love to you and dad. Salutations to A. F.

yrs

- E -

Nijinsky danced 'L'après-midi d'un faune' at Covent Garden on 1 March 1913. Ralph Seymour, who published Poetry in Chicago, proposed to publish Pound's translations of Arnaut Daniel by subscription in a fine limited edition, but the project was in the end cancelled due to insufficient interest.

⊹≔≕⊹

423. TLS

[March 1913]

10 Church Walk Kensington, W. [London]

Dear Dad:

I'm going south in a few weeks time, Sirmione via. Paris, to get bathed and sunned and in general newly equipped for the dam bore of continuing to live.

Unless there's some further unforseen accident I'll be able to send you the same cheque that you sent back last year. June is the best time for London and you'd better plan to come then. <besides any other month may be inconvenient.> <I won't be back much before then & July is too far off to count on.> I don't think I can fly over the hundred. second and return on the Mauretania wont be much more than that if you get round trip. I'd like to ask mother but that'll have to wait. If she came evrything would have to be done just a bit better. Any how I cant do the double fandango this year.

Have been pounding this machine for days, time for grub .
Love to mother, salutations to A. F. and co/
Yrs
Ez.

━╼━━╾━

424. TLS

[early April 1913]

19[*sic*] Church Walk. Kensington, W. [London]

Dear Mother:

Tell Aunt Frank not to worry about the soap, it's sent for her to keep clean with. I've no intention of having her pay for it.

has Ellis GOT the job, your clipping only says he is trying to get it. personally I've no objection. Denmark is a good spell off. And his effect on London wont commence for some little time as there are several steps of diplomatic progress to be traversed before he gets to Synt Jymes. And as I'm the last person he'd apply to have as first secretary I don't see that I can be expected to put on a wedding garland to see him united to the North Sea or whatever it is. He really belongs at the Hague tribunal.

One Robert Frost has escaped from the U.S. and is to be published here. I like him and his stuff. Dine with Hewlett tonight. Yeats only coming as far as Paris <(toward Italy.)>

F M H returning here in a day or so. You will have found the things in Poetry for March and April. Hope you've sent the 'Fortnightly' on to Tagore.

Tell dad that Kipling is 'gaga', retired to some village or other, never heard of in London. Also that I'm not publishing any book about travel in France. thank heaven. He can get any number of Mead's translations and books from the library or he can subscribe to the Quest . . I'haven't any to send him.

Suppose I ought to be at something useful have done nothing but converse with aspirants to literary and scholastic labours for the past week

Love to you and dad. Sorry I can't ask both of you to come over in June. Think the voyage may freshen him up a bit.

yrs
-E -

*Pound's '***things in Poetry*** for March and April' were 'A Few Don'ts by an Imagiste', (preceded by F. S. Flint's 'Imagisme', actually drafted by Pound), and his 'Contemporania', a dozen poems which would go into* Lustra. *His review of* **Frost's** *A Boy's* Will *would be in* Poetry *in May.*

━╼━━╾━

425. ACS

[mid-April 1913]

[Sirmione]

Dear Dad:

Perfectly willing to meet Wright. (re. Mencken) when he comes to London. Tho' I shan't be there until June.

Sorry you're not coming over – but I suppose you know best what suits the times & seasons.

As I'm already in Sirmione, mother's suggestion that I cross the Atlantic instead is a bit impractical. – Besides I <u>do</u> <u>love</u> ocean travel.

Have met the lot of the younger french poets, on my way thru' Paris. – Romains, Vildrac, Duhamel, Arcos. etc.

W. R. has been doing some more music. I like the way he has set 'The Return', better than the way he has done the Troubadour things.

Love to you & mother.

Let me know when Wright is coming, or send him my address & tell him to write.

Yrs
. E .

426. ALS [*letterhead*] Albergo Restaurant 'Bella Venezia'

[c.10 May 1913]

[Venice]

Dear Mother:

Your remarks on 'low diet & sedentary life' are ludicrously inappropriate – if that's any comfort to you.

As to the cup of joy I dare say I do as well as most in face of the spectacle of human imbecility.

As to practicality . I should think with the two specimens you hold up to me, you'd be about through with your moralization on that subject. Surely the elder generation (A. F. & T. C. P.) attended to this worlds commerce with a certain assiduity, & camped not in the fields of the muses.

I don't suppose America has more fools per acre than other countries - still your programme of the Ethical society presents no new argument for my return.

All Venice went to a rather interesting concert at 'La Fenice' on Wednesday - and I also, thanks to Signora Brass for the entrance is mostly by invitation. I don't know whether you remember the very beautiful 18$^{\underline{th}}$ century theatre. but it's a place where you might meet anyone from Goethe to Rossini.

I enclose what I believe to be a Donattello Madonna. and an interior which I don't think you saw. - at least I wasn't with you if you did see it.

I can't be bothered to read a novel in 54 vols. besides I know the man who translated 'Jean Christophe' - and moreover its a popular craze so I suppose something *must* be wrong, with it.

Have you tried Butler. 'Way of All Flesh' & his 'Diary', I think, that's what they call it.

I shall go to Munich next week & thence to London

Love to you & dad.

Salutations to A. F.

Lovingly

. E .

The Doolittles. are here. pere et mere. also Hilda & Richard.

+≻━≺+

427. ALS

[late May 1913]

10 Church Walk [London]

Dearest Mother:

Am glad to be back. Room all full of green trees & sunlight, weather quite up to anything I've found in Italy or France.

Met an interesting & agreeable set of americans in Paris & should have been taken to the Van Vorsts if I hadn't been hurrying back.

Seymour is waiting for the 'Patria Mia' mss. & it will be out this fall.

The Arnaut is, he thinks, about ½ subscribed already.

The Quarterly Review has accepted my article on The troubadours. – if I'll make a few alterations. (i.e. Remove most of the useful information & stuff in a few gaudy generalities.)

I'm very much bucked as the Quarterly is the one venerable & self respecting organ that's left. or at least, it's the most 'weighty' & the contributors are all supposed to wear white beards eight feet long.

W. R. Is coming over to give a concert here, next week.

Love to you & dad.

. E .

The 'Patria Mia' mss. was mislaid in Seymour's office and not published by him until 1950 when it resurfaced.

+≻━≺+

428. TLS

[3 June 1913]

10 Church Walk. [London]

Dear Dad:

Thanks for your cheerful letter. If there is any joy in having found one's 'maximum utility'. I should think you might have it, with your assylum for the protection of the unfortunate. As for T. C. it is rather fine to see the old bird still holding out, still thinking he'll do something, and that he has some shreds of influence.

I'll try to get you a copy of Frost. I'm using mine at present to boom him and get his name stuck about. He has done a 'Death of the Farm Hand' since the book that is to my mind better than anything in it. I shall have that in the Smart Set or in Poetry before long.

Whitman is a hard nutt . 'The leaves of Grass' is the book. It is impossible to read it without swearing at the author almost continuously. Begin on the 'Songs of Parting' perhaps on the last one which is called 'So Long !', that has I suppose nearly all of him in it.

We had a terribly litterary dinner on saturday. Tagore, his son and daughter-in-law, Hewlett, May Sinclair, Prothero (edt. Quartely Rev.). Evelyn Underhill (author of divers fat books on mysticism) D and myself.

Tagore and Hewlett in combination are mildly amusing. (I believe Hewlett's 'Lore of Persephone' is good , but haven't yet seen it .

Tagore lectured very finely last night. I enclose a note from Koli Mohan Ghose, who has been translating Kabir with me. The translation comes out in the Calcutta 'Modern Rev' this month.

Prothero is doing my article on Troubadours in the Quarterly, as I think, I wrote.

Am finishing the Patria Mia, book, for Seymour and doing a tale of Bertrans de Born.

Hope Aug. Poetry, will have some stuff by a chap. named Cannell whom I rooted up in paris, a philadelphian.

W. R. is playing at Mrs Fowler's, Friday before his pub. concert.

W. G. Lawrence down from Oxford yesterday, good fellow, going out to India next winter.

Am playing tennis with Hueffer in the afternoons.

I'm promised that I shall meet De Gourmont and Anatole France, intime, next time I go to Paris, that also pleases me.

'Ortus ' means, birth, or 'springing out', same root in 'orient'

'Strachey' is actually the edtr. of 'The Spectator' but I use him at the type of male prude, somewhere between Tony Comstock and Hen. van Dyke. Even in America we've nothing that conveys his exact shade of meaning. I've adopted the classic latin manner mentioning people by name.

Love to you and mother. Salutations to the entourage. Cheer up ye' aint dead yet. And as Tourgueneff says, most everything else is curable.

yours,
. E .

Tagore was giving a series of five lectures at Caxton Hall, beginning on 19 May with 'The Relation of the Individual and the Universe'. His 2 June lecture was on 'The Problem of Evil'. 'Ortus' was one of the 'Contemporania' in Poetry *in April. John St. Loe* **Strachey** *figured in another in the group, 'Salutation the Second', in a line excised from some English collected editions.*

+≻━≺+

429. ALS

[after 7 June 1913]

[London]

Dear Mother:

Re/ yrs: & dad's letters – questions – etc.

May Sinclair is rather like an acorn + a New England conscience.

Will send on the Modern Review as soon as I get a spare copy.

Richard has come as far back as Paris.

The Hueffer's have had a garden party with everybody one has ever met.

Katharin Heyman has had a musical party full of countesses & operas being rehearsed etc.

I get free seats for Irish players, & pay off my social obligations.

Will Lawrence is taking me to the Oxford Cambridge cricket at Lords' on Tuesday.

I shall see the new Russian ballets on Monday & Friday.

- I enclose W. R. program – a bit late.

Now time for tennis if I expect to get it thru' before tea time.

Love to you & dad,
- E

In the **Modern Review** *(Calcutta) in June appeared 'Certain Poems of Kabir. Translated by Kali Mohan Ghose and Ezra Pound'.*

+≻━≺+

430. ALS

[after 26 June 1913]

10 Ch. Wk. [London]

Dear Mother.

Have survived the enclosed . . J'etait bien loin de ma montagne. .

What respectability !!! gawd.!! - some what palliated by the presence of various friends.

I saw Lady Gregory the other evening. she said you had been very good to invite her to tea, & that this last time when she was in Phila. . she was only there three days & had lost your address.

I don't know what else. We play tennis at Hueffers. more or less every day.

Have been rushing around for Wright. you'll have to take in the 'Smart Set' to watch me supporting my friends.

Cannell & his wife are lodged just below me, & another Parisian colonist is settled just over the way.

May Sinclair has a party on Saturday. & Mrs Brunton (who did my last portrait) a luncheon. ditto.

I'm dining with W. L. George. (short stories.) in a few moments. & with Helen of Troy to morrow.

The Chi 'Tribune' for May 11th might divert you. vide. edt. page.

Guess I'd better be cutting along to dinner.

Love to you & dad,

. E .

Enclosed was the invitation to a Garden Party on Thursday, 26th June from 'The Master of the Temple and Mrs Woods'.

+≡≡+

431. ALS

[late July 1913]

Daisy Meadow Brasted, Kent

Dear Mother

Am down here for a few days. Manning & I have the place to ourselves today. He is still writing the same romance.

Weather sunny & uncertain. Place covered with roses & poppies & woods dry to walk in.

I can't remember what I wrote last. I expect the new poems to come out in Nov. at least I'm getting the <u>mss</u> into shape. & playing tennis.

Yeats & I retire to some country place or other for the months of Nov. Dec. Jan. - running up to London for a day or so per. week.

Cannell goes back to Paris today. Have had some very well written stuff from D. H. Lawrence. (not W. G. ditto.) for the. S. S.

Quarterly has paid $75 & will print in Oct. I suppose

Miss Lowell gives me hopes for the future of America. She says her brother is as intellegent as she is so there may even be some hope for Harvard.

I may take over the lit page in the new Freewoman but the matter is not yet settled

Frost has done some new Eng. narrative poems. dull but with some quality.

Cournos is writing on contemporary american painters. I'm getting turned into a dam'd editorial bureau. 'Poetry' has a new Yeats for Oct. & me again for Nov. I suppose.

Don't know that there's much else in process.

Love to you & dad,

E. P.

*The collection of **new poems** he was getting into shape did not in fact come out until it had grown into* Lustra *(1916). As for his 'getting turned into a **dam'd editorial bureau**', he was being a very active Foreign Correspondent for* Poetry, *was also finding work for* Smart Set, *and was about to begin his association with* The New Freewoman *(later* The Egoist*).*

432. TLS

(19 August 1913)

10 Church Walk [London]

Dear Mother,

Yes, I suppose A. F. was at about the end of her tether.

As for things here, I am fairly placid and busy. The Freewoman has turned over three columns to me, so I'm a sort of editor, I buy the poetry and do the notices. Which means to say I can amuse my self drawing invidious comparisons between the intellegence of my friends and the utter imbecility of my enemies.

Also we are running a translation from De Gourmont which will shock you beyond all bounds.

I begin 'The Approach to Paris' in the New Age, next week. A dissection of contemporary poetry in France.

Bill Williams little book is as far as 'proofs'.

I have been enjoying Miss Lowell's society - sister of Harvard president and the astronomer and the Lowell lectures, and quite able to dispense with that background.

I like Fletcher very much, vide revs. of his books to appear in N. F. and Poetry.

Richard in town for a week. W. R., the Hirshes, Hilda, all in paris, whither the Cannells have returned.

F. M. H. off to the sea-shore. His stuff in the last Poetry very nice, tho' it had to be chopped to fit that minute space.

I dare say you've seen the Smart Set with its new batch of contributors. I paw over a certain ammount of stuff for them, fit mostly for rejection, F. Gregg Wilkinson turned up with its husband two weeks ago, with a rather pleasing youth in their train, one Rogers who has had a couple of plays on in Phila. at the little theatre. Very ingenuous.

This is supposed to be THE desertedest season but people keep running thru town in relays, so its not precicely a desolation. There is no doubt that London is the one spot in the world where continuous residence is in any way bearable.

D. up for a few days, between visits.

Yeats has found a farm, just a little too far out but I suppose we'll land on it in Nov.

Miss Lowell says she caught Henry James saying decent things about me, I don't know precicely what, but the news is consoling, as he is one of the six intellegent people on the island. F. M. H. is doing such a delightful book about H. J.'s work. O, but delightful.

Have been out once, and now Richard wants his dinner so I close,

Love to you and dad

. E .

*Aunt Frank, Frances Weston (latterly Beyea), had just died. The translation from **de** Gourmont being serialized in the New Freewoman was 'The Horses of Diomedes' (1897). Pound's **'Approach to Paris'**, a series of seven articles, ran in the New Age from 4 September to 16 October 1913. William Carlos Williams' **'little book'** of poems was The Tempers, published by Elkin Mathews with an 'Introductory Note' by Pound who arranged the publication.*

⊹══⊹

433. TLS

30 / 8 / '13

10 Church Walk [London]

Dear Dad

Glad you think seriously of coming over. Quiller-Couches' 'Book of Victorian Verse' is no good. The man is an imbecile. His 'Book of English Verse' is good only so far as it is cribbed from Palgrave and the other anthologists. In the modern book he has left out a number of good men. included apes, and chosen very badly from the authors whom he has used. I wish I had forbidden him to use my stuff and may ask for its withdrawal from the second edtn. Yeats says the book wont run to a second edtn. and that it aint worth while, so I may not bother. <The two poems of mine are 'Ballad for Gloom' & Portrait sonnet from Exultations p. 25>

My <new> edtn. with mathews contains no new poems . simply the four little books bound as two.

No I dont write the editorials on the Freewoman that's Miss Marsden, I suppose.

I am concerned with litterchure.

Enclosed card from Yeats with view of <our> winter domocile.

<Yes. I've seen the Smart Set. for Aug.>

I'll send you New Age series. dont bother. I dont know much of anything except that I have been rushing hither and yon, to divers plays and writing a lot of prose . etc.

Hilda back in London. I believe her family arrives next week.

farewell supper to Tagore, last tuesday. Motored for a couple of hundred miles with Miss Lowell at front end of the week.

My mind is on too many things for me to collect it into an orderly chronicle.

Love to you and mother.

E. P.

Amy Lowell had motored Pound to the Cotswolds and Oxford on the 24th.

⊬⊐━⊏⊬

434. ALS

6 / 9 / '13

[London]

Dear Mother,

Have been ripping out my series for the N. Age. = necessary reading etc.

Have just done a summary of it for Poetry.

Compository faculty about ready to quit work. William's book in final proofs arrived yesterday for my attention.

N. A., Freewoman, Poetry, proofs etc. keep one occupied.

'Lustra' may come out in Oct.

Hilda, & family here, also Pa & Ma Proctor, both the latter I have not seen yet.

Have only 1½ more articles to do for N. A. so that wad is fairly worked off.

am thinking of publishing a small anthology of les jeunes.

Have some of D's new sketches to adorn my walls. which same do please me.

The rest of my activities you can follow fairly well in print.

A bientot –

. E .

Love to you & dad.

---

435. TLS

(30 September 1913)

10 Church Walk, W.[London]

Dear Dad,

If mother really wants to come over I can find $150, that ought to pay her passage decently. The only question is, when does she want to come.

I shall be in the country from Nov. 1 to. Feb. 1. . March is rough crossing. She might start in April?

Wright is hoppless but he keeps on paying. the more I have to do with americans the less do I think there is any chance of the damn place ever being fit for inhabitation save by blacks, red indians and Russian jews .

Have just been to the Isle of Wight to stay with Upward. He is intellegent . Have you read his 'The New Word'. I may be able to send you 'The Divine Mystery' when it comes out.

Have been away for several days, and the papers are piled on my desk. Mostly bother.

More anon.

E P.

---

436. TLS

13 / 10 / '13

10 Ch. Wk. [London]

Dear Mother,

Wrote you a letter about a week ago but it was too dull to send. My days are as full as the weaver's coal scuttle. Nothing of any particular importance. F. M. H. is back so I have a house to live in as well as a place to sleep.

My other pass-times you can gather from my printed stuff.

I have taken to watching the dances at the Cabaret, which is a mildly amusing spectacle even if it has not managed to make itself into the temple of the arts that it set out to be.

The exhibit of old spanish masters now at the Grafton is the finest lot I have seen outside Madrid. Goya, Velasquez, Zurbaran, Valdez Leal, El Greco, all very well represented.

You'll find Giles 'Hist of Chinese, Literature' a very interesting book. Upward has sort of started me off in that direction. I have also embarked on a french translation of Confucius and Mencius. Tagore's 'The Gardener' is out, and I have reviewed in for the N. F.

The Miss Mapel are going to the far east at the end of the month.

Have seen Mrs Fenollosa (relict of the Fennolosa who has written on Chinese art, and who has had so much to do with the Freer collection) and Sarogini Naidu (of Hyderabad, authoress of divers poems,) remarkable rather as having been done in english by a bramin who has broken purdah.

Etc. etc. it is sufficiently difficult to collect one's wits for the purposes of coherent articles, let alone trying to remember at the end of a week, what one has done during the course of it.

Dicky Green dropped in a week or so ago, did I write that? I fed him chop suey and he daparted in a cloud of content.

Saw pop Shelling in the museum for a few minutes, The weather has been warm enough to sit out in the Gardens, quite up till now. etc.

love to you and dad
E. P.

*The **Cabaret** Theatre Club, also known as The Cave of the Golden Calf, with decorations by Epstein and Wyndham Lewis among others, was a nightclub opened in 1912 by Mrs Frida Strindberg. Pound's **review** of Tagore's* The Gardener *was in the* New Freewoman *of 1 November 1913. 'Pop Shelling' was Felix E. Schelling, Professor of English in the University of Pennsylvania, 'mine ancient professorial enemy', as Pound described him to Dorothy.*

437. ALS

30 October 1913

[London]

Dear Dad

Have I written before to ask you if you could find among my papers a sketch called 'Crime a la mode'

Anyhow. if you can manage to find it, Id like you to send it along. Send any sort of thing you find . short stories etc. provided you dont run to more than 20 cents postage.

I may be doing french poets for the Quarterly. (it won't appear for ages)

Don't know that there's much else. to recount

Love to you & mother.
. E .

PS. It is Oct 30.
at the threshold of my 98th yr. I salute you.
Did I thank you for the 2 quid. or did I only send thanks via mother.
    anyhow. here's to it -

yrs

. E .

+===+

438. TLS

[late October/ early November 1913]

10 Church Walk. Kensington, W [London]

Dear Mother,

I plan to spend my birthday largesse in the purchase of four luxurious under-shirts. Or rather I had planned so to do, if however, the bloody gardsman who borrowed my luxurious hat from the Cabaret cloak room (NOT by accident) does not return the same, I shall probably divert certain shekles from the yeager.

Upward's 'Divine Mystery' is just out, Garden City Press, Letchworth.

His 'the New Word' has been out some time, the library may have the anonymous edtn.

My stay in Stone cottage will not be in the least profitable. I detest the country. Yeats will amuse me part of the time and bore me to death with psychical research the rest. I regard the visit as a duty to posterity.

Current Opinion is an awful sheet. Merely the cheapest rehash of the cheapest journalistic opinion. <u>ma che</u>! No periodical is ever much good. Am sending the Quarterly which is at least respectable. I hope you don't think I READ the periodicals I appear in.

I am fully aware of the New Age's limitations. Still the editor is a good fellow - his literary taste, or at least that of the paper is decided by his innamorata, which is unfortunate. Most of the papers bad manners, etc . . . . .

I seem to spend most of my time attending to other peoples affairs, weaning young poetettes from obscurity into the glowing pages of divers rotten publications etc.

Besieging the Home Office to let that ass Kemp stay in the country for his own good if not for its.

Conducting a literary kindergarten for the aspiring etc@@etc.

Richard and Hilda were decently married last week, or the week before, as you have doubtless been notified. Brigit Patmore is very ill but they have decided to let her live, which is a mercy as there are none too many charming people on the planet.

Met Lady Low in Bond St, Friday, 'returned from the jaws of death', just back.

The old Spanish masters show is the best loan exhibit, I have yet seen. The post-Impressionist show is also interesting.

Epstein is a great sculptor. I wish he would wash. but I believe Michael Angelo NEVER did, so I suppose it is part of the tradition. Also it is nearly impossible to appear clean in London, perhaps he does remove some of the grime.

Anyhow it is settled that you come over in the Spring. If dad can't come then, we'll try to arrange that for the year after. I shall come back here from Sussex. (mail address will be here all the time as I shall be up each monday.) You will come over in April, at least you will plan to be here for May and June. Once here you can hang out at Duchess St. quite as cheaply as you could at home.

I shall go to a Welsh lake later in the season instead of going to Garda in the spring. having been in the country thru' the winter I shall probably not need Spring cleaning.

If I am to get anything done this day I must be off and at it.

Love to you and dad

E. P.

*Yeats was taking Pound with him to **Stone Cottage**, in the country near Coleman's Hatch in Sussex, for conversation and companionship, to act as secretary, and to read to him after dark. The two poets would spend ten weeks there, from the second week of November through to mid-January 1914. The '**innamorata**' of A. R. Orage, the editor of the New Age, was Beatrice Hasting. Harry Hibbard **Kemp** (1883–1960), known as 'the Kansas poet' and 'the tramp poet', had stowed away on a boat from New York and been arrested and jailed in Southampton. The Home Secretary's eventual decision was not to deport him.*

✢

439. ALS

[mid-November 1913]

Stone Cottage | Coleman's Hatch | Sussex

Dear Dad.

It is fine wild country here and I suppose I will benefit accordingly. London seems reasonably far off and one is glad of the quiet.

Yeats is doing various books. he wants my Daemonalitas. will you try to find it along with the other thing I asked for . = 'Daemonalitas' by the Rev. Father Sinistrari of Ameno'. paper cover, not very large.

W. B. Y. is just starting for the post so I conclude this. Have turned the N. F. over to Richard, and am trying to shove 'Poetry' onto F. M. H. so I may be free to do what I hang please. Don't know that much will come of it. Any how

I'll have three calm months in this place & will return to the 'bewilderingly briliant life of the capital' with forces & cantankerousness renewed.

Hope you'll see Yeats when he gets to the U. S. A.

Love to you & mother –

Wild moorland here with curious dark colours. etc. Am reading Confucius in my lighter moments.

Yours

. E .

—⊨—◄—

440. ALS

(26 November 1913)

[London]

Dear Dad,

Re /. mexico. I at least am d–n glad to see Lord Cowdray getting it in the neck.

I think everybody - at least the people who know - sees the show merely as a duel between Cowdray & Rock feller, and no one cares a rap which one of 'em gets fried in his own juice. - or 'oil' to be more exact .

Cowdray has been driven more or less into his hole. - at least I hope he has. - one doesn't know. His connection with the solem gag of the english press – or part of it – 'The Times' etc. gets him detested in my particular corner of the world.

We've been chortling over Tagore's getting the nobel prize.

I[t] was a very nice slap in the jaw for Gosse & the stodges who kept Tagore off the Academic Committee. when W. B. Y. proposed him. we have had gay & unhallowed mirth since the Nobel decision.

It means a lot for the reform party in India - Tagore's prestige with the jacks in office, etc.

That mildest of men is registered in Calcutta as. 'suspect no.12 class b.' because he wouldn't fire my amiable friend Kali Mohon.

He had taken the young man from a violent political campaign. made him a teacher - the only possible way to keep him out of politics. - and then the 'authorities' ordered him to turn K. M. out. god bless our beaurocricy.

of course 'Ulster' & the Dublin strike are the two topics of the moment. & nobody knows enough what the result will be, to hold any coherent views.

yrs ever

E. P.

A columnist in the New Age *for 30 October 1913 noted the involvement of Lord* **Cowdray**, *'a type of omnivorous capitalist', in Mexican affairs and especially in its oil wells in* *competition with American financial magnates, among whom it named Rockefeller. In* **Ulster** *the Protestant Ulster Volunteers were organizing to prevent the British Parliament granting Home Rule to Ireland. In* **Dublin** *a bitter industrial dispute between 20,000 workers and 300 employers, with the right to unionize a burning issue, had begun in August and would not end until January 1914.*

+⟩═══⟨+

441. ALS

(5 December 1913)

10 Church Walk [London]

Dear Dad:

I believe the country is agreeing with me - Yeats is very good company.

He thanks you for invitation.

Major Pond is arranging his tour & if the Wyncote club wants him to lecture they should apply to Pond.

Thanks for the book. rec'd. That story should be in the trunk of things I left when I was home last. - that is if I didn't destroy it.

The Glebe - 96 Fifth Ave - is publishing 'Des Imagistes' an anthology in Feb. 1914. - write for prospectus.

I think I wrote that I am to have Prof. Fenollosa's valuable mss. to edit & finish a book on the Japanese drama & an anthology of chinese poets.

It is a very great opportunity . as not only Fenollosa but the two authorities of the Japanese Imperial court have prepared the stuff, & been at great expense in gathering the materials.

If you get Fenollosa's 'Epochs of Chinese & Japanese Art'. you'll get some idea of what his work means. & of his unique opportunity.

Richard has taken on the N. F. so I'm fairly free to work on the Fenollosa mss when it arrives.

Like every thing worth having it has come out of a clear sky without any effort on my part.

Love to you & mother.

Greetings to T. C. P. if he arrives.

Yours

. E .

Pound began working at once on the book on the **Japanese drama** *which would be published in January 1917 as* 'Noh' or Accomplishment. A Study of the Classical Stage of Japan *by Ernest Fenollosa and Ezra Pound. His small anthology of* **Chinese poetry** *was published in April 1915 as* Cathay, *then incorporated into* Lustra *in 1916.* **Richard Aldington** *had been formally appointed Assistant Editor of the* New Freewoman.

+⟩═══⟨+

442. TLS

Christmas [1913]

Stone Cottage | Coleman's Hatch | Sussex

Dear Mother

Have just come in from a decently long walk. Clear and cold longitude 12 latitude 77 or viceversa. I believe it is about 44 @1 really.

Yeats is better company than anyone in London so I am not bored here. We find we have room to fence in the study when the weather is bad.

I am not sending you any Xmas decorations as I take it you are coming over in the late spring and my Xmas goes into transportation. I'd like more or less to know what date suits you as I may fit in a trip to Paris before you come. I think I suggested the end of April so that you could stay on into the season. You'd better come this year as I shall be less and less in touch with people as I get more to do, or as I find it less necessary to be in London, at least I hope so

This machine is very good (Standard, Corona) the only really portable sort, it is part of my rake off from Poetry. It ought to fairly good @ £10/10.

I dont know that there's much else, we read mss. plays for the Abbey, and sources for Yeats' ghost book. and I am deciphering Fenollosa's heiroglyphics.

Fletcher has some wierd stuff in this number of Poetry. I hear from Bill Williams now and again Seymour said he'd send on the Arnaut before Xmas but he obviously hasn't.

Love to you and dad, and salutations to whom they are fitting .

. E .

Poetry had awarded its £50 prize for the best poem published in the magazine in 1913 to Yeats, who had accepted £10 while proposing that the rest be given to Pound. Pound spent his £40 on the typewriter, and on two small sculptures by Gaudier-Brzeska.

443. TLS

4 January 1914

Stone Cottage, Sussex (mail Church Walk)

Dear Dad

1 Eagle recd. safely, thank you. Best wishes for the new year.

China is interesting, VERY. make sure which chinese government is giving you the job and then blaze away.

Am just back from London and piled high with letters which are mostly other peoples business.

I believe the whole dinner committee is to be invited down to Blunts some-time during the month. I wrote didnt I, that we were arranging to give a dinner in honour of Wilfrid Scawen Blunt? Vid my note on Status rerum in Poetry if you dont know of him.

Brzeska is doing a memorial relequaire . for the occasion. He has some nice stuff on exhibit now in London. I dont know that there's much else new. Love to you and mother. Appropriate sentiments re/A. E. Pound whom I vaguely remember as being thinner than any other of the males on the Chippewa farm. I thought he was dead ten years ago. Your clipping says Alfred not Albert.

Shall inspect the Loomis remains at some convenient season. You arent very explicit but I guess I can find something or other.

Hilda complains that you have abandoned her since she became a decent married woman. Dont know what else. Yeats sails on the 29th.

Salaam . And send on your Chinaman as soon as you like.

yours

. E P.

4 - 1- '14

*Homer Pound's **Chinaman** was Far-san T. Sung (1883–1940). As Inspector-General of Mints in the new Republic of China he had visited the Philadelphia Mint, met Pound's father, and offered him the possibility of working in China. When he met Pound in London shortly after this he was optimistic about finding a position for him also in Peking. Pound arranged the publication in the Egoist of Sung's essay, 'The Causes and Remedy of Poverty in China', and wrote an introductory note to the first of three instalments in March 1914.*

⊣⇒⇐⊢

444. ALS

[January 1914]

[Sussex?]

Dear Mother

It is rather late in the day to go in to the whole question of realism in art.

I am profoundly pained to hear that you prefer Marie Corelli to Stendhal but I can not help it.

As for Tagore, you may comfort yrself with the reflection that it was Tagore who poked my 'contemporania' down the Chicago gullet. - or at least read it aloud to that board of imbeciles on 'Poetry' & told 'em how good the stuff was.

I do not wish to be mayor of Cincinnati nor of Dayton Ohio.

I do very well where I am, London may not be the Paradiso Terrestre but it is at least some centuries nearer it than is St Louis.

I believe Sussex agrees with me quite nicely.

Yrs.

E .

+≡≡≡≡+

445. TLS

[19 January 1914]

10 CH"WK. [London]

Dear Dad

Have seen Sung. pleasant chap. He seems fairly sure of fixing you in Pekin, and optimistic about yours truly. We may yet be a united family.

Presentation to Blunt yesterday, will send printed account. am just back and settling in London and rushed to death, more in a day or so.

. E P

Love to you and mother.

+≡≡≡≡+

446. TLS

[23 January 1914]

10 Church Walk, Kensington W [London]

Dear Mother

Here's the Blunt festivity. The proto arranged as follows

Blunt

Yeats   E.P.

Sturge Moore   Richard

Victor Plarr   Flint

Yeats disguised by influenza and glasses. The rest quite recognizable. Manning had to go back to lincolnshire and Masefield's wife wouldn't let him out. We were fed upon roast peacock in feathers which went very well with the iron-studded barricades on the stairway and other mediaeval relics and Burne-jones tapestry.

Hulme lectured at the QUEST last night on futurism and post impressionism, followed by fervent harangues from Wyndham Lewis and myself.

W. B. Y. is coming to Wyncote for the night if he lectures in or about Philadelphia. He will let you know.

There'll be a longer account of the Blunt show in the Egoist and Cournos is sending it to the Boston Transcript.

Have enough of Brzeska's stuff in my room to give it an air. He is going to sculp me as soon as we get time.

Coburn has done a very fine photo-portrait which I shall use in my next book if I ever have a next book.

Monro has just taken a batch of stuff for the next No. of POETRY AND DRAMA.

Yone Noguchi dined with me on Tuesday, interesting litterateur of the second order Dont like him so well as Sung, or Coomaraswami, .Still you neednt repeat this, as the acquaintance may grow and there's no telling when one will want to go to Japan.

Dined at the Fowlers yesterday before Hulme's lecture.

More anon

Love to you and dad

Ez

Eight of Pound's Lustra *poems were in the March* **Poetry and Drama**.

+>==<+

447. TLS

(January 1914)

10 Church Walk , Kensington. W. [London]

Dear Mother

I dont know that it much matters when you come, take the months that suit you. I dont know that there is very much of a formal season. I think you ought to be here during June. The F.M.H. garden party is alway about July 1st. then people begin clearing out. but I dont know that it matters The Fowlers will go to the country as early as possible, I dare say you might be invited down to the cottage, but I dont know. Its always cram packed.

this <above> letter is divers days old I shall go on with another one.

Cournos is sailing for America in a few days. He will call on dad.

He has just written a history of American painting and I want him to see our honoured progenetrix by Page.

Also I want him to meet Whiteside. And dad may as well introduce him to Rogers (Inquirer) and Menken, and anybody he thinks may be useful. Ledger etc.

I dont know that there''s anything more. I sent a longish letter yesterday.

I think I was saying in the first part of this scrawl that the F.M.H. tennis court and garden stays open fairly late in the summer. Only they've now got a cottage and may go away earlier this year that usually.

Anyhow, come when you like. I enclose a rather better view of the cottage. At least it gives a better idea of the setting .

Love to you and dad.

. E .

╬══╬

448. TLS

[before 18 February 1914]

10 Church Walk, Kensington, W [London]

Dear Mother

I am taking a small flat around the corner, in a couple of weeks. I shall have a gas range to play with, and hope thereby to free myself from part of the necessity of restaurants.

Please send me the receipts and specifications and directions for pan-cakes, waffles, fried chicken à la Lucy, that brown hard fry with gravy. Also cream-soups, tomato and potato . and any other of the simple pleasures of the poor that you think I can cope with.

When you come over I shall probably insist on your bringing an American ice cream freezer, unless by some miracle I find that they can be obtained here.

The flat is

5 Holland Place Chambers

Kensington, W.

Mrs. Langley is going to look after me there for a while at least, so I wont have any fuss about service.

They say it will be in order by the 18th I think you'll be safe to answer this note to that address, tho' of course anything sent here will reach me.

Yours

.E.

╬══╬

449. TLS

[February 1914]

[London]

Dear dad,

Do not bark, scratch or bite. Those parodies of Richard's are very good and he signed 'em at my special request. They are the only printed parodies of me that are any good, tho' Manning has done some nice ones.

320

No one whom I hadn't had under my own jurisdiction could have done the job so well. They attest a definite manner and do not in the least affect one's enjoyment of the originals. I was delighted with them.

Max Beerbohm said yesterday that he is doing a caricature of your only son. That IS immortality, I hope the Italian air wont put him off it, he goes back there in a few days.

Unless d'Annunzio makes some fuss, I shall translate 'La Figlia d'Iorio' with dramatic production assured. Miss Darragh may also do one of the Japanese plays if it proves stageable.

I suppose I shall get mearried some time in April, but you needn't mention the matter. There will be no fuss. I think mother may as well come in June or when ever it was that she wanted to. I mean there is no use her 'getting here for the registration' or anything of that sort. Besides every thing will be unarranged and out of order We wont be either in or out of the flat etc. etc. & D. is going to Italy for March.

Also there's no chance of your coming until later etc. etc. .

You needn't mention the matter to Yeats. I shall write to him in due course
yrs with love
. E .

*Richard Aldington's **parodies** of Pound's 'Contemporania' were in the* Egoist *in January. 'La Figlia di Jorio' (1904), a play by Gabriele D'Annunzio (1863–1938).*

+≈≈+

450. TLS

22 February 1914

10 Church Walk, Kensington. W. [London]

Dear Mother

I dare say I <u>am</u> going to be married. The family has ordered the invitations and stuff for curtains etc. In which case I shall <u>not</u> come to America and if you want to inspect us you will have to come over here.

I know who Lord Cowdray is, but I dont know anything about Pearson of Barrington. If you know that thoroughly disgraceful scoundrel you would have done well to have introduced him to me years ago. I should find him most useful. There is no crime he would not commit. Of course I knew Cowdray was 'a' Mr Pearson.

No I have not met Grierson. We have written and have invited each other to dinner or tea or something but that is as far as it got. He did a good book of American before the war reminiscences.

You are right in supposing that Yeats is not for exhibition. He will want a peaceful evening. If he cares to drive you can arrange that after he arrives.

I suppose when Gribbell does finally get into the senate, I shall get a job in this rotten embassy. The Supply of Y.M.C.A. secretaries will have run out by then, or let us hope so.

Think of belonging to a nation that gets itself represented by Page and VanDyke. It, to put it mildly, it borders on the disgusting.

Barrie did not give the £50,000 to the shakleton expedition. He has denied the slander.

Love to you & Dad
E. P.

22 - 2 - '14

*In 1914, Walter Hines **Page** (1855–1918) was US Ambassador to the Court of Saint James, and Henry **Van Dyke** (1952–33) was US Minister to Holland and Luxembourg. The report that **J. M. Barrie**, the author of* Peter Pan, *had donated £50,000 to Shackleton's Polar Expedition was formally denied and informally confirmed, Barrie having wanted to remain anonymous.*

+⊨══⊨+

451. TLS

28 February 1914

10 Church Walk [London]
going to 5 Holland Place Chambers (Kensington W.)
on Monday

Dear Dad

I'm sending you Tagore's prose book, which I haven't had time to read, and now that the Fenollosa stuff is here I shant get time to read. Also I can easily borrow a copy and I've heard part of it in his lectures.

Eva Fowler is going to lend us Daisy Meadow right up to the end of May.

Met the laureate at lunch yesterday and found him disarming. He is having me down in March sometime or other, he lives just out of Oxford.

He displayed a flattering familiarity with my works, said I had a great future and then having no better or more fitting way of spending his evening he went on to dine with the king.

He is almost as charming as Blunt or possibly more so. I think he has more sense of humour. He called his job 'this professorship'.

I enclose a note from Mrs Woods, nothing in it, only I think mother was asking about her.

The papers are full of Wyndham Lewis' cubist room that he has just done for Lady Drogheda. I don't know that I have written of him but he is more or less one of the gang here at least he is the most 'advanced' of the painters and very clever and thoroughly enigmatic.

Brzeska is using up a ton of Pentelicon for my head. vide Egoist, you'll find the mad outline drawing very interesting AFTER, you've had it on the wall for a week or two. The tactile values in the that drawy cats paw etc. also the composition.

Epstein is stronger but Epstein is twenty years older. Brzeska is exactly like some artist out of the Italian renaissance.

Guess that's about the extent of the present despatches.

love to you and mother

.E P.

28 - 2 -14

Tagore's prose book was Sādhanā: The Realisation of Life. A Series of Lectures *(1913). The poet* laureate *was Robert Bridges (1844–1930).* **Henri Gaudier-Brzeska** *was transforming the half-ton block of marble Pound had supplied him with into what would become known as the 'Hieratic Head of Ezra Pound', now in the Raymond and Patsy Nasher Sculpture Center, Dallas, Texas.*

452. ALS

[March 1914]

[London]

Dear Mother:

I enclose these curious announcements of the pre. nuptual reception.

I think you and dad may may as well write again to Dorothy - - saying nothing about the earlier letters you sent a year ago.

The family is being very nice & I have heard from divers outlying members.

yrs

. E .

I don't think there's any use of your coming over for the ceremony for we shall go away for a little - immediately after - so I think June is your best time.

Yours

. E .

Please forward the enclosed I haven't the addresses –

The **enclosures** *were the formal printed invitations to the reception on the Saturday preceding the wedding ceremony on Monday, 20 April 1914.*

453. TLS

16 March 1914

5 Holland Place Chambers | Kensington, London. W.

Dear Mother

Thanks for the receipts, re sauces etc. I am rather vague about 'dozens' I should think five half dozens of anything would probably do us for some time to come.

I presume D will have the appropriate sentiments. She is a very well behaved person. I dont know about dozens either I suppose one wants a dozen tea spoons . .

About your earlier letter. I believe D has some sort of chronometer. When she gets back from Rome I'll enquire whether or no it works. The D'Annunzio play hasn't materialized. If it comes I expect it will be almost as bad as Barrie but one would get paid for it.

I've finished with the Jap job for the Quarterly I shall not come to America. The 'ceremony' will be the week after the reception, quite private.

I suppose we'd better have 'dozens' the young Langley only comes in once a day so there are two meals to be considered <between wash-ups.> You say 'there are' so and so many. So I suppose it is merely a question of sending not of outlay, in which latter case I should say half dozens.

I dont see why anybody's photographs should be exhibited to the Pullmans but I drift constantly further from certain points of view.

Neither do I wish to meet Barrie. I am going down to Oxford to see the poet laureate tomorrow and that will be sufficient ordeal. He is one of the most charming men I have ever met but how in god's name
. . . .

Oh well I dont suppose he has ever had any call to think about anything but smoothe lawns and dicky-birds. I mean it will be a tour de force If I manage to pass the entire day without saying something that I really think instead of drifting along in a mild quasi-silent acquiescence. Of course so far as passivistes are concerned he is far and away the best of the lot. <u>ma</u>!!!!! <u>che</u>!! Anyhow he has studied his art (on the edges) and made a few experiments (along well sanctioned lines).

He has all the delightful qualities that make efficient literary criticism impossible in England.

Wyndham Lewis is starting a new quarterly 'Blast' which will be the sole intellegent publication in England. You will thoroughly detest it.

Brzeska appears to be making a mess of my bust.

May sinclair is moving to St John's Wood and bequeathing me a very comfortable arm chair. The Miss Maple are in India, being shown about Calcutta by Ghose etc. anyhow they are storing some oriental carpets with me, so the floors will be doubly covered.

I have translated another Jap play . read half of James 'Tragic Muses' which is excellent. etc. etc.

Love to you and dad

E. P.

16 - 3- '14

+>==≡+

454. TLS

(25 March 1914)

[London]

Dear Dad

I thought grand ma Pound's letter to you very charming.

I have been rushed to death. Imagiste Anthology is out as I dare say you know. I enclose an interview, rather inexact, and also old Bridges' letter.

I have done a few notes on Yeats and Hueffer for Poetry, and am on another fenollosa article, you'll have to wait for the August quarterly to find out more or less what its about.

Richard and I are going down to old Blunt's for a couple of days, starting tomorrow.

Brzeska has about finished my symbolic bust . .

The Egoist has got another lease of life . not that I care much about it . , still it's a place to publish Joyce and the few good things that no one else dares publish . .

Mr Shakespear is 'a solicitor' that'd be a 'lawyer' in the U.S. Both families are anglo-indian' (NO, not half breeds)

Am glad Julia Wells has appeared somewhere, everyone seemed to have lost track of them. Please tell her that she and Matilda should have had invitations to the 'party' if I'd had any idea of their addresses, same applies to Margaret Snively.

'Daisy Meadow' is Mrs Fowlers cottage in Kent . very pleasant. . (The Chart, Brasted, Kent)

You can find out something about Fenollosa in the preface to his 'History of Chinese and Japanese art.'

Cousrnos seems dammmm glad to get back to England.

D gets back on Monday.

Guess thats all before the mail goes.

Love to you and mother.

- E P -

Pound reviewed **Yeats'** Responsibilities *in* Poetry *in May as 'The Later Yeats', and* **Hueffer's** Collected Poems *in the June number under the heading 'Mr Hueffer and the*

*Prose Tradition in Verse'. The Fenollosa article, 'The Classical Drama of Japan',
appeared in* Quarterly Review *in October 1914.*

+➤—◆—◄+

455. TLS

12 April 1914

5 Holland Place Chambers | Kensington . | London . W.

Dear Mother

I don't know what I've written and what I haven't. The wedding is on the
20th. of April. Then we go to the country.

I am going to lecture on Imagisme on May 30 at the Cubist Academy, the
Ormond St. Rooms.

Walter is giving a concert here on June 3.

Monck wants to put on the Nishikigi, one of the Fenollosa plays at Norwich
in June. So I may go up there. but I don't see that that matters.

I enclose your ticket, you'd better come for the last week in May. The fare to
Norwich wont break you even if we all go up for a week.

The siller is come but it came in my absence and the Express man wouldn't
leave it with the concierge so it has gone back to the office and will I suppose
come again on Tuesday, the rest of the time being hollidays.

I should like the original cutting from the Millwaukee paper anent the splicin'.

Various letters this morning from Chester and Rex Henderson. etc.

I rec'd five copies of The Century this a.m. Gord help all poor sailors on a
night like this.

I enclose a note from Mrs Woods. . What else? Poetry is printing the Jap play,
in May, I suppose. D and I are going to Stone Cottage after all, as it will be less
bother than Daisy Meadow.

Yeats is back, just back I shall see him tomorrow. I suppose he didn't get to
Wyncote?. I think he got ill at the end of his visit to the U.S.

I ought to get off a couple of articles in the midst of various matters.
Furniture etc.

love to you and dad.
E.

12 - 4 - '14

In its May number Poetry *printed 'Nishikigi', translated from the Japanese of Motokiyo
by Ernest Fenollosa, and edited by Pound. 'Nishigishi' is based on the tale of a woman
who for three years paid no heed to a man's declarations of his love, and who relented
only when he had died of despair. In the play their still troubled spirits meet a century on
and are finally united.*

+➤—◆—◄+

456. TLS

[before 20 April 1914]

5 Holland Place Chambers | Kensington . W. [London]

Dear Mother

Package arrived O.K.

D seems pleased with necklaces, and wore the coral the same evening to the new Shaw play, with an aunt and uncle whom I'd only met once and who are rather pleasing.

Christianity and all that thereto appartains is in England so detestable that I dont suppose she will ever use what our dear friend Lower termed 'the symbol of your faith'.

I will write to my grandmother shortly, as soon as I get a chance, these last few days are rather full of detail. Especially as most of the beneficii have come as cheques.

Cousin Will Wadsworth descended with £10 and I believe Cousin Clara is sending some silver. F. M. H. has endowed us with some very nice chairs.

I've written to Aunt Florence.

Must make an end of this and get out.

Love to you and dad.

E.

*The **new Shaw play** would have been* Misalliance.

+≻━≺+

456a. ACS [*cardhead*] 12, Brunswick Gardens, Kensington.

[20 April 1914]

[London]

Salutations.

Ceremony legalized

Love

D. P.

E. P.

+≻━≺+

457. TLS

[May 1914]

Stone Cottage | Coleman's Hatch | .Sussex .

Dear Dad

Right O! Mother is to go to 8 Duchess St. W. I'll arrange for that . . . if she hasn't sailed before this reaches you. Which I dare say she will have.

One never knows when a boat train will arrive. Of course I will do my best to meet her and she had better telephone from Liverpool or where ever she lands.

Dorothy wants to write a letter of welcome but there seems so slight a chance of even this note reaching you before she mother sails that I have told D. not to bother.

And mind you rent that house and follow after. We have been down here for a little over a fortnight and I have been plugging into the Fenollosa mss. at a great rate . .

That beastly magazine in Chicago will print one of the plays fairly soon and then you'll see what they are like.

I want to send this off by the first mail, so I wont run on very much.

We were married on the twentieth, I think I wrote but dont remember.

Of course if mother arrives at some impossible hour she must come straight to 5 H.P.C.

tell her to try and telegraph from Liverpool

yours

E. P.

The Duchess St. Adress is co Miss Withey 8 Duchess St. London. W.
Near Oxford Circus, and off Portland Place.

----

458. TLS

[May 1914]

Stone Cottage | Coleman's Hatch Sussex

Dear Mother

Your change of plan is very disconcerting. I suppose you'll come in the Autumn or sometime or other or if you rent the house.

It is quite certain that I shall not come to America. London is much more amusing. The Nishikigi is in the May 'poetry' with two bad misprints p. 41 'pricket's horn' is wrongly put 'cricket's'. Page 45 'faint substance' is wrongly put 'faith' substance.

Anyhow it ought to give dad some idea of the Fenollosa stuff which he has been wanting.

We have got through the larger chunk of our month here very quickly. return to London on Monday.

Can T.C.P. do anything about the embassy? Surely the present Dorcas society administration will finish at the next election??? anyhow? Won't it? Of course one can't tell from this side, and seeing very little news.

I don't see how I can invite both you and dad. There simply aint the transportation.

I have got through a lot more Fenollosa but dont know when or where it will appear.

I wonder if you have ever seen some paint tubes and brushes that I acquired ages since. The paint will be dried past utility I suppose but I'd be very glad if you would copy the names on the tubes, the names of the colours, as they were a carefully selected scale which I have forgotten. If they are illegible you might get Whiteside to give you the list of his seven colour series . s.v.p.

Also I suppose the brushes are so light that they could be sent for tuppence.

I asked the N.A. to send dad my article on Upward but dont know whether its out, or if they'e sent it.

D. says you'd better come over.

We have bothe eaten a great deal and are monstrously fat from rurality. (not corpulent). I suppose it isnt actually disfiguring yet. And we go back to town before it is likely to become so.

Enclosed from Richard re/ affairs in London. ref. to Imagiste Anthology.

Have done nothing much else except my lecture for the 30th.

I shall probably take up with 'Poetry and Drama' (a quarterly that used to be the Poetry Review =) when I get back to London.

Dont know that there's much else. I continue to discover young poets.

> Love to you and dad, and salutations to the elect.
>
> Yrs
>
> E. P.

Pound's 'Allen **Upward** *Serious' was in the* New Age *for 23 April 1914.* Poetry & Drama *published two poems by Pound in June, 'Fan-Piece for her Imperial Lord' and 'Ts'ai Ch'h', and another in December, 'Dead Ione', but nothing more.*

+>==<+

459. TLS

15 June 1914

5 Holland Place Chambers | Kensington W. [London]

Dear Mother

Right O.

No Church Walk wouldn't do, besides it is full. Cournos has my old room.

I have just written a note to Miss Withey. 8 Duchess St. Portland Place. W. (just off Oxford Circus).

Details in case your boat arrives at 3. A.M. I don't know what one can do in August but I reckon we can find something or other.

Glad dad has determined to come too.

I dont know when I am likely to write molasses and sugar, I should say vaguely 'never',. However there are plenty of people doing it so you won't lack for verses, pretty pretty verses like the sitting-in-the-tree birds

'tell me not in mournful wish-wash
life's a sort of sugared dish-wash'
and all that sort of thing.

My soul's nose is scratching itself on the stars
I use the clouds as a hanky.
Blow ye winds heigho.

or

'cluck, my chicken,
how i love the farmyard. a sonata in four acts.

Le mouvement vorticiste is well under weigh. BLAST is I believe, really coming out this week. Delicate sensitive work.

Suffragettes are blowing up most everything else. I really dont know that there's much other news. Various people come to tea, or feed us dinner. Poetry for July will possibly have some poems you wont like in it.

Etc.

This will catch you just about as you are starting so I wont run on.

D. sends her best salutations to both of you.

yrs.

E. P.

15 - 6 - '14

*The **Vorticist movement** led by Wyndham Lewis was primarily concerned with the visual arts, but included literature also. Lewis's over-sized magazine BLAST printed Vorticist manifestos, writings and designs. Pound contributed 'Salutation the Third' with other 'Lustra', and 'Vortex', a prose manifesto. The August (not July) number of Poetry printed 'Το Καλον', 'The Study in Aesthetics', 'The Bellaires', 'Salvationists', 'Amitiés', 'Ladies', 'The Seeing Eye', and 'Abu Salammamm: A Song of Empire'—all but the last were included in Lustra (1916).*

460. TLS

[c.12 July 1914]

5 Holland Place Chambers | Kensington. London. W

Dear Dad

How would you expect me to be writing letters to U.S.A. when it was decently supposed that you were en route.

We now expect you on the 28 or 29th. Directions re/ Duchess St. still hold.

I dare say you'll have London mostly to yourselves during August, but as you say that dont matter, all right.

I dont see that there's much to write.

BLAST IS out. You can get what other news there is on arrival.

Blast dinner on Tuesday is occupying my spare moments as Lewis has gone to Paris for the interim and left me to run the thing.

Vorticism is sweeping the land. Blast is positively the largest periodical ever printed.

etc. come on over and dont expect me to stand here talkin.

D. sends love to you both.

Love to you & mother

E. P.

In the summer of 1914, Isabel and Homer Pound visited Ezra and London. Homer returned to his work at the Mint in Philadelphia about the end of July; Isabel stayed on, and would sail for New York from Liverpool in mid-October.

4

War Years: 1914–18

World War One broke out at the beginning of August: following the assassination of its Archduke at Sarajevo, Austria-Hungary declared war on Serbia; its ally Germany declared war on Russia on 1ˢᵗ August, and on the 3ʳᵈ invaded Belgium and declared war on France; Great Britain and its empire declared war on Germany on 4ᵗʰ August, and against Austria-Hungary on the 10ᵗʰ. Austria-Hungary and Germany were joined by Turkey (in November), and by Bulgaria (in October 1915); Britain and France, in addition to their dominions and colonies, were joined by Japan (immediately), by Italy (in May 1915), and by the USA (in April 1917).

461. ALS [*embossed letterhead*] 5, Holland Place Chambers, Kensington, W.

7 September 1914

[London]

Dear Dad

Sorry you had such a hell of a trip.

Hower it seems unlikely that it will occur again.

We are all down at Aldebrugh for a fortnight, as I dare say mother has written.

She'll be glad to get the $100 as the steamship Co wont hold a passage except for full payment in . . advance.

You probably get more war news than we do

There is no other news. The Fortnightly Review for Sept 1. contains my article on 'Vorticism'.

I've corrected proofs of the Quarterly article. & am finishing up another batch of the Fenollosa's notes & translations

guess thats about the lot

yrs

E. P.

7 / 9 / '14

[*Dorothy's hand*] My best love to you

DOROTHY.

462. ALS [*embossed letterhead*] 5, Holland Place Chambers, Kensington, W.
[after 22 September 1914]

[London]

Dear Dad,

I haven't written because I thought mother was keeping you posted. - same
re/ the £5 from Liverpool. - which I did think I wrote about.

re/ . letter to E.P.D.P.

yes come again this autumn if you like but DONT return 3$^{\underline{d}}$ class.

Brzeska has written from the front or near it, at least in shell range.

May Sinclair is with the red X in Belgium.

Have done a few notes for Poetry. found a new good poet named Eliot.
shaken down some more Japanese play notes & got in a few cheques.

guess thats the lot.

love

E. P. D. P.

Don't know how mother is making out, - hope she isn't bored to death. - I can't
knock off work and look after her - and as before said London at this season is
not gay. - let alone its being war time

yrs

.E P.

*Gaudier-Brzeska had enlisted as a volunteer in the French army in August. T. S. **Eliot**
introduced himself to Pound on 22 September. Pound's '**few notes for Poetry**' were
probably 'The Audience' in the October number.*

+>—-—=+

463. ALS [*embossed letterhead*] 5, Holland Place Chambers, Kensington, W.
Wednesday [c.14 October 1914]

[London]

Dear Mother:

It has seemed very natural to have you here. & quite odd now without you.

I'm glad you've got comfortably into Chester.

Had a delightful day yesterday with Dolmetsch - his clavicords virginals,
harpsicords etc.

wish you could have heard his ancient music

Be good & dont get into a muddle.

yrs

.E P.

your letter from Chester has no address on it. hence I send this to the Steamer.

+>—-—=+

464. ALS

Friday (16 October 1914)

[London]

Dear Mother.

The enclosed came directed to me.

Also Cook sent an announcement of the sailing of your boat & what trains would leave London – That I do not enclose as it would be no use.

I forward a letter from H. L. P. no particular events to record here.

Yeats to tea wednesday, Wadsworth in yesterday.

<u>mss</u> of <3^d> Jap. article back from typists to be worked on.

Hope you have enjoyed Chester as much as you expected to you.

Love from us both & bon voyage.

E. P.

465. TLS [*embossed letterhead*] 5, Holland Place Chambers, Kensington, W.

24 / 10 /'14

[London]

Dear Dad

Dont know that there's much new. Find Dolmetsch very interesting, and have commisioned a clavicord. Hope to be able to pay for it by the time it is finished.

Am stirring up a college of Arts, prospectus in next Egoist.

<u>Noh</u> article in Quarterly Rev. for October. London not yet dynamited by the Deutschers.

Enc. yours to mother which arrived after her sailing. She seems to have enjoyed Chester and to expect pleasant Xing.

Have sent off mss. of another Jap article to north American review, don't know that they'll print it.

Am reading Boissier's 'Fin du Paganisme' and dont see that there's much chance of my having anything else to do for some time.

Brzeska's sister heard from him on the 7th. that's ten days later than his 2nd. note to me.

Walter over for a concert, that is to say he played with the orchestra at Queens hall, last night. Yeats back in town.

Wilenski has sent in a good article of contemporary german poetry, for Poetry.

Eliot has sent in a good poem for same.

guess that's the lot.

Love from us both.

E.P. D.P.

Yeats' wedding present to the Pounds had been a cheque, and, after commissioning the **clavichord**, *Pound told Yeats that he hoped it would 'flower into deathless music—at least into an image of more gracious & stately times'.*

The ambitious 'prospectus' for The **College of Arts** *was published in the* Egoist *on 2 November. It would offer, particularly to American students wishing to study abroad and cut off by the war from Vienna or Prague, 'contact with artists of established position, creative minds, men for the most part who have already suffered in the cause of their art'; and it would 'aim at an intellectual status no lower than that attained by the courts of the Italian Renaissance'. The faculty would include: Gaudier-Brzeska (sculpture); Wyndham Lewis (painting); Edward Wadsworth (design); Reginald Wilenski (portraiture and history of painting); Arnold Dolmetsch (ancient music); Felix Salmond ('cello); K. R. Heyman (piano); Ezra Pound (comparative poetry); Ivan Korshune (John Cournos), (Russian novelists); Zinaida Vangerowa (Russian contemporary thought); Alvin Langdon Coburn (photography); Mrs Dolmetsch (XVI century dances). The College did not materialise.*

The '<u>Noh</u>* **article***' in the* Quarterly Review *was a long study of 'The Classical Drama of Japan', edited from the Fenollosa manuscripts, and including complete translations of 'Kinuta' amd 'Hagoromo'. In expanded form, it would become Part III of Pound's 'Noh' or Accomplishment (1916/1917). The other 'Jap. Article' did not appear in* North American Review.

*Eliot's '***good poem***' was 'The Love Song of J. Alfred Prufrock'. Harriet Monroe found it lacking in vitality, but at Pound's insistence did publish it in* Poetry *in June 1915.*

⊹⇒═⇐⊹

466. ALS [*embossed letterhead*] 5, Holland Place Chambers, Kensington, W.

2 November 1914

[London]

Dear Dad.

We have heard again from Gaudier. He was O. K. on oct 25th.

May Sinclair has got back from Belgium. having been in Antwerp.

Wadsworth is drilling in some home-defense corps. Cunninghame Graham is going to the U. S. A. to buy horses.

Hulme is being trained to be a gunner & may have already gone to the front.

I have been busy with this College of Arts propaganda.

Guess that's about all

Love to you & mother.
E. P.

2 / 11 / '14

D. P. requests me to state that the chocolates were duly delivered on Oct. 30th. Thank you.

⊹⇒═⇐⊹

467. ALS [*embossed letterhead*] 5, Holland Place Chambers, Kensington, W.
(9 November 1914)

[London]

Dear Mother:

Sorry you had such a bad trip home. Hope you are O.K. again. Dad said you had recovered.

Last news from Brzeska on the 27ᵗʰ Oct .- he was then O.K., bored. doing an essay for BLAST & cutting statues with his jack knife & an entrenching tool.

Miss Sinclair is back. & her diary will probably make amusing reading.

I think I wrote that Yeats & we are going down to Stone Cottage for Jan & Feb.

Wadsworth is doing wood-cuts. Lewis decorating Hueffer's study.

I enclose observer summary of the week - which I believe you used to follow.

I am reading Bossier's 'La Fin du Paganisme' which is very entertaining.

The early christians were as bad as the present lot.

Have met the Dulacs since you were here. He is interesting when he can be got to talk.

Love from us both.

E. P.

+⤞⤝+

468. ALS [*embossed letterhead*] 5, Holland Place Chambers, Kensington, W.
[30 November 1914]

[London]

Dear Dad:

Am sending some C. o A. circulars by same post.

Have busted into Fenollosa's chinese notes. - (not Japanese.) & found some fine stuff. that has kept me going for the past ten days.

Yeats in night before last, etc. etc. Have been mostly absorbed in the Chinese stuff - very fine. You'll see it in time. Have sent some to 'Poetry'.

War losing interest. have stopped taking in the paper. Wadsworth has several new woodcuts & a daughter. Lewis has a new studio. Dolmetsch is about to have a concert .

C o A has taken £ 10-10. via Coburn.

Brzeska is slightly wounded. & in sole possession of an abandoned vialla. having the time of his life apparently .

Love to you & mother.

EP. D.P.

'*Exile's Letter, From the Chinese of Rihaku (Li Po)*' *would appear in* Poetry *in March 1915.* Cathay, *containing thirteen poems **from the Chinese** (including '*Exile's Letter*'), along with Pound's previously published version of the Anglo-Saxon '*Seafarer*', would be published by Elkin Mathews in April 1915.*

+▰▱◀+

469. ALS [*embossed letterhead*] 5, Holland Place Chambers, Kensington, W.
[December 1914]

[London]

Dear Mother:
Your's to hand. Sorry you tried to bathe - don't do it again.

———

Bulletins announce Cracow in flames. Dont know that there's much nearer news. Gaudier has been named for promotion to be Sergeant - Mr & Mrs Dolmetsch & Brigit in to tea yesterday.

Ask dad to send those notices of the Col of Arts to the <u>press</u>. How many more does he want.

'Poetry & Drama' is stopping at Xmas & I dare say the Egoist wont last much longer.

Hilda back from the country - looking more robust.

Have finished 'Boissier'. Lewis installed in new studio. Wadsworth doing more wood-cuts. Yeats in Ireland.

Dolmetsch very intelegent & considerable addition to life.

Am cogitating still another article on the 'Noh'. hope dad has been able to get the October 'Quarterly' from the library. I haven't a spare copy and as all the stuff will someday be in a book there's no use spending 6 shillings on spare magazines.

As for 'Julian's' they haven't turned out an artist for the last 30 years.

Love to you both.
E P

'*Cracow in flames*' *was an exaggeration. The battle of Cracow, 12–26 November 1914, in which the occupying Austria-Hungarian army were attacked by Russian forces, was fought out in the country around the city.* '**Julian's**', *a Paris art academy, at which Pound's Wabash friend, Fred Vance, had studied (as mentioned in 'Three Cantos. II' (1917)).*

+▰▱◀+

470. ALS [*embossed letterhead*] 5, Holland Place Chambers, Kensington, W.
(December 1914)

[London]

Dear Dad:

Don't suppose there's much comment to be made re/ T. C. P. – I suppose he was about ready.

Heard from Brzeska yesterday. He is back in the trenches, apparently not very active. I imagine he is on the border S. E of Rheims, tho he is, of course, not allowed to say.

Cambell. (Joseph) is over from Ireland & is coming in this evening.

I go on with the Chinese.

Do you ever see the St. Louis 'Mirror' if so you might pass it on this way. a chap called Webster Ford is writing good verse in it .

Everyone here is surviving and in health.

D. P. doing black & white designs.

Wadsworth woodcuts. Lewis cogitating another BLAST.

Guess that's about all.

> Love to you & mother.
> E. P.

*Pound's grandfather, **Thaddeus Coleman Pound**, died 21 November 1914, penniless in Chicago. He was however honoured in obituaries and eulogies for his earlier services to the State of Wisconsin, as member of its Assembly, Lieutenant-Governor, and representative in Congress. 'Webster Ford' was the pseudonym being used by Edgar Lee Masters for his 'Spoon River' poems.*

471. ALS [*embossed letterhead*] 5, Holland Place Chambers, Kensington, W.
20 - 12 – '14

[London]

Dear Dad

Merry Xmas such as it is. Thanks for Xmas donations from you and mother received.

Have got a good little book out of Fenollosa's Chinese notes.

Second BLAST well under weigh.

Have done another imagiste article. This time for the undignified 'T. P.' however the revenues demand it .

Dolmetsch concert a success. Saw G. B. S. there he looks extinct. like a doddering copy of Tolstoy - it was quite a shock to see the change in his once alert appearance.

Dinner with M. Sinclair & some dull Belgians Friday.

Have met a very interesting Capt. Baker. full of stray facts about India & Cashmere. - very intelligent - also interested in Chinese.

Walter has gone back to Paris. Lewis having afternoons - on Saturdays.

Cambell still here. I wonder if you can get anything of his from the library. 'Mearing Stones'. 'Judgment' are two of the books.

Plarr has brought out a little book on Dowson which I've not yet seen.

Love to you & mother & Xmas greetings to the family at Toiga.

yrs

E. P.

BLAST *no.2, a 'War Number', would not appear until July 1915. Pound's '**Imagisme** and England. A Vindication and an Anthology', would appear in 'T P's Weekly for 20 February 1915. About* **Captain Guy Baker** *he would write in a 1918 essay: 'A wild man comes into my room and talks of piles of turquoises in a boat, a sort of shop-house-boat east of Cashmere. His talk is full of the colour of the Orient. Then I find he is living over an old-clothes shop in Bow.' (Literary Essays p. 436) Baker's anecdotes figure at the end of Canto 19.*

472. ALS [*embossed letterhead*] 5, Holland Place Chambers, Kensington, W.
24 Dec. 1914

[London]

Dear Mother:

A package arrived two days ago with two chest protectors & various implements with which D was much pleased.

Saw Orage monday. he asked tenderly after father said that he liked him & that he was very intelligent.

I am doing a new series of articles for the New Age - beginning with the new year. Will send them on. I'm doing Dolmetsch. vorticism. Epstein etc.

Plarr has just brought out a charming book on Dowson. have spent the morning reviewing it for Poetry.

Have had an offer for a book on Noh or on troubadours but it was not good enough so I have refused.

Heard from Gaudier this A.M. he's in a wet trench on the Aisne.

Have done an article on Imagisme for T. P.

as I want to finish the N A series before I go off to the country. I am fairly busy for the moment.

'Poetry & Drama' is to stop for a year.

That is, I think, nearly all the news.

7 column of violent abuse of BLAST just arrived from New Zealand. Madame Strindberg said to be lecturing on Vorticism in America. Victorious Christmas.

yrs

. EP .

The 'new series for the New Age' consisted of seven articles under the general heading 'Affirmations'. Pound's review of **Plarr's Ernest Dowson**: Reminiscences, Unpublished Letters and Marginalia *(Elkin Mathews, 1915), would be in* Poetry *in April 1915. Pound's letter, dated '21/12/'14', in reply to the* **abuse of** BLAST *no.1, would be printed in the offending magazine,* Triad *(Wellington, NZ), in March 1915, preceded by some further editorial comment from Frank Morton, characterising* BLAST *as 'the lunatic organ of the Vorticists', and characterising Pound as 'one of the queerest fakes that ever came within the field of criticism'. Pound's reply began: 'It is an excellent and honourable thing to be condemned in company with Cezanne and Picasso'.*

+ >—<— +

473. ALS [*embossed letterhead*] 5, Holland Place Chambers, Kensington, W.

30/ 12/ '14

[London]

Dear Dad.

Mathews is publishing a little book of Chinese Poems in March.

'The Drama' a Chicgo ¼^{ly}. is printing a big wad of Jap plays (5 or 6) & notes. probably in May.

Greetings of the season. 'Victorious Xmas' & New Year. etc.

Offered that book to E. M. yesterday. & signed the contract this A.M. The war seems to have waked him up.

Will send you N. Age. Orge asked affectionately after you last monday.

Love to you & mother.

EP

New year greetings to family at Tioga.

Drama *would publish in May 1915 'The Classical Stage of Japan: Ernest Fenollosa's Work on the Japanese "Noh"', containing translations of seven plays—in expanded form this would become Parts I and II of* 'Noh' or Accomplishment *(1916/1917).*

+ >—<— +

474. TLS

16 January 1915

Stone Cottage | Coleman's Hatch | Sussex

Dear Dad,

Have been down here, as you know, naturally there is nothing to write.

I suppose you get the New Age, I have ordered it sent you. Am scribbling those articles. Have read a big dull book on Macchiavelli, by Villari. Yeats is doing his autobiography. D. is working on a cover design for another edition of Ripostes.

Heard from Gaudier, via Mrs Shakespear, yesterday. He was O.K. on the 9th., has been promoted to corporal, has less hard work, has been 25 days without dry place to sleep or time to wash, now however back out of front line for two weeks rest.

We are having a great gale of wind, woke last night suspecting it was an earthquake.

Love to you & mother

Yrs,

E. P.

16 / 1 / '15

The 'big dull book' was The Life and Times of Niccolo Machiavelli *(1892), by Pasquale Villari (1827–1917).*

⊹══╾┹

475. ALS

1 February 1915

Stone Cottage [Sussex]

Dear Mother

I don't know that there's much news in this wild region

We are reading Doughty's 'Arabia–Deserta' a fine book. and also a lot of dam'd translations of icelandic sagas.

W. B. Y. has done some poems & is rebeginning a dam'd play.

Gaudier has, as I think I wrote, been promoted he was O.K. a few days ago.

Vorticism is to acquire a sort of hall near Park Lane, according to last accounts.

My next batch of poems is to be in Poetry in March.

My other diversions you will find in the New Age as it appears.

Love to you & dad.

E. P.

Feb 1st.

Pound was reading aloud in the evenings **Doughty's Travels in Arabia Deserta** *to save Yeats's eyes. Vorticism's '**sort of hall**' was for Wyndham Lewis's Rebel Arts Centre, set up in dissidence from Roger Fry's Omega Workshops. It would be bombed in a Zeppelin raid and burnt out in September. Pound's '**batch of poems**' for the March* Poetry *included 'Provincia Deserta' and 'The Coming of War: Actaeon'.*

---

476. ALS

7 February 1915

Stone Cottage | Coleman's Hatch | Sussex

Dear Mother:

I keep forgetting, I met old Wadsworth before I left London, & he wanted to know all about all the american ditto. Wanted 'Wadsworth Family in America'.

I told him I didn't think the book could be bought, but that we could easily lend him our copy.

Unless you know of ditto. for sale will you mail me our copy (to London).

W. B. Y. has gone up to town for 3 days. So we are placid and uneventful.

I have read a number of eighteenth century works from the cottage book shelves - a horrible era. - very like the century magazine of today.

W. B. Y. & us still swamped in sagas. and he is begining a play - Gaudier still alive, & damp.

We are completely cut off from the world here.

regiment came over the hill the other day & drank up our cider. otherwise the war has not yet penetrated this county.

Eliot is the only new discovery. I dare say something of his will get printed sooner or later & give him a designation.

Salutations to H L P. D wants to thank him for one florin. recd.

He seems worried about your health. I hope your weariness of the return voyage has done away with itself by now. That ocean is a mistake.

Love to you & dad.

E. P.

Feb. 7.

---

477. ALS
Feb 12ᵗʰ [1915]

Stone Cottage | Colemans Hatch | Sussex

Dear Mother:

Have just corrected proofs of my chinese book. & sent typed mss of same to father.

D. has made a very good cover design for another issue of repostes.

will send copy when I get one to spare. The sole proof & has gone back to Mathews.

Gaudier. O.K. on Feb 4ᵗʰ.

This A.M. whole battery of artillery deployed for our benefit on the heath before Stone Cottage. That's about as near as we'll get to the war zone. I reckon.

Sunday, Feb. 14
No change -

By the time I get back to London I shall have spent 6½ months out of the last 13, in rural surroundings, - which is all that can be reasonably expected. - even if I do it free. No news. Have found a few sane paragraphs in Eliphas Levi. Doughty's 'Arabia Deserta' still occupies the evenings.

Love to you & Dad.
E. P.

Eliphas Levi (Alphonse Louis Constant, 1810–75), French occultist, author of several works on ritual magic and mystery, and an influence upon the Hermetic Order of the Golden Dawn of which Yeats was a member.

+>==<+

478. ALS
[?late February 1915]

Stone Cottage | Coleman's Hatch | Sussex

Dear Dad:

It seems unlikely that the germans will blow up this island. & not beyond probability that they will sink a few ocean liners.

Besides, as I have pointed out before there is nothing for me to do in America. Neither the pig faced Gribbel nor the goatheaded Curtis is likely to pay me for doing good work - or bad either for that matter. Nor does the spectacle of the American magazine world allure me.

Yeats just reads out that an American boat (cotton boat) has hit a german mine. I dont suppose Wilson has guts enough to send over the navy - even if my glorious fatherland has still got one. - It would be exhillerating but very imprudent. Besides I dont know that a german conquest would do any real harm.

However it ought to have been swifter in its progress if it was to be painless. etc- etc.

I have as yet seen little desire on the part of the great American people, in peace _or_ war, to have me amongst 'em.

Besides you know quite well that _you_ prefer London, & your life is less wrapt up in the arts than mine is.

I sent a letter to grandmother some weeks ago but addressed it to 2020 Estangh St. I now find they have moved to the next block. I wonder if she got it.?

Enclose proposed cover for the chinese book. it is not to be this colour.

We go up to London at the beginning of next week. I dare say you will have the March poetry by the time you get this note.

Thanks for the wad of magazines. W. B. Y. has got one act of his play liyed out. I don't know that there is much more to say. Will send you D's cover for 'Ripostes'. she has done one or two new pictures. And so on.

Love to you & mother. & don't worry about the island. its still anchored & the bank of England still keeps open.

yrs

E. P.

+>==·==<+

479. ALS

(6 March 1915)

5 H. P. C [London]

Dear Mother:

Came back to town on Monday & promptly came down with influenza. Whence I am by now again up on end.

Recd. a fat batch of Times Chronicles this morning.

Naturally I have not collected much news during the week.

The 'London Group' is having a large show. Huge canvass by Lewis. Gaudier's sketches from the trenches. etc.

That's about all the news I have imbibed.

The Medico says I may go forth into the outer world on Monday - more anon.

Love to you & dad

.E P.

+>==·==<+

480. ALS [*embossed letterhead*] 5, Holland Place Chambers, Kensington, W.
16 March 1915

[London]

Dear Dad.

Here's D's cover for the new edtn. of Ripostes.

There's a lot of good stuff ready for next Blast. which I have seen at Lewis' this P. M.

Quinn has written me to know where he can get a good Brzeska statue.

I am sending you a bundle of letters to me from various people. = which same I want <u>kept</u>. I send them because some few of them may amuse you & mother.

Cournos just in. Hopeful about getting his book of translations from 'Sologub, published soon.

yrs
.E.
Love to you & mother

16 / 3 / 15

481. ALS [*embossed letterhead*] 5, Holland Place Chambers, Kensington, W.
(6 April 1915)

[London]

Deer Dad

Recd. $10. in letter from mother. for which same, our dutiful salutations.

D. rolled up your sketch with some others unfinished, & some bad ones as a wrapper & it will be sent as soon as the P.O. reopens. (this being Easter monday.)

Thanks for the Hamilton clipping. 'How very like Prexy Stryker' !!!!!!!

Have had a Chilean, & Mexican painter & a most interesting Jap. together with Epstein & Capt. Baxer in here to tea various days of this week.

Jap. interested in dancing, & helpful & interested in 'Noh' work.

Woodward has sent in a criticism of the Wilson administration violent enough to please the New Age where it will shortly appear.

I plan to bring out another small anthology in the autumn. Eliot, Webster Ford. Goldring, etc.

vol of 'Cathay' sent last week.

Hueffer gone to the country for a month.

Spring not yet too apparent.

Tuesday.

Recd. great wad of dam'd papers representing almost complete waste of 7c. postage & the general depravity of America.

Coz. wants to know whether Billy Sunday is a black man? The invention of newspapers was a great evil though the invention of hell was probably worse.

Barnard's museum laudable. but the other sculptor sheer muck.

Basta.

yrs

E. P.

The 'Jap interested in dancing' and in the Noh was Michio Ito(w) (1893–1961)–he would dance the part of the hawk in Yeats's At the Hawk's Well. Pound's **Catholic Anthology** *would be published by Elkin Mathews in November.* **Billy Sunday** *(1862–1935), the celebrated American evangelist and revivalist preacher, was not 'a black man'. Dorothy was known as '***Coz***' in her family circle.*

⊬⊐═⊏⊣

482. ALS [*embossed letterhead*] 5, Holland Place Chambers, Kensington, W.

(6 May 1915)

[London]

Dear Dad:

Have rec'd various attentions (chiefly medical <u>via</u> the american mails.). in return. 'Times' & Woodwards article. Also have transmitted yr. order to Mathews.

Wedding aniversary cheque goes into ' Jo jo'. So we get the work of art & Gaudier the cash. = no waste. & plenty of monument.

Enclose some prints. that may entertain you.

I dare say D. Has told what news there is - will write later

yrs

E. P.

'Jo jo' was Gaudier-Brzeska's 'Boy with a Coney'.

⊬⊐═⊏⊣

483. TLS [*embossed letterhead*] 5, Holland Place Chambers, Kensington, W.

16 May 1915

[London]

Dear Dad

I dont think anything in particular has happened since I wrote, save the general events which you will see in the papers. <u>Itow</u> is the last item of interest

346

he is now dancing at the Coliseum but his work is naturally much too delicate to show on a huge stage. We are going down to the S. Kensington museum this p.m. to discuss Shang bronzes and the dance positions in the statues of Siva. He has written to Japan for books about the Noh. He is the first Jap I have met who has any intensity. Long faced not usual pie-faced type.

Vorticist show at the Dorè gallery to take pace in June, D working at an oil picture. 'Blast' in hands of the printer AT last. also promised for June. Be sure and get Edgar Master's 'Spoon River Anthology', it is the best home grown product America has seen for SOME time.

Walter is over and his playing is much stronger and richer than it was some years ago, or even last year. He has however written nothing new.

We dined with the Dulacs on Wednesday. or Thursday.

Musical at Mrs Fowlers on Tuesday. Have got Coria a job in Langleys grocery shop, his family, as I think I wrote, destitute from Mexican revolutionettes.

Love to you and mother.

yrs

E. P.

May 16th

+≻═━≺+

484. TLS [*embossed letterhead*] 5, Holland Place Chambers, Kensington, W.

23 May 1915

[London]

Dear Mother

I think it is unlikely that we shall seek refuge in America. True they wont have Americans in the English Army yet, and that I am unlikely therefore to enter active service, but it is still possible that I may find some indirect work to do.

Apart from war considerations it should be granted that I have a career or something of that sort to consider, or at least an income to make and that a trip to America would not in the least assist in the process.

I am working on a long poem. I think I sent the 'Times' review of Cathay. There is a faint chance of my getting a paper to run. D is at work on a picture for the coming show. Blast exists in proofs so you may expect it in a month or six weeks.

Eliot down from Oxford yesterday, very intelligent. Kreymborg, the starter of the Glebe, has started something else and has written over for stuff and suggestions, but has not mentioned the name of his magazine.

Mencken's correspondence is amusing. I suppose the enclosed small blast is partly his work, he has sent me a packet to distribute. It is an amazingly comprehensive analysis of contemporary American literature.

You will by now have received various missives containing thanks for two batches of medicine, the wedding anniversary gift, the Wadsworth family history. Do you want the latter returned now or after the war. Old Wad was very appreciative of the attention.

The Wisconsin, legislature has sent me a document relating to T. C.'s demise.

The Cheltenham school board sent me a year ago a document relating to a donation of books from father. Am I expected to write an oration in return?

Hilda's infant died, so dont send it a christening spoon, or embarrass Mrs Doolittle with enquiries. Hilda is, I believe recovering quite nicely. They have gone to Hampstead and now reside there beyond the reach of any known form of transport and in excellent air. As Gaudier, it (i.e residence in Hampsted) is good for Richard, he will no longer be tormented by doubt.

Etchells is back in London again. Hueffer is in the country but I will convey your appreciations when he gets back. The book is very good. I trust the faculty of my rotten University will read and digest it. The preface contains a number of statements similar to those which I have made repeatedly any time for the last ten years.

I have been reading various volumes of Henry James. If your unfortunate continent had only familiarized itself more fully with his excellent works it would be a far pleasanter, a far more possible habitat.

I recommend father to get Stendhal's 'Chartreuse de Parme', I suppose there is a translation. He will enjoy the opening chapters and need not bother to finish it.

The day is most excellent and I shall now go out to enjoy it.

Love to you and dad.

E. P.

May 23rd 1915

> '**I am working on a long poem**'—*this may be the earliest mention of Pound's beginning seriously on his Cantos. **T. S. Eliot** was at Oxford on a Harvard Travelling Fellowship for the academic year 1914–15, working on his doctoral thesis on the philosopher F. H. Bradley. **Kreymborg's** new magazine was to be called* Others (1915–19); *he had published* Des Imagistes *as an issue of* The Glebe *in February 1914.* **Hueffer's book** *was* When Blood is Their Argument: An Analysis of Prussian Culture (1915). *Its critique of Prussian 'Kultur' chimed with Pound's holding that 'Kultur' responsible for the way literature was taught, or, in his view, mistaught, during his time as a student at the University of Pennsylvania.*

⊣━━⊢

1. Isabel Weston Pound

2. Homer Loomis Pound

3. Ezra in uniform of Cheltenham Military Academy, *c.* 1900

4. Aunt Frank

5. Family group, Alhambra Palace, July 1902 – Aunt Frank, Mrs Miller,
Homer, Isabel, Ezra

6. Ezra at Hamilton College, *c.* 1905

7. Isabel Pound, 'a proud Presbyterian peacock' (letter no. 195)

8. Homer at the Mint, 1896

9. Dorothy and Ezra, *c.* 1913

10. Blunt presentation, January 1914 (see letter no. 446) – Victor Plarr, Sturge Moore, W. B. Yeats, Wilfred Scawen Blunt, E. P., Richard Aldington, Frank Flint

11. EP, 1916 – this print inscribed with a line from EP's A Lume Spento was shown by IWP and HLP to Harding Weston, Isabel's aged father then in an Old Soldiers Home, in 1926

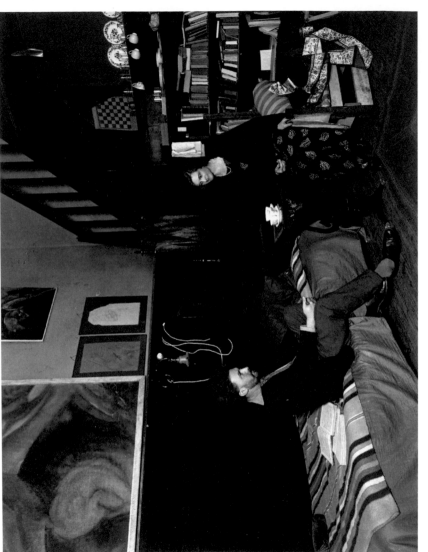

12. EP and DP in their Paris studio, c. 1922

13. Homer Pound in the 1920s

14. EP and Mary at Gais, 1927 (see letter no. 798)

15. Isabel Pound in Rapallo, 1935

16. The How(e) coat of arms

485. ALS [*embossed letterhead*] 5, Holland Place Chambers, Kensington, W.
[after 31 May 1915]

[London]

Dear Dad

The arrival of Zeppelins seems to have filled London with a quiet content-
ment. We have hopes that they'll get the church at the corner, but it is obvious
that they they will have no effect on the nerves of the inhabitants.

I have been agitating the question of a good weekly paper - nothing yet
settled very little else done

Walter gave a concert this P.M. & cleared up a little money.

Has 'Drama' come out? with the Noh plays.?

Kreymborg is starting a new magazine of sorts & has some of my stuff for it.

The Irish Players are over, but haven't much news.

Had a pleasant note from Schelling re/ 'Cathay'.

Eliot has done a few amusing poems. I have done a satire (vide Kreymborg's
venture). & a long provençal rigmarole.

Love to you & mother,

- E -

D. has had a photo - kodak snap taken- await results.

The first **Zeppelin** *air raid on London was on 31 May 1915. Pound's animus against 'the
church at the corner' was due to his not appreciating the playing of its bells. The* **'Irish
Players'***, with whom Yeats was much involved, were from the Abbey Theatre in Dublin.
For Pound's reply to Felix* **Schelling's** *'pleasant note' see his* Selected Letters: 1907–41
(letter no. 71). Three of Eliot's **'amusing poems'** *were published in* Poetry *in October—
'The Boston Evening Transcript', 'Aunt Helen', and 'Cousin Nancy'. Pound's own
'satire' was probably 'L' Homme Moyen Sensuel', first published in the* Little Review *in
September 1917, with a note that it was 'written in 1915'. (Six short poems from* Lustra
were included in Kreymborg's Others *in November 1915.) The* **'provençal rigmarole'**
would have been 'Near Perigord', published in Poetry *in December.*

486. TLS [*embossed letterhead*] 5, Holland Place Chambers, Kensington, W.
June 11th 1915

[London]

Dear dad

Coz after many tribulations has succeded in getting herself KodakVs, and
then the only one that comes out is one with her tongue out.

I enclose cards to the VORTICIST show. also press cutting. May raise a
katalog later., you wont be able to get in for the private view, as it was yesterday,

so there's no use making a special trip for it, still you'll be glad to know it was a very pleasant occasion.

Mother's letter to D rec'd this AM.M., and thanks for same are here inclosed. Damn Mrs Lorrrrrimer's tea party.

I have just written a note on Willie Bryan's tactful resignation, I suppose you'll be recrossing the Atlantic as a bold volunteer in another six weeks time. Oh the rotterdamn dutch and the gotterdamn dutch and the other dammmmm dutch of the dutch compaignee!!!

The note as printed this evening is rather better that Woody Willie's 'Tew prowd tew fite.' talk. Roosevelt is dead right in his first manifesto about America's duty to civilization.

Gaudier is getting very tired of the trenches its time someone came in and hurried matters. Bravo for the Dagos. I hope they'll get to Trieste before Joyce starves to death.

I believe Alfred Kreymborg, once of the Glebe is starting a new magazinelet called others, in which you will shortly find some stuff by yrs. truly. A few animadversions on old women (of the male sex).

Orrick Johns and Eliot have both sent me in some good poems. Masters, as you say, is good stuff.

A young chap called Bodenheim sent me letter and some verse this a.m.

I've got 1500 dollars pledged toward taking on a weekly paper, but it cant be done under 2500, so I suppose it wont come off . . . at least not yet a while.

A chap was in last week who thought he could find £1000 to do the thing in style but he hasn't yet put it over. Also Belloc was very nice about it and interested in the scheme. We do need an intelligent weekly. Belloc is about gord almighty in the publishing world at this moment, after years of fight.

There is a show of Whistlers at Colnaghi's but not a particularly good one. I dont know that there's much else to report. I have been busy rushing about re/ the Weekly project.

Eliot is intelligent which is a comfort, and Lewis does not bore one.

Love to you and mother, regards to grandmother and the Feet.

E. P.

I'll ask Wadsworth to have another shot at me some day soon!!

Extra by DP = O. S. has begun a new novel – [*in DP's hand*]

The first, and only, **Vorticist** *Exhibition had opened at the Doré Gallery in May.* **William Jennings Bryan** *had just resigned as* **President Woodrow Wilson's** *Secretary of State fearing, wrongly, that Wilson was preparing the US to enter the war. On 7th May, a German submarine had torpedoed the British registered Cunard passenger liner 'Lusitania' within sight of the Irish coast, causing the loss of nearly 1200 lives, 128 of them US citizens. There were calls for America to declare war on Germany; Wilson, in the 'note' Pound refers to, had made a formal protest to the German government about its violation of the laws of war; and Bryan, who was determined to maintain US neutrality at all costs, had mistaken that for a move towards war. Pound addressed the issue of*

US neutrality in the New Age in September and October, making clear his view that the
US should be with the Allies for the sake of civilization. Theodore Roosevelt, a leading
campaigner for American involvement in the war, had written in January to Sir Edward
Grey, Britain's Foreign Secretary, dissociating himself from the Wilson-Bryan policy of
neutrality. Italy entered the war on the side of the Allies in May 1915. **'Oh the rotterdamn dutch'**, variant of traditional drinking song. 'O. S.', Dorothy's mother, Olivia
Shakespear.

---

487. **TLS** [*embossed letterhead*] 5, Holland Place Chambers, Kensington, W.
(30 June 1915)

[London]

Dear Dad.

Brzeska has been killed, which is pretty disgusting, though I suppose it is a
marvel it hasn't happened before.

Walter is over, vide enclosed. He goes back to Paris after a final show on
Friday. Hueffer in this morning, has done another book, on France, and is now
asked for information about the Euphrates, heaven knows why.

Both his novel and the book on Germany are doing well. Mrs H. has out a
new novel also.

'Blast' is supposed to be being printed, I suppose you'll get a copy in due
season. I will send one along.

Have sent two long poems to U.S.A. one to 'Others' and one to 'Poetry'.

'DRAMA' is out as I suppose you have discovered by now. seven plays etc.

Chap, named Waley, from Museum, in last night to see Fenollosa mss.
Etchells back in town. Lewis flourishing. Why do you spend money on
such rot as the Century Magazine??????? gosh!!! Current Opinion is silly but
entertaining. . . . a sort of perpetual softening of the brain with a few
contemporary facts still visible.

Very interesting show of chinese jade etc. at the 'Burlington Fine Arts'.

Eliot has suddenly married a very charming young woman.

Love to you & mother,
dont know that there's much more on the bulletins
E. P.

Pound wrote to John Quinn on 13 July: '[Gaudier]-**Brzeska** was shot in the head in a
charge at Neuville St Vaast on June 5th. News got here about the 28th. died at once. I
believe.' **Hueffer's novel** was The Good Soldier. '**Mrs H**', Violet Hunt. No **long poem**
appeared in Others; 'Near Perigord' was in the December Poetry. T. S. **Eliot** married
Vivien(ne) Haigh-Wood on 28 June, without forewarning to his family or friends.

---

488. ALS [*embossed letterhead*] 5, Holland Place Chambers, Kensington, W.

[1915]

[London]

Dear Dad:

As you go through New York, do try to see John Quinn. (business address 31 Nassau St.) he has just ordered 20 copies of <u>Blast</u> for private use & he is some human being.

I dare say he is very busy all day. You might ask him to dine.

Say at 'Mouquins' (forget the address. 6th ave. about 34th st.) or at the 5th ave. restaurant (entrance on 24th st.)

They are both good, if I remember rightly. & not too exhausting (cashiely.). or better the Brevoort.?

hurriedly

E. P.

Love to mother.

⊰━━⊱

489. ALS [*embossed letterhead*] 5, Holland Place Chambers, Kensington, W.

[c.10 September 1915]

[London]

Dear Dad

I am busy writing 30 page letters to Quinn.

There may be a magazine.

There certainly will be a Vorticist show in New York – Lane [*word censored*] to publish my book on Gaudier.

The new anthology has gone to the press. D. is away in Malvern hills for a week with her family.

Zeps. got the old rebel art centre in [*word censored*] too late to do any damage.

I'm offering 5 shillings for the first <u>boche</u> who get either the church steeple or the vicar of Kensington. 10 for the bishop of London

You might drop a line to John Quinn 31 Nassau St. N. Y. Say you want prospectuses to distribute <u>if</u> or as soon as they are printed.

How many subscribers <u>can</u> you rope in?

Monthly magazine. edited by E. P. committee. Yeats Hueffer, DeGourmont. Quinn.

contributors everybody of importance.

Joyce. Lewis. etc. Cunningham Graham. etc.

Q. thinks he may be able to swing it. By the way if I should want to go to france I must show that 'I have been American for 3 generations'.

can you get copies of birth certificates of me. you & T.C.P.
& send them to me or will it cost too much

Love to you & mother. & grandmother

yrs

E. P.

I am decently registered

P.S. that statement from the Winsconsin legislature will do for T.C.P. all right. I think.

so dont bother about his.

*The official censor scissored out the location of the **Rebel Art Centre**, and with it the word(s) following 'Lane' on the other side of the sheet. Pound's **Gaudier-Brzeska**. A Memoir . . . Including the Published Writings of the Sculptor, and a Selection from his Letters, with Thirty-eight Illustrations, would be published by Lane in London and New York in April 1916. Pound's efforts to edit **a magazine** of his own came to nothing. '**H.H.S.**' (in following letter) is Dorothy's father, Henry Hope Shakespear.*

+⟩——⟨+

490. TLS [*embossed letterhead*] 5, Holland Place Chambers, Kensington, W.

25 September 1915

[London]

Dear Dad

Miscio Itow says he is going to the U.S. next week. I have given him a note of introduction to you. I hope you can put him up for a week. You will find him interesting, as soon as you can understand his english. I am very fond of him. He is samurai, not the round moon faced type of jap.

He has a good engangement in New York, I dont know that he is likely to come to Phila. but you can have him over for a week after he finishes with his theatre work. You can talk Noh. etc. I believe he has translated my hokku into Japanese. etc.

You can show him the mint, etc . . . You might also take him out to see Ames or C. G. Child at the University. I dont know that any of the other men would interest him or be interested.

I enclose a note from Schelling, some months old.

Anthology in the press. Lane is to publish the book on Gaudier as soon as I get it ready. We have just come back from five days at Daisy Meadow with the Fowlers.

Wadsworth doing two-colour wood cuts. Have done a few more 'Cathay' and am at work on a very long poem.

War stagnating, no excitement. No.one disturbed by Zeps. save concierges, catetakers and people of that sort. I believe one Zep was almost over the church at the corner, I offer five shillings to the first german who will bust up that damn bellfry or murder the vicar. Otherwise they seem unlikely to be of any real use to the community. Bomb very near H.H.S's office. , got nothing but an old bicycle shed.

Hueffer up in town on leave yeaterday, fed us at his club along with the Mastermans. No one seemed to have much news.

Fine report from a cousin of Fowlers that one zep had been brought down plump into the river, down stream 'somewhere in england'. Pleasant if true. Scott now in command of 'the fortress of London' is a good chap according to all acounts. I have met him twice, but once at a rather formal luncheon. he is the 'paint before gunnery' man. I wonder if that yarn has reached America or if I have told it you.

Etc. I must rush out and get in again before lunch.

Love to you and mother.

E. P.

25 Sept.

*Re. **Scott**, see letter no. 269.*

⊹⊱══⊰⊹

491. **TLS** [*embossed letterhead*] 5, Holland Place Chambers, Kensington, W.

[c.18 October 1915]

[London]

Dear Dad

Thanks for your alfred-david, sorry it cost you so much.

Itow is not going to America. The stinking swine of a company broke their contract with him. He is doing the enclosed in a studio up the road, DuLac and Ricketts have made him proper costumes, historic, from jap prints. etc. so it will be a fine show, proper 'Noh' movements etc.

'The birth of the dragon' is a choreograph of my own done about two years ago. I will send you translations of the sword-dance-poems later.

Book on Brzeska has gone off to the printers re-corrected in mss. I suppose it will come out in Jan.

The anthology has been corrected in proofs and ought to be ready in a couple of weeks.

Kreymborg writes me that there is something about Gaudier and myself in the Oct. 'Current Opinion', please send me a copy at once, as I want to stir up John Lane to do a full size portfolio of the drawings as well as the book on the sculpture.

Any american cuttings, showing interest in the matter will be of use.

I have not had a spare moment for weeks and don't expect any for three weeks more. I think we have had another Zep raid since I last wrote.

Love to you & mother. more anon.

E. P

*Homer Pound had sent an **affidavit**, drawn up by Woodward for a fee of $2.75, in the hope that it would serve to secure the permit to go over to France—see letter of c.10 September above. Pound published 'Sword-Dance and Spear-Dance. Texts of the Poems used with **Michio Itow's Dances**', in the New Age in December.*

+≥—+—≤+

492. TLS [*embossed letterhead*] 5, Holland Place Chambers, Kensington, W.

[c.30 October 1915]

[London]

Dear Dad

Thanks for the £2. received.

have just got model of cover design for Brzeska book. very fine model of his green stone charm.

Also have turned in the last of the photographs for the book. It has been some work to get them all right. I suppose the book will be along fairly soon now.

Lionel Johnson book out.

Had a letter from Christine Logie (as was), she had seen a notice of the Gaudier book. Wanted news from America, said she hadn't heard from the Chesters for a long time. Sent her regards to you and mother. She is apparently living just outside London.

Itow's dances are going finely. especially the Noh stuff and the sword-dances. He is going to try to give the play of Kumasaka, not exactly as the Noh actors would do, but as the Kiogen actors. It ought to be very interesting.

Yeats has finished a new play. Dolmetsch has brought out a book on old music. Hueffer up in town on leave for a few days.

Benington photographed D. when he came to do Gaudier's 'Birds'. I hope it turns out well, in which case you will at last get your picture.

When the consignment of stuff finally goes over to Quinn you must run over to N.Y and see what's been going on.

The back cover for the anthology was originally a snow storm, and the front cover was faked up to go with it.

Will send you the Gaudier book and anthology as soon as they are ready.

Lewis is fussing to go into the army. It seems a great waste.

I have done an obituary on De Gourmont for the 'Fortnightly' but heaven knows when they'll print it. His death is a great loss to everybody, and a particular loss to me as he had been so interested in the projected magazine.

Am reading Gaudier's books. One very interesting one on ancient Egypt.

We are going down to dine with Yeats this evening.

Have sent an article on Joyce to 'Drama', it will be out either in Nov. or Feb. number.

also some stray notes on things in general.

Guess that's about all, save a stray dull article in the new Age.

Love to you and mother. D. sends hers also.

yrs

E.

Pound had edited and written a preface for **Poetical Works of Lionel Johnson,** *just published by Elkin Mathews. His preface was not used in the American edition published by the Macmillan Company of New York.* **Yeats'** *'new play' was probably* The Player Queen *which he had begun in 1910, and did not in fact finish until 1919.* **Dolmetsch's book** *was* The Interpretation of the Music of the XVIth and XVIIth Centuries— *Pound reviewed it in the Egoist in July 1917, under the title 'Vers Libre and Arnold Dolmetsch'. Fortnightly Review published his* **obituary tribute to de Gourmont** *in December; he wrote another for the January* Poetry. *His review of* **Joyce's** Exiles, *'Mr. James Joyce and the Modern Stage, A Play and Some Considerations', appeared in* Drama *in February. Pound had been trying for some months to interest theatre agents in the play, without success. His* '**dull article**' *in the* New Age *was headed 'This Super-Neutrality'.*

⊹═⊹

493. TLS [*embossed letterhead*] 5, Holland Place Chambers, Kensington, W.

12–11- '15

[London]

Dear Dad

One of Gaudier's statues and various drawings are now safely lodged in the South Kensington museum. . . . after some negotiation. The illustrations for the book are coming out finely.

Itow is attracting attention. I enclose a photo. . . . which does not represent his personality 'off'.

Coburn has done so fine photos. of him. The half-tone of the enclosed is very poor. Will you however forward it to T.B. Hinckley, 'The Drama' 6018 Jackson Park Ave. Chicago. as I have sent him some notes on Itow etc. and he may as well see it.

The 'Seafarer' is being translated into Japanese and Chinese, I dont know that the job will get finished, but Utchiyama seems intelligent and he may go on with it, and other things.

We may go down to Stone Cottage after Xmas. nothing settled.

Love to you and mother. Salutations to the family at Tioga.

D. sends love.

yrs

E. P.

+>=-=<+

494. ALS

27 November 1915

[London]

Dear Dad

That imbecile Mathews has sent you a bill with your 2 copies of the Cat. Anth.

Please pay no attention to same as he should not have sent it. said copies belonging not to him but to your faithful offspring.

D. wrote yesterday so there isn't much news.

Bloody fools have put a purple cover on the <u>anth</u>. instead of a grey one. <u>ma</u> <u>che</u>!

Windows to be washed. I must turn out.

Love to you & mother.

E. P.

27. 11- '15

+>=-=<+

495. ALS [*embossed letterhead*] 5, Holland Place Chambers, Kensington, W.

[early December 1915]

[London]

Dear Dad –

yrs rec'd. 'M. B.' is a chap named Bodenheim. – Maxwell Bodenheim. (address him c/o 'Poetry' Chicago) I did not feel that his full name would appeal to the English public at this moment. He says his people are jews from Alsace. I think he may do some fairly good stuff. Monro's. stuff is good.

357

E. P. gets nothing out of it except the satisfaction of getting Eliot's poems into print . . between covers.

Also it will cheer up Bill (Williams).

Otherwise its not worth doing

Yours

E. P.

Love to you & mother.

Maxwell Bodenheim was a contributor to Catholic Anthology 1914–15. *Eliot was the lead contributor, with five poems including 'The Love Song of J. Alfred Prufrock' and 'Portrait of a Lady'. One of* **William Carlos Williams'** *two poems was 'The Wanderer', which (in his words) was his 'first "long" poem, which in turn led to* Paterson'.

+⊨═⊨+

496. ALS [*embossed letterhead*] 5, Holland Place Chambers, Kensington, W.

(17 December 1915)

[London]

Dear Mother:

I think we are going to Stone Cottage on Tuesday for a few weeks.

Am being translated into French. - somewhat - & slightly into Japanese.

Did a longish new poem yesterday.

Yeats has finished a play & done a couple of short things.

Wadsworth is shaved & looks in his a-a uniform as if he had never been out of a navy.

Lewis has enlisted -. That about takes the lot.

When is our disgusting country going to send the fleet to Trieste or Fiume or the Dardanelles.

It may be such rotten junk that it cant face german guns. but even the tubs that were used in the Spanish war ought to be good enough to fight austrians.

I dare say you have the Dec. 'Poetry'.

Have been reading Roscoe's 'Life of Leo X.'. wich is a fair fat book.

The illustrations for the Brzeska book have been very well done. I'm still waiting for proofs. of text

Eliot has got a job in London after Xmas

Henry James is very ill

They say that everyone in France who had heart trouble has died of the worry.

Stuart Merrill died this week or last. Taillade has been ill but recovered.

I suppose we will go to France after the war. if it ever ends.

V.H. has been in for the evening
it is now time to retire.

Love to you & dad.

yrs

E. P.

You might find 'Zeppelin Night' by V.H. & F.M.H. entertaining.

Eliot was about to move from teaching at the Grammar School at High Wycombe, midway between London and Oxford, to be a Junior Master at Highgate Junior School in north London.

+≡≡≡+

497. **ALS** [*embossed letterhead*] 5, Holland Place Chambers, Kensington, W.

(18 December 1915)

[London]

Dear Dad

Glad you like the Perigord poem. You will improve it considerably if you blot out the first 2 lines of part III (page 118).

Begin that section with 'Bewildering etc' I ought to have done it in <u>mss.</u> as I know cant get proofs from Chicago. The lines are unnecessary & detract a good deal from the vividness of that part of the poem.

Vilanelle. is the name of an old verse form. with rhymes & a refrain. I wanted the effect of a recurrence of a theme & meant 'Vilanelle' to mean generally the feel of the vilanelle form in a modern subject. I think I have missed fire. I wanted to convey the <u>'sense - the feel 'that something critical is happening to some one else at a distance'</u>

It is a perfectly definite emotion.

I have however only succeded in giving the impression that <u>I</u> was disappointed by their absence. It's not good enough.

The 2 opening lines of second paragraph of division 1. ought to be expanded and made to dominate the rest.

As it is they pass unnoticed. & the end isn't sufficiently prepared for.

We must have another try at it.

Wish you could get over - they won't take Americans in the British Army - so I am likely to be here until the war is over.

Perhaps you could get over this summer. The boats wont be crowded.

Perhaps you can jack up the Vilanelle. if you insert after the words 'diverse forces' the lines

'How do I know?

oh I know well enough'.

For them there is something afoot'.

As for me

I had over-prepared. Etc.

I did a goodish poem about 4 pages . day before yesterday.

Reply to Hagedorns antique sonnet on Cabaret Dancer.

Also 6 small versions from Florentis Christianus' versions of greek anthology.

Mlle DePratz (from Aubeterre) is translating, or rather she and I together are putting some of my stuff into French. She is a friend of Judith Gautier & of Laurent Tailhade. & seems to think I am more wanted in Paris than here.

At least she says the stuff will 'go' & that Tailhade will like it.

Now that DeGourmont is dead there is no one whom I would rather please.

Poor Henry James has had two strokes - Mlle DePratz says that everyone in France who had heart trouble has died of the strain.

James will never walk again they say.

De Gourmont & Stuart Merril are as much killed by the war as was Brzeska.

I am scribbling because I swopped my typewriter for a new model this morning & it hasn't come yet. I can't afford it, but I think it will be an ultimate economy. The new model seems more durable. The old one works out at about £3 per. Year. I think 2 more years would probably have finished it.

The new one ought to last nearly forever as they've improved it a lot.

This is Saturday - we go down to Stone Cottage on Tuesday. - but go on addressing letters here. as we may only be gone 3 weeks - in which case we go down again later.

Lewis has enrolled. He is 31. - They have called up unmarried men from 19–23 today.

I think Italy has done more than people generally think.

Rummel is in Paris. T.P. not much use.

If you like the 'Perigord' you would probably like Browning's 'Sordello' - It takes a bit of reading. The historical background is all lucidly put in Sismondi's 'Italian Republics' (I think that's it.) - anyhow its Sismondi & I think it is in Everyman's Library for 25 cents. Then you have to remember that Taurello = Salinguerra etc. & that R. B. calls his people first by their front name & then by their last.

It is a great work & worth the trouble of hacking it out.

I began to get it on about the 6th reading - though individual passages come up all right on the first reading.

It is probably the greatest poem in English. Certainly the best long poem in English since Chaucer. You'll have to read it sometime as my big long endless poem that I am now struggling with, starts off with a barrel full of allusions to 'Sordello' – which will intrigue you if you haven't read the other.

I must have the lot typed out & send it you as a much belated Xmas. – though I dare say the present version needs a lot done to it.

It will be two months at least before I can send it. - I suppose - as I dont want to muddle my mind now in the Vth canto - by typing the first three cantos - and

I dont want to leave the only copy with a typist while I'm out of town. Besides you may as well have a shot at 'Sordello' first.

Ebbene. Merry Xmas & happy New Year to you both.

& salutations to the folks at Tioga.

& to Miss Thurston & Miss Moran.

yrs

E. P.

you'll have got your 'anthology' by now & the 'De Gourmont'

---

*The first two lines of '**Near Perigord**. III' as printed in* Poetry *in December 1915 were: 'I loved a woman. The stars fell from heaven. / And always our two natures were in strife.' The lines did not appear in* Lustra, *or in later collections. The new lines for '**Villanelle**' were printed in* Lustra, *and in later collections. Pound's '**To a Friend Writing on Cabaret Dancers**', a reply to Herman Hagedorn's 'The Cabaret Dancer' (in the December* Poetry), *was first published in* Lustra.

+>=—=<+

498. TLS

Dec 31. [1915]

Stone Cottage, Address London as usual.

Dear Mother

Rec'd I pair of slippers and £2., for which my ringraziamenti.

There is, natuarally, no news. The Egoist is to publish Joyce's novel in volume, I think. And may serialize Lewis' novel.

Yeats has gone up to London for the day. It is raining. We are reading Landor and the autobiography of Herbert of Cherbury, both with enjoyment

Rec_d also 3/3 from Japan, for 1 copy of Guido. Letter from C. T. Chester. etc.

Otherwise no events since my letter to H.L. P.

Happy New Year to you both.

yrs

.E.

---

*Six commercial publishers having declined to publish **Joyce's** A Portrait of the Artist as a Young Man, Harriet Shaw Weaver had decided that The Egoist Limited would bring it out in volume form, and would serialize Lewis's Tarr. Pound helped raise the £50 to be paid to each of the authors, and as part of the arrangement offered The Egoist, for free, a series of twelve articles and his twelve 'Dialogues of Fontenelle', translated from Bernard de Fontenelle's Nouveaux dialogues des morts (1683).*

+>=—=<+

499. ALS

[? February 1916]

[London]

Dear Dad

Milton Bronner who used to be in Ky. is now in new york.
address

310 Windsor Place Brooklyn – N.Y.

I dare say he passes through Phila. now and then.

He has written some poetry – I'd be glad if you could send me a vol. of it if you can find one. I don't know that it is published in a book or only in magazines. He has written several favorable notices of me.

You might put him up for the night or give him dinner if he is in Phila.

Yrs

.E.

500. TLS

[February 1916]

Stone Cottage [Sussex]

Dear Dad.

Your letter, with Sanborn's, recd. also note from 'New Republic', It is a rotten dull, stupid and vulgar rag and I hope you will waste neither time nor money on it. Plump dullness, german temperament, general debility. If you have further communication with the virtuous Tobey you can tell him he is running with a dead and decrepit aggregation, from me. Go back to Kate Douglas Wiggin.

Yeats is going to do an introduction for three of my Jap. plays, which his sister's press is now printing. He has done a play of his own on the Noh model, and is preparing a new new dramatic movement, plays which wont need a stage, and which wont need a thousand people for 150 nights to pay the expenses of production. His play and a brief skit of mine will be done in Lady Cunard's big room, in, I suppose, April.

The Egoist is to publish Joyce's novel in volume form. They begin to serialize Lewis' 'Tarr' in April, and there prefatory articles by Lewis and myself in the March number. I have also done some amusing dialogues from Fontenelle, and shall start that series in the May Egoist. You can spread the news. The paper has forked up £50 each to Joyce and Lewis in consideration of which I think it ought to [be] encouraged, and trust you will put the news about a bit.

mention the coming serials and the volume to anyone you happen to be writing to. press etc.

Yeats seems to expect the new drama to do something, at least there will be no compromise, actors will wear masks, scenery will be mostly imagined, at most a cloth or a screen, and the dominion of Belasco and the chews will no longer be coterminus with the known and inhabitable world.

I will send you some announcement slips of the new phase of the Egoist's existence. reorganization,

We have all been up to London for a week, and are now back here for, I suppose, another three. I suppose the Brzeska book will be out fairly soon now.

We have both ordered passports @ 8 / 4 each, (8 shillings and four pence). All england save London has been put off bounds. The Home Office has kindly saved me from the depredations of the Sussex authorites, as we had been here some time without finding out that we ought to have registered. Finally managed to get identified. Yeats took a few shots at it. got a letter from the poet laureate which would have hanged all three of us in any country in Europe, a perfect extacy of timidity on old Bridges part, derived from reading Conan Doyle.

I have finished Roscoe's 'Leo X.', and we are also through Heroditus, and mostly through Landor.

Love to you & mother.

. E .

*Pound was finishing off his versions of the **Japanese 'Noh' plays**, and Yeats, excited by their non-naturalistic form of drama, had arranged for four of them to be published by his sisters' Cuala Press as* Certain Noble Plays of Japan: From the Manuscripts of Ernest Fenollosa, Chosen and Finished by Ezra Pound, with an Introduction by William Butler Yeats . . . MCMXVI. **Yeats's own 'noble play'** *was* At the Hawk's Well; *the **'brief skit'** was not performed with it, and was forgotten until 1987 when Donald Gallup and the Friends of the University of Toledo Libraries published it in a small collection of Pound's* Plays Modelled on the Noh (1916). *In the **Egoist** for* **1ˢᵗ March** *1916 Pound had one article, 'Meditatio', opposing censorship of the kind both Joyce and Lewis had endured, though without directly referring to either* Portrait *or* Tarr.

*As US citizens Ezra and Dorothy Pound were officially aliens, and as such were **required to register** with the local police; further, because Stone Cottage was in an area used for military training they were, according to wartime regulations, aliens in a prohibited area. The police had called to question them at Stone Cottage; Pound had been summoned before a Sussex magistrate on suspicion of being a foreign spy; Robert Bridges, the Poet Laureate, in his reply to Yeats had asked what evidence there was in the latter's letter to prove that any of them were who they claimed to be; Charles Masterman, a friend in the Cabinet, had had a word with the Home Office; they had gone up to the American Embassy and obtained parchment passports; and in the end the Sussex authorities were appeased.*

501. ALS

Feb 27 [1916]

Stone Cottage [Sussex]

Dear Mother:

The summer that lasted most of January is over.

Deeper snow than I have yet seen in England.

We go back to Town after another week. Yeats has it in his head that we are to take a fortnight at Bath later in the spring & see if we can discover any monuments of Landor's occupation.

I have done some more Jap plays. as perhaps I wrote. 3 or 4 are to be done in a book with an introduction by W B.Y.

I shall also edit a small book of his fathers letters. some of which are diverting.

R. & Hilda are going to Devonshire for a while, so we hear.

I think I wrote that I had done some dialogues of Fontenelle for the Egoist & that the paper is to try to wake up a little.

Yeats thinks he is going to startle the elect with a performance of his own celtic Noh and a farce of mine in a month or so.

At least his new scheme is better than the jew theatre - I dont know how much better. I dare say it will end in a riot of mask makers & musicians.

Am reading Leonardo's note books, McCurdy's selection. = some fine things in it.

Love

.E.

Passages of the Letters of John Butler Yeats: Selected by Ezra Pound, *with Pound's* '*Editor's Note' dated 'May 20*[th]*, 1916', would be published by Cuala Press in 1917.*

+‡══►‡+

502. ALS

March 1st [1916]

Stone Cottage [Sussex]

going back to London on Monday

Dear Dad.

No force used on Sandburg.

Sordello needs about six readings. also get Sismondi's History of Italian Republics. & read book 1. The historical back ground is in that.

Scheme of poem roughly.

Sordello - parentage uncertain grows up at Goito

Wins contest in poetry at Mantua (easy walk's distance
    Ed. Williams.& I did it on foot.)
Becomes official minstrell to Palma
Taurello Salinguerra (cf. the late T. C. P.)
    his character.
Schemes of Papal & Imperial parties.
Various parentheses by Browning.
Sordello's parentage discovered
Sordello offered leadership of party he don't believe in
Dies, having refused it.
'Beneath his foot the imperial badge'
    or some such line.
fine bits
descriptions of castle at Goito etc.

————

analysis of S. temperament.

————

various jems on route, but not a simple poem by some distance.

————

Don't remember any thing about Radcliff.

Mother's letter to D. says he was at Tagore dinner. I dare say it's all right. What sized object is he? You might send details if there's any reason why I should recall him.

Voluminous letters from Quinn yesterday & today. you should get notice of Vorticist show in N. Y. in a couple of months time.

Love to you & mother

Yrs

E. P.

+⟫===⟪+

503. TLS [*embossed letterhead*] 5, Holland Place Chambers, Kensington, W.

7 April 1916

[London]

Dear Dad

Still rushed to the limit. Gaudier book out next week, finally. Mathews going to bring out my new poems in September. Starts in May, such is the condition of printers.

Jap plays being printed. Yeats introduction not yet finished, so don't know when book will be ready.

Lady Cunard has sole copy of my dialogue play. Have written to her for a copy, to get a few made.

Yeats play a success on Tuesday. not yet quite in order, whole scheme of things too new. Royalty presented with a fine view of the bosom of my best pants during preliminary arrangement of scene.

My play supposedly to be done next month at Claridges. Am trying to do a couple more.

Don't you worry about Quinn. He is the father of his country and a white man, also the busyest man in N.Y. he'll get round to you some time. At present he is paying the rent of half the good artists in Europe.

He has sent me an order for Lewis stuff on top of the Gaudier, and is paying the freight on vorticist show to be held in N.Y. sometime, as soon as I can arrange it. He is also offering me funds to remake the Egoist. I can't accept it however unless or until I am sure they will let me do what I want with the paper. This is for you alone, as he forbids me mention his name in connection with this matter. It might interfere with the bigger scheme. He had 4000 dollars pledged for the big scheme, but I think that had better wait till after the war. There was to be 10,000 dollars in all, for me to blow, on the chance of making a go [*of*] it. I am not sure that remaking the Egoist won't be more economical, and that I can't make [*it*] into something as quickly as I could found a new monthly. However I don't yet know that they'll agree to renovation.

What else?

Lewis off at Dover. Gunner Lewis learning to gun. Wadsworth potting at Zepps. He goes off in a torpedo boat to pot the Belgian coast pretty soon.

Itow still here and likely to stay. He is the hawk in Yeats' play. Koumé and Fugita, two very charming and high-up japs also contribute to one's enjoyment of life. Koumé of Daiymio family. His father has two Noh stages in the back yard etc. He is a fine chap, looks a little like a miniature of Bill Williams. Fugita, evidently son of a much used general judging from family photos. He is a satirist with no end of humour and great talent. Koumé did the Hagoromo. <vide my translation Quarterly Review> the tennin part, before the Mikado at the age of seven. The flying movements of the dance are most exquisite. They are a very fine pair of humans.

Quinn has just sent me Roosevelt's book damning Wilson. Uncle Sam is cutting a damn rotten figure. The Italian penny comics. show Wilson and Sam singing plaintively under the Kaiser's window and getting piss pots dumped into their hats in return, and it is not very far off the mark. The root of the matter is ignorance, black Liberian ignorance.

I spent the week before last, or last week, I forget which, in bed result of over work and the blizzard. 80 big trees down in the park. Counted twenty from bus-top first day I went down to Piccadilly. Then three days of hot spring, now cold again.

Well, all this plugging type writer takes it out of me, all same, writing articles.
ring off. love to you and mother.

Yrs

E. P.

7 – 4 –'16

Theodore Roosevelt's Fear God and Take Your Own Part *(1916) was a collection of
speeches and articles.*

+⇒⇐+

504. ALS [*embossed letterhead*] 5, Holland Place Chambers, Kensington, W.
April 9, 1916

[London]

Dear Mother:

I don't know where anything is, or what questions I am expected to answer.
I have a vague idea I haven't written to you for about six months.

I am very busy arranging my next vol. of poems what is to go out & what
stay in it etc. I enclose some more Chinese.

Koumé is doing the Kumasaka dance-part. for us this evening in his studio.

The Gaudier comes out this week.

I have selected old Yeats' letters to W. B. Y. to the latters liking.

Am doing some 'Noh' of my own - don't know that they'll ever get finished.

DuLac is a great addition to life - He is better at everything else than at
painting - His masks & costumes for 'Hawk's Well' were magnificent.

There is no use your reading Lewis' novel in the Egoist. it will only make you
throw fits.

The Fontenelle was great fun to do - and most sane & charming. First
number next month.

I've still a pile of stuff to get through with.

Love to you & Dad.

. E .

+⇒⇐+

505. TLS [*embossed letterhead*] 5, Holland Place Chambers, Kensington, W.
Sunday 7. May 1916.

[London]

Dear Dad.

They have begun printing my new vol of poems. 'Lustra' Took the mss. to
Mathews Monday. He rushed at once to the phone telephoned for the paper.

Then telephoned the printer to appear instanter before him. Fine large type, and photggravure of the Coburn ¾ face photo.

I am scurrying through the end of my prose book 'This Generation' for Marshall, 331 Fourth Ave, New York.

I dont know whether papers can be sent through except from the publishing office. I have mailed you the April Egoist and will mail May at once. If you dont receive them you'll have to subscribe direct. I cant ask them to send you a subscription. I can only mail you my spare copy. Begin with April, as Lewis' novel began then. My Fontenelle starts this month (May number).

I enclose further notice of the Gaudier.

Love to you & mother

Yrs

. E.

'This Generation' was to be a collection of Pound's essays from periodicals dealing with contemporary art and literature. Terms had been agreed with a new publisher in New York, John Marshall, and the sole copy of the manuscript was mailed to him about this date; Marshall, however, decamped to Canada, the manuscript disappeared, and the project lapsed for the time being.

---

506. TLS [*embossed letterhead*] 5, Holland Place Chambers, Kensington, W.

25 / 5 / '16

[London]

Dear Mother

D. took to the violet pin very much and wears it most of the time. I dont know what she may have said about mauve, she likes the pin. It is redish purpleish colours she dislikes.

Have just finished reading Butler's 'The Way of All Flesh', most entertaining.

We rec'd a fine Whistler lithograph two days ago, delayed wedding present. Was amused at old bookseller asking six pence for a second hand copy of a booklet printed at five pence, still in print, he said 'everything costs more now'. Naturally I paid the six pence.

I think at last I have got a correct invoice of the vorticist show, from the packers, so I hope it will really get started before the end of July.

I have finished up most of my jobs.

/ / / / / /

Tell dad not to worry about the Borston transcript. They had a large halfpage about the Gaudier on April 8.

Am going down past the bank tomorrow will look in on Kent if I have time.

Yeats was very much surprised by the Irish outbreak. He knows Pearse and has always said Pearse would manage to get himself hanged, however Pearse has got himself shot instead. The whole lot of imbeciles were of course fooled by German promises.

I found both John Quinn and James Joyce sentenced to five years imprisonment in the same list, however they seem to have been duplicate Johns and Jameses, as Joyce is safe in Zurich and J.Q. in New York. <Waley even heard a rumour that Yeats himself had been shot - but having just seen him in Museum St, was able to contradict it.>

John Marshall, 331 Fourth Ave. is to bring out Joyce's novel as well as my prose book. I shall send him mss. of Eliot's poems in a few days.

yrs

. E .

The 'Irish outbreak' was the Easter Rising led by Patrick Pearse of the Irish Republican Brotherhood, and James Connolly of the Sinn Féin. In this attempt to seize Irish independence there was some serious fighting around the Dublin General Post Office before the rebellion was put down by the British authorities, and its leaders executed.

+≍+

507. TLS [*embossed letterhead*] 5, Holland Place Chambers, Kensington, W.

(June 1916)

[London]

Dear Mother

Thanks for the £1/ but don't be alarmed about the food supply. The small increase in prices, a stray penny here and there, is infinitely less than the postage on packets of anything would be. Eggs is went down again. I don't notice any difference in expenditure, whatever there is can easily be made up by dining 'in' one more night per week instead of going down town to Bellotti.

I enclose Konody's tactful rev. of Gaudier. Poor chap he took a long time to think it out. He had to have something that wouldn't committ him. He was afraid of my uncertain fury and equally afraid of the dealers in ancient and moribund styles.

Have made final arrangements for 'Lustra' today. Two editions, one unabridged and one slightly smaller. Also sent Quinn material for a bigger American vol., to be made up of Lustra and selections from Canzoni and Ripostes. He thinks he may be able to get the MacMillan Co. to take up all my stuff. I don't know that he will manage it. Watt here is trying the English MacM. with the big Noh book.

Monro is called up for service on Saturday. Rodker has been arrested for conscientiously objecting. We hope it will teach him sense. He has a faint excuse in his polish descent, but he has no excuse for being an ass. Yeats has gone to Ireland for a week or ten days. Hueffer up sunday on leave.

369

Orage has asked me to do another series of articles on prose writers of last half century, James, Butler, Galdos, Turgenev, etc. at least we have arranged something of the sort. We dine with Koume tonight at the Japanese club.

Met W. H. Davis last week and liked him. He was the 'super-tramp', but since he has had a pension from the government his poetry has greatly improved.

Can dad send on the Transcript <u>attack</u>? Specimens of assininity not rare but nearly always diverting. Prominent London ass confessed two weeks ago that he had been trying to ruin my career for sometime and here I 'was more like a rock than ever'. Poor chap! The only compliment he could have paid me. And his ex-boss is down and out also.

Your admired (Miss.) K. Buss is a discipular imbecile, but you needn't mention the fact in public, her lucubrations may be of some use. Encourage her to go on. She did have sense enough to quote the 'Gaudier' instead of trying to say anything on her own which IS a beginning of wisdom. The poor old chap on the times was a lot more worried.

Besides she will annoy a lot of people, and that is to be counted to her eternal credit.

Lewis has been made bombardier. i.e. a sort of lance corporal of artillery.

Yrs

. E .

Elkin Mathews was to publish two editions of **Lustra**—*the advertised edition which would not print thirteen of the poems Pound had wanted to include, and a second edition, to be sold as it were under the counter, which would include all but four of the banned poems. This was because Mathews' printer, Clowes, had found offensive a number of poems in the collection, and had refused absolutely to print those four. Mathews had agreed with the printer about the offending poems, reflecting that 'not only men come into this shop, but* <u>ladies</u>'; *but then he compromised to the extent of having 200 copies of the less bowdlerised edition printed for those who dared to ask for it. The* '**bigger American volume**', *also entitled* Lustra, *would include all thirteen poems excluded from the advertised English edition, along with the selection of earlier poems, and also 'Three Cantos of a Poem of Some Length'.*

No '**series of articles on prose writers of last half century**' *appeared in the* New Age. *Pound's next series for Orage would begin in July 1917.* **W. H. Davies** *(1871–1940) published* Autobiography *of a Super-Tramp in 1908.* **Kate Buss**, *an American admirer of Pound's work, would review* Lustra *in the* Boston Evening Transcript *of 6 December 1916.*

⊬══⊬

508. ALS [*embossed letterhead*] 5, Holland Place Chambers, Kensington, W.
19 / 6 / 1916

[London]

Dear Dad:

Dont try to buy these Cuala's as they are too expensive. Let others do so.

I have some sort of offer from MacMillan for the big Fenollosa book. Shall find out just what it is this. P.M.

Wadsworth goes soon to Salonika - Lustra set up. will send an <u>adv.</u> soon.

Love to you & mother

E. P.

+>====<+

509. TLS [*embossed letterhead*] 5, Holland Place Chambers, Kensington, W.
20 / 6 / '16

[London]

Dear Dad.

I am 'up to my eyes'. MacMillan have agreed to publish a big vol. of the Fenollosa plays, as soon as I choose to send in mss. (that is for both Eng. and the U.S.A.). 'Lustra' is getting published with only a few omissions. Lady Cunard is being very kind in hunting up supplies for Joyce, who is still stranded in Zurich. We have been given free run of the Aldwych for the opera season. Began on Tristan last night and take the Magic Flute this evening. Beecham conducts very finely. Wagner is a bum artist. We expect more pleasure from the Mozart. They have collected some excellent singers and one or two who act extremely well.

Getting placed with MacMillan <u>here</u>, is quite a step onward. I dont suppose it will begin to be remunerative for some time, but still it is a sort of Bank of England firm. Quinn has offered his services in getting the U.S. MacM's, to run all my stuff on your side of the ditch. I sent off his two Gaudier Statures yesterday.

I may have to go to Dublin to manage the Abbey theatre for a few months this autumn.

Dulac has done a most noble caricature of yours truly. I will send a reproduction if there ever is one. That's all I can think of at the moment.

Am doing a brief note on W. H. Davies for 'Poetry'

E P

[*stamped with seal made for Pound by Dulac, with his initials 'EP' made to look like a Chinese ideogram*]

'Noh' or Accomplishment | A Study of the Classical Stage of Japan *would be published by Macmillan and Co. in London in January 1917, and by Alfred A. Knopf in*

*New York in June. Altogether **Lady Cunard** and Pound raised about £200 for Joyce in the summer of 1916. The free run of the **opera** season was thanks to Sir Thomas Beecham who was 'en liason' with Lady Cunard.*

+=====+

1916

20/6/16

Dear Dad.

I am " up to my eyes " . MacMillan have agreed to publish a big vol. of the Fenollosa plays , as soon as I choose to send in mss. (that is for both Eng. and the U.S.A.). "Lustra" is getting published with only a few omissions. Lady Cunard xxxxxxxxxxxxxxxxxxxxxxxxxxxxxxxxxxxxx she is being very kind in hunting up supplies for Joyce , who is still stranded in Zurich . We have been given free run of the xxxxxxx Aldwych for the opera season . Began on Tristan last night and take the Magic Flute this evening . Beecham conducts very finely . Wagner is a bum artist . We expect more pleasure from the Mozart . They have collected some excellent singers and one or two who act extremely well .

Getting placed with MacMillan here , is quite a step onward . I dont suppose it will begin to be remuner -ative for some time , but still it is a sort of Bank of England firm . Quinn has offered his services in getting the U.S. Mac M's , to run all my stuff on your side of the ditch . I sent off his two "audier Statures yesterday .

I may have to go to Dublin to manage the Abbey theatre for a few months this autumn.

Dulac has done a most noble caricature of yours truly . I will send a reproduction if there ever is one. That's all I can think of at the moment.
                                   W.H
Am doing a brief note on Davies   for " Poetry "

509. TLS, EP to HLP from London, 20 June 1916.

510. TLS [*embossed letterhead*] 5, Holland Place Chambers, Kensington, W.
22 June 1916

[London]

Dear Mother:

I enclose the last review of the Gaudier. Wadsworth has just been in, new naval uniform. He sails for Lemnos tomorrow. He is in the 'information'.

I may have to go to Dublin to manage the Abbey theatre this autumn. At least I've said I 'd go for four months if they cant get anyone else.

My next job is to get the big Jap book ready for MacMillan.

Have sent in revised proofs of Lustra.

Jean de Bosschere in yesterday, much impressed with the Lewis's and the Gaudier's. He says Figueire will certainly bring out a french translation of the Gaudier Book after the war if the firm is still publishing. Also that they have nothing so good in france, or nothing like Lewis work.

Am sending some of de Bosschere's stuff to Poetry with a note. He paints also.

Shall be too busy with the big Noh book to be very communicative for some time.

yrs
E. P.

22 – 6 – '16

511. TLS [*embossed letterhead*] 5, Holland Place Chambers, Kensington, W.
16 July 1916

[London]

Dear Mother

Did I write my thanks for the pyjamas. If not here it is with due expansion. 'Lustra' announcemtns you will have rec'd. I have done '12 Occupations' from DeBosschere's 'Metiers Divins'. Mathews is bringing it out with De B's sketches. Also have made a stab at one of LaForgue's 'Moralites Legendaires'. Quinn writes that the vorticist show has arrived in N.Y. De Bosschere and DuLac about the sole remaining inhabitants. Called on Mrs Clifford this p.m. for the first time in years. Dining with DuLac tomorrow. Lady Cunard has promised that Joyce shall not starve and stirred up various people about him. Lewis is still Bombadier.

Have been reading Congreve and also a life of Voltaire. Nothing but a long course of the latter can save America from a perpetual susseccion of Wilsons and a perpetuation of our national infamy.

The news from France and Italy is most excellent. Now time to go forth for food.

yrs

. E .

16 / 7 / '16

Pound's 'Divagation from Jules Laforgue', 'Our Tetrarchal Précieuse'—a treatment of Herod and Salome—would first appear in the Little Review *in July 1918.*

+⟩━•━⟨+

512. **TLS** [*embossed letterhead*] 5, Holland Place Chambers, Kensington, W.

July 31. [1916]

[London]

Dear Mother

It has now turned grilling hot after a novemberish July. Am very bust doing the big Noh book for Macmillan.

Dulac and I think of doing a book on prePericlean sculpture. He has collected and taken a lot of photos.

Mary Moorse's address is Mrs J. F. Cross, 32 Elmwood Ave. East Orange. N.Y.

Itow is, I believe sailing for N.Y. on Saturday. at least that is the present opinion. Have been fencing with Koume every morning and getting some much needed exercise. He is very young and quick and has had training in Japanese fencing, so he has learned our very quickly.

Heard Mozart's 'Seraglio' last week.

Tell Dad not to bother to send me the Smart Set, they usually send me a free copy. from the office. I see there is to be a new affair called the 'Seven Arts', I wonder if it will be any good.

Aug 1. = better send this

yrs

E. P.

Love to you & dad

+⟩━•━⟨+

513. ALS [*embossed letterhead*] 5, Holland Place Chambers, Kensington, W.
[1916]

[London]

Dear Dad,

Here is the faint <u>mss</u>. . of the new jap play.
The other three you have seen In 'Poetry', 'Drama' 'Quarterly Rev.'.
They are all 'set up' but I haven't a spare set of proofs

yrs
E. P.

*The '**new jap play**' would have been the fourth of the* Certain Noble Plays *being
printed by the Cuala Press, i.e. 'Kagekiyo'.*

514. TLS [*embossed letterhead*] 5, Holland Place Chambers, Kensington, W.
18 – 8 - 16

[London]

Dear Dad

If you go to spending 1200 dollars remaking that house you'll get stuck, and
never have any loose change for the rest of your days. It would however be
perfectly cheap and easy to make it into TWO appartments. All you need do is
to box in the front stairs and cut a door where the first stained glass window is.
You can have the two extra steps below that landing on the out side. Vide
drawing.

[2 sketches here]

Cost of actual change, very little. Expense would be putting stove and sink in
present servants room, and bath in present passage to kitchen. Which expenses
you would get back out of first six months rent. You could keep a store room
on third floor. You couldn't rent those top rooms for much, and it would
certainly not be easy to transform them or reach them by seperate stair.

You could of course box in the entrance. but you would lose almost a room
on the second floor. I should certainly advise you to get a tenant for the second
and third floors before you go skylarking into a three deck institution.

What do you propose to do about heating? Let the second floor flat heat by
gas?

The first floor has no servants room, unless you keep the back half of the
second floor. That would leave you a bath also. and the new kitchen could go
on the third floor. That is the easiest alteration to make and there would be
NO expense apart from the gas range on the third floor, plus sink etc. AND the
new front door. Much the most sensible plan. Even if you dont think you are

going to have a servant. one small extra room is no harm. Second flat could then have all third floor if desired.

Expenditure of 1200 to start with, very risky. I should think second kitchen would be best on third floor, but it could go where the little sewing room is, and your old bed room next it would be dining room. Thats as you like.

Re / a letter of long time back. NO, I dont remember anything about Professor what's his name, nor any music.

People who want 'Lustra' can very well order it direct from Mathews, as directed on the circular. No one but the publisher can send printed books out of the country anyhow, so even if it weren't a bore for me to tie up parcels, it would be necessary for them to order from Mathews. I am getting extra photogravures of the portrait, but I dont know that they can be sent. There's no hurry. If I give the old toad another month he may have the book out.

MacMillan have started printing the big Noh book. Have rec'd sample page. Mrs Fenollosa says she has some more chinese stuff for me to go at.

Cuala book should be ready quite soon.

I have not seen the N.Y. Times. nor Sun, revs. of the Gaudier. I think I sent you the enclosed from the Chronicle. It is the last I have seen.

> Yrs
> E. P.

---

515. TLS [*embossed letterhead*] 5, Holland Place Chambers, Kensington, W.

31 August 1916

[London]

Dear Mother

Yrs. of Aug. the umpth. undated, to hand. I dont understand what it is (??? Polio??) that is dividing so many families. Nor yet N. F. prohibiting the import of children.?????????

Have rec'd a note from 10 Downing St. to say that the govt. recognizes Joyce's literary merit and will send him £100. Quinn is making a fine haul of vorticist drawings and pictures. So Lewis wont go bankrupt etc.

If I am reduced to beggary I shall at least have spent the year doing some good to the arts, at their source.

There appears to be no one left to look after but myself.

Mrs Fenollosa writes that there are more Chinese mss. for me to attack. Yeats has just wired that he is back, and will be in this evening, so I shall probably know whether I've to go to Dublin.

D. has just done a new picture. Those desiring the Cuala edition of the four Noh plays had better order at once. vide enclosed. I have nearly finished with the Chinese part of the Fenollosa stuff already rec'd.

Dulac has been in and tuned the clavocord. I think I told you he had done an excellent caricature of E. P. He will probably burst out as THE portrait painter before very long. or at least into some new role that the vulgo dont yet expect.

We are naturally pleased with Roumania.

Itow has arrived safely in N.Y. . I dare say you'll see him sooner or later.

Love to you and dad.

E. P.

Aug 31 1916

*The '**note from 10 Downing St**' would have stated that Prime Minister Asquith had granted a Civil List award to Joyce. Lady Cunard, at Pound's instigation, and with support from Yeats, had spoken with Edward Marsh who was 'in some way in charge of these grants'. **Roumania** had declared war on Austria-Hungary on August 27 when its troops crossed the border into Transylvania.*

+┠═══┨+

516. **TLS** [*embossed letterhead*] 5, Holland Place Chambers, Kensington, W.

19 September 1916

[London]

Dear Dad

Have forgotten when I last wrote and what about. Had copy of 'Noble Plays of Japan' sent you yesterday. Have turned in the proofs of the larger Macmillan book.

Quinn says he has seen you. but offered no comment as the information was contained in a cablegram. He has cut in for several £100 of vorticist pictures. which I suppose you will see sometime or other. Have met various new people here. Tucked in a few good dinners. We are going down to Stratford for a couple of days next week.

It is about time you came over again. Did Joe Cochran get into the State Assembly?

Your copies of LUSTRA should have arrived by about now.

Flinders Petrie did a book on Egyptian Sculpture, called Arts and Crafts of Ancient Egypt. The illustrations are good. Havent yet had time to read the text.

Dulac, as I have written, is the mainstay of one's comfort. DeBosschere has 'a message'. Have heard the phrase before but never yet met the actuality. It is extremely curious.

The phrase is used loosely. ad nauseam. De Bosschere has got it in a queer sort way. I dont mean that he is an artist of anything like Joyce's or Lewis's callibre, but there is something or other figiting around in his carcass and trying to get out in expression.

377

Curious perception of the inanity and ant like multiplicity of human activity, industrial etc, wholly mechanical and without any conscious reason. Multitude of grotesque molecules infinitely active, incessantly doing this that and the other, making things they dont use etc. etc. etc. senselessly bailing out boats, making hat pins, carrying satchels,

Lewis has been recommended for commission.

Have a good new Hokusai print hung up to the left of me.

The rest of the news is doubtless in the newspapers and is good.

Love to you and mother.

E. P.

19 – 9 – '16

E Pound.

+≻━≺+

517. TLS [*embossed letterhead*] 5, Holland Place Chambers, Kensington, W.

(22 September) [1916]

[London]

Dear Dad

Re/ the house, and your questions. I really dont see that there is much to add. It seems to me that to turn it into three flats at great expense would be wild speculation and only produce three sets of discomfort.

Certainly NOT. unless you get some one to take at least one of the flats on a ten years lease before you begin alterations.

It is perfectly easy to make two flats as I suggested, at a cost of very few dollars. i.e. second front door where stained glass stair window now is. Board partition up inside banisters, leaving 'em as ornament to ground floor hall.

Leave inside step to floor in case you want to re convert. Put extra step outside on poarch.

Give second flat that side of poarch and the side lawn. back to where fence used to come.

Kitchenette in old sewing room. If the Shelleys or some one amiable too[k] the upstairs they might use back stairs for milk etc.

Back division means simply double locking door into back hall. Also it leaves a bath of sorts on each side of the division. This is good enough, at least until you see whether the scheme works and whether you really <u>can</u> get a tenent.

[*sketch here*]

I could about do the partition myself if I were there. New door will need carpenter.

Of course they neednt have the run of the back stairs unless it is convenient, or unless they are amiable. But it would do until you found they were going to

378

stay, and until you were sure of clearing the cost of an outside stair to the second floor kitchen.

Guess that's about the lot.

As said, I have sent on 'Certain Noble Plays' and 'Lustra'. The Macmillan book is corrected in its first proofs.

Coburn and I have invented 'vortography'. I haven't yet see[n] the results, He will bring them in tomorrow morning. They looked damn well on the ground glass and he says the results are O.K.

The idea is that one no longer need photograph what is in front of the camera, but that one can use ones elements of design. i.e. take the elements of design from what is in front of the camera, shut out what you dont want, twist the 'elements' onto the part of plate where you want 'em, and then fire.

I think we are in for some lark. AND the possibilities are seemingly unlimited.

The apparatus is a bit heavy at present, but I think we can lighten up in time.

I think I wrote that the government had sent Joyce £100 in recognition of his literary merit. Some government! And a long time before the U.S.A. will arrive at a like state of intelligence.

Receipts this week £5/5 for perfidious article on Nevinson's show of war pictures, for English 'Vogue'. Poetry ought to send on some soon for the Sept. stuff. How do you like the second Voltaire poem ?

I wonder if the Seven Arts imbeciles are going to print my translation of Voltaire on jews. You might ask 'em to let you see the mss. if they aren't using it. It wipes the pants off the Pentateuch all right enough.

Neither England or America have yet learned the lesson of honesty from Voltaire. Jefferson probably read him, but the rest of America has absorbed only Rousseau's rhetoric, and Montesquieu who is inexact and rehtorical though right in his general drift.

I dont think there is a decent translation of Voltaire Co. Hamley wrote a short life of him, published by Blackwood in 1877. it might interest you. Hamley is tainted by his period but his facts are interesting.

I wonder if there is a decent translation of Confucius. I've Pauthier's french version. NOT the odes, but the 'Four Books'. The sayings.

He was certainly a much nicer man than St Paul.

Am trying to arrange a Lewis show at the Leicester Gallery, dont know that it will come off.

Love to you and mother. Guess that's all at the moment. Have ordered a new pair of bags and got a new pair of brogans.

E P.

Ezra Pound

'**Vortography**' *was photography using an arrangement of mirrors to produce refracted or superimposed images in a kaleidoscopic or 'Cubist' manner. Coburn exhibited his vortographs at the Camera Club in February 1917. The '**second Voltaire poem**' was 'To*

Madame du Chatelet', the second of Pound's 'Impressions of François-Marie Arouet (de Voltaire)', included in Lustra. His '**Voltaire on jews**' would have been 'Genesis, or, The First Book in the Bible', first printed in the Little Review in November 1918. The Confucian '**Four Books**' are 'The Analects, or Sayings of Confucius', 'The Great Digest', 'The Doctrine of the Mean' (Pound's 'Unwobbling Pivot'), and 'The Book of Mencius'.

518. **TLS** [*embossed letterhead*] 5, Holland Place Chambers, Kensington, W.
(27 September) [1916]

[London]

Dear Dad

My real acquaintance with Quinn is by letter. I met him twice only in New York and not intimately. Once at a full table after supper, and secondly when he invited five of us to Coney for an outing.

The real acquaintance began when he wrote me about getting him one of Gaudier's statues.

He is all right.

We have today come back from a delightful visit to Mrs Leggett at Stratford. She has dug out an elizabethan house that belonged to Shakespeare's (WM. Shx's) daughter. It was until a few years ago embedded in a shell of Victorian plaster. Full of Elizabethan fittings etc. very diverting.

Lady Cunard has just this instant sent in an opera for me to translate, (i.e. the libretto). It is just about in time. Shall get £40 or £50 for the job, and possibly survive the winter. 'Poetry' is getting very lean in its pocket.

Blighters only sent me 65 dollars for Sept. instead of 100. However they've paid the rent for several years so I suppose it must be put up with, as they 'aint got no more'.

Do see what you can do about the suppression of Dreisser's book. Strangle Ellis and Sunday and the Comstock family, and abolish the Christian superstition or do something to cleanse the country you live in.

Love to you and mother.

EP
E. Pound

Pound and Dorothy had stayed in Hall's Croft in Stratford-on-Avon, and slept, as Dorothy wrote to IWP, 'in a wonderful old four-poster, in a wonderful room, which was the bedroom of Shakespeare's daughter Susanna'. Pound was commissioned to **translate the libretto** *of Massenet's 'Cendrillon'.* **Dreiser's** *The Genius had been withdrawn from sale by its publishers following an attack upon it as 'immoral' by Comstock's successor, John S. Sumner. A protest was being organised by H. L. Mencken.*

519. TLS [*embossed letterhead*] 5, Holland Place Chambers, Kensington, W.

(12 October 1916)

[London]

Dear Dad

Have finished first typed copy of the libretto but have not yet recovered command of my intelligence.

Two copies of Lustra and one copy 'Noble plays of Jpaan' should have reached you. If they dont, please notify me. I shall devote the money order to personal uses unless I hear to the contrary.

I shall send you copies of the photogravure of the coburn photo. after the war when one is permitted to send photos about indiscriminately.

Have done a review for the Times, but it is not in todays 'Literary Supplement' so I dont know whether it is merely delayed or whether the adverse element in the office has managed to get it chucked.

Re/ 'Heather'. The title is put on it to show that the poem is a simple statement of facts occurring to the speaker, but that these facts do not occur on same plane with his feet which are solidly planted in a climate producing Heather and not leopards etc.

you can picture it thus.

[*sketch here*]

Man has come to put up gas bracket just over me.

more anon

E Pound

Pound's **review** *of William Morton Fullerton's* The American Crisis and the War *appeared in the* Times Literary Supplement *of 19 October 1916.* '**Heather**', *a poem in* Lustra.

+⇒—⇒+

520. TLS [*embossed letterhead*] 5, Holland Place Chambers, Kensington, W.

19 Oct. 1916

[London]

Dear Dad

Had my first article in the 'Times' (Literary Supplement) this a.m. I dont know that it will go any further. It would be considerable help if they should decide to give me any sort of regular allotment.

Of course I shall not come to America. On the whole I have spent more time in Philadelphia than you have in London. AND you rather want to see more of London AND I have no desire whatsoever to gaze on the Schulykill River. And America offers me no means of livlihood, AND its an intellectual and artistic desert. AND no one has yet shot Woodrow Wilson. And Hughes is not an interesting alternative.

Re/ your question as to who has invited me to dinner. Dulac invites me most. also the Shakespears and Tuckers. and Mrs Wadsworth fed us in celebration of the sale of Ed. Wad's sale of two pictures to Quinn. Ed. Wad. being at Mudros off 'Tino'. . For the rest the Principessa di Monaco is the Principessa di Monaco, she is also a niece of Heine's, which is considerably more of a distinction. Mrs Leggett whom we were with at Stratford is an American whose daughters have married various englishmen, she has just dug out a very old house at Stratford, which belonged to Shakespeare's daughter (Wm. Shx. in this case). It had been embedded in Victorian plaster, etc. it is much better preserved and much more interesting than any of the 'show places' in Stratford.

Beecham who has given me the libretto to do is Sir Thomas B. the best conductor in England and a very good musician. I believe he 'keeps up' half musical England and is paying for the opera which he conducts, I dont suppose even a full house such as they had Saturday pays for all the expenses.

Birrel who helped about the suppression of Lustra is Augustine Birrel, essayist, and sometime secretary for Ireland, and various other things in the cabinet.

Chemborg or Shamborg or whatever his name is had better borrow the vorticist show from Quinn and exhibit in in Philadelphia

enough for the moment

yrs

Ezra Pound

I think the full signature is now required on letters to neutral countries. at least it is to Switzerland - hence this formality.

.E.

When Elkin Mathews was being fearful that he might be prosecuted for publishing some of the poems in Lustra, **Augustine Birrell**, *who could speak for the Home Office (which would have to launch any prosecution), assured him that it was 'simply out of the question that any of the poems are exposed to the risk of prosecution for indecency'.*

+>=+=<+

521. TLS [*embossed letterhead*] 5, Holland Place Chambers, Kensington, W.

31 October 1916

[London]

Dear Mother

Thanks for the birthday money order.

Of course I shall not return to America this winter, and there seems no reason why I should ever return. Only a large salary would induce one, and I hope I shall not be offered a large salary as I should then feel some compunction about not accepting it, and it becomes more and more apparent that America is NOT a place to live in or go to.

Old Beecham is dead and Goosens has been conducting in place of T. B. so I have not yet finished the revising of the libretto.

The last sheets of the music appendix for the Macmillan Noh book, have come, so that's nearly done with.

Review copies of 'Lustra' have reached the press so the attacks will be starting any time now.

The Quarterly has a general damnation of all living poets in the current number. I haven't read it through. A very good ad. for the Catholic Anthology and more than I should have expected.

Hope Eliot will have a book out in the spring. Lewis has been sent on to Exeter to train as an officer so his life will be more comfortable for the next few months.

Dined at Claridges with the Principessa on sunday evening, met an ex-Italian-ambassador-to-Washington (one Mayor des Planches) and a few other nuts.

Yeats is buying the ruin of an Irish castle so I suppose he will in time disappear from the world.

We are having this small triangular room papered, it is at present in a state of transition smelling of paint and dilapidation.

Love to you and dad.

yr

Ezra Pound

31 Oct 1916

Met old Wedmore in Mathews' the other day. Dont know that therese anything else.

Catholic Anthology *was reviewed by Arthur Waugh in the October* Quarterly Review. *He characterised Eliot's poetry as that of 'a drunken helot', a phrase Pound mocked by calling his enthusiastic review of* Prufrock and Other Observations *in the* Egoist *in June 1917, 'Drunken Helots and Mr. Eliot'.*

+——◆——+

522. TLS [*embossed letterhead*] 5, Holland Place Chambers, Kensington, W.

15 November 1916

[London]

Dear Mother

It seems very difficult to get it into your head that I earn my living, or such living as I do earn, by being in London. AND that to go to America would be to lose all I have gained or at least set me back two or three years. Nothing is done save by personal contact. Nothing is printed or agreed on. I should not have done the Gaudier, or the Noh, or would my poems be in print. if I had been on the wrong side of the Atlantic. This reason is perfectly plain and practical.

Add to it the fact that I loathe the American state of mind, and also that I certainly shall not cross the Atlantic except in the Mauretania or something as large and as swift.

I did not realize that you and father were seriously offering me the fare across. I appreciate it but I have no desire to see a country that elects W. Wilson. The size of the vote for Hughes was gratifying. It was more than I had expected. BUT STILL. . . . . .

That dirty dish rag W. W. has also made it next to impossible for people to get pass-ports back to civilization. I have no desire to be stuck in America for an indefinite period of years.

The Hughes vote leave one however some hope. The country may not be forever uninhabitable. I <u>had</u> given up all thought of seeing the place again. I feel a little differently since the election.

A Japanese invasion is the only thing that will civilize the West. I suppose it is too much to hope for.

Europe at present is much too interesting to leave. I wish they give dad a job in the Embassy here as a reward for his ages of service. There'd be some sense in that. But I suppose it is out of the question.

The paper hangers have also been here, putting the enclosed on the triangle room. They didn't bring enough and the space over the mantle is still green and the paper hanger's boards are still here awaiting his return.

The Dulacs and Mrs Patmos are coming in this P.M. Christine ex-Logie is coming tomorrow. A chap named Frederic Chamberlain is coming Friday. I met him at Lady Low's, he is doing a life of Queen Elizabeth and expects it it take the remaining years of his life.

The Newark 250th aniversay committee say they are sending me £10 for a poem.

Hilda sailed for America last week. I dont know whether Richard has been sent out yet or not. Lewis is in an Officers Training Corps.

Roberts writes from the front much as Gaudier did. He is in the field artillery. Wadsworth is still in the East.

Granville is starting a new monthly. Very small as yet, but it will pay something. This is the sort of thing which is not copped by the absent.

Have done a few reviews for the International Journal of Ethics, and may do them an essay on DeGourmont.

Be calm.

Love to you & dad,
E. P.

Ezra Pound

15 - 11 –'16

Newark, *New Jersey, had held a competition for poems upon the city's 250*[th] *anniversary, and had awarded Pound one of the ten $50 prizes (after the top three) for his 72-line entry, 'To a City Sending Him Advertisements'.* **Charles Granville's** *new monthly was to be called* Future—*Pound would be a frequent contributor till its demise in 1919. Gallup records no reviews or contributions by Pound to the* **International Journal of Ethics**.

⊹⊱━━⊰⊹

523. ALS [*embossed letterhead*] 5, Holland Place Chambers, Kensington, W.

13 December 1916

[London]

Dear Dad:

You must not exaggerate! The Newark affair is $50 not £50 and the blighters havent sent it yet. Though they said it would start on Nov 10th.

As for a lecture tour in America. People usually do it after they have got old & soft in the head and no use for anything else. It is a symptom of decay which I do not look forward to with any pleasure. A bad end which I presume awaits me in my indigent old age.

Still. you should put your question to Pond not to Pound. He arranges these things for his unfortunate well paid victims.

Best Xmas to you & mother. Hilda has not gone to America after all. which explains why you have not heard from her

Have finished the libretto & am doing another longish essay on De Gourmont.

You better treat youself to a set of Landor $8.75. and worth it. We have just done so. also found a fine set of Aeschylus with latin crib on the 3 penny stall. day before yesterday. & have added them.

New wall paper. goes well in the room also new hearth mat of verdant green.

Capn. Baker just back after two years in the east.

Lewis through most of his exams. for artillery commission.

No word from Quinn since September.

Love to you & mother
E. P.

Ezra Pound

13 - 12 –'16

At Stone Cottage in the New Year Pound would be reading to Yeats from **Landor's** Imaginary Conversations; *and he would contribute an article on Landor to Granville's* Future *in November 1917. In an article on* **Aeschylus** *in the* Egoist *in early 1919 Pound described the set he had bought:*

the Thomas Stanley Greek and Latin edition, with Saml. Butler's notes, Cambridge, 'typis ac sumptibus academicis'. 1811—once a guinea or half-a-guinea per volume, half leather, but now mercifully, since people no longer read Latin, picked up at 2s. for the set (eight volumes in all) rather less than the price of their postage. Quartos in excellent type.

‡‡‡‡

524. ALS [*embossed letterhead*] 5, Holland Place Chambers, Kensington, W.

16 Dec 1916

[London]

Dear Mother.

We have been smothered in fog for a week. - good news from Verdun this a.m.

Coburn's show of vortographs is set for February. I don't know that there is much other news.

Lewis has passed all his exams. rather well.

Hueffer has gone back to France.

A chap named Montsier was in week before last to interview me for the Adam's Syndicate. I believe its the N. Y. Sun. & other papers.

Koumé made an excellent Buddha at the Italian Red X benefit tableaux last week.

Have you heard anything of Itow in america. I hear he is doing excellently.

MacMillan say the Noh book will be out early next year.

There is no news since my last to dad, as we have hardly been out of the house; save to dine with the Dulac's on Thursday.

Waley reports that a Japanes magazine about Noh. has an article with my name forged at the bottom.

De Bosschère is doing a critique of me for the Egoist - with a caricature appended.

Do you get the rag. I can't send single copies now

Manning is at the front, as I think I wrote.

Cuala press has paid up £5 royalties.

Re. the £30 you mention. I certainly don't want it till dad has paid off that note in the Jenkintown Bank. It is a waste paying interest on it. at a high rate. & only getting a low rate on deposits.

I think from pesent indications I shall manage for another year of war all right enough and it dont look as if the Hun could hold out for much longer than that. Thanks all the same.

Love to you & dad.

.E.

Ezra Pound
5 Holland Place Chambers.

De Bosschère's critique was spread over the January and February 1917 issues of the Egoist.

+⊨═⊨+

525. **ALS** [*embossed letterhead*] 5, Holland Place Chambers, Kensington, W.
4 January 1917

[London]

Dear Mother:

Old Wedmore is a chap who used to write delicate prose stuff in the 90's - Look him up in Mosher's catalogue - pirated editions -

Georgie Hyde-Lees is in the operating room at some hospital or other. being very competent & useful.

Her family has just rented its house & is departing for the sea coast.

Koume was Buddha in the Italia Red X benefit. Am my self roped in for for a show in benefit of prisoners in Germany.

Sir Thomas has stumped up handsomely for the libretto. & times are easier.

Have had carbons made of begining of long poem & will send it on shortly.

Or rather I'll enclose it.

Love to you & dad.

yrs

Ezra Pound

4 - 1 – '17.

+⊨═⊨+

526. **ALS**

[c.4 January 1917]

[London]

Dear Dad.

Here's the first 3 cantos of the long poem.

Send me your first impressions & second impessions as soon as you can.

I don't want you to show it about until it's printed or until I have decided on the final form of some of this

Yrs

E.

Homer Pound to EP, 10 January 1917:

Well, this morning came the P O E M.

It took my attention – on the train – and I was in town almost before I knew it - It was a cool clear morning – I walked along the street with my

387

head up – and felt the stimulus of the spirit – that breathed out of the MSS. I have been very busy all day – but at odd times have taken a fly – at the Poem. You wish a first impression – Well – In reading it I can feel its sweep – and it is as I imagine like one going up in an Airship – The Mechanician has honored me with a seat – and we are soon up in the pure azure – Time and space are nothing – We sweep the whole world – and just as we lose ourselves – he drops me out – and here I am just pegging away – and it will be some time before the next Mss – comes – I thank you for the compliment, My opinion does not seem of much value – but I am glad that in that little room – in London a son of mine can lose himself in such matters – but but –may I be permitted to suggest that as this poem is not for the Yahoos – for after the first word it soars way above the crowd – so use a different word than "hang" It seems to me "Listen-all" - - would be a better word – ask D – if I am not right . . . . . I will read the poem more carefully when I get home this evening – Of course there are many words and names that I do not understand as you well know – but nevertheless it gives one a desire to see the places – I wish, some day we can go over them together –

The opening line of the cantos Pound had sent was, 'Hang it all, there can be but the one "Sordello"'.

⇥═══⇤

527. **TL** [*embossed letterhead*] 5, Holland Place Chambers, Kensington, W.

[c.5 January 1917]

[London]

Dear Dad

I wonder if you could let me know what latin books of mine I left in America. At the present moment I want two small volumes of my set of Ovid. Two little brown books 3½ by 5½ inches, probably no lettering left on the back. Front page begins: P.Ovidii.

They aren't very valuable, but they are of a convenient size, and the postage cant come to much. Otherwise I might get a new set.

If you've nothing better to do, you might send me a list of all my foreign books, as they are no use to you. Some of them may be worth mailing over. Some I probably have duplicated here.

I mailed the first three cantos of POEM yesterday or the day before. Hope it reaches you safely. It is a bit of a chaw, but remember it is only a beginning of a much longer affair and that some of its incomprehensible places will be elucidated later on. (I hope.)

I want very much to know what you make of it, both as a whole (i.e. the lot sent) and in detail.

So write at length on the matter.

Quinn cables that he has been very busy. Forgot Lewis installment of cash for pictures and even had to cable that at the last minute.

+≻══≺+

528. ALS [*embossed letterhead*] 5, Holland Place Chambers, Kensington, W.

24 – 1 '17

[London]

Dear Dad

After five months silence I have just had 36 page letter from Quinn.

He was delighted with you and mother, and says you must see him when you next go to New York. He really liked you, all right. Both of you.

He seems to be doing jolly well for me. The vorticist show is open as you doubtless know.

Have been answering the 36 pages, and doing other letters it entailed.

So this is only a scribble.

Various bundles of papers have arrived from you.

Yrs

Ezra Pound.

> **The Vorticist exhibition** *of works collected and shipped to New York by Pound, and organised there by John Quinn, ran from 10 to 31 January 1917.*

+≻══≺+

529. TLS [*embossed letterhead*] 5, Holland Place Chambers, Kensington, W.

27 January 1917

[London]

Dear Dad

The Times has run to two columns on the 'Noh' book. I am having a copy sent you.

Quinn seems to have nearly fixed up a deal with a New York publisher called A.A.Knopf, , 220 W. 42 220 W. 42nd. St. .

He will probably bring out Lustra or rather a larger vol. containing Lustra and most of the earlier poems.

They may want you to send them copies of Personae and Exultations, on loan.

I cant send marked copies from here without special permit etc.

Also Quinn or Knopf may want to see your copy of 'Noh', as I haven't a spare copy to send them.

They will presumably write to you for what they want,
Love to you and mother.
Yrs
E.

Ezra Pound

27 - I - 17

The Times Literary Supplement *review of* 'Noh' *or* Accomplishment *was in the issue of 25 January 1917 under the heading 'Japanese Mysteries'.*

⊢══━╫

530. TLS [*embossed letterhead*] 5, Holland Place Chambers, Kensington, W.

4 March 1917

[London]

Dear Dad

There is not much to write. There have been various commendatory notices of 'Noh', but none of any interest as none of the reviewers know anything about the subject, and all of them fall back on lengthy quotations from the book. I had the 'Times' sent you or at least ordered it sent.

Joyce's novel has had a column in the Times and a damd silly page from H. G. Wells in the 'Nation', all of which ought to help its sales. I hope you have it by now. i.e. the novel 'A Portrait of the Artist as a young Man.', and also the earlier book of stories 'Dubliners.'.

Rodker has just done an unpleasant tale with something in it. Am trying it on the Smart Set.

Quinn appears to have made satisfactory arrangements with Knopf.

Alfred A. Knopf

220 W. 42nd. St., New York

I trust you will give them all the help you can, lending them copies of Personae and Exultations, if they want them, seeing mss. is arranged according to my directions (as in my letters to them), and correcting proofs. etc. You might drop him a card saying that I have mentioned the matter to you, and that you are ready to help.

I shall want to see one set of proofs, better the first set. I think you will be able to do the revise quite as well as I could. That will save a month or six weeks in the printing.

Knopf not the American Macmillan is handling 'Noh' in America.

The book of Poems is to be Lustra with earlier poems, selected.

I doubt if Lane has any more circulars of the Gaudier. I have a vague recollection of having asked him about it, some time ago.

None of my books from the list mother has made, can be sent now. A lot of things seem to have disappeared, but it dont matter. I shall want the Agricola sometime, but not now.

Remembrances to grandmother and folks at Tioga.

If Miss T. wants a copy of Lustra unabridged she had better send her M.O. to Elkin at once. I saw a copy of the numbered edition in Charing X. Rd. a few days ago marked £1/1. Man said he had put up one for 10/6 a few days before and sold it the same day, so thought he might as well try it higher.

Elkin still has a few copies left. He has however the right to advance the price on the last few dozen, so the modest sum of 5 shillings wont avail much longer.

Boston Transcript had a page on the Cuala 'Noh' book. about five weeks ago. Not interesting.

(opus of K. M. Buss, 44 Bradlee Rd. Medford Mass.)

recon thats about all,

Love to you & mother.
E. P.

Ezra Pound.

4 / 3 / '17

+>—+—<+

531. TLS [*embossed letterhead*] 5, Holland Place Chambers, Kensington, W.<8>

27 / 3 / '17

[London]

Dear Dad

It is extremely kind of Quinn to want me to get forty dollars out of one copy of 'A Lume Spento', and I should certainly like him to have a copy but there simply <u>aint</u> any copies. I figure that your copy cost you from 20 to 40 dollars a month for about the first two years I was in London, and when I consider that you sent on the cash without any grumbling, I dont feel that you should be made to give up your copy even for Quinn.

I dont think he would have made the offer unless he had thought it was 'an extra copy', which he specifically calls it in his letter.

If he merely wants to spend money on me he is now having a chance re/ a proposed magazine arrangement. If on the other hand he really wants a copy of A.L.S. I think it just possible that he might be able to get one from either from

F. S. Flint

17 Canonbury Park

Canonbury, London N.

or from Mrs Alice Herbert,

35 Avonmore Rd.

London W.16.

at least I know that both of these people once had copies, if they still have them I imagine that they would sell them for 15 dollars. I think either of them would probably jump at it.

There is, or was, also a chap in St Louis, but I've forgotten his name. And Quinn's friend King has a copy which he bought on a book stall, but he is a collector also and may want to keep it.

Possibly Mrs H.Adams who once lived at

> 5 Cumberland Terrace
>
> Regents Park, London W.

has a copy.

Possibly Ernest Rhys (co/ Dent and Co.) has a copy, (he probably would be glad of £ 3/3). I cant at the moment think of anyone else who **has**. That is who would sell unless perhaps they were dam'd hard up.

Of course IF you could find a <u>spare</u> copy it would be wholly another story. In that case Quinn ought to have it. I think we'd better leave it that IF I can find a copy Quinn shall have it for what it costs me. In the mean time you'd better keep yours.

He might try W. C. Williams, 9 Ridge Rd. Rutherford, N.J.
or Mrs V.Jordan (Viola Baxter as was) 81 Pallisade Ave. Bogota N.J.
probably either of them could do with 25 dollars.

/ / / / / /

That's that.

Hueffer has been in all the afternoon. Back on leave. We have jawed a little about the front, and a good deal about french prose.

It is very pleasant to see him again, as there is really nobody else with whom one can talk about books.

The Egoist is going to publish Eliot's poems. Joyce's novel has been excellently reviewed in the Times, by Brock, and in the Nation by H. G. Wells.

The Sketch has reproduced a couple of vortographs. I must have it sent you. They are badly chosen, about the worst in the show, <u>ma che</u>! The head might be fairly good, but was done straight into the light on a dull day. Then Coburn was ill for a month just before the show, and there was no time to do a better one.

Bennington has done a good photo of D. which will be sent you after the war.

I think Iris Barry may write some good prose if given time. Young Rodker has sent me a novel, extremely unpleasant, but showing energy. I have sent it on to Mencken with a recommendation.

Lewis has done some short sketches.

That is about the length of 'current notes on contemporary litterchure'.

I believe I am in excellent health. Have just put in a hard week at the Museum.

Love to you and mother. Will answer her letter shortly.

Tell her I believe I have met Clive Bell, but there are a lot of those washed-out Fry-ites, and I cant tell one from the other. A sort of male Dorcas-society.

yours
E.

Ezra Pound

27 / 3 / ’17

*Brock, i.e. Arthur Clutton-Brock (1868–1924). For Pound's letters to **Iris Barry** in 1916 see his* Selected Letters—*they were mainly about her poems.* ***Dorcas societies,*** *commonly associated with a church, supplied clothing to the poor—not an apt analogy for the male members of the Bloomsbury Group.*

⊹⊱━⊰⊹

532. TLS [*embossed letterhead*] 5, Holland Place Chambers, Kensington, W.

6 April 1917

[London]

Dear Dad

Thanks for the £3, or for my half of it. Whatever ability I have for arranging words into sentences should be employed at this instant on something other than family correspondence. I haven't enough for both.

My last activity is the reviewing of the assenine works of contemporary theologians. I dont know how long it will last, but it is entertaining. Blighters blowing off whole bookfulls about God. The one subject on which all men are equally, abyssmally and incurably ignorant. It's a graft that might well be finished off.

Get the <u>May</u> number of the 'Little Review ' pub.

31 W. 14 th St. New York.

there may be something in it.

Wells is a sloppy sort of animal, would decorate a butcher's shop to advantage. Mixture of vulgarity and vigorous intellect, which sometimes works, and equally often does NOT.

Joyce is a very great prose writer. The content of contemporary novelists is for the most part purely factitious.

Joyce is set on reality. His style is certainly remarkable in a language like english where there are hardly any prose writers, he is one of the few who write as well as the French masters. There is no mush. I think you will find hardly a word wasted in the whole of his writing. Beyond. that he is one of the half dozen living people who have even thought about <u>anything</u>. Dunghills like Chesterton burble, others merely mop off a surface. Others are incurably ignorant and incapable of any save the most rudimentary form of perception.

He is the first man writing english since Hardy and Henry James who has been able to enter their class.

He is the first irishman who has ever given any indication of what Dublin is really like. A book like his had it been promptly published and read by the right people might have prevented the rising. He has hit problems so fundamental that I am told the book might have been set in Belgium and been true, with merely a few substitutions, as for example some other row than the Parnell question.

Where in English will you get anything better done than that dinner scene?

He writes as Durer painted. And MY GAWD how he wipes the floor with the Sainte Foi Catolique in that sermon!!! The scarlet woman of the Capitoline needs a new cloak after he is done with her.

Have written a few things in prose. You may see them sometime.

More anon. Love to you and mother, and greetings to family at Tioga.

Yours

Ezra Pound

6 - 4 - 1917

*Gallup does not record any reviews of **contemporary theologians***. *In the May number of the **Little Review** there would be an 'Editorial' by Pound, accepting the post of Foreign Editor, and two contributions, 'Pierrots: Scène courte mais typique (After the "Pierrots" of Jules Laforgue)'—this signed with the pseudonym 'John Hall'—and a prose 'pavanne', 'Jodindranath Mawhwor's Occupation'.*

✛⇒✦⇐✛

533. ALS [*embossed letterhead*] 5, Holland Place Chambers, Kensington, W.<8>

<note numeral in address>

27 April 1917

[London]

Dear Dad:

Quinn sent on £8 for copy of 'A Lume Spento'.

I am doing something with 'The Little Review' 31 W 14th St. New York.

Haven't yet heard from Quinn, so dont know whether he will back me up in it, or whether he will think it too small.

He has been most ample in other offers re' my books etc.

What has Homer married??

The long poem is coming out in Poetry. Thru' June. July. Aug.

Quinn has fixed up the book publication in New York.

The censor encloses this slip. re. money order. I think you were referring, however, to m. o. in your other letter. Sent as anniversary present??

394

Have written to Q. to see if he can get me a war job.

Embassy has 'no instructions'. consulate ditto.

Lane sent you all the prospecti there were left.

Eliot's poems are in proof.

etc. .etc.

Yeats is in Ireland for a few weeks

remember me to grandmother - regards affection.

DeBosscher has got a three years contract to illustrate books for Heinemann.

my head is about as alive as a pan cake at the moment.

Love to you and mother.

more anon.

yrs

Ezra Pound

27 – 4 – '17

'**Homer**' here is Pound's cousin, Homer Foote. The US had just entered the war.

+>==<+

534. TLS [*embossed letterhead*] 5, Holland Place Chambers, Kensington, W.>8<

9 May 1917

[London]

Dear Dad:

Your allied colleagues make a bad shot at diagnosing a lead <u>half-crown</u>. vide the reverse of sheet.

You will by now have rec'd notice from Little Review that I am editor of half of it. I trust you will rake in a few thousand subscribers and start us on the roads of prosperity. Quinn is paying contributors, or rather paying me to pay them. I have some damn good stuff for the next four or five numbers. Yeats, Lewis, Eliot, E. P.

I think Eliot may take on part of the Egoist, and brace it up. . . . a much needed brace.

You may have seen Quinn on Joyce in Vanity Fair for May, a fine boom for all of us. . . . . also the amazingly good press Joyce is getting. I have been very busy arranging detail of the Review, and, therefore have not written for some time. Have still a hunk of work to get through.

LITTLE REVIEW, 31 W. 14th. St. NEW YORK

'Poetry' is printing my long poem in three chunks, June, July, August.

Also Knopf may want your copy, as he may include it in the vol. of Poems. I wrote Quinn to ask you for it. I haven't a spare copy at the moment, and my clear copy was lent when I wrote to Q. so yours was the quickest available.

The Cuala Press edition of old J. B. Yeats letters edited by your son, is out. It is also damd expensive. I get only one copy. Will try to send you a set of the proof-sheets as soon as I can spare mine.

I trust you will send your subscription 1.50 to Little Review promptly and cheerfully. I MUST get in enough subscriptions SOON, so as to enlarge the format. It is now 32 pages, and <u>must</u> be 64 really to succede (commercially). Literary success is (OF COURSE) <u>ASSURED</u> by the effulgence of certain contributors.

more anon. Love to your and mother.

Ezra Pound

9 / 5 / '17

The letter is typed on the verso of a letter to Pound from the London Mint informing him 'that the representation of a coin enclosed is a counterfeit florin manufactured of base metal, and is of no value.' **Eliot** *became Assistant Editor of the* Egoist *in June.*

✠══✠

535. TLS [*embossed letterhead*] 5, Holland Place Chambers, Kensington, W.>8<

15 May 1917

[London]

Dear Dad

After all our struggles. Quinn sent the wrong proofs of Lustra to Knopf. So a lot of poems have been omitted from the galley proofs, which I am returning today. or Tomorrow

I enclose a list of errors in the proofs, and also a list of the OMISSIONS.

I shan't see the final proofs, so it devolves on you to see that ALL THESE ERRORS get corrected, and ALL the poems mentioned get included.

(The Temperaments is optional, but I want it in at least 150 copies, even if Knopf leaves it out of the public edition.)

If you dont want your 'Personae' and 'Exultations' spoiled, perhaps you'll copy.

'In Durence'

and 'Piere Vidal Old' (including the prefatory note) and let the printer work from your type script.

As you know S. Maynard refuse to give up the poems in Provence. These two poems however aren't in their book. They will give the note of the earlier work and permit the Knopf vol. to have the feel of completeness.

With the THREE CANTOS added, the book will be stronger than it would with the S. Maynard poems. and the Cantos omitted.

Poetry is printing one canto a month. through June, July, Aug.

that will finish in time for Knopf. to use the poem.

Magazine is going strong. Sent off some live stuff for July. number this a.m.

Am exhausted with proof correcting, so close.

Love to you and mother.

yrs

EP

Ezra Pound

15 – 5 – '17

LIST OF ERRORS IN LUSTRA GALLEY PROOFS

Galley no.	should read		
2.	songs	not sons	['Commission']
2	a young sapling		['Dance Figure']
3.	bus-stops	not bus-tops	['FurtherInstructions']
3	É not E in ITÉ		
3	be'a'! not be 'a!'		['The Study in Aesthetics']
	word set close, number for note		
	comes before ! mark.		
5.	W.B.Y.	not N.B.Y.	['Amitiés']
5.	Bub title to be separate from first of 'Amities'.		
6.	of	not for Midons Aelis	['"Dompna pois . . ."']
6.	delete full stop.		
8.	In PAPYRUS'		
	Spring not to be written in caps.		
	Spring not SPRING		
	Poem sic. PAPYRUS		
	Spring.....		
	Too long.....		
	Gongula........		
8.	too	not to	
8.	turquoise	not turquois	['Women Before a Shop']
9.	bel	not el	['Our Contemporaries']
	bistre	not listre	[" "]
	; at end of line.		
10.	Heard	not And	['Provincia Deserta']
	tingeing	not tinging	[" "]
12	Emperor	not Emepror	['The River Song']
13	in to	not into	
14.	Have	not had	
15.	line space.		
16	St Circ	not St. Cire	['Near Perigord']
17.	comma		
	indent Papiol		[" "]
21. stet.	un e duo		['To a Friend . . . Cabaret Dancers']

22.   remove sub dedications etc. Have a sub title page,
    CANZONI , first published 1911
    or <u>Earlier Poems</u>. Before 1912.

24.   <u>thick</u>   not think
    add quotes '   '

27   <u>come</u> to be inserted
    <u>your</u>   not our

29   end line in middle of word word , <u>loveli-</u> *['Apparuit']*

33.   addition to 'footnote'*['Salve Pontifex'* : 'Balderdash but let it stay
    for the rhythm.'*]*

LIST OF POEMS OMITTED FROM GALLEY PROOFS AND TO BE
    INSERTED IN LUSTRA

Poem.	to be inserted.	
1. Salutation Second	before 'The Spring '	gal 1½
2. Commission	" 'A Pact '	' 1½
3. The New Cake of Soap	" ' Salvationists'	4
4. Epitaph	' Arides'	' 4
4 b. The Temperaments	after ' The Bath Tub'	gal 4.

    (this in limited numbered edition if you choose.)

5. Meditatio	before ' To Dives'	gal 5.
6. Phyllidula	' ' Coda '	gal 5
7. The Patterns		
8. The Seeing Eye	' Ancora	gal 5.
9. ἱμέρρω	' Shop Girl	' 8
10. Ancient Music _____	' Epitaphs	' 9.
11. The Lake Isle /		
12. Pagani's Nov. 8.	' Cabaret Dancers,	' 20

13. Impressions of Francois Arouet.
        1.,2 = and 3
        as the end of of ' Lustra ' proper.   gal 22.

14. In Durence   (From Personae)
15. Piere Vidal Old (From Exultations)
      EARLIER POEMS published before 1912
      was headed Canzoni
      as beginning of 'sub. Section   gal. 22
16. THREE CANTOS   with sub title pages to itself
          as conclusion to the whole volume.

Note the 13. Arouet . is in three parts.
    1.   Phyllidula and the Spoils of Gouvernet
    2.   To Madame du Chatelet
    3.   To Madame Lullin.

If I sent you an <u>emended</u> copy before, follow it. if not you can use the enclosed.
Starred poems in this list enclosed under cover. to Knopff.

In Apparuit. galley 29.

        line ends.

              about it, loveli-

  est of all things. etc.

to divide on the syllable. as in Ripostes.

Galley 33 have added a few words to footnote.

You can check the page proofs from these lists, as well as from my corrected 'galleys'.

Titles in square brackets are editorial additions. 'The Temperaments' was not included in the 'public edition', but was printed in the sixty copies 'for private circulation', fitted in (out of place) as the last of the 'Lustra' poems.

✦━━✦

536. **TLS** [*embossed letterhead*] 5, Holland Place Chambers, Kensington, W.

23 May 1917

                                   [London]

Dear Dad:

Don't you worry about my pay from the Little Review. I get paid all right, and everyone in my section gets paid, and it is a great comfort. The 'L.R.' after May 1st. will be quite a different affair from the L. R. before that date.

You just busy yourself enlarging the subscription list. The more subscribers the sooner we enlarge the size, and the more you get per number for you exalted nickel and dime.

/ /

Have completely rewritten my long poem, cut it down six pages. See that Knopf uses the new mss.

I sent it this a.m. to Quinn. You will get the proofs to correct. I shant see 'em. There are various queer points that I have specially marked 'stet' or 'O.K.' so that they shant be mistaken for slips, of the typewriter.

I began the revision on Saturday about 11.15 p.m. it is now Tuesday morning.

As starting on an article for Aug. L. R. so will desist.

Love to you and mother. I seem to have lost her mss. cook. book. You might ask her to send on receptts and directions for corn-bread, and the various flapjacks.

                           Yours

                           E. P.

Ezra Pound

23 / 5 / 1917

may send you a duplicate copy of new version of poem if I have time to make it. Let 'Poetry' alone. i.e. let 'em use the version they've got. don't tell 'em I've done a new one.

+=⚬=+

537. TLS [*embossed letterhead*] 5, Holland Place Chambers, Kensington, W.
24 July 1917

[London]

Dear Mother

Your phrase 'many of' my 'friends' in connection with the inhabitants of your native village is rather inexact. Neither the multitudinousness nor their amicality are of so marked a shade that the untempered noun and adjective can truly be applied in conjunction. If Miss K. notifies me of her presence in London I shall invite her to tea in due course, but I do not think America Red X. units are very likely to be sent on pleasure trips to the capital, at least not many. Nor will George, if he is now over here get a commission in the Army or any other job. Those employed by our government will be selected from the inhabitants of Missouri and on the basis of a complete ignorance of all Europe. They will also be appointed in Washington and not via the American embassies. Still George may have friends at home.

It is a pity that Wilson and the Kaiser, Teddy and Hindenburg, and a few other picked specimens cant all be put in a bull ring, cut each others throats and finish . the job altogether, it has been going on long enough.

Why you send me hymn tunes I do not know.

There was a long review of 'Noh' in the Morning Post yesterday, I'll send a copy sometime. Lewis is convalescing. D. has returned from the land. I have done a short series on Provincialism for the New Age, and am beginning a longer one, i.e. presumably called 'Studies in Contemporary Mentality'. I begin on July 12. I forget whether dad can get the N.A. in America, or whether I have to send it from here.

Am doing 'Elizabethan Classicists' in the Egoist, beginning Sept.

Love to you & dad.

E

Ezra Pound
24 / 7 / '17

Wyndham Lewis was convalescing from trench fever in a military hospital in France. Dorothy Pound had been with relations in Dorset and had written of cows and crops, of haymaking and hoeing up thistles. Four articles under the heading **'Provincialism the Enemy'** *appeared in the* New Age *in July and August; the* **longer series,** *studying the* *mentality of the nation as revealed in its magazines, would run to nineteen articles between August 1917 and January 1918.*

---

538. TLS [*embossed letterhead*] 5, Holland Place Chambers, Kensington, W. <8>
25 July 1917

[London]

Dear Dad:

Here are the copies of the Post review. I havent sent you the press because one cant bother the censor indefinitely, at least I dont feel that one should.

Will you send one of the enclosed to Quinn, one to Knopf, and one to Mrs Fenollosa, Spring Hill, Mobile Co. Alabama.

There have been a lot a press notice, but as no one knows anything about the subject, the revieweres have for the most part done about a column of quotations from the book itself, which is not interesting to reread, whatever its adv. value.

Wrote to mother yesterday, since when there is no news.

Yrs

E.

Ezra Pound

25 / 7 / '17

---

539. TLS [*embossed letterhead*] 5, Holland Place Chambers, Kensington, W.
Aug 23 1917

[London]

Dear Dad:

I dont quite know what 'feelings' you want me to run up. It is of course pleasing to see the stars and stripes and the union jack amorously entwined on the same flag pole at the British Museum. As you know an Anglo-Franco-American alliance has been in my eyes a desirable thing for a long time. America had sunk lower than the mud, and everything I had written on the subject had been suppressed. I dont know how much impressed I can now be at the sight of America doing what England has been doing all along. I dont know (now that one can scarcely read the communiques from the front for boredom with the same phrases repeated year after year) I dont know what waves of emotion a Billion dollars is expected to raise. Simply, America is doing what she damn well ought to do, and what so far as I can see, she ought to have begun doing sooner. (Until I have seen all the diplomatic correspondence I am not in a position to assert this 'ought' scientifically.

I shall never believe in rhetoricians nor in Wilson nor in any man who slops the language as he does. I do not favour conscription, but I indubitably benefit (personally) by the present American system of it.

It is ironical that both Homer and David should go, and that I who care something for civilization should be left at my typewriter. It must be especially bitter for Florence who certainly dont give a curse whether London and Paris and all that they mean, are destroyed or not.

An intelligent government would of course preserve people like Lewis and myself. Lewis is however in the thick of it.

I don't think Wilson tried to make America understand the war, before he came in, and I don't much believe America knows what the conflict means. However I am thankful she is in. (On the other hand, she never would have recovered if she hadn't come in.).

As I am for the present definitely left out, through no act of my own, or through no neglect of my own, I think it would ill become me to go about shouting magniloquently about the glory of war. Just as it is not Mr Rockfellow's business to do so.

America is fighting on my side, probably for reasons not in the least my own. That is about as far as I get with it.

Conscription is perhaps effective, and perhaps preserves some of the right people, it is however unprincipled. The people who flop from abject cowardice into servile prussianism all at one gulp do not impress me.

It may be excused as 'necessity' but that excuse serves the Germans in Belgium.

IF it was necessary, to have such a law to keep down the German reservists in America, THEN well and good. But I do not wish to gulp down ideas until I KNOW.

Certainly the bosche must be beaten. That proposition is of more importance to me than what America now does. The greater part she takes in it, the better for her.

I see nothing to do but keep quiet. I would have had America in two or three years ago with a volunteer army. And I suppose I should now be taking less interest in mundane affairs, unless I had been rejected for eyesight or given some job where my brains instead of my hide were of use. (It is not however the habit of democracies to use my sort of intelligence.).

I shall not write against conscription, or do anything to impede the executive in the least. Besides I should have done it months ago if I had been going to.

So long as I am myself 'too old tew fight' I cant see that it is decent for me to flag-wave.

Neither can the acts of America to date, fill me with any feeling in excess of what one feels for the French and English troops that have been in the field since the start. <That is to say I care for America merely as I care for Australia

or any other part of 'the Allies' who are 'my country'. I am glad that America is now part if it. So is Siam.>

I have never taken any stock in Russia. I can only hope she wont make too hellish a mess of her front. They are and always have been a stupid and uninteresting people. Coming from one barbarism I can not be expected to take interest in another.

Re/ the Review. I do not expect to 'get' anything 'out of it'. <apart from my stipend> It is not the business of 'literature to exploit or 'get things out of' people.

One's job consists in putting down what one thinks clearly and with no regard to the local prejudices or temporal prejudices of the proletariat or public or whatever it is called.

If there can be printed in America a paper that can be read in Paris or London without boredom one might have a sensation of gratification. Up to now America has produced local gazettes. Harpers and that boiling are too far in the past to mention. The New Republic is punk, ditto Seven Arts, in a different way. Poetry has escaped in a small corner, and this was NOT due to the Chicago board.

As Lewis has said (July number) 'Matter which has not sufficient mind to permeate it grows. . . . gangrenous and rotten.'.

That is the American 'world (or rather village) of letters.'.

The shock of hearing that ideas, not current in Omaha, exist is probably too much for America . . . infant industries . . . infant mentalities.

There is no need of people 'adopting' other ideas. I dont see how I can be much clearer than I am in the end of my Poggio dialogue.

I shall print DeGourmonts last letter to me, in Dec. You can also refer to a poem of mine 'The Rest', and may get a clue from it.

Lower's poem on the chapel on the hike-pike is an example of what one is going <u>away from</u>. One at least disinfects oneself. One releases the microbes of W. D. Howells and Co. I dont know what else one can be expected to do.

The blight of Tertullian, Calvin and co. is probably an eternal disease of mankind. Also the American dullness, once of Century, Harper, now of New Republic, Dial, (creeping over Harriet's part of Poetry). One wants relief from this stifling.

Fortunately I am over here. Otherwise I should get entoiled in endless controversy over things that do not matter. And get nothing done.

Look at the correspondence in the L. R. . . . yelling that we give them 'invention instead of interpretation'. i.e. creation instead of gas . . . . .

It was perhaps a mistake to join up with an American paper at all. Nothing can be done except in London or Paris. One can not turn a province into a capital, and the province is always a series of impotent and diminishing ecchoes.

One/ can not however stop merely because people have not yet read DeGourmont, or Anatole, or the Classics, or anything except St Paul and Robt. W. Chambers.

/ / /

One would also like to give people something better than the Shaw, Wells, Bennet, generation, daft on abstract ideas, and the last two, sunk in vulgarity.

As for American literature, the odour of decayed thought is almost tangible in the Seven Arts and New Republic. (The first article in the Seven Arts you sent me, was an exception, the man (wrong) but <u>trying</u> to see for himself. Let us even grant he succeedes.

That is better than the old gang of magazines. But the magazine <of Arts> itself is punk. Dead thought. Hilda had a flash in her first poems. Eliot invented. Williams has done one poem. Masters applied a method to matter that he had seen first hand, BUT he has flopped back into cliché, current magazine opinions etc.

The rest dont KNOW anything, (Alice Corbin, is perhaps an exception she also has done one or two good things). the whole scope of their ambition is to 'get something accepted', NOT to get something said.

Lewis, Joyce, Eliot, Romains (not Romain Rolland) do think. This active chemical in the mind is the thing worth preserving. It must have its court yard.

They <these men> do not perpetually go on pawing over other-peoples cast off thoughts.

The long prose of Hueffers <to begin in Jan.> is also active, in a rather gentler way, but still, living.

Yeats again made his own place. He didn't simply produce to supply a market demand.

There is no earthly need of agreeing with what people think. But there is a need that some people should be capable of thinking, not merely of pawing over thought already formed. AND they should have space and licence to do it.

Of course all intellectual freedom is loathed in America. Tolerance has never existed there, save as between rival sets of so called Christians, with a look askance at Catholicism. Catholicism <u>is</u> perhaps the worst and the Church of England the most comic. If I could believe the Quaker's banned music because church music is so damn bad, I should really view them with approval.

Bar their asceticism (partly a fake?) they seem to have some admirable, (Confucian?) ideas. Perhaps Quakerism tempered with classic mythology would give one a working hypothesis.

This has got long enough

Yours

E.

Ezra Pound

Homer and David Foote were sons of Pound's aunt Florence, a teacher of music. Pound was 'left out, through no act . . . through no neglect', having volunteered for National Service in England, only to have the Board decide that he had neither the manual nor the clerical skills they were looking for; and having found the US authorities in London not interested in recruiting him to the American war effort.

The '**Poggio dialogue**' was 'Aux étuves de Weisbaden, A.D. 1451', published in July's Little Review. **De Gourmont's 'last letter'** to Pound, as well as being printed in the December Little Review, was included in his essay, 'Remy de Gourmont, a Distinction'. The letter, written in June 1915, was a response to Pound's seeking de Gourmont's collaboration in a magazine aiming to bring together the best American, English, and French writing, in order to advance mutual understanding. De Gourmont had written:

> There is in every country a nucleus of good minds, of open minds, and they should be given some relief from the stale stuff of the magazines, something to give them confidence in themselves and to be a support. As you say, the first thing is to lead them to respect French individualism, that feeling for liberty which some among us possess to a high degree. They can understand that in theology. Why do they not understand it in art, in poetry, in literature, in philosophy. They must be made to see—if they do not see it already—that French individualism can, when necessary, put itself under the most severe disciplines.
>
> Doubtless to conquer the American is not all you intend. The aim of the Mercure has been to allow to those who deserve it the freedom to write what they think—the sole pleasure of a writer.

'**The Rest**', one of the earliest 'Lustra' poems, first appeared in Poetry in November 1913. '**Harriet**' is Harriet Monroe; '**Anatole**' is Anatole France; '**Hilda**' is Hilda Doolittle ('HD'). **Hueffer's 'long prose**' was 'Women and Men', appearing in instalments in Little Review.

+≈≈+

540. TLS [*embossed letterhead*] 5, Holland Place Chambers, Kensington, W.
31 August 1917

[London]

Dear Mother:

Glad you were entertained at Kape Kawd. One of the views with the old Kawdgers was quite amusing.

Have just sent off final proofs of Fontenelle, for the Egoist booklet. AND mss. of 'Pavannes and Divisions' to Knopf. it is a collection of various prose things, there seems some chance of his printing it.

He has bound American edition of 'Noh' very nicely. Little Review going strong. Arthur Symons has sent in a one act play, apparently prefering to have it in the L.R. and not be paid, than to send it elsewhere ('Drama' is what I suggested) and get payment.

Joyce is having his eyes operated on. Thinks his next novel will be ready for combined publication in Egoist and L.R. by January.

That will bring the L.R. list of contributors into pretty good shape. Yeats, Lady Gregory, Hueffer, Symons, May Sinclair, Lewis, Joyce, Eliot. Hope to get to the French stuff in due course. Waley has done some Po Chu-I. I hope in time for Oct. number.

Want a few £100 more to spend on contributors. and increase of format.

/ / /

I have been long meaning to ask Dad to get me a couple of glasses-cases from Keith. They do not appear to exist in England except in alligator skin or gold. One of mine is lost, and I set down a statue on the other, to the some detriment of it and contents. I have remended it a bit, but it is unsatisfactory.

He can send me a couple of the one piece steel nose grips too, if he likes. the kind which have no cork or tortoise shell, but simply hollow steel pieces that set on the nose.

All the english models of this sort of thing seem clumsy. In fact tooth brushes etc. all these minor forms of conveniece are in the U.S. superior. It does not constitute civilization, any more than a kitchen constitutes as house. But still . . .

/ / /

Am running in the New Age 'Studies in Contemporary Mentality', about ten or twelve articles.

/ / /

We are dining with old Ionides, this evening. He is of the imperial greek constinople emperors, and once sacked a pascha, friend of Whistler and Dumaurier, etc.

Dinner with Mrs Fowler tomorrow. Old Galton and various people seem pleased with the L.R. I value his opinion of prose as much as any one's

Time to start on preparations for exit.

Yrs
E.

Ezra Pound

31 – 8 – 17

Pound's **Dialogues of Fontenelle** *were published by The Egoist Ltd. in October 1917.*

+≻═≺+

541. TLS [*embossed letterhead*] 5, Holland Place Chambers, Kensington, W.

29 October 1917

[London]

Dear Dad

Am over my head in work. Have asked Egoist to continue your sub. and to send you 2 Fontenelles, from me.

N. Age articles may come out in book, so have not bothered with sending you the current numbers, but will try to get a file.

Old Upward thinks he is going to have a weekly, opulence for us all etc. I will believe when it really comes off.

Yeats married Georgie Hyde-Lees a week ago Saturday. Mother will remember her.

Lewis back on a ten days leave.

Granville in yesterday looking for copy. He will probably use some selections of the long poem in his paper 'The Future'. He has paid up a few guineas during the last year.

I am naturally waiting to see the American edtn. of Lustra, and to hear result of negotiations on prose book. Newark Committee paid up the Fifty dollars all right . enough.

Thanks very much for the glasses cases and bridges. Cournos. I have not seen for some time.

I dont know anything about Noh plays in N.Y. I dont expect to make anything out of them, anyhow.

Baker has been out of hospital, and generally adding to life, but may have to go back in again, as formalities demand etc. . . .

Rest of Hueffer's mss. came yesterday.

Have been meaning to answer mother's letter for some days, will get round to it in time.

Yrs
E.

Thanks for her offer of clothes – I have all the pyjamas I can wear at present. Will write to her re the rest.

Ezra Pound

29 - 10 – '17

+>——=+

542. TLS [*embossed letterhead*] 5, Holland Place Chambers, Kensington, W.

3 November 1917

[London]

Dear Mother

Thanks very much for your birthday donation. I have been on my head with work, and am just beginning to see daylight somewhere above me.

Quinn has been invaluable in getting Lustra thru press in N.Y. (Copies have not arrived here yet) Also in getting prose book arranged.

Lewis is back on a few days leave, with attendant turmoil of arrangements etc. and everything to be done instanter.

I have writ. father re/ N.Age, articles. They may go into a booklet. At any rate will transmit 'em in time.

Have ordered Egoist continued to him.

Re/ Wardrobe. I certainly dont need any more pyjamas. Socks are the only thing I can think of at the moment. Always useful .

Dad has forwarded some slips. re/ bonds. Really!!!!!

You can put the 150 into 'em if you like. But I'd rather H. L. P. used it to come over here on after the war.

I suppose I shall have another look at N.Y. about then. If all goes well with the L.R. etc. etc.

at least I feel the time approaching when I could stand another inspection of the eastern margin of the country .

Mr Wm. Beitler, First Pres. Ch. etc. is a curiously illiterate person. I thought the letter was from an indian (Bengal) student until I got to the end. Curious baboo or pidgeon idiom that he employs.

I desire the Newark Committee to be encouraged , but I do NOT wish the volume underlinecirculated. It is a chapter of my life that I would have unknown, save in Newark, and for practical purposes .

I should of course 'justify' my action if challenged but I would like the subject tactfully dropped. Not obtruded upon the attention of the elect.

My attitude, i.e my real attitude, should be concealed hermetically from Mr W. Wack, who might be used for higher things later.

Have ordered copies of Fontenelle sent on.

'Pavannes and Divisions' will include it, and about all the rest of my prose for the last few years that I want kept . save a few things not yet out in the L.R. and some information re/ troubadours not ready for the press.

A swine on the Open Court, or some such rag has the Fenollosa essay on Chinese character, promised to print, but damn slow.

Drama has another brief article, accepted.

Last long job. the french anthology no. for Feb. L.R. it will make a good chunk of another book.

    oh well.

love to you and Dad.
E.

Ezra Pound

3 / II / 17

---

*The '**swine on Open Court**' was its editor Paul Carus. Carus did not publish the essay, 'The Chinese Written Character as a Medium for Poetry', by Ernest Fenollosa and Ezra Pound', which first appeared in instalments in the* Little Review *in 1919.* **Drama** *apparently did not publish the 'brief article, accepted'. The '**french anthology**', Pound's 'A Study in French Poets', filled most of the February number of the* Little Review, *and made up 'a good chunk' of* Instigations *(1920).*

⊹═══⊹

543. TLS [*embossed letterhead*] 5, Holland Place Chambers, Kensington, W. <8>
18 November 1917

[London]

Dear Dad:

Peace and be still, re the Gaudier drawings of me. The photo. of the drawing was made by Dulac, and as he naturally did not charge me for the job I could naturally not insist on his making more prints than suited him. The thing went to Knopf, via the Chief censor, as I have a special permit for sending mss. and stuff needful for my books.

The thing is to be used in the brochure about me, so you will ultimately get several, and enough. Besides Knopf will surely let you have all the pulls you want.

Quinn has certainly contrived to get Lustra very well printed. There are numerous misprints all the same. I thought you were to have page proofs. However none of the slips are very terrible.

Beecham has put on a wonderful production of Figaro, but the opera is to close down fairly soon

I have had 'Fontenelle' sent you and ordered Egoist.

Lewis has got his leave extended, and may be attached to the Canadian staff for drawing. At least I hope so.

I have turned out endless scribble during the past week. N Age etc.

I have survived my brithday comfortable. Met Cunningham Graham this p.m. at Mrs Dummett's. etc etc. Granville is reprinting parts of three cantos in 'The Future' etc.

Quinn has sent me books by Mencken and A. Lowell.

Love to you & mother

Yours

E.

Ezra Pound

18 – 11 – 17

The **brochure** *was 'T. S. Eliot's Ezra Pound, His Metric and Poetry', published by Knopf in January 1918 in connection with Knopf's edition of 'Lustra'.*

+≕≕+

544. TLS [*letterhead*] The Little Review, London Office:-

5 Holland Place Chambers, W.8.

Dec 24 th. 1917

Dear Mother:

I am quite aware it is, and has long been time, for me to write to you. I have been doing ten and twelve hours a day rewriting 'Arnaut Daniel', and hope some of it may be fit to read. And I have been writing music criticism as one man, and art criticism as another, etc. etc. and going to concerts takes time.

Lewis is in town for a little. He is do war record paintings for the Canadians for a few months, at any rate.

We have brought out Lewis stories here so the psychic diseases of the late slimy Comstock's boot lickers, and of the unfortunate republic will not hinder that very much.

Dont know that there is much else to report, Yeats is at Forest Row. Baker has gone to Bath to see if it will cure his rheumatism.

Fist chapter of Joyce's new novel has come, and is most excellent, though not intended for servant girls in the suburbs or the jejune mind generally.

The Egoist is bringing out 'Tarr' here. in book form.

Make my salutations to family.

Love to you and dad, and Xmas greeting, as per. order.

> Yrs
> E.

Ezra Pound

Pound was radically revising his translations of the canzoni *of* **Arnaut Daniel** *which were not published in 1913 due to the Chicago publisher's entering into a new partnership. He was writing* **music criticism** *as 'William Atheling', and* **art criticism** *as 'B. H. Dias', both for the* New Age.

Wyndham Lewis's story, 'Cantleman's Spring Mate', had been published in October's Little Review, *and the issue had then been suppressed by the US postal authorities under the Comstock law, on the ground of the alleged obscenity of the story. In early November that story, together with 'The Ideal Giant' and 'The Code of a Herdsman', were 'Privately printed for the London Office of the Little Review', i.e. by Pound, in an edition of 200 copies.* **Joyce's new novel** *was* Ulysses, *which was to be serialized in the* Little Review, *and to get suppressed more than once.*

---

545. TLS [*embossed letterhead*] 5, Holland Place Chambers, Kensington, W.

24 January 1918

[London]

Dear Dad

Will get around to writing letters in a year or so. Have sent off the 'Arnaut' to Rev. C. C. Bubb 2077 E. 36 th. St. Cleveland Ohio. Dare say he will print it in time, and send you a copy.

Granville was Stephen Swift & Co. in the days of his glory. He has just sold 'The Future' and got a commission in the Naval auxilliaries. His son was killed at the front some months ago. Swift published my Guido Cavalcanti and

Ripostes. also spotted up £100. before they went bust. Had agreed to give me £100 per year advance on royalties for ten years.

Some of Granville's own poems are coming out in Poetry before long. Naturally NOT the best, as I sent the proofs of his book to H M and she has probably chosen unwisely.

Still hear from Mencken. He has sent me 'Pistols for Two' by 'Hatteras'.

The new <u>diseuse</u>, Raymonde Collignon is, I think, going to do Walter's settings of the troubadour songs.

Have I thanked you for Xmas, £2/??????? If not, this is it.

Wadsworth is back from the eastern Meditaranean.

Hueffer in town on 48 hours leave. Heard from a chap named Busha. americanus. hopes to get to London. is now at Winchester.

Have had promising story from a chap called Windeler.

Am doing art and music critiques under pseudonyms, paying the rent. rather entertaining work. ||<u>NOT to be mentioned.</u>|| It may be I have at last found a moderately easy way to earn my daily. Bloody queer what a man will do for money. MUSIC!!!!

'The Future' is printing some chunks out of the long poem. Lewis is painting for the Canadian war records. Expects to return from front with his sketches fairly soon, and do picture here.

Joyce's new novel beginning to come in, chapter at a time. Have sent new batch of my poems to Harriet. Really.!!!! when the hell I am supposed to write letters . . . eat. . . . sleep . . . etc . . .

Going to concerts is easy, but it occupies space.

Go to see the Collignon through some of the Provencal music tomorrow p.m. I think she may really revive the whole thing. At least she is about the only singer I've ever heard who gives me the impression of being able to do the job right.

Yone Noguchi has just writ from Japan for review copy of Gaudier book. Says he reviewed my 'Noh' last spring and that it is now well known in Japan.

Koumé is engaged to the half-jap daughter of Capt. Brinkley author of the Japanese Series. The best books on Japan that have been done.

Love to mother. Will write to her. . . . . .

Salutations to the family at Tioga.

E

Have also heard from a lecturer called Griffis = ? one of the luminaries of 'Sarah's' intellectual horizon??? He <u>dont</u> mention Sarah - says he knew Fenollosa in Japan

Ezra Pound

24 - 1 - '18

*The '**Arnaut**' manuscript—apparently the only copy—never reached Rev. Charles Clinch Bubb, and was presumed lost at sea, 'submarined'. B. Cyril **Windeler's** story, 'Elimus', was printed in the April Little Review. Pound had sent to Harriet Monroe '**two series***

. . . one mediaeval', i.e. 'Langue d'Oc', and the other 'Moeurs Contemporaines' (see Pound's Selected Letters *no. 141). She would declare both series 'unprintable', and they would appear in the* Little Review *in May. No poems by Pound would be published in* Poetry *in 1918.*

┼──────┼

546. TLS [*embossed letterhead*] 5, Holland Place Chambers, Kensington, W. <8>
17 February 1918

[London]

Dear Mother:

Dont know that there is much to write. We are meeting Lewis for dinner this evening. Am continuing to write weekly criticism of painting and music. Dolmetsch in Friday to tune the clavicord; says he is goin to come some evening and teach a few large pianists something about music, they not to know where they are being brought.

Am working again at troubadour music. Have found the right singer (Raymonde Collignon), we have been down to the museum digging at mss. and also sent off some drafts to Walter.

I hear the brochure on me is in print. No copy has yet arrived. Knopf might send one NOW even if he cant send a few dozen.

Wadsworth is probably to be stationed in England.

The L. Review should keep you au courant with most of my motions. I am very sorry to hear of Quinn's illness. Am sending off a story by a new man, Windeler, in a day or so. Yeats family says it is going to Ireland shortly, we have just declined to be dragged down to Oxford for the week.

You should look up Dolmetsch two books of reprints of early English music. Especially Henry Lawes, who really knew something about settings.

I dare say my next book will be made up from my music criticism. Q says Pavannes is in the press. The Arnaut Daniel has gone to Bubb, as I think I wrote.

Love to you and dad.

.E.

Ezra Pound
17 – 2 – '18

Yeats and his wife were then living in **Oxford***.*

┼──────┼

547. **TLS** [*embossed letterhead*] 5, Holland Place Chambers, Kensington, W.
23 February 1918

[London]

Dear Dad <re your letter undated>

Very sorry you have been down with RHEUmatizzzzzzzzz. Hope its over.

Dont know what was matter with L. R. save ubiquitous and ancient disease or <u>Poverta,</u> about which out firend Guido Cavalcanti made such unpleasant remarks. (in a Canzone, not in one of the ballate I translated.)

I dont know how much you put up. HOPE they've returned. it, now they have a fat guarantee (1600 simoleans acc. Q's last letter.)

Q. keeps volcaning. Cable yesterday re/ Eliot, and Q. cant possibly be out or hospital yet.

Thanks for clipping from Ledger. Author made one true remark without intending to do so. Q. also sends Reedy's with longer article. He has done me an excellent turn with. that brochure. Haven't yet recd. a copy, but believe it is on the way.

I must take a little time off and get through a bit of work. Hope you are all right by time this reaches you.

Love to you and mother.

E.

Ezra Pound
23 / 2 / '18

*John Quinn had persuaded some wealthy patrons to join with him in **a guarantee fund** for the* Little Review. *Babette Deutsch had contributed 'Ezra Pound, Vorticist', a review of* Lustra, *to* **Reedy's Mirror** *for 21 December 1917.*

548. **TLS** [*embossed letterhead*] 5, Holland Place Chambers, Kensington, W.
30 / 3 / 18

[London]

Dear Dad

I shudder to suggest the number, the egregious number of words I have slapped thru this machine during the pastt two weeks.

H. W. Wack may have got me hitched to the Newark Sunday Call. In which case you will be able to have voluminous weekly data of my activities mental and otherwise.

There is, I think, nothing to say beyond the fact that I am hitting this instrument, and that the hit will in due course be registered, and you will be able to inspect them.

Sent back proofs of Pavannes (forty yards of em.) at the beginning of this week.

Have also been vaccinated. That at least appertains to my private unpublic life.

The 'Future' says you have subscribed, so you will see my monthly outburst on current literature in their columns.

Macmillan has lent me the complete edition of James, so there is reading matter in the house 'to go on with'.

I wonder if the March L.R. is suppressed yet. It is a very active number.

Love to you and mother.

Yrs

E.

Ezra Pound

Just one article by Pound appeared in the **Newark Sunday Call**, *and that was 'Henry James—The Last Phase', on 12 June 1918. (See letter of 12 June 1918 for further details.) The* **proofs** *were for* Pavannes and Divisions, *a collection of Pound's periodical 'sketches and essays' being published by Knopf. Pound was preparing a special* **Henry James** *number of the* Little Review *and working on a lengthy appreciation of James' entire oeuvre, 'a Baedecker to a continent' as he termed it.*

+≻══≺+

549. ALS [*letterhead*] The Little Review, London Office:-

5 Holland Place Chambers, W.8.

Monday evening 15 / 4 / 1918

Reverend Progenitors:

I did one article this a.m. I have conversed with two editors. I have been to a press view of a show (art) I have just done another article. I have sent 12.000 words to Newark since - oh well during about 3 weeks. et.c. Thanks for aniversary commemoration. will cash it shortly. Friday I recast & Saturday I retyped & revised about 3000 words of a Laforgue fantasia - condensed from 5500. am I expected to pour forth my soul at greater pace –

Your Wisconsonian friend has not yet called or written

Q's brochure is here & in process of distribution am working on my H. J. number which should leave here by end of June. -

God be with you

Yours

E.

Ezra Pound
This is not the quiet life demanded by the loftiest literature

The 'Laforgue fantasia' was 'Our Tetrarchal Précieuse', first mentioned 16 July 1916.

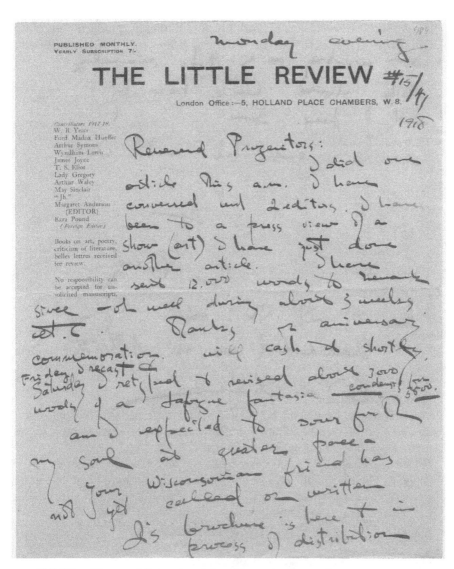

549. ALS, EP to 'Reverend Progenitors', London, 15 April 1918, *first page*

550. ALS [*letterhead*] The Little Review, London Office:-

5 Holland Place Chambers, W.8.

12 May 1918

Dear Dad:

There are 42 vols of H James. when I emerge from the hind end will resuscitate my personal correspondence.

Have had good letter from Jules Romains & Stanton of the Mercure. re. Feb. L. R.

Hope to get the French end in working order during next months

Gaudier Show open. various good things I hadn't seen have been lent by people who knew him before I did.

Love to you & mother

E

Ezra Pound

> The **Gaudier-Brzeska show** *at the Leicester Gallery was reviewed by Pound, as 'B. H. Dias', in the* New Age *of 23 May 1918.*

+⟩===⟨+

551. TLS [*embossed letterhead*] 5, Holland Place Chambers, Kensington, W.

26 May 1918

[London]

Dear Mother

Have at last finished my long scrawl on James, and sent off same. Feeling the weight off my boozoom. Not yet filled with a desire for further use of typewriter.

Awaiting May number L. R.

Various literary events which you will in due time deduce from its pages. Favorable recption of Feb. no. in France. Romains, old Mockel, Stanton of the Mercure etc. Hope for further importations.

More poems from Eliot, and others said to be on the way from Yeats.

Suppose 'Pavannes' will rech you fairly soon. Should have another vol. of essays ready by end of year.

Gaudier show open as I think I wrote

Love to you & dad.

E.

Ezra Pound

26 - 5 - 18

*The **February number** of the* Little Review *carried Pound's 'A Study in French Poets'.* ***Four poems** by **Eliot** were in the September number:* 'Sweeney Among the Nightingales', 'Whispers of Immortality', 'Dans le Restaurant', *and* 'Mr Eliot's Sunday Morning Service'.

+>=—=<+

552. T&ALS [*embossed letterhead*] 5, Holland Place Chambers, Kensington, W.

12 June 1918

[London]

Dear Dad:

Revive your waning confidance in my fiscal situation. The first year of the war knocked my intake gally-helly, or else it coincided with a slump. The second year I got back to 50% of pre war gate receipts and have since got back to par, also paid off increments or whatever it is that accumulates. So I dare say the two branches of our eminent house have about the same status. At any rate I take at least half of what you do, and D's supplies are her own. and were equal to mine <pre-war>. I know she has just declined offer of H. H. S. to make up any deficit due to drop in dividends. Also she had £100 from a defuncted aunt a few months back. <gone in war-bonds by now.>

Have just laid in a new overcoat and am sitting in a just completed maxima cum laude pair of pants; have iron-fibre shirts (six) from the Buckingham Place factory due in tomorrow. (esteemed shirts, as you may see from voucher.). Have also purchased some new shorts from same firm, so sections of me will be clothed rather better than at dates previous.

You can have either the next book (probably prose) or the 'Cantos' dedicated to you, if there are ever enough of them. Might have had a sub-dedication in front of them in the Knopf vol. if I had thought.

As you dont say what the article in the Newark Call was, how the hell can I tell whether it was the first. They have five. I have rec'd cheque for one, but have not had any copy of the paper. I asked them to send it you, or to notify you of appearance of articles.

Jules Romains is coming on as French edtr. of the L. Rev. Yeats on his way back to London. Says he has more mss. for L. R. Stanton has written something for the Mercure, you might watch for it, if there is a library near by that gets the Mercure. It will be in Stanton's notes on American Lit.

You must come over as soon as the war stops, perhaps I can come back to N.Y. with you; that depends on how the L. R. and various other matters stand. Very largely on whether Quinn thinks there is anything to be got out of it. (I think he is a bit fed up with the American office of that organ at the present moment.).

Heaven knows when there will be an end, but I dont think there will be much travel for pleasure before then. I may come back to drill with the middle aged levies.

Shall naturally leave the latch string out for Homer and David if they come via this island. Busha not got to London yet.

Hope you feel more cheery on your 6oieth. than on the day you wrote. If your job was writing you would be just about getting into the swing of it, don't try your Methusalem game on me, you are a long way from the bone-yard.

I dont in the least know which article Newark has printed. There is one on H. James, one on Joyce, one Hebridean music, one on new poetry and one on something else, forget what. War restrictions have chopped off that job. (Rather a relief as it means writing much too much per week.)

Have hopes of my music criticism, as practical cash assest, and a non-interferer with anything else. NO editor has yet found a way of harnessing music to guild socialism or the Arch Bishfake of Canterburry or the question of tarriff or prep. rep.

May number has made hash of three of my poems. I wish someone would occasionally <u>look</u> at the proofs. brush by with a duster, etc.

Love to you & mother

E

Ezra Pound

12 - 6 - 18

Also dont let mother worry about food scares. I have never seen such chops as the two now in the kitchen. I think it must have been an Amy Lowell among sheep.

The food restrictions cant restrict much except human anacondas. - at least we are always on the verge of forgetting to use coupons before they run out.

.E.

Pound's next volume of essays, Instigations *(1920), carried the* **dedication** *'To / My Father / Homer L. Pound'. In August Homer Pound recovered from the* **Newark Sunday Call** *the articles not used—'Hueffer—Joyce—New Poetry—UnEnglish'—together with photos of Pound, Raymonde Collignon, and Joyce, also not used. Only the Henry James article had been used. (See further letter of c.20 September 1918.) In the* **May number of Little Review,** *in 'Avril' (in 'Langue d'Oc'), the last line of the fourth stanza was also printed in place of the last line of the third stanza; then in the 'Moeurs Contemporaines' series, in 'Stele', all but the last word of the fourth line was missing, together with the following line of Greek which it translates; and in 'I Vecchii', a line which doesn't belong intruded to the detriment of the sense, and was then repeated, and repeated again.*

⊹⟫═⟪⊹

553. **ALS** [*letterhead*] The Little Review, London Office:-

5 Holland Place Chambers, W.8.

18 July 18

Dear Dad:

Out pourings fairly rapid. N. Age. – new series on greek for Egoist. Oct. L. R. sent off today with greetings from Mockel. edtr: of 'La Wallonie' a Little Review that published Mallarmé, Verlaine, Maeterlinck & Co. From '85 - 92.

New Yeats & DeBosschère poems. also some De B. line blocks, Rec'd £2 for U.S. troops.

Can you find out any thing about Rev. C. C. Bubb 2077 E. 36th St. Cleveland.

Blighter shd. hv. recd my Arnaut Daniel mss. but haven't heard from him for months.

Is he a vile hun. & interned or hung ? ?

———

A skunk named P. Carus edtr. of a damn thing called the 'Monist' & 'the Open Court' has stolen a Fenollosa mss.

address La Salle. Ill.

If you can get anyone to knife him. - do so.

I don't know many people in them there parts - put a price on his pelt & warn the neighbors.

Haven't rec'd any information from Newark Sunday Call. - one check has come but no copy of article.

I want a couple of copies don't know date.

Aldington is out of firing line - or was with influenza - Dare say he is back for present now.

Lewis still here doing picture of gun-pit.

Pacify mother by saying I have new pants. new waist coat. new hat. 6 new shirts - & a thicker new full suit in the making.

Also a typist three days a week so that I shall have less mechanical waste of time. & can use my lofty intelligence for more intelligent matters than swatting a Corona. .

News good to night.

Love to you & mother.

E

Ezra Pound
[*D's hand*]
Dorothy Pound   Love, D.

---

*Pound's **series on greek for Egoist** consisted of three articles under the heading 'Early Translators of Homer', and a further three under the heading 'Hellenist Series'. Four of the articles—on 'Hugues Salel', 'Andreas Divus', and 'Aeschylus'—were reprinted* together as 'Translators of Greek' in Instigations. A short fifth article, 'Sappho', consisted simply of an English and a Spanish translation of her 'Hymn to Aphrodite', and was not reprinted; nor was a final, fairly general article.

The '**typist three days a week**' was Iseult Gonne, to whom Yeats had proposed marriage in 1917 when he despaired of marrying her mother, Maud Gonne the Irish revolutionary. Yeats had secured work for Iseult as a librarian in the London School of Oriental Studies, but there was an idea it might be better for her if she could secure work as a typist. Since she left London to be in Dublin with her mother in November the arrangement with Pound did not continue long. Her letters to Pound from Dublin are evidence that she had fallen in love with him and wanted to be with him; his letters to her were destroyed by Francis Stuart whom she married in 1920. The predictable conclusions have been drawn about Pound having entered into a passionate 'affaire' with Iseult in 1918, and this, though unproven, is certainly one possibility. What is beyond doubt is that at the end of 1918 Pound and Iseult were apart, and that Pound stayed with Dorothy.

554. TLS [embossed letterhead] 5, Holland Place Chambers, Kensington, W.
27 July 1918

[London]

Dear Mother:

Very busy. Dont know that there is much to report, save output of questionably valuable mss. The L. R. gets a fair share.

Dulac up in town for a few days, in to dine yesterday. Lewis still here painting. W. B.Y. in Ireland.

Am having a solid suit of clothes constructed by an ancient and established tailor. Continue to inspect art and music for the rent.

The present situation in France rather excludes minor events.

Am dining this p.m. with the illigitimate line of the House of Hanover. Image of the early Georges still preserved in one countenence.

Have started my long essay on DeGourmont. Collected a few quid on Imagiste Anthology. etc. Also despatched mss. for Oct. L. R. dealing with La Wallonie.

Love to you & Dad.

E.

Ezra Pound
27 - 7 - '18

The 2nd battle of the Marne, 15–20 July, was the final German offensive in which their army advanced to within forty miles of Paris, only to be forced to retreat by the French. The initiative was now with the Allies.

555. **TLS** [*embossed letterhead*] 5, Holland Place Chambers, Kensington, W.

17 Aug, 1918

[London]

Dear Dad:

You wrote a few weeks ago that some chap on the Phila Press, wanted to know what I thought of his article. I didn't know what you meant, wondered if it was a spiel of year before last or what . . . . . I see by the wrapper on Pavannes that the Press has had something more in it . . . .

Haven't yet seen the article so cant send detailed critique to possible author.

A stranger has sent me the N. Y. Times, very amiable on July 21st.

Have escaped going to Persia with some commission or other, but have had several crowded days, finishing work etc. so as to be able to leave.

Have planted some propaganda in the N. Age for the U.S. A. prop. dept. . . . . . Hope they'll recognize it as such. Turned out seven article last week and seven this. No, eight, have just done another.

What the hell is the American 'Bookman'. They've got a new edtr. who invites my contibution.

Am pleased with get up of Pavannes. Knopf seems to think he'll be ready to do another prose vol. in autumn of next year.

The 'Future' prints 40,000 of next issue. Have you got 'Tarr' yet?

You might look at Lytton Strachey's 'Eminent Victorians'. This machine still warm with favourable review of it.

Yeats has been over for a few days. Wadsworth in last sunday.

Love to you & mother
E

Ezra Pound

The 21ˢᵗ July **New York Times** *Book Review had carried an unsigned article under the heading, 'Ezra Pound, Poet of the State of Idaho'.*

Pound, as he told John Quinn, had gone to the US Embassy in London 'to point out'—this was in the hope of preventing T. S. Eliot being called up—'that if it was a war for civilization (not merely for democracy) it was folly to shoot, or have shot one of the six or seven Americans capable of contributing to civilization or understanding the word'. He had then felt that, 'as a sop' to the Embassy, he ought to offer his own services to his country, and had been sent to the propaganda department where he was given pamphlets to place with London papers. Then he had a note from the Embassy asking, would he 'go to Persia by Monday', in connection with a commission 'to feed the starving Persian'. He made his preparations to do that, getting ahead with his articles for the Egoist and the New Age, arranging Instigations, and marking out 'two or three months work for a copyist'. He waited to hear from the head of the commission, at last was asked to call him at Claridge's, missed him there, and decided that after all he would not go to Persia. His propaganda in the New Age was a series of six articles in August and September under the heading 'What America Has to Live Down'.

Pound reviewed **Lytton Strachey's** **Eminent Victorians** *in the October* Future.

+>≡≍+

556. TLS [*embossed letterhead*] 5, Holland Place Chambers, Kensington, W.
[c.20 September 1918]

[London]

UNFortunate Man:

I do not know whether you have made a hash of the Newark matter or not, or whether you have stopped me getting about 40 dollars.

I sent five articles, I have been paid for one. (I do not know which one, as you have not told me.)

Neither do I know whether Stalter is a swine. He may merely be a man rushed to death as I am. The paper restrictions cut in on the paper, and naturally outside stuff like mine would be the first to lay over.

As he had accepted the stuff he would probably have tried to use it after the war. Now that you have inserted your care, he can go back on things.

Don't however worry. IF you can sell the stuff to one of the reporters who looks in on you from time to time, DO SO.

You are in an excellent position, as you can say with perfect truth that you butted in, and that you had no filial sanction.

Some of the sprigs ought to be able to get the stuff into sunday ledger or something of that sort.

At least the NEW POETRY article ought to be got off on someone.

I dont want the bloody things here.

The Joyce has appeared. in 'The Future'.

If you cant get the stuff into Phila. paper. try the Bookman with the New Poetry. FIRST. and after that the other scribbles.

IF you can collect anything on the bloody stuff, DO so, DEW so.

It was written AT LENGTH to fill space. only you neednt say that. I dont care if it is cut, ONLY it ought to be sold and forgotten. or perhaps its guts cut out, if it has any, and conserved.

Thank god I dont have to do it every week. Hope to have a new book of verse before forever.

London Times has a col. on Pavannes, favorable, yesterday. Will send it on if I can get a spare copy.

Dont bother about the Newark affair.

There is a chap named Roymond, ex mayor of the city who has written me re- pavannes. Only man on record who has read the Spirit of Romance. You can find his name in the aniversary book.

Had note from David. Busha called when I was out, and have had not answer to my note to him.

Love to you and mother. will write sometime or other.

Yrs.

E.

Dont tell. the Reporter any thing save that you wrote to <u>an</u> editor without my order - saying send stuff to you & that it is now on yr. hands. I can remember the name of the chap you said hd. done article. At any rate. if you hadn't broken in - I shd. not have got anything for the stuff till <u>God knows when</u>. So damage isn't Lawge but cash it in if you can

Yrs

E

The **Times** Literary Supplement *of 19 September 1918 reviewed* Pavannes and Divisions *under the heading 'Diversities and Provocations'.*

†⪢━◄┼

557. **TLS** [*embossed letterhead*] 5, Holland Place Chambers, Kensington, W.

3 Nov. 1918

[London]

Dear Dad:

Have again heard from Busha, but he hasn't yet showed up.

Enclosed from Michelson will show that my remarks about that tainted oyster Van Dyke bring comfort to the afflicted.

Have seen only criticism send by J. Q. once called 'E.P. proseur,' one 'Poet of St. of Idaho' and one 'Who does Idaho proud'.

Have never seen Mordell's article. nor his brother.

Hope mother is all right again.

Have sent off a condensed 'Arnaut Daniel' to Bubb. First mss. was submarined last Feb.

Have finished my new note on Gourmont. Also had N. Age sent you.

Also done a new <u>oeuvre</u> on Propertius. Have sent it to that imbecile Harriet as I need money. She will probably die in spasms. I hear she is delerious over the Jepson article, and will be seeking vengence. Still I need the cash for the Propertius. It is her last chance to maintain connection.

Quinn will certainly not back the L. Review after April, so something has got to be devised. Misses A. and H. have NOT show tact to him-ward.

Hope to have a new vol. verse started for press before long.

The Gourmont is the last piece for the next prose vol. which Knopf plans to bring out in autumn 1919.

Atheling and Dias continue their activities, as you will see in N. Age. (this information is NOT for dispersal.). Atheling is acquiring a definite position of his own.

Love to you & mother.

E

Ezra Pound

> *Max* **Michelson** *may have been comforted by Pound's savagely satirical treatment of Henry Van Dyke in 'L'Homme Moyen Sensuel' (in the* Little Review *of September 1917, reprinted in* Pavannes and Divisions*).* **'Ezra Pound: Proseur'**, *by Louis Untermeyer, a disapproving review of* Pavannes and Divisions, *was in* New Republic *of 17 August 1918. The condensed* **'Arnaut Daniel'** *did not see the light, apparently because the Rev. Bubb's private press had suspended operations. The* **new oeuvre on Propertius'** *was* Homage to Sextus Propertius. *Harriet Monroe printed just four of its twelve sections, and would not have the indecorous rest in* Poetry, *in part on grounds of taste, and in part because a Professor of Latin in Chicago advised her that, considered as a translation, it was full of errors. Pound would retort that his poem was no more a translation than Fitzgerald's* Omar Khayyám, *and break off the connection. Edgar* **Jepson**, *commissioned by Harriet Monroe to write on American poetry, had written an attack on* Poetry's *prize poets; when Miss Monroe rejected his article, Pound had it printed in the* Little Review *and appended a note critical of the other magazine's suppression of Jepson's dissenting views.* **Misses** *Anderson and Heap were the editors of the* Little Review. *Pound's* **new volume of verse** *would be* Quia Pauper Amavi, *to be published by* The Egoist Ltd. *in October 1919—it would collect 'Langue d'Oc', 'Moeurs Contemporaines', 'Three Cantos', and 'Homage to Sextus Propertius'.*

✢━━✢

558. TLS [*embossed letterhead*] 5, Holland Place Chambers, Kensington, W.

6 November 1918

[London]

Dear Dad

I'm not trying to hold you up for forty dollars, nor do I think you have done me out of it. But I do think it strengthens your hand in trying to get Mordel or someone to help you unload the stuff elsewhere.

I am not prepared to burst into rage against the Newark people. They are no worse than other editors, and what can one expect of newspaper men when America has so long tolerated such a bunch of shits, snots, and punks, as her 'representative men of letters' 'great authors' 'prominent authors' etc.

Orage (R.H.C.) on the state of the copyright law in this weeks new age is very sound.

Sorry to hear of Gib Doolittle's death. And of Miss Whitechurch's.

Still expect to hear from Busha. Will write to mother. I did, I think, thank your for birthday postal order, thanks again. (No, I cant have written about it as it is in yr. yesterday's letter.)

Apples 2/- each in the shop at the corner, but other food is reasonable.

Bloody Hell, about not knowing what I am rushed to death on.

Rapidly becoming star music critic. concerts, reports on same. Art shows, monthly lit. Article in 'Future' and other trifles.

Also must start some sort of permanent and paying magazine here as soon as war stops and paper restrictions go off.

Thanks for bunch of clippings. Dont know which is better. See and hear nothing, or receive constant testimony to local imbecility.

Italian kid drawings interesting, but as his father is a sculptor one cant tell how much is kid and how much hot house training.

Love to you & mother
E

Ezra Pound

6 – ii – '18

+══+

559. TLS [*embossed letterhead*] 5, Holland Place Chambers, Kensington, W.

15 Nov. 1918

[London]

Dear Mother:

Am suffering from cold contracted on Monday in observing the ceremonies of armistice. Have not yet succombed to influenza. Spent some hours in drizzle spectating the crowds on bus-tops, George Rex et Imperator, also in drizzle in open carriage, looking happy. I should think for the first time in his life, not the usual official grin, but a certain suitable satisfaction. Large crowds before the palace, even going to the extent of declaring that he was a jolly good fellow. Also long rows of guns down the Mall. Ring dances in Trafalgar Square, etc. Also at least one banner inscribed 'Gott mit uns'. and another indicating that William had at last found the Better 'Ole.

Lewis states that on Tuesday evening the sole drunken member of the police force was carried triumphantly round and round Piccadilly circus.

I am glad the main hostilities are obsolescent. But the process of extracting payment from the Hun pfennig by pfennig will continue I suppose for some time.

As dad shd. now receive the N. Age he will see that I have been enjoying Rosing's Russian, and the K. Fraser Hebridean music. The latter family was taken on sunday to the flat of the former (in bed with flu.) and the Wild Isles were shouted down the hall way for his benefit.

425

Otherwise the events are mainly public, and presumably reported at length in the Phila. papers.

Dont suppose anythin personal can happen before end of armistice. Paper restrictions are about as personal as any public affair can be for me.

Have sent off my Gourmont notes to the L. R. N.Age is printing a few more A. Daniel things, I presume next issue.

Suppose Busha, Sandburg, and various others will now get leave and show up.

Must wash and go forth to a concert.

Yrs

Love to you & dad.

E.

Ezra Pound

15. Nov 1918

The **armistice** *had brought hostilities between Germany and the Allies to an end at 11.00 a.m. on 11 November.*

5

London, Paris: 1918–24

560. TLS [*embossed letterhead*] 5, Holland Place Chambers, Kensington, W.
4. Dec. 1918

[London]

Dear Mother

Had a good view of Foch on sunday. Have been extremely busy. Article for
N. theatrical quarterly sunday. 2000 on Lady Gregory's new. vol. translations
yesterday. Rosing's full Moussorgsky programme last night.

Chance of starting a Quarterly review here, seems good, as soon as paper
and periodical restrictions go off. Probably begin with a May number. Part of
the cash to hand. Encellent flying man as business mgr.

DeBosschere private view coming on Friday. etc. Did you once write to
me about an American painter called Noble?? Dont know anything about
him save that he is coming on Thursday and is not fooled by certain puffed
figures.

'George' Mrs W.B.Y. has been ill, but reported better. Dulac back in town,
Richard back on ten days leave. As the N. Age now arrives you have some
indication of my weekly round. Mathews thinks March will be the month for
next vol. poems. He hasnt seen mss. dont know whether he will flee in tailless
terror.

Out burst in a typically American organ called 'Pep' (pub. Newspaper
Enterprise Assn. W. 3d. St. And Lakeside, Cleveland. Oo.)

Ernest Finlay edtr. I want father to send him copies Little Review containing
articles on tarriff and copyright. AND to keep Finlay poked up into action
over it.

Prop. Dept. here reports that my N. Age articles have gone on to Senate
committee, with other arguments. Something may be done. At least provisional
measure, to last for six months after signing of peace. Ought to be made
permanent.

Why the hell the inhabitants cant attend to these matters for themselves.
I dont know.

Have two vols. Swinburne's letters just in, expect to use for Books Current
next month.

Dont know what else there is to report.

Love to you & dad

E

Ezra Pound

*Pound's article for the **new theatrical quarterly**, Theatre-Craft, called for 'small and simplified theatres' suited to 'Michio Itow's dancing' and 'Raymonde Collignon's exquisite art'. The article on **Lady Gregory's** The Kiltartan Poetry Book was in December's Future. **Richard** was Richard Aldington. Instead of Pound's next volume Elkin **Mathews** would publish, in June 1920,* Umbra: The Early Poems of Ezra Pound | All that he now wishes to keep in circulation from 'Personae', 'Exultations', 'Ripostes' etc. With translations from Guido Cavalcanti and Arnaut Daniel and poems by the late T. E.Hulme. *Pound's November **outburst** in PEP, 'The Highbrow— How he looks on American newspapers', was in response to its editor's asking him, 'For the love of all, Ezra, tell me quick what newspaper published in these forty-eight backwoods of America you do approve, and why'. Pound's review of the edition of **Swinburne's letters** appeared in the February* Future.

---

561. TLS [*embossed letterhead*] 5, Holland Place Chambers, Kensington, W.

[5 December 1918]

[London]

Dear Dad:

Thanks for Xmas letter duly recd. this 5th day of Dec. (enclosure £4)

Am dead with various labours.

will write later.

Misses A. and H. have been extremely untactful in their relations to J. Q. so have themselves to thank if L. R. goes bust. They have been a great relief to me, in their readiness to print the best they can get; relief after dealing with imbecile in Chicago. BUT their dealings with J. Q. have not been signalised by excess of tact.

Hope to start a new Quarterly here in the spring.

Do see that all the L. R. different numbers containing copyright stuff go to Emmett Finlay 'PEP' Newspaper Enterprse Assn. West Third and Lakeside Cleveland Ohio.

write him to keep the matter agitated. DON'T bother Quinn with it, but stir up any one else you think of. First N. Age article have got as far as Senate Committee. etc.

let me sleep.

Yrs

E. Pound

---

562. TLS [*embossed letterhead*] 5, Holland Place Chambers, Kensington, W.
6 December 1918

[London]

Dear Dad:

Thanks for Mordell's books and the Hailey clipping. IF you have the misfortune to meet Mordell tell him I said I was very glad to receive them.

(that is fairly true. It ends my curiosity re/ what you had been writing about. Now. NOW that we are alone, let me confess that Mordell's stuff IS absolutely THE most unimportant and provincial I have seen since the local bard in Crawfordsville assured me that Shakespeare would live as a wit but not as a poet.

Mordell is either wrong or else so bloody obvious that he ought to be denied pen and paper. (Dont deny him pen and paper. It is useful to have him advertising one in the Press).

Bloody idiot. Everyone knows that Dante is full of mediaeval lumber. The point is that he is full of indestructable beauty. Vide The Spirit of Romance for want of a better guide book.

Mordell's style utterly unreadable. So much for his burble about unimportance of style, form etc.

No, mon cher, leave him alone. Be polite to him, but dont waste your time looking for sense in his writings.

His 'waning of lit. vals.' is, if I remember, prevented. (I.e. forestalled by two lines in the Spirit of Romance, re/ relative permanence of literary works.) Rest of him seems to be twaddle. Montgommery country is quite large enough to contain, surround and engulph him. Article on me, rather incoherent, and of no interest save in so far as it is so many inches of newspaper devoted to advertisment.

Lady Gregory's new book (Cuala Press, too expensive) has good things in it. Am reading Swinburne's letters, two vols. with interest. Perfectly normal and amiable young man. Dare say the later letters will be dull enough. He is quite good on Landor. Forget whether you have got that set of Landor yet. Think you wrote you had it. Cant think of anything more worth your reading.

Chance of new Quarterly seems good.

more anon.

four art shows. today none good.

Love to you & mother

E

Ezra Pound
6 Dec 1918

*Pound is evidently commenting on Albert **Mordell**'s* Dante and Other Waning Classics *(1915). Pound's parents also lived in **Montgomery County**, Pennsylvania.*

563. TLS [*embossed letterhead*] 5, Holland Place Chambers, Kensington, W.

19 Dec 1918

[London]

Dear Mother

Sumptuous Xmas packet of brushes, sashes etc. duly rec'd, and herewith thanks for same.

Am engaged in promoting a quarterly review for the sepulture of various corpses. Have part of the funds arranged. Your president is said to be arriving next week. Ed. Wad. has been told to paint him in act of landing.

Dad can observe part of my weekly activities in the 'New Age'. Dulac back in town; Windeler about, also Lewis, and Ed. Wad. Chance of life beginning again if some fool dont try to prevent the Russian cannibals from eating the remains of the Hun.

Reported relaxation of paper restrictions etc. Manning has turned up again, appears about twice weekly. Old Plarr has let loose on subject of Strasbourg, 11 stanzas in yesterdays Times. He was on the walls there in '70 at the age of seven and saw the Gallifet charge. Jepson read an amusing paper at Poets Club dinner last evening. Dining with the aged Ionides this p.m. (reminisences of Whistler, B-Jones and co.).

Have various things in hand for 1st. quarterly. The Little Rev. being full up till April number. last of my second vol. with them.

Does dad know anything of Marianne Moore, who seems to be writing very good stuff. 14 St. Lukes Place N.Y.

Harriet writes that poor Michelson has gone off his head I don't wonder. poor devil had sense of literary quality and values. If he had got here, he would presumably have been all right, but Chicago has claimed her victim.

Harriet has bust up my Propertius series, but is paying a decent price for the four things she is printing. Have sent the rest to Mencken; will reassemble them in Quarterly.

Harriet is an ass; but one may as well get what cash possible out of her.

She has returned that article on American poets, apparently. It is not good enough for the Little Review. at least I cant remember what I wrote, but think it was too diffuse and hurried. It is not to be printed unless I am paid something for it. (I don't care how much or how little) Dad might write to the 'Pagan' 7. E. 15 th. St. New York. and ask what their rates are, saying he has mss. of mine.

(I am not supposed to know anything about his offering it to them.) Dont suppose they can pay much.

Greetings of the season

Love to you & Dad,

E

Ezra Pound.

Victor Plarr's reminiscences of 'the Gallifet charge' figure in Pound's canto 16. None of the 'Propertius series' appeared in Mencken's Smart Set. *Various sections were printed separately in the* New Age *in 1919, but the poem was first properly assembled in* Quia Pauper Amavi *(1919). The* **quarterly** *Pound was projecting did not materialise.*

564. TLS [*embossed letterhead*] 5, Holland Place Chambers, Kensington, W.
27 December 1918

[London]

Dear Mother:

Succeded in cooking excellent turkey with superlation of perfect achieve-ment. Have been to one or two dances, fed F. Manning & Capt. Baker and Col. Lawrence on said large fowl.

You may have seen that an englishman was with Sherif Feisul and had been making an Arabian kingdom. Thought it must be the brother of my friend W.G Lawrence, killed early in the war; wrote to enquire, and my conjecture proved to be right.

Did not get much information about Arabia from Col. T. E. L. he was rather exhausted with struggles with big wigs, and Syrian deputations from Manchester. And more ready to know what had happened in London during the last nine years.

He left in the midst of Provencal metric, trying to collect his political faculties to deal with Lloyd George next morning.

Lawrence is all for Arabia for the Arabs. Feisul has promised to collect all the oral songs of the desert. The Turks have set £20,000 on Lawrence's head or rather £10,000 on the head, and £20,000 on the whole carcass.

Think I wrote you that old Birrel had written a very appreciative note re H. James number of Little Review.

Have £110 towards new quarterly, and some copy in hand.

Love to you & dad.

E.

Ezra Pound
27. 12. 1918

565. TLS

10 Jan. 1919

[London]

Dear Dad:

Kittens will grow into cats. Santa Claus, is less objectionable than the Xtn. Churches, but less durable and more cloudy. I still remember a black and yaller dawg and an Apple Tree.

Hecht and all that sort of writing are cloacae, and necessary. Until the Muznik family is honestly described, diagnosed it won't be cured. This sort of thing may be more a part of sociology than of literature, but no, the two things touch.

The good writing is the honest writing. However even Hecht has left the U.S.A., has been here for the last five days, on way to continent.

'American number' came yesterday, I find I am utterly unable to read it; so don't yet know how 'punk' it is.

Wharton Storck's announcement of his Contemptary Verse, is the worst piece of dung I have yet seen. It is complete waste of time, and nerve force keeping in touch with America at all ... i. e. so far as art or literature is concerned.

I was caught by 'Poetry' some years ago. Can't be helped. time wasted. Hope if I get the Quarterly to be able to cut off communications with U.S. magazines altogether. Nothing in any of 'em, only hoaxes, and mental dishonesty, and boobisms.

Can't combine the different magazines. Anderson uncombinable. Marsden a block. New Age wd. lose its subscribers, who care for politics, if it took up literature too seriously. It is primarily a political paper.

I had perfectly clear vision years ago (1908) when I left for Gib. || folly of nostalgic sentiment, plus fly-paper of belief in 'New' growing great country etc., made attractive by Harriets cheques, and decent ideals of her first announcements, etc. gradual immersion in idiotic attempt to get America either to do or at least to accept good stuff.

Suppose, not much harm done ... can't tell ... any how, no use going on with it.

If anyone in America did do anything good, he, she or it would come here.

Barnum was the real the reel Murkhn expression.

Quite a number of 'nice' amiable people, but passive and mostly illiterate, utterly unorganized. At any rate no use so far as supporting the arts or permitting discrimination is concerned.

Ought to be left in peace like other placid cattle, and not bothered about altitude of their perceptivity.

Hecht very illuminating. Born in Russia, Chicago police reporter who wanted to be a conjurer in earlier life. AND the prose hope of Chicago ... with serious moments and an interest in style.

Other 'best thing in the country'. Bill Williams half inarticulate, but solid. Marianne Moore, almost unintelligible, lesser Eliot.

Ignorance's desire to remain undisturbed in itself. etc. etc.

Michelson has gone off his head, was trying to get over here. etc. etc.

You are lucky to have a job which makes it unnecessary for you to come into any contact with 'the American world of letters' etc.

There are plenty of pleasanter things in life.

Damned mania for reforming things, due to my presbyterian training, I suppose, otherwise I might not have begun trying to improve America's'??? questionable quantity of brain-substitute.

/ / /

Oh well. Rodker, is trying to start a press, and Granville is ready to start a new publishing firm with a weekly and monthly (the latter devoted to my ideas on literature, so far as compatible with circulation.

Lewis' picture best in Canadian war memorial exhibit, but a compromise.

Several poems by Eliot for Quarterly, also my Propertius, Manning ready to work for it.

Getting my next prose book into final shape. Lewis' own exhibit scheduled for end of month. Rosing's series of concerts begins next week.

Hecht says he has done a 'story' for Chicago Daily News. (verity <u>not</u> essential), you may look out for it.

O. S. just in, sends love to you both. Thanks for 'lovely little book.'

Aldington very bored with army now the war is over. etc.

Eliot's father just dead, dont know whether he will be going to America or not, will ask him to look you up, if he does.

Yeats has just asked me to be godfather 'if it is a male'.

November L. R. mostly drawer sweepings, not good as a number, but cant trust M.A. to construct anything.

The two 'em have nerve, and that is commendable, but there the thing seems to end. (dont pass on this grumble.)

Love to you and mother.

E

Ezra Pound

The December Little Review *was an '**American number**'. Pound was about to give up as Foreign Editor, and John Rodker would replace him. **Charles Wharton Stork** edited the monthly* Contemporary Verse: The All-poetry Magazine for America. ***Rodker's* Ovid Press** *would first publish a Gaudier-Brzeska* Portfolio of Reproductions; *then Pound's* Fourth Canto *as a private edition in October 1919;* Fifteen Drawings of Wyndham Lewis *in January 1920; T. S. Eliot's* Ara Vos Prec *in February 1920; and* Hugh Selwyn Mauberley *by EP in June 1920. **Granville's** new scheme did not materialise.*

+≻━≺+

566. **TLS** [*embossed letterhead*] 5, Holland Place Chambers, Kensington, W.

23. Jan. 1919

[London]

Dear Mother

Have just got my mss. for 'Instigations' into shape, all save last four pages, for which I am waiting for printed copy in next Egoist, and have dumped same on O.S. for purposes of correction of slips.

Shall send it to Knopf soon.

I woulder if father can find out whether Knopf has received mss. of Eliot's book. and possible cable me if it has NOT been recd. Dont cable if it has.

Want father to correct first proofs of Instigations, if he will, page proofs to be sent me. here.

As he gets the N. Age you have some indication of my weekly activities.

Granville hopes to get a publishing business into shape in about a weeks time; expects to use me as the literary prestige of the business and wants to bring out four or five books. Beginning with import of Pavannes. There was quite a good translation, or rather adaptation from Zenophon by him in N. Age of last week.

Hecht, the prose hope of Chicago, has passed through this village, with the click and shatter of cinematography, a portent of modernity.

Manning is doing a story for the proposed Quarterly. Have recd. fathers letter with Morley's entertaining article. also enclosed from David.

Love to you & dad.

E.

Instigations of Ezra Pound, Together with An Essay on the Chinese Written Character by Ernest Fenollosa, *would be published by Boni and Liveright in New York in April 1920. It would bring together his 'Study of French Poets', 'Henry James', 'Remy de Gourmont'—those from the* Little Review; *essays on Eliot, Joyce, Lewis, and other contemporaries; 'pavannes' from Laforgue and Voltaire; an essay with a selection of his translations from Arnaut Daniel; and his work on 'Translators of Greek' from the* Egoist. **Eliot's book** *was his* Poems *to be published by Knopf in February 1920.*

+══+

567. **TLS** [*embossed letterhead*] 5, Holland Place Chambers, Kensington, W.

27 Jan 1919

[London]

Dear Dad:

Do you suppose you could write 'literary' criticism or do a summary of American book production?

I know it sounds a bit wild? but after all you have as much sense as a lot of four-flushers who burble in the Murkhn Press.

Quite likely you haven't the flow of pen-language, but you are sober and industrious and have read more than most of the newspaper critics. I mean more solid literature.

I have been offered a salary . . . will believe in it when I see the offices of the company and cheques and due appurtenences. To edit lit. section of a weekly. Shouldn't mention it until you hear from me that the capitalists have deposited their deposits. etc. Still there might be an opening for a sober and energetic American. Low rates of payment, etc.

Still . . . . . iff . . . . With a few years practice you might develop enough pencraft to enable you to live here. NOT YET, but still . . . IF I do get the bloomin' job I shall have to have assistance of some sort, and may as well begin within the family circle.

Dont want flourishes, simply sober statement of what current books have anything to 'em; and what it is they have.

At any rate take a sunday a.m. off and send me a 300 work review of one book, and a 500 word rev. of another.

You are not too old to learn the job. At first you will probably find it difficult to write 1000 words at a go. That is the normal state if the writer is honest. I find now that 2000 words come as easily as 600 used to. That is all a matter of accustomedness.

/ / /

Even if the proposed weekly dont come off; something or other will probably come off some time; and you wont have wasted the effort.

You probably need a change of sabath recreation ANYHOW.

America badly needs someone who will really be honest, who will hunt for the best books, impartially. AND who wont try to force a village pump standard on others.

After all, a careful study of my works will give you a better critical basis than most of the reviewers possess. And you have certainly read me more carefully and attentively than anyone else, even where you disagree.

Naturally you wont be able to make much to start with. BUT still.

You might get an occasional joy ride out of it during the first year or so, and something better afterwards. No use for frivolity. It is a drug on the market. Simply put down a sane opinion on say a book of Dreisers. Not what somebody thinks you ought to think but what you really do think. All same you would chalk up results of assay on your little blackboard; no swank, no curelycues.

This bottle has so much silver in it; such and such fineness.

Dont worry about lack of technical minutae. Dont see why you shouldn't do as well at it as I do at music criticism. (about as practical a line as I have struck)

My music crit. all based on general feel of the thing. Good crit. probably is based on general feel. Rest all manner of ones exposition.

Have a shot at it. Cant do any harm.

Yours

E.

---

568. TLS [*embossed letterhead*] 5, Holland Place Chambers, Kensington, W.

2 February 1919

[London]

Dear Dad

I dont think the 'articles' are good enough to print unless one has the excuse of being paid for doing them. Better send 'em back <to me>; destroy the James, which has been done in the L. R., and send back the others.

As for booze. Say rather personal liberty has been done in. Having got rid, supposedly of Prussianism, oppression, tyranny, you are in for a worse era. Already the Tertullians are crying out for a divine right to interfere in the local government of other parts of the earth.

The principles of the founders of the U.S. chucked away for a bit of doctrinaireism. Whole thing done. by people with no knowledge of history, no sense of the difficulty of maintaining liberty. The half-baked think personal liberty was discovered by G. Washington or at most by French Revolution or O. Cromwell. They 'forget' i.e. they have never heard that it existed under the Spanish <u>cortes</u> before they were suppressed in Chas. V.'s time; or that it existed in Rome before the Empire. Brutus, Cato etc. being only characters in the play of Wm. S. a playwright patronised by Henry Irving.

D. has suggested for the first time that I should 'give up' America.

Having always been 'free' the American has no proportionate sense of the value of personal liberty or the difficulty of maintaining it for any long period, i.e. for more than a century.

Established in one form, (e.g. emancipation of niggers) it begins to be undermined in others. However you are a frivolous people. The senator from North Dakota already wants to start of Carrie Nation crusade against the rest of the world. One idea at a time being all that most heads can carry without spilling something.

'Efficiency' the shibboleth of Prussia, the Prussian excuse from 'governing' is taken up by the cranks who now say America will be so 'efficient' that England will have to go dry in self defense. Same old desire to victimize someone or something.

The unfortunate founder of your religion was a profound genius in his perception that no scheme wd. work without a basis of good will (charity in the gentle sense, tolerance), but he was merely an ordinary young man in NOT seeing that Xtianity wd. become a curse through its not containing safeguards against aggressiveness. Hence its utility to a weakened Rome. etc. etc.

Confucianism has, I think, never made martyrs, & has stolen no man's land on pretense that it was doing him good.

———

Enclose Busha's letters.

Love to you & mother.
E.

2 Feb. 1919.

The 'articles' were probably those not used by the Newark Sunday Call—*see letter of 30 March 1918. 'As for booze', the manufacture, sale, or carriage of alcoholic drink was about to be prohibited by the 18th Amendment of the Constitution of the United States—the Prohibition Era would last from January 1920 to December 1933.* **Carrie Nation** *was a leading anti-liquor crusader.*

╪══╪

569. **TLS** *[embossed letterhead]* 5, Holland Place Chambers, Kensington, W.

25 March 1919

[London]

Dear Dad:

Whitman is all right. I dont need a new copy, have excellent imprint for which I paid 8 pence.

Will write you more about him sometime. He wrote badly a good deal of the time but ultimately got a technique. Most of the Memories of Lincoln is well written, only one bad patch.

Plenty of meat all through him. Bill Williams much nearer him, really, than I am.

Re/ Propertius. That fool in Chicago has utterly queered the thing by printing mostly the prologue, in which there are too many names for the number of pages she has used.

Still it holds down the american copyright, and protects me from some of the thieves whom the U.S. so kindly fosters and protects by barbarism of sneak law.

Wait till you get the whole thing, and see if allusions dont sink into scale.

I dont grant that reders of latin will necessarily get more from the latin than you do from the English. MacKail presumably reads the language, yet if you look at his notes in his History of Latin Literature (my copy somewhere in the house???, or get from library) you will see that he has been a complete ASS, seen no irony in Propertius, read him entirely through Burne-Jones, Vita Nuova, Victorian slosh and Xtn sentimentality.

I have perhaps overemphasized the correspondences between Augustan Rome and the present, but still there is a great deal unchanged, and some of the most modern lights are the most literal in their interpretation of the latin.

Dont expect you to get portrait from the excerpted left foot and right ear.

Hope the whole opus will give as much Rome as Cathay gave China.

Most readers have got little from Propertius save Emeralds and Chrysolites and a charming cadence. Have not observed him twisting the tails of official versifiers, Horace and Virgil. Augustus living spit of Wilson,

one wants to remember Ovid off among the Gaetae for no published reason. General flood of official rhetoric, as now flood of journalism.

Ovid and Propertius really up against thing very much as one is now - and similarity does not apply to any other known period of history.

Athens was never the centre of a great world, never metropolitan, as Rome was, with weekly post to Britain and mss. reproduced by slave scriptoria almost as rapidly as now by press. At least book publication almost as rapid and efficient.

Horace presumably read as soon in England then as Kipling wd. be now in New York.

Wonder if Myres 'Dawn of History' wd. entertain you. Has some good phrases, not very well written as a whole, but not very long either.

Also Maine's 'Ancient Law', a heavier and long established work.

Also re names in Propertius, I dont see that one need know anything about any of them to get the general sense of any passage.

Suppose Hector, and Achilles, and Troy, and Helen, together with Bacchus, Apollo, Persephone, are fairly familiar.

Place names dont hold up the sense much:

Aetna, Thebes, etc.

Callimachus, and Philetas, really the only obscure ones, Mausoleum, a fairly common term, named after said Mausolus, etc.

/ / /

Am hoping to get to South of France before long.

I, apparently can go quite well, as N. Age wants some work done. Probably have to get a death certificate for D.

New Poems have gone to press. Moring and Egoist, not as per enclosed announcement. Rodker was too slow in getting the press. He has the Gaudier drawings for first of series. I shall give him something to print in late autumn presumably.

Have not heard from Quinn for months, dare say he is fed up.

Richard has stirred up Liverlight's agent, and thinks they will apply for mss. of Instigations. Knopf has given out.

etc.

Weather has been damnable here. Sun at the moment.

Love to you and mother.

E. Pound

25 - 3 - 19

Harriet Monroe had printed in the March Poetry *only parts 1, 2, 3, and 6 of '**Homage to Sextus Propertius**'. J. W. Mackail's* **Latin Literature** *(1899) was a popular upper school and university manual.* **Ovid** *was banished by Augustus for some undeclared offence to the remote edge of the empire and spent his last years in sad exile. Sir John L. Myres (1869–1954) published* **The Dawn of History** *in 1911; Sir Henry Sumner Maine (1822–88) published* **Ancient Law** *in 1861.*

A clerk in the US Consulate in London had told Pound he should go home and take up his duties as an American citizen, and was threatening to stop his passport in order to prevent him travelling to **France**. *Pound, according to this clerk, could be allowed to go only if he had business there—so he would declare his writing a new series, 'Pastiche. The Regional', for the* New Age, *to be his business; he was further told that Dorothy could not go with him unless she were ill, hence the ironic '**death certificate for D.**'.*

The volume of **new poems** *would be* Quia Pauper Amavi, *to be printed by Alexander Moring's De La More Press, and published by the Egoist Ltd., in October 1919. It would collect 'Langue d'Oc', 'Moeurs Contemporaines', 'Three Cantos', and 'Homage to Sextus Propertius'.*

+⊱───⊰+

570. TLS [*embossed letterhead*] 5, Holland Place Chambers, Kensington, W.
[?April 1919]

[London]

Dear Dad

Will you ask W. E. Keith, 41 S. 18th. to send my correct prescription to Melson Wingate, (ex. Phila optician) as per enclosed envelope.

/ / /

Hale is a bleating ass and Harriet Monroe another. If any one tackles you, you can point out the kind of ass Hale is from the following.

1. <u>insolito</u> (<u>un</u> accustomed) could not be rendered by 'when they have got over the strangeness' a thing is 'solitus', 'accustomed' <u>when</u> <u>one</u> <u>has</u> <u>got</u> <u>over</u> the strangeness'

it is 'unaccustomed' <u>before</u> one has got over the strangeness' therefore whatever I did, I certainly did <u>not</u> make that error.

2. He is an ass about 'Punic'; English audience is perfectly familiar with 'Tyrrian' for purple. The use of 'Punic' for dark red or dark reddish purple, is a latin elegance lepidum elegantium and perfectly proper to introduce into English, I believe Ovid and Horace also use it. Teubner emphasises it by using a cap. P. in his text of Propertius. It simply is not so hackneyed as Tyrrian.

3. He <Hale> is probably wrong, in other matters, on which argument wd. be possible. As a mere matter of utter inaccuracy and utter insensitiveness to relation of latin to english.

'My lady' no more renders the latin 'puella'; than the B. V. M. would render 'Diana of the Ephesians' or Aphrodite Anadyomene. The cliché phrase in

439

english reeks with all sorts of mediaeval and pre-raphaelite victorian associations not to be found in the latin.

Note under it all that my poem never for a moment pretends to translate.

The fragment <which> that stick Harriet has printed is unintelligible and Hale is to be pardoned for part of attitude. BUT he is an ass.

If he had seen the whole poem it might (though it also might <u>not</u> have dawned upon him) that even I, a person quite capable of forgetting the Marcian aquaduct, <an object as familiar to Propertius as the Schuylkill bridge to a West Philadelphian,> would scarcely have thought I found mention of Wordsworth, or a parodied line of Yeats in the work of Sex. Aur. Propertius, or even in so late an author as Statius

(I dont propose to argue with the monkey house. If this letter amuses Morley, he can, if he so chooses avenge my reputation. It dont much matter.)

Also if I have forced the meaning of 'tacta' (which I <very likely> have not) Hale has to add three words not in latin to explain his sentimentality and I have not in <u>any</u> case forced the meaning beyond the character of Propertius as displayed in the Vth. book, in the poem on Cynthia's drive to Lanuvium.

As Hale has nothing by his syntactical accuracy to stand on he had better lie down. Wholly apart from all questions of living English, literature, etc. He is not even sound in his own door-yard. He is typical example of sort of intervening mentality that prevents the classics from circulating.

I dont seriously suggest that Morley shd. answer him; but he might keep these points up his sleeve if he reviews 'Quia Pauper Amavi', which the Egoist will send him.

This better than belated slap at Hale.

Have been asked to give a lecture in Newcastle on Tyne in Nov. for £15/15.

yours
E

Ezra Pound.

In the April number of Poetry *Harriet Monroe had printed a set of sarcastic corrections of 'Homage to Sextus Propertius' by* **W. G. Hale** *(1848–1928), Professor of Latin at the University of Chicago. Professor Hale had considered Pound's work not as a poem in its own right but simply as an academic translation, and had found in it so many 'blunders' as to be forced to conclude that 'If Mr. Pound were a professor of Latin, there would be nothing left for him but suicide'.*

571. TLS [*embossed letterhead*] 5, Holland Place Chambers, Kensington, W.
[?April 1919]

[London]

Dear Dad:

Here is a draft <with a few annotations for you> of Fourth Canto; not to be shown to anyone (save I. W. P. if she wishes to see it) Wont be printed until there is another bundle of three; Fifth is begun.

Have some hope of getting South. At least we have our passports, and a job lot of French bank notes.

Dulac's father is finding us a place in Toulouse. Hope Eliot can also come out. Time I had a let up; time he had a let up.

Will write.

Love to you & mother,
E.

Ezra Pound

Ezra and Dorothy crossed to France on 22 April 1919, and the next day went on by train to Toulouse which they would make their base for the following three months.

<hr>

572. ALS

30 May 1919.

Toulouse / address for U.S.Mail – London

Dear Dad:

Have been resting a month // Nothing doing. // Course of trip Nimes, Beaucaire, Tarascon, Avignon, St Remy, Les Baux, Arles, Carcasonne, indicated by post cards. Old Dulac, father of Edmond Dulac, painter, very hospitable to us here. // Will be here another months, then mountains, presumably, then Excideuil (near Perigord) then a week or so in Paris // Am to lecture in Newcastle in Nov. so that dates return.

Quinn heard from. 'Instigations' said to be placed with Liverlight, at better rate than wd. have been with Knopf.

Proofs of part of 'Quia P. A.' came yesterday. Also £10/- from a british quarterly - which may develop. Also small cheque from Knopf. // so feel may be able to hold out here, according to schedual planned. D. much better. Also suppose rest has done me good.

Will look up Wallace when I go north // We came straight thru Paris on way here, stopping only between trains. (tea with Miss Mapel.)

Hope Eliot will join us somewhere for a few weeks .

Think you might take your next vacation in Paris // about next year things shd. favour transport // (unless you prefer London.) –

Five eagles in gardens here // old abe- and dollar models // Also double decked owls with remarkable optics. Other features to be found in Baedecker //

not yet up to much descriptive effervesence // Have ground out 3 articles for Orage and the one for 'Art & Letters' but no 'flow' yet. // No hurry about it. // also pen slower than machine.

Colour on the Garonne very fine now & again. D. pleased with Nimes.

Love to you & mother.

· E ·

+⟩━⟨+

573. ALS

13 July 1919

Montréjeau

Dear Dad:

Thanks very much for suggestion of $50. but I'd rather you kept it & made sure of getting over here next summer. Drafts on any English bank are good here. // drafts & cheques more acceptable, in fact, than English money. to the tune of 1 franc per £. // but I am without other address, than care New Age ,. 38 Cursitor St. London E.C. 4., as the Shx are away during Sept. & there is no one to forward mail from H.P.C.

wherefore, I suggest that at any rate you dont ship any cash until you get a fixed address, <u>and</u>. bis, encore & repeatedly, IF there is any question about yr. doing or not doing both, retain said 50 strips as a nest egg & lay the same on a Cunarder or other transporting vessel, airspip, or other modus - some time next summer.

I think Paris will do as well as any where, as your vacation is so short, wd. be rather a waste of it to try to get to Italy. Better to see one place more thoroughly.

Dont in the least know what I am going to do, or where be, after Sept. // or rather, know I shall probably be in London in Oct, and suppose will stay in England three months, unless - - - etc. conjecture vain & dependent on what arrangements I make re periodicals etc.

Band outside & greased pole being erected in the place of the cattle market outside window, cross-eyed man has been lathering it with salad oil, now surrounded by kids. // They are having their fête today (13th) instead of tomorrow which is Market day.

Excellent veal in these parts. D. sketching mountain tops daily. go back to Toulouse later this week & thence northward to Excideuil. (Perigeux, Hauteforte, Dordoigne)

Have sent Orage largish package of random reflections which will reach you in N.A. in time.)

They have now run up a hoop with four live geese, (squawk), a chicken, & a dead rabbit to top of said greased pole.

discussions, grins, indignations, final decision to allow geese to descend until the time of ascent of pole approaches more closely - band. etc. kids. etc.

dare say I'd better close - as the post office dont work tomorrow.

Love to you & mother.

.E.

13 July 1919

+>——=+

574. ALS

16 July [1919]

Montréjeau

Dear Mother:

It is very good of you to think of sending $50. but I think it had better be saved & used to transport H.L.P. to Paris next summer. Dont suppose you can both come? - Anyhow it strikes me it wd. be better for you to come to Italy the year after??

Dad has such short time that wd. be waste for him to spend more than necessary in actual travel. He cd. see Paris in a fortnight.

I dont yet know how much or if I shall be settled in Paris, etc. etc.

For Italy you wd. be able to come to Genoa by boat, Mediterranean is not nausibond. // trip costs no more than to Cherbourg or Liverpool - but it wd. completely use up H.L.'s holiday.

Other scheme wd. be for you to come to Italy next spring & join H.L.P. in Paris & return with him in July or Aug.

IF. we <D. & I> get to Italy in May. - you cd. bring very light baggage & have H. bring the rest to Paris.

All of which is somewhat in the air at present my dates are. Excideuil. about July 25. Angers Aug. 25. Paris Sept., London October.

Lecture in the northern wilds Nov. 3rd.

Suppose, I shd. then be in London until after Xmas - but even that is uncertain.

Monck now wants to proceed with production of 'Nishikigi' that he had proposed before the war.

'Q.P.A.' shd be out soon. shd. have been out six weeks ago.

'Instigations' presumably on its way to print. Haven't yet rec'd contract but Q. says it is under weigh. Hope Boni will get the 'Chinese Written Character' mss. from the Little Review. Dad might cast an eye on the matter; at least make sure that L.R. has <u>mss</u>. or has forwarded it, or is ready to forward it when Liverlight is ready for it.

Better. Will he drop a line to Liverlight reminding him that the <u>mss</u>. is part of 'Instigations' & that be shd. get it from. M.C.A. - if he has not already done so.

Quinn is off on vacation, so dont want to bother him about it.

All this was clearly stated on <u>mss</u> of Instigations as sent, but one never is sure enough in these matters.

D. has sketched various peaks & clouds. We go back to Toulouse this p.m. Shall be sorry to see the last of old Dulac whom I like very much. // also feel very much at home in Toulouse - but dont suppose I shall ever have good enough reason to settle there for so long again. Venice, Verona, Sirmio wd. always be more attractive when there weren't impediments of international nature.

Hope Eliot will get out next month. Rodker is apparently doing good work with his press. I think I sent you the announcements. 'Ovid Press'. - portfolios. Gaudier, Lewis, poems, Eliot, Rodker, E. P. // excellent labour shd. be advertised.

Romains writes that he expects to be in Paris in Sept.

Love to you & Dad

Any signs of life in the N.Y. branch of the Wad. family!

Yrs

. E .

+‑⊨‑≒+

575. ALS

21 July 1919

Toulouse – in state of about to pack up.

Dear Mother,

£11. has arrived, for which my thanks.

Note from Dad, saying one from you is imminent, but yours not yet here.

You will by the time you get this have my suggestion of best use for the £11.

I shall, naturally cash draft recd. & as naturally spend it; but shall hope to be able to lay hold of equivalent sum, if needed for transport of my august progenitor next year.

Have just done another three N. Age articles.

Have I sent you these cards of Montsegur & Rocafixada? Walks of four weeks ago. Hope to walk for another week from Excideuil. Eliot probably coming out in august.

Feel very much at home here & shall be sorry to leave.

more anon.

Yours with love

E

21 - 7 – '19

+>==+

576. ALS

23 July 1919

[Toulouse]

Dear Mother:

Here is the final debris -

Did I send father F.T. Sung's letter. I meant to, but cant find it, so possibly it has been sent.

Our possessions seem to be going into our luggage cases, despite contrary appearances.

nothing remains but a sulphur bath, the police, a final meal with the Dulac's, the despatch of two vols. of Michaud's Hist. of Crusades. to 5 H.P.C. etc.

Trust new series of Dordoigne p.c. will now vary the tone of my correspondence

Nothing, has happened since the day before yesterday.

Love to you & dad,

. E .

23 – 7 – 19

Sung's letter, dated 'Peking / Mar 16, 19', is printed in Ezra Pound's Chinese Friends (ed. Zhaoming Qian). There is nothing in it of importance.

+>==+

577. ALS

[7 August 1919]

[Excideuil]

[attached to letter from Dorothy to Isabel Pound]

P. S.

Have no desire to see any American publications of whatever nature. Have given orders that no books or periodicals in any language be forwarded.

Thanks for the offer, but please do not waste postage trying to fulfill it.

Hope you enjoy Maine. Distinct recollection of purchasing fire-works, among valued souvenirs of a virtuous youth
    much too virtuous in fact, but wisdom only comes with the years.
Love to you & dad.
. E .

+⇒⇐+

578. ALS [*letterhead*] G$^{\underline{d}}$ Hotel de Bordeaux

22 August 1919

[Bordeaux | Brive]

On our way north - with contemplated delays. Malamort & Aubazine one hopes, tomorrow. Then back here & to Orleans for a few days. & then Paris.

Eliot has been with us for a week or so.

Observe a real hotel with stationary // usual paucity of ideas fitting in similar circumstance. Prospect of sulphur baths later in the p.m. Strong odour excellent cigar in this smoking or writing room.

Probably get back to London 1$^{\underline{st}}$ Sept. or thereabouts - as one month Paris now appears about as expensive as two months next spring.

Also various small arrangements possible in London - announcements later if anything comes of them.

Sumptuous lunch pressing me further & further toward an equally sumptuous somnolence.

Brive: Cathedral 11$^{\underline{th}}$ century restored; aged houses – good stone cutting // newly furbished as junction Paris: Toulouse, Bordeaux-Lyons

Etc.

Walking tour Thiviers: Brantome: Bourdeilles.

Eliot went on to the Fonts de Gaume, & Les Eyzies grottes - prehistoric painting & sculpture. Must take a week to same, sometime. Vide a few remarks in the Gaudier-Brz.
Love to you & dad -
Will expect letters in London - no address. for present to which same could be
sent
yrs
. E .

+⇒⇐+

446

579. ALS

3. Sept. [1919]

3 rue de Beaune Paris

Dear Dad:

We go to London next week.

Saw Wallace, brief amiable chat, switched in between two scheduled 'calls'.

He had very little to say – naturally – I also had very little to say. -

He computed your age correctly, said he had known you when he & you were both younger than I am etc.

He struck me as very very tired, offered to do anything he could for me; but there was nothing I wanted done; cant bother him about imbecilities of passport beaureau and such trifles.

Have seen Vanderpyl; am lunching today with Mockel (La Wallonie) meeting some painters on Thursday.

Miss I. Mapel lunched with us two days ago. Her sister has gone back to W. Va. and she is in act of packing.

Discovered my old suit case that I swapped with them for trunk which you may remember my returning to U. S. A. with in yr. of grace 1906.

We have also come in for a rather charming old Spanish wall mirrour which she can't carry home. Hope to get it to London intact.

Paris is a very pleasing city; am exploring it properly for the first time; first time I have been completely idle & without ties to some one quarter; we have a large room from which we see the Seine & Pont Royal and a corner of the Louvre & windows of rue de Rivoli, on the opposite side.

Mildly expensive, but Excideuil has been an economy.

Food here rather cheaper than in London; not so good as in the South.

Have also seen Valette (Edtr. Mercure de France) he talked for about an hour in a very small quiet voice.

Intelligent but resigned.

Knows what is wrong but also knows that even a dis proportionate effort would probably fail to rectify it very much.

He has done a big job in making the Mercure, & his personality explains the result.

Fleicitate mother on her £100 – only I still think Sirmio a better spring resort than Wyncote; and apart from familial ties there is each year less reason for my coming to America; the literary horizon grows bleaker & bleaker –

Familial ties, I may point out pull equally east as west

Mail can go to 5 H. P. C. from now on.

———

Give my regards to Sylvester.

———

447

Must get a move on if I am to get to Mockel's for lunch.

yours

love to you & mother.

E

3 Sep^t. 1919.

*Ezra and Dorothy were staying at the Hotel Elysée on the Left Bank. Hugh C. **Wallace**, US Ambassador to France, had known Homer when he was registering mining claims in Hailey, Idaho, around the time Ezra was born there. In spite of Pound's not wanting to 'bother him about imbecilities of passport bureau', he had to go back the next day for a note directing the Consulate to issue the visas and permits for their return to London.*

---

580. TLS [*embossed letterhead*] 5, Holland Place Chambers, Kensington, W.

15 September 1919

[London]

Dear Dad:

Hope the enclosed will keep Boni in order. You can forward it it him.

Got back Thursday, but Dulac asked us dont to the country on Friday, and as the trip from Paris had been tiring we went; shd. have sent you the enclosed then, but forgot to do so. Dare say it is not too late.

Have seen Orage, Moring, rec. letter from Quinn, etc. and now want to breathe before diner.

Love to you and mother, more later

. E .

15 Sept

---

581. TLS [*embossed letterhead*] 5, Holland Place Chambers, Kensington, W.

15 October 1919

[London]

Dear Dad

Of course as Quinn is correcting the mss. it will probably be all right as he wd. make sure of the French, or have it assured, BUTTTT all the same, so far as I can remember, I never suggested that you should correct more than one set of proofs and that the second shd. be sent to me.

Boni himself is on this side or was.

Q. P. Amavi shd. have reached you. Special edition will follow.

Am now selecting and arranging early poems for decennial orgy, Mathews and Poetry Book Shop, (Harold Monroe) are issuing the book together.

Have been a dramatic critic for three weeks, official style of same being Marius David Adkins, don't know that it will last, but hope it will pay the rent.

Have been back a month, and no time to breathe YET. more anon.

Love to you & mother

E

15 Oct. 1919

Have you seen any of Hueffer's novels on the American cinema. He says the cinema rights are paying his keep. Shd. like to know if you see the films.

Pound's 'decennial orgy'—i.e. Umbra. The Early Poems of Ezra Pound. All that he now wishes to keep in circulation from 'Personae', 'Exultations', 'Ripostes', etc. With translations from Guido Cavalcanti and Arnaut Daniel and poems by the late T. E. Hulme—would be published by Elkin Mathews in June 1920 (without Monro's Poetry Book Shop). 'Marius David Adkins' was dropped as music critic of The Outlook *after just two reviews, for failing to flatter the play in one, and the leading actress in the other.*

---

582. TLS [*embossed letterhead*] 5, Holland Place Chambers, Kensington, W.

[late October 1919]

[London]

Dear Dad:

Enjoyed old Skidmore's treatise on 'Reality' also interested in beginning of Comarette's 'Aes Signatum' rec. this a. m.

As far as I have read he has not considered the possibility of the bars being weights; tho' he does say the weights of the bars vary, which wd. be against their being weights, but not absolutely conclusive if there are only a dozen of them.

As for their commercial use. Has he any argument against the hypothesis that they were traveler's samples. This wd. account for their being smaller that the big ingots.

Possibly a very wild guess, but wd. give reason for breaking, possibly to test properties of given sample of metal for casting.

The analogy of the minature sets of china dishes, traveler's samples often supposed to be doll's dishes made for toys, is two thousand years late. But the results might well puzzle an antiquarian.

In case of the broken bars (chinese laundry ticket) it wd. be interesting to know if fragments of same bar are found together; or if EVER two pieces of same have been found in different place and later fitted together.

Have vague idea that two joinable fragments of broken ring or metal have at times been used as means of certain identification of messengers etc. even more certain than a seal which can be duplicated.

Later custom of betrothal by broken six-pence.

Lot of weights, I think at Nimes, with official insignia showing them to be legal weight, hence the possible ' romanom'.

All of which is sheer amateurish guessing . . . evidently not wilder than some of the learned Hunjectures which C. has analyzed.

C. argument against the very plausible theory of scarificial or ceremonial use, i.e. artistic ornament, wd. be rather for the commercial sample view, firm wd. naturally want to make sample look attractive; show its ability to take form with finesse.

Quia pauper amavi. Pauper refers to subject. I am the pauper. The 'poor' whom you imagine me to love wd. be accusative plural, and your sentence wd. read Quia pauperos amavi.

Ovid remarks that he has wirrtten, been able to write his Art of love because he was unable to pay. He says if a man needs merely say 'I will pay' he can dispense with other qualifications, notably with intelligence.

The Black cock is naturally a symbolical, black magical cock and not a Plymoth rock rooster hunting pebbles on the stern and cock-bound <hide-bound> coast.

The worm of the procession had three large antennae, and I hope to develop the motive later, text clearly states that this vermiform object circulated in the crowd at Church of St. Nicholas in Toulouse. Not merely mediaeval but black central African superstition and voodoo energy squalling infant, general mirk and

epileptic religious hog wash with chief totem being magnificently swung over whole.

Cock in barn-yard wd. not give hypernatural atmosphere to the passage. I prefer them purely apparitional.

Boni ad. seems to contain some common sense. Hope the public will follow sound advice Boni has given 'em.

Love to you & mother

E. P.

remember me to Mrs. S. A. Pound

*T. Louis **Comparette** (1868–1922), author of the 60-page study Aes Signatum (1919), was Curator of the Museum of the Philadelphia Mint. 'Aes signatum' (stamped bronze), a form of currency in ancient Rome, is a piece of bronze of measured quality and weight, bearing an official stamp. '**The Black cock**', and '**The worm of the procession**', are images in Pound's 'Fourth Canto', privately printed by John Rodker in October 1919.*

583. **TLS** [*embossed letterhead*] 5, Holland Place Chambers, Kensington, W.
[2 November 1919]

[London]

Dear Mother:

I go up to Newcastle tomorrow a. m.; hope to arrive before complete con-gelation. Nothing of particular importance to communicate.

Lewis portrait will probably be photographed sometime, and then you will get better idea than from description. He is doing a fine thing for the Imperial war memorial, 8 ft. by 12.

D. is working up her Pyranees sketches extremely well.

Yeats family over from Ireland. W. B. still enveloped in celto-spiritist fog.

Rosing again in form at yesterdays concert.

Those idiots Liverlight Ltd. have sent my proofs by express instead of post, result that letter has arrived but proofs have not.

If they try to wriggle on their contract or put in charge for delay the matter will have to be taken up. Have you Will Wadsworth's address. I cant bother Quinn further, but Will was once a lawyer, he probably is yet as it is only five years since be sent me notice of his setting up with someone in law office.

NOTHING to be done until Liverlight's first accounts come in, i.e. in about a years time.

Please

Ask H. L. P. not to write to Quinn re my affairs save in case of necessity, as Q. is extremely busy and not, I think, in real health.

Have been offered £300 toward starting a new magazine on practical lines, but it will require from £800 to £1500 to start it on lines really practical, so I don't know that anything is likely to come of it. The plan is only a week old.

Neither is it particularly interesting to start a magazine on practical lines. Sole hope being that one might be able to get some good work into it without the public's finding one out that it was there.

Love to you & dad,

. E .

Managed to pass Oct. 30 without remembering it. (as usual).

Pound was to lecture on the troubadour poets to the **Newcastle** *Literary and Philo-sophical Society on Monday 3 November. The audience would number 714 persons. In his 'Art Notes' in the* New Age *of 11 December 1919 'B. H. Dias' wrote, 'Wyndham Lewis'* **portrait** *of Ezra Pound rises with the dignity of a classic stele to the god of gardens amid the bundles of market garden produce at the Goupil Gallery'.*

584. TLS [*embossed letterhead*] 5, Holland Place Chambers, Kensington, W.

21 / 11 / '19

[London]

Dear Dad:

Thanks for £2/. I have sent 7d. to Eliphants or Ollypants as requested.

No proofs have reached me. If they'd use the post instead of rushing around to Express companies, worst known swindlers on earth, I might have had proofs three or four weeks ago. Even now they'd probably save time by sending me proofs by post.

Idea of using express too baroque to permit discussion. 'Express'!!! Christ all hemlock! it means years and years.

Why not freight? why not charter a yacht?

The hundred copies of Knopfs brochure were sent by express, required special permit to import & took months.

/ / / /

I cant get the N.Age for nothing . Also they pay very little not through ill will but because they cant. If you'll start an american subscription list or get it put on sale in the leading book stores you might increase my screw. Not that it matters.

Dont know that there's much news.

Will try to collect you a few notices of Q. P. A.

Love to you and mother.

E. P.

*The **brochure** would have been T. S. Eliot's 1917* Ezra Pound. His Metric and Poetry.

━━━

585. TLS [*embossed letterhead*] 5, Holland Place Chambers, Kensington, W.

Nov. 22 1919

[London]

Dear Dad:

I have started up your sub. to N. Age again.

I want you to PHONE to Liveright. No proofs have YET come. I cant make out whether they were sent by express or by post. Hammer into Liveright that express is idiotic. When Knopf sent the brochure by express it took months.

IF proofs have not been sent by post, a set ought to be sent by post NOW.

I suspect < naturally you will not let them know I suspect this.> they are trying some game, and going to try to crib some of my royalties on grounds of my being responsible for delay. I take no responsibility for any delay due to EXPRESS. Pure idiocy on their part. As for 'insuring' proofs; the proofs have no value whatever; the speed in transmission is all that counts. Type being set up, proofs can be replaced quite easily.

/ / /

Secondly. As Liveright never answers a letter. Please phone that I have three new cantos done. THUS there is enough matter for American edition of poems, as follows.

Homage	to Propertius
Langue	D'Oc.
Moeurs	Contemporaines
Cantos	IV, V, and VI. (possibly VI and VII, by time matter is settled
	Same size vol as English Q. P. A.

Liveright's agent wrote asking if they cd. import Q. P. A., you understand that the first three cantos are in Knopf's 'Lustra', therefore the English sheets of Q. P. A. can not be sold in America.

/ / /

IF Liveright dont give you an answer re poems, within a fortnight, and if they cant be lucid about the proofs of Instigations ; then take up matter of Poems with Knopf. Letter wd. do for that.

Terms for either Liveright or Knopf, to be royalty of 15%, and I shd. like you to ask (quite naievely) for an advance on royalties. Try it on. Especially with Knopf. Simply say to Liveright if he wants the poems 'Are you prepared to make an advance on royalties.'

The money is really just as good to me at one time or another, but they shd. be got into proper state of subjection.

In dealing with Knopf if it comes to that, imply that Liveright has not been approached about poems, but that you are coming to him to see if he is prepared to better than Liveright. Liveright gives 15% on Instigations. Therefore Knopf shd. give 15% AND pay 100 dollars of it in advance.

Procedure therefore as follows.

1. PHONE to Liveright.

2. Delay of two weeks, for suitable and satisfactory answer re/ proofs, and offer on poems. < Possibly take time to send me Liverights answer if they propose anything.>

3. If Liveright unsatisfactory, first letter to Knopf. 'Do you want poems' Q. P. A. with new cantos for old. book to be called 'Homage to Sextus Propertius' and the Propertius series to come first in the vol.

4. Second letter to Knopf. 'What terms do you offer?'

Then refer the matter to me for final sanction.

/ / / / /

Wadsworth's Vorticist architecture, the last bomb here. Lewis portrait to be reproduced, will send it you. Press very favourable on it.

D. back from Oxford today.
Love to you & mother
E

22 – II - 19
Large turkey now in kitchen
Rodker printing Lewis portfolio. & Eliot poems handsomely.

+≻━━≺+

586. TLS [*embossed letterhead*] 5, Holland Place Chambers, Kensington, W.

[c.25 November 1919]

[London]

Dear Dad:

Have just heard from Liveright. They want the vol. of poems; so you needn't bother about those negotiations exposed in my note of Saturday.

Proofs haven't come. Am writing to Fleischmann, so you needn't bother about anything. Phone, if you have time, to suggest sending another set of proofs by post, even now.

/ / / / /

Dear Mother:

Tell Server studios are very hard to get here; BUT not absolutely impossible. If he will send me particulars of what he wants; size, price, number of rooms, studio to live in or only to work in, etc. in full detail, I will keep a look out for one, BUT I cant promise anything, nor have I time to rush about to agents, save the two just near here.

I dont suppose he expects to hold classes. Wadsworth had the studio the Albert Memorial was made in. Enormous and cheap, as too big for any ordinary use. If S. wanted it mostly for summer, it might do. Winter fuel makes it expensive. Heaven help him if he expects anything small & cheap.

Love to you & dad
E

+≻━━≺+

587. TLS [*embossed letterhead*] 5, Holland Place Chambers, Kensington, W.

13 December 1919

[London]

Dear Dad:

Spent last week proof-correcting 'Instigations'; this a.m. bought up some french francs @ 40 to the £; should have done so last week @44; but still feel 'better' as have this sort of start toward getting south of the channel, in the spring.

Had tea with Editor of the Times, whom I met before he was so large and monumental a figure. Suppose he has had more to do with smash-up of Austria and creation of various 'younger nations' than any other one man. A personified monocle whom I have known (very slightly) for ten years has been appointed ambassador to Prague, (Prague was once in Bohemia, suppose it is still in the same part of map.) Lewis 'imperial' picture has had a good press. Too hurriedly done to be really 'IT'.

Met a Jap attaché at tea, today, who had known Fenollosa and confirmed what I have heard of E. F., starting Japs on track of knowing their own art etc. etc.

Have done cantos 5, 6, and 7, each more incomprehensible than the one preceding it; dont know what's to be done about it. Liveright says he is ready to bring out vol. of poems. Shall put the Propertius first and follow by 'Langue d'oc' and Cantos IV to VII., book about same size as Q. P. A.

Early poems, with title 'Umbra' shd. be out, here, in spring. Best out of early vols, Mathews and Poetry Book Shop combining to print this edition.

Give my rememberances to folks at Tioga. Have been reading works of Thos. Jefferson (no connection between two ideas). Wider knowledge of TJ's life and opinions would be a good pill for the Murkhn Peepul; however the little school text books will probabably go on telling the little lies some swine thinks ought to be told to the unfortunate young.

Rosing concert today, Tinayre on Friday, Tinyare going to continent and then to U. S. A. (Yves Tinayre) hear him and tell him who you are if he gets to Phila.

Yeats starts for U. S. sometime in Jan.

Is Leonard Wood all that's left of the G. O. P.??

Love to you & mother

E. P

13 – 12 - '19

General **Leonard Wood** (1860–1927), with the endorsement of his friend Theodore Roosevelt. was a contender for the Republican nomination in the 1920 Presidential election. The nomination went to Warren G. Harding.

The **editor of** The Times was H. Wickham Steed.

588. TLS [*embossed letterhead*] 5, Holland Place Chambers, Kensington, W.

24 December 1919

[London]

Dear Mother.

Merry Xmas. But why the devil, dad, whom I have just written a fairly stiff letter; should go and pay those cadging L. R. females twenty dollars, just because Europe owes America ninety billion dollars, and the English £ is therefore worth very little, beats me.

And why the hell he expects me to pay them in dollars what I have recd. in £ also beats me.

Thanks for Asia with note on Lawrence.

If I had paid them £30 they wd. probably have got even more money out of him. Which is a comforting thought, no, hardly. I was a bloody fool to pay them anything. I could perfectly well have charged them £30 for the Chinese mss. which they didn't print when I sent it, and only use now in the hope of annoying me.

Even that silly old fool in Chicago has done what they have never done, i.e. sent some acknowledgement of my having done something for her hopeless fool of magazine.

They got stuff out of me, <stuff I paid for with money I could have kept for myself to Q's perfect satisfaction,> work out of me, money out of Quinn because I was pushing the paper. Their final return is to do my pore old father out of 24 dollars. O glorious females.

Quinn warned me out a full year before I quit. I know that the thing led nowhere, but wanted certain stuff in print and went on, for the sake of certain things I considered worth while.

If dad wants an eye opener, let him try to get a refund out of them. They will of course say they haven't any money, which will probably be true.

The only formal answer is that I recd in £.and paid in £. and the £ I recd were no more valuable & no less so than those I sent to them.

yrs

E

24 Dec. 1919

Note I dont complain of the two years in connection with L. R. I dont want a word in public. They have their points. But this last turn is playing it too low. I had my fun, it cost a certain amount. It cost Quinn a damn sight more than it was worth to him or possibly to me. I have had to write excuses for those females by the page and ream, to keep Q. from busting up the whole thing. I only hope this last affair wont reach him. He was sick enough with them two years ago. He wd. be very much annoyed to know that they had let dad in.

yrs

E

+≡≡+

589. ALS [*embossed letterhead*] 5, Holland Place Chambers, Kensington, W.

24 December 1919

[London]

Dear Mother:

   Please get yourself a Xmas or Twelfth Night box of 'Ackers' with this 'rectification of error'

Yrs
E

It is too small to cash here.

24 Dec 1919.

+≽══≼+

590. TLS [*embossed letterhead*] 5, Holland Place Chambers, Kensington, W.

14 January 1920

[London]

Dear Dad:

   Thanks for letter and enclosures of T. C. P. Seems a chance that my finances may be eased a bit shortly; shall possibly be able to halve your loss with you on cheque in £. But I DEW THINK them females played you for a 'rube'.

   Note from Boni saying all corrected proofs recd. so book may appear sometime.

   I do not think American politics particularly inviting, at any rate don't see why I shd. waste my life on them with no prospect of having any effect. I certainly don't want to live in Washington with present gang or any likeley successors thereto. Imagine having to meet and converse once a month with some of our leading darks. (Intellectual darks. I doan mind dem wot is brack outsaade)

   The editor of the Times said he wd. be delighted to have my 'collaboration'. That is an exceedingly urbane phrase which he has picked up on the continent. We agreed that music was the only safe and possible subject I cd. treat without causing riots. But I don't think he had guaged the extent of possible oppositions, at any rate the head of the music dept. is alledged to have fallen ill (probably at the prospect) and nothing has yet happened. I like Steed very much. Also think it no inconsiderable advance that the Times shd. be edited by a man who knows there are countries in Europe not included in Brit. Empire.

   He once got a thing of mine into the Lit. Sup. (when he was foreign edtr. not Boss edtr.) but edtr. of said Sup. returned from absence and stopped that little game.

   I have a good stiff punch in 'L'Art Libre' for Jan. 1. It has been very well translated, but being in French and as I have only one copy, will not send it to you. All goes to show that it is very difficult from the episcopat to keep ALL the lids down ALL the time.

Article for France-Amerique dont seems to have come out yet.

I enclose communication from the Internationale of Arts, letters, etc.

Have told N. A. to change address to Wyncote.

Some of Baker's collection of Lewis, and some of the Gaudier charcoals which I have given the S. Kensington museum are now on show in the East Hall there.

love to you and mother.

Salute the cousinage in Tioga and Montana.

yrs

E

14 – I - '20

*In L'Art Libre of January 1 was Pound's 'Londres et Ses Environs. Un petit guide pour l'étranger bien intentionné'. There were articles also in the February and April numbers. Captain Guy **Baker** had died in the so-called Spanish 'flu epidemic which swept the globe at the end of the war.*

+≈≈≈+

591. **TLS** [*embossed letterhead*] 5, Holland Place Chambers, Kensington, W.

14 January 1920

[London]

Dear Mother:

Have just turned up an old letter of Dad's wherein he suggests that I shd. write to Homer and congratulate him on birth of a male heir. The profound meditations arroused in me by this fact completely inhibit all processes of verbal expression.

If I write what comes into my head. !!!!!!! No, the declaration, 'Rather unto thee than unto me' wd. not increase the warmth of interfamilial feelings. I am, as usual, perfectly willing to be amiable. BUTTTT

I hope it makes Homer happy. Beyond that I can not go.

When I am really opulent (Greek Kalends) I shall set up a stud farm.

I hope Homer can afford it; and that he derives pleasure from the presence of it, its bottles, it diapers, its damp pieces of biscuit; it . . . if it takes after its father . . . damp pieces of white peppermint candy . . . etc.

Perhaps on the theme of egg biscuit and peppermint I might wax more eloquent. Tiens, c'est une idee.

Voici, enclos. The humble literary effort of your devoted son.

Have four new super-shirts of elegant cut; such as inspire the respect of the august makers thereof (WING, <u>of</u> Piccadilly) otherwise the domestic status is very much as it was when I last wrote.

Am leading a life of pleasure and indigence, practice none of the democratic virtues; and am feeling reasonably fit; have sunk far enough into the metropolis to feel glad I have come back to it. My sympathies go out to the unfortunate family Yeats, now on the unsympathetic boozumm of the execrable and · · · · · · · · · · · Atlantic. Hope father will show George over the Mint if she turns up and asks to see it.

D. seems to think we may get to Italy in the spring. At any rate Mrs. Eden has assured her that there is some food in Venice, contrary to published reports.

A man filled with virtue says he is paying me some moneys this week. The statement has all the characteristics of improbability.

Johns writes me that my last ode to the Virgin Republic will appear in the 'next' issue of Much Ado. The editor thereof will probably be deported, and I shall be asked to return my passport to the Embassy after this fatal event.

It is a great pity that Th. Jefferson is not taught in American schools.

Yrs

E.

14 - I –1920

*Pound did scrawl a note to his cousin, **Homer Foote**. recalling his having been apparently brought up 'on biscuit and peppermint sticks'. Pound's '**ode to the Virgin Republic**' was a 38-line satiric 'Canticle', sent to the editor of Much Ado, Harry Turner, apparently not intended for publication, and not reprinted by Pound. It began, 'LIGHT OF THE WORLD! My country 'tis of thee, / Where booze is banned and letters are not free'.*

+⟫——⟪+

592. **TLS** [*embossed letterhead*] 5, Holland Place Chambers, Kensington, W

21 January 1920

[London]

Dear Dad:

From the pie faced liar who runs the North American Review, and dont even apologize for his lies when they are shown him, to the nigger on the Boston Transcript, to the poor well meaning fool in Chicago with her noble voice from the gutter; there is not one editorial office in the U. S., that wdn't be relieved by my demise (opportunity for a few more columns). There is not one bean-fed mucker in the lot who wd. pay me a day labourers wages.

What they want is VanDyke, and they get it. I think possibly Quinn and Bronner have gone into the matter at closer range than you have. Bronner said he thought at first I was wrong, but came round after trying to place an article.

I have undoubtedly had good press notices from time to time.

What your bog of a country wont provide is the office boys fifteen dollars per week. And bloody lucky for me that I can get on without it.

459

I never denied there were a lot of parasites ready to make use of anything I had done, and flood the market with dilutations. The pork headed Century that turned down some of my best stuff, now ready to print a ten percent dilutation, oh YUS.

Also chance for sale, possibly, if I shd. stop inventing anything, and do immitations of my old stuff. Even that is doubtful.

However. L'Art Libre seems glad to get my stuff, and I like the way they have translated the first article. Bosschere seems to think that now the war is over there shd. be no difficulty in placing my stuff on the continent.

Trouble being that, as on N. A., the rates are low and one has to do rather too much for ones mental health.

D. has made a fawncy bag for I. W. P., suppose she will receive it in time.

Love to you & mother

. E .

21 - I -1920

The owner and editor of the **North American Review** *was Col. George Harvey (1864–1928); William Stanley Braithwaite (1978–62), a black poet and anthologist, had attacked Pound and* Poetry *in the* **Boston Transcript** *in 1916; the 'poor well meaning fool in* **Chicago***' was Harriet Monroe, founder and editor of* Poetry.

593. TLS [*embossed letterhead*] 5, Holland Place Chambers, Kensington, W

1 February 1920

[London]

My Dear Parent:

If you are feeling like being useful and clever, and if you wd. care to see me in our arid fatherland; you might cogitate the following.

Rennert (a poor thing without backbone) said in 1911 that he wd. accept Spirit of Romance, Guido, and Arnaut Daniel as substitute for Doctors Thesis.

I dont care much about the Ph.D. or about coming to America. But IF the university chose to confer the degree it might facilitate my getting a decent guarantee for a lecture tour out of Pond or some other swine.

What I suggest is, that when Instigations comes out, you see Rennert, then your acquaintance Smith, then Schelling, and find out on what terms they wd. give me the Ph. D. 'in consideration of my published work'. Remember I had done <u>nearly</u> all the class work required before I left in 1907.

There is AMPLE evidence of my haveing since then done a damn sight more than wd. have been necessary to take the degree.

They will buzz 'regulations' and formalities at you. Perhaps you cd. get Woodward to go in your place. At any rate go to see Woodward first and see if you can cook something between you.

Tell Woodward that Rennert proposed me for fellowship in 1911 or '12 but being a natural worm he backed down when someone objected that I wasn't going to be a professor.

That is sheer piffle as the foundation is for the 'advancement of learning' and not for the making of professors.

I think Woodward, who after all spent six years in that bonehose will be a better man to see these corpses than you wd. Only see that he is really posted re/ my 'works'.

yours

E

Love to you & mother

1 / 2 / 1920

+⊱━⊰+

594. TLS [*embossed letterhead*] 5, Holland Place Chambers, Kensington, W

22 February 1920

[London]

Dear Dad:

Have a shot at C. H. Douglas' 'Economic Democracy' when the U.S. edtn. comes out. Dont know anything about photo in Van. Fair. What is it alleged to be there for??

Have been plugging this keyboard since yesterday a.m. no Head left. Fine Epstein show now on.

Turner has a letter of mine in 'Much Ado' for Feb.

'Umbra' has got as far as having a sample page in the right kind of type.

Managed a meeting between Douglas and Keynes on Thursday last. Douglas the real mind. Keynes fairly courageous in his book, but has invented whole Roman Apostolick Church of economics, just as bad as the old Whore of Babylon.

H.D. has gone to Greece. Have had an ambiguous message from Mme. Cilokowska which may mean that DesFueilles has really done the translation of 'Noh' . . or it may mean that he has only translated a bloomin' article for 'France- Amerique.'

Booked for tea with Edgar Jepson this p.m. good chap . . finest collection of jade in England got by intelligence not opulence.

Love to you and mother.

E.P

22 – 2 – '20

461

Pound, who was just discovering Douglas' economic thought, had enthusiastically recommended **Economic Democracy** *in his letter in* Much Ado *of 2 February.* **Jepson** *is remembered as 'a lover of jade' in canto 74.*

+——=+

595. **TLS** [*embossed letterhead*] 5, Holland Place Chambers, Kensington, W
April 18 1920

[London]

Dear Dad:

I think I wrote you that Padre Jose (Spain 1906) turned up here a couple of years ago. He is still here, visible at concerts, etc. very amiable.

Have just stopped destroying enclosed post card. refers to an article I have written for 'Hermes' a Spanish magazine devoted to litterchure.

We start for Venice a week from tomorrow Italian Embassy has taken the burden of visas off my shoulders, and the tickets are being prepared. So it seems possible we may get off.

How do you feel about Paris in July, or last week in July there and first week in August here.

/ / /

Have had a cable from the Dial which I take to mean that I am now part of the show. Enclose tentative stationary. Dont know that they want the connection mentioned in America. Possibilities of vendetta ????

Hope you have recd. Eng. Review

There is a good review of Eliot in todays Observer.

/ /

Rodker has sent in proofs of first part of my new opusculus.

Accompaniments to four XIIth century songs, seems to be about ready for publisher.

Etc.

Love to you & mother

. E .

18 / 4 / 1920

Padre José *Maria de Elizondo's conversation is echoed in canto 81. Pound's article in* **Hermes** *was a brief eclectic survey of English literature from Chaucer to Imagisme and after. Pound had agreed to be European agent for the* **Dial**, *and would be very active in seeking contributions and advising its wealthy young editors, Scofield Thayer and James Sibley Watson; but Thayer did not want Pound's name to appear on the Dial's masthead, nor even on the letterheads of his London Agency. In the* **English Review** *for April 1920 there was a substantial appreciation of Pound's work by May Sinclair—it would be printed also in the* North American Review *in May. His* **'new opusculus'** *was Hugh Selwyn Mauberley. Pound was working on the words and Agnes Bedford on the accom-*

*paniments for the '**XIIth century songs**' which would be published in December 1920 as* Five Troubadour Songs.

+≻━━≺+

596. TLS [*embossed letterhead*] 5, Holland Place Chambers, Kensington, W
[24 April 1920]

[London]

Dear Dad

Am sending you 'Mauberley', my new poems, advance sheets. I dont want you to show it to people YET.

Because 1.

I want the Dial to print cantos IV–VII, they probably want something of mine, and wd. certainly <u>prefer</u> short poems to the cantos. Therefore I want them to remain in ingornace of the fact that there are any short poems, until the cantos have had a full chance.

If they saw the short poems firt, they wd. probably want to print them <u>instead</u> of cantos. It wd. get my name into the Magazine, for less money, and in more convenient way. . Therefore please lie low about 'Mauberly' until you hear from me.

2. Re Boni and Liveright. I suppose they will write about the U. S. edition of Propertius when they send 'Instigations'. Am not sure I want 'Mauberley' in that vol. tho' Boni very likely would.

/ / / /

I got your anniversary present, and acknowledged it in a stern and unmannerly letter on international exchange.

This is Saturday. We are supposed to leave Monday a.m. and there is a devil of a lot to do.

Love to you & mother
E

Better have these sheets <u>bound</u> . They are ~~worth~~
Thought you wd. like to see em without waiting for 'em to be bound here.

+≻━━≺+

597. AC

[*postmark* 29 April 1920]

[Venice]

Arrived . sunny side up.

Price, in the ascendent. Have fine 1 room in the Pilsen-Manin which we cant afford.

Co. Thos. Cook.

463

Ezra and Dorothy had crossed to Paris on the 26th, and gone on to Venice on the 28th, intending to spend a month there. However, due to Dorothy's suffering a 'quasi-complete disintegration' in Venice, they were retreating after ten days to Sirmione on Lake Garda.

---

598. ACS

9 May. 1920

Albergo Pilsen-Manin Venice

We go to Verona tomorrow & then on to Sirmione in a few days. Discovered a Greek church here yesterday with some very fine paintings. Suppose its in Baedecker but never happened to go into it before. The poor parson, greek speaking no Italian but having been seven years in U.S.A. - very bored with Venice; says there are no greeks left here: conducted us thru the ex-episcopal mansion & conversed for an hour . . .

Grand canal empty, no lights in windows, no gondola but ours out last night. Prices fantastic, but equalized by the lire being 77 to the £ Eng.

Food remarkably good here. In fact you might recommend the hotel to anyone who can dispense with windows on Grand canal which, by the way, one doesn't usually get when one goes to Grand Hotel. There being only a certain number per house. Met three sets of acquainted Inglese on Friday, but they have since disappeared. The 'International' (picture show) is supposed to be going to open but one cant stay forever waiting for them to decide when.

yrs
. E .

---

599. ALS

20 May 1920

Hotel Eden Sirmione

Dear Dad:

Weather warm, new variety of emerald green larger lizard apparent.

Will you let the Trial = I mean <u>The Dial</u> 152 W. 15th St. have the sheets of 'Mauberley' to look at.

You can say you want 'em back, and that any poems they want can be typed, so that your copy needn't be messed at the printers.

Say the book is to be out shortly . . - i.e. is at the binders.

Dial is printing Canto IV but needs dynamite.

When I get another 7. N. A. articles off my chest, shall be free to enjoy the remnant of the summer.

Some chance that Joyce will come over here for a week.

Love to you & mother,

. E .

D. will send an olive tree in <u>time</u>.

20 - 5 - 20

Pound's **New Age** *articles made up his highly mannered family memoir, 'Indiscretions; or, Une revue de deux mondes'. In 1922, when the articles were about to be published as a book in Paris, his father protested to Ezra, 'HAVE A HEART', and asked him not to bring up old family gossip and old scandals about his grandfather and other men now dead; and 'Of course Mother objects to the whole thing', he added. They felt the family was being exposed to public gaze in an unseemly fashion.*

+≻══≺+

600. ALS

22 May [1920]

Sirmione

Dear Dad:

Sorry Grandmother is ill.

Dare say this lake <u>wd</u>. do her good if it weren't so far off. Am sending her a p. c. or rather will put several in an envelope if I can find a variety; they are a bit thinned by war.

Wish Woodward had confided his European address; suppose he'll be gone before you can send him mine.

This business about my not having any work for Ph.D. is a quibble. The requirement is 24 units & Thesis. The 12 units credited for M.A. count toward Ph.D. or did when I took them.

For the next 12 units they shd. have record of my entering the courses, i.e. attendance for one year at 12 hrs per week while Fellow in Romanics.

One doesn't take the exam on these courses until one comes up for degree, and the units presumably aren't put on the book.

The point is that I have complied or nearly so, with the requirements for physical presence in their gehenna.

Barker's concluding sentence, is a fine piece of conclusion <u>not</u> implied by preceding statements in his letter, but psychologically interesting.

Do note that what I have asked for is (as Woodward's letter shows he realizes) a statement of the minimum of the Universities demands i.e. what it still asks me to do before I can receive its (fundamentally useless) sanction to exist.

The parentheses in this note are, obviously, for you & G. C. W. The statement that it (Ph.D.) is only given 'in course' is formally correct.

But about the only ounce in their pound of flesh <u>wd</u>. be (in order for me to be strictly 'in course'), <u>wd</u>. be for me to come to <u>Phila</u>. and physically present myself for examination on the 12 hours of class work. (lecture attendance) suffered in winter of 1906-7).

The point is, do the blackguards want to hang up on that mere formality, <u>despite</u> my record of published work. Remember this is as much an enquiry into the psychology of the University // scientifically valuable as a record of the Spirit of the Age // as a desire on my part to possess a futile decoration which I shd. use only about once in 10 years.

It will be quite as <u>valuable</u> to learn that they will accord no credit <u>whatever</u> on my last 12 years work, as to receive any leniencies or courtesies they might offer.

W. Barker's last sentence spreads pages 'between the lines'.

However, let G. C. W. have his shot when he returns. - shd. like to see the 'gownsman's' remarks. Never mind about the N. American review.

============

Note that W. Bark. seems to think I asked for a degree & was refused at some period ? ?

Or does he mean <u>he</u> asked for the degree for me.

I never came up for exam on my second year of Post grad. work.

But find out if you can what Barker means by 'Faculty refusing to recommend the Board of Trustees the issue of mandamus'

If it means that Barker asked for the writ. it is highly interesting & very sporting of him to have done so.

<u>But</u>, I dont see what effect it wd. have on an honorary degree – <u>Unless</u>, as is more than probable there more niggers in that wood pile than are showing their sleek black heads.

There'd be a high mortality list (apoplectic mostly) if I <u>shd</u> return & continue my studies <u>in</u> <u>course</u>. Have they considered <u>that</u> contingency?

It might pay me as 'copy'.

A refusal on religious grounds wd., for example, be stupendous.

Possibly if Woodward cd. see Rennert, it wd. be the best next move. Rennert will presumably profess good will, but has no back bone, & loathes all forms of disputation.

Love to you & mother –

Tub here is 32 miles long, but perhaps I shall get to the 3d floor some day.

Yrs
E .

In his letter of 1 February 1920 Pound had prompted his father to sound out professors Rennert and Schelling at the University of Pennsylvania about the award of the PhD. On 31 March, Homer reported that he had 'had a talk with Prof. Schelling, and he promised me to do all he could on your behalf'. However Schelling then advised the Faculty that 'Mr Pound . . . has done none of the work demanded' for the degree, and on 3 April

Wharton Barker, a banker friend of Homer Pound and a Trustee of the University, wrote this letter to Homer:

My dear Mr Homer L. Pound:-

The record of your son's work at the University of Pennsylvania, when he sought the degree of Ph.D. has been placed in my hands. I have given it careful consideration, and the action of the Faculty in refusing to recommend to the Board of Trustees the issue of mandamus for grant of degree, was a just refusal, of course an honorary degree is now out of the question. I regret more than I can tell you that I am obliged to find the facts as stated.

Yours very truly,
Wharton Barker

Barker wrote again to Homer on 3 May 1920, replying to his letter of 30th April:

The record of Mr. Ezra Pound when a student at the University I cannot show to you, but can say that he was denied the degree of Ph.D. not because of conduct, but because of what the professors thought was neglect of the work undertaken by him. I regret very much to be obliged to make this statement because I would like to see your son's desire and your ambition for him gratified.

Pound himself wrote to Barker in August, along similar lines to his letter above, but mentioning also the resentment he had aroused as a graduate student by showing his dissent from Professor Schelling's 'as it then seemed to me, narrow prejudice against the right of contemporary literature to exist'; and further, that Professor Penniman would 'never forgive me for wanting to think, and for preferring the search for sound criteria to a parroting of dead men's opinion'. Barker replied:

I do not think the action you and your father would like to have the University of Pennsylvania authorities take possible so long as the relations with the members of the faculty are what you describe them to be. I am sure that an honorary degree such as has been suggested the Trustees of the University of Pennsylvania would not be conferred upon you so long as Dr. Penniman and Dr. Schelling are in opposition.

*HLP had written that they were putting a bathroom into their **third floor**, in order to rent it out.*

601. ALS

28 - May [1920]

Hotel Eden Sirmione

Dear Dad:

Thanks for note, (14th May), amazing speed considering Italian strikes.

Instigations shd. have been sent to 5 Holland Pl. Chambers. - however, as it hasn't been, please have it sent. co. Mrs. Shakespear, 12 Brunswick Gdns. London W. 8.

All further mail shd. go to 5 H. P. C.

I shall be in Paris by the time you get this - if you do get it.

Have just had letter from Woodward which appears to have taken 12 days to come from Naples.

Have sent grandmother a card from here, & D is trying to do her a sketch, but the paint don't seem to be working well. - so god knows if she'll ever get it. - Glad grandmother is improved.

Bathing here doing D. good. // am scribbling articles for Orage & it interferes with my leisure. Joyce hopes to spend next week here with us – salvo incidenti - which means if the bloody trains run. // It is not precisely the year for travel.

Love to you & mother

E

Joyce reached Sirmione on 8 June, and left on the 10th. Ezra and Dorothy set out for Paris that day, and remained there until about 21 July.

+⊱━⊰+

602. TLS [*letterhead*] The Dial *Agency*, 5, Holland Place Chambers, London, W.8.

8 August 1920

[London]

Dear Dad:

This machine has been in constant action since my return.

Thanks for letter re Mary Felton of dark and delectable memory.

New news: Joseph Conrad sends in messages of interest in Dial

Mss. of Benedict Arnold Bennett dispatched to N.Y.

Yeats autobiography said to be approaching New stuff by Eliot, Morrand, Soupault.

Etc.

Shall get back to private life in a few moths time. I 'OPE.

Can Chris. Morley do anything for Dial. It is a good show, he'd better come in on it.

Also any others with sense. Get him up, show him the list. Tell him NOT to mention my name or say who is the active European agent. No use in scaring the heckers.

Love to you & mother
E

8. 8. 1920

+⊨══⊨+

603. TLS

20 August 1920

[London]

[*beginning missing*]

Large box of varia to hand. D. writing, very pleased.

Does that leaf from Govt. employee's paper mean that 'retirment bill', plus pension is passed, or is the fancy cover a pipe dream?

New striped chair cover, new cuorderoy cushion to swankify my new chair of all work. Have just come back from three days in Mrs Fowler's cottage. Still ending up various Dial jobs and translations.

Dad might bring enc. Ovid press circular to attention of Sunwise Turn, and the other book shops. Also Elkin Mathews is bringing out a special edition of 'Umbra' 100 signed copies @ 25/ (cheaper for U.S. than here with exchange where it now is.

Thick paper and grey boards with parchment back and gilt top.

Signed copies of Mauberley all gone, save two or three velum copies, bound in full parchment at £3/3.

Have heard from Liveright, re new vol poems for spring.

Etc. havent yet really had time to breathe. Think I wrote the five troubadour songs music are in the press.

Love to you & dad.
E. P.

20 Aug. 1920 -

Homer wrote on 17 August: 'the U.S. has passed a Pension Act. At the age of 65 Dad can retire—on pension of $720 per year. In the mean time the Gov. deducts 2¼ per cent for pay to go to that fund—amounts to about $5. per month. So three years from now prepare for it.' In fact Homer would not feel able to retire until June 1928. Boosey & Co. would publish in December **Five Troubadour Songs** | *With the original Provençal words | and English words adapted by Ezra Pound from Chaucer | Arranged by Agnes Bedford.*

+⊨═⊨+

604. TLS [embossed letterhead] 5, Holland Place Chambers, Kensington, W
(1 September 1920)

[London]

Dear Dad:

Very glad about the pension. . Not much to it, but if you rent the house on a ten years lease you and I.P. cd. live over here, or in France on the double result.

Suppose Homer F. is capable and wd. look after the real estate in yr. absence.

/ / /

Wot d'ye mean 'as near t- t- truth?

Didn't the bitch-bulls <u>all</u> have the sore-horne, and maggots crawlin in the crater of the cavity: And, as to Thadeus ::::: waaaal Hirmam . . . wot is t be sed?

The french is from Rabelais and indicates that the habits of small boys have been for some ages the same. I really cant look up the passage at the moment. But if you guess right and verify the same from nature you wont be far out on the total.

/ / /

Do you mean as near to the truth as <u>I</u> can get? or as can be <u>gotted</u>.

[*ms*]Yeats appears to approve rather vigorously of parts of Mauberley -

Haven't yet been assassinated by some of the near-sitters.

D. gone to sea bord for a week or so.

Mannings new novel, great stuff. Hope Dial will get on with it.

H.D. sailed this a.m. for N.Y.

Love to you & mother.

& hoping to see you in a few years time if there is still a Europe to come to.

Yrs

E

Homer had questioned the accuracy of various details in Indiscretions, *including Pound's writing of his grandfather's farming, that 'the fad for clipping the horns of milk-cows exercised maleficent influence upon both the farm and the milk-route'. Pound had quoted a passage from the beginning of chapter 11 of* **Rabelais'** Gargantua and Pantagruel. **Manning's new novel** *was 'The Gilded Coach', of which the first hundred pages were seen, and admired, by the Dial's editors; but they would not begin serialising it until they had the complete novel in hand, and Manning never did finish it.*

605. ACS [*cardhead*] The Dial, 152 W. 13th St. New York
22 September 1920

[London]

Will write when I get time to breathe.
Sending fueilles libre.
Take it 'Hermes' is unintelligible being in Spanish.

Yrs
. E .

22. 9 - 1920

In Les Feuilles Libres. Lettres et Arts *in August had appeared translations by Ludmila Savitzky of five poems from* Lustra.

+⊱——⊰+

606. TLS [*embossed letterhead*] 5, Holland Place Chambers, Kensington, W
30 Sept 1920

[London]

Dear Mother:
So long since I wrote that it is utterly impossible to begin anywhere in particular. Ref/ Dial.
We meant down to Lacock Abbey for four days, 14th century cloisters, charter of Henry III left there in 1225 still in the tower room, etc. Family name Talbot, vide. works of Wm. Shx. et al. Got a little tennis, etc.
Dicky Green turned up here a fortnight ago, escaped meeting the Virgin Mary, but found a S. African cow puncher here, the latter very much shocked at his nearly asking Dicky how the hell one now managed in U. S. since the pubs closed, but Dicky got in first with some jaw about Pilgrim Fathers, and Dennis was save the ambarassment. Fortunately the B. V. M. had left, otherwise Dicky is much too deaf to have ever found out that she wasn't D.; whom he wanted so much to meet, and did finally.
Dicky is taking home a large photo. of the Prince of Wales whom he considers a most estimable young man.
Ethelwyn Snively also arrived on these shores and is again departed, amiable and unchanged.
My article has at least appeared in Hermes of Bilbao, at last I write for an editor really named Jesus. (Jesus de Sarria) whom the Padre assures me is <u>muy liberal</u>; several lines in my second article have been altered slightly por miedo del obispo, i.e. the bishop of Bilbao, who is still supposed to be very powerful.
Did I send you 'Feuilles Libres' with the Savitzky note.?

L Intran, has quarter col. on Sept. Dial. various new items, for latter. Shane Leslie etc. coming in.

Have you seen Bill Williams new book?

Concert Season starts, for me, today. Marquesita is starrig in the Beggars Opera. Eliot's book of essays gone to press, proofs passed.

Sent mss. of new vol. poems to Liveright two days ago. Also mss. of Cantos V-VII to dad.

Yrs

E

Dorothy's cousin Charles Talbot was living in **Lacock Abbey**. *There is a reference to this visit in canto 80.* **L'Intransigeant** *was a Paris daily news sheet.* **Williams'** *new book was* Kora in Hell: Improvisations *(1920). In his 'Prologue', dated 1918, Williams, aiming to define his own poetic against Pound's practice, had declared that 'E. P. is the best enemy United States verse has', and Pound had retorted, in colourful language and at length, that the reverse was nearer the truth, yet had closed his letter by telling Williams, 'Have written to Dial that you are the best thing in the country'.* **Eliot's book** *was* The Sacred Wood *– Ezra and Dorothy had helped correct the proofs. Pound's own* **new volume of poems** *would be* Poems 1918–21 | Including Three Portraits | and Four Cantos: *the 'portraits' were 'Homage to Sextus Propertius', 'Langue d'Oc' with 'Moeurs Contemporaines', and 'Hugh Selwyn Mauberley'; the cantos were the 'Fourth', 'Fifth', 'Sixth', and 'Seventh'.*

✦━━✦

607. ALS [*embossed letterhead*] 5, Holland Place Chambers, Kensington, W

7 <u>Oct</u>. (1920)

[London]

Dear Mother.

Apart from August arriving two months late to the gt. peril of provisions & decayable stores, don't know that there is much to write apart from what shows on the Dial.

Am expecting to expand into a work room round the corner, as flats <u>one</u> size larger don't exist

Mathers back from France, Etchells from villegiatura.

Have sent copy for 'Three Portraits' to Liveright.

Proust is doing a preface for Morand's next book. etc.

Looked over some other American publications yesterday and found 'em chiefly filled from the swill pail. – dead flabby; second to tenth rate importations – Britis journalism watered down.

Lowell & Van W. Brooks seem to me additions & good ones to Dial contingent.

Bosschère has done some fine work – <u>not</u> his popular pot boilings - but the real stuff wont reproduce so that's that's.

Love to you & dad

E .

Concerts begun again but nothing very notable yet.

+⊨═══⊨+

608. TLS [*embossed letterhead*] 5, Holland Place Chambers, Kensington, W
31 Oct. [1920]

[London]

Dear Parents,

Doan you taawk teh me abaht niggurs; Ah wuz present three naits ago when Mr Roland Hayes de celebrated neegrooo tennuh wuz persented with a luminated address by the ex-mayor of Battuhsee in company with sum thirty abyssinian shieks an potentates and ethiopes and other African's in burrnooses <& fezzes>, an a very impressive cerimony, verhy simple and verrhy fine in de dressing down room of the Wigmo hall after a very fine concert which I hope to commemurate in the New Age in a week or so.

He doan ax no lee way from the remainin white hopes, he sing Go dahn Moses and he sing 'Manon' and all de high toff music and ah hopes fer to see him again.

Have also seen Lindsay. He has his points. He remembered H. L. P. with warmth.

Thanks for £3/ arrived on my natal kalends, yesterday. Also £7/5/4 which the noble Quinn had nobly wrenched from the Drama League; both arriving to mark the anniversary of my descent into the vale of tears.

O boy, when Mr Hayes comes to Phila. you jes' goa an' heah him sing.

Think 'Old John Brown' about the best of Lindsay's stuff.

But the Hayes performance, and the old black shieks had more guts I think.

Most of my activities will reach you via Dial or N. Age. (even this Hayes concert wd. probably have done so.)

I hope Leo P. proves a more suitable neighbor than the Sheip contingent, I see he is in the same line as Soloman Jerome Levi Sheip. Cigar boxes. Is Mr Kunkle still opposite, and Lower's bedroom still lined with pink satin, and Miss Annie Heacock still waving sufferage banners, and Bean still at the livery stable and Chris Myers shoeing horses, and the Luskin's increasing, and Freckles still druggist, and daddy Yarnel . . . no, he had gone out of biz. I suppose the Larzeleres haven't got any fatter, and that Jim Bryan is still the local cut up; and Billy Webbs hair still parted in the middle. And Mrs Bean still shampooing ladies hair. And McClure still living on the fat of the church, and the Curtisses and Gribbles, and Oh God, and Mrs Wade still as kittenish, and Gertie Hark and

Mamie Washburn still supporting the Presbyterian church with pristine religious fervour.

Joe is I suppose a pillar of the Phila. Bar. And Tommy drunk aboard a temperance battleship in Singapore; and Wes Pulman still contemplating an artistic career.

Whiteside has not turned up hhere.

AND so on.

Got in £4 or £5 worth of song books on Friday; dont know when there will be any visible results . . .. may come also via N. Age.

Letter from Bill Williams, yesterday. etc.

Love to you & dad

&

many happy returns of the day, also of the ? 25th nov.?

is it not

Yrs

E

'William Atheling' reviewed **Roland Hayes'** *performances enthusiastically in the* New Age *of 25 November 1920, and of 23 December 1920.* '**John Brown** *(To be sung by a leader and chorus)' is the second part of Vachel Lindsay's 'Booker Washington Trilogy'.*

+⇒—=+

609. TLS [*embossed letterhead*] 5, Holland Place Chambers, Kensington, W
26 Nov. (1920)

[London]

Chere Madame:

(et Monsieur ton epoux)

This is, or yesterday was, I believe your three thousandth or something anniversary, HENCE my congratulations. Many happy returns, peace, and prosperity.

Thank Dad for admirable summing up of Wilson in N. American. I have long been saying the same. I hope Mr. Harding is a nice man, and that he will throw over his friends, as amiably as possible.

Am just sending off translation of corking Morand story of Constantinople. Proofs of troubadour music, in more advanced state, now here. D. gone to Oxford for a few days.

Read large slice of my works yesterday in some hall Monro takes for instruction of the masses.

Concert audience looks more intelligent than theatre audience, audience for dancers considerably more alive looking, poetry obviously the art for the poor. Curiously sogged and inert mass in hall, perfectly docile, sober, etc. looked as if they wd. have stood anything.

/ / /

Yeats has had his tonsils removed, and it seems to have done him good. Looking very fit.

Hueffer back in town, getting over results of his hardships, expecting an offspring from present incumbent; and most valliantly going head on against the old gang, Gosse et cie.

Rodker has given birth to a daughter; Mop (now mated to celebrated economist of wrong school) also expectant, also Iseult, mated to an irish adolescent non-political, Phyllis also mated, to an architect, no results visible but then she's only been married a fortnight. The Morning Post, I believe, talking of over population.

etc

Love to you & Dad

E

Pound's translation of Paul **Morand's** *story, 'Turkish Night' was in the September* Dial. *Stella Bowen was about to give birth to a daughter by* **Hueffer;** *Mary Butts had given birth to a daughter by* **Rodker;** *Margaret ('* **Mop** *'), married to the economist G. D. H. Cole, was expecting;* **Phyllis** *Reid had just married Harry Birnstingl.*

✜══✝

610. **TLS** [*embossed letterhead*] 5, Holland Place Chambers, Kensington, W

13 December 1920

[London]

Dear Dad:

I enclose portrait of Mr Roland Hayes, the most congenial American I have for some time encountered.

Mr La'renc B. Brown is less congenial but most culchurd, assiduous reader of the Dial. Montague Ring, is I learn the daughter of the first black Othello, who played with, I think it was, Keene. Have not met Montague, but I hear that I should meet 'Emma' who is a real contralto.

Hayes is really good. Has taken to the Hebridean music with gusto. and so on.

Yours recd. re/ Elwood Pound the far–beyond-seer, is he writing on akasic tablets or wott-all.

The new book of five troubadour songs, with Agnes Bedfords accompaniments is out. Very good, I believe, except one page full of misprints, chiefly [?].

I hope to get France before long, and to work again with Walter. Though shall, presumably go south now, and get back to Paris, if all goes well, by May. Cant yet feel it is going to happen. Go on sending letters here.

Will send section Five of Hueffers Eng. Rev. stuff, you will get No. IV. in the Dial. probably Jan. or Feb. He is doing a whole book.

Some of it may go into N. Y. Post. Also long poem of his is coming out in Poetry in March or Apr.

Snow and black frost here.

Am sitting to Lewis again tomorrow a.m.

Love to you & mother.

congratulations on yr 37th.

E

Enclosed was a flier for a Wigmore Hall concert by **Roland Hayes**: *'On account of the* ENORMOUS SUCCESS *of his* RECENT RECITALS 1 *and in response to many requests |* ROLAND HAYES | The Celebrated Negro Tenor | will give a THIRD RECITAL . . . . At the Piano: **Lawrence B. Brown**.' *One of the songs in his programme was by* **Montague Ring**, *the pseudonym of the British composer Amanda Christina Elizabeth Aldridge (1866–1956), daughter of the actor Ira Frederick Aldridge.* **Hueffer's English Review stuff** *was an instalment of his* Thus to Revisit: Some Reminiscences *(1921). His* **'long poem'** *was 'A House', which appeared in the March* Poetry, *and which would be awarded its $100 prize as the best poem of the year.*

⊹══⊹

611. ALS [*embossed letterhead*] 5, Holland Place Chambers, Kensington, W

20 December 1920

[London]

Dear Mother:

Does 'Ls' in yr. last refer to Luskins or Larzeleres? – otherwise refs are lucid.

Transmit my pontifical beneficences to Joe Cochran & the widdy woman.

Where is the great Tom C.?

Younger british composers are n.g. – bad as the georgian poets.

Scheduled to leave for Avignon via Paris in Jan. if I don't drop dead or get discovered assassinating some prominent & unpopular person – or gt. literary calamity.

Weather better today, saw Hayes again on Sat. – good boy. He has had another concert & says his expenses are cleared for a 3rd. Judith Litante, the other promising singer. Rubinstein technically great, but unsatisfactory pianist.

Am preparing second set of airs to follow the Five Troubadour songs now pub. by Boosey.

New passports £3 each.

Tea at Steeds (Edtr. 'Times') on Sat. he seems to think the Empire in as bad a state as I do.

Fowlers yesterday. Jim Fairfax back from austrailia – improved but not sufficiently.

E. P. Mathers defective in thyroids consigned to Canary Isles.

Harold Monroe's new book (on Mod. Poetry) better than might be expected.

New Tweeds eminently satisfactory. –

Is yo. friend M. Van Vorst in Paris.?

Season's greetings. Turkey ordered for Sat. –

Did Whiteside get over here last year? – Is he coming this. Expect to be in Paris from Apr 20 – onwards till further notice.

Love to you & dad

E

20. Dec 1920.

*'Aetheling' praised **Judith Litante's** singing in the* New Age *on 11 November, and again on 23 December. No **'second set of airs'** appeared; but Pound had been working for some time with Agnes Bedford's help at finding the music in the words of poems by Villon and Cavalcanti, and was moving towards composing his first opera, 'Le Testament [de Villon]'.*

+⊨==◁+

612. **TLS** [*embossed letterhead*] 5, Holland Place Chambers, Kensington, W

27 Dec 1920

[London]

Dear Dad:

Thanks for Saturnalian three quid duly recd.

We are in action of closing up; have presumably rented the flat; and are in some sort of trajectory toward Orange or Avignon.

Dinner with Hueffer yesterday; offspring and new wife doing well. Ditto re/ Rodker family. Flint also refurbished with deceased w's sister; an improvement I think.

Have you read C. H. Douglas' two books on economics? Lunched in standard oil stronghold last week. Hamilton alumni meeting; Lee '93, now British Lawyer, Peck '13 doing some post grad work at Oxford, and myself together with Lee's son, and a rather pleasing chap called Drayton.

Think it is about time you began to read french in your off hours, the language isn't horribly difficult to read. Certainly France is only remaining country where your pension wd. be of much use. Dont waste time trying to pronounce correctly, that comes when one is in a country. Besides two thirds of the books one wants to read are in French.

Etc.

Love to you & mother

. E .

The flat at 5 Holland Park Chambers would be taken over by Agnes Bedford. C. H.
Douglas' two books on economics were: Economic Democracy (1920), and Credit-
Power and Democracy (1920). His Social Credit followed in 1924.

Ezra and Dorothy set out from London in early January, spent ten days in Paris, then
on the 18ᵗʰ went down by train to St. Raphaël on the Mediterranean coast.

---

613. ACS [*cardhead*] The Dial

30 January 1921

[St. Raphaël]

Just to remind you of the so valuable state of Literature (americo – european
in this the 1921ˢᵗ year of grace.

Contrasted with the so passionate purple ink of the Mediterranian – Tyre
having doubtless yielded the suitable dyes = this being Jan 30ᵗʰ. the sawbath &
we still at St Raphael

Carnival supposed to be going on at Nice – evidence here of a few small boys
in false faces

Yrs

E

This note is written across Pound's Dial *postcard on which are listed 36 European*
authors whose contributions or promises of collaboration he had secured.

---

614. ALS

Feb. 3 and 5. (1921)

St Raphaël

Dear Dad:

No, I don't advise you to buy European money of any kind - not unless you
are a dam'd sight cleverer than the people who work that shell game as a
profession. You'll be 'ad. - of course i̲f̲ I'd turned all my £ into francs 3 ½ weeks
ago - & turned it all back ten days ago I'd have made 1000 f̲r̲. minus about 200
that the banks wd. have charged me for the change. - As it is I was dam'd lucky
to get 60 per £ in Paris. & possibly lost by changing some money last week
instead of this. - But it is no job for an amateur.

Everybody in Vienna is gambling on the Kroner - but I advise you to stick to
poker, roulette, 3 card monté, & things you r̲e̲a̲l̲l̲y̲ d̲e̲w̲ know about.

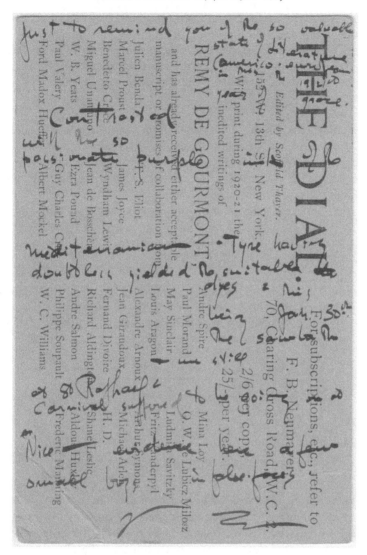

613. ACS, EP to HLP, [St. Raphaël], 30 January 1921.

The only way to be happy is to refrain from reading the papers. Hueffer is probably right in buying a farm - so that in case of crash he will be sure of his food supply - only as you know - farmiculture isn't in my line.

The ex Mrs. H. whom you met is still living on Campden Hill - or was when I left the village // These things do happen - one receives the parties on alternate days - it is after all a personal matter between the combatants.

I see – (by private communique from Mencken) that that bright star Elmer Chubb is agitating for the suppression of religious tollerance by constitutional amendment // so the Dear ole U.S.A. is to the fore as usual in intellectual matters. Wilson's reign being one of the most retrograde in history & one in which most ground has been lost in the way of personal liberty.

Saturday Feb. 5.
Took yesterday off & inspected Cannes - which - apart from very small hump of old town - is rubbish, & Nice which has more guts than wd. have or might have been expected. - quite an habitable place -but for distraction rather than repose - still quite a possible place to live for a season. - probably not this one - Italy begins about halfway between here & Nice.

Dare say we shall plunge into the Samoa-like wilderness again next week.

Love to you & mother

E

Elmer Chubb, a fictitious poet invented with satirical intent by Edgar Lee Masters, with H. L. Mencken cheering him on; at this time he was the supposed author of sonnets fulsomely praising the reforming zeal of William Jennings Bryan, the Anti-Saloon League, etc.

∗══✦

615. ALS

[*after* 21 March 1921]

Hotel Terminus St. Raphaël

Honoured Progenitor:

Thanks for the fr. 125 (?$10) (or $7.50 acc. to date you bot em. I suspect Mr. Gimbel made something - but that don't affect the quality of my appreciation // I don't on the whole think you ought to do these things it is pleasant to receive & blessed doubtless to give - but I think the family intakes are now about even & that on the whole I am having the easier time of it. // not of course, that you cd. spend yr. money better - if you are bent on blowing it - or that I have any surety of continuing to earn anything whatever.

The proof that I know something about economics lies in the fact that I lead considerably more of a life than Rockefeller & Morgan & various other pods who <u>have</u> large sums written down on paper to their credit - & that on the hole I enjoy a fair share of liberty & do extremely little that I wdnt. do if I had a ballance equal to theirs. Even if I had such a ballance it wd. benefit others far more than it wd. me. // Also if one wanted to interrup more interesting cerebrations one might attune oneself to the game of percentages as one does to art values, or other matters of interest. (interest <u>vs</u> usury, if you want so to formulate it.)

if one lives to be 98 - perhaps the <u>last</u> eight years of ones life might be devoted to the accretion of a bank ballance // in a well ordered life there shd. be no time to do so before then. // I am not even sure that those eight years cant be better employed - will let you know when & if I get there. // I dont, in the interim, envy Vanderlip.

I am very sorry that Desmond Fitzgerald has been copped // but it had to come sooner or later - one has expected it for a year. There was a fine paragraph on him in an article in the Mercure de France (Vepres Irlandaises) some months ago. The Irish have every right to their liberty save what they might have by being more civilized, instead of less civilized than their despots. // You may remember a contrast of Irish & English ministers in one of my N. A. articles yr. before last. (Fitzgerald & Balfour were the originals of the paragraph.).

Dial costs 46 cents to print, why the hell shdnt. Thayer charge 50 for it. He makes the public a present of several $1000. each month. Even now only the direct subscribers are paying for material cost of what they get in paper & print. Thus much for trying to make a civilization in Armour & Co.'s front yard. Geo. Horace will never understand why people do this sort of thing. Wallace is said to be at Cannes. Don't know that I am called upon to bid him a kind adieu. Despite what people say, I think Harding shd. be less of a calamity than Wilson – if only for the reason that one can hardly conceive of anyone's being 'more'.

Give my regards to 'Jake'.

Love to you & mother

E .

Desmond Fitzgerald of the Sinn Fein was arrested by the British in March. He would be released later in the year following the signing of the Anglo-Irish Treaty which created the Irish Free State as a self-governing dominion within the British Empire. Geo. Horace Lorimer, a Wyncote neighbour of Pound's parents, was editor of the Saturday Evening Post.

616. ALS

2 / April / 1921

St Raphaël

Dear Mother:

We go back to Paris, presumably next week – mail to go via London.

I have had another & longer letter from Thomas Hardy - who has on this evidence - managed to read my 'Propertius' & 'H S M' - without thinking too badly of them.

I continue to play tennis. Last night there was a local fête, with four tambours & small flutes. - tambour about 3 feet deep, carried slung over left elbow, & played with one stick, while performer works stops of flute with fingers of left hand

etc.
very sober
& serious

———

Cristian is translating 'Moeurs Contemporaines' into french <u>very</u> <u>slowly</u>. Hope it will be finished before I leave // He is also supposed to be doing a note for Dial, on some new french books. – Cocteau's 'Carte Blanche' only serious work I have attempted to peruse lately, & that not very serious.

The postal rates have riz.

copper coins still mixed - Luxembourg, Tunis, IndoChine - with regular supply of Ital, Span & Portuguese.

Notes from 25 centimes up – very ragged paper – but not so scarce as they were - mostly local. - <u>Nice</u> issues <u>10 c</u>. in al<u>uminum</u>.

Have seen perhaps a dozen silver coins in last two years. (i.e. on continent.) plenty in Eng.

D. continues to sketch –

Thats about all.

Love to you & dad.
E .

Thomas Hardy, in a letter dated 18 March 1921, had written that, being 'old fashioned', he considered 'lucidity a virtue in poetry', but assumed that was not what Pound was after; still, would it not be more helpful to a reader, he suggested, to call the poem 'Sextus Propertius soliloquizes or something of the sort'. **Christian**, *pseudonym of Georges Herbiet, was a French artist and writer who ran a bookshop in St. Raphaël.*

+⇒=+

617. ALS

20 April 1921

Hotel du Pas de Calais | 59 rue des Saints Peres [Paris]

Dear Dad:

Comfortably fixed here - slightly too expensive but hardly worth the trouble to move - You can still write via England & save postage. Have seen Mrs Whiteside & Esther - also various new lights.

Cocteau intelligent - profile a bit like Bill Williams. Picabia, intelligent.

Cros burried in govt. office, but doing good work.

Joyce's 'Circe' chapter here in typescript. - magnificent = a new Inferno - in full sail.

Yrs

E

Love to mother

20. 4 – 1921

+⟩═⟨+

618. ALS

24 April [1921]

59 rue de Saints Peres [Paris]

Dear Mother:

Have had my Time fairly full since arrival. Dial connection ending July 1st.

Brancusi a fine sculptor, Cocteau living spit of Bill W^{ms} from certain angles.

Picabia very much alive, <u>etc.</u> swarms of lesser literati & arterati - Cros calm as ever. - Morand out of town - various new books that will in due time be reported.

Sorry Dad has been laid up for so long. - Hope he is really over it & not too bored with U. S. M.

Lewis has produced a new paper of no gt. interest - He is having a show in London - Joyce next chapter great stuff. - fr. trans of Port of A. - is finished. - Have various invitations to contribute to various reviews fr. & cyzoslovak but no visible sinecure.

Love

E .

While in Paris the previous July, Pound had persuaded Rodker's mother-in-law, Ludmila Bloch-Savitsky, to translate into French Joyce's **A Portrait of the Artist as a Young Man.** *The* **Dial connection** *had been terminated by Scofield Thayer. Lewis's* **new paper** *was* The Tyro. A Review of the Arts of Painting Sculpture and Design, *of which there would be just two numbers, and to which Pound had not been invited to contribute.*

+≥──=≼+

619. TLS

9ᵗʰ May. [1921]

59 rue des Sts. Peres. | Paris VI

Dear Dad:

Have lost count of time, various reasons, including exploration of this excellent city. Picabia, Cocteau, reorganization of Lit. Rev. in hopes of real number in July. Brancusi photos . . . only sculpture I have come up against since Gaudier's death, save some of Epsteins.

Have seen the Whitesides on occasion. Joyce being published here, Ulysses in English, Portrait in French.

Lewis coming over, and Eliot for a little.

Various nibbles at 'Noh', but dont see that they are likely to come to much, difficulty of translation into french being considerable. Still may be some indirect amusement.

Cocteau, Jean Hugo, (family much amused at my having one of their blue china bowls) Picabia, Cros, Morand, all either have turned in copy or promised it for L. R.

Also various other people here whose names wdnt convey much to you.

Don't know how long it will take us to get how much settled.

Are in light high room with balcony – only there isn't enough of it.

Have knocked off an article on Brancusi, & one on general conditions here.

Love to you & mother .

E.

*Pound's **article on Brancusi** appeared in the Autumn number of the* Little Review.

+≥──=≼+

620. TLS

11 May 1921

59 rue des Sts Peres | Paris VI (mail to this address)

Dear Mother:

The ambassadour to the Ct. of St Jim is a dirty dog, a fosterer of liars and an animal with whom I have no desire for intercourse of any description.

Garvey is on the right tack, my friend Hayes has just been recd. at Buckingham Palace; we damn well owed poor little George some pleasure in return for the bother of having Wilson messing around the building; for the moment the negro seems to be quite as likely as any white or pallid segment of the American people to qualify in the art ring. The French govt. was about to decorate the black painter Tanner, when the Washington govt. fearful lest white inability be so indicated requested the Elysee to not.

My recollections of nearly all the niggers I have ever known are quite pleasant: I can't say as much or anything like it for whites, presbyterian and other. the blacks have better voices, better muscles, better complections, and I believe more good will, in general a better and more kindly nature, and are less inclined to prohibit the pleasures of others; frankly after 35 years among anglo-saxons I am not in the least convinced that they are superior to any other race whatsoever; the Egyptians were dusk to duskish and they have left some of the best sculpture we possess.

The jew and negro are the only two races who can imbibe Xianity without becoming detestable; I don't know that this is an argument in their favour. etc.

Thanks for the Garvey clipping.

I dont, en passant, know any sounder investment (even commercially) - than the first edition of Ulysses. Of course possibility that our foetid and paternal post office will stop yr. copy in the mail, just to prove that you are free citizens of a once-called free country.

Pass it on to the gt. intellectuals Wood and Penniman.

etc. love to you and dad

E

+⟩══⟨+

621. TLS

31 May 1921

59 rue des Sts. Peres, PARIS VIe.

Dear Mother:

D. is very grateful for offer of large topaz, BUT present state of French post office is rather serious obstacle. I believe all sorts of packets are opened, and they decline to insure ANY registration to foreign countries, so perhaps you had better not try to send the ring until there is some surer mode of conveyance.

I know you think non-arrival of watch cocks is kussedness, but I have not seen any decent ones, the craze has run its length, and the cheap shops are full of obviously faked cocks that have never been in watches, and that have not the clean cutting of the old cocks. Obviously stamped out in softer metal, by machine. IF we do find any good ones they will be sent you, probably Mrs Whiteside cd. be persuaded to carry 'em.

Walter loudly aplauded at his concert yesterday.

No fer gods sake don't send any books, unless perhaps you can find my Hamilton College hymnal, which has in it two pages I want to see. You might even detach the pages, one of Luthers 'Ein Fest Burg' and one or two others of plain songs (Draw nigh Emanuel,) and perhaps two others, I dont clearly remember. I want to see the arrangements.

Tell dad I had to use considerable energy to keep out of that Voices by Marg. Wilkinson. Bitch unable to comprehend that I did NOT wish to be present.

Old Hueffer has been very amiable in his last book 'Thus to Revisit'.

Lewis goes back to London today (unless he dont.) Rodker staying on here for a bit.

31 <u>May</u>
May as well send this W. R. second concert success. Watch the Lit. Review

Yrs

E

Love to you & dad.

Watch cocks: *thin rounds of brass, intricately carved or engraved, fitted into watches to cover the balance wheels, mainly 16th to 19th centuries. In Hueffer's* **Thus To Revisit** *(1921) there is a chapter of friendly appreciation of Pound and the Imagists, which concludes with an image of Pound as a 'Rufous Terror', like Orc in Blake's* America, *a force of heroic vitality impacting upon his contemporaries.*

⊹══⊹

622. TLS

28 June 1921

59 rue des Saints Peres | Paris VI

Dear Dad:

Since writing, so far as I remember, I have translated all of Gourmont's 'Physique de l'Amour', written a supplementary chapter for U.S. edtn. and written an essay for Les Ecrits Nouveau, in something approaching french, or at least with words recognizable as belonging to that langwidge rather than to yourn.

Have also been to Fontainbleau for a day, and to Montmartre for two evenings, party on on tonight, lunching with Knopf tomorrow. etc. Raymond over from London. also Rodker. DeBosschere has been. Christian up from St. Raphael.

New Cocteau Ballet 'Les Marries de la Tour Eifel' very entertaining. I get in free. Sherwood Anderson here; also Rosenfeld, music critic of Dial. Djuna reported on the high seas. Recd. 'Playboy with photo'. Arthur Symons over from London a fortnight ago. etc.

O. S. here, D. supposedly returning with her to London next week to visit her progenitor and other branches of the domestic souche.

I shall be here during July; have vague invitation to go to Brittany, sometime, I suppose in Aug.

Has the N.Y. Eve Post., printed an article of mine, which they are supposed to be about to? Shd. like a copy when it appears.

Love to you & mother

E

28 June 1921

*Pound's **supplementary chapter** was appended as 'Translator's Postscript' to* The Natural Philosophy of Love, *his translation of Remy de Gourmont's* Physique de l'Amour; essai sur l'instinct sexuel *(1903), when it was published by Boni and Liveright in New York in August 1922, and by the Casanova Society in London in 1926. The title of his **essay in Les Écrits Nouveaux** (August/September 1921) was 'Le major C.-H. Douglas et la situation en Angleterre'. An editorial note remarked: 'We have respected the exotic flavours [les savoureux exotismes] of this article written directly in French'. The* Literary Review [of the N. Y. **Evening Post**] *would print Pound's 'Parisian Literature' on 13 August.*

⊢⪤⊣

623. TLS

30 July 1921

[Paris]

Dear Dad:

Have finished trans. Gourmont, also postscript, trans of which latter into french has been accepted by Mercure de France. ditto. article on C. H. Douglas by Ecrits Nouveaux. Have you recd. Philao Thibaou?

Quinn here, rather daft on acquisition, but affable. Has fed me several times. Thayer here, more intelligent than might be thought from contents of Dial. Have also done him a long letter on Paris.

By time you get this Cantos shd. have appeared in Dial. (cantos V-VII)

Am working with sort of secretary on longish opus. Succeeded also in dancing the tango for fisrt time last sabath eve. shall have another try tomorrow.

Heat has been a record here, something like 100 in shade on Thursday. Only I never can keep track with the centigrade thermomenter of where it is in detail. However it really is warm. Figure reduced to adolescent line.

D. writes it has also been d---d hot in London. where she is visiting her progenitor. Think I wrote O. S. had been with us here during June. Long letter from Hueffer this a. m. etc.

Pansaers has just deposited a five hundred page vol. on musical history. etc. Have also met various Dial contributors, Cowley, Cummings, also Kreymborg, and his little lot. (he said he had seen you sometime or other and that you had been affable.)

Picabia, Cocteau etc. out of town. I like Marcel Duchamp, painter who has mostly given it up in favour of chess, he annihilated me, after I had cleaned up the rest, and Kreymborg polished him off a few days later. A. K. being an international, and Duchamp having done several books on the game.

The last Proust is excellent, you will in time see brief ref. to it in Dial.

Let me know if Pilhao dont arrive.

Love to you and mother, and rememberances to family at Tioga, love to grandmother.

Liveright has paid up for translation of Gourmont, but says nothing definite about time of printing my poems.

> Yrs
> E .

In August, **Le Pilhaou-Thibaou | Supplément illustré de '391'**, *a Dadaesque 'revue' edited by Picabia, included Christian's translation of 'Moeurs Contemporaines'. In his 'Paris Letter', dated 'September, 1921', published in* The Dial *in October, Pound wrote at some length about 'The new* **Proust**', *i.e.* Le Côté de Guermantes II, *and* Sodome et Gomorrhe I.

⊹⇒⇐⊹

624. ALS

27. Aug. [1921]

59 Sts Peres

Dear Dad:

Yrs to hand. Nothing to be done about excess of metal in U.S. // all part of credit system // C. H. Douglas on the right line. Take a century or so to get thru' peoples heads. // Have article in 'Ecrits Nouveaux' probably in Sept. // also one due in 'Mercure de France'.

Liveright announces 'Poems' & trans of Gourmont for this autumn.

Pilhao is the gesture of the right hand, & Thibaou is the gesture of the left hand.

J.Q. gone back. I think rested somewhat by vacation. Have got thru' a longish job of which I write you later if it ever appears.

D. comes back on Monday, or is expected to. dined with Whitesides night before last.

Love to you & mother. You will get other news in Dial article. Thanks for N.Y. Post fragments.

> Love
> E .

⊹⇒⇐⊹

625. TLS

Sept. 18th. [1921]

59 rue des Saints Peres | Paris VI.

Dear Mother:

D. much pleased with the topaz ring, which really becomes her, as many rings dont. Cocteau coming back to Paris in a few days. W. L. here for a week.

Did I send copy of article in 'Mercure'? translation rather poor. Bassoon decorative, also seems to be good for the lungs. Various other french essays of mine supposed to be about to appear. Liveright's catalogue announces Poems and the Gourmont. 'Ulysses' about half printed. College hymnal was recd. in due course. Have taken a studio but not sure present tenent will be evicted with much promptitude.

etc.

Yeats has given birth to a son. Otherwise population remains static. J.Q. has returned to N.Y.

etc.

Love to you & dad

E

*Dorothy Pound wrote to Isabel Pound on 20 September: 'Ezra got his **bassoon** the day I came back! It is very handsome to look at, and he is learning to make very nice noises on it, with some rather queer ones in between times! I believe he has grown broader across the lungs already. He will be a soloist always . . rather than in an orchestra!'*

626. ALS

22 Oct. [1921]

59 rue des Saints Peres [Paris]

Dear Mother:

Thanks for birthday letter & enclosure (fr. 200), just received.

The bassoon slumbers. I have been over to London for a week; english race terminates below the cervical ganglion. // Lewis painting better than I had expected from drawings & photo. - Yeats somnolent. Hueffer about as usual. // Wadsworth family enriched by decease of earlier branches. - nothing very startling to report.

Koumé left a card here two days ago so I suppose I shall see him soon. – Demuth also in Paris.

Eliot has been ordered away for 3 months rest. It is high time. -

I saw a copy of Kreymborgs article at Eliots - dont see why I should waste a year of my life lecturing - unless the price offered was high enough to give one three years rest after it.

I remember dad's struggle to get a largish high school put up. - Don't suppose anyone is now offering him a vote of thanks???

Thanks for offer of blankets – I don't much think it is worth while shipping them. They are probably cheaper here, - in any case <u>don't</u> send 'em <u>now</u>, as we haven't yet got into the studio - & don't know <u>how</u> long present tenent can wangle her extension, et. bloody cetera. Shd. be glad if they wd. settle matter, either to let us in <u>now</u> or to leave us free till April or June, – as I want to spend Jan. Feb. Mar. in the south.

Love to you & dad.

E

And thanks again for reminder of the tie.

+≻═≺+

627. ALS

Dec. 3d [1921]

70 bis rue Notre Dame des Champs | Paris VI

Dear Dad:

Have been constantly busy since getting in here, cleaning, building furniture. having <u>cheminee</u> in back room rebuilt at landlords expense. Also Mrs. N. C. Mc Cormac of Chykaago in here doing a small bust of me - photos to follow etc.

Dont know when I last wrote. / / Stove heats studio about 20 ft. cube

we have got to point of dining at home. change after 9 months of restaurants.

will try to send longer letter in time.

Have built two armchairs kitch tabl. chinese dining table. - also wash stand, & stool plus shelves, screws etc. - see the end approaching.

Love to you & mother.

E.

Tell I. W. P. that D's address is that at the head of this letter - & that she sends the salutations to you both, being here present.

Two rows of building keep off noise of street.

Pound's letter included several rough sketches of the studio and its situation. He described it more clearly in a letter to his grandmother in February: 'We are up the hill from the river here, and the air good; two gardens between the studio and the road so it is quiet enough; and the big Luxembourg Gardens just two minutes to the east, also the rue Vavin with very good shops for meat, cakes, bread etc. just at hand, so life is very convenient'. The 'gardens' were courtyards between no. 70 and the two ranges of studios

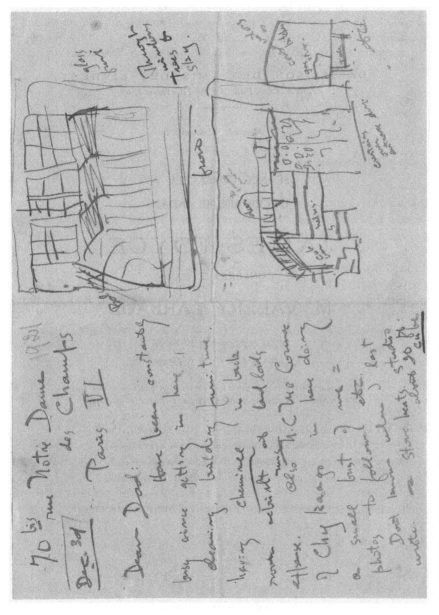

627. ALS, EP to HLP, from Paris, December 3 [1921].

behind it and parallel to the street. Like the many artist's studios off rue Notre Dame des Champs, 70 bis had a front wall of glass, a large open interior, and little else. In her letter of 20 September to Isabel, Dorothy Pound wrote that the studio 'has a little room off it, a littler one up a staircase (the latter in *the studio) and then a cupboardy kind of place across the hall where we shall have some kind of cooking apparatus'. In the event Ezra cooked on a spirit lamp in the main room; they used the ex-kitchen as a box-room, the little downstairs room as a dressing room, and the littler upstairs room as a bedroom. Their lease was for three years, until October 1924.*

+══+

628. TLS

Xmas [25 December 1921]

70 bis, rue Notre Dame des Champs | Paris VI e.

Dear Dad:

We now buy the Tribune every morning to see whether Cousin Tom's wild cat has et up General Foch. I think D. sent you earlier clipping.

Much needed gaiety, as she is still in hospital; has lost tip bone of left forefinger from a whitlow or some damn thing of that sort.

It is very disthracting. By the time I get out to the hospital and back (its at Neuilly) there is not a great deal of time to get this place in order or proceed with anything else.

The joke about the wildcat is that in Cocteau's ballet 'Les Mariés de la Tour Eifel' there is a wedding Party interrupted by a LION, every body runs but the noble old general who advances somewhat gingerly toward the animal but finally, on the third roar skeedaddles; retun of lion with good pussy air and one boot in its mouth; grief on part of the company. However all ends happily, the aged general returns in one boot and one sock.

The ballet cant have got to Montana.

Quinn writes that Liveright has sailed for YURUP. Mrs Joyce nearly killed by motor bus last week. Caught between it an lamp post, but nothing apparently broken.

News seems lacking in amenity. Thanks for yr. compliments on 'Poems' Liveright has printed them with all the pomps. Thought I'd translated most of the greek and odd bits for you.???

Further explanations forwarded on demand.

Monday:

Thanks for 200 exact, fr. recd. Have also heard from Liveright, who has got to London, and says he is about to descend on Paris.

Dont know what we can do about warm climate. Harding ought to make you consul to Nice, or Monte Carlo. He seems to be gettin on fairly well, for an American president.

Love to you and mother. Tell her to 'wait an' see'; one shdn't give out press notices on these matters at half-cock.

Hope the felx. flier is still flexible after so many years wait.

More anon

E

Pound's **Poems 1918–21** *had just been published by Boni and Liveright in New York. Homer had written to him: 'Delighted—new poems—Liveright—You in class by yourself'. Re the **flexible flier**, see letter of 6 February 1898.*

┼══╾═╾┼

629. TLS

8 Jan.1922

70 bis. rue Notre Dame des Champs | VIe. [Paris]

Dear Mother

Wish Ferdy had brought the KAT here, it looks very amiable.

Re/ dad's questions. When, if ever, I retire, I shall put for Italy or the Riviera. I dont see much point in Paris unless one is actually in the city. There are pleasant hills about the edge of it, but I dont know anything about the cost of living in them.

At Excideuil one wd. be too burried. No water. At Sirmio one can go into Venice for the day or week end. One can get easily to Verona, Brescia, Mantua. (Vicenza, Padua). Verona is about 45 minutes on train, and Brescia about 30. Boat about 20 to Desenzano. And I suppose the cost of living will remain less in Italy than in France.

I shall never see you again if you go to California. Everyone goes to Venice off and on. And Milan is not out of reach. You wd. be within an hour or so of enough interesting place to fill your vacations for a number of years. And anyone you wanted to see wd. come down from Venice.

Dad cd. have a boat and fish, as well as his garden. And the villains of the village are well disposed. Old uncle Menegatti has retired there. I think you wd. pick up a certain amount of the lingo in time. The chap at the albergo della Pace speaks yank.

However. Copies of Vanity Fair and Youth not common in Paris. Does either of the descriptors say anything of any interest.

Liveright has been here. I like him. Have arranged to do some more translations.

Don't know where Server attempted to see me. Certainly left no card or address, if his attempt carried him as far as the Pas de Calais.

Eliot here, with new poem in semi-existence. Met Picasso for first time on New Years ever.

493

D. considerably better.

Love to you both
E

8 Jan.

In January's **Vanity Fair** *there was an article on Pound by John Peale Bishop. Eliot's* **'new poem in semi-existence'** *would become, with considerable help from Pound,* The Waste Land.

+‡═‡+

630. TLS

19 Feb [1922]

70 bis [Paris]

Dear Dad:

Carpet slippers recd., for which much thanks to you or mother or both as the case may be.

Am trying to write crit. of Joyce's 732 pages, and some other jobs tidied up before going to Italy. Your name has been presented as a 'SPESHULIST' to the Oirish nation, in the person of one of the acting cabinet, and presumably listed. I was at a sort of final dinner of the convention here, about thirty people and three of the cabinet. May have written to you of Desmond Fitzgerald, who was one of our original dinner gang in London in 1909.

D. much better. Much pleased with shawl which finally got here.

Have idea for another book for H. B. L., have done thirty page sort of sketch to be filled in. etcn etc. et bloody cetera.

Cd. do with an auxilliary corps.

Will see about house in Sirmione when and if I get there.

Love to you and mother. Press notices not yet recd. from London. You might send me anything interesting, if it isn't too much bother. Also small bottle of sal Hepatica which I cant find in Paris, if that are NOT too much ditto. Winters much lighter here than in London.

Menegatti is the uncle of the proprietor of the hotel that was in 1910, and who has since retired to private life (i.e. the uncle) in Sirmio.

E .

Pound's articles boosting **Joyce's** Ulysses *appeared in the* Dial *and* Mercure de France *in June. The International* **Irish** *Race Congress in support of the provisional government of the Irish Free State had taken place in Paris in mid-January. The* **press notices** *would be of* Poems 1918–21 *published in New York at the beginning of December 1921.*

+‡═‡+

631. TLS

[March 1922]

70 bis, rue Notre Dame des Champs | Paris VI

Dear Dad:

Sorry you are feeling 'low', and that mother is down with cold.

Am not financially worried for the moment, bar calamity - shd. be O.K. for some months. Wish I cd. pension you off at once, but there are no signs of that state of affairs being immediately imminent.

Dial has sent me 50 bones for VIIIth Canto. which you may, therefore, see some time in the not infinitely distant future.

I will look up price of real estate in Italy. Cant, of course judge whether the soil is suitable for corn, peas, etc.

I find the writings of Confucius very refreshing; have french translation, wonder if there is a good trans. in english. Think you wd. enjoy same if it exists. If not I will make one for you.

(any more orders.?)

Have one more article to correct, and then shd. be at leisure to do what I like for next few months. Unless interrupted. Liveright has just suggested the trans. of a damn poor novel I am trying to switch him onto something fit to read.

Observer review brought in orders for 136 copies of Ulysses, last tuesday, 136 in one day at 15 bones the copy. So that for Mr Sumner and his rum-hounds.

Yrs

E

send this now | love to you & mother

+>==<+

632. TLS

Wednesday, 22 Mars [1922]

70 bis, rue N. D. des Champs | Paris VI

Dear Mother:

Dad's letter of Mar. 10 to hand; also howl from Mencken.

My Article on Joyce is to appear in Mercure de France sometime or other before long. Also Canto VIII has been paid for by Dial. Will forward N. Age on Bel Esprit. as soon as possible.

Visas for Italy in order, and we shd. leave on Monday. 7 members of B. E. enrolled, four reserves who oughtnt to be allowed to pay double. 4 certainties not yet heard from. and various letters out.

Rune of Hospitality, is not mine. Dont know why Finger chooses to print it over my name. but the ways of barbary are inexplicable.

Fine weather until day before yesterday, since when equinox and snow flurries. . . .

Winter easier than in London.

ETC.

G. B. Shaw now write me two post cards a week, complaining of the high price of Ulysses.

the 150 edtn. is sold out, only the de luxe copies remaining; none sent to U.S. as there has been no need to risk their seizure by the idiots.

Love to you & Dad
E .

B. E. was Bel Esprit, a scheme being organised by Pound and Natalie Barney to establish a fund guaranteed by thirty donors who would pledge $50 a year, the prime purpose of the fund being, in Pound's view, to provide Eliot with an annual subsidy of £300 ($1500) so that he could give up his day job in Lloyds Bank and devote his whole time to literature. A French beneficiary was to have been Paul Valéry.

---

633. ACS

29 March [1922]

Genoa

Thus far. <u>not</u> waiting for conference.

supposed to go to Carrara day after tomorrow

Hotel = Royal Aquila (??) did you stop here in 1902?

seems familiar – either from then or from 1908

not going to Campo Santo either - but will try the one at Pisa.

Trip from Paris not exactly restful – but its over -

Sun O.K. & wind still cold
E

*There was to be a major economic **conference** in Genoa in April, involving the allied powers and Russia, in pursuit of a post-war settlement of international trade.*

---

634. ALS

11 April [1922]

Siena | address via London

Dear Dad:

Have had an order for translations of Morand - at least Llona says go ahead it will be O.K. so I am damaging this end of my vacation in hope of clearing the other

I think this place is probably better than the Lago for all year. They say it's as cold now as it ever is that it is O. K. all summer.

There's a motor buss to Florence & you are only a couple of slow hours from Rome.

garden wd. grow here better than further north - also enough of a city – cinema etc. to keep you from depression of winter.

(at the Lago you wd of course have Verona in reach - but more change of temperature, winter & summer.

hills very fine, & air very clear here. farming centre – trottin' hosses exercised on the sabath on the <u>Lizza</u>.

They are bldng. new houses outside old wall. etc.

Was worried by announcement in Paris Chic. Trib. saw on way here. re Dougherty's decision on pensions for competitively [?] only. - Dose that cut your throat? possibly not irrevocable

Here yr. lack of Italian cd. be less isolating, as there is steady flow of Eng. speaking. animals -

Will make further report when I have seen Perugia.

This certainly better climate than anywhere in france. - not sure it isn't the best general climate I know of. Food - at least in this Pension, excellent. evidently easier to get good produce than in north Italy. also the wine better - which is one way of judging soil - the only way <u>I</u> have.

Certainly a garden here wd. be more satisfactory than further north.

Rome itself no use as all year residence.

Views very pleasant. = not so dramatic as Sirmione. but more ways of getting out of the town - this a city that is all edge, five minutes to get into fields, gardens in sort of V under our window; Sirmione a fishing village with few hotels.

etc. more anon.

Love to you & mother

E .

---

635. ALS

12 April [1922]

Siena

Dear Dad:

If you hear a rumour of my demise please DO NOT contradict it. I send you this note so that you and mother need not be worried.

I want a little repose. - If any enquiries reach you please reply simply that you have heard NO details.

You will naturally <u>not</u> be expected to answer questions at such a sad moment.

I shall rise again, at a suitable time. Possibly in six weeks
only <u>don't</u> spoil the lark.
I am telling the only people likely to pained - let the rest warble.
yours
E .

Pound was about to post to Margaret Anderson of the Little Review *on the 14*[th]*, Good Friday, a postcard signed 'D. Pound' but in John Rodker's hand, announcing his death and saying that photos of his death-mask were on their way to her. The photos were in fact of the life-mask taken by Nancy Cox McCormack.*

---

636. ALS

[after 12 April 1922]

Siena

Deard Dad:
<u>Giv' him</u>? <u>GIVE</u> him? <u>say</u> Homer, dew yew want tew go East & sell a mine.
No. I dont know anything about Mason - also I'm dead – don't disturb me for a while.
I might jess barely get Mason a copy for $100. (one hundred bones.) only it is not very likely. The last copy as you know fetched $40. some years ago and there jess' ain't any more.
Also the Quinzaine has disappeared. No on' has a copy. Don't part with either for less than $100.00
'Ulysses' probably being held till some safe means of getting it by the bigoted slaves of the U. S. Customs house is found.
Money will probably be returned if no way is found to get the book by the presbyterian frontier
Thanks for l.400. recd. - what am I to do, open an acc. for you with the Creditogesellschaft. // I think America is probably as safe a place for capitalists to invest their surplus // Can't tell a damn thing about European finance. save that it is ALL false. and <u>lire</u> cheaper now than 2 years ago, though not much so.
Am meditating depositing any American cheques I get in the Jenk. Trust. Co. // dont know any thing about Continental banks.
I bank with the Equitable Trust Co. of N.Y. – Paris Branch. –
but it is all a gamble. Relation of the dollar to Suchard Chocolate about the only unchanged internat. phenom.
People who spend all their time gambling on exchange, bound to beat the amateur.
All you can be sure of is that the $. will buy <u>some</u> francs or <u>lire</u>. any time.

The garden under this window very calm.
ETC.

Yrs

E

Apparently Mason had expected to be given a copy of A Lume Spento, *but that was now changing hands at elevated prices, and Pound was reminded of one of Homer's own stories of Hailey, Idaho, recalled in* Indiscretions: *'the man who sawed wood one week and when subsequently invited to repeat the operation (ten days' interval), said: "Saaw wud? Saaaw WUD!! Say, [Homer], dew yew wanter gao East an' sell-a-mine? I got ten-thousan'-in-the bank".'*

┼>══<┼

637. ALS

22 May [1922]

Hotel Savoia Venice

Dear Dad.

We are blowing ourselves for a fortnight – rooms on Gd. Canal. next door to Hotel Danieli.

Balcony six feet away from it. - can't go on indefinitely - but Sirmione is supposed - to be cheap enough to balance it.

Have had fine trip. Cortona, Perugia, Assisi, Spello, Ancona, Rimini, Ravenna.

By all means don't spend money on Little Review.

The women are all right but they ought to get in help for the arts from the outside. - If you want to spend money spend it on Bel Esprit. - only I can't see that you have any to spare.

At present I am a more worth & important object than any thing else the L. R. can offer.

Joyce is provided for.

am trying to get Eliot out of the bank.

When I see you I will analyze L. Rev. - too much bother to write.

Also wait for my Bel Esprit manifesto.

in mean time remember that I'm dead

Love to you & mother

E

22 May.

┼>══<┼

499

638. TLS

[c.16 Jul 1922]

70 bis, rue Notre Dame des Champs Paris VI

Dear Dad:

Have been some time getting round to this note. Liked Milan very much, two group shops <young men> with galleries for exhibits, ready apparently to show what I tell 'em, and general air of being alive. Came back so that Koume cd. have his show here, it went very well. Sent a note to Chas. Wadsworth co/ Equitable but he isn't known there. Have you his address?

The Bel Esprit is also apparently in action. 22 of the 30 pledges recd. and the first years £300 either in hand or promised. The U. S. Authors club sent on 200 bones from its Carnegie fund, last week.

Louis Berman, the gt. gland sleuth has been here for a fortnight. Landed on door step the night I got back from It. He has been tackling Joyce (some tackle) and studying the higher types.

Frank Bacon also turned up last week. Was damn glad to see him, after twelve years. Had just used part of his biography in my cantos (Canto X.)

Have now a rough draft of 9, 10, 11, 12, 13. IX may swell out into two.

Berman has gland-analyzed the busts of the characters quite nicely. (I had an article in N. Age on him.) I send copy under sep. cov.

Finger, as you say, seems to have seen daylight.

D. got off to London on the 13th. and reports safe arrival.

Love to you & mother.

E .

About yr. questions regarding Italy. I suppose Siena is as good a place as any for permanent residence. Mountains enough presumably to keep it bearable in summer, and far enough south to make winter comfortable.

You dont want to live in big city like Milan (any how it wd. cost twice as much). Siena costs about half Venetian prices. Every place has some objectionable feature at some time of the year. I shd. think Siena for base wd. do. It is near a lot of places. etc. Only thing is for you to look abaht for yourself.

I don't know whether I go to Milan or Japan when my three, six, nine, year lease here is up. Or whether one cd. ever do without some kind of a corner in Paris. etc.

I don't much believe the oriental expedition, I mean I don't feel it coming off. And shd. feel lonesome out of Europe.

Painters are coming in here thursday to redo the lower half of the studio in deep sea blue. Present mud-green being 'impossible'. Have also had the glass-side of the house cleaned.

E

⊹══╍═⊹

639. TLS

20 Aug 1922

70 bis, rue Notre Dame des Champs | Paris VI e.

Dear Mother:

Flood of people during the last week fortnight, month. Cant remember
when I wrote. Hope one Speiser will call on dad on his return to Phila. he has
been in twice, and bought a Brancusi, etc. Lewis, Rodker. etc. Etchells over
from London, etc. etc. Ought to be getting off next letter to Dial. Watson has
been here. Leger is doing interesting painting. Koume's stuff still here on the
wall. Bosschere, Llona, VanDeym, etc. everone in and out of Paris.

Dial letter will probably be as interesting as this.

Brancusi's yesterday. He working to finish up the pedestals for Quinn's purchases. Frank Bacon turned up here, as I think I wrote. Have various materials
for my Malatesta canto lying about.

Also various useless representatives of bad american periodicals have looked
in.

D. is in Devon for a few weeks.

Love to you & dad,

E .

640. TLS

2 Sep. [1922]

70 bis, N.D. d C. VI [Paris]

Dear Dad:

Cant remember when I wrote or what I said. Been a flood of people. Your
Miss Stukey turned up in a restaurant last week. Claims to have introd. the
Bhharronesse to the Little Review.

etc. Brancusi finishing up pedestals for Quinn, then goes to Roumania. Bill
Wms. has sent in an interesting mss. for proposed series of prose booklets.
Dont know that it will come off.

Various Murkns traveling, have stopped. Watson of Dial, Bishop of Van. Fair,
Washburn of Century Co. etc. also one Speiser of Phila. who has promised to
look in on you. Seems a good chap.

Mlle. De Pratz is in Judith Gautiers old apartment, with various relics of the
great Theophile, general period not unlike 24 E. 47th. in the earlier stages.

Am plugging along on my Malatesta canto, may run into two cantos; the
four to follow it, are blocked in.

Have also ground out a few prose articles. .

Etc. Hilda & her mother supposed to be arriving in Paris tomorrow.

Some sons of bitches in London are trying to cheat me over the Morand translations. my beau père says litigation, even if successful wd. cost more than the job's worth - However I expect to survive.

Eliot's new Quarterly has got to the point of having stamped stationary.

Love to you and mother
Also - regards to folks at Tioga.

E .

The 'Bhharronesse' was Baroness Else von Freytag Loringhoven—her writing appeared frequently in the Little Review. *W. C. Williams'* **interesting mss.** *was his experimental* The Great American Novel. *Pound was commissioning six* **prose booklets** *to be published by William Bird at his Three Mountains Press, the series to constitute an inquest into the state of prose after Ulysses. The series would include Pound's* Indiscretions, *Ford's* Women and Men, *Williams'* The Great American Novel, *Hemingway's* In Our Time, *also* England *by Bride Scratton (writing under her maiden name, B. M. G. Adams), and* Elimus, *a story of 'a young emigrant's disappointments in Canada', by B. Cyril Windeler, a British wool merchant.*

Pound's **translations** *of Paul Morand's short fictions,* Ouvert la Nuit *and* Tendres Stocks, *had been approved by Morand whose English was good, and by Victor Llona, a professional translator; nevertheless, when their reader found fault with the translations, Chapman and Dodd, the London publishers who had commissioned them, refused to publish them. Pound did receive the £25 due to him – while the reader received £10. Eliot's* **new quarterly** *was* The Criterion.

641. TLS

3 Oct. [1922]

70 bis N.D. de C. Paris VI

Dear Dad:

The opera ballet has, as they say, no future in it. The grape vine twist sounds all right, but for the last ole amendment. whereanent. What the dooce are Flinn's initials, and does he want it sent to the Mint or to his private address. I suggest Cointreau rather than Benediction as it comes in a square bottle and might possibly be taken for books. Shall I try him a large bottle, or send ½ and then if that gets through try again.

The Mint address might make it liklier to get through, but it might also complicate Flinn's life if detected.

I am pluggin along on my Malatesta cantos; will take years an years and years at the present rate. For the rest vide Dial. also Three Mts. Press, as per announcement sent you.

Hem. has gone to Constantinople, fer to see the war etc. D. busy painting up the walls etc. in this shack.

She saw Wm. Wad. in London. He said when he was in Paris he saw in the paper that we were in Italy. So that's that. He said he was goin ter see Belle when he got back to them states.

No Walker or Williamson has turned up. Met Miss Stuckey who said she was going to call. but hasn't yet appeared

Love to you & mother

E .

+>==+==<+

642. TLS

[October 1922]

70 bis, N.D. des Champs Paris VI

Dear Mother:

Thanks for letter. Dare say Ellis was beaten by something worse. Like Churchill getting turned out of Dundee by a 'dry'. However. Present him with my regrets, and tell him I hope it will learn him something. If he had read my works more carefully, it wdnt. have happened to him.

HOWever. Hueffer over here for month. They and the Golijewskis, in last night. Gol. an ex russian general of the ole regime. Large amt. of jaw between him and F.M.H. Bill Bird syndicating a spiel on the opera, may meet your eye.

Dont know what is to be said about Wyncote's discovery of me. General reference is to Whistler's Gentle Art. re some Paris show of his work.

Of course a reading of Q.P.A. wd. be more enlightening to the rural audience than the G.F. but for that one can, I suppose, wait, the dawn of a long distant future.

Possibly the Universitaires are taking up that side of the matter. Ref. Yeats on 'their Catullus'.

Seem to have been fairly active for some weeks. Various XVth. century wash-lists are turning up. Saw Brancusi yesterday, very active. Hueffer has finished a new novel, and also a long pome which is to be shot at me Monday.

Missed seeing ole King (who put me up for three or four days in N.Y. in 1910.) tried to find him yesterday. but find he is sailing today.

Criterion meritorious but a bit dull. (vide enclosure).

Hem. gone to Lausanne to look at the thieves and liars.

Dining with Dave O'Neil on Sunday. (vide Kreymborg anthologies)

Oh yes. Hawley Chester turned up week before last. With a funny little broad-faced wife, both with large grins. Hawley same as ever, save that he has got to look rather like Frank Bacon (same business marine insurance).

Also: Miss Williamson and Miss Stuckey have called.
Hawley with various bits of news re T. Cochran et al.
Love to you & Dad.
. E .

*In the 1922 elections, **Winston Churchill**, who had been MP for Dundee since 1908, was soundly defeated by a prohibitionist candidate. For Yeats' **'their Catullus'** see 'The Scholars' in* The Wild Swans at Coole *(1919). The **Lausanne Conference** was about the post-war settlement with Turkey.*

---

643. ACS

24. Oct. [1922]

[Paris]

Still here.
no news.
E

---

644. TLS

30 October 1922

70 bis, N. D. de C. [Paris]

Dear Dad:

Your cheque to hand, on the minute. Thanks for same. Am plugging on my next batch of Cantos. Dont know what else is to be expected of me during the oncoming year. (Any suggestions??)

Stimulated by the number of things the adolescent Rudin does not comprehend, I have spent two days chipping a block of marble, myself. It will not be a chef d'oeuvre, but I have even less respect for bad sculpture than I had before I tried stone cutting.

Very interesting evening at S'oiseau Bill's last night. Lincoln Steffens talked for about an hour on the Russian revolution, most of which he had seen, and of Lenin whom he knows, apparently, fairly well. Expect to see more of Steffins, damn good chap.

Hem. back from Constantinople, fed up even with the Turks. Dirty job of selling munitions to irresponsible nations. One line Lloyd Geo. has never left. i.e. no policy that runs agin the sale of guns. (probably don't know it himself. .??? why be charitable.)

Padraic Colum just arrived in Paris, will be here a week, then goes to Hawai, govt. job studying Hawaian folk lore.

Eliot's new Quarterly very good, in octogenarian way. Will be more intelligent than Dial, but possibly no more lively. Why don't you tell the Dial to ginger up. Even Watson compains that it is dull. Cant expect a stolid family magazine to play the giddy goat. Thery're losing a great deal of money on it. in noble endeavour to do something - they aren't quite certain what.

Liveright is paying my rent. Dial runs to about 300 bones per year. plus poem.

Love to you & mother

E.

*S'oiseau Bill, for Bill Bird. Horace **Liveright** had contracted in January 1922 to pay Pound a non-repayable advance of $500 a year to translate French books of Liveright's choosing, and Pound saw this as a way to take care of his rent.*

+≡——≡+

645. TLS

25 dec. [1922]

70 bis N. D. d. C. [Paris] VI

Dear Mother:

D. wrote you last week, just as I was about getting round to doing so.

Have got three of the Malatesta cantos into some sort of shape; attempt to avoid going away with huge mass of notes. Donth know how many more will be needed to deal with S. M.; sevral cantos blocked in, to follow the Malatesta section.

Also article sent off to Dial re/ Cocteau's Antigone et etc., which you will see in due time.

Magnificent lunch with Nathalie and Mrs Brooks yesterday, really remarkable food. Turkey 'truffe' etc.

We are due to leave on Friday, if D. has finished with dentist. (U. o. P. grad. and I believe fairly efficient.)

Rodker has been over.

Article of mine, probably deformed, supposed to be in Jan. Criterion. without my proof corrections.

The O Niels gone to Switzerland. Various people possibly descending on Rapallo.

Xmas pudding by hand from N. C. McCormack, Rome; also food and drink left by J. J. yesterday p.m.; so the edible side of the season is arriving in due order. Have also seen Rooshian players, very rooshian, Hueffer gone to Cap Ferrat. Yeats, as you may have seen, made a sennatorrrr of the new Irish hell-for-leather.

greetings of the season.

love to you and dad,

Oh yes, Dr Augustus Baldwin Wadsworth, left a card, or rather two cards, but no address, two or three weeks ago, since when no further trace or indication of him

D. has finished her designs series of ten for Windeler's Elimus, for the 3 Mts. Press. . vrey good, for the most part.

Series of ten.

Yrs

E

Pound's first contribution to Eliot's **Criterion**, *'On Criticism in General', did appear in the January number*

<hr>

646. ALS

[January 1923]

Hotel Mignon | Rapallo

Dear Dad:

Very sorry you have been ill again. Damn that s.o.b. Dougherty.

Thanks very much for cheque. Recon this place about solves the orful problem of 'where to spend January' wish you were here. – Sea one side facing east or south east, and olive yards the other, also palms & oranges.

Am chewing along on Malatesta - also tennis - also Salel's 'Iliad' which I found in Paris in Dec. after six years' wait.

Berman also here - and a lunatic ex-athlete called 'Stretter', who plays tennis rather better than the gland-sleuth.

Dont buy francs for the moment: - perhaps too late for lire. If you got any of the latter at (54 fr. per 100 lire.) you did well.

It cant be done now. - Dare say they havent changed so much in relation to the $. at any rate one might as well try roulette or 3 card monte.

I have sent a rough draft of 4 more cantos to Watson. hope to have them printable by midsummer.

Liveright is paying for this trip.

Dont suppose he can afford to pay two members of same family for NOT translating french litterchure.

Little Review says it is ready for more eruptions. Dont make out whether they just have printed a new number, or are hoping to.

All printed matter gets stopped for me at 70 bis.

Bel Esprit going slowly. Probably Paris branch will get Paul Valery's fund in shape before the bloated U.S. unbuckles for T.S.E.

There'll be a Dial letter or so - & then the cantos - containing about what I have to say.

Going up to Monte Fiore this p.m. unless obstructed.

Love to you & mother –

& take it easy - or be as aisy as ye can. glad you're not in Oirland

E

*The '4 **more cantos**' sent to Watson of the Dial were drafts of the Malatesta cantos, still far from their final form. There was civil war in the Irish Free State.*

+≒═╡+

647. ALS

19 Jan [1923]

Hotel Mignon | Rapallo | address Paris 70bis

Dear Mother:

Can you tell me how ill dad has been. His letter is not very specific. Neither cd. I make out from the newspaper clipping (recd. Paris during Dec.) what was happening re/his pension (if any.)

Have you <u>any</u> idea what you cd. get as annuity on yr. joint lives, from procedes of house etc.

I don't see that I can do much as my income is still extremely unsteady & has no settled element.

This place is very pleasant - but dont know how the sea air <u>wd.</u> affect one in the long run.

If you were coming suddenly I still think Sirmione is about the best shot.

So long as the exchange lasts Domenico will feed one for about a dollar a day.

I might manage to rent a place that you cd. use for the year & in which I cd. stop for 3 months a year But the arrangement is about hopeless unless you have at least $ 500 a year sure & solid.

I take it I cd. probably - in emergency - make up the difference between that and the actual cost of life.

BUT I don't know that you have that much apart from the problematic pension. No use Dad's busting himself waiting for a gang of Christian Pro-hibitionists - Unless there is some chance of something occuring during his lifetime.

If you can send me any definite statement I'll go to Sirmione this spring - after Rimini & definitely look for some possible habitation.

Bar new armageddons - it wd. of course be better to <u>have</u> a pension.

I dont know what the actual rents are; nor how the exchange will work; nor whether it wd. be necessary to shift for a month or so each year

507

Cant take an <u>old</u> place - without probability of ants in walls etc. and the newer villas at S. are in limited number. Probably a year round lease there wd. be cheaper than here - where there is a sort of all year season. ETCetterer. There is also the bloody cost of transport (transatlantic) to be figured on.

Also Italian taxes - if one is figuring to the tenth decimal. The French tax is fairly light on people with low rents. I dont know how the Italian tax works ETC.

At any rate let me know something definite re/ resources & re/ dad's state of health.

Love

E.

+⟫━━⟪+

648. ALS

24 Feb [1923]

Rome

Dear Mother:

I Continue work in Vatican library.

Have discovered that Soranzo still exists.

Expect to do a little cross country plunge next week.

Have seen the puppet show twice. excellent <u>possibilities</u>

Have met several amiable literati - also Giacomo Boni Chief of the scavators - who lives up on the hill inside the forum enclosure. Etc.- results - I mean mine - scheduled for July Dial - unless something intervenes.

Rome. about the tail end of Europe –

I was perfectly right 21 years ago in deciding against it.

glad to look at it once again - but it is not habitable.

Week <u>filled,</u> & I suppose profitable.

Love to you & dad.

E

The 'cross country plunge' would involve crossing Italy from Florence to Rimini and to Venice and visiting libraries and archives in the search for documents relating to Sigismondo Malatesta and his wars and times. Dorothy would make a separate tour with Stella Bowen.

+⟫━━⟪+

649. AL

2 Marzo [1923]

Firenze.

Madre mia cara.

Il sua lettera ittallana recivuta -

Si sbaglia molto nelle detaglie della lingua – ma anch' io mi sbaglio piu. e l'ortografia mi scapa sempre.

Siamo qui arrivato di Roma – via orvieto – dove siamo reposato la notte.

lettera – dev' essere feminile?? o no? sempe questo questione di sesso!

mi duole che il padre non puote scender' il collino? quel di Wyncote.? magari. Cosa poss 'io scriverte?

Ho lavorato a Roma – studiando nel Vaticano – sotto l'ombra di San Pietro.

Sono arrivato in Firenza – ho parlato con librao Olschki (bello nome, proprio Fiorentino).

Ho parlato a Roma con l'avvocato Pam (Max) amico di Quinn. etc.

Non ricevo il Dial – ni altra materia stampata – quando io sono in viggio – e perche non posso ben capire lo che dice lei al fine de la sua lettera.

Intendo essaminare l'archivi qui – e poi andarme a Cesena.

D. fara un piccol viggio con Stella – moglie actuale di Hueffer – per rivedere le gallerie di Perugia – Siena, etc. – poi ritorna ella a Rapallo.

arrivata l'ora della cena.

addio.

Con tanto rispetto –

il devoto suo figlio[1]

+⊨⊩+

---

[1] 2 March (1923)   Firenze

My dear Mother,

I have received your letter in Italian.

Many details in your use of the language are wrong – but I make even more mistakes, and spelling always escapes me.

We have arrived here from Rome – via Orvieto – where we rested for the night.

Letter must be feminine?? or not? Always this problem of sex!

I am sorry Father can't walk down the hill? The one in Wyncote? I wish he could. What can I write you about? I have worked in Rome – studying in the Vatican – in the shade of St. Peters.

I have reached Florence – I have spoken with the bookdealer Olschki (a beautiful name, truly Florentine).

In Rome I spoke with the lawyer Pam (Max) friend of Quinn's. etc.

I do not get the Dial – nor other printed matter – when I am travelling – and I don't understand what you want to say at the end of your letter.

I intend to examine the archives here and then go to Cesena.

D. will make a short trip with Stella – present wife of Hueffer – to revisit the galleries of Perugia – Siena, etc. then she returns to Rapallo.

It's time for dinner. Good-by

with deep respect

your devoted son.

650. AC

30 / 3 / 23

[Venice]

once again -
always worth it –
exhausted & glad the library is shut till tuesday. found Divus Iliad this p.m. –
mate to odysea I got in Paris 17 years ago.

+⊨═══╪+

651. TLS

24 April, [1923]

70 bis N.D. des Champs [Paris]

Dear Dad:
  Blue kimono just come, D, much pleased with same,
  Enclosure inaccurate, hope to ship cantos soon, Hueffer's Book and Bill
Williams both corrected for press so 3 Mts, should have them off its wheel soon.
  Am still in whirl of work. hope to get to surface in month or so,
                          love to you and mother,
New typewriter rather a comfort, Underwood portable, runs easier and feels
more solid, also ribbon don't curl up (yet)
                          Yrs
                          E
Hem back from Ruhr, and Marse Henry (Stretter) back from Italy, Seldes here;
and S'Oiseau Bill in good form

+⊨═══╪+

652. TLS

11 May [1923]

70 bis, [Paris]

Dear Mother
  re/ one or two things in yr, last. If you're breaking up house keeping, I want
you to keep your grandmother's portrait <Page>, the How Arms, the chess-
men, and one or two books, Cost of transport wont overweigh the value of
same.
  Large pictures can be shipped rolled. In which case the other old lady wd. act
as wrapping to the really fine Wadsworth female.
  Am playing this machine several hours daily, It leaves one very little to say,

510

S Oiseau is preparing de looks edtn, of Malatesta at 25 dollars a shot; with still more valued edtn at 50 bones, Streater at work on special capitals,

Samle page will follw in due course. Several copies already sold.

Four of the Three Mts, books off the press, but not yet from the binder's.

Le cher Walter again in evidence. Enormous technique. Picabia's vernisage Monday <u>evening</u>. Tell dad he is not expected to order a copy of the Cantos at 25 bones. One will be provided for him. The edtn, will be limited to 50 copies at that rate and 10 at from 50 to 100

Guess Bill will print the highest priced one on rolled zinc, with pearl studs.

Love

E

The *'de looks edtn'* would *grow into* A DRAFT OF XVI CANTOS of EZRA POUND for the Beginning of a Poem of some Length now first made into a Book with Initials by HENRY STRATER, *printed by William Bird at his Three Mountains Press in Paris between May and December 1924.*

+===+

653. TLS

19 May '23

70 bis, N.D. de C, [Paris]

Dear Dad

Unanswered letter from you somewhere in this stack. See daylight, probably wrongly <i.e. hope ungrounded.>, a few days hence.

Haven't seen 'interview' you speak of. There was note in N.Y. Herald here, which I sent you; but the N.Y. edition, for New York was intended to be fuller. Shd, like to know what the kid put across. (send it on if you have it, s,v,p,)

3 more Three Mts, press books are about ready, now at binders.

Edtn. de luxe of Cantos, planned. Marse Henry designing opulent capitals. Don't try to buy one, its too xpensive. Will send you one in the autumn IF it gets done.

Green number of Litl, Rev, looks less like a mausoleum than Dial and Criterion. The Leger picture comes up extremely well.

Tell mother I shall not, presumably, visit Godjeff or Gotchoff at his institute.

The old black man is a male of the species. His john the baptist Ouspensky looks too much like the late skunk president Wilson to be acceptable.

Gotcheff holds his vodka like a reel gent. I think they need pupils. Ouspensky earns his pay answering fool questions from American ex-flappers who want to know ALL about the cosmos.

Gotcheff is a damn good cook; or had one, and supervised the food himself with <u>maestria</u> the night I dined with 'em here, last winter. I still think Confucius about as good a guide as one can want in this vale of imbecilities.

????

As for mothers remarks on INJUNS, I see some son of a bitch of a typical goddam american commissioner has just forbinnen 'em to dance. Comissioner Burke. Really the way the dung comes to the surface in them there states is too too . . . yes, precisely, too too.

And I see that 'Old Posey' big chief, of the posey piutes. is to be shot for not going to prayers.

And Harding is going to <be> a new Christo: lincoln, sitting in the black house weeping because the national troops have got to go out and to shoot the jin-swillers.

Bill S oiseau is doing a book on wine; so as to teach the escaped WHAT to drink, in order to keep the best vineyards working. Expect to correct his mss, next week, or this.

MacAlmon coming on, Hem, coming on. Prose hopes. Some of D's designs for Elimus, very good.

Pleasant luncheon at Princesse Bassiano's last sunday with all the stars on our bill, Larbaud and various nouvelle revue francaise knuts, having to listen to Cocteau, who was in rather good form.

Joyce has had 13 teeth out and an operation on his other eye; his nerves being somewhat relieved after removal of dental explosives.

Brancusi doing more birds; worried because he has to move out of his studio in a years time and has three years work he wants to finish first.

Picabia's show NOT very good, he looking very tired and subdued.

ETC.

D. at moment putting coat of ultramarine on heraldric but hitherto unpainted chairs.

Love to you & mother

E

╌═══╌

654. TLS

26 May 1923

70 bis, N.D. des Champs, [Paris]

Dear Mother

You all dun ax who be Marse Henry; youall better look at de clippins youall dun send in dishyear directum. Marse Henry be Marse Henry Hyacinth Strater.

The little Review, in person of J H to lunch yesterday.

Reported that dad had been looking tres chic on his last visit to N.Y.

Also various data re them there united States.

Private view, or "premier" of Chauve Souris, a few night ago. Some of it good. Dont know whether you saw it in U.S.?

Finished that damn translation for Liveright day before yesterday. Have done enough typing to last me for some time, Not yet fully recovered controll of my vocabulary.

love to you and dad.

E

Photo passpote, enclosed. somewhat solid.

Jane Heap of the Little Review *signed herself **jh**.* **Chauve Souris** *was a touring revue. The '**damn translation**' would be published by Boni and Liveright in November as* The Call of the Road *by Edouard Estaunié, the translation being credited to 'Hiram Janus'.*

⊹⊱══⊰⊹

655. TL

6 June 1923

70 bis [Paris]

Dear Mother

We appreciate the invitation to spend the summer; especially as there ain't any. At least it hasn't got here yet. However we escaped the winter so I suppose it's kif-kif.

Cost of travel too high; also H.H.S. is ill and D. may have to go over and relieve O.S. in looking after him. Any how she is going to London sometime.

Cost of trip <to U.S.> equals I suppose a year's leisure. What about the quota of immigrants.?

Prize clipping from Times Chronicle 'all the stars on our bill'. Have seen one satelite of Curtis press, southern 'gentleman', very slippery article. I dont imagine Geo, H, will butt into my sunlight very extensively.

Little Review, including Mina Loy, present in Paris. Leger has just been in, full of energy. Hem, Bob and S'Oiseau all in Spain. Marse Henry doing well on the Caps.

Rodker seemed pleased with reception in Wyncote; sole apparent oasis in American desert. I dare say he is back in London by now.

Love to you and dad. Sorry the aerial service isn't cheaper.

Sorry I see no way of arranging visit.

D. sends saluti.

Am working on Kung canto.

⊹⊱══⊰⊹

656. TLS

Thursday, about the 21st, June 1923

70 bis, N.D. de C, [Paris]

Dear Dad:

I'm doing a canto on Kung; don't know about english translations of him. I have Pauthier's french translation of the Four Books; and a latin translation of the Odes (an anthology of earlier poetry that K, is said to have collected. The Bowmen of Shu, is supposed to be somewhere in that Anthology.

His idea of beginning in the middle i.e. on oneself is excellent. The exact reverse of Christianchurchism which teaches: thou shalt attend to thy neighbor's business before thou attendest to thine own.

Have just heard another infamy of your friends the Bok's.

I read about Burke <Indian Komissioner> in Paris Chicago Tribune before seeing note in L.R.

L.R. here present. Jane <u>apparently</u> vigorous, but not so solid as she appears. Margaret not such an ass as jh and others might lead one to think.

D. went to London Tuesday. H.H.S. seems to be rather ill. He's 72 and has been working full bust.

About the white races. Apart from one's few dozen friends, I don't know that they'd be much loss. Saw Siki done out of a decision last Saturday; then a very grave polite and gentlemanly coon so determined not to let the umpire call him on a foul that he simply refrained from hitting his opponent.

Hem.had his opera glasses on Siki, s'oiseau was on the other side of the ring, and we all three had good seats, and could see NO foul. Siki very amusing, and perfectly aware that the cards were stacked.

The Princess Bassiano is one of those agreeable american ex-flappers married to an Eyetalian; don't know that much more can be reported, very well behaved, gave us excellent lunch, in midst of good and very bad literary company, after which Cocteau entertained, thereby reducing the 'nouvelle revue francaise' to silence (which they ought to be kept in permanently).

She enthused over Eliot for half an hour, was going to do something for Bel Esprit, and has since mislaid the matter (like any other sassiety enthusiast.) The cartoons being the only part of american publication that mirror the age and people.

MacAlmon is publishing his friends' books here. He is coming on. Makes no stand about his series being litterchure. He says I won't touch anything but young Flauberts and that verybody cant be a young Falubs, so he will publish his friends. He has however chosen a good list. Bill Williams, Mina Loy, and Hem.

I like Mina very much. (personally, I mean she has also brought me an intersting mss, sort of vers libre novel.

Mac, Hem and S oiseau back from Sapin, full of bullfights.

Have been down with bloody annoying cold, but am much better.

Collins book <Doc. looks at lit.> sounds, from review, as if it might contain some sense. Buggle Wuggle or whatever it is you have sent, Mumbo Jumbo just same old backwash Shaw: Mencken stunt.

I suppose there are a lot of people that need to be told they are idiots, in words of one syllable.

Having got close enought to Shaw to know, at first hand that he is a bloody bottomless fool, merely an ass unqualifiedly an ass, a nincompoop; one is unlikely to be taken in by a thiner verson of the same type of mind. Research of the obvious.

There's a point at which even Pres, Harding ceases to be a joke.

Will send you a copy of July Criterion, as soon as I get it. It is to contain the Malatesta.

Other cantos lying here on desk unfinished. Including Hell and the Honest Sailor.

Love to you and mother
E .

The 'canto on Kung' became canto 13. Robert McAlmon's Contact Editions was publishing Hemingway's Three Stories & Ten Poems, William Carlos Williams' Spring & All, and Mina Loy's Lunar Baedeker. The tale of 'the honest sailor' is told in canto 12; 'Hell' is in cantos 14 and 15.

+≻═≺+

657. TLS

Sunday July 8 [1923]

70 bis, Notre Dame des Champs | Paris VI

Dear Mother:

It's very nice of you to want us, BUT, and there are a lot of buts, and the expense of the trip, and the horror of America, and the incidental expenses London to Canadian port 120 dollars don't by any means cover cost of trip from here to Wyncote.

I should like to see the house once again but think of what one has to go through to get to it.

Mr Shakespear died on Friday, so D, will stay on in London with her mother, I suppose, rather longer than usual. I may go over later. He has been ill since middle of April getting steadily weaker; apparently with no pain.

I will do what I can for the Parker-Monroes.

Harriet of the latter patronymic arrived here Friday evening.

Little Review contingent on deck; bringing out next number here.

I enclose some very bad proofs of D's <good> designs for 'Elimus'

Letter from Dad sometime ago speaks of my letter in Playboy. Cant remember any letter to Playboy; what's it about. And who wrote it????

We are using eight Leger cuts in next L. R. and he has done a magnifique cover, adapted from designs for his Ballet Negre. Etc.

Still waiting for July Criterion, will send it when I get it.

Also may start work on mediaeval music again.

George Antheil appears to be a bright spark. Your bitch of an acquaintance Mrs Bok has I believe done him dirt, all because Mr Strogoff or whats his name got a divorce. Wonderful example of Phila mind. One musician divorces so you break your word to another.

Antheil also approves of my orchestration, so I naturally think him a genius. Nobody but a genius COULD approve of my orchestration. (don't tell anybody Antheil approves, it will ruin his chances with American audience. He appears to have drawn great crowds in Berlin, Budapesth, etc,)

Love to you & dad.

E

*The wealthy **Mrs Bok** had supported the young Antheil's studies in Philadelphia in the expectation that he would become a virtuoso concert pianist; when he decided to be a composer instead she withdrew her support, saying he needed to prove he had it in him. (In 1925 she would send a cheque to cover the expenses of the first performance of his 'Ballet Mécanique'.) In the Fall of 1923 Antheil would go over the **orchestration** of Pound's opera, Le Testament, developing under Pound's direction its very advanced micro-rhythms and fractional metrics.*

+══+

658. TLS

1 Aug, [1923]

70 bis, [Paris]

Dear Mother

Yrs to hand. Re/ London, I dont know anything about your 'failures'. You may have been trying to do something incompatible with the climate.

Old H. H. S. is said to have liked you very much. He probably wd,nt, have thought of mentioning the fact, but then he so seldom mentioned anything. I heard of it accidentally three years or six years later.

The fiancee of the cousin of my cousin arrived, with replica of herself having different lable. It is a LONG way from here to Utah.

Mrs Mac Cormac back in town, has done bust of Mussolini; unusual summer inrush of americans. They do no convince one that the country's future will arrive in our time.

Cantos IX to XII are in July Criterion. Am revising the earlier one for S Oiseau's edition.

Hem, returns to Toronto in a few weeks.

Were various other things I intended to write or answer. May get round to it in time.

Ah, dad's letter discovered at last. 3 Mts, paris built on various hills, Mt Parnasse, St Genvieve and Martre.

Yes that damn call of the road is the one I did for Liveright. Hoped he was going to use pseudonym. The author is an ape. However its a way of paying the rent. I couldn't refuse to do it, as L. had gone on paying me all last year without deciding what he wanted

Who is 'Smiley' of the Ledger. Dont understand allusion.

Price of three Mts, books is 2 dollars, simple ordinary cheque on Jenk, Trust Co or other U.S. bank to Paris office brings the book.

I am not a bookstall. S oiseau has a factotum to tie up packages. Etc

Love to you both,

E.

+≻═≺+

659. TL

24 Aug [1923]

70 bis, N. D. De C, [Paris] VI

Dear Dad:

Am continuing musical research. Young Antheil is due to play us some Stravinsky on Tuesday. Have knocked some more Canti into shape, now on fifth on from Malatesta, and have revised earlier part of the pome.

I did not send you copy of Criterion, supposed you wd, see it on news stand sooner than copy wd, arrive via Paris.

Dont know that there is much else to report. Hem sails fer Toronto on Sunday. Toronto 'Star'.

The Joyce family back in Paris. And J. J. launched on another work. Cal'lated to take the hide off a few more sons of bitches.

Strater gone to bedside of his grandmother in N.Y. so designs for my edtn, de luxe are delayed. Also Bill S Oiseau off on vacation.

Quinn may be coming over next month

+≻═≺+

660. TLS

30 Aug, 1923

70 bis, [Paris]

Dear Mother

Thanks for the fr 100 enclosed in dad's letter. All the same I dont think you ought to. Since the death of D's aunt last year she has had rather more than before; so that our combined intake is now probably more than yours. Not but what I appreciate the koind intention.

As to American weekly and other papers, critical articles are usually (I mean out of what you send 95 or more %) mere bosh. The stuff is written by people who know nothing about the matter; unsuall incapable of thought, or if by chance they do know or think AND say anything they get chucked at once (recent case of Gorman).

It is waste of postage to send em also waste of my time, as I always look through the damn stuff to see if you have marked anything or found anything of interest.

Joyce is back and started on new opus.

Antheil played through his piano sonatas for us night before last and is doing his mechanisms this evening. He is very solid. Next phase of music for those fed up with era of Debussy. Am trying to collect my wits for an article or manifesto on subject.

Am reading a bad book of C, Borgia; also a large encyclopedia got out by french conservatoire. That's about that.

Hueffer due back here Monday.

Have found a good chinese restaurant. Hem, gone to Canada. N. Cox MacCormac gone to London. Deplacements, Villegiatures.

D. sends her love,

E

⊹⊱──⊰⊹

661. TCS

[c.10 September 1923]

[Paris]

Hueffer back, has read me mss, of new novel 'Some Do Not', best he has done since Good Soldier, or A Call.

Joyce back (with fat czeco slovak brother in law. Antheil going over mss of opera with me. Bill Wms. says he is arriving, sometime this winter. S. Oiseau in Venice. J. Q. wrote he was coming but the distinguished client was shot accidentally (or otherwise) while out hunting last week, so I don't know whether or not he will arrive. We have a new Leger 'projet' waiting to be framed. That's about that.

ever

E

+⊨=⊨⊨+

662. ALS

3 oct. [1923]

[Paris]

Have been meaning to write.
Quinn here. Ford starting new monthly review with large prospects.
Have done article on Antheil – presumably for Criterion.
etc.
announcement of review shd. follow
various deplacements & people in Paris

love to you & dad,

E

Ford was starting his Transatlantic Review. *Pound's* **article**, *'George Antheil', would appear in the* Criterion *in April 1924.*

+⊨=⊨⊨+

663. TLS

[October 1923]

[Paris]

Dear Dad.

Various things going on. J.Q. here, or rather gone to Berlin for three days. Ford projecting new review that ought to be good if it materializes.

Antheil active. Bill still preparing that edition de luxe, which however, appears nearer than it did.

Have finished canto XVI, that is fifth after the Malatesta, having rewritten beginning of poem, and condensed three cantos into two.

Experimenting on some violin pieces. Antheil has done one damn good piano and violin sonata, and begun another.

Is Homer still playing the fiddle, or has he subsided into commerce?

D. in London clearing up things; think she has found a flat that will do for O.S.

Think I wrote that they are putting on the Arne opera in London and that Raymonde (Collignon) is to have leading part; at last.

Wot'ells??

Dudley Murphy, whom I met in venice in 1908, he being then eleven; turned up a few days ago. His dad is a painter, he is trying to make cinema into art. ETC.

Have at last got a copy of Cumming's 'The Enormous Room'; interesting in a way, but dont seem able to get on with it very fast.

Leger's ballet negre, opens on Thursday, three nights here, then it goes to N.Y. Covers on current Little Rev, are from L's designs for the costumes.

I was very glad to get that photo. of gt,grnd mthr's portrait. Think I have already said thanks.

E P.

*Pound was involved with **Dudley Murphy**, Fernand Léger, Man Ray, and Antheil, in a 'vorticist film-experiment' to be called Ballet mécanique.*

⊹⟫━⟪⊹

664. TL

22 Nov, [1923]

70 bis, [Paris]

Dear Dad:

Best wishes for yr anniversary; also hopes for the 'raise'.

Antheil has played his own stuff with the Berlin Philharmonic; but he is not publishing, he is twenty two and wants to wait a bit.

He and Olga are doing both violin sonatas here on 11 Dec, (will send you programme and poster) but the second sonata is NOT yet quite finished. I dare say these will be published in time.

There are pianola rolls of his 'Mechanisms' which are nearly impossible to do by hand.

My 20 page article on him is due for April Criterion.

There shd, be about 8 pages of his music in the second number of the Transatlantic

My opera is called 'Le Testament'

D, due back next week.

Am getting free dinner from some bloody litterary society this p.m.

love to you and mother.

DONT send me a Harding medal.

Thanks for the Mexican gold dollar. recd. long ago.

⊹⟫━⟪⊹

665. TLS

8 Dec. 1923

[Paris]

Dear Dad

Re yr queery (verso) the answer is mainly in the negative. Vide duplicate with different headlines.

George <u>was</u> making hell's own merry noise, lambasting the bass and yelling the violin part of his second sonata. The Sweede, who is not a musician came down; I did nothing to calm his feelings. Neither did the concierge or the proprietaire, who both know that he gives parties and plays his damn pyano and dances over my head until 3 a, m,; so he went for consolation to the police.

The commissaire de ditto asked me to call at his bureau; after ¾ hour argument he wrote in his ledger. 'Monsieur declares that in his quality of compositeur de musique it is necessary that he make of noise.'

A few days later just as G and O were ending a rehearsal of Sonata No I, the Sweede began hammering on the floor.

George played De Wacht am Rhein, and the noise above ceased instantly. It has not been repeated.

yrs
E .

Etc.

Miss Stukey in yesterday for "comp" tickets.

several errors in this cutting also . but nearer the facts than yr. last envoi.

Love
E

Pound had installed a piano in his studio to enable Antheil and Olga Rudge to rehearse for their 11 December concert in the Salle du Conservatoire. The unfortunate Swedish neighbour lived overhead. The fragmentary **cutting** *stated, 'These young men are cousins of Mr. Homer L. Pound of Wyncote, and he is awaiting a later letter giving fuller accounts of what happened.'*

+≥—≤+

666. TLS

6 Jan, [1924]

70 bis, [Paris]

Dear Dad

Left hospital this a.m.; no operation, must stay on diet a while.

Booked sleeper for Rapallo, tuesday a.m.

Thanks very much for the 600 lire (only you oughtn't to go on sending cash. I think we now have more than you have . . . but thanks for the spirit.

Thanks for the magnificent hair brushes.

The wooly bed slippers of two years ago that I dont use here in studio, were most useful in hospital.

More from Rapallo; got all I can do to finish off before leaving.

Will copy violin piece for Homer some time. Season's greetings to all at Tioga,

Love to you and mother

E .

Pound had been in the American hospital at Neuilly since December 23 with an attack of appendicitis.

+⊱━⊰+

667. ALS

29 Jan. [1924]

Hotel Mignon Rapallo

Dear Dad:

Long time since I wrote you letter of any length. Don't know where I was or whether there is much to report. Have had some tennis today & am supposed to be on the mend.

Certain amount of work in Paris. Nov. & Dec. preparing concert - general executive functions etc.

Also. I suppose I have learned a good deal of musical technique - actual mode of representing sounds on paper - or possibly I havent -

also, work on vorticism film - experiment interesting - but probably Murphy hasn't brains enough to finish the job in my absence or without pushing.

Bird is still preparing the de luxe CANTOS.

Baldy Bacon is F.S. Bacon. he visited us in Wyncote once or twice. also turned up in Paris last year 2 days after I had typed out that canto. There is a hell (2 cantos) & war (one canto.) & the honest sailor ½ of that canto - that you haven't yet seen - reserved - for the book.

Article on Antheil supposed to appear in April Criterion - heaven knows if it will.

Also a note on Joyce - for which Der Querschnitt has thanked me – but I don't know whether they mean to print it.

A new music theatre in Paris has asked about doing my opera - but I can't do anything about it before I get back to Paris - it means more work than I want to take on at present - also I want to be sure of their capacity to do it.

(D. recd yr. letter 2 days ago. & will answer it.)

E.

Nancy C. MacCormac has had my mask cast in bronze. She is having a show in Paris in spring - we expect to see her here for a day or so. en route.

Bill Wms has arrived in Paris. vide enclosure. Hem is expected back shortly. His opinion of Canada not likely to be printed anywhere save in Africa.

Natalie has paid for private performance of Antheils 5 instrument symphony - it seems to have gone well. (18th Jan.) & he may be doing orchestra score for 1st violin sonata. - orch. to replace piano. = Subject of conversation between mother & Mrs E. K. Bok if they happen to meet.

Love to you & mother.

E .

Natalie is Natalie Barney.

+━━+

668. ALS

4 Feb. [1924]

Hotel Mignon Rapallo | (you can write to this address.

Dear Mother:

Not much to report Sandford here with us. He & D. doing sketches. I am still doing nothing, but have played a few sets of weak tennis

Enclose notice of George. - perhaps if he comes to America this autumn you might put him up for a few weeks - while he prepares his concerts. You wd. get the music free - very different from Walter's.

Natalie had his symphony for 5 instruments done <u>chez elle</u> a fortnight ago - with good results.

Dont know where Mrs Pullman is & shdn't recognize her if I met her. I don't suppose you have her exact address??

Haven't yet seen second no. Transatlantic it is supposed to be on sale in the U.S - but is not apparently procurable here. G.& I are doing the music section.

Also - as I think I said. my article on G.due in April Criterion.

otherwise - nothing to be expected of me till Soiseau gets round to issuing the <u>deluxe</u>

Love to you & dad.

E .

+━━+

669. ALS

5 Feb. [1924]

Hotel Mignon Rapallo

Dear Dad:

Felt for some time in Paris that I was being bad correspondent -

possibly too late to remedy the matter now - as I haven't yet collected my wits & certainly never will be able to sort out what I have written you from what I did not write.No great amount of news here

Surf high today. clouds heavy. probably no tennis. The <u>chien</u> <u>policier</u> pups are very lively & very lionine - they are the chief ornament of the limited 'front' at the moment.

Met Bechofer, old new age writer, on front two days ago - he had no news in particular save that Orage has gone to America with the Gurdjieff gang. - I suppose Orage is pretty well worn out - he always had Theosophic kink - you might see him - or then again he may be entirely submerged in the Gurdjeff-Ouspensky hash. I haven't. seen him in Paris - he was at Fontainbleu. (for about two years, I think.)

Enclosed Ref. from Mt Allegro. L. Holt may have mentioned the latter to you.

Berman walked up there with us last year. We haven't tried the climb yet this year.

Ciao.

E

⊣⟩══⟨⊢

670. ALS

10 Feb. [1924]

Hotel Mignon | Rapallo

Dear Mother:

Estaunie is a bad writer; I couldn't escape the translation. but escaped signing - & got my years leisure to do the Malatesta –

That's that - now 'fergit it' & lets hope the act will pass into general oblivion.

The Xmas gifts that arrived were. 1. brushes - 2. mocassins (my size, not D's. = much more opportune as she has a new pr. bed slippers & I hadn't. 3. lire 600. . I suppose the shawl will arrive in Paris in due time in any case D. sends thanks.

Precisely. O. R. is niece of Bayes (Mr. or Mrs.) & Bayes takes very good photos of animals. wild. (apart from which – oh well. - he takes excellent photos.

Re. house. yes I shd. like to pay you a visit before you leave it – But the voyage west over the Atlantic is so <u>much</u> longer than the voyage east. And apart from Oak Lodge the American Scene. & the Amurkn a'mosphere are so little inviting.

At present our only plans are to have as few plans as possible - & not to feel that we <u>have</u> <u>to</u> do anything in particular.

Have sent p.c. to various people. - never quite sure that the Foote address is still 2020 Estaugh. Sorry David is laid up.

Am sending card to Will W.

Hope Dad's diet is not as rigorous as mine has been. Let me know if anything passable <u>is</u> settled about pensions.

We hope to look for some sort of villa – or at least possible situation for one – sometime – neither too remote – too hot nor too cold. etc.

Love to you & dad
E .

O. R. is Olga Rudge.

+≻═≺+

671. AC

[after 23 February 1924]

[Rapallo]

Woodrow gone.
peace to his ashes.
& damn the passports he bequeathed.
At any rate he wasn't an oil grafter.

Woodrow Wilson died 23 February 1924.

+≻═≺+

672. ALS

12 March [1924]

Address. | Hotel Mignon | Rapallo

Dear Dad:

Sorry to hear of Mrs. Warrens death. please convey my sympathies to Mr W.

We have come 2000 feet up to Monte Allegro - partly to escape press of visitors in Rapallo - go back at end of week & thence to interior - Mignon address probably best for rest of our stay in Italy.

Am much better - have been trying to do a bit more music. have in fact done some remains to be seen whether it is any good

Re/. silk shawl - it hadn't arrived when we left Paris Jan. 8th concierge is instructed to forward nothing but letters & D. will write to her to know whether package arrived.

New Transatlantic (3$^{d.}$ number, here with my (Treatise on Harmony) title of which F. has distorted on his cover. - F. writing every weenk in Paris Tribune Sunday Supplement.

Little Rev. I shant see probably till I get back to Paris.

California whale has not yet penetrated Italy.

Bill Williams somewhere in the vicinity but haven't yet seen him. –Bunting <1> & OBrien <2> have both arrived on this hill crest from Rapallo. during the week - (for tea only)

1. Ex sub-edtr. Transatlantic 2. Short story collector.

Old Ionides 'memories' seem to be being read - O. S. took 'em down from dictation or rather poked old L.I. into some sort of coherent narration.

D. sends love to you both.

Anch'io

E

Hemingway, apparently under the impression Pound was still in hospital, had sent him a telegram at the end of January: 'Rushing two hundred pound California bathing beauty your bedside hem'.

+≡≡≡+

673. ALS

25 March. [1924]

address. Hotel Mignon | Rapallo

Firenze

Dear Dad:

Your letter with news of your mothers death came this a.m. She seems to have made about as good an end as any one could. in the fulness of time. and no long illness.

I sent her a card from Rapallo – don't know that she got it. – never sure of their address -

Sorry Homer is out of job - Am here - in palazzo. with huge rooms & bath - Musicians treated better than poets - Have been trying to finish new violin suite in time for Olga's London concert.

Did finish it yesterday but am not sure it is finished <u>right</u>. Am not yet well enough to work at long stretch -

Have also other music that I want to do.

Bill W^{ms} may be here in Florence - left word for him at Cooks this a.m.

D. & I hope to go up into the hills south of Venice in April - Use Rapallo address. until further notice - the hotel will forward mail.

News of L. Holt's wedding arrived before we left Rapallo. Enclose Nancy C. McC notices.

Have recd. bill for 25 centimes tax from French govt. – prize bureaucratic imbecility.

for rest. Criterion & Transatlantic should bring you my news.

Love to you & mother. & take my

regrets to Aunt Florence – for grandmother's death.

yrs

E

*Homer's **mother**, Susan Angevine Loomis Pound, died 29 February 1924. Pound's '**Fiddle** **Music**: First Suite' would be performed by Olga Rudge in London in May, and in Paris in July. The VIth movement was reproduced in* Transatlantic Review *in August.*

+⊨⊷═⊶⊩+

674. ALS

10 April [1924]

Florence | address Mignon | Rapallo

Dear Dad:

Lunched with Berenson monday - ditto with Loeser (friend of J.Q.) last week - both in mag. villas with old ahrt abaht 'em - Went up to Fiesole today to avoid lunching with A.G. etc. -

good room here at Hot. Berchielli - overlooking Arno - old houses & ponte Vecchio - have also had certain amt. of music. Lever Quartetto in 2 concerts & Pizetti in private.

Have collected certain amt. reading matter to occupy projected month at Assisi - D. wanting to paint there.

proof of <u>Prospectus</u> of Bird's edtn - of Cantos - has arrived & been returned with suggestions re modification -

Enc. card - supposed to indicate arrival of shawl at 70bis.

Probably <u>not</u> settling in Florence - decision against it seems to be coagulating.

bath about ready - more anon.

E .

*Isabel Pound would ask, 'Should I know **A. G.**?'*

+⊨⊷═⊶⊩+

675. ALS

[c.1 May 1924]

Hotel Belle Arti | Perugia

Dear Dad:

Going to Assisi next week. Paris by June 1st // after May 20th send mail Paris. Hem. has good story in April Transatlantic.

This note mainly to ask if you know any thing about American Presidents - I have what I need on Wash. & Jefferson but that's about all. - I don't care a damn about their public eye wash. I want facts indicative of personality.

Is there anything in yr. old vols. of Grant's Life. - or Blaine's '20 years of congress.' – or did you pick up anything when you were in Washington or from T.C.P. that threw any light on Garfield – Arthur – G. C. - or whomever happened before Garfield. Lincoln?? (forget dates. . Johnson, Grant, ? Hayes. - Garfield - forget if there were any others. -

Can you look over books in Phila library. -

Jefferson's letters I have read. He was probably the only civilized man who ever held down the job.

(of course it is now accepted that Lincoln was J.X^t. & not human. - so I'm not counting him.)

Tyler - Harrison 1st possibly Monroe. might be the brighter spots in the annals of national bad taste.

I can't remeber the names of a lot of 'em. There was a Johnny named Polk & two bums called Adams / / anny how it wd. be more interesting for you to read such of their correspondence as is printed - than to read the pollyanay de nos jours -

I believe Grover has written his own life - but suppose the book's bunk & designed to tell the young to be industrious.

Any how the earlier occupants are more likely to be interesting

By the way ole C. T. C. has written to me. if you see him – ask 'em why he dont get some artist to paint something like the enclosed on the walls of the Wyncote Church - connect religion with life - once again. - expense tribling - difficulty lies in finding the artist - real requirement is a painter who has excreted the XIX th century.

Love to you & mother
E P.

*G. C. would be Grover Cleveland; **C. T. C.** would be Carlos Tracy Chester.*

+≥==≤+

676. AL

[c.8 May 1924]

Perugia. | 1923

Dear Dad:

going on with that idea of reviving amurkn ahrt. I have written to the ancient Chester -

I think the next step 1. is for you to see him & the new parson - whom you report susceptible to the litterchure of the last decade.

2. get me a diagram of the decoratable spaces in the ch. - there were laurel root letters back of pulpit? & a window. main space?? over slide partitions at back - but also walls about the large windows. [*sketch*] etc.

it wd. be a great lark to get these presbyterian heckers to do something useful. - as 'ad' value it wd. be unequal'd & unheard of -

& if people are going to continue living on that undesirable continent they ought to institute the rudiments of civ. some time.

I don't imagine they wd. pay an artist plumbers wages - but don't worry about that - you get the dimensions - & see if I can get a design to fit the space.

a painter wd. be bound to be done in a contest with a session - don't let that worry you -

you go ahead and get diagram of the space - & the main measurements - i.e. to give one general idea of size & scale necessary.

& don't worry about the local millionaires and big bottoms -

I wd. almost insist as an initial condition that neither Bok or Curtis be asked to contribute.

The idea that nothing can be done without vast wealths is

[*rest missing*]

+≻━≺+

677. ALS

12 / 5 / '24

Assisi

Dear Dad:

D. still doing sketches of frescos in church here. & of mountains.-

When you answer write to Paris address. - we go back to Perugia at end of week & thence slowly northward.

No time yet for news of London concert. - (Saturday.) - Have been reading large work on the Este. & various rubbish found in hotel book case - about ready for my typewriter 'wanct again'.

an thaat is about thaat, I reckon.

'Arsen Lupin' famous french 'Raffles' - i.e. most famous thief in cheap fiction. April Transatlantic quite good - May less interesting. Sill ole Ford is making quite a good come back.

Long letter from Hem - on vicicitudes of Paris.

Love to you & mother.

E .

*Pound had contributed a 'communication', 'Death of **Arsène Lupin**', to the April* Transatlantic Review.

---

678. ALS

16 / 5 / 24

Assisi

Dear Dad:

Recon I have sent you this gate before - however its a good gate; thank god we are due to motor back to it tomorrow.

Assisi all right for 3 days - but not for life.

George & Olga have had their London concert - apparently success with audience / press so far (5 notices) uniformally <u>un</u>favorable - which is as it should be. G. has been staying with Mrs S. who seems pleased both with him & his music - Don't know whether he is in precipitate exit to U. S. A. or whether I shall see him in Paris.

Have read vast work on Ferrara - & blocked out course of a few more cantos.

Some of Henry's designs are good - I dont care for the one Bill is using as an ad. but I am pleased quite definitely with some of the others.

Shd have been in Paris to make final selection etc - but still. – it will be a fairly good looking book. - you are <u>NOT</u> expected to subscribe - an exemplaire will reach you in due course.

Am begining to want typewriter again = sign of awakening energy.

Love to you & mother.

E

---

679. ALS

[after 16 May 1924]

Albergo Belle Arti | Perugia

Dear Mother:

Here's the caravansary on edge of hill. Town much more air'd than Assisi. D' busy painting.

Have found some old music XV century in library & spent few days copying.

Tell Dad - if people kick at price of XVI cantos he can remind 'em that A Lume Spento was pub^d. @ $1. & that he sold a copy for $40 & that J.Q. sold same again for $52.50.

As those are the only terms in which the native can think.

Reassure dad that he will get his copy when it is printed - without any further action on his part. I haven't any more announcements here.

Note on Antheil is in Criterion - we start northward in a day or so.

Love to you & dad,

E .

+≻━≺+

680. ALS

28 Maggio [1924]

Mignon. Rapallo | address Paris

Dear Dad:

Re/ yrs.14$^{\underline{th}}$ inst. THAT (i.e. uninterestingness of U.S. presd$^{\underline{ts}}$.) is PREcisely the point. - I hope, with a few well chosen phrases, to rub it in.

only I want an almost infinite number of facts to select from.

Sorry I did not know T. C. P. The curious similarities of style; due to certain lack of beating about bushes, amuse me considerably.

About best phrase in this stuff is 'as it costs the govt. about $20.000 per head to exterminates the red warriors' etc. wd be cheaper to educate.

Sorry he burnt his papers. - they might have had educational value for yrs. truly.

Is there any way of finding out exactly what T. C. did re/ indians, river traffic. & irrigation??

Do you know definitely what he did in way of originating & putting through legislation.

Cd. you write a brief life of him for me.?? - Perfectly simple statement of facts that you know.

Why did he die broke or nearly so? booze?? or optimism? or final philosophic indifference

Re. exectutives, I have one or two plums. Geo. W's death - Jefferson trying to get a gardner who cd. play the french horn in quartette after dinner. (wanted to import one along with a clavicord) Shd. like something of the Lincoln family that hadn't been worn to death & that didn't feature J. Christ too heavily - also Grant.

The row of duds begins early with Mr. Adams.

———

Letter re/ church to hand – also -

———

531

Do you know name of Arthur's son. There might be various Arthurs in Paris. Who was this Robertson. an injun commissioner or zummat?

Where did she get the name Angevine (always thought it was Ang<u>e</u>line) Angevine much more interesting - from Anjou - but how did she get it?? what french impetus?? & Susan: I thought it was Selina - however thaats that.

Re church - photo idea excellent - send me photos of four sides - & statement of what material the painted wd. have to paint <u>on</u>. dare say photo wd. show. - also dimensions - base dimension wd. do as photo wd probably show scale.

Sorry I can't follow Clarence's filial example. - but that side of my character ain't never deeeveloped - (nor has the correspondingly receptive side of yours, I shd imagine.)

fact that the wood has not been painted is interesting?? have they been varnished - or is wood open to first coat of colour.

Wet yesterday - fine today – hope to get a few sets of tennis before going back to Paris. NOW

Love to you & mother

E

*Homer Pound's reply to Ezra's request (about 1 May 1924) for the lowdown on American presidents had begun, 'I can conceive of no more **uninteresting** thing to write about'. He had however taken 'from your grandfather's old scrap book several leaves . . . they may give you light on Garfield and McKinley'; and he thought to mention that the son of President Arthur—'the one who appointed me as Register of the U S Land Office at Hailey Idaho—was living in Paris, and that Pound 'might look him up and get a story from him'. The **best phrase** from Thaddeus Coleman Pound's papers went into canto 22, along with some other details about him. Jefferson's wanting **a gardener who could play the French horn** became a detail in canto 21.*

*In another letter, Homer had reported that Mr Chester was very pleased and 'quite worked up about' Pound's suggestions for the decoration of the **church**; he himself would 'get the exact measurements and have the space photographed'. Clarence Chester's '**filial example**' was sending his father 'a check each month—so he does not have to worry' in his old age.*

In the course of this letter Homer wrote: 'Last Sunday evening at church I was looking at the west window and the thought came into my mind, how I wish I could put a beautiful window in memory of Mother—Then Monday I get your letter—'.

━━━

681. ALS

[c.31 May 1924]

Rapallo | supposedly last day

Dear Dad.

Re. memorial window. D. thinks of doing design -

I don't know whether you met Hulme. & a Mrs Kibblewhite in London. - anyhow. - old house where we used to meet in 1908-09. is part of stained glass works.

Thought it might be possible to send you D's design & essential parts of glass. & have glass set up. & <u>leaded</u> according to plan. in U.S.A. - This might bring cost into reason.

Want actual width & height of <u>small</u> windows that make part of large ones - NO intention of doing whole window - but might manage a small pannel - in this way - I suppose the sub divisions are about - 16 inches by 30 - ??? [*sketch*] however let me have size & will go into question of cost. - the glass without the lead wd. be quite easy to ship. & the design wd. cost nothing. etc. -

Yrs

E

＋━━━＋

682. TLS

[c.11 June 1924]

[Paris]

Dear Dad:

Ef yew see Ford; feed him; but dont fer Gawd's sake put any money into the Transatlantic Review. It may be all right, it may even succeed BUT it is no place for a poor man to put his money. The amt, needed to make it go, ANNYhow wd be so large that anything you cd, put in wd, be useless.

Ford left Paris before I got back, so has no letters of introd, or yr, address; but he may drift up.

E P

＋━━━＋

683. TLS

(19 June 1924)

[Paris]

DEER DAD

Program for July concert is ready; remains to be seen if we can get a hall.

2. XV century piece, I dug up in Perugia,
2. Javanese fiddle chunes.
1. fanfare, violin and tambourin, By E.P. to celebrate George's entrance O. R.
G, to do his six piano sonatas.
O. R. to do my fiddle suite.

both of em to repeat his 2nd, viol, and pianny sonata
and then the Finale, G's new 4 tette. which looks damn good. Have only hear
the lst, violin part, to date.

I seem to be writing a book an musiKKK.

To hold essay on G.A.; Atheling's select aphorisms. and the Theory of Harmony, small scrap from Trans, At. and continuation of same; with some mathematical loops.

However. . . . nawthin certun.

Love to you & mother

E

*The invitations to the **July concert** read:*

M. et Mme. Ezra Pound vous invitent

À une audition privée de

MUSIQUE AMERICAINE

(Declaration of Independence)

À la

SALLE PLEYEL

22, rue Rochechouart (9ᵉ)

le

7 Juillet à 9 heures du soir

Exécutants: *Olga Rudge & George Antheil*

*Pound's '**book an musiKKK**', Antheil and The Treatise on Harmony, would be
published by Bird's Three Mountains Press in October.*

+≥─≡+

684. TLS

21 June or theyreabahts. [1924]

70 bis [Paris]

Dear Dad

Thanks for letter, very interesting, and interesting packets re T. C. P. Looks as
if he wd. make a canto also paper money, had just summarized Marco Polo's
note on Kublai Khans issue of paper currency.

NEXT The OIRISH, bedad, have sent me a foot square of paste board calling
me an Emmynent son av my counthry (we suppose its intended as a compliment) as the rest of the engraving invoites me to be a guest bedad of their
Nation; during the national barbaric games and horse show (in gaelic)

The naygotiations are pending. Its the young naytions that commit this sort
of imprudence. D. has cut off the Erse postage stamps for the grocer's boy, and
George has drawn pictures on the envayloop.

534

We have the Salle Playel for the 7th, July. After skirmish. The Conservatoire being full of its annual competitions; and the Salle Gaveau to be filled with renovating workmen on the 1st, July.

D. has finished a half yard of mountains, etc.

Enclose clipping a marvel of inaccuracy.

T.C.P. stuff very interesting.

Have not yet finished translation of the XV century music for the show. Members of quartette not yet found, ETC

Joyce has had another operation on his eye, but is up and about again. Now seems certain that Kume was killed in Jap earthquake. At least they have published obituary notices.

ETC.   more anon.

Love to you and mother

E

*In his packets re T. C. P. Homer had enclosed 'a piece of scrip', the **paper money** issued by his father's lumber company and valid only in the company store. 'The town was flooded with it at one time', he wrote, 'and it was finally decided that it was not legal and State outlawed it I understand'. Pound would frequently refer to this company scrip as evidence that different forms of money were possible. Canto 18 begins with Pound's summary of Marco Polo's account of **Kublai Khan's currency**.*

*Pound had been invited to be an official 'Guest of the Nation' at the **Irish** Free State's Tailteann Games, at which there would be performances, displays and contests of all kinds, from a horse show to literary awards. Pound's **negotiations** were over issues of censorship and passports—receiving satisfaction on neither matter, he would refuse the invitation.*

+⊨=⊨+

685. TLS

[June/July 1924]

[Paris]

Dear Dad

Am sending you concert poster registered post. Think you might get some sunday paper to reproduce it, as Sandford's design is very good (though the damn block maker got it screwed cock eyed onto the block (about two centimetres off centre).

The team is all American, Antheil born in Trenton N. J. and Olga also from the U. S. Antheil and I both known in the U. S. (first Paris appearance). Music news.

Yrs,

E

I enclose programme

It ought to go, I mean reprod, of poster, as NEW ART AND NEW MUSIC etc

+>==<+

686. TLS

13 July, '24

70 bis. [Paris]

Dear Dad:

Yrs, of 3d, inst. to hand. Have just finished or I hope finished preparing my book on George for the press. At least it is typed and corrected, unless I think of something to add, before Bill S Oiseau gets back from Spain.

I have sent you most of the clippings, I think all, that have yet come out. Not the English ones, which I haven't or haven't in duplicate. The Islanders didn't like it; that is the press didn't, the audience seems to have enjoyed itself, at least according to eight or ten reports.

I have nothing to do with the Little Review; you can try telling jane to go to hell if you think it will have any effect.

Enclose some more souvenir currency.

Thanks, but dont send the Burrrrns till I get settled in my <u>next</u> abode; dont know when that will be; am having a special book-case trunk constructed, but there will be no room for new acquisitions.

D. left for London Thursday. Ford back, have only seen him for one moment at concert. Hear Quinn very ill with cyrosis.

Am not the least sure I shall go to Ireland;

The present passport system is an infamy, it is all the fault of the U.S. govt; but I see no reason of entering into friendly personal relations with any govt. that supports the system. If the Irish choose to waive the utterly assenine regulations, I will consider going over; but they've got see that the French authorities also waive 'em for my return.

Certain necessities one has to submit to; one cant, that is, waste one's time, avoiding a law however imbecile, or however much contempt one has for the swine who made it; but a pleasure trip is another matter.

Mind, I dont think, the Irish govt. will or probably could manage this matter.

I understand that Rep, Bloom of N.Y. is getting into action. I trust all other members of both houses will die of the plague AT ONCE.

There ought to be general campaign pledge to vote for no representative, senator or other, who tolerates the present idiotic restrictions. (I haven't time to organize it).

I am sorry Coolidge lost his son; but for the rest I dont believe his any more intelligent than any of the rest, or rather, he probably has sense enough to be honest. that's something.

Speiser called one day when I was out and D. in middle of packing; also arrived at concert with wife and two sons; had no chance to damn him for not starting Phila. campaign on pissports.

The Washington Y.M.C.A. sharks are so goddam ignorant they dont know europe existed without pissports for mostly a century.

Miss Stukey at concert. Had few moments talk about nothing in particular before it started.

ETC,

love to you and mother.

E

+⊨—⊨+

687. TLS

12th of Aug, or thereabouts. 1924

70 bis. [Paris]

Dear Dad

Sorry you weren't here yesterday to meet C.E.S. Wood who struck Idaho about 1878 and remembers 'ole man Hailey, as a stage driver in Boise, when there warn't no Hailey as a place, and Boise was barracks.

He seems en route for California in a hurry, but hopes to meet you some time. We didn't get to the subject of Idaho until about two minutes before he had to leave for the Opera . . So I haven't many details, save the names of a few injun wars which I have already forgotten.

He has written several vols. of verse, rather Whitmanian it wd, seem.

Linc. Steffens back from Italy, Emma Goldman also adorning the corner café. I suppose the Dome is becoming the centre of universal activity.

My book on George A. is in press, as I probably wrote you.

Enclose card from Miro. vide reprod of his picture Farm in last years Lit. Rev. D. says it is wet in Devon.

Thanks for the long notice of J. Q's demise.

There is one error in reprod of the VIth figure of fiddle music, in copy in transatlantic.

5th line, 3d, bar 4th and 5th notes should be sixteenths instead of eights.

was hurriedly copying it on piece of paper that wd, reproduce legibly. George seems to think the whole suite will be published shortly.

I have not, as you will have gathered, been to Dublin.

Here are some more olympik stamps for mothers philatelic friends. If they'd yelled sooner I cd, have sent a few million marks in same manner. German postage has now gone back to ten pfennigs.

537

I appear to have lost 160 fr. by not cashing a cheq last week. the quid is now only 80.

etc.

Love to you and mother

E

*Charles Erskine Scott **Wood** (1852–1944), soldier, attorney, civil libertarian, author, fought in the Nez Perce war in 1877, was present at the surrender of Chief Joseph, and afterwards became his friend. (Was also a supporter of Emma Goldman.) John **Quinn** died 28 July 1924.*

688. TLS

21 Aug, 1924

70 bis, N.D. des Champs [Paris]

Dear Mother:

Why dont you send on the C. E. monitor. I am not interested in notices of my books, as nobody in America knows anything about that matter, and the mag. writers are gathered from the slime of even whatsoever society there is;

but I am interested in <u>all</u> the notices of the music, as this has practical end, i.e. ultimate production of the opera.

Give my best to Tommy Cochran.

Another of the 100 dollar edtn. of Cantos has sold. The book is about half printed, and about one third of the edtn. subscribed.

I do NOT approve of Miss Stikey's teacher Lhote. He is the last of pea time, a complete foozle, no bloody use for anything. I have never expressed any approval of him

Hospital reports favourably on my innards.

Corrected proofs of the 'Antheil' have gone back to the printer. ETC.

transatlantic review has a new lot of jack and will presumably continue.

I am supposed to start editing the musical supplement with more controll. If you know anyone not a gawd damn fool who wants to send in copy on the subject, let em blaze away.

Old Wood says he will try to see dad. I had all the Chief Joseph campaign from him at lunch three days ago.

Love to you & dad,

E .

689. TLS

End of August [1924]

70 bis. [Paris]

Dear Dad

Yrs of 21st, inst to hand this a.m.

am just back from a short walking trip (six days) another one, in the Vienne (i.e. about Poitiers) found a couple of good towns and a good inn.

Ask the 'Episcopal' if he wants a 200 dollar psalter. Bill is thinking of doing a big one after he gets to the end of the Cantos.

Will send you a set of Antheil proofs in a week or so.

Re/ Victrola. Olga went to see a phono company about ten days ago but the cost of records is too high. Will wait until one is paid for submitting to the indignity.

N. C. MacCormac has been told to turn the bust over to you. It had not entered the Q. collection at the time of his death. Dont communicate with the executors about it, as that might raise questions.

But you should get it IN TIME. Effort should be made to keep Q's collection intact and IN AMERICA. I am in correspondence with the estate; but dont know what will or can be done about the matter.

The Seurat circus picture goes to the Louvre that is all I know <u>definitely</u> about the arrangements.

Went to print show while Bill corrected a sheet of Canto V. and saw various other bits of later cantos. It looks like a very fine bit of printing.

D. due back sometime next week. (this is sat.)

Rodker in yesterday on way through Paris; no news in especial.

Conditions: country districts O.K.; magnificent feeds 8 francs and 7 fr 50. City of Tours ruined, slum property. Result of industrialism, i.e. I suppose a munitions factory and morocain troops.

Rural france is O.K. though

I have lost track of the general rascality of conferences. The original treaty was an infamy, and I dont know how they are going to wiggle out. The Daily Mail is already wailing about the Dawes plan.

I dont propose to bother about the matter as my advice is not likely to be asked or taken.

I propose to devote the last years of my life, if I live to be over 98, to the quiet and systematic slaughter of bureaucrats. Apart from that I shall try to have no political ideas.

I find my friend Weyman knew ole Comperet. Weyman was one in the neumismatic museum in N. Y.

ETC.

Sunday - after various interruptions -

Love to you & mother

E

*Homer Pound had asked, 'Why not have a **victrola** record made of your "fiddle music"
then we could hear it over here'. Germany had defaulted on the heavy reparations
imposed on it under the Treaty of Versailles; France and Belgium, in retaliation, had
occupied the Ruhr; **The Dawes plan** was an attempt to enable Germany to resume
payments.*

---

690. TLS

4 Sept. [1924]

[Paris]

Dear Dad

Re yrs of July 3. I suppose that copy of Burns is NOT the 'Kilmarnock'
edition. It is more likely to be an American edition, IF there were American
editions. The matter of the date is important.

I believe a 'Kilmarnock' is worth enough to give you both six months
vacation. I think I saw a notice of a copy sold for 500 pounds sterling. It may
have been dollars, but I think it was 'quid'.

Will you send me a description of the title page, and state what condition the
vol. is in.

My health seems O.K. at last. Dont want to whoop over it yet.

You may be able to find out val. of the Burns from some local dealer,
but DONT sell it till you have consulted me. Send me description, accurate
measure of page. state of binding, etc. Unlikely to be the valuable edition.

Have had tennis with Hem. this a.m.

D. due back today.

                          love to you ad mother.

                                    E

---

691. TLS

12 Sept. [1924]

70 bis, rue Notre Damn des Champs | Paris VI

Dear Dad

Book on Music has gone into final proofs and is, I suppose, being printed.
Will send on copy shortly.

Cantos being very magnificently done, but job goes slowly. Am dining with
new backer of transatlantic this evening.

Young Joyce learning to sing. His dad seems to want him to learn the bass
role in my Villon. J. J. back from coast, eye not yet in shape; but well otherwise.

Ford doing his memories of J. Conrad. etc. Have purchased a new trunk and traveling book'case.

D. back, as I think I wrote. England very wet and generally undesirable as place of residence. etc. Have planted various possessions of various friends in preparation of coming mobilization.

McAlmon has done a very good description of U.S. west, called the Village. will also send you that when it appears. I play tennis two or three times a week with Hem. Leger, back from Italy; has discovered Carpaccio. Picabia and Satie preparing a ballet. Have seen Misses Holt and Stukey peRAM-bulating the streets. George A. supposed to be doing orchestral works. O.R. practicing Mozart.

Love to you & mother

E .

Ezra and Dorothy left Paris for Italy towards the end of September. **Antheil and The Treatise on Harmony** *would be published in October by Bird's Three Mountains Press.*

6

Rapallo: 1924–29

692. TLS

7 Oct. [1924]

Mignon, Rapallo

CHAW
Terbaccer with DAW
 - es
Dear Dad:

There was an article in the N.Y. "Nation" on George and me, by Henrietta Straus, sometime in, I suppose, September, or possibly the end of Aug. I should like to see it if you can get hold of a copy.

I continue to play tennis here. Mrs S. goes back to London next week, if she can get a wagon lit. The Bill Yeats family is considering a trip to Italy sometime in the fewchar. Bob McAlmon says he is going to stop off here on his way south, etc.

That being about the size of the nooz. CHAW terbaccer wif DAWes.

Love to you and mother. Salutations to the Feet.

E

*Charles Gates **Dawes** had been elected to serve as Vice-President to Calvin Coolidge.*

693. ALS

14 Oct. [1924]

Hotel Mignon | Rapallo

Dear Mother:

D just back from dip in the gulph of Tigullio - summer at last. O. S. here with us. will write of last week in Paris sometime soon.

Tell dad. I met very fine Cherokee chief just before leaving.

E

694. TLS

15 Oct, '24

Hotel.Mignon, Rapallo,

Dear Dad:

I am very glad to have the 'Burns' and shall certainly keep it. It is not of any commercial value, evidently a reprint; and is put in the traveling book case as a personal souvenir. Vwoila! Thanks.

Had fairly strenuous two weeks before pulling out of Paris. Old Dunning who lived across the garden fell ill, and had no one to look after him. Also emerged from all hospitals he was put in, and collapsed shortly after, and had to be replaced. As to doctors I tried American french, one turk (excellent chap whom I hope to see again), and finally a Cherokee chief, three hours before my departure, whom I also hope to see again. It also transpired that Dunning had written a very fine book of poems during the last year. I have sent the mss. to Liveright and hope he will act on it.

George A. began a new violin sonata, I think a considerable advance, or probably an advance on the others. My book on G. A. is out, and copies shd. reach you as soon as this does. Anatole died a few hours after we left, there was a storm on the channel. Brussof the Rhooshun poet croked. The stone of my sapphire ring disappeared while I was helping the porter shift my book-box on the Gare de Lion platform. I told Dorothy to stay and look for it while I went to register the baggage, but thought it had got wrenched out while lifting the box from the taxi. When I got back to the platform she had gone. I was annoyed with her for giving up the search so quickly. She had however found the stone, covered with mud at that. So it is back in its setting. Olga's taxi ran into a tree a few days before that. Hem's lawyer in St. Louis has been trying, apparently, to swipe all Hem's hard-earned. G.A. had been very ill and worried about other matters. et cetterer. Howeffer . . . . the sun is warm here; I have been playing tennis and doing nothing else, since arrival, sunday. D. bathed in the gulf yesterday.

The title page of the Cantos has been set up; but the book wont be done for two or three months, yet.

We have taken an extra room here, ... oh yes, the other contretemps was that we got here and found the hotel closed. The management being still on auto ride, returning from Naples. So we slept the first night next door.

The Transatlantic is stewing along; also contributed its mite to final con-fusion, as the Fanelli music mss. wouldn't 'reproduce' and F. was howling about for something else, more or less as one was driving to the station. Also various bits of copy hadn't come in. Etc.

Ole Sadakichi Hartmann has sent me a copy of his Confucius' a sort of play . badly written, but I think rather beautiful and interesting.

I also started a violin (solo) sonata but did <u>not</u> finish it, owing to various of the details given above.

Rapallo empty and tranquil. Have bought a new racquet. Rode of the tennis club, and a chap named Washburn (am. novelist, I believe, though I have never located any of his work) still here.

O. S. came to Paris on the 8th. and is here with us for I suppose about a month.

Wish you were also. Rode offers to build us a house for a reasonable price; but I don't want to settle just yet. I have a magnificent new RED trunk, quintuple splendour, that and the traveling book case, D's trunk and various suit cases seem to contain most of the necessaries, racquet, type-write, bassoon, in fact about everything save the clavicord and a few woiks of Aht.

I feel that the north side of the alps is an error, useful only to make one glad to get to this side. An error I hope not to repeat.

Love to you and mother. Hope to see you before long.

E

Ralph Cheever **Dunning** *was an opium addict, and Pound had bought from the Cherokee chief a cold-cream jar of raw opium which he left with Hemingway to be given to Dunning in case of another crisis. Liveright did not publish Dunning's poems; but Pound did get a number of them published in* Poetry, The Dial, Transatlantic Review, *and his own* Exile; *in 1929 a collection, under the title* Windfalls, *would be published by Edward W. Titus in Paris 'at the Sign of the Black Manikin'. Pound contributed 'The Unpublished Work of* **Fanelli**' *to the November number of Ford's* Transatlantic Review, *along with two brief notes which may have filled in for the music mss.*

<hr />

695. TLS [*letterhead*] John F. Dryden. Unites States Senate

23 October 1924

[Rapallo]

Dear Dad:

Have shaped up some more cantos; and sent you carbons of two that are more or less finished. Re / Victrola: have they an agency over here; some place where George and Olga could play the stuff for the records? IF one is going to have a record made of the stuff it ought to be made of the stuff AS PLAYED by the originators, and under the composer's direction.

Dont try to <u>send</u> anything for my 39th, except good wishes. Am apparently in xcellent health, at any rate playing good hard tennis daily, and feeling very fit. Greetings to Aunt F. I never can keep their address, I suppose it is still 2020? Give her one of the copies of ANTHEIL; and I'll send you another to replace it. Or rather, I am writing to Bird to send her one in yr. care.

The 'bust' isn't a bust but a bronze <u>mask</u>; of which I think you have photo. It is a pussn'l, souvenir, and has no value in commerce, not being for sale. It is in the U.S. so you will have no customs formalities.

Sun still O.K. here; took sea bath a few days ago; D. has been in, most days.

Rode who runs the tennis club here is an ex-sea capn. who is excellent antidote for Conrad. He says sailing is NO life; he had fifteen years of it, seven in command.

love to you and mother
E

23 / 10 / '24

*John F. Dryden (1839–1911) had been a New Jersey Senator, 1902–7. The **carbons** were of cantos XVIII ('Kublai') and XIX ('Sabotage?'), with a note saying 'Not for publication: domestic use only. There are only XVI in the book.'*

⊣⊱⊰⊢

696. TLS

25 Oct 1924

[Hotel] Mignon [Rapallo]

Dear Dad

D. has idea you asked for extra copy of enclosed. Haven't your letter at top of my pile of papers, but send it? cutting annyhow.

Sun magnificent today. Thought yesterday we were in for 5 days rain, but courts ought to be dry in another hour. Must start on another LONG hunk of Canti, like the Sigismundo having used up the chop-chop in the five now drafted. (2 of which I have sent you.)

As you say U.S. presidents do not present ALL the features required for the full mind. Am using a bit of Jefferson in the XX or thereabouts.

etc.

love to you and mother.

D. and O.S. send salutations to you both.

D. thanks for yr. long letter and will answer same sho'otly.

Will write to mother myself; seem to have sent my last half dozen notes to you and none to her.

E

⊣⊱⊰⊢

697. TLS

30 Oct, 1924

Hotel Mignon, Rapallo

Dear Mother:

Compliments due you that your son has lived 39 years without being hanged. D. pointed out at dinner that there was no capital punishment in Italy, so that the present state of non-suspension had some chance of continuing, if I refrained from recrossing the alps.

Am, as I have written to father, again in apparently good health; nothing visibly wrong save half of one toe nail, remnant of walking tour.

Mario (son of the hotel) took us up to the top of the 'vetta' in excellent car, this p.m., rained this a.m. so there was no dust and proper panorama from the summit.

Also got a little tennis, after descent. Have here a reasonable amount of quiet and time to read.

Think I have sent dad most of the news. Hotel still undergoing repairs and we three are the only people in it save the owners, so there are no interruptions. The reasons for NOT taking a house or apartment seem to increase. At least there is no pressing hurry. The new magnificent RED swank trunk and the traveling book-case seem to hold most of essentials of comfort.

And the out look from the front windows here being an asset. One also has excellent windows in Perugia. Cant keep up three establishments.

Have been through the last half of Dant's Hell; and acquired a little more greek during the past fortnight; real comforts of idleness, after the hurley-burley or hurloo-burloo of Paris.

Nearest neighbors being H.D and the McAlmons, somewhere in Suisse. I suppose this state of tranquility can't last, but it is very comfortable while it does.

Shall now retire for the night.

Love to you and dad.

E

+≻═≺+

698. TLS

1 Nov. 1924

[Hotel] Mignon, Rapallo

Dear Mother:

Here are some post war souvenirs; came as wrapping to a packet of lux that D, got yesterday.

Sun and wind today; and smoke, I suppose from charcoal burning, on the hill side. I mean one sees it going up in various spots on the hill side.

Events here are reduced to a minimum, it either rains or does not; mostly has not for the three weeks we have been here.

Have sent Dad two cantos; and done more, not yet in shape to send. Am, as I possibly wrote him, ready for another long chunk; and trying to find some bhloomin historic character who can be used as illustration of intelligent constructivity. Private life being another requisite. S. M. amply possessed of both; but other figures being often fatally difficient.

love to you and dad

E

✦━━✦

699. TLS

12 Nov. [1924]

[Hotel] Mignon, | Rapallo

Dear Mother

Have come on notice of a volume of Dolly Madison's Letters. Also some ambiguous remarks about John Tyler's daughter in law, no name given; having written letters to her sister.

Presumably using name Tyler.

Can you get hold of either volume, and send it me if it contains anything of interest.

Am, as I wrote father some time ago; looking for matierial for American History, NOT doctored to suit school text books.

Old T. Jefferson has some excellent passages. The Tyler administration shd. be entertaining. Have got one good line from T.C.P. re / the cost of shooting Indians.

The way the notice of Tyler matter is worded, D. Maddison might have married Tyler's son; and there may be only one book. Have vague impression that she was Mrs Maddison . . . however . . . even that wouldn't have prevented her making a 2nd. splice.

O.S. departed last night, safely put into through reserved sleeper, after considerable doubt as to which of various published timetables, labled NOVEMBRE, was in accord with actual working of the railway.

A gent wants to translate my book on George into bosche. Remains to be seen whether he will get it done.

transatlantic prints 12 of Dunning's poems in last number.

Mr Munson is said to be about to print an article on me in a new effort called the 'Guardian' pubd. in Phila. have not yet seen a copy.

Mr Edwin Seaver of Woodstock, Ulster Co, N.Y. is printing a well disposed undersized magazine. i.e. the right size; the big one getting fatty degeneration in such early stages of bigness. Dont know that he has yet had any contents, but he has hopes.

Love to you and dad

E

*Dolley Madison (1768–1849), a noted Washington hostess, was the wife of James Madison, 4th President. Elizabeth Priscilla Cooper **Tyler** (1816–89), was daughter-in-law of the 10th President, John Tyler, and his official White House hostess and First Lady 1842–4. Gorham **Munson**'s 'Another Aspect of Ezra Pound' appeared in the* Guardian, *1 November 1924. **Edwin Seaver** (1900–87) was to be literary editor of the just established* Daily Worker, *and would help found* New Masses *in 1926.*

+〓〓+

700. TLS

29 Nov. [1924]

Rapallo

Dear Dad:

Had not gathered from previous letters that mother had been so ill. Very glad to know she is up again. Also Homer's offspring, can't read her name Laoe??? Laoenie???

The 'Inquist' is the series of six book printed by Bill. The Cantos are advertised for end of THIS year. Exhibition of sample pages now going on in Paris.

As to Cantos 18-19; there aint no key. Simplest paralell, I can give is radio where you tell who is talking by the noise they make. If your copies are properly punctuated they shd. show where each voice begins and ends. It is NOT a radio.

You hear various people letting cats out of bags at maximum speed. Armaments, finance etc. A 'great editor' at least edt. of the woilds best known news sheet, a president of a new nation, or one then in the making, a salesman of battleships, etc. with bits of biography of a distinguished financier, etc.

mostly things you 'oughtn't to know', not if you are to be a good quiet citizen. That's all.

Who made the bhloody war? The cantos belong rather to the hell section of the poem; though I am not sorting it out in the Dantescan manner, cantos 1-33 hell, next 33 purgatory, and next 33 paradise.

Am leaving the reader, in most cases, to infer what he is getting. Though re/ two cantos there will be a very narrow margin for error. as you will see, I think, from the book.

Love to you & mother

E .

+〓〓+

701. TLS

3 Dec. [1924]

Mignon, Rapallo

Dear Mother

As it rained yesterday on 'St Bibiana' we are supposed to be in for quaranta giorni of rain. Six bust strings in my new racquet.

Have played a bit chess with McLean a chap here whom I may get started on a new publishing scheme. McAlmon due tomorrow or next day. After which I suppose we must pull ourselves together and trek for Sicilia.

Glad to hear from dad that you are up and about again. I did not realize that you had been seriously ill. Last impression I had was that you were visiting the Waaadswuffs or zummat o that sort.

Dont know that there is much news. have had a good deal of tennis. Sample pages of the Cantos, binding etc. are being exhibited in the rue de l Odeon. I think I sent dad a notice. Am continuing labour on further chunks of the opus.

Talk of Yeats and Mrs Y, coming out to Sicily in Jan.

love to you and dad.

E.

---

702. ACS

20 Dec. [1924]

[Taormina]

Sun. & snow on Etna – not exactly like sul verso
Xmas, Buoni
E

---

703. ALS

21. Dec. 1924.

Taormina | (go on sending mail to Mignon. Rapallo

Dear Dad.

Hyhyer we arur. 700 ft. up mountain with enclosed below. & Etna with snow ½ way down. on the other side. (D. working on same from large room balcony) results later.).

Yeats & Mrs. due in Siracuse about Jan. 6.

Have read bk. 7. of ovids Fasti & walked a bit on mountaing behind the town. since arrival here.

Saw Byington for a few minutes in Naples. - whole office working on immigrant forms. & more forms. great day for the paper trade when them bastards in washington discovered the paper form in triplicate and hextuplicate

Naples dirty. - perhaps less so than 20 years ago - but quite so, quite so.

————

Food in this hotel O.K. & roof balcony very good place for D. to work - gk. theatre one side – sea - stub of italy in front. & Etna. etc.

Some conversation here with a Thesophic scotch 'mason' with danish name from Honolulu.

Knudson - now gone

ETC.

Taormina a bit small for continued residence.

As to Byington (as mother will probably want news). he was very affable. is now consul general. seemed to remember Aunt F. (possibly official memory). is married has five offspring - one ill at the moment.).

A liner was due to sail & immegrant business busying whole office. (D. passport attended to with due dispatch.) at least as far as the Naples office goes.). B. said it had taken him some time to inherit his grandfathers job. South America & England intervening.

22. Dec.
Warm enough for sun bath this a.m.

Happy new year to you & mother. Suppose it will take this about 3 weeks to arrive?

Love
E

+⊱⊰+

704. ALS

28 Dec (1924)

Taormina

Dear Mother:

The 3 magi with a red light on bamboo pole went out to look for little J. at 2. a.m. Xmas - later procession with angels. & little J. - & various fireworks - some I think fabricated by local quarrymen.

ending with pin-wheels. two feet across. at about 4.30 a.m. also band, bagpipes, & large bon-fire of several large whole tree stumps.

return to normalcy - great deal of food in this excellent Hotel (Naumachie.) found M. Snively's name in guest book at Mola that spike of town on next rock behind castello – higher but looks about level in post card.

Yeats & Mrs. due in Siracuse on the 9th – we are due to go there in a day or so. Etc.

good deal of glare = glad of my ray filtre goggles. Have read Ovids 'Fasti' & done not much else.

D. done sketches of Etna. Wine & apples good – oranges & figs too sweet & tasteless.

Buone feste. bon anno

E .

+⟩━·━⟨+

705. ALS

3 Jan (1925)

H. Roma Siracusa

Jan 7. dinner 2 hrs. long or more with director of local museum & 30 members of inn-keepers family.

Bread made with sesame - otherwise food of southern Europe. - cats & pigeons gather fragments in dining room.

This a.m. went to gymnasium. (per. enc.) Papyrus said to grow only here & in Egypt.

Good deal of ruin – sea. Etna visible when weather is clear.

Not exactly habitable place. - port full of boats - unloading wheat loading in stone ballast. etc.

sample of wheat & papyrus. enc.

Love to you & mother,

E. P.

address. Rapallo

Thanks for note book. Did I acknowledge your 100 lire? if not Thanks fer them. also.

Love to you & mother

E

+⟩━·━⟨+

706. ALS

16 Jan [1925]

Palermo

Very fine harbour – mountains. etc. difficulty about tennis – unless one pays 120 fr. per day at Swynk hotel -

W. B. Y. & Mrs. still here -

551

Comfortable rooms top floor – Not yet very settled in mine -
Fine trip here. i.e. as per scenery
Castrogiovanni – Vale of Enna – an'-so-on - have done a small amt. of work –
Plenty for D. to paint if she can find a place to paint it from.

Yrs

E

＋＝＜＝＝⫶

707. ALS

Pension Suisse 65 Via Cavour | Palermo.
(But go on writing to Rapallo.)

23 Jan [1925]

Dear Dad:

Haven't yet got Sicily sorted out – Taormina british suburb in splendid cite. Siracusa near, too near Tangiers, but interesting for a few days - i.e. city - outside it mostly greek desolation & a few ruins.

Homesick Swiss in second hotel we tried - had been hall clerk on Broadway. etc - so glad to see someone who had seen N.Y. Paris, London & heard of Ostend that he took us for ½ price - i.e. offered it -
Etc -

Have used Yeats typewriter to get through a bit of work – W.B.Y. went up toward Naples yesterday. etc. .

This town has a few good coffe & icce cream shops - & appearence of modernity in spots.

W.B.Y. tried theatre - I stood it for 14 minutes - have motored out to Cefalu. D. sent cards - I think mosaics - & one bit of very old masonry on the hill.

Am expecting some sort of copy of Cantos, sometime.

D. has had one shot at the port here - plenty for her to do – difficulty to find unfleesome spot to do it from - apart from roof of pension - fine old house.
Etc.

Love to you & mother

E .

Pound later recalled 'Yeats wanting me to speak some verse aloud in the old out-of-door Greek theatre at Siracusa, and being annoyed when I bellowed [Sappho's Greek] and refused to spout English poesy.'

＋＝＜＝＝⫶

708. ALS

28 / 1 /'25

Palermo | address Rapallo

Dear Dad:

I recon' it'll be Rapallo - Im sorry you have been ill again.

This country <Sicily> is interesting . but not exactly habitable - A few <u>de looks</u> hotels; and a British suburb at Taormina

rest of it. I think rather better for 3 weeks xcursion. However - one had to explore. We are due to go to Girgente tomorrow. said to be hell & the promised land . by various differing travelers.

NO - fer gawds sake dont <u>send</u> anything. when you get round to coming . bring anything you think the U.S. can spare. - at present even small postal packets have to be fetched from central post office - a bhloody bore. (possibly local infection, for Palermo only.)

Will send card to Inglis - Don't know that there is much to write apart from wotz in the guide books.

Yeats was supposed to be resting - after struggles in Irish senate – bombs - windows busted by machine guns & other celtic & twilit excitements.

Instead of resting he was rather exhaustedly trying to finish a book.

Slightly disintegrating effect on his surroundings -

I have typed to end on Canto XX. & recd. copy of Bill's edtn. I-XVI - special proofs. Too late to correct any thing - only one error that matters / head should be <u>heads</u> on p. 58 line 10.

head<u>s</u> rose. = snake head<u>s</u> not the single head of Medusa herself.

you will probably find 2 of them there cantos a bit strong. (pungent)

but I think they are only what is needed. I wd. have gone further if I had seen any way of doing it.

Is Nancy going to sculp that squeezed lemon???

Eliot writes that he wants to print some more cantos in his mausoleum. Don't know that he will when he sees 'em.

The head of the Paris Sera has declared in favor of Jazz. - George has finished new opus – mostly for xilophones. ETC.

General result is rather in favour of North Italy.

Have gathered a few books from local publisher - ETC: Hope you will be getting your Cantos . about now.

That will give you something to go on with. & ask questions about.

Straters work & Bills printing come up better than I had expected.

Have very faint recollection of Morgan - //. sorry he has gone. / ?? Flynn is still on deck isn't he?

I enclose curious & friendly letter from Saunders - who turned up in Paris summer before last.

Harbour here very fine - possibly better than Gib. shd. like to see latter again for comparison.

Love to you & mother & keep well.

The worst of the winter ought to be over

. E .

Homer Pound had sent a photo of **Nancy** *Cox McCormack and mentioned that 'she was doing a bust of George Wallace'.* **Morgan** *had been Engraver at the Mint.*

⊹══⊱⊱

709. ALS

[30–1 January 1925]

[Palermo]

Dear Mother:

Most of these books can go - give 'em to Miss Warren - or give her those she wants & send the rest to Learys.

Keeping only the few specially marked.

31 Jan - We have been to Girgenti & got back to Palermo 5½ hours at 9 miles (nine) per hour -

Sicily shd be done either with rook-sac only - or with full luxe - 200 lire a day.

Thanks for making out this list but most of the books ought to be scrapped.

Hope dad is up again & feeling fit

The climate of Sicily is not on the whole an improvement on Rapallo - unless one cd. live on a shelf - (very small shelf of rock) in Taormina - this trip interesting but hardly restful

Rc. yr. Acad. Pol. Science. Prof. Pigou's name on the list rather damages the prestige of the possibly well intentioned body. to say nothing of Nansen - well known crook.

Saluti -

Love to you & dad.

Why does Idaho couple me with Goozling Bogling??

The Academy of Political Science was set up by Columbia University in 1880 'to promote objective, scholarly analyses of political, social and economic issues'. Arthur Cecil **Pigou** *(1877–1956) was Professor of Political Economy at Cambridge University and an influential voice in British economic policy. The Norwegian Fridtjof* **Nansen** *(1861–1930), the most prominent bearer of that name in 1925, was well known as an explorer of the Arctic, as a scientist, as a statesman and diplomat, as an active proponent of the League of Nations, as a mobilizer of relief programmes for prisoners of war and famine victims,*

and as the first League of Nations High Commissioner for Refugees. He was awarded the
Nobel Prize for Peace in 1922.

+⇒—⇐+

710. ALS

[February 1925]

[Palermo]

Dear Mother:

Please sell or give away <u>all</u> the books <u>crossed</u> <u>off</u>. from this list[1]:

I no longer want most of them; & need none. & they are not worth transport; & I dont want to clutter up shelves. – even if. I had 'em.

The stuff accumulates <u>too</u> rapidly. . I have to dump & dump.

The books <u>left</u> on the list - can be packed & brought when you come.

I think Rapallo is about as good a port as one is likely to find.

Keep the manuscripts. & bring em when you come when I get some sort of
pied de terre.

E

+⇒—⇐+

711. ALS [*letterhead*] Hotel Pension Terminus, Roma

11 Feb. (1925)

[Rome]

Dear Mother

We have fetched up here for a week. I think the brown curtains across the
Piazza are the Pension Michel that we went to in the year two.

---

[1] The list in IWP's hand is headed 'E.P.'s Books in Trunk'. Among the books crossed off by EP are
several Grammars—Greek, Latin, French, Danish, German, Portugese, Spanish—and a Greek-English
Lexicon. Then there are old course books crossed of Galdos' *Doñas Perfectas*, Marcus Aurelius' *Thoughts*,
Cicero's *De Senectute*, *Extraits des Chroniqueurs Français*, *Specimens of Old French*, Ronsard's *Poésies*, *Poesia*
di Metastasio, *Le Rime di Petrarca*, Molière's *Comédies*, *Obras* de Camoës. Also crossed off are a number
of French novels – Dumas' *La Tulipe Noire*, *Les Trois Mousquetaires* and *Scènes de la Vie Parisienne*, Hugo's
Notre Dame de Paris, Mérimée's *Carmen*, Balzac's *Du Mariage*. Books in English crossed off include More's
Utopia, *Poems of Ossian*, *Winter's Wreath* by Mrs Hemans, Cowper's *The Task*, Sterne's *A Sentimental*
Journey, and Young's *Night Thoughts*.

Books marked 'Keep' are: Wilde's *Salomé*, Jean Beck's *La Musique des Troubadours*, *Poema del Cid*,
Kristian vom Troyes, *Die Lais der Marie de France*, *Aucassin und Nicolette*, Rodolphi Agricolae, Giosuè
Carducci and *The City of Dreadful Night*.

There is a question mark beside *Modern Woman* by F. Farr, also beside *Astrology* and 'Old Shakespeare'.

Also in the trunk were copies of *Book News* and *Forum*—EP asked for his contributions to these
to be cut out; and copies of *Personae*, *Exultations*, *Provença*, and 'San Trovaso MSS.'—EP marked these
'Keep—or send now to Rapallo'.

Anny how we struck a bad pension that had been recommended to us in Naples, & left; & a good place here where we had only intended to stay the night so we are here for a week & omit Pisa. // Cant remember where I left off Sicily. will send on a guidebook - it was two months work instead of six months repose. Went to Nisini's today & am taking bronze head of self (Nancy Cox's bronze founder) back to Rapallo

Have also collected some reading matter for next Rapallese months.

Looked in on the fish again in Napoli and collected D's passport.

My present intention is not to pass any frontiers until the abomination is ameliorated.

Passage to America is too high to encourage transit for brief tour.

Weather here in Rome seems quite good. & city from this angle of incidence seems habitable - which it did not two years ago from Piazza di Spagna quarter.

I suppose you cant give me any data of how you want to live in Rapallo - small cottage with place for dad to grow corn??

Amiable note from Tauchnitz - dont know that it will come to anything. - probably not -

Bill & Robt. combining in Paris to print & more or less publish.

Have done a little general reading for the Florentine canto. IF . that is to say . reading with an idea to their being Florentine cantos if the facts warrant or possible a canto - singular if they dont.

Cheerful letter from Strater; who is surviving N.Y. - as I haven't his $6000 a year free of work, I dont however see how I am to afford the Xperiment.

I have never said american life was impossible for an artist who held enough Tobacco stock.

I hope dad has recovered fully by now. esprit et corps.

Love to you both

E .

Bill Bird and Robert McAlmon co-operated in bringing out Contact Collection of Contemporary Writers *(1925). The facts warranted less than a full* '**Florentine canto**'—*just the part of canto XXI devoted to the Medici.*

+⊨=⫤+

712. ALS

15. Feb. [1925]

Rome | address H. Mignon | Rapallo.

Dear Dad:

The Eyetalian govt. is assisting in experiments with a new type of locomotive that saves a great deal of power. (runs on naptha, & then has totally new system of application.).

Do you want to sell it to Baldwins. you understand that as it <u>saves</u> coal it will take money out of coal interests pocket & that it will <u>not</u> be a simple matter to place it.

(study the two last cantos I sent you).

Question is whether Baldwin is coal-owned; or whether <u>they</u> could buck the coal interests in placing such an engine

all the patents. etc. are in order. If you have a preliminary talk with Baldwin – <u>all</u> you can say is 'Can you buck the coal interest, by a better type of non coal burning engine.'

Don't try to discus the mechanics of the thing.

Simply say the results of Ital. govt. tests will be forwarded <u>if</u> they wish. (tests taking place - will have taken place, I think by time you get this.

If you want printed matter in Italian, I can have that sent you.

Realize it is far more a question of finance than of mechanics. - but Baldwin may be just out of range - any how he sells engines out side the U.S. & may still be self-contained (i.e. not have to rent money.).

Remember he must buy through us (I mean don't tell <u>him</u> that - but keep it in mind.). this is not a charity bureau.

You can cable me at Rapallo if B. is interested. don't bother to cable unless the answer is affirmative

Yours

E

P.S. above all dont show any undue interest in the matter & don't try to persuade 'em. Either they want it or they don't.

It is a financial question - Depends whether the rail ways are pledged to give themselves money via coal - or whether they aint.

etc

That also to stay in your own mind

The less said in first interview the better.

Do they or do they <u>not</u> want the enginccring details.

I am acting for the engineer. The ital govt. is not concerned in sale to foreign countries.

*The **Baldwin** Locomotive Works in Philadelphia had already developed a non-coal burning Diesel-electric locomotive. When Homer Pound spoke to Mr DeKrafft the Treasurer of Baldwins, he was told 'they were doing something with oil, not Naptha', but would consult their expert and write to Ezra.*

+⇥⇤+

713. TLS

26 / 2 / 1925

Mignon | Rapallo

Dear Dad

Glad to hear from I.W.P. that you are again on deck and in full blarst.

Is this G. Carson the chap whose smelter I plunged on, in 1910??

If so send him my compliments, and say that I have backed a few winners in my time and am glad to hear his big peanut roaster has won out. He probably wont remember me. I saw the tall guy from I think Ohio, with the DDDEEEEEEP bass voice.

This Carson thing, IF is the same may, might make a good prelude if you try Baldwin on that locomotive. Say the smelter was the only other machine I ever took any interest in.

    more anong. Am bak here in Rap. not having had typewriter in Sicil. various arrears.

I see they are paying the Senators more.

yours

E.

always takes 10 – 15 years after

George Campbell **Carson**, *a wandering prospector known as 'Desert rat', invented a successful copper-smelting furnace.*

⊬⊏⊐⊬

714. TLS

27 Feb. [1925]

Hotel Mignon | Rapallo

Dear Dad:

Be'ohld S.E. <Muss> in the lions' den. Lend the cards to Nancy Cox, especially the "nice pussy". One of the cubs used to be in the vestibule or somewhere when she was doing the bust.

Did you ever get the dictatorial family in its bath <(sea bath)>; refer that also to Nancy.

The Herald says something about Civil Servants bill; but nothing definite. Also Calidge hadn't signed.

Lemme know DEEtails; you might even cable if it goes through.

ALSO say what it means. detail.

There are usually five cubs in that cage; dont know that they were there the day of the photo. One spends time jumping off that log onto whatever.

Am plugging through arrears of correspondence, not having had this machine in Sicily. One days tennis here, and rest of time wet, sort of young tornado last night. Not cold.

ETC, love to you and mother, and send news of bill.

E

At the beginning of March 1925, Ezra and Dorothy began renting the roof-top apartment of via Marsala 12—'int. 5' signifying 5th floor, a climb of 100 steps or more when the lift was not working. Dorothy described it in a letter to Isabel Pound: 'We've got two rooms to sit in, and a very large terrazza—all facing the sea and to ourselves—which will make still another during suitable weather—a bedroom facing to the mountains, another little one, which we use as dressing room, and then a kitchen and a bathroom.' She was wondering whether she would be able to have a little roof garden.

⊹⊱⊰⊹

715. TLS

address for letters
BUT CONTINUE TO SEND PACKETS TO HOTEL MIGNON

10 March 1925

Via Marsala 12 | int. 5. | Rapallo

Dear Dad:

Vast surprise yesterday when the elevator suddenly began to function. Having signed special clause in lease that we couldn't go to law if it didn't. And it having been out of whack when we inspected the building.

Cant make out from Paris N.Y. Herald etc. whether them there damn senators and that lemon faced president have passed your bill, or only given 'emselves more pay.

We have here a large flag pole, and could I suppose put a tent on the roof. Electric coffee in the a.m. gas not yet heating bath.

So far, it looks as if this were the most comfortable quarters we have had. Enclose another post card indicating exact locus. Back windows get all the view to that side, as building is higher than the old houses behind it. Card I sent saturday shows how we front on the bay, and the mediterranean ocean fer that matter.

Recd. Idaho matter; thanks. Also letter from Mrs T.

D. has just started for walk up to Monte Allegro with a sister in law of the McLeans (the other amurkn resident inhabitants of Rapallo)

Wotells? At any rate there is room for you to sit down if you arrive suddenly

I think it is about the best position in Rapallo; and very convenient, as we still feed at the Mignon, which we couldn't conveniently have done if we we[re] up the hill.

Tennis club also quite near.

Oh yes. The ?? Warenhauser story: Didn't he get permission to build a railway, and keep the trees, and then cut a belt of timber two miles wide?

You might send me particulars; what railway, etc. .

what Warenhauser (if it was Warenhauser?) and in fact any information thereabout that you have time and inclination to send.

Did I say that ole Chas Erskine Wood sent on regrets at not having been able to go to Phila. en route to Calif.??

Tell mother we duly went to Naples aquarium, 3 times or 4.

I enclose Byington's pussnl attention to other detail.

I note in mother's letter that Catherine Cochran as was is buyin' modern aht. Tell her to have a shot at the Wyndham's lewis things (i.e. the dozen good ones) in Quinn's collection if it comes up for sale; or to let me arrange for her to get some new ones straight from W.L.

They are the best value now in europe. Unless she wants to go in for sure things at really high prices: Rousseau, Picasso, etc.

Probably NOT known in U.S. that one can still get very fine Picasso etchings quite cheap, if one knows where. (Probably not at prices I paid for mine five years ago; but still)

Do you know any of the blokes connected with this new Guggenheim endowment? I see there is one at Swarthmore. Antheil ought to come within the scope of same.

ETC.

Love

E

The 'Warenhauser story' went into canto XXII. Homer's opinion, as he told Ezra, was that 'Weranhauser' was 'strictly honest', and 'as for cutting the trees two miles wide, its just as likely to be your grandfather as any one else'. Friedrich Weyerhaeuser (1834–1914) was born in Germany and emigrated to America in 1852. Homer wrote that in 1925 the Weyerhaeuser Lumber Co. 'is one of the largest in this Country and I understand controls and owns more timber than any other company'.

+⊨⇒═⊨+

716. TLS

Via Marsala 12, INT 5. | Rapallo
(an dont leave out the INT.)

18 Marzo. (1925)

Dear Dad and Mother:

Thanks for going to Baldwin. Will forward results of govt. tests when the govt. gets round to 'em.

You can live here on 100 seeds a month; and whatever you get from house wd. be velvet an xtras.

We pay 600 lire a month, and this place is supposed to be furnished. All the necessary things are here. We are buying guyser and a few ornaments. That is about 25 dollars per month.

YES I shd. like you to bring all the books on this list, save the french bible.

The edtr. of the Atlantic is a bloody idiot and an ignoramus to boot. He ought to be chucked into the swill pail, and all his family, race, cousins an connections. However, America as a hole is going collectively bug-house. Lets hope you escape before it sinks.

The springs for new arm chair have arrove. The weather has escaped at last from universal european blizzard. Etc.

Did you instruct O.S. to send on 'Bosis incident'. Poor Lauro; I didn't tell him to go to America, but I expect the visit will cure him and prevent its becoming a habit.

Hem's book is being pub, by Liveright.

George being very active. New Xilophony about to be done; and opera and ballet in construction. Etc.

yours

E

Re / Bosis: Has he kissed Calvin on both cheeks; or made love to Mrs Coolidge??

+⇥⇤+

717. TLS

25 March 1925

Via Marsala 12, int 5. | Rapallo

Dear Dad: 1.

Zarlatti is supposed to be coming up to Spezia for his tests, shortly, and to see me pussnly. Tests will evidently take some time. He is not worried about the electric oil engine, as he thinks his can beat it.

Mother's remarks re/ Baldwin wd. tend to show that it is self-contained, and 'aint had to rent anny money lately.'

2.

Maj. Unwin says he will take me up hill to the villa where he had a flat, comfortable, etc, and quite cheap. Place in sight of tennis court. Haven't yet decided which of several we see from out shore windows.

Wot ells. Have typed out most of seven cantos, taking it up to XXIII.

Bill Bird is making flying trip to U.S.; dont know if he will have time to see you. Only had word from him as he was sailing.

561

D. still actively reno-rummagifying; place getting into order. rain yesterday and today, and more coming up the harbour.

Nothing more to be done about Zarlatti for the present. You can even forget his name, conveniently, until I write again.

What ever else I had in mind to write, has escaped. Have had three weeks steady sun and tennis, up to yesterday.

Am reading young Bosis' translation of Sophocles, which is quite good, very clear and restrained.

Etc.

Love to you and mother

E

+══──═+

718. TLS

2 April [1925]

Via Marsala 12, int 5 | Rapallo

Dear Dad:

Law looks all right, (recd. the text of same) only trouble is the Kongerus who avent parsd it. Blarst their bhloody gizzards.

looks as if you bust loose the day it finally goes through.

HAVE YOU recd. Cantos, YET, and ef not, why not??

Liveright says Instigations is out er print; so hang onto whatever copy or copies you have. Dont lend except to people you can trust, or to whom there is some special reason. Liveright SAYS he will-try to find copy for Dr Aydelotte, if not, you may hear either from him, Moe, or me.

Any how they are to be lent copy if they need it.

ETC. weather brightening up.

Love to you and mother.

E

+══──═+

719. TLS

[April 1925]

Via Marsala 12 int 5 | Rapallo

Dear Dad:

I must have got the Weranhauser from an obituary article on him in some paper. He died a year or so ago????

His dealings with the govt. were purrfekly legal. The senate was fool enough to tell him he cd. have the trees, and not to specify how wide the road wuz to BEE.

I remember your once saying that he et up pore ole T.C.

That's how I came to notice the name when I saw it in the paper or magazine or whatever it was. Dont know what it was, most of these things come from you, sunday Times or clippings. If I kept it it is with my archives in Paris, and heaven knows when I shall see it again.

Food here not expensive. I suppose you can get a place for 25 bucks a month. We eat at the Mignon for about 8 or 9 a week, each; because we are too lazy to use the three kinds of range in the kitchen. But this is not a necessary expense. It is merely a rest.

morning coffee here, on electric kettle.

I dont know WHY the HELL you haven't got your copy of Cantos, unless Bill is taking it to America himself to save risk of loss in post.

Will write to Three mts. AT once.

I haven't yet got my second copy, supposed to be still at Binders. French books are issued unbound, everybody then binds his own, i.e. has it bound to suit his own taste, IF he wants it enough to bind it.

Thus there are no wholesale binders, as in Eng. and U.S., or rather very few, and the chaps that can do these de looks jobs are slow as coal tar, and used to finishing one copy at a time.

It works out better for public, i mean in distributing new writers. In Eng, and U.S. one pays 75 cents for ten cents worth of binding every time one buys a book. The ang-sax race is NOT very intelligent, and no one is going to tell 'em this, as it is cash for booblishers, and also helps on author's royalty (for what is worth)

now time to dine.

Love to you & mother

E

Compliment H. on cross word success

*The **cross word success** was Homer Foote's.*

╬══╬

720. TLS

29 April [1925]

via Marsala 12 int 5 [Rapallo]

Dear Dad:

Thanks l. it. 100 recd.

Hope bronzette has arrived o.k. there shd. be NO. charges save whatever the goddamd u.s. govt imposes. Lemme know wot they are and I will refund or protest or both.

The seccertary-an-typist of the 3 Mts. reports copy of CANTOS shipped to you. If you haven't recd. by the time you get this, respond and will start tracer.

If you get 2 copies put the second into cold storage until instructions arrive concerning its destiny.

Please send me six copies of the speshul Hailey Hawk or wotever its called.

ALSO TELL LIVERIGHT it is coming out. Tell him the name of the paper, and its address. or tell them to notify him. (dont say I said so.)

Weather here stormy, get tennis between showers.

Hope I have at last found a bookseller in Genova who will send on the stuff I want for work.

D. has ordered the complete H. James, so the place will be stocked with something in the way of reading matter.

I did not mention the bronzette as I wanted it to B a surprise, hope you have by now solved the enigma.

Mr Walsh threatens to send me his new Quarterly from Paris. Mr Hemingway writes from time to time. Mr Strater is in N.Y., I suppose painting WORSE, but he seems happy.

The Gd uff, dott. Pres of the R. Soc. Ven. has written in to know about provencal music; stirred thereto by Dazzi of Cesena. the bibliotecario of the Malatestiana.

There is some talk of a collected edtn of my pomes, i.e. all except the Cantos in one convenient vol. I dont know that anything will come of it; part of the stuff is still tied up by earlier contracts. et cetterer.

The governing class of germany does not wish the place to be a republic. I hope the argument wont extend to Rapallo, if it does I shall hope to retire to. . . . ???

I suppose Granada or Valencia.

Love to you and mother. Oh yes giv me regards to Jake.

yours

E

The Times-News-Miner *of* **Hailey**, *Idaho, was to feature Pound in May. Ernest* **Walsh** *and Ethel Moorhead were about to dedicate the first number of their magazine,* This Quarter, *to 'Ezra Pound, who by his creative work, his editorship of several magazines, his helpful friendship for young and unknown artists, his many and untiring efforts to win better appreciation of what is first-rate in art, comes first to our mind as meriting the gratitude of this generation'.*

⊣≡⊢

721. TLS [on 'Ezra Pound' letterhead]

[c.May 1925]

Rapallo | via Marsala, 12 int. 5

Yeas mong vieux;

I intended Cantos XIV and XV to give an accurate picture of the spiritual state of England in the years 1919 and following. Including Mr Wilson. They were written before the Harding Coolidge period, or I shd. have devoted a line or two to the mushiness of the former and the cant of the latter.

Coolidge writes better than Woodie, but the common-sense bluff or pose can be as bad almost as the mealymouthed blah. It is more efficient, a better implement. The silliness and triviality of the murkn mind. Woodie so conceited he didn't feel it necessary to know anything about Europe. Cal, ditto re economics.

The ang-sax race as a whole or hole, very insensitive to mental rot and decomposition. Eng. much worse than U.S.

England insensitive to mental decay. U.S. silly, incomparable shallowness and triviality.

Glad to see ole Elihu has balled 'em out. If his ole brother Square had been alive, recon Elihu wd. have been pushed onto it sooner.

If you can find any better or more efficient way of expressing the state of things, please notify yrs. tly.

re condition of copy recd. You can clean the pages with bread, and the parchment of cover with slightly moist sponge.

Bill was away from Paris when the copy was shipped.

Am not writing for the mentally infirm. Nor have I any interest in keeping up the consecrated humbugs of the ang. sax woild.

Canto XVII deals with a sort of paradiso terrestre. XVIII and XIX, I think you have. Geryon, fraude. You can look it up in yr. Dante . the minor hell of rascality.

XX lotophagoi; further sort of paradiso . or something in that direction.

then some narrative. Medici and Este.

This Quarter, a new magazine shd. reach you in time. There is some stuff abaht me by Mina, in CHARM a murkn monthly. and in Poetry for May. by Arriet.

love to you and mother

E

Elihu Root *had just published his* Men and Policies: Addresses *(1925). His brother, Oren Root, like their father, had been Professor of Mathematics at Hamilton College, where they were known in turn as 'Square Root'. Harriet Monroe's article in* **Poetry** *was headed simply 'Ezra Pound'.*

722. TLS [on 'Ezra Pound' letterhead]

6 June [1925]

Rapallo | via Marsala, 12 int. 5

Dear Dad:

You by now know or shd. know that the Bronze is a cast of a stone carving by Gaudier.

Nisini who cast it, is all right, evidently. I asked him to ship it, as I had very little time in Rome, especially after that which it took to make the casting. Nisini evidently took the bronze to a shipper who has soaked us, you, etc. 3 dollars ten cents.

When however you deduct charges for FORMS. The goddam govts. all use forms now, and that leads to bootlegging, etc. brobably six affidavits to be made out etc.

How much did the bloody robbers charge you on the Cantos.??

I am not going to refund that.

Straters address is 1 Lexington Ave. N. York

ONE Lexington Ave.

Saw Walsh in Bologna, also Carnivalli. Walsh ready to print Antheil's music in This Quarter, also bits of my uproar if the magazine continues.

Saw Linati and Ferrieri in Milan, pleasant evening, very warm in Milan, good trip, glad to get back here,

If you haven't recd, a copy of THIS QUARTER or cant find one on sale, lemme know and I will send one along to you.

Editor wrote me he HAD sent you one.

Love to you and mother.

E

723. TLS

10 June. [1925]

[Rapallo]

Dear mother:

Weather here rather pleasant, hot in mid day want wool in evening, various mason, carpenter, tentmaker, putting up large awning on roof and preparing to sling mosquito net in bed room.

D. did one rather good copy of background of XIV century picture in Cesena, Dazzi and Marchetti both apparently pleased to see us. Dazzi doing pleasant sort of verse. Linati has also done a more lively bit of work that his former, shall try to have it traduced for T.Quart.

At present I want photos. of machinery and spare parts. Wonder if you know where to get em FREE. I dont intend, and dont want anyone else to spend anything on said photos.; also they have got to be good composition AS photos as well as representing good shapes in machinery.

Beekly is dead other wise he might be turned onto U. S. Mint. Spose Jake is too old. Want photos with HARD edge, not muzzy, arty.

All credit to photographer and sourse of machine. Most photos of machines try to give too much, too many parts of machine, or all of it at once. NO use for present purpose.

Etc. love to you and dad.

E

*Pound would pursue his '**Machine Art**' project through the next two or three years. It was prepared at first as an article for* This Quarter, *but the magazine ceased publication upon the death of Ernest Walsh before it could appear there. In 1927 Pascal Covici of Chicago agreed to publish the book Pound had submitted, but changed his mind in 1928 after moving to New York and entering into a new partnership. 'Machines', an introductory note to a selection of 15 photographs, would appear in Samuel Putnam's* New Review *(Paris) in 1931. The surviving 'Machine Art' materials were published in* Ezra Pound's, Machine Art and Other Writings. The Lost Thought of the Italian Years. Essays *selected and edited, and with an introduction by Maria Luisa Ardizzone (Duke University Press, 1996).*

+≒═≒+

724. TLS [on 'Ezra Pound' letterhead]

[mid-June 1925]

Rapallo | via Marsala, 12 int. 5

Dear Dad:

If the asst. engraver is a decent chap and a friend of yours I suppose he can have a copy of the faun. I mean the next time I go to Rome whenever that is. It wd. cost him about ten dollars as I dont want to make money out of the affair and am willing to distribute the object to those who can appreciate it; though not to dealers and speculators.

The Hailey paper not here yet. I send you one from the Adriatic. Shall try not to be too hard on you, but also shall INSIST (for all the bhloomin good that is likely to do) that you do NOT ressurect any more of my juvenalia and distribute same to the press, even of recondite mountain villages.

Letter from O.S. states that the Hailey paper shows me as an inhabitant of the village as well as in present state of preservation.

You can forward the Testa di Ponte to Blackfoot collection if you like. Wonder if they run to a copy of the Cantos. They'll have a Tennesee trial if they do. Yaas, I wrote to Mrs Trego, but recon the epistle rather stumped her, as no reply has been forthcoming.

love to you and mother

E

*The **Blackfoot collection** was probably the Susie and Byrd Trego Collection now in the Library of Idaho State University, Pocatello—a local history collection formed while they owned the Blackfoot, Idaho, newspaper. From Pound's letter to Mrs Trego it appears that she had written an article about him in their paper. '**Tennessee trial**': a reference to the trial about to be staged in Dayton, Tennessee, in which John Scopes, a high school teacher, would be charged with illegally teaching the theory of evolution. William Jennings Bryan, the chief prosecutor, was leading a fundamentalist crusade to have Darwin banned from the nation's classrooms, and the State of Tennessee had made it unlawful 'to teach any theory that denies the story of divine creation as taught by the Bible and to teach instead that man was descended from a lower order of animals'.*

+⊱══⊰+

725. TLS [on 'Ezra Pound' letterhead]

20 Giugno [1925]

Rapallo | via Marsala, 12 int. 5

Goshdratangoldingitall;

Ef yew go an dig up enny more of my infantile perductions and print 'em. To say nothing of NOT even dating the damn things!!!!!!!

Una vez yo ti coja!!

Also you might correct a few other errors before they are sanctioned by time.

    1. I did not live Arnold Bennet in Paris or elsewhere; knew him very slightly and dined ONCE at his flat.

    Probably printers error or something.

    I stayed with Rummel in Paris

    2. Knew Hewlett in England not in Italy.

    3. Never attended the Dante lectures in Florence.

Thanks for the photos. Wot ells?

Six sets of tennis yesterday; that seems to be about the size of the nooz. Miro is having a show in Paris. Hem supposed to be going to Spain to likk bulls, having bust his hand in prize fight in Paris.

    L ile des Bardes, by Simone Tery arrived yesterday, all erbout Uncle Willyum Yeats, and James Jheezus Joyce, etc. Journalism seems much the same in Paris and Hailey.

    Wot ells? Bill Bird still in Denmark or somewhere, his assistants continue to muddle. First I get Ford's copy of Cantos, then I get one marked 'Printed for R. McAlmon, etc. So you can count yourself as fortunate in having recd. one at all. Various people haven't.

Various people have written books. Mr Antheil is not an artist and licherary critiKK. as you probably know. Some damn fool has just gone and given more money to the Sorbonne instead of to the right people; all this endowment of institooshuns of alledged learning and nothing to the people who make the stuff for the god dam profs. to learn.

D. having washed in gulf of Tigullo wants her lunch, also sends salutations. Had a waterspout here in the bay two days ago, jess like pixtures of 'em.

love to you & mother

E

Homer Pound had provided the Hailey Times-News-Miner *with 'The Mourn of Life', a piece of light verse written c.1906, and with 'Ambition', a truly 'infantile perduction'. In the long feature article entitled 'Hailey Sends Literary Genius out into the World of Letters' there were more inaccuracies than the ones noticed both here and in a good tempered letter to Cunningham of the* Times-News-Miner. *In the latter Pound wrote that 'None of these errors is of any consequence'; and he laid the blame for the publication of 'several undergraduate exuberances that I should have preferred not to see in print' upon H.L.P.*

726. TLS [on 'Ezra Pound' letterhead]

23 June [1925]

Rapallo | via Marsala, 12 int. 5

Dear Dad:

Various enclosures recd. Have sent a note to Cunningham telling him not to worry about the article, as you are to blame for his having printed stuff that oughtn't to be in it.

I dont think Walsh is likely to have copy of the photo. He certainly wont have more than the one used by the printer. Man Ray being a Hartist painter etc. that takes photos of people to pay his rent, not simply fer pleasure, Have seen the Charm article so you needn't bother to send it.

As Man has never got anything out of me fer takin the photo in the firs' place I dont imagine he will be dying to make free copies; an his prices are aimed at the ploots.

Hoepli (book shop) has just sent on a pile of historical stuff, don't know that any of it is much use. Wot ells?

Friend of D's has just met Esther Heacock in Svizzerland. McAmon has brought out a miscellany of depressing Contemporary writers, including yr. offspring. It is Called Contact. C.C.W.

Walsh is supposed to be goin to print some of Antheils music, in next number, sizeable wad not merely a sample page of mss.

Rain yesterday, five sets of tennis today.

love to you & mother.

E

Contact Collection of Contemporary Writers included Djuna Barnes, Bryher, Mary Butts, Norman Douglas, Havelock Ellis, F. M. Ford, Wallace Gould, Hemingway, Marsden Hartley, H. D., John Herrman, James Joyce, Mina Loy, Robert McAlmon, Ezra Pound, Dorothy Richardson, May Sinclair, Edith Sitwell, Gertrude Stein, W. C. Williams.

━━━

727. TLS [on 'Ezra Pound' letterhead]

[24 June 1925]

Rapallo | via Marsala, 12 int. 5

Dear Mother.

Re/ books, you can now send on the lot in a case if you want the room. I am in no hurry, but as we now have some sort of supposedly permanent locale there is no reason fer not sending them.

I dont mind the portrait being LOANED TO Will Wadsworth (young Will), so long as he is ready to send it to me on demand: i, e, if he wd. like it; only I dont want to give it away. Might in twenty years time have a place that needed a little ancestral adornment.

Crockery, no, apart from the few plates you did yourself. Much better cash in things of sort. Risk, of breakage, cost of shipping, etc . . . too great.

As to books. I sent you once a list of those worth sending me.

If you've lost it, I have also lost or burried the list of what there is. May be able to find it.

Love

E

━━━

728. TLS [on 'Ezra Pound' letterhead]

7 July [1925]

Rapallo | via Marsala, 12 int. 5

Dear Mother:

Fine triumph for Marcus Garvey, here on the Sawbath; fete and procession postponed from friday because of rain; many rockets, very handsome, and a procession, wif a fihn BIG BLACK Jheezus wif a big gol' sash in de front, and den a l'li skinny po'h sote of white Jheezus a follerin after, and then mama in all her best clothes.

Marcus he don' say dat Jheezus Chri'se wuz a black man, an now we know it.

British fleet leaking oil into the front yard, and increasing the amount of tennis. Fleet's parson an the episcopal admiral comin' back for more this p.m.

Believe T. Quarter is going to print a fairly large wad of George's music. Otherwise no headlines. Death of Eric Satie reported, but am not sure it mayn't be a hoax, as there is very little obit. matter and that only in two papers out of four I have seen from Paris.

love to you & dad

E

Rapallo's annual festival in honour of the Madonna of Montallegro, 1–3 July, culminates in a grand fireworks display. Olga Rudge gave birth to Pound's daughter, Maria Rudge, on 9 July at Bressanone-Brixen in the Alto Adige. Around the end of July, Pound was with her in Bressanone when they placed the baby with foster parents in nearby Gais.

+≻━━≺+

729. TLS [on 'Ezra Pound' letterhead]

11 July [1925]

Rapallo | via Marsala, 12 int. 5

Dear Dad:

Thanks for photo of Wissota Power House.

That's the sort of thing. good composition. Want ALSO photos of individual parts of magazines. Full credit to factory using them, or making them.

Enclose note from Corriere. Quotations not abs. accurate. But better than that god damn fool writing in Bookman. Thanks for sending it.

Dinner with the bhloomin admiral on Tuesday, very good meal, full battle-ship style, nawthin like it this side of the interstices of Oxford colleges.

The bloomin navy came out one set ahead on three days tennis. Light cruisers in today, with crack team aboard, so awaiting a complete smotheration later today. The local dagos beat em at water polo.

love to you & mother

E

+≻━━≺+

730. **TLS** [on 'Ezra Pound' letterhead]

8 Aug. [1925]

Rapallo | via Marsala, 12 int. 5

REEspected Progenitors:

The card of Medal Press magnificent. I note it is the Royle Mint. Why cant the Uncle Sam mint do something as good in the way of photos of its internul workings.

After all the issue of the mag. ought to regard mainly amurikun machinery. Wot else is there in the country save howlin luncay and . . .. .???

Get Jake to take the photos. give him new lease of life.

Dont think the other photos. you mention have yet arrived. the 'Medal press.' is a post card.

??? What was Baldwin electric supposed to send???

Cesena is near Rimini, near Ravenna.

No they do not speak english.

Most of yr. letter (I.W.P.) unintelligible as it evidently refers to effects of my demand for photos. of machinery, which have not yet been made visible here.

Love

E.

have been up to Milan, struggling with printers who I hope will print anthill's moozik.

+⊨==⊨+

731. **TLS**

11 Aug. [1925]

Rapallo | via Marsala, 12 int. 5

Dear Dad:

The Sellers photos are magnificent, and JUST what I want.

Give me particulars. Sellers are?? makers of machinery??

Who took the photos??

Is there any way of finding out what the individual photos are. I shall tell Walsh to use the whole 15.

If cant get separate lables, shall simply catalog them as 1 to 15. Sellers and Co. Spare parts.

But shd. like to know wot the bloomin leetle machine is.

The photos MUCH better than the Rile Mint, post card.

I want this number to be American Art.

Does I.W.P.'s question re Baldwin electric. mean that they are sending some photos.

This fifteen is RIGHT.

DEElighted.

Can we get anything equally good of some big out door machinery? For contrast.

Not harbour cranes WITH ROMANTIC CLOUDS IN THE BAK SIDE.

Also let me know the name of the chap who provided you with the photos. Want list of collaborators. Man who finds a lot of photos like this Sellers lot deserves just as big a lable as one who rehashes a last months magazine article under impression he is creating something. In fak a good deal larger one.

Baldwin wd. be good ground.

Ships more dangerous. But the engine room of same shd. provide something.?? Cramp?

Or cd. Althouse get something from big steamship lines. Are there any American lines? I hate to adv. a company that puts up with the XVIIIth amendment, and makes no fight against visas. But still . . .

Maybe we can stick to the soil. Pumps, drain pipes, something Mr Kipling hasnt enthused about.

Has Jake seen this lot. Can you start HIM doing bits of Mint. A govt. that will elect Wilson, Harding and Coolidge in succession dont deserve recognition, But then the govt. dont know the Mint has any insides so it dont matter.

These Sellers photos are EXACTLY right. It is the clear hard edge, emphasis on the FORM of the machine and parts that one wants.

The NOSE of the big dies, for example, excellent shape. photos, of detail of the coin press, especially at point where the force is concentrated.

NOT the damn detail of the <u>coin</u>, sentimental symbolism. Miss Murphy the belle of the bowery, Liberty before she was lost.

Love to you & mother

E

+≈≈+

732. TLS [on 'Ezra Pound' letterhead]

24 Aug. [1925]

Rapallo | via Marsala, 12 int. 5

My Dear Isabelle:

Have yew gawt your frien' Mrs Bok'z address? Dont know whether she ever recd. my brochure on Antheil; but she appears to be about to behave very well toward G. A.

Has her bloomin institewt developed to the point where it can supply me with a decent bass and a decent contralto (neither of whom admire ppPuccini) capable of singing the note indicated and holding it for the TIME indicated.

Also are they going to use my 'Harmony' as a text book, or can they get a prof. capable of understanding it OR disproving it. If the contains error I shd.

be very glad to know it; up to the present no one has been able to find any. La Societe Philotechnique has just made me an associe on the strength of it They've been going since 1795.

Have sent off T.Q.'s advance payment for printing of the Antheil supplement. We may give some sort of show in Milan this autumn. G. thinks he can get the opera done in Vienna.

Have already written to dad re/ photos. of Sellers machinery, excellent lot. want about 35 more, of same grade, but dif. subj. matter.

Love

E

*Mrs **Bok** was paying the expenses for the performance of Antheil's Ballet mécanique'.*
Pound was seeking singers for his own opera, Le Testament.

+>===<+

733. TLS [on 'Ezra Pound' letterhead]

[early September 1925]

Rapallo | via Marsala, 12 int. 5

Dear dad:

Perhaps you-d better forward the enclosed two pages to Wellman Seaver Morgan. Cleveland Ohio.

With whatever persuasive measures you can use. The 4 photos, besides having been rolled, are NOt as good as the Sellers. backgrounds too gray, will be even dimmer in reprod.

Also too much in each photo. gets out of sculpture into architecture. Wd. rather reserve the architectural side for later issue.

As I say in the letter. I cant pay for the photos no fund available, but I can send 'em the blocks after we have used them, if the blocks wd. be of use to them for later advertising. At least I see nothing to prevent this.

There is enough in this crane for a whole issue, IF they can get an intelligent photographer as Sellers did. Otherwise, keep on. Try a steam whistle or a farm tractor, or whateFFFFFer. Why cant you get the coining rpress?? Govt. secret?

E

Wellman Seaver Morgan were a major engineering company.

+>===<+

734. **TLS** [on 'Ezra Pound' letterhead]

12 Sept. 1925

Rapallo | via Marsala, 12 int. 5

Dear Dad:

I dont imagine that ole bunk vendor Willie Ellis will turn up here. Dont, however warn him off; if he does arrive he will get a jolt in the cerebrum (i.e. supposing he has any mental organism above the medulla)

Walsh has been here. also deelighted with Sellers photos. So you can tell C.S. that their appearance is assured, and I will try to put in any remarks that will give compensatory publicity to him and his company (not that the litterary woild is a very heavy buyer of hydraulic hoists or wotever they are.)

Dont worry about Harpers; dead bodies decay. Dont know about Sept. Poetry having anything <u>about</u> me, they are supposed to be printing my boost of pore ole Dunning.

You oughtnt to see Harpers, you ought to read books; better for the mind and nerves.

Cant pay your taxes for you. Its a hell of a country. However it takes several generations to learn that. Wot culture it HAD is drifting this way. F.F.V. on the other wing of the gulf of Tigullio even runs to corn and mint juleps.

95 dollar school tax, HELL, that fer havin the washerwoman's son taught the world was made in seven days , and then saved by a pigeon.

Looks like its about time fer you to turn bolshie. OR high Tory.

I will send you copy of This Quarter. Have already seen proofs of the Antheil musical supplement.

I hear Mrs Bok is going to give G.A. <u>some</u> boost during the comin' season. Ef yew see her give her my compliments on her sperited action.

((Tell [*name blotted out*] to put on my opry if she wants to do somethin reely useful (not that the booblik wd. like the opry . . . but then wot dew we care abaht the booblik.)

If you get the opry decently produced Ill give you royalty on the profits. (As Bill Bird sez, god ferbid that I shd. tell publishers how to make money.))

Liveright hopes to do a collected edtn. of my poems in one vol. i.e. every-thing up to Cantos. Dont talk YET as there may be several hitches. Have long wanted collected edtn.

Tell the QUILL bk. shp. to order T. Quarter, and both it and Centaur to PAY up to Walsh when they sell T.Q. if they want it to continue.

My article on murkn arht will be about 2 lines long. or maybe a complete silence. Let the photos dew the woik.

love to you and mother.

E .

The September **Poetry** *did print Pound's 'Mr Dunning's Poetry'.* **FFV**, *'First family of Virginia'; by extension, those who consider themselves the best society. A parental hand blotted out the reference to Mrs Bok—'am quite sure', Homer wrote, 'if I called her by the name you use that that would end all your chances'.*

---

735. **TLS** [on 'Ezra Pound' letterhead]

14 Sept. 1925

Rapallo | via Marsala, 12 int. 5

No, my dear Dad:

The last lines are not Keats, nor me, they are Dunning. That's why I wrote the bhloomin article; breaking my more or less vow that I'd be damned if I ever wrote another line of prose.

That's WHY I am trying to find some god damn publisher or editor with sense enough to print the rest of Dunning's mss.

If you like the quotation drop a line to Cheever at 70 bis rue N.D. des Champs. He is now 48 and has not had the hell of a lot of glory.

D's birthday today. 9 new plants fer the roof; funny lookin articles; not my province, herbage.

More hail day before yesterday than have ever seen all at once.

etc.

Love to you & mother

E

Pound had closed his article with these lines:

> Ease me of jealousies and hates that wait
> About my soul to spoil it unaware.
> Soothe me with sights of beauty and the great,
> And reconcile my smallness to despair.
> Heal me of hate, the curse of lonely kings—
> While yet a last chord as an echo rings,
> Let peace descend now ere the air be dumb,
> O music, while thy memory yet clings
> Whose power is more than wine or opium.

---

736. TLS [on 'Ezra Pound' letterhead]

1 Oct. 1925

Rapallo | via Marsala, 12 int. 5

Dear Dad:

Shd. be writing this to mother, but for little erand (as usual,) enclosed.

Fortnight of excursions. The Sayres motored me down most of the way to Florence, where I looked into archivio. Since when Miss Barney, and Mrs Brookes have stopped off here in one relay, and Nancy Cunard in another.

Mrs S. due on Thursday next, or rather she goes through and D. gets into same train, and they go to Perugia for fortnight while I go to Modena for a bit of a job. Stopping off in Milan.

Mrs. S, not having seen Perugia and Assisi. Went with D. to Chiavari yesterday to get her winter outfit. Now investigating thermisifoni eletrici, as means of staving off possible cold snaps in Jan N.

Walsh ill again, but expects to proceed to Milan and get his next number printed. The music supplement, said to be now in the post.

Ditto a couple of drawings by Wnd. Lewis; though I suppose he will probably keep em to make part of his problematical show, and send em when it is over.

McLean's struggling into house too far up hill.

Will you (re/ enclosure) next time you are in the vicinity of Keith's, get me two steel nose pieces, the kind with the hole in, and no cork or other funny biznis. ALSO GET copy of my prescriptions, which I seem to have lost somewhere between Paris and London. I know it pretty well by heart, but can never remember whether the axis for cylinder in left eye is 125 or 135 I think it is 125, but wd. rather be sure. If Keith hasn't a copy on his record, can you apply to Dr Pyle. sorry to bother.

Get mother a box of Ackers with the change, or floral tribute, as you prefer.

Florence a poor city, but tower decorated with little oil lights, for the 20 Settembre, very decorative.

Wot ells??

Liveright is publishing Hem's. book. ought to be out by now. Linati very active, has translated one story of Hem's, and done two more articles in Corriere, one on J.J. and one on Carnevalli. etceterer.

love to you & mother.

E

577

737. ACS

17 October 1925

[Venice]

> yrs recd . . . 17 Oct
> thanks for photos. etc
> waiting at Rapallo
> going back in a week –
> Venice in Oct – something new.
>
> love to you & mother
>
> E

+══+

738. TLS [on 'Ezra Pound' letterhead]

23 Oct.1925

Rapallo | via Marsala, 12 int. 5

Dear Dad:

Back to the keyboard. Venice rather different in Oct. Looked at Este, and the hills thurabats, dont think I shall shift to that side of Italy, though I like it very much, conveniences for habitation no so plentiful.

Recd. two lots of photos. They are dran good photos. esp. Brown pyrometer. But they dont touch the Sellers lot.

TOO much in em that is not forced by necessity.

The good forms are in the parts of the machine where the energy is concentrated. Practically NO machines show high grade formal composition; the minute they hitch different functions, or etc, or have parts NOT included in the concentration of the power, they get ugly, thoughtless,

might just as well be one shape as another.

Neither the pyro, nor the level, is an ENERGY condenser.

They are not really machines at all, only measurers.

WOT about the coin presses, are they govt. secret or zummat?

What I am gettin at is; MUST distinguish between machinery, motor parts, and mere stati[c] structure. The static structure in machines, really part of architecture and employs no extra principle. Governed purely by form and taste.

Its the mobile parts, and the parts REQUIRED to keem them in their orbits or loci. that I am interested in.

Wot about Cramps machines for making battle ships. NOT the ships.

Farm machinery not much good, any farm machine being usuall two hundred small machines of same sort hitched into one big one with no regard to appearance.

In any case the regard to appearance is merely dilletantism. The beauty comes from the efficiency at one point (vortex).

Have now four more canti on the way, (beyond the three that are supposed to be in press for T.Quart.)

Have grub up some material on last trip, and have a case of book comin from Venice. etc.

love to you & mother

E

D. & O.S. presumably in Siena. due back shortly – any photos of <u>detail</u> of big printing press. ??

---

739. TLS [on 'Ezra Pound' letterhead]

24 Oct. [1925]

Rapallo | via Marsala, 12 int. 5

Dear Mother:

Thanks for birthday frivolities recd. Also thank dad for prescription and glasses-nose pieces from Kieth.

Expect D. and OS. back from Siena today or tomorrow.

Have got new raccogliatore for notes, as Canti [X]XII to XXIII are about finished and need holder to themselves. Am going on to XXIV etc.

Proofs of the T. Quarter section recd.

Dunning in hospital again. Gaudier Embracers has got as far as Genoa; dont know whether I have to go for it, or whether it will be brought to door.

Books from Livrt. forwarded by mistake to Venice. Heaven knows when they'll get back. Need copy of pomes 1917 to make up collected edtn.: spose it will arrive in time.

Fine weather, and tennis yesterday but court still soggy. Ploughing thru mass of books collected on last trip. ETc.

fambly returned - after enjoyable Trip. am sending few scraps I collected in Venice.

E

---

740. TLS [on 'Ezra Pound' letterhead]

23 Nov. [1925]

Rapallo | via Marsala, 12 int. 5

Dear Dad:

Thanks for photo of press. I wasn't grousing about the LEVEL. BUT Sellers' photos are so MUCH better than any of the others.

I dont care a kuss what the press cost. CAN you persuade 'em to PHOTO the DETAILS of it.

A whole show like that in one photo. shows the ARCHITECTURE much more than the mechanics. NOT the least interested in the architecture (for the moment) want to distinguish clearly between machines and architecture. I.E. the very essence of the machine; the parts that move ;

the problems of static stuff are as old as Vitruvius. I mean questions of proportion, balance for the_eye (as in distinction for balance in mechanic).

This aint lack of gratitude to you or inquirer; merely I know what I want, and the clearer I make it by the photos, the less need for blah; and the more different from other collections of photos. of machinery, architecture, etc.

AND, among the DETAILS of machines, I want the PARTS THAT MOVE; also the sockets in which the moving parts move ; the points where the energy concentrates.

Ram that into Rogers or whoever else is still on the INQ.

(they can get a cheap and easy sunday page, out of T.Q. later. . . .

I dont want em to start BEFORE.

Etc. am reading H.J.'s prefaces, and his later novels. A wise ole bird; too bad I didn't know as much before he died as I now know.

love to you & mother

E

Homer had sent photos of the printing press used by the Philadelphia Inquirer, 'the largest press of its kind in the world' and known as 'the Wood Press'.

+‡===‡+

741. TLS [on 'Ezra Pound' letterhead]

24 Nov. [1925]

Rapallo | via Marsala, 12 int. 5

Dear Mother:

Enc. D. on terazza (together with the foot of the fambly).

No, have not seen the Spring Little Review 'view (machine number); send it on, s.v.p. if you have a copy (not on sale here).

NOW about possessions. I distinctly want the portrait of g.g. Wadsworth. I dont care about the Howe portrait, though Uncle Ezra is amusing; and I shouldnt chuck mother Howe on the ash heep. I don't imagine Ford will pay a high price for anything. except possibly the clock (to which he is welcome)

Hannah's embroidery is a pleasant souvenir; not to be sold cheap.

THE ARMS I DISTINCTLY WANT. Let Henry have a photo of 'em with note that they belong to us, and that reference to same will be found in

Longfellow's tales of Wayside inn. (you can look up passage, I dont travel with the text).

In fact <I suggest> the cleverest approach to H. F. wd. be to have the arms photod. and send him a print. (small one, let him pay if wants enlargement, but let him suggest it. Send the quotation from the Tales of W. S. Inn. and the photo. saying simply it might interest him to see what the decor. was in Long-feller's day. But dont sell. NOT fer any price less than 20.000 bucks which he wont pay.

His acquaintance might be made profitable, though I doubt it. But can do no harm to acquaint him with something that is NOT for sale, and to do this before you offer him other trinkets. Say nothing about sale in opening epistle. (others will have done so.

The clock he might buy for a slightly higher price than some antique dealer. . . . I dont believe he wd. be a particularly good market for anything else. Though there is possible chance on grandma Howe if you can prove she is daughter of the 'host'. I imagine she was grand daughter;

Anyhow, clock is too cumbersome to ship. Not so the portraits and arms.

Have you, or are you likely to find the lists of books that you sent, and that I returned to you, with the items I want marked,

NO HURRY ABOUT THIS, so far z I'm concerned.

Value the Page portrait of grandmother W. at 25,000 bucks.

There is NO point in selling it unless it brings enough for dad to retire on. ABSOLOOTLY NONE. at that point I shdnt. object. but anything less than that seems to me futile. Besides the thing has its definite value. I dont know the trade price for Page at the moment, but he was certainly a damn good painter, the best of his time in America. and quite as good as a lot of so called master-pieces in the european galleries. Dont undervalue it, and dont sell without consulting me. That and the arms, I definitely want.

and strongly object to sale of them, unless it means something solid, i.e. chance for dad to quit work.

No sign of the P. Monroes. I fergit just who P.M. is. Grandson of HIRAM or wot't'ell??

Love

E

*Great-grandmother Wadsworth was Mary Wadsworth (b. 1808) who married Hiram Parker. This **Henry Ford** was the current proprietor of the Wayside Inn. Pound had previously referred to the How **coat of arms** in letters 187 and 362. William **Page** (1811–85) was 'known for his sedate portraits' (Encyclopaedia Britannica).*

+≡=≡+

742. TLS [on 'Ezra Pound' letterhead]

26 Nov. 1925

Rapallo | via Marsala, 12 int. 5

Dear Dad:

Snappy thanksgiving. I spose the enc. is worth about one hindfoot of a murkn Turkey at present rates. Get a new necktie fer yerself and half pound of Ackers for mother. and save a lot of international banking.

Nooz? Eliot reported at La Turbie, just above Monte Carlo; dunno if he'll get as far as this. Wot ells? Jawg making feverish and contradictory plans for spending Mrs B's money giving concerts everywhere from Tokyo to the North Pole.

Walsh trying to get a eyetalian printer to deliver magazine ON TIME. (wot an idea. An Italian might, but a PRINTER!!!!!!

etc.

Crisp cold bracing weather. And the new electric heater somewhere between here an the factory.

Thanks fer nooz that Pocatello is forestalling the fundamentalist movement.

love to you and mother

Ezra

743. TLS [on 'Ezra Pound' letterhead]

28 Nov. 1925 & 2 Dec.

Rapallo | via Marsala, 12 int. 5

Dear Dad:

Thanks for ancient mss. recd. Glad the Venetian leather comes in handy. Middle size one is for I.W.P. as per lable enclosed in it. If the customs criminals haven't removed same.

I (re/ poems you mention in yrs. Nov. 13th) can't remember anything of 'Man' but four lines, and dont think I <can> reprint 'god' as a rhyme for 'board' at this stage of the game. howeffer noble the sentiments may be.

I haven't a copy of the Whistler poem here. If you choose to copy it out and send it me, I will reconsider it. I had some reason for rejecting it from Lustra; but don't quite remember what. Its just possible that it might fit the present collection.

The things I'm throwing out are the 'soft' stuff, and the metrical exercises. At least what I once bluffed myself into believing were something more than exercises but which no longer convince me that I had anything to say when I wrote 'em; or anything but a general feeling that it wuz time I wrote a pome.

'mass of dolts' is too mild. Even the Chicago edtn. of the Tribune is pointing out that the contemporary an contemptible am. cit. has bitched most of the fundamentals on which the country was founded, and used to be respected. 'Trial by jury' gone, etc. on acc. that terbaccer chewin son of syphilitic bitch Mr Volstead.

As for knocking Europe back into 18th. century frontier regulations; that started with Wilson (both he and Harding ought to have been jailed, for different reasons)

Coolidge ought to travel a bit, so as to learn a few things not known at Pike's corners. Cal isn't a crook so far as I know. The hole country giving thanks for that small favour.

Oh well. I still hope that no democrat will ever sit in the Whitehouse.

But I wish they'd make Tom Jefferson's works compulsory in the schools.

An git a Mitchell in the state dept. to clean em up.

The second number of T, Quart. is still bein' printed. The photos. are for NO, 3.

Mrs S. gone back to Lunnon.

Very hard to get a just formula: BUT if the res publica means anything at all it ought to mean 'The Public convenience'.

that is what Jefferson and Co, tried to make it mean. And no nation has ever so betrayed itself (save possibly in a complete collapse under invasion) in so short a time as America during the past ten years.

A law that has to enforces itself by illegal means is an abomination.

The anonymous tyranny of anonymous non entities working by paper forms, has NONE of the advantages of individual tyranny, and I imagine it has ALL of its evils. (though I may exaggerate in this latter).

You might send me sample copies of several 'serious' american weeklies, telling me by letter what gangs the represent.

I believe the New Republic stinks of something, but forget what. Is there ANY republican weekly? Woterbaht the 'Hamilton, jefferson, assn.' that one heard a little of and then didn't.

The nation, I meen the peepul are what? 60% solid bone, 15% criminal, and 5% cranks. The five percent run the show for the profit of the 15%

or do I exaggerate. are there 19 just men in the gomorrah. (not includin wille ellis.)

When I say 'weeklies' I mean unillustrated papers printing articles alledged to be critical, or to deal with ideas.

<u>etc</u>

broke in verse about here.

love to you & mother.

E

Homer had urged Pound to include in his collected poems the verse at the end of A Lume Spento, *of which the first quatrain runs, 'For* **man** *is a skinfull of wine / But his soul is* *a hole full of God / And the song of all time blows thru him / As wind thru a knot-holed board.' Neither that poem, nor 'To* **Whistler** *American', were included in* Personae *(1926). The phrase* '**mass of dolts**' *is from the latter poem. The* **Volstead** *Act of 1920 had reinforced Prohibition.*

⊹═══⊱

744. TLS [on 'Ezra Pound' letterhead]

24 Dec. [1925]

Rapallo | via Marsala, 12 int. 5

Merry Xmas, and so forth.

Dear Dad:

Next time you hear Roland Hayes, you go roun' back an speak to the boy. Tell him I told you to, and take him my greetings. Ask him about songs of the Hebrides.

The photos. of the level are A.1. as photos. but the level isn't strictly a machine. That's all. I am going to use the photos.

Ought to have sent Xmas greetings to the Feet. Dont quite know what the fambly consists of.

I keep tellin you that the machine photos, aren't in No. 2 of T. Quarter, but for No. 3. however, I spose they'll get along in TIME.

Mrs McCormac is in Spain doing Primo de Rivera (while he lasts).

The bronze of me aint a work of art, its a cast. Value depends on how long I've been dead and how many sentimental nincompoops have written eronious statements concerning my sufferings, and the nobility of my character.

D. is in Cairo, when last heard from she had been there '24 hours without a flee' but didn't expect it to last.

Eliot has just been here for four days. has at last escaped from Lloyds' Bank and is more alive than might have been expected, from the circumstances or from the damn magazine he edits.

Have probably said more in my letter to you than I shall in T. Q. re/ the photos. taint my job.

Send me a list of the Feet. with ages and addresses.

Have had enough cold weather to make trip to Switzerland unnecessary;

tennis court, at least one of the courts in shape again today. Chap named Severi, plays decent game, here to do portrait of old Hauptmann (Gerhardt). Took Possum Eliot to tea with Beerbohm yesterday. etc. Mr Chamberlain at the Casino, and Max hoping Lloyd George will not defile our immediate shores.

Have recd. elegantly engraved Xmas cards from the Garbage Man (Lo Spazzino del Caro): augura buone feste e Buon anno. F. M. Ford and others. Hem. supposed to be breakin his neck in the Ausstrian mts.

love to you and mother

EP

Alongside 'D. is in Cairo' Isabel Pound noted, 'Sailed from Genoa Thursday Dec. 17 arrived in Cairo Monday Dec 21'. (In fact Dorothy had sailed on the 'Esperia' from Genoa on 10 December and had arrived in Cairo on 14 December.) T. S. Eliot had left Lloyds Bank to join Faber & Gwyer, publishers.

+≈+≈+

745. TLS [on 'Ezra Pound' letterhead]

11 Jan. [1926]

Rapallo | via Marsala, 12 int. 5

Dear Mother:

Thanks for enc. list of books. The ornage leather Spanish books arrived O.K. thanks. Re/list. I have marked AT THE FRONT those that I shd. be glad to receive here any time you like to send 'em. and at the hind end, those that I don't want thrown away i.e. send 'em when you bust up house keeping.

If you are going to send a box SOON, send it now, so that it will arrive before I go up to Paris in the sprung.

Various things I miss from the list???

Newell's old french romances,

Whistler's 'Gentle Art' among others.

Farnell's Troubadours, probably in London.

However, after so long a space of time . . .. . .

Am working on concert version of about half my Villon. in case we manage to do it in Paris; Tinayre ready to sing four short chunks and one very long chunk. now looking for a deep sea BASS; preferably old Radford.

About this book list; looks to me like list of books in parlour book case, rather than my own lot.

seem to be vurry few furrin books in it. However . . . not a matter fer blood an tears.

D. seems to be enjoying pyramids.

Walsh about off his head with delays of Milan shipment of T.Q. reported finished.

Think I reported Fitzgerald's brief visit. etc.

Bacon has sent on a lot of photos. of hoists. etc. to supplement dad's lot.

One tennis court fruz, so that sun makes it soft. Weather however very good.

Love to you and dad

E

+≈+≈+

746. TLS

17 Jan. Sunday [1926]

Via Marsala 12/5 Rapallo

Dear Dad:

Sorry to hear of mother's accidents, though you dont say what . .

No, not much trouble about heat, new arrangement of oil (patent oil) in thing like hot water radiator heated by electricity. sometimes burns out fuse . . . but warms, except on phenomenal days. ten inches ice reported from Venice, and half metre of snow from Milan. Things, as the cook shop says 'never before seen in this world.'

Sun this a.m. and occasional warm days between the cold.

D. seems to be enjoying Cairo and pyramids, she had chosen a good winter for the south.

I have about polished off the concert version of various chunks of the opry, that I hope to give (i.e. concert) sometime toward summer.

T.Q. at last out.

Sent you little tune for Homer's fiddle yesterday or friday.

Cant remember whether I wrote to you or to D. re/ Fitzgerald.

Best story is the apochryphal one of Fitz. at Bucknm palace.

Mary: And what did you do in the gt. war?

Fitz: Time.

As matter of fact wot happened wuz:

The ever tactful George: Were you in the army?

Fitz (not going to be high-hatted). Not in the British army.

That reprod. you saw: of the four gT, minds??? possibly reprod of a reprod??? ole J. Q. somewhere in the pixture???

Send my regards to the Coomans, where be they an wot be they adoin'??

Cant believe much in Waldo Frank. believe his brother is edtr.?? ne c'est pas.

Dont worry about my buyin bank stock. Just as well to know where a bank is.

White pigeon gone; evidently lost from one flock goin south, and took up with another. Habits do not fit these birds for domestic use. I enclose somethin for the meat bill. wot 'ells? I think your name is on T. Quart. list, and that paper may arrive in time. Post very slow over holidays.

Suppose I shall settle in for another go at literchure, after month of musical swat.

Have at last bought a metronome, possibly the most gawdamdest instrument of irritation ever invented by man but highly instructive.

Love to you an mother

E

recd. G. & S. note book very neat & handy. Thanks.

Homer Pound had been sent by the Coomans a photo cut from a New York paper, Town and Country, *showing F. M. Ford, Joyce, and Pound—the original, taken in Paris, had included John Quinn. Homer had recommended that Pound read an article by **Waldo Frank** in* Harper's.

+≻═≺+

747. TLS [on 'Ezra Pound' letterhead]

2 Feb. [1926]

Rapallo | via Marsala, 12 int. 5

Dear Mother:

Recd. (for D.P.) one oriental drapery, containing also one enamel broach or pin. Drapery emitting THE most enormous and foul stench of mice ever known to man, has been hung on terazza. Hope it will have disinfected itself by the time D. gets back from Cairo.

Enclose Paris Tribune on T.Q.; also panorama. Rapallo, San Michaele Pagana, Mta. Marcherita, Porto Fino. pin hole indicating our approx. location. Church in fore, is St.Ambrogio, about a mile up hill to the east. Monte Allegro wd. be off to the rt. hand corner of the card.

Have been hammering out concert version of about half the opry. Now more or less in shape. Old Radford can't officiate, helas, as he is on for Haendel feste, in Narth of Hengland. Gotter look fer another bass fish. Send on yer Otter Cans. Wot ells. Louvre has kindly consented to accept J. Q.'s gift of Seurat's Circus.

Bill Wm's new book. In American Grain recd. better have a look at it.

Dad's letter re/ Feet. Recd.

love to you and dad.
wet sirocco, but not bad.
E

+≻═≺+

748. TLS [on 'Ezra Pound' letterhead]

2 March 1926

Rapallo | via Marsala, 12 int. 5

Dear Mother:

Sorry to hear from Dad that you have had a fall of some sort, and also hurt your hand, (H. not very specific as to how, when etc.)

I enc. a few kodak shots. Have just got back from week in Pisa, Livourno etc. D. returned yesterday, has had about enough Egypt, interesting place, but not very habitable. I believe she sent you a packet from Cairo which shd. arrive in due time.

Have had ceiling painted, and am starting reform of the flat. I.E. eliminating the furniture we get throwD in wif de rent.

Sent on proofs of two Villon songs, about ten days ago.

Komroff, Liv's boss printer or zummat, says the proofs of new edtn. are on the way.

Rodker has a new book out, in french as he hasn't a brit. publisher. This time the job is well done.

Hope you are feeling O.K. again. Tell Dad. His eyetalian citharistria or she-flutist can play that chune I sent Homer for the fiddle. It shd. go very well on a flute (though in principle one should NOT write flute music for the fiddle.)

As to the time. That 5/8 has taken about fourteen years to discover. i.e. neither Walter, nor Agnes, nor even young Jarge, had managed, for one reason or another to find out that most of my rhythms do not fit bars of two, three or four EVEN or equal notes; or rather they had ALL found out that, but none of em hit the simple division of two longs and a short (or the various equivalents)

You will see the two Villon songs split into all sorts of bars; but the lot I have just fixed up for the June show has been, tentatively at least, laid out largely in 5/8.

So thaa's thaat.

Etc.

Love to you and dad.

E

The 'proofs of two Villon songs' were for Two Songs from Ezra Pound's Opera Le Testament. Paroles de Villon. 1. Ythier's Song: Mort J'appelle. 2. Le Galant: Je renye amours, *engraved in Paris in preparation for the July concert. The other 'proofs for new edition' were for* Personae (1926).

+≻—≺+

749. TLS [on 'Ezra Pound' letterhead]

3 March 1926

Rapallo | via Marsala, 12 int. 5

Dear dad:

This is how Pisa looks from top of tower, or rather the country going north, as the Tower and Duomo etc. are just on the edge, as you may remember.

I remember I got a lire back from Brownell for not going into Campo Santo. Just as well, I wanted the lire then; and I shouldn't have recognized the Mino da Fiesole 'Isotta'.

588

D. back, somewhat worn by trip; or at least dessicated with Egypt, and disliking sea travel.

We have started making this flat more habitable, chiefly attempting to eliminate or conceal the 'furnished' element. . .

Answered most of yr. letter in my letter to Isabel yesterday or day before.

It'z only people who DONT sing and play the fiddle who have to stop and think about music. No man with a LLLovely tenor voice ever composed anything. (Joyce, might look like a Xception, but he has let his voice go to hell, and taken to litterchure. Poor devil, having very bad time with his eyes.

'Josephine' as I said to I. W. P. can try that air on her flute.

Re/ teeth. O. S. is going into nursing home for ten days, re/ hers.

Re/ eyetalians, wot became of 'Virgeen'? is she running for female alderman on the demmy ticket in the 17th. ward??

Really [--- ---] america; the more bunk I read about the [--- --- ---] you people elect in that forsaken country.[2] Ellis Island, Volstead, thieving pie faced prohibitionists, etc . . . .

itz enoufh to make a cat. . . . . (let us say: spew.)

Thank heaven Burbank has come out for a little honesty.

I hope your retirement bill goes through now, and at last.

Re/ Two Worlds, I never have the addresses of these bloody papers. But whenever you see that ad. I wish you wd. send a p.c. to the editor of the paper printing the ad. calling him a liar or words to that effect.

Funny T. and Kownty, cutting Quinn out of that Photo. while running article on his show in same issue.

Weather fine here, tennis going again. The Riviera show, must have been entertaining, and that there she-jew Suzanne, having won, now dying of scare.

I see some Swiss firm of N.Y. chewelers are offering to put a wrist watch on the statchew of liberty

Rot. They ought to take down that statue.

It represents a NASTY unamerican french idea, imported from Paris with the express aim of corrupting the descendents of the Salem witch burners; fundamentalists, tennessee anti-Darwinian apes, and the remainder of the GREAT majority of the PLAIN (yes, undoubtedly plain) 100 purcent murkns.

(Parenthesis: have recently read some selections from the Talmud. Never disliked jews before; but as it now seems that they were responsible for Christianity, I dare say they deserve all the kicks they get.

I wonder if there is a decent English translation of Confucius. I have a good french trans. and have just bought a goodish little book on C. in Italian. Think you might find the character sympathetic.

---

[2] Several words in this sentence heavily crossed out, probably by parental hand.

Bhudism bunk, and all monotheistic religions ROTTEN, damned, and nasty. Jew, Xtian, and Mohemedan. all fanatic, and all based on liars. The greeks at least had a sense of form.

Pore ole J.C. Trying to but up Jew-ism. & now gettin blamed for the same old thing in possibly worse form.

ETC.

love to you and mother

E

Josephine Tropea, 'an Italian girl', Homer had written, 'now a fine young lady and clerk in a Candy shop', who remembered 'that you gave her some medals down at the Mission'. Luther Burbank (1849–1926) followed Darwin's lead in investigating natural selection in plants and had become a famed plant breeder and naturalist. In January 1926, in an article entitled 'Why I am an Infidel', he had declared himself a believer in the revelations of science and was being attacked as anti-religious. **Two Worlds**, *edited and published by Samuel Roth, carried Pound's name as a contributor on its masthead, without his permission. Roth would become notorious for pirating Joyce's* Ulysses *in his next magazine,* Two Worlds Monthly. *Suzanne Lenglen (1899–1938), who dominated women's tennis in her time, turned professional in 1926.*

---

750. Western Union Cablegram

RAPALLO 23 | MAR 4 1926

To H L Pound / U S Mint Philadelphia Stati Uniti America
ISSUE INJUNCTION IMMEDIATELY PREVENTING TWO WORLDS PRINTING ANYTHING OVER MY NAME

EZRA

Homer Pound took advice from a lawyer and wrote back the same day:

Sorry I cannot carry out your instructions—with the facts—as I have none to swear by . . . . I could not make an affidavit that the 'Two Worlds' were about to publish something that would be injurious *to you. . . . If they should print anything that would be of* injury *to you, you could bring suit to recover damages.*

---

751. TLS [on 'Ezra Pound' letterhead]

4 March [1926]

Rapallo | via Marsala, 12 int. 5

Satire, my dear Homer; SATIRE!!! Wotcher mean by satire?!?

Those are just the simple facts (cantos 18, 19) wot have taken me a number of years to collect.

And all of 'em by word of mouth or from the original actors. Carrranza, Massarich, Griffiths, the edtr. of the Times, the owner of Vicars.

Just the simple facts, [-----------] and [----------]³ or his pug dog Mr Louse do NOT tell the trusting public.

Baymont is Lamont of Morgans. Benkensdorf, Griffeths Mensdorf, & unknowns, but perfectly real people; the ones that happened to be THERE.

Dont talk to me about satire. This is how it is. What you read in the papers is what you are supposed to believe. Only trouble is that the FACTS are so damn hard to get at.

You understand the NAMES dont matter; what I am trying to give is the STATE of rascality and wangle. <not the "news">

I cabled you this a.m. to issue injunction against that son of a jew bitch Roth. And hope you have done so. I'll boil his damn liver in vinegar if I ever get with in boot shot of him.

Price tells me he is hard to get at as he (Roth) merely has desk room at the given address and only shows up there to get his mail.

I will of course refund on the injunction. I dont imagine it will come to over 25 bucks. I note the scoundrel has not signed his threat, but merely typed TWO WORLDS in place of signature.

The reason for McAlmon etc, is that the U.S. has passed thru a period of maximum infamy, and the sooner people get used to printing facts instead of lies, the sooner the air will be cleared.

Hope mother is better and that your retirement is going thru. Jake ought to be given chloriform; then taken out and preserved. I dont wish him harm, but he is a bad example; I shd. cloriform him painlessly, and then let him wake up in some pleasant place, where there wuz no choo choo car to take him away.

As I wrote you, the shawl arrived, also enamel pin. The shawl has been on the terazza for two weeks and still STINKS, oh STINKS.

Re Mac. very different from the Sherwood Anderson, and all the other people mixing sex and saccherine. Kill off all the rest of of if you like, and if you want to restrict the output,

The others put in what they think will sell. Mac puts it down as he sees it. Very different form of activity. Chunk of Mac in NO, 2, T.Q. not his best.

I dont know why you shd. be bothered about these matters, you haven't the leisure to do anything about it, and s'far as I know, you are in no position to carry on campaigns of enlightenment. At your time of life, you ought to have a bit of leisure to enjoy yourself. I hope those bastards will pass th retirement bill.

I dont know that there IS anything to be done. J.C. undoubtedly had a great "influence", but after 2000 years, we see that he tried to kill judaism, and that

---

³ Several words blanked out by parents.

the racial force was too strong, they changed the lable, and all the worst features cropped up again: hence your fundamentalists, emigration commissioners, heresy and blasphemy tirals; muddle of private and public affairs, etc.

If you took out all the american legislators and officials and shot 'em; they'd only have another set the week after; just as damned imbecile. Hence ones disbelief in violence.

Here I am waisting time, when I ought to be writing something for my 17 faithful readers.

> love to you and mother, and hope she is in shape again
>
> E

Cantos 17, 18 and 19 had appeared in This Quarter, *and Homer had commented, 'I readily see that the 18ᵗʰ is a satire on our times'. The names which 'don't matter' relate to canto 19: Venustiano* **Carranza** *(1859–1920) was a leader of the 1913–15 Mexican Revolution;* **Massarich** *is Tómaš Masaryk (1850–1937), philosopher-statesman and first president of the Czech-Slovak republic—referred to as 'the old kindly professor' in the canto; Arthur* **Griffith**—*referred to as 'the stubby little man'—was a Sinn Fein leader; the editor of the* **Times** *at the time in question was Henry Wickham Steed; the owner of* **Vickers** *the armaments manufacturers was Sir Basil Zaharoff (1849?–1933), referred to in canto 18 as 'Zenos Metevsky'; Thomas* **Lamont** *(1870–1948) was a junior partner in J. P. Morgan & Co.; Count Albert von* **Mensdorf**-*Pouilly-Dietrichstein (1861–1945), referred to in canto 19 as 'Wurmsdorf', had been Austro-Hungarian ambassador in London, 1904–14. '***Mac***' is Robert McAlmon.*

+=—=+

752. TLS [on 'Ezra Pound' letterhead]

13 March 1926

Rapallo | via Marsala, 12 int. 5

Dear Mother

Don't you worry about my spring. Nine sets of tennis yesterday, and still upright this a.m.

Past fortnight largely occupied in making interior more habitable; building framework inside the place to occult the furniture also various other devices; gold ceiling in salotto;

ancient table needing acres of sandpaper, and then two tons of molten lava to fill the worm holes; etc. have built a walnut book case; and distended a gross ream of tapestry.

Mr. McAlmon's style is fortunately better than that of ole Havelock; and steadily improving; in fact he is almost my one remaining comfort in the woild of letters.

Wm. James gt. asset was being his father's son and Henry's brother; but he probably died ignorant of both these advantages.

Opry? chances of production?? When? Opry's git produced in time. Its chance of gettin produced sometime is almost a dead cert. Successful composers usually wait from ten to forty years. Unknown composers, indefinitely. Even Debusy and D'Annunzio working acc. plan, waited about ten years to get on San Sebastian. Glad I saw it in 1910. Hasn't been much chance since then. Tho it has just been done again in Milan. However, that isn't a real opry; just a play with fine chunks of musical interlude.

The word anaGOGical is explained somewhere or other. The Greek word originally means 'leading up to'; I shd. think you might take it as meaning: leading up to a sense of things in general.

But as I haven't looked at that passage in Dante's prose for some time; wont swear that he uses it in this exact sense. However it is in the Commedia, a third strata of meaning. The literal, i.e. Dant havin vision, or going through hell etc; the allegory, states of mind depicted, the anagogy: the general significance.

Thanks for ole Skidmore's letter; am sending him a line, and a p,c,

Present my compliments to the ex-Whiteside; with 'auguri'.

Just looked at the clipping re/ Stavinsky. 'Most Russian of the works' etc. Strav. being a pole. However. . . . . .

Do you think I had beeter sign my moozik 'Poundowsky' or 'Poundievski'. I haff no obschehiun zo lonk ass tey tond vandt me to shanche de notes.

Wd probably speed up the production, several years.

Stowkowski has read my book on Antheil; reported much discouraged by it.

These wise guys that are out for eliminating melody have got a nice leetle job cut out for themselves. Wonder what they REALLY told that jack-ass reporter they were tryin' to do.

Am still lookin for a basso with a bass voice. Old Radford is took for the Haendelfest in June. I don't want a camouflaged barrytone.

If you happen to meet any of the nobs, tell 'em to send a couple of spies an secret service men to the June concert.

Have corrected first proofs of collected edtn. Hope the post delivers 'em to Liv

love to you and dad

E

Isabel Pound had written: 'I find T. Q. depressing and your Cantos bewildering——In Spirit of Romance p.115 is **anagogical**. *I have yet to find the meaning of the word.'* **Stravinsky** *was of course Russian.*

+⊱━⊰+

753. TLS [on 'Ezra Pound' letterhead]

17 March [1926]

Rapallo | via Marsala, 12 int. 5

Dear Dad:

Roth is not worth the powder; no use suing for damages as he has no money. Any connection or supposed connection with his magazine is detrimental.

I object to it because it further muddles the distinction between things already muddled enough by the jackass law 211 U. S. penal. Not interested in muck or Mark Twain or smutty post cards;

but object to literature being censured by idiots.

Probably cheapest thing to do is for you to write promptly to any paper printing Roth's ads.

I DONT WANT TO AS I HAVE ALWAYS MADE POINT OF IGNORING THE EXISTENCE OF THE GOD DAMN THINGS. or for other reasons dont want to recognize them.

If you dont mind: Floowing form. My son, Ezra Pound now in italy does not see current publication regularly, has asked me to write to any paper printing ads. of TWO Worlds; stating that he is not a contirbuting edtr. of same, and has no connection whatever with Mr Roth or any of his activities; and that Mr Roth is perfectly well aware of the fact.

and start on THE DOUBLE DEALER, 204 Baronne St. New Orleans

Also in case of Vanity Fair and New Republic, ad p,s, to effect that I am asking you to start proceedings for lible, if they <u>persist</u> in publishing after receiving repeated denials of Roth statement.

(You need NOT add that you do NOT propose to fulfill my request.)

Reckon thats about that. Went to Genoa yesterday and ordered new suit a few shirts, etc, also purchased a pr. slippers.

Next room in hand of 'colorista'; good man, specializes in 'finto marmo e finto legno' but am not calling upon that part of his talents. Have also bought small table, antico, about two feet high and looking like a small elephant.

Rest of aptmnt. more or less veiled in various devices of me-yown con-skruktion. Dont know why we have delayed it so long. Also electric fixtures, of predecessor, in course of elimination.

love to you & mother.

E

Hope she is O. K. again.

'finto marmo and finto legno': painted to look like marble or like wood.

754. TLS [on 'Ezra Pound' letterhead]

24 March [1926]

Rapallo | via Marsala, 12 int. 5

Dear Dad:

Old Mathews died several years ago. Dare say his books were sold for up-keep of his wife and young darther. There are plenty of copies of Canzoni to be had for 63 cents; so reckon the dedicace is priced at $14.37. If you want any MORE of my autografts I can arrange to supply you (to almost any extent, at $13.47 each or even less.

The Quinzaine IS however hard to get. But don't you go investing and waiting for a rise.

Mother's last letter very wild. Have destroyed my reply to it.

Don't of course TELL Centaur that my books, while WORTH infinitely more, can be bought for a great deal less.

Neumayer regularly kept a copy of Lustra in the window at 5 dollars, while buying at 5 shillings.

Letter from Joyce this a.m. so his eyes are working again.

Also note from Mencken suggesting that I submit something for Murkn Murkury. Wot ells; day in Genova, tailor etc.

D. has been under the weather, but up again yesterday.

Three aged tennis players, tournament breed have been livening up local court. Wot ells?

Mother's ideas about my joining a crook company (T.Worlds) very curious. Really is dif. between some jackass braying ABOUT one, and being part of a swindle . . . . however . . .

also her historic anectdotes re Small Maynard, Irish Lawyers, Ernest Rhys . . . etc. . . . . WHERE did she get the thin film of fantasy on which to build orl that there superskrukchure.

Glad to see that the drys arc gittin a bit of hell in the senate. Hope they and the rest of the assassins of the republic will all die of Brights disease; with two hundred thousand other bureaucrats. otherwise, spirit calm; weather outside equinoxial, ETC.

Walsh vurry pleased with machine photos (yours and those sent in by Baldy Bacon)

also music sup. of opry numbers projected. (for No 4 or 5.) Joyce's kid aint a basso after all. J.J. always said he ought to be a tenor; and now he is.

Will send on Centaur address. <to Walsh> The scoundrely british printers of No. 1. have held up a lot of Walsh's mail. Sent him estimate of 7000 fr. and bill for 17,000 fr.

(but were unable to give much account of ANY reason why it shd. be more than 11.000 at outside . . . etc . . . so is it.

There are honest englishmen, but never safe to assume that a briton is honest
TILL YOU KNOW.

love to you & mother

E

+⊨═⊨+

755. TLS [on 'Ezra Pound' letterhead]

14 April 1926 and May 1st

Rapallo | via Marsala, 12 int. 5

Dear Dad:

Yrs 2nd. inst. recd. Advise you consult me before buying OR selling
incunabulae (such as Blast, etc. or my woiks.) Red BLAST <u>very</u> hard to get.
Shdnt. sell less than 50 bucks UNLESS YOU HAVE several copies.

I dont even know whether Lewis himself can lay hold of copies of it. If there
is any profiteering on it, he ought to benefit.

Suits of clothes here cost from 500 lire to 1680 . depending on how much
cut is desired. Suits in quite durable material can be had for 500 to 600. The cut
above that is pure swank, tariff on English cloth, etc.

Have purchased new holder for increasing mess of mss. of Cantos.

<u>May 1st.</u>

Evidently started this note some days ago. No nooz, save change of address
(for letters)

mail dept. Equitable Trust Co. 23 rue de la Paix, PARIS.

Believe Eliot and family are going to arrive here and occupate this flat in my
absinthe.

Soc. Musicale Independante, giving George's Quattuor a Cordes on
Whenzday. with Damn-rosch and the murkn lambastador on deck.

Still waiting for Liv's proofs. not that there is any speshul.

Mr Lavezzo reports that the noo cupboard is to arrive shortly and that he is
'sending in the same time the Principessa di S.Faustiono's two Bureus.'

McAlmon finding London deader than ever. Mr. Hemingway said to have
bagged large contract with Scribner, and his friends all gloomily praying for his
soul and the remains of his wits.

Mr. Bird gone to Spitzbergen. Mr Rummel, as I think I reported months ago,
has recd. the order of Leopold.

Have you seen any complete list of the Guggenheim awards? Shd. like to know if ANY of it has gone to anyone good.

etc. Love to you and mother

E

+>=·=<+

756. TLS

24 April. [1926]

[Rapallo]

Dear Dad:

Glad to know Isabel is all right again. Hope your BILL gocs through AT LAST. High time. Also hope to get my page proofs before I go to Paris. Enclose sample of new suit. At LAST in order, after long struggle with genoese tailor.

Stink of murex still invading the village, despite contrary wind. No gt. news.

Have been reading a lot of stuff re/ early Xtians. A rum lot; jews mostly to blame. Wot ever may be said agin the kawfliks they seems to have been less idiotic than the early heretics. But a rum business altogether; state of mind very like W.j.Bryan, Tennessee and the rest of that middle western hell.

Appears to be not a flees difference between mod. cath and prots. However. Very little in it that is likely to be any use; except that I have found clear definition of Manicheans; and, as I always thought, there is very little trace of 'em in 12th. century Provence. Etc.

Confucius the only one of the alledgeded doctors and sages who seems to have had real good sense. Shall have to look up the Quakers one of these days. Ever since I went into Kensington Church eleven years ago I have understood that the quakers forbade music on purely aesthetic grounds. John Fox or Mr Quake or whoever was the first one, must have an 'ear' and been simply unable to bear it.

Also vast perspective of human psychology in a word-derivation I have just hit on. Ennui, from the gk. word 'ennoia' meaning 'a thought'.

Little or no news from the outer world. A lioness went out for a walk in Alesandria the other day, without eating anyone; and has now her pixture in the 'Domenica del Corriere'.

I keep looking about the village for suitable habitations for you. What's your opinion on stairs and hills? The sea front is of course more expensive than the back. As the valley is small and alluvial, I don't know about healthiness of it, at least on lower floors. Question of how far IN or OUT of village you wd. care to be; etc, etc. dare say there is time enough.

The five flights to this flat are too much when the allegator don't work; and it now mostly dont, as I refused to have a janitor and family planted in the rest of the top. alledgedly to keep it in order but in reality to destroy the sacred quiet of the terzza. Etc.

Love to you and mother, and saluti to the Feet. I dont know how H. is to make a living, I have never understood how anyone does; unless they have the knack of selling things. A bit late in the day for him now, I suppose. How old is he? 36?

Olga is having a concert in Rome, with Casella at the pyano. Doing the small tune I sent you for Homer, with the acc. I have since rigged up. At least I have been told it is on the pogram.

Have heard of a chap called Robert Maitland, who may do the bass for me in Paris.

etc

E

---

757. TLS

29 April 1926

[Rapallo]

Dear Dad:

Thanks 1. pr. cuff-buttons (pat. No. 99564327890) recd. Have I, at my time of life, got to start wearing CUFFS!!!!?

Z-matter of fac' I believe D. wants 'em for some similar purpose, so they wont be wasted.

Tribute to my solution of the collar problem, deep and hearfelt some years ago in Place de'l'Opera. enormous bearded Frenchman well on in years, stopping on middle island between busses remarking:

Ça! CA c'est Intelligent!!

on which he grabbed his own immaculate collar and tie and shook it with ineffable disgust.

We grinned at each other and passed. but I think I wd. recognize him again, anywhere.

ETC. Two of the best Lewis drawings from J.Q. ruins have arrived safely, save that a good deal of black pastel has been knoched off the 'Red Duet'; however the pair of drawings are now reasonable safe.

Nooz not very heavy. Hope to get my Collected edtn. proofs before I start for Paris.

You better send letters to me care Equitable Trust Co. Mail Dept. 23 rue de la Paix, PARIS any thing mailed on or after May 10th. If for any reason we dont get started, post is almost as quick via Paris as to Genova direct. Have a new. mss. holder. That's about all the lictherary progress I can report.

Report that Am. Library in Paris had barred Mencken's Green Mercury, proves false. They'd merely put it in inner room to keep it from being swiped from the magazine desk. It appears a fairly halmless sheet; quotations of local moronism about the best feature.

McAlmon is thinking about going back for a look at the psychopatich wards. Hope you'll meet him if he does.

Can not regard Communism as cure for national imbecility, but the New Masses looks to me about only murkn publication worth the 25 cents per issue.

love to you & mother
E

┼═══┼

758. TLS

13 May [1926]

[Rapallo]

Dear Mother:

Have just been down to Rome for few days, heard a lot of modern moozik. The Satie (vid. prog. enc) being the best by far and nothing else as good as G.A.

Casella very good conductor, no nonsense; very competent; also clever in his own compositions, though the ones I heard were not very important.

Tinayre had a show in Paris last week; also G.A's quartette done in concert of mod. stuff.

Damrosch has taken George's symphony, so you may be able to hear it in the autumn.

G. due to have big orchestral show in Paris on June 12.

Think I already wrote that mail was to be sent to Paris. co/ Equitable Trust Co. 23 rue de la Paix. Wot ells??

Mrs Bok almost unique case of someone with money showing some sense in use of it. Guggenheim show seems to be bunk; at least the short list of beneficiaries that appeared in Paris Trib. contained no mention of anyone of any interest or more than shool-medal talent.

Met Respighi also in Rome; rather sympathetic figure. Eliots also present, with collateral branches.

Just recd. Mencken's statement re/ his boot to the Boston smut-hounds. If dad hasn't seen it, he might write to Mercury for it.

etc.

also various things to tidy up before leaving this village.

Love to you and dad.
E

┼═══┼

759. ALS [*letter head*] Hotel Restaurant, Foyot, Paris

[7 June 1926]

[Paris]

Dear Dad:
    Absolutely rushed copying parts etc.
    D writing today.

Love to you both

E

Pound was copying **parts** *for the concert performance of* Le Testament *on 29 June.* **Dorothy** *wrote: 'Some of the songs have had to have new accompaniments for concert platform, and one has had to be slightly altered for Tinayre's voice, and so on: all meaning making new copies'. Enclosed with the following 8 June note will have been the announcement for* **Antheil's** *concert at the Champs Elysées theatre on the 19th.*

⊹⊱══⊰⊹

760. ALS

8 June [1926]

[Paris]

Dear Dad.
    will send announcements of <u>my</u> show soon.
    In mean time start your press friends on the enclosed.
    Record <u>shows</u> for U.S. music in Europe.
    other news re G. A. has possibly reached you Damrosch doing G's symphony this autumn.
    Am. Guild composer. etc etc = am somewhat busy

Love

.E.

⊹⊱══⊰⊹

761. AL

[c.20 June 1926]

[Paris]

    Champs Elysees biggest theatre in Paris crowded for GA. People sitting on strapontins.
    Landslide pro Antheil.
    busy as hell
    Mrs G. giving most of A's work in private series vide verso.

600

*The **verso** was an invitation:*

Mrs. Christian Gross
at home
1, Ave. Charles Floquet
Vendredi 25 Juin 1926
Musique à 3h.30 précis de l'après midi

Symphony
For 5 instruments 1922–23
George Antheil
Conductor
Vladimir Golschmann

Sonate d'Église 1926
Virgil Thomson

+⟩━━⟨+

762. ALS

13 July [1926]

Foyot [Paris]

Dear Dad

Just wrote a line to mother. Still busy clearing up.

Re. enclosed recd. by post from Italy some days ago, possibly some weeks ago.

Does your firend Willie think he's the second coming of Christ? Or wot- t- ell.

Yours

E

P.S. D. says it came six weeks ago. in any case I took no action in the matter. Being in Paris I did not rush off to Genoa - in search of the mahatma

+⟩━━⟨+

763. ALS [*letter head*] Hotel Restaurant, Foyot, Paris

11 Aug [1926]

[Paris]

Dear Mother,

Will get round to answering a letter or so, in time.

Not much <u>nooz</u>. supposedly the quiet season.

Hem due back in a few days.

Have eaten a few meals and wasted a few dozen sheets of various sorts of paper.

    an thaats about that

Love to you & dad.

also corrected one more set of Liveright's proofs. & met his ex. ex. officio printing expert

    August a great month for mental paralysis.

yrs
E

---

764. ALS

29 Aug. [1926]

Foyot [Paris]

Dear Mother:

    No nooz in speshul. Hem. & Antheil back in Paris.

    Just met a man named Borie who says dad caught him reading the New Republic.

    dont seem to be a great many hours per diem. =

    every time I sit down it is an hour later etc.

    Hem done a new nuvvle. Have you tried his 'Torrents of Spring' or the passing of a great race?

♩ ♫♩ | ♩ ♩ ♩♩ | etc

    Found time for a hair cut yesterday & have had a pr. pants pressed.

    Picabia is prepared to do a fresco if needed.

Love to you & dad.
E

---

765. ALS [*letter head*] Hotel Restaurant, Foyot, Paris

11 Oct [= September?] [1926]

Paris

Dear Dad

    next generation (male) arrived.

    Both D & it appear to be doing well.

Ford going to U.S. to lecture in October.
Have told him you wd. probably be glad to put him up.
more anon,

yrs
E

Dorothy Pound gave birth to her son Omar in the American Hospital at Neuilly on the 10th of September. On the 11th Pound went to the Mairie at Neuilly to register the birth, 'sur déclaration du père'. Dorothy wrote to 'Dear E. P.'s Parents': 'We name him [Omar], to keep up the poetic tradition. It seems to suit him admirably also. He appears small, neat, very philosophic, and at present the eyes, dark blue, are also in the picture. He has a comical crop of dark brown hair, increasing. I hope you won't be too shocked to hear he is not to return with us to Rapallo just at present. He has already been deposited, in a nice cradle (chosen by my mama) in a little-house-with-garden just outside Paris. Madame Collignon has two children of her own and knows all about bottles and milk and such like. . . . . I am anxious to get back now to Rapallo and the terrazza .'

---

766. TLS

Sometime in October (1926)

Via Marsala 12/5 [Rapallo]

Dear Dad:

Damn glad to be back here. Had week in horspital before leaving Paris, and then a bit of rest. Now supposed to be o.k.; had all the possible taps, tests, analyses etc. and supposed to be suffering from health, but completely exhauseted.

Thanks for American Mercury; seems to be about the best thing in the place. Do you get it regiler? If not you mayzwell subscribe, and I will pay half the sub. (dead bloody broke fer the moment, will take me three months to ketch up.)

Bhloody glad to be back here. Wore aht, completely.

Will, with the less complicated schedule get round to writing more fully, than has been poss. in Paris.

Oh yuss. The Barnes foundation have sent me copies of their journal. Barnes seems to be on the right track, doing what J.Q. might have. He himself writes much better than his staff.

Their address is Merion Pa. They wd. prob. send you the journal. (I have only nos. 1 and 2. of the second vol.; if you can get the first vol. send it on to me after reading it.

Young jawg has been down with pneumonia, very ill, but was up and about again before I left Paris. Shd. be nooz of his Saturday show in the paper that orter rive this a.m.

Invitation from Convegno in Milan for Antheil concert in Jan or Feb.
etc

yours fer repose, love to mother
E

*In 1922, Albert C. Barnes (1872–1951) established the **Barnes Foundation** in a suburb of Philadelphia 'to promote the advancement of education and the appreciation of the fine arts'.*

┼══┼

767. TLS

Sunday 24 or 25 Oct. [1926]

Via Marsala 12 int 5 | Rapallo

Dear Mother

Gt. relief to get back here. Air one can breathe etc. Mare grosso, messing up front in fine style; relieving my mind about town improvements, and danger of anything being built between us and sea.

Slowly catching up with varia neglected in Paris. No particular nooz. Waiting Liveright's volume.

My note on Jawg appears in current Oct. Criterion.

Letter from Carnevalli this a.m.

Robt. has started for Panama. Hem. in Spain,

etc. Love to you and dad.
E

┼══┼

768. TLS

27 Oct 1926

[Rapallo]

Dear Dad:

Correspondence has been rather fragmentary during summer. Have been very busy, learned a lot about writing fugues, but not enough to be any use YET. etc.

Books I want for next preparation of canti haven't come. Have spent past week having fool ideas about starting a magazine; WITHOUT interference for ONCE. Dont know that I shall get round to doing it. Have you any suggestions?

Small note on young Jawg appears in current Criterion.

A greek author says there is no door tight enough to keep out a cat.

The danish dentist offers to bring me a lion cub from Africa where he is going as soon as he gets a permit.

Otherwise the day has been without incident. Sea now calm after having churned up a good deal of rock during past week.

Love to you & mother. Also pass on my salutations to the Feet.

E

<hr />

769. TLS

29 Oct. [1926]

Via Marsala 12 int 5. [Rapallo]

Dear Mother

Birthday letter recd. have plenty of neckties had already ordered noo pr. gray flannel pants this a.m. and will deevote yr. 5/ to them as I am SHORT. (Not serious, but temporary. Howeffer my credit good in village.

Thanks for timely.

Re garage difficulty. Wot I suggess, IS that you do as people do here when they live on the 'illside. Namely BURROW a garage IN from the road level. as you cant poss. make drive into 'grounds' of Oak Lodge.

[*diagrams*]

not quite so large; but a lot of houses on hillside HERE have their garages burrowed or BLASTED out beside the front gates.

Thus garage fits UNDER the front lawn with no damn damnage to outlook from front poarch. Offer to build or dig one for a serious buyer, or get plan and estimate. a few beams and a wash of concrete do the job.

Chartres no go as architecture, too damn gothic, may work on the green arrival, but have seen too much really good stuff to swallow it. Best thing in Chartres wuz the lion cubs in the circus. My earliest memories are the dawg kennel in Chippewaw, and sliding outer the haymow. onto my PROboscis.

an that's that.

also Sary Vessels killink a mouse with a oat-shovel

Is my garage plan clear or do you want it EEEllllaborated?? and precicified??

etc. love to you and dad. Nice warm mist and swish, salt over everything, submarine

but not wintry.

etc.

E

<hr />

770. **TLS** [on 'Ezra Pound' letterhead]

15 Nov. [1926]

Rapallo | via Marsala, 12 int. 5

Dear Dad:

Am rather thinking of starting a magazine. Pore Walsh has died off; so dare say T. Q. will come to a stop after Moorhead has brought out a sort of memorial number to Walsh. All of which xplains why your machine photos haven't yet appeared.

At present am looking for contributors. Mac A, is in panama. Hem sez he has something. Must have at least three items of interest before I cast myself upon the waves.

As per recent letter: lemme know if you get the Am. Mercury; if not, go ahead and subscribe, read it and then forward to me. I will refund you the subscrimption.

Several people seem cheered at prospect of unfettered publication. That's about as far as it has got. Neumayer wants 100 copies as starter. I don't know whether you want to ask your friend at the Centaur or whats is nyme book shop, how many he thinks he can use. (sale price 50 cents. format small.)

Difficulty of Transatlantic, and T.Q. was they never cd. get any money out of american book shops. They wd. order copies but never pay.

I don't know that the centaur was one of the defaulters but I heard general howl against american dealers. You might let me know if you have any way of keeping an eye on one or two depots. If I can get a sort of supervisor in a few vast cities it might simplify this side of problem.

If I start, I shall have absolOOT controll; no more combinations or compromises.

As I have writ no prose for three years; I seem to have a sort of head of steam up; for the editorial part of the show. also Cantos to print.

I take it you know of no noo rizink cheeniuses in Montago. Co. or on the banks of the Schuylkill???

Still a few poems by ole Dunning, unprinted. Shall have civil war with les jeunes, the day I print 'em; but it all helps the general shindy.

Did I tell the New Masses to send you a sub. or sample. I have read their six months issues with care. About the livest wire now functioning.

At any rate both it and the Am. Merc. have stuff in 'em one can read. McNaught is am imbecile. I spose nothing else has awakened. Old mags. still dead as they were in 1874??

Ole Harriet occas. gets something decent but smothers it in afternoon tea.

Hope Liv. will have sent you new vol. by time this reaches you.

Have hopes of bringing out another lot of Cantos de luxe next autumn.

Looked at Instigations a few nights ago. Excellent work, ought to be better known.

etc. love to you & mother.

E

+≽═╼+

771. TLS [on 'Ezra Pound' letterhead]

17 Nov. [1926]

Rapallo | via Marsala, 12 int. 5

Dear Dad:

Have been looking over letters recd. in Paris during rush. Think I have answered most points. You mention, by the way, being about to send a article by J. W. Crawford. Same has never turned up.

Harriet did not send her book, but I imagine it is merely reprint of her articles in Poetry.

Dont bother about sending Stork. (Chas Wharton)

I read your friend Rose's sixth cousins uncles poetry. It is poetic. You can pass that on, if you think it will comfort him. Shows feeling, etc. all as it shd. be. (this you need NOT pass on ONLY it isn't interesting ENOUGH) I dont want him to send on mss. for my review if I start one.

Plenty of excellent family doctors, whose cases do NOT make articles for medical journal.

Two fotos. of y,v,t, reached here this a.m. taken some forty yeahs ago.

Bill Bird aint been arrested fer stealin the narth pole after all. Apart from which there is small news, but excellent sun, after three weeks rain.

vado giocar' al tennis.

love to you & mother

E

+≽═╼+

772. TLS [on 'Ezra Pound' letterhead]

18 Nov. [1926]

Rapallo | via Marsala, 12 int. 5

Dear Dad:

Re/ your enervé epistle of 3d. inst. Omar born 10 Sept. My illness nothing whatever to do with it. Source of supplies presumably sound. Dutch East India 6%, some of it. I spose that is O.K. <or as solid as anything is a world of crazy finance.>

Much more sensible that infant shd. be reared near some sort of proper medical attendance. i.e. American hospital, than here. Where I have vivid recollection of Berman looking for sterilized food, and finding fly down neck of Strater's infant's bottle.

Re/ this Quarter, you have by now my letter, and news of Walsh's death.

Let Barnes outfit alone, for present. He evidently has a kink somewhere in his make up. I believe one of his faculty, Buermeyer, died recently in N.Y. in curious circumstances. Send me any data you come upon. But I recon you better not go to visit his gallery without invitation. (J.Q. never wd. say anything about him, but cursed violently at mention of his name.)

I had nothing to do with Quinn sale in Paris. Met Brummer whom I like (most marvelous accent, especially over the phone.)

Yes, send on the books any time you like.

Yes. D. in perfect health.

83 bucks a month wd. go quite a way here AS LONG AS THE LIRE STAYS ABOUT WHERE IT IS. Or if they stabilize anywhere above 22 lire to the dollar. They talk of stabilizing at 23 or 24.

I mean I live on about $10 per week, save when having a bust out. Naturally dead broke now, after five months in Paris.

Don't remember meeting Patterson . but one meets a lot of people without knowing who they are, and forgets very quickly unless some reason for recalling them.

?? your Package to D.??? two photos recd. yesterday, or do you mean larger package??

I take it we are to expect you in person about this time next year, or in June 1929 unless some change occurs in Wash. D.C. As I take it, (or at any rate hope) you are hale an hearty, despite truss.

I sent a letter from Paris on 10 or 11 Sept. so dont quite know why you shd. still have been in state of uncertainty, on 3d. Nov.

love to you & mother

E

In his letter of 3 November, Homer Pound had written that it had been 'weary waiting' for any word about Dorothy and Omar:

> *What puzzled Dad was the fact that the Newspapers knew what he had been named before we had a letter from D. and none from you. Why? Young Wallis was in Paris and came home and told his parents about it, and then Mama happens to meet Mrs. W. at a womans meeting—I heard that a western paper had it &&&/ Will you please give me the date of* <u>Omar's birth</u>? *. . . It was also a great relief to your Mother to hear from you. You know by this time that it takes very little to give her a nervous spell, but I trust she will recover, and become reconciled to the way you have given over the matter of rearing the boy. Seems very queer to us, but*

I suppose it is something we cannot do anything about. <u>BUT</u> I take it that was really what upset you.

Homer had written again on 10 November: 'I must confess we are puzzled as to why you leave all reference to D. and Omar out of your letters—Mama will get a nervous spell unless she hears something soon. She is making various little things for him.'

*Joseph **Brummer**, a New York art dealer, had been in charge of the sale of John Quinn's extensive collection of art works and manuscripts. Under a Pension bill which had been before Congress for some years Homer, if he continued at the Mint until he was 70 (in 1928), would retire on $1000 a year, or $83 a month.*

+‖⇒⋅⇐‖+

773. TLS [on 'Ezra Pound' letterhead]

19 or 20 nov. [1926]

Rapallo | via Marsala, 12 int. 5

Dear Dad

Answered most of yr. questions yesterday. Sorry you seem to have been worrying; not like you to worry.

In any case no expected calamity ever arrives. Them that arrives is on-expected; and usually a blessing in disguise. Them that etc . . . in short anything that falls on ones head is not what one expects to have fall, so foreboding is at a discount.

In any case, DONT. you have enough bothers of your own.

re/ package. A package for D. or rather O. arrove that's all right.

Etc. Joyce now struggling with Roth. Miss Moorhead struggling with Walsh's papers, for new number T.Q.

Rain, marvelous and abundant, never been nothink like it. Understand O. doing O.K.

so thass that.

love to you and mother

E

+‖⇒⋅⇐‖+

774. TLS [on 'Ezra Pound' letterhead]

23 Nov. [1926]

Rapallo | via Marsala, 12 int. 5

Dear Mother

No doubt Annie Heacok has seen things in her time (one doesn't know just what) but no doubt the chronicle of her nights will be LURID. Will it, do you think, git by the p.o. censors??

As to school children, the purpose of adult literature is rather to transmit those things which it takes a bit more time to find out, so to speak faculties for comparison of experience that are denied the quarter-baked mind of the primary school infant. But as the American mind in 98 2/3% of the known cases, coagulates at the 7th, grade primary school stage, doubtless the licherary efforts of the infants you mention will find large field of consumption.

Omar is not up for adoption by the local worthies, if that is what you mean to suggest.

If on the otherhand your information is meant to indicate that the ancient neosaurian race that used to inhabit Wyncote about the years 1895 to 1900 is in the act of dying out, I can but regard you as over optimistic; much as I might like to accept the idea, I must insist on a wider survey.

Miss Draper's program seems about the same as what it was in London eight years ago.

Do I take it that Wille was so excited by Ford's simple outbreak that he at once rushed to the --- no we can hardly believe it --- telephone, and put through a call on that account and no other.??!!

Or had he some scheme for saving Ford from the yawning jaws of Tartarus, before it were yet too late?

D. sez she is about to write. It has rained for five weeks, we shall all crumble if it continues another ten days; the flesh falls from the bone; the nazal passages are encrusted with salt. The spray sweeps over the terazza; it bursts fifty feet into the air over the breakwater; it is undoubtedly the last phase of an already decrepit planet. Nothing but the new promenade (concrete) has prevented the front from sinking below the gulf of Tigullio; as it is the steam roller goes out in dry moments and all the loose stone is mashed in where the sea and pulizia civile have heaved it.

Mr Chute has arrived from England, with his beard redder and his tonsure even less visible.

Am reading Mozart's letters, etc. etc. and editing the non extant review. in vacuuo

love to you & dad

E

Isabel Pound had written on 11 November:

> *Progress of the Arts in Wyncote represented by Miss Annie Heacocks memoires, a choral society conducted by the brother of your early banjo instructor, Smith of Jenkintown and the Womens club. Various school children are writing verse and drama later some attempt journalism but the popular business is advertising. How such acquire sufficient income for family needs is marvellous. Most everyone has a car. [She went on:] Mrs. Jim Heacock adopted a handsome infant now five years old. Harold Washburn having only one child adopted a second. That method of*

augmenting the family is popular. There are six such cases just about us. They are secured while quite young and the earlier connection is forgotten, so ignored.

Ruth Draper (1884–1956), an American actress internationally renowned as a performer of dramatic monologues. '**Willie**', referred to by Isabel Pound as 'W.T.', had by her account 'telephoned from Swarthmore that Ford was quoted in N. Y. World as to the three great Americans, H. James EP &&'.

+⫯⊨⫯+

775. **TLS** [on 'Ezra Pound' letterhead]

22 Dec. [1926]

Rapallo | via Marsala, 12 int. 5

Dear Progenitors:

D. wrote me to git you all a decent present while I wuz in Rome; but having muddled transmission; the chq. which shd. have been paid me by AM. Exp. CO. in Rome, arrived HERE after I got bak. so I counted my strips of macaroni, and bought neither your present nor a new pr. of pyjamas. in Rome.

However: the bronze of the Gaudier embracers is gt. success, very fine, and shone like a Brancush; it is has gone off to Windeler;

and ought to about square my account with him.

This place is now adorned, Cat and Water Carrier contemplating the marble Embracers from op. ends of the two rooms.

Also the two Lewis, and the two Gaudier drawings, filling bed room.

[diagram]

rough sketch of aptment, rather out of proportion. For anybody desirous of NOT owning anything, I seem to become less competent yearly. Still haven't got Clavicord, and rather want it, here. I mean increasingly regret its being still in London, after five years. Also H. H. S's Amati cello, that I might experiment on.

Cable from Liv's make-up mgr. (named also Gross) that my Collected pomes have been mailed from N.Y. I told 'em to send you a copy. If you haven't got it by now, KICK.

Jarge not having Olgas address, O, ditto, re/ Jarge, (both of them having mine) am doing some wild telegraphing to get her to Budapesth in time for a concert. next fortnight.

Prospects of review improving. It has at any rate called one entertaining mss. into being. A sketch by Monsieur Hickok that wdnt. have been writ, but for prospect of review's being about to be.

You better read Benjamin Constant's 'Adolphe' in preparation for Rodker's treatment of same theme under 20th, instead of 18th. century conditions. Or maybe both wd. horrorfy you. Anyhow the B. Constant is worth reading.

Rosanov is prob. not for Wyncote.

The greatest calamity in history has fallen upon pore Bill Williams. Noo Masses printed a mss. without telling him, and it cost him 5000 dollars.

LIFE is stranger than fiction, and immagination always gets left behind.

Yours, with love and Xmas greetings,

E

New Masses *had published William Carlos Williams' story 'The Five Dollar Guy', about a local oil man indecently propositioning a woman friend of his, without realising that Williams had written it using their real names. The oil man sued for $15,000 dollars, and Williams had to settle out of court at a cost of $5000 which he did not have.*

776. TLS [on 'Ezra Pound' letterhead]

22 Dec. [1926]

Rapallo | via Marsala, 12 int. 5

Dear Dad:

re. enclosure just recd. from you. Wot is wrong with it?!!!!!

Nearly everything except the small idea in the middle. It is a mess. It has too many words that don't function, cotton stuffed in to fill the cracks of the metre; lines stuffed in to rhyme at the end.

Comes of trying to write a sonnet, NOT because the subject needed a sonnet, but just for sake of making a sonnet; subject balooned out to fill the shape.

I did one of these every day for a year as exercise; some were worse than others.

To say nothing of its being a BUNK, non musical conception. I mean it is the way someone thinks about moozik when they dont know NAWTHINK about it.

It wont, as a job, stand inspection anywhere.

Where'd you be if you passed stuff as 909 when it was anywhere from 607 to 750.

It <the enclosed> is so bad that you cant emend it anywhere. Even strengthening the end to

'Daring to hold the sea beneath thy hands'

is still pompous, and archaic.

Forging the sunlight in bands,
Daring to hold the sea beneath thy hands.

Besides there are two hundred thousand kids doing as well or better.

Look : 'scroll the poets make'.

equals 'poet's scroll.'

scroll is a dead word, like a high hat of six years ago.

Too indefinite for poet. The dreams may be too indef. for poet <?? unlikely>,
but the musical execution is probably more precise than words.

whole thing a muddle of unformed idea.

'Melodies 'hardly' 'woven'. melody being a single line or thread. well, pass it.
it may not be false, but it aint a phrase that hits a bulls eye.

It is like a 'subject for a painting'. Difference between thinking about making
the picture, and really DOING it.

Besides is is so in the english tradition or talking 'about' the matter.

———

Thanks for magazines. My own review seems to be coming on. Hickok has
sent a cheery description of his last voyage.

etc. more anon. wrote to mother this a.m.

go on

MAN PLAYING IN THE HALF LIGHT

[*see facsimile overleaf*]

sitting beneath cloud of soul
forges sunlight into strips,
carves clouds, paints upon air,
dares even hold sea under hands.
dares even hold down force of sea
with hands

i.e. there is matter for 20 or 23 words. the sonnet contains 100 (or 104 with
bloomink echo.)

I dont say the 24 words make a poem. to make a poem one wd. have to beat
em into shape, give some better order, etc. and movement.

———

Yes, do see Centaur shop. The price will be 50 cents. I mean they are to sell it
for that. what discount will they expect. How many copies can they take, and
can you trust em to PAY?

etc.

E

╪══╪

777. TL [on 'Ezra Pound' letterhead]

[1926]

Rapallo | via Marsala, 12 int. 5

[*fragment only*]

After all the bunk that has been talked about 'democracy' etc. very good thing
for people to begin analyzing the disease.

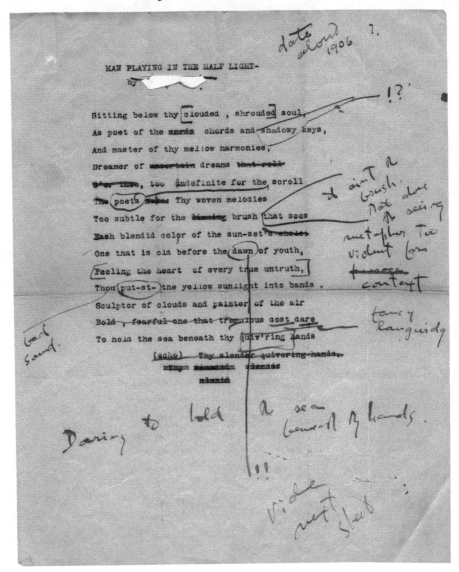

Poem with EP's ms. Comments enclosed in 776. EP to HLP, from Rapallo, 22 December [1926].

Macchiavelli believed in democracy because he never really seen one.

Now, probably no thinking man disbelieves in the need of an aristocracy, only there AINT any to be had; and the quality of the candidates in NOT encouraging.

Moorhead's picture of the Asquith LLoyd George era is also worth printing, though not pleasant reading for convalescents. Hang it all one must have some report of what goes on in alledgedly civilized countries. Otherwise we might believe the Daily Mail's account of it.

This kind of stuff is written, like Miss Beasley's suppressed memoirs, for people who are seriously considering the state of thing; it is not a box of Acker's chocolates. I don't recommend a book on kidney disease, as light reading either; but I shouldn't think of supporting a govt. that suppressed medical publications. Personally I shd. find a book on the kidneys more interesting than Lormier's bunk, or the sunday supplements you send over (all written by people who no next to nothing. I mean just that, the whole of the stuff is written by people who half-know, quarter-know, one 40th know; and are therefore absolutely untrustworthy in everything they say.

Gertrude **Beasley** *(1892–1928), a Texas schoolteacher and international lecturer, published her frank memoir,* My First Thirty Years, *in Paris in 1925. Considered shockingly sensational it was banned in Britain and America.*

+⤜⤛+

778. TLS

1 Jan. 1927

[Rapallo]

Dear Dad and mother:

1. re the Noo Masses. No need to send it as I subscribe. As to joining revolution; surely you can use your own bright wits and relieve me of necessity of arguing these minor matters. And if you wish to quote me in yr. reply, you might say that I 'thought I heard a revolution rumbling along vagule somewhere in the REAR'

not exactly following, or showing intelligence enough to adopt my ideas with any precision, but allowing for margin of error due to any mass action etc. . . . .

Some of the things that used to be so 'mysterious when Douglas (C.H.) wrote 'm) are now I suppose clearer, since Henry Ford has wrote 'em in his autobiog. etc. etc.

Thanks for photo of uncle E.

As to 'Stratford' magazine, I encede you and think NOTHING of it.

Etc. good tennis weather, for the week. and so forth.

E

Henry Ford, founder of the Ford Motor Co., published his autobiography, My Life and Work, *in 1922.* **'uncle E.'** *was IWP's uncle Ezra Brown Weston, husband of Aunt Frank*

+⤜⤛+

779. TLS [on 'Ezra Pound' letterhead]

2 Jan 1927

Rapallo | via Marsala, 12 int. 5

Dear Dad:

Re/ that trunk full of books, do see how much it is going to cost before you decide to send 'em. I dont know whether they are books you read yourselves. One ought to have books here, but still, some proportion between cost of sending 'em, etc, as to whether it is worth while; as to whether same cash spent on new lot??? etc.

Anyhow, if you're hard up, consider the matter carefully; also what they'd fetch if sold. Believe Leary's is no more, but suppose there is some second hand book shop in Phila. Etc.

at any rate, do nothing rash.

Wrote an article this a.m.; can't tell whether I ought to have a review, or pack the stuff into articles and try to sell 'em. Or whether there is enough intelligence in your beloved fatherland to form a rational public. Never found the native scene precisely crowded with competent citizens. Perhaps one fools oneself into believing that they exist.

etc.

yrs
E

I havent Fords. N.Y. address. but you cd. reach him care Mrs J.R. Foster 300 W. 49th N.Y.

780. TLS [on 'Ezra Pound' letterhead]

8 Jan: 1927

Rapallo | via Marsala, 12 int. 5

Dear Dad:

Pressure reduced. You might use this or part of it getting mother a Xmas present, and the rest on coal bill, or anything you find handy. Sorry there isnt a 'naught'(o) at the end of it.

Young chap called Adrian Stokes has drifted into the village, with large trunk full of highbrow books (Spengler etc.) which I am swallowing. in return for tips on the XV century.

Weather now fine, about every other day. Bacon and young Price are investigating printing terms in N.Y

Problem of mag. is WOTTER put in it. Possibly no need for yet another.
Love to you & mother

E

<hr>

781. TLS

11 Jan. (1927)

[Rapallo]

Dear Dad:

'Count Bruga' arrove this a.m. so we can count the day a dead loss, as I have wasted it on said book, tripe but amusing in spots. Has interrupted my reading of Spengler, who is also tripe, but of a larger order.

At least Spengler does recall a lot of things one had forgotten. Was interested in opening chapters and even thought of doing a refutation. Only the sort of job one ought to be PAID for, and paid large, especially as I don't see anyone else capable of covering the field (in murkn or henglish)

However, guess I'd better stick to me-yown jawb. As S, seems to mean by 'The West' a lot of thing I dislike, I shd. like to accept his infantine belief that they are 'declining', but still. . . . .

Don't think you need bother about reading the book, especially as you aren't in shape to combat the mass of its misinformation. Wot 'ells??

Young Jawg preparing for concert in Budapesth, at least he is 'sposed to be doin' so.

Etc. love to you and mother.

E

Count Bruga *(1926), a novel by Ben Hecht. Pound was reading* **Oswald Spengler's** *recently translated* The Decline of the West.

<hr>

782. TLS [on 'Ezra Pound' letterhead]

[before 21 January 1927]

Rapallo | via Marsala, 12 int. 5

Dear Mother:

Yes, I recon you'd better send the trunk full of books, as listed. There is considerably more than 25 dollars worth.

Dont remember 'girandolle'.

Whatever you do; DONT use the 450 to pay debts with. Put in bank or in bonds.

The Page portrait is the one unabandonable treasure; and the Hanah H. little embroidery is worth transport; i,e more interesting in fably than out.

Am preparing magazine for press; been in bed a week with tonsillitis; typing on lap in bed. Hope to be out by tomorrow. Tired, and dont want to get more so, so close. Love to you and dad

Nex day.
Jore-ake is gone, but still fatigued, and plenty to do getting NO. 1. ready for press.

Olga and Jawg due to give concert in Budapesth on 28th. One Adrian Stokes, and one Beaumont Wadsworth, both turned up in Rapallo . . . . . now becoming licherary centre of yourup.

Ed. Wad and Windeler have brought out very pretty, 18th, century copper plate book of mediterranean ships. wot ells.

Nacherly review entails lot of correspondence. Keep me from getting too far out of 'touch' with general stupidity.

Price wrote on Jan. 4 that Ford was due for grand bust out in Herald Tribune (N.Y.) on the 8th. re/ glory an immortality.

etc.

Will possibly resume communiques when I git the review orf me ands.

love to you & dad.

E

*Pound's little **magazine**, Exile, would run to four numbers: no. 1 was printed in Dijon and published in Paris in February 1927; because of difficulties obtaining copyright in the US no. 2 was published by Pascal Covici in Chicago in Autumn 1927; no. 3 also in Chicago in Spring 1928; and no. 4 by Covici in New York in Autumn 1928. John **Price** was American agent for the magazine. Ford Madox **Ford**'s 'Ezra' was in the New York Herald Tribune Book Review on 9 January 1927.*

+‡==‡+

783. TLS

24 Jan. [1927]

[Rapallo]

Dear Dad:
Hesper, Vesper, the evenink star; adest, is to; that is to say, has arrove.

1st, number of the review has gone to press. Yes, I want the Centaur to order from Price, but wanted you to prod 'em into ordering a decent quantity, NOW,

I want to get in orders, or estimate as to what the order will be, so as to know how many to print. Having no central depot, and NOT intending to warehouse a lot of copies, for envental use.

Have seen the Ford review; and sent him the Grande Cordon of the Order of St.Michael and Ananias.

You might send any other reviews you see. Horace has sent me a fat book on Napoleon, and Stokes, and P.B.Wadsworth, now in Rapallo have toted in others. Clear, cold weather.

etc.

love to you & mother

E

*Homer Pound had asked the meaning of '**Hesper** adest' in 'Cantus Planus', a poem in Personae (1926).*

✛══✛

784. TLS

10 Feb. 1927

[Rapallo]

Dear Dad:

Sorry the chap on the Record is a friend of yours. I broke my long habit, and responded to Edtr. telling him which 17 kinds of a god damn fool he had go to write his reviews.

If you see Craven, and like him, give him a poultice, and tell him he shd. look up his DATES.

Orl rite; guess you may as well send on the trunk of books. Think I said so before.

Am correcting proofs. No. 1. of 'The Exile' (i.e. my noo review. name not to be DIvulged until Price gets it registered. Also been thru lot of mss.

Ole Dunning has sent in a damn good poem for No.2.

Have REJECTED a lot of mss. Also have writ you re/ Ct. Bruga. wot ells.

Jawg and Olga said to have played very well in Budapesth.

No. the N.Y. Times did not send copy,

Mr Gorman writes like zif he'd swallowed a porkenpine. Has heard I'm a hell ov a important writer, dont know why, but feels mission to EXplain it to others.

Ford sent me copy of Tribune article, but duplicates useful. Etc. More remarkable item is that Horace had put in an 'ad' whether by his own wish or whether he had it blackmailed out of him by the trib, ad. agent, I dunno.

Covici of Kichago writes that he wants to wake up. Have given him a perfectly good chance. Wot ells?

Jawg possibly looking in here during the week; recd. one fool letter from him with Florentine postmark.

Of course if Kichago CAN be stirred up to fight N.York it is all to the good.

A gent. named Saml. Putnam seems like he'z lookink fer a shindy; at any rate he poked up Covici; remains to be seen if Cov. will take action.

I want a queit life till I get my next vol. of Canti into shape. UGH!!

Thank Aunt F. for Omar calendar, have been meaning to write to her; but rather heavy correspondence, now, with all the buddink authors; and all the ole stags that have to be poked up.

Bill Bird & spouse thru here in auto. Mc Tavish cleaned up quarter millione (250.000 francs) at Monte.

etc.

love to you and mother

E.P.

Craven had reviewed Personae *in the Philadelphia* Record, *and had told Homer that he had 'read it all through carefully and what he wrote was his impressions—had not read any other review'. Herbert* **Gorman** *had written 'Ezra Pound, An Embattled Poet' in the* New York Times Book Review *of 23 January.*

⊬═══⊬

785. TLS

18 Feb. [1927]

Rap[allo]

Dear Mother:

Young Jawg thru here early this week. Has had show in Budapesth with Olga, and they're having another in Rome tomorrow. He then goes to N.Y. He may take refuge in Wyncote fer a few days before show. Also says you and dad are to have best box in the house if you go over to N.Y. for concert.

Have sent back second proofs of the review this p.m. Enclosed cover proof, not accepted, but substance of cover will be as announced thereon. WOT ells.

New Masses say they want to print me on Jawg. and somebody on 'Me on Jawg' and a review of Personae. etc. Wot ells.

Nacherly voluminous correspondence re/ revista. A little decent tennis. Harold Loeb here for a day; and a stray admiral making decent four. Loeb seems improved since his 'Broom' period.

Fine poem from Dunning for No.2. as think I reported.

Good deal of flurry, as O. was giving concert on 23d. and Jawg turned up unexpected, with passage fer N.Y. taken for 24th. from Cherbourg. etc. etc.

Also Milan ready, but no time to fit it in, due to Ferrieri being an ass, and not getting mobilized sooner.

Etc.

Love to you and dad

E

D. sends salutations

New Masses *published Pound's 'Workshop Orchestration', an article proposing that Antheil's 'Ballet Mechanique', through its grasp of 'longer durations', showed how the noise of a machine shop might be time-spaced, 'so that the eight-hour day shall have its rhythm; so that the men at the machines shall be demechanized, and work not like robots, but like the members of an orchestra.'*

---

786. TL [on 'Ezra Pound' letterhead]

[c.4 March 1927]

Rapallo | via Marsala, 12 int. 5

Dear Dad:

La petite Olga has pulled this on her own; without M. Antheil's assistance. Wot ells.

I keep chucking out mss. from 'sanctum' of Exile.

Enc. from Walter.

Note from G. Yeats, that W.B. will presumably send on ms, for Exile 2.

SECOND EPISTLE:

Dear Mother:

Yrs. 11th. ult. recd. Yes. The murkn. peepul have probably developed to the pt. where the great question of Nestle's vs. breast feeding, will hold their attention. I recommend the question be thoroughly gone into in all ladies literary socs. did Longfellow. . . . use pasteurized etc. Great stuff and at just the right level fer the murkn. intelligentzia.

Enclosed was a cutting from the Paris edition of the New York Herald *of 4 March 1927:*

> ROME, Wednesday.—Unusual honor was accorded to Miss Olga Rudge, American violinist, recently when Premier Mussolini invited her to play for him at his home in Via Rasella. . . . . The program included Beethoven's Romanza, a sonata by Mozart, opus 15, and a sonata by Veracini. Mussolini complimented Miss Rudge on her technique and unusual feeling. saying that it was rare to find such depth and precision of tone 'especially in a woman'.

---

787. TLS

21 March 1927

[Rapallo]

Dear Mother:

Cable from Pascal Covici of Chicago this a.m. saying he
WILL PUBLISH ANTHEIL AND ADOLPHE AND MACHINE ART ALSO
MAGAZINE THIRD ISSUE PLEASE RUSH COPY OF ANTHEIL AND
OTHER MANUSCRIPTS WHEN READY

So thass, that. Looks like another convert. Nothing said about terms, but
Saml. Putnam (claiming NO connection with pub. firm of that name) sez. Mr
Covici is on the square.

House has been fairly active getting off. mss. and 'preparing same for printer
etc. since 9 a.m.

If Walsh's relicts can be moved to restore the machine photos, that means
that they will at last get printed after so long delay.

Omar reported to be doing well. pleased with change of weather. Reckon
that's about the nooz fer one day.

love to you & dad.

E

788. TL

3 April [1927]

[Rapallo]

Dear Dad:

It is a wise father that knows his own sons. I THINK Mr Wescott is in error.
Does he say who his mother was? Have not yet observed any signs of heredity
from the male side in Mr W.; but am open to mendelian proof. What else does
Mr W. say in his 'book'??

WHY THE HELL shd. you pay 3 dollars for another copy of Indiscretions?????
I ferget wot it is published at, but if you insist on having more copies send me a
dollar and half each for as many as you want.

Price hadn't recd. <u>exile</u> when he last wrote, it was sent from France, or at
least from Dijon on March 10th.

D. is O.K. preparing to take Omar to England with her for visit.

Olga gave Mozart recital with old Consolo in Florence last week; and is going
up to Berenson's for week-end. Hem. and Hickok passed through here in a
Ford, on way to Rimini and San Marino.

Had a little decent tennis yesterday and day before. Looks like storm today.
One battleship, italyan, in harbour. Very few Exile cards left. Did I write that

Covici sez he will publish my ANTHEIL - 'Antheil' means new edtn. of the book, plus a little more matter. Rodker's Adolphe, 3d. issue Exile; and book on Art and Machines, IF I can ever get the photos. back from Walsh's ruins.

Don't stir up Price re/ Covici and Exile, until arrangements are completed for transfer. I think cable may be an error and mean 'AFTER 3d. issue'.

Ford writes from Toulon, hopes to come down here for a day or so. Wants me to lecture in U.S.A.; but looks like a rum show to me.

Why shd. I be crucified to save 100 million sons of bitches ready to reelect Coolidge support Volstead, tolerate Bryan, and in general keep up the god awful mess they do keep up.

Besides you cant save 'em from themselves, and they wdnt. be 'appy if they wuz.

Rodker is preparing to print Canti XVII-XXVI; and has the mss. for nine of them in hand. I suppose I get another one done by August, or sometime.

Don't take these fulminations with too deep a depression, it is time for lunch, and I shall now descend to sea front to partake of same.

Homer Pound had been reading Glenway **Wescott***'s* The Grandmothers *(1927), a story of nineteenth century Wisconsin, and had remarked that Wescott 'claims to be one of your boys', possibly because he was then living in Paris.*

⊹⊱⊰⊹

789. TLS [on 'Ezra Pound' letterhead]

10 April 1927

Rapallo | via Marsala, 12 int. 5

Dear Dad:

Cold day, high wind; battle ship in front yard; corso floreale dawdling along the front.

Recd. Am. Mercury; W. Work; and Mr Wescott's nuvvle.

Mencken has one good item called 'Training of a Journalist'

Wot ells?? nawthink much. Am.Merc's account of America looks as zif it wuz getting steadily worse.

Have read Finlay's Hist. of Byzantine Empire, dull with occasional items of interest.

Note that Lamberton is 100% murkn. also pixture of LOGS in Canada.

Suppose if I got started on another canto, or hadn't forgotten all the moozik I learned last summer I might feel better. At present am feeling inactive.

Hats 35 and 40 dollars INDEED. Can do better than that here.

What you might do to assist editorial functions wd. be to indicate ANY tract or group of POSSIBLE intelligence in the U.S.A. Do you ever see a serious publication.

Mencken gets an item about once in every three numbers. Have you any opinion of how the New Masses carries? C.W. Wood appears to cerebrate from time to time.

Am looking round for a sensitive spot; some part of the murkn consciousness where a jab wd. be felt. Does it exist??

Have you read Elmer Gentry or Gantry or whatever its called? Is it any good; or merely the olde olde story?

Have things changed during the past years or are they still as they were in 1910? Etc.

Sorry to bother you with questions; but very little nooz here.

As you don't know what's in Cantos XVII-XXV; I suppose you have no STRONG ideas re/ what ought to go into the next ten;

apart from Nero's having remarked that he wished the Roman people had only one neck.

even that simplification seems to present complications.

The modern universal remedy is One millyun dollars, but those that have 'em seem unable to do anything of the least interest with same.:: so there is prob. a fallacy in that remedy also.

Ford sez he is coming down here in a week or so; perhaps I can pump him re/ N.Y.

ole Steev has telegraphed from Shy:kago re/ some kind of lecture bureau; but looks very flimsy to me.

I haff no more g,d, idea WHAT the american is capable of understanding, even when put in the simplest terms than how you wd. teach calculus to an esquimaux.

HAVE THEY ANY insides to their heads? I mean; is there any reason to suppose that those one hasn't met are any more intelligent than those that one HAS?

On looking into Personae yesterday, was surprised I hadn't been shot before leaving England. Only supposition is that no reader understood half what he read, or that reading of work was strictly limited. As W.B.Y. says: The only reason we are here is because they dont know we exist; if they had the least idea what we thought they wd. abolish us all.

Await your reactions to 'Exile'.

Oh yes, did I write that had lunch with Max Beerbohm last Thursday; largely occupied in recollecting members of prewar England. Cunninghame Graham turned up just as we were leaving. Still decorative but showing wear. Had been looking after ranch in Venezuela . and also digging supposed lit. talent out of Caucasian circus rider.

Also heard from Henry Newbolt, very affable. About to spot up for using some poems in a sort of Anthology. Naturally argument about WHICH.

Defended his choice in part by saying Robt. Bridges also approved of the pomes. Obviously I have a very select set of readers.

Had I but had 'a natural talent for sycophancy' I might have 'gone far'.

Mac George, our local retired colonel, knew Lawrence in Arabia . adds footnote about the chief in command saying: Take em away

Lawrence: But these Arabs are friendly

C. i C. 'Take 'em away.

Etc. McG. much interested in the Lawrence stuff and in 'Asia.'

Etc. getting on for dinner time; probably shd. have postponed writing this till after same; might have got a little more sparkle into it. A relapse into cold weather is fatal in Italy;

everything runs on the sun.

love to you and mother

E

Elmer Gantry (1927), *a novel by Sinclair Lewis.*

⊹⟨≡⟩⊹

790. TLS [on 'Ezra Pound' letterhead]

11 April '27

Rapallo | via Marsala, 12 int. 5

Dear Dad:

Have written a line to Cousin Charles. Sorry you have been ill; ditto re the small FOOTE. You might by the way send me a list of the young Feet and Wads. for future ref/- The local Doc. says I am O.K.; rather good specimen, English born in China, and returned via Africa.

/ / /

Afraid the whole damn poem is rather obscure, especially in fragments. Have I ever given you outline of main scheme ::: or whatever it is?

    1. rather like, or unlike subject and response and counter subject in fugue.

        A.   A. Live man goes down into world of Dead

        C.   B. the 'repeat in history'

        B.   C. the 'magic moment' or moment of metamorphosis,

               bust thru from quotidien into 'divine or permanent

               world'. Gods etc.

In Canto XX, fragment in Exile. Nicolo d'Este' in sort of delirium after execution of Parisina and Ugo. (for facts vide, I spose, the Encyclopedia Britan.)

      'And the Marchese

        was nearly off his head' after it all

Various things keep cropping up in the poem

The original world of gods; the Trojan war,

Helen on the wall of Troy with the old men fed up with whole show and suggesting she be sent back to Greece.

Rome founded by survivors of Troy. Here ref/ to legendary founding of Este (condit (founded) Atesten Este)

Then in the delirium, Nicolo remembers or thinks he is watching death of
Roland. Elvira on wall of Toro (subject rhyme with Helen on Wall) (epi purgos,
on wall) peur de la hasle (afraid of sunburn)
Neestho (translated in text: let her go back)
[H]o bios :: life
    cosi Elena vi[d]i : thus I saw Helen
        (misquote of Dante)
The whole reminiscence jumbled or 'candied' in Nicolo's delirium. Take that as
a sort of bounding surface from which one gives the main subject of the Canto
the lotophagoi: lotus eaters, or respectable dope smokers; and general paradiso
:::: You have had a hell in Canti XIV, XV; purgatorio in XVI etc.
the 'nel fuoco' is from St Francis 'cantico'
    'my new spouse placeth me in the flame of love'
Then the remarks of the opium smoker about the men who sailed under
Ulysses
voce profondo : with deep voice
and then resumé of Odyssey; or rather of the main parts of Ulysses' voyage up
to death of all his crew.
for Elpenor, vide Canto I.
Ear wax, ear's plugged so they couldn't hear the sirens.
Neson amumona, literally the narrow island; bull-field where Apollo's cattle are
kept.
Ligur aoide: keen or sharp singing. (sirens)
      song with an edge on it.
   that gets most of the foreign quotations.
Tan mare fustes: is Roland's remark to moor who comes up to finish him off,
as nearly as I can remember his sword is broken, but he smashes the moor
over the head with his horn (olifans :: elephant : olifant tusk; and then dies
grumbling because he has damaged the ornaments on the horn and broken it.
Tan mare fustes; colloquial: you came at at a bad moment. Current cabaret
song now; J'en ai marre: I'm fed up.
    Any more ke-weschuns???

    As to the Rodker: I rather think he gets more into the 90 pages (that make
the complete nouvelle) than most novelists get into 300. However . . . .
    Give my regards to Ingles; tell him he is to keep you in order. Wot 'id young
Jack bust his hip for?
                Love to you and mother
                      E

John Rodker's Adolphe 1920 was being published in Exile.

791. TLS [on 'Ezra Pound' letterhead]

3. April 1927

Rapallo | via Marsala, 12 int. 5

Dear Mother

Sorry to hear you have been ill. But relieved to hear you are recovering. Glad dad enjoyed the concert. N.Y. apparently aware of Jawg's arrival. Ford has just been here for a week. Wants me to lexture in U.S.A. but as yet no sufficient guarantee has arrived. F. haz sure done noble; ramming my woiks into that desert alkali.

I have got to page 24 in my book on machines for Covici. At least he SEZ he wants it. I have recovered the photos. so seems some chance of their being utilized at last.

Book will permit me to comment on EL RIVETOR.

Price's xperience with customs will by now have convinced him that the govt, ought to be anihilated. Have you ever heard of a congressman named Vestal? One honest man in that nest of scoundrels. Is anything known of him?

Wot ells.

love to you & dad

E

You shd have omar's photo by now -

EL RIVETOR, 'that charming cartoon which greeted Mr Antheil's performance in New York (April 1927)'—EP in 'The Acoustic of Machinery', one of his 'Machine Art' drafts (Machine Art & Other Writings (1996), p. 72). '**Price's xperience**', as reported by Homer, had been with the Postal authorities rather than with Customs. The first number of Exile had 'Passed through O. K. . . . NO duty charge'. (But see Letter 794). However, 'there should be at least 4 numbers a year to entitle the magazine to 2 Class postage; and as for copyright, 'the whole contents of the magazine should be sent them, and it should be printed over here, under the present rulings'. 'No use damning them for it', Homer commented, 'they simply have to do as the law says.' Albert H. **Vestal** (1875–1932), Chair of the House Committee on Patents, was forwarding several bills to reform the copyright laws.

Isabel and Homer had been longing to see a **photo of Omar**, and Dorothy had finally sent one, the first, on the 16th. 'I hope you like him: brown eyes after mother', she wrote; and the grandparents liked it so much they had it enlarged and gave copies to their friends, and sent one to Ezra.

792. TLS [on 'Ezra Pound' letterhead]

1 May 1927

Rapallo | via Marsala, 12 int. 5

Dear Dad:

Thanks very much for the dinner. The rest of your honoured epistle Xpresses my own sentiments but as Ford has been so nobly selling my stock in America, AND as he has given several lectures himself I cd. hardly put it so simply. <D. also of yr. opinion>

I cant see that a lecture tour wd. be justified unless there were a surety of clearing up say 10,000 dollars (which there aint). Less than that wd. be no use as capital and wd. probably go in extra expenses, and one be no further along at the end of it, save for six months' wasted time.

The opera is another matter, but it dont need a HUGE house, and whether America will take anything that isn't put on a BIG CIRCUS ree-mains to be SAW.

I have written out about thirty pages of letter press to go with the machine photos. but whether Covici will print it, remains also to be SAW. I dunno if its good enough. Out of rabbit of writing prose.<he sez he wantzit but he aint saw it yet.>

Voluminous edt. notes for Xile get reduced to a page or two. or disappear.

This is nothing to weep about. If I pull off the long poem, that's enough.

Glad mother is better. Weather here also fogged up.

Yes I recd. book, two worlds, and murk-ury. Thanks

Roth is less a scoundrel than the LAW. I dont imagine his stealing those poems takes anything out of my particular pocket, but the same dont apply to about 40 other people whose work he has swiped.

an thaat's that. If you happen to see Sellers tell him I have recovered the photos. and am making another effort to make use of them ; but may not be sufficiently intelligent to put it over. Xplain that the demise of late regretted Walsh has caused delay.

love to you & mother

E

+=—=+

793. TLS [on 'Ezra Pound' letterhead]

Satrdy. May the 7th, 12 and the somethingth p.m.

Rapallo | via Marsala, 12 int. 5

Dear Dad:

Have just shipped the Machine text and photos. to Covici, and eaten half a chicken. So thaa's thaat. Cov. sez he wants book; but remains to be sawn if he does when he seeZit.

Yr. hnrd epistle to hand. I can not answer fer Jawg's answering letters. he mostly dont till he gets excited and busts in 20 pages.

I dont imagine he took the critiques to heart. Nobody has had as much 'space' on a concert since Adam invented the BANjo.

It now remain to see whether E.P. will finish another book by the 15th. Probably KNOT. Why should he?

The multiplicity of new reviews is a good sign; even if the reviews are bad. The more people find out about our goddam copyright and customs house the better, and the sooner they'll be dead.

Also any sign that anybody is not lying down flat and accepting the Century, and Mencken, etc. is also to the good. Thankful hearts are uplifted even when I return 'em their mss.

love to you and mother.

E

+≔≕+

794. TLS [on 'Ezra Pound' letterhead]

11 May [1927]

Rapallo | via Marsala, 12 int. 5

Dear Dad -

Price reports that he has finally rescued Exile from the sonzofbitches in the N.Y. customs. Two murders on his block that evening, but he fails to state whether any of the cutoms house is yet dead. One can but hope. Have been looking through T.C.P relics and find that he suggested doing something or other re/ Mississippi floods.

Do you know anything about a paper called the 'Nation'? What pollyticks etc? I may be writing a few articles somewhere or other. Get a few things off my chest so they wont disthract my mind from matter of importance. But shd. like to take prelim. precaution of knowing where one can call WHO a s.o.b.

Bill Bird has got a letter from Otto Kahn saying he will tell Metropolitan I have writ a opera; but I don't imagine anything will come of it.

Exile No.2 is prepared but am waiting to find out whether it can be printed in the U.S. or whether it has to be bootlegged. The first number printed in the U.S. will possibly contain a short history of the murkn. bureaucracy.

I see somebody in China suggesting that every embassy shd. have an educated man attached to it to establish 'cultural relations' or zummat. tell that to the illiterate senate. Mrs Trigo sez Borah is such a nice man: and the papers say he is studying Spanish.

Sfar as I'm concerned you can switch off Murkn. Murk. and try some other paper for a while. I reckon I've about got Murk. range. Shd. like to see copy of New Yorker, Nation (don't buy 'em specially for me) or any other serious pubctn. you use. Does 'Outlook' still exist. Don't seem to be much brain in the country. Difficult to understand after living over here for so long, where the literate element occasionally has a stab at public matters.

New Statesman sent me two quid. stg. last week don't yet know what they printed. I wrote in anger.

Cant remember what I had on my mind; wuz intending to write you ABOUT something. Enc. clipping from Nouvelles Literaires. Linati also due for another shot in the 'Corriere'.

Flowers sprouting on terazza. Sun fit to bathe in. Wot ells? Rodker reports two capitals designed for next vol. cantos. How he is to sell it, I don't know as most of the subscribers to Vol. one, are either broke, or enraged with EITHER me or J.R.

However . . . . .

Exile No. 1. seems to have cleared expenses. and a few copies still stored for future ref.

etc. love to you and mother

E

*Otto Kahn was a generous patron of the New York Metropolitan Opera. Exile no. 2 contained two brief items by Pound that could be considered notes towards 'a short history of the murkn bureaucracy', i.e. 'Prolegomena', and 'Note re 1ˢᵗ Number'. Pound would initiate a correspondence with Idaho Senator William **Borah** in 1933. The* **New Statesman** *had published a long letter from Pound under the heading 'American Book Pirates'.*

+⊨=◄+

795. ALS

June 1st [1927]

Venice

& extremely busy. will resume correspondence with outer world sometime about July 4th.

Rodker waiting for Cantos.

Covici publishing 2nd SECOND exile

book Trunk in Rapallo

your damn fool shipper sent it via NAPLES.

As I take it you paid to Genoa. can you put in claim - or at least STRONG censure. I have no typewriter here. & cant compose suitable diatribe in ink-

Love to you & mother

E

Just recd. George's apologies for not visiting you - he was very fatigued. concert so soon after his pneumonia. He is invited for Frankfurt festival

Dont worry about Lewis - all large fauna shd. be preserved.

*Homer Pound had seen Wyndham **Lewis**'s severe critique of Pound as 'The Revolutionary Simpleton' in his magazine* The Enemy.

+>=<=+

796. ALS

15 June [1927]

Venice

Dear Mother.

Cant correspond without typewriter.

Book trunk is at last delivered to Hotel Mignon.

Great deal to do here. 3 libraries. Am supposed to have finished Canto XXVI. - so Rodker will have it in time for the new vol.

I enclose some animals.

Love to you & dad.

Dont suppose your Monros will be in Milan in July or Aug. are they completely illiterate?

I mean what are they supposed to see me for. Naturally connection with making money in any way shd inspire respect & curiousity on my part. Has P.M. suggested my taking active part in his bizniz or wot??

I dont otherwise see why it is my place to do anything but admit 'em if they turn up in Rapallo.

where I shall be probably in August.

D. has prob. written you that she has transferred the egregious Omar to London.

I have a little difficulty in placing the P. Monro.? Hirams grandson on the distaff side ??

What's he interested in except the value of his time??

Peace be with you.

Venice rather puts one off the belief that anybody's time is of such vawst importance

Love to you & dad

E

Dorothy had written from London to Isabel Pound:

Omar's address is now London. I fetched him from Paris yesterday: Mother and I went up to the [Norland] nurseries this morning, and he seemed quite happy: certainly much less tired than his Mama! . . . He is out nearly all day in the pram in the garden and taken each morning into Kensington Gardens.

They are all so nice, and business-like at his place, that I feel very content to have him there.

┼╾╍╼╫

797. ALS

3 July [1927]

Venice | but address Rapallo

Dear Dad -

Thanks for enlargement - comes up very well.

No. I don't want you to sell the coat of arms. - Will try to send you $50. for it, before Xmas. if you want to cash in.

Sell him the chess men, if he wants to buy something.

Was busy finishing vol. II of cantos.

Have had more trouble with my tripes, hope it is the end of it. however rather disthracting. - Doc. don't regard it as serious,

Also gathering 'material' for further canti = slow process.

I think the charge on trunk was 237 lire.

But haven't the voucher, as Papa Amante paid it for me in Rapallo, & I shall pay him when I get back.

I had to send him the papers nacherly.

thought I told you how much it was in my letter.

However if your receipt is to Genoa or Naples it means that you paid the distance. whichever was furthest.

Put in a claim for 273 lire.

Somewhat warm this a.m. - wot ells??

very convenient to have Dazzi here in Querini (biblioteca). Also chap: named Favai – painter who plays chess.

Castelani. painter whom I met in Cesena, has also come up to the local great city. = making progress.

Stokes has gone back to England.

About the antiques. The things I <u>don't</u> want sold are gt. grandmothers portrait; the arms, & the little embroidery by Hannah Howe (unless you have already sold this last.)

Glad to hear mother is really well.

will try to resume correspondence when I get back to typewriter.

Love to you & mother.

E

┼╾╍╼╫

798. TLS [on 'Ezra Pound' letterhead]

26 July 1927

Rapallo | via Marsala, 12 int. 5

Dear Dad:

Enclose another member of the family. Also canto 26.

Re mother's epistle recd. on return here. I have not read Millay's King's Henchman, and she will please NOT send me a copy.

more anon; various arrears awaiting attention.

E

Pound was just back from a visit to his daughter Maria at Gais.

799. TLS [on 'Ezra Pound' letterhead]

29 July [1927]

Rapallo | via Marsala, 12 int. 5

Dear Dad:

Havent done much but clear up desk, etc, since ruturn.

1.   Rodker is said to be getting on with edtn. of Cantos; D, having seen six designs for the caps. etc.

2.   Covici reports, new edtn. of the Antheil to be out in Aug.

3.   2nd. Exile for Sept.

4.   Likes the Machine book very much, and is going to gather in some more photos to see if he can beat the lot already collected.

/ / / / thass thaat.

Will you in return for enclosed two bucks please
purchase FOUR copies of <u>Town and Country</u> for May 15th.

Will you please send ONE, complete marked copy to Mrs Dalliba John, 11 Lungarno Guicciardini, Firenze, Italy.

One complete copy and two cut out double pages with picture and notice re/ Olga, here to me. She is on way to Salzburg, but dont know what her address will be by end of Aug.; hence want 'em sent here, rather than direct.

The book trunk contained a hell of a lot I didn't want, but some of it may come in useful and several of the items I had not asked for I am very glad to have, so thass that.

Some of the stuff OUGHT to have been sold, even if for 50 cents . . . . hwoeffer . . . . I never wd. have paid for shipping the early vols. of Poetry, but find it interesting to look back at that distant epoch, and mebbe it will come in handy.

ETC.

Love to you & mother

E

<hr />

800. TLS

2 Sept. 1927

[Rapallo]

Dear Dad:

As all my prose woiks except Pavannes and a few unbound copies of the Gaudier are out of print, spose you run erbaht and find someone (old dull firm) ready to do a four or five vol. edtn. of my woiks (prose) properly sorted out into Mediaeval, French modern, yanko-british modern, frivolacious, traductions, etc.

Covici, as you know, is sposed to be on the job. He has enough to keep him employed for a bit.

What you can do is to ask a few questions; and also get me catalogues of a few old firms; I want to see who handles this heavier variety.

Also git me, please, a list, full list, of woiks included in Doc. Eliot's 'book-shelf' five foot shelf.

that is fer another propoise, but precedes the other request.

Re/ pubshrs. rule out Macmillan, Knopf, and new wildcat or dishonest firms, Selzer, Boni and Boni. Selzer dishonest, and Boni hardly sound.

Appleton, Lippincott, Scribner,? Methuen, Constable. (dunno if the latter exists in america), Holt.

be issued in uniform size, binding - every six months until finished.

Etc.

love to you and mother.

E

Oh yes, about David. I shd. be very glad to see him. Why the hell dont you or didn't you give him my address?? I shant be in Paris. Can put him up for a week here if he wants to come down, or can get leave of absinthe.

as you haven't given me his Paris address, I dont know how I am expected to communicate with him.

am writing to Paris Tribune, to see if they will put in ad. for him

*Over the following five years Pound put much effort into preparing **a collected edition of his prose writings**. The Aquila Press agreed in 1929 to publish his Collected Prose, as well as his edition of Guido Cavalcanti's poetry, and his translation of the Confucian Odes, but the press failed before completing the first of these undertakings, the Cavalcanti edition. Other publishers would show interest in the collected prose project—Caresse*

Crosby's Black Sun Press, Hamish Hamilton—then in 1932 George and Mary Oppen, with Louis Zukofsky as editorial adviser, would bring out the first volume of a proposed twelve volumes, after which they would run out of capital and that would be the end of the project. '**Dr. Eliot's Five Foot Shelf**' or The Harvard Classics, a 51 volume anthology of world literature selected by Charles W. Eliot in 1909 while President of Harvard.

+≥—•—≥+

801. TLS

4 Sept. [1927]

[Rapallo]

Dear Mother:

Dad was asking about what magazines to send.

The New Yorker is no good; just same old flitter as Vanity Fair, and usual junk.

I have seen enough of the Mercury to get forumula, dont buy it on my account. On the otherhand, if you buy it, send it, as Carnevali still likes to see it. He is bed ridden for life in a country hospital outside Bologna, and glad to get reading matter.

Wot I suggess, is a different mag. each month, less boring and gives on more diversified view of the national idiocy.

'Asia' does have something in it, and not wholly concerned with delivering canned tripe.

No, on the whole, send the Mercury if you buy it at all direct to

EMANUEL CARNEVALI

Il Cavaletto | BAZZANO | privincia di Bologna | Italy.

That will save one lot of postage, and I wont be tempted to waste time on it.

Thanks for photos recd.

love to you & dad

E

+≥—•—≥+

802. TLS [on 'Ezra Pound' letterhead]

7 Sept. [1927]

Rapallo | via Marsala, 12 int. 5

Dear Dad:

Will you forward the enclosed to Aunt Florence in order to show that I have taken what measures are possible in order to get in touch with D.F.

Apart from which there is no news in particular since I last wrote. Might have been simpler to provide the noble militaire with my address before he started.

11th Sept.

The above appeared some days ago. No nooz of Mr D. Foote as yet. I dont know of any further measures I can take. I hear some of the band is going to Nice. which aza matr ov act is not much easier to get to or from than Paris. Etc.

Canto 27. has gone toward the printer, who says the paper for book is sposed to be on way from Italy to London.

Am blocking in Cantos 28-30 but they wont affect the present volume.

Otherwise waiting for manifestations from Covici. and various other lines are out, awaiting nibbles. all seems to move very slowly; BUT . . . I dare say one has got accelerated to too great a degree.

Having a printer (as let us say Darantiere) under ones hand, spoils one for slow processes of publication.

Fine ole equinoxial gale getting up. 2 bits of brit. navy in harbour, also a supply ship. Local team beat 'em at water polo this morning 3 to 0.

However the natives have little do do save swim.

Jawg writes me that he has a ballet finished, with decoration by Miro; you may have heard me mention Miro years ago. Spanish painter; some reprods in Little Rev. or elsewhere.

Some talk of Russian Ballet putting it on. In fact a 'promise' but Jawg is so hopetimistic . . . in any case nothing definite or soon.

Thanks for the enlargements, did I thank you for em before.? D, also encloses her thanks.

Have been rereading H. James 'Europeans' and 'Aspern Papers' very good author. Also, I think it pays to read him in the revised edition. at least I dont remember these being as good when I read 'em in earlier form.

Various forms of herbage sprouting on the 'roof' (in pots . . . not from chinks in masonry)

Omar records birthday on[e] yesterday; he sends you his best regards. We recd. statement from his official spokesman that he wd. not run for the presidency at either this election or that in four years time. He trusts that Calvin wont either. He thinks Borah's chances are low.

Yours

E

Pound's letter of 1 November 1927 is in response to the following letter from his father. (Pound's letter(s) 'of the 2 & 8th' are missing, presumed lost.)

Oct.19 (1927)

Dear Son,

Yours of the 2 & 8th here. <u>Thanks</u>. Now do not mistake your old Dad. Had no idea you would invest in Book Shelf, but in order to get you the information, had to go to the Main Office here, and there Dad had a lecture on the importance of the shelf &&&. Dad has always had some sort of notion about the matter as you seem to have. The <u>Waste</u> <u>Basket</u> will serve you. <u>Jews</u> = Why does Ezra hate the Jews? was asked me, and I had to say I did not know, so I am pleased to hear from you regarding that matter. I may remind you that some years ago I had to tell that <u>August</u> body that meets in the Witherspoon Bldg, what the Hebrews were doing down town for the children &&&. Why if it was not for them (the jews) here in Phila – this old town would be a desert. They are the ballast in this old ship, but I must confess I had an idea that you desired to get out of their hands & <u>But, but</u>. &&

Why not send me a copy of your latest portrait by Stowitz = We want to know <u>who</u> the Principino <u>is</u>??

Regarding the Gaudier book. I have loaned Mr. Sears my copy, and expect to hear from him in a week or so. You wrote that it was prose = you desired published? = Will get in touch with Jeanne Foster, but would like to know how you got her to take an intcrest in you and who she is? Did you think that Dad was not competent to act as your Agent?

Lovingly,
Dad

Well maybe I am not up to such matters?

+➤═◄═►═◄+

803. TLS [on 'Ezra Pound' letterhead]

1 Nov. 1927

Rapallo | via Marsala, 12 int. 5

Dear Dad:

Very amiable of Mr Harriman, to whom I trust you will transmit this epistle. I don't care how mad it makes him if it carries a germ of thought.

I had never heard of Sears and Co. till this a.m.; that is not remarkable as they are almost the worst type of parasitic printing house, and have no single book on their list that is printed for any reason save that of gouging the most possible cash out of public for the least possible return, in mental stimulus.

Yes, they print several classics, but only those on which copyright has expired, and for which they pay nothing to the creators. (Poe, or Flaubert).

They are parasites, and parasites, and yet again parasites. Their contemporary stuff is on a level with Curtis, Lorimer, or other vermin. It leaves the booblick just where it finds it.

That Mr H. has derived pleasure from my work, or from any other piece of decent writing shows or may show that he has got his own head an inch above that of his printer's foreman, but it also shows that he ought to have it jacked up still further. It shows that he is getting something <u>out of</u> literature, or is merely being amiable to you whom he has met personally.

The presenting of 'what is modern' means taking a risk on not having immediate sales, or on not having sales at all.

Any firm, obviously has to cover its expenses, and make a profit. But I decline to meet a man or write out verses for a man whose firm MERELY DOES NOTHING save act as parasite. If there were one or two authors on their list it wd. be different. Heaven knows Liveright prints tripe, but he prints something else as well, so also Knopf, Harper, etc. but this Sears list is amazingly complete in its parasitism.

I don't care what he does, but he has got to do something. He has got to do what they make people do here in Italy when they give concerts, even if they play dead men's music, i.e. pay in a small percentage for the upkeep of the living.

A certain percent, say, for argument, merely one fourth of one percent of their profits on dead stuff have got to go to the upkeep of living, non-commercial writers;

or they have got to get out and work for the new Vestal copyright law, i.e. law against theft, as now permitted by our dastardly copyright bluff.

or they have got to think up some way of giving a small return, or making a small contribution to the mental existence of the race.

yrs.

E

Nov. 1.

There endeth the epistle for transmission to Harriman, pass it on. I dare say it won't draw blood and tears. One has to educate ones periphery. It is slow going. He prob. thinks his damn firm an innocent corporation. Ahj!!!

Jeanne is a friend of Quinn's, thought you had met her. At any rate, I suggested she start a lit. agency, for pushing live stuff, and having placed matter in her hands, I have to behave as I wd. with any other agent. (She's now asst. edtr. on Bookman or some other dead rag, etc. etc,)

Nancy Cox was in N.Y. last time I heard of her. No reason why she shdn't pretend she was writing to us, (if she does). I don't suppose she can 'write', but don't tell Harriman, that. I don't recall that she ever actually sent us a letter worth reprinting, so they prob. aren't actual copies of correspondence. She's a good girl. As you know, she made a very nice brass head of yr. aff. offspring.

Thanks very much for the 5 bucks, which you shdn't have sent.

I can't get up any interest in Mr Monroe, but he is welcome to call if he happens to be in Rapallo. Every time a real murkn. business man comes here with his breezy, vacuous geniality, it postpones my unprojected trip to the U.S.

Jews!!!! oooo sez I 'ates the jews? Ask him why he thinks I 'ate the jews. I hate SOME JEWS but I have greater contempt for Christians. Look wot they dun to america: Bryan, Wilson, Volstead, all goyim. horrible goyim. Curtis, Lorrimer, american womens clubs, all the tripe, all goyim.

Of course some jews are unpleasant, ask any jew if they aint.

Haven't yet recd. photo. of protrait by Stowitz; suppose he is east of Suez, by now.

If your friend wuz a jew himself, or if you meet an elder in ISraEL, ask him whether he don't want me to write an article on Goyim, for 'Zion' or for the Jewish World.

Stokes just come to take us to lunch.

The 'Principino' is the Prince of San Faustino head of the Bourbon del Monte tribe. His maw was Miss something of somewhere, back in heaven knows when. He lives a few doors off on the cliffs. I think we get a free trip to Firenze on thursday.

am now going to lunch.

E

J. H. Sears & Co. were publishers in New York. Jeanne Foster was assistant editor of the American Review of Reviews

+⊨⊨+

804. TLS [on 'Ezra Pound' letterhead]

11 Nov. 1927

Rapallo | via Marsala, 12 int. 5

Dear Mother:

Very nice trip to Firenze, fine weather down and while there, caugh in mist on Bracco pass coming back.

Worked like dog while there. By miracle found and bought copy of non extant first edition. of Guido, (a.d. 1527).

yesterday sent off TA HIO to Hughes; wrote and sent off article to the Nation. in p.m. did yet another article. etc.

tremendous tempest. also played a little tennis in high wind. etc.

Payson Loomis arrived here during absence. Has ordered one of the new 100 dollar Cantos. Oh yes, sample pages of that recd.

P.L. also brought some pomes, some of which I shall send on to Cov. for 3d. issue Exile.

Stokes and Kent, in on Weds. evening. all three of the young for dinner. so at last there is evidently a new generation beginning to sprout.

Stokes working on book on XV century, Malatesta etc. has published a Ariadne and 'Dawn in the West'.

etc.

wot ells. Omar cutting back teeth. wot ells.

TA HIO is the first book of Confucius, in case I haven't said so before.

Glad to see am. elections have gone wet, but wish pestilence wd kill 80 percent of present american bureaucracy.

love to you & dad

E

Pound had bought from Orioli a copy of the first printed edition of the works of **Guido Cavalcanti**, *and would shortly begin to put together his own ambitious edition of Cavalcanti's poems, to consist of a 'Critical Text, with Translation and Commentary and Notes by Ezra Pound', together with facsimiles of the original manuscripts. Pound's* **Ta Hio**. *The Great Learning Newly Rendered into the American Language, was to be published in April 1928 by Glenn Hughes at the University of Washington Bookstore, Seattle. The article in the* **Nation** *on 30 November 1927 was headed 'The Passport Nuisance'. Of* **Payson Loomis** *Dorothy wrote to Isabel Pound, 'a most charming but determined young man . . . We called him cousin. He's gone to study in Paris'. In Paris he succeeded A. R. Orage as translator to Gurdjieff at La Prieuré. In the 1928 presidential election the Democratic candidate Al Smith, a* **'wet'**, *was calling for the end of Prohibition, but the 18th Amendment would not be repealed until 1933.*

+==+

805. TLS [on 'Ezra Pound' letterhead]

16 Nov. [1927]

Rapallo | via Marsala, 12 int. 5

Dear Dad -

Yes, I get the magzines. At least sfar as I know. Haven't read the fascist article yet, but in general way I shd. think the name Seldes wd. guarantee its being hogwash.

I thought I did answer re/ the Coat of Arms. Tell him to go to hell. The coat stays in the family. It aint his coat.

Jeanne means well. Personality in question is however none of their damn business and not for sale.

Money for sewers. HELL!!

As to lectures, let 'em go on talking, usually the points they raise as inducement are the best deterrents. Much better than I cd. think up on my own.

Have shoved off a lot of mss. during past week time enough to discuss same when it gets printed.

Now hope to do Guido with full text in reprod of original mss. etc. have got the fine cut out of the way, and HOPE to git on with the Guido. wot ells.

The enc. had the usual photo and Art. 211. am sending 211 elsewhere. Wot ells.

Ringtailed gyascutus!! awl rite.

Any indications that Idaho wants me to succede Mr Bore-er?
The senate needs instruction worse 'n the ladies clubs??

E

Homer had sent Pound a copy of the November Harper's *and recommended that he read an article on '**Fasctisti**'. **Jeanne** Foster had suggested that Pound undertake a lecture tour in America. Homer was having to find $400 for the connection to the new **sewer** system, this with the house up for sale but no buyer in prospect. The **enclosed** may have been an interview in the Paris edition of the* Chicago Tribune *of 1 November 1927, in which Pound denounced the 'Idiocy of U. S. Mail Act' and had Article 211 of the criminal code printed. The interview was accompanied by a **photo** of Nancy Cox McCormack's life mask of Pound.*

<hr />

806. TLS

22 Nov. (1927)

[Rapallo]

Dear Mother:

No, thanks vurry much, don't think I can stand sunday supplements regularly. Have now made my little inspection of Eng. and Am. state of contemporary mentality. Evidently once in seven or ten years is enUFF.

Glad to have clippings of anything of interest and an OCcasional whole literary supplement. Regular supply wastes too much time. Journalism -- same thing poured out week after week, water on backs of ducks, may keep em damp but don't change organism.

Yes, if prose works (mine) once put in order might ultimately penetrate, and then the lives of your goddam neighbors Curtis, Lormier etc. wd. become more difficult, and resurrence of such diseases as Wilson, Bryan, Harding, Vilstead wd. be less frequent.

No man who has read a book will read certain sorts of tripe. However, ça s'appelle civilization, very slow in the making.

The whole prose recast shd. not appear until 'How to Read' has been printed, that is a sort of pivot, or whatchercall it, Any how, that gives the central idea, or ideas, and the until-now apparently random and scattered work all falls into shape, and one sees, or shd. see wot is related to wot and why the stuff is not merely inconsequent notes.

Briony are islands in the Adriatic other side of Venice, said to enjoy (like California) gt. nacherl a'vantages, but supposed to be gtly. polluted by golf-links and the golfisch booblik.

Mr. Loomis departed for Gurdjeff instichoot. (10 bucks a week and all found) must say the cheapness of the board looks a'zif the dear ole black man was in earnest and not merely out for oof.

M. Stokes has villa up hill, and M. Kent still in residence.

The last Hungarian, M. Josef Bard, stopping at Marsala (hotel) next door. Vide Harpers and Forum for his occasional essays, also novel now in press.

Rapallo repidly becoming the intellexshul centre of yourup, but don't mention the matter yet. There are several people who wd. render the seafront less agreeable.

Comment on Guido now attaining VASTY bulk. Must check my meoentum and stop writing prose efer . a while.

etc.

love to you and dad

E

'**How to Read**' *would appear first in three parts in* New York Herald Tribune Books *in January 1929. In a note in* Literary Essays of Ezra Pound *(1954) the essay is dated '1928 or '27'. In 1932 it was printed first, as 'Prolegomena 1', in the first (and only) volume of the proposed collected edition of his prose.* **Joseph Bard**, *described by Dorothy as 'a young Hungarian, full of languages, and writing in English', had written* Shipwreck in Europe *(1928), a novel which Pound would contrast with William Carlos Williams'* Voyage to Pagany *(1928): 'the particular equation of the Vienna milieu has had recent treatment "from the other end on" in Joseph Bard's* Shipwreck in Europe, *more sprightly and probably less deeply concerned with the salvation of the protagonist' ('Dr Williams' Position'). Bard introduced Pound to the work of the German anthropologist Leo Frobenius and to his concept of 'paideuma'.*

⊬⊱⊰⊦

807. TLS [on 'Ezra Pound' letterhead]

1 Dec.'27

Rapallo | via Marsala, 12 int. 5

Dear Dad:

Yrs. 11th inst. to hand.

Wrote to yr. esteamed Hamham or wots his name yesterday, he wuz enquiring wot wuz wrong with Sears.

Have tried to keep it in words of one syllable. Bad commerce to put their standard so low.

Lay off, s.v.p. such shows as Random house. Remember Covici WANTS to do the job. Small amateur firms are no use. for the business NOW.

Bad to <u>offer</u> the thing to people who may want it. Random cdnt. handle it ennyhaow.

Thanks for zeal.

Pussnly I dunno about paying mortgages. Might be better to invest (unless mortgage was eating large interest.) You can get seven percent on Brazil coffee bonds; labelled 7 ½ but cost 106.

However . . . . ef you've done it you've done it. Complimenti, if it makes you feel easier.

Prob. too late in life for you to take to finance. Wotcher pay on the mortgage 6%?

If you do sell house, fer Krizake do take advice of someone who knows at LEAST as much about investment as I do, before you park the profits.

Not that there'z any use in a amateur's trying to be clever, when the banks aint jess gawt nothink else to dew.

About collected edtn. Nothing is any use save some ole firm like Harper. Until one of that kind is ready, there is no use running counter to Horace's jedgement as to state of market.

Yaas, I hear Deah Wyndham wuz in new yok. Don't worry pore ole Wyndham has his troubles.

Have recd. copies of Cap. designs for XVII:XXVII; and like them very much.

Rodker has run wild and threatens to print three or four copies on veritable bullshide or sheeps hide or whatever at $250 each.

Tell that chap to go to hell about the coat of arms.

The chess men are another story. I dunno wot they are worth, but if you can cash in for double their value I can't see any great objection. I shd. like to have 'em . . . . but it aint a necessity.

The coat of arms, seems to me to belong in the family. Shdn't sell ones family tombstones. etc

Young Loomis that turned up here, very nice chap.

Yes, good trip to Firenze. Think I reported. La Principessa lent me copy Revelry last night. Seems rather gentle and rosy coloured pixture of Washington life. Can't believe thur evuh wuz such a refining feminine inflooenz in life of late presidential mess.

You may find me in the nooz sometime in a month or so.

Apart from which, there are supposed to be latent.

1 CANTOS, vol. 2. :: that at any rate is in process of being printed.

2 Exile 2. 'according to Covici'

3 Machine Art. ditto.

4 Pamphlet or pamphlet plus?? Hughes.

5 New Guido de luxe, Faber and Gw. say yes IF they can sell few copies to murka. Horace has writ to em asking how much. an' thaaas thaaat.

<Probably about all the traffic will stand for moment Cov thinks 2 vols a year about limit consumption capacity>

Plus one or two articles, one in proofs, so I suppose the 'Nation' means to print it some time.

Exile three; in typescript in this desk, very great improvement on early numbers IF le sieur Cov. ever gits orf the mark.

Glad to hear mother's so well.

Sure, hell yes, we receive magazines. Muss. not yet interferred with my reading matter. an thats that

love to you & mother & complimenti re H 3d

E

Revelry, *a novel by Samuel Hopkins Adams (1871–1958), based on the scandals of the Harding administration.* **In the news**, *probably on account of the announcement in the January 1928 number of the* Dial *that Pound had accepted its $2000 Award for 1927. Faber & Gwyer would find that Pound's desiderata for a* **de luxe** *edition of Guido Cavalcanti were proving too expensive, and also that neither Horace Liveright nor any other American publisher would agree to co-publish.*

808. ALS

16 Dec. [1927]

[in hospital, San Pier d'Arena]

Dear Dad:

Went down to Firenze & did a bit of work in libraries, for G. Cavalc. - backside swoll again - Have now, I presume, had the fistula finally dealt with -

Doc, in Venice, thought it unnecessary but Lusena, here, said it wd, never have come right until operated - - not supposed to be grave – but merely a bore. -

The job was done this a.m. & burning sensation now (2.45 p.m.) dying down.

Sent you announcements of new Cantos yesterday.

Exile No. 2. recd, here on Wednsday.

and No. 3 shipped off yesterday.

Also will find some canti in the Dial

No, I dont get the Nation. regularly, shd. be glad if youd send it <u>when</u> you <u>have</u> it.

Letter of mine has, or will appear.

Consul & part of staff, in Firenze where I applied for new passport on Monday - seemed pleased to hear I was registering kick -

Imagine any pore gordam official condemned to READ a application form - Takes 1 ¼ hrs to fill it out.

This a.m. is supposed to be one hell of a big whale -
Papa Amanti knew him during war. & he is said to know his job - enny how - hope he has demonstrated it in present instance -

---

This is his nuova spidale at San Pier d'Arena –

The head of nerve dept has flat under me in Rapallo - & is interested in Cantos - already been in to nquire –

====================

Bard at work on 2nd contract for Harper novel –

ect

E

*Pound's '**kick**' in the* Nation *of 30 November 1927 was headed 'The Passport Nuisance'. In the* Nation *of 14 December there was his **letter** declaring,*

> *For next President I want no man who is not lucidly and clearly and with no trace or shadow of ambiguity against the following abuses: (1) Bureaucratic encroachment on the individual, as the asinine Eighteenth Amendment, passport and visa stupidities, arbitrary injustice from customs officials; (2) Article 211 of the Penal Code, and all such muddleheadedness in any laws whatsoever; (3) the thieving copyright law.*

---

809. TLS

27 Dec. [1927]

[Rapallo]

Dear Dad:

Am up and about again. Recd. copy Am. Merc. also of Nation.

Have had 3 canti to correct in proofs. Wot ells. Dining at villa Barata this evening.

D. has recd. 10 bucks. xmas for offspring, for which our thanks.

Wot ells.? Nawthink much new I reckon.

Bard's novel here in proofs. Harper having cut the lurid sections. I dont know that it is made for wyncote, either.

Tell mother I shall be glad to Katherine Cochran as was; don't imagine she will have made much of 'Reidy the stiff'. . . . but still. . . .

Wotz bekum of Tom an' Joe?

Love to you and mother. Sent off a couple of very small packets ten days ago. Hope same arrove.

E

The '*3 canti in proofs*' would have been 'Part of Canto XXVII' and 'Canto XXII' for The Dial, *and* 'Part of Canto XXIII' for Exile no.3.

⊹⊱⊰⊹

810. TLS [on 'Ezra Pound | *res publica, the public convenience*' letterhead]

4 Jan. [1928]

Rapallo | via Marsala, 12 int. 5

Dear Dad

Desmond Fitzgerald, minister of defense, and commander in chief of the Oirish army has just been in, he is leaving fer the U.S. with the presidint in a few days time. As he is on ofishul bizniz, with every moment occupied, I said it wd. be suiting for you to call on him rather than him on you.

He will endeavor to telephone you when he gets to Phila. upon which you are to look in on him in his hotel.

more anon. Rather busy at moment.

E.P

yr. leter of 17th dec. recd.

⊹⊱⊰⊹

811. TLS [on 'Ezra Pound | *res publica, the public convenience*' letterhead]

8 Jan. 28

Rapallo | via Marsala, 12 int. 5

Dear Dad:

Recd. seven spanish dollars, or bill for same on continental congress. Also other contents of pckg. Thank you

Fitz. turned up here on Wednesday, as I rather hurriedly reported. If he does find the time to phone you, you might remember that he is the triple decked hero, much more so than Mr Lawrence 'of Arabia'.

Wot ells? Recd. proofs of a few cantos. Have packed up a small section of the Guido critique. Cold spell has let up. Wish I cd. be sure it was over. Now poss. to lunch out in the sun.

Bard and young Stokes the chief local sources of conversation.

Painter been in flat touching up north side of settin room. weather chief source of amusement.

love to you & mother

E

⊹⊱⊰⊹

812. **TLS** [on 'Ezra Pound | *res publica, the public convenience*' letterhead]
13 Friday, Jan. '28

Rapallo | via Marsala, 12 int. 5

Respected Progenitor:

Re/ Dial. It is the sort of news one prefers to believe after cashing the chq. same passed into lire early this week, and no protest has yet reached the local authorities.

I have not yet seen the Dial itself. nor Eliot's review. As you do not comment on latter I purrzoom E. has fulfilled Hem's prediction and been 'cautious'.

If you divide 2000 by 20 or twenty five you will arrive at some estimate of the valoo of licherchoor <per year> in the by-your-wife-so-respected market. It is of course a great thing for the country that a lot of sonsofbitches can make forchoons, and the benefactors who preserves these inferior species of biped are of course entitled to gratitood from those who like to see certain kinds of formenifera preserved.

Don't pick on the Dial, there are worse things.

and so forth.

A little more paint has been put on the settin room. The weather is warmer. The Chi. trib. reports death of Th. Hardy on Front page, and Death of Famous English Race Horse, in same size headlines on the back page. The curator of the Tate has let several millyun pund worth of Turner water colours be wet, but the Savoy cat has saved 2, millyun bottles of booz. <from flood> It is a great pity two hundred thousand Eng. and American politicians were not in the cellar of the Tate Gallery. and kept there. Not that I am crazy about Turner, but still . . . . . .

　　　　ETC.

My doc. sez I am going on O.K.: hope he knowz hiz bizniz.

Rodker reports several sales of Cantos.

Price reports Exile selling in N.Y.

Anything in particular you wd. like to have reported in Vol. III of the Cantos?

Perhaps mother wd. like me to devote a little space to the life of Cyrus K. Curtis and his LLLove ov the Human Race?

Jining in the euneevursal cho-russ of praise.

So I see Scribners is also going in for Quaker Oats and Mr Aiken. cheers!!

Mr Aiken is a fine specimen of wide open space robustezza. waal, waal, waal. Aint life jes' wonnerful. Hear dear Walter is at last having some pop. success. Apart from crosses from the royal Belgiums.

　　etc.

love
E

*Conrad **Aiken's** short story, 'Your Obituary, Well Written', was in the November 1927
issue of* Scribner's Magazine. ***Eliot's review*** *of* Personae *(1926) in the January* Dial
had the title 'Isolated Superiority', and was subtly qualified in its appreciation.

---

813. **TLS** [on 'Ezra Pound | *res publica, the public convenience*' letterhead]
22 Jan. [1928]

Rapallo | via Marsala, 12 int. 5

Dear Mother:

Recd. Scribners' false alarm. WHY these transports. Not till the last member
of the Scribner fambly is dead of diabetes will the product of their skunk-
perfumery plus sugar be altered.

Blah, and more of it. Aiken is a second rater. Hem. has a facility for doing all
sorts of stuff. Do fer xt's sake LOOK before you hurrah. Van Dine does a
barefaced immitation Doyle, all right as efficient example of cheapest form of
'tec', but for the boobconsumption they have to bblurb it as literature.

<Recd Time, Harpers Scriblers>

Whay the hell cant they do as every sane person does, read a 'tec' as a tec and
admit it.

Merely the worst form of deadhead gradually becomes extinct, or if not
worst form, at least certain definitely dated forms of blah disappear because the
god damnd imbeciles that produce 'em die, and the same brand of fool starts
diluting the fashions of a later period. But the deelightful quality of half-baked
pink-lemonade continues.

The spirichool home of Hen. Vandyke is the same ole firm. etc.

Wot ells? recd. Gertie Bell's letters. D. has begun 'em. Hope she'll find me the
quotation I want as illustration of spirit of hempire. If not I'll have to quote it
from memory.

Trying as the Dial is, it does occasionally print something decent. The
Mercury occasionally, at rarer and rarer intervals does print a socio-pl. article.

BUT the rest uv 'em. Pewk.

Asia is another question. having no literary pretense.

Wot. ells. Bard gone to London yesterday. Sez. he will bring back my
clavicord.

DONT call the Dial 'my own country'. The Dial is two young men, existing
in spite of the U.S.A. The country has got a LONG way to go, before can
be regarded as wanting anything fit to read. It howletch for lollypops, and
Chitaqua lecturers.

Do keep these things separate in yr. mind.

The Jan. Dial has one decent short story. Epstein has shown up very well in
the trial of the N.Y. custom house.

Have had bee-yewteeful catalogue of year befo last's show, from Brancusi.

Did I write that Gretchen Green, Tagore's ex-secretary was stationed some-where in Pa. and might look in on you

??

Etc.

E

*'S. S. **Van Dine**' was the narrator and supposed author of the Philo Vance murder mysteries, of which 'The Greene Murder Case' was then appearing in* Scribner's Magazine. *Conan **Doyle**, author of 'Sherlock Holmes' murder mysteries. Pound was probably hoping that Dorothy would find in **Gertrude Bell's letters** a quotation corresponding to a sentence he had cut out of an obituary article in the* New York Times *of 18 July 1926: 'she had a profound sympathy for the national aspirations of the Arabs and was firmly convinced that, when it was not inimical to her own interests, Great Britain should endeavour to carry out her war-time pledges made to the Arabs'. Pound would quote that in canto 52 in 1938: 'I think wrote Miss Bell to her mama / that when not against the interests of Empire / we shd/ keep our pledges to Arabs'.*

*　**Jacob Epstein** had given expert testimony on Brancusi's behalf in a famous test case that had begun in 1926 when US Customs would not recognize Brancusi's 'Bird in Flight' as a work of art, regarding it instead as 'a manufacture in metal' on which tax was due at 40% of its value, and refusing to release it until Brancusi paid the $240 duty. Brancusi sued for return of his money and won, the court's verdict being delivered in January 1928.*

+≡≡≡+

814. TLS [on 'Ezra Pound | *res publica, the public convenience*' letterhead]
25 Jan. [1928]

Rapallo | via Marsala, 12 int. 5

Dear Dad:

DO'mestik trouble!!! waal, waaaaal, waaaaaal. Ef a author sticks to wot he knows something about!!! Dear Fordie ought to a authority on that subject.

Have sent card to Ingle. Am supposed to be through with medicos. at least Lusena sez, final cure. Not quite closed up yet, but supposed to be finish of the matter. Lusena is one large size A.1. celebrated big pot, with extensive war record etc. so don't think I shd. have had any better attention even from Ingle.

Lauro Bsis friend Santana turned up yesterday. Being useful re/ Guido. Have no copy of letter sent to Dial.

Enc. sample morning's mail.

Wot'er you being operated FOR. Sedentary pursuits or wot?

Mine I think I stated was superficial fistula. following a couple of posterior abcessae. None of 'em supposed to be serious, but all a demnition bore.

Hope you see Fitz. Papers here full of Cosgrove.
love to you & mother
E

William T. Cosgrave, *the first President of the Irish Free State, was at this time touring the United States and Canada to rouse support for the new state.*

+≡=≡+

815. TLS

1 Feb. [1928]

V, Mars. 12/5 [Rapallo]

Dear Dad:

Enc. teleg. from Monsieur Coogan. Also clip. from Paris Chi. Trib.

Article on part of Guido is due in March Dial. Various other matters suspended, at least mail dont seem to arrive.

Hughes, as I think I said, is printing the TA HIO, 20 copies of which shd. reach you, in, I spose six months time.

Am looking at empty apartments here, for you, whenever I see sign 'to let'. Wot ells.

Kitty Heyman having succes with Scriabine concerts in Paris.

Yeats has been fairly ill. Due here on 17th inst.

Olga stopping off at Sta Margherita, goes on to Paris tomorrow.

Cournos in hospital in Switzerland. Contribution for Exile recd. from him this a.m.

Orrick Johns in Firenze. Haven't seen him, he was in hospital in Sicily last winter, then instead of coming here, he had to go to France to buy a new wooden leg.

Bill Bird talks of restarting his press.

I return at last a photo found in book trunk; have you any idea who it is? dem-d if I have.

'Nation' been sitting on an article of mine for months.

Love to you and mother.
E.

Stokes' family also arrived here, staying at 'the Bristol'

D. having a shiny bronze of Gaudier's 'Embracers' cast in Rome

Mould is there, had one bronze made when I was there two years ago.

Pound's article, 'Where is American Culture?', appeared in Nation *in April 1928. It was critical of the inefficiency in promoting American culture—due largely to their bureaucratic systems—of such cultural foundations as the Carnegie Libraries and the Morgan*

Library, the Curtis and the Juilliard music foundations, and the Barnes and the Guggenheim art foundations.

+⊱══⊰+

816. TLS [on 'Ezra Pound | *res publica, the public convenience*' letterhead]

1 March (1928)

Rapallo | via Marsala, 12 int. 5

Dear Mother:

Yeats has been here for a week or so, probably about ten days. Probably settling here. for part of year.

I enclose last thing in eyetalyan elegance. Dont know what the nooz is. Agent tells me there is to be a new British edtn collected poems, annotated by Eliot.

Telegram from N.Y. lecture bureau, prob. nothing likely to come of it.

The local young tennis terror wants me to enter Alassio tournament with him in the doubles. Not that I am back on my game yet. but still complete paralysis not set in. Slight lumbago for past few days.

Wot th ell.

D. is up a mountain with a returned missionary. Yes Chinese book arrived, berry interestin'. returned missionary promises us a descendent of Confucius in a month or so, who will prob. be able to decipher it.

Various dambloody amurkn magazines recd fer which, thanks. Have spent the p.m. playing chess in the bosch cafe. am still a little disthracted between that and William. not that there is anything of importance to relate.

Hope dad is O.K. again.

Antheil is supposed to have finished a jazz opera, not to be in good health, and has been asked to do music for one of W. B. Y.'s plays for Dublin theatre.

What V. Hunt book? (Flurried Years was sent me, not by authoress, some time ago). etc.

E

The **new British edition**, to be published in November 1928, would be a Selected Poems, 'edited with an Introduction by T. S. Eliot', but without further annotation. Pound would not approve of Eliot's omitting several of the epigrams from Lustra, and the whole of Homage to Sextus Propertius; nor would he approve of his including five early poems which he had himself excluded from Personae (1926). The '**local young tennis terror**' was Giuseppe Bacigalupo, who would become the Pounds' doctor and friend. The **Chinese book** was a 'screen book' consisting of eight ink paintings, each accompanied by a poem in Chinese and another in Japanese, the paintings representing eight classic views about the banks of the Xiao and Xiang rivers in South China. Canto 49, the 'Seven Lakes' canto, would be drawn from this book—see letter **827**. **Antheil** was *composing the music for the Abbey Theatre's June 1928 production of Yeats's* The Only Jealousy of Emer.

⊹⊱══⊰⊹

817. TLS [on 'Ezra Pound | *res publica, the public convenience*' letterhead]

21 March [1928]

Rapallo | via Marsala, 12 int. 5

Dear Dad:

Record snow storm on hand. Recd. your letter containing notes from DeVoto, and the noble perfesser of moozik.

Don't know why DeV. hadn't got my letter to him when he wrote. Praps. Harper saw postmark and thought it wd. be bad for morale of one of their authors to receive communique from europe.

FER GARDZAKE learn thrift and waste no more postage sending Harper's monthly sawdust across the Atlantic. IF by a miracle it shd. contain anything cut out the paragraph, but don't send the whole magazine. Glad to have the Nation.

Spring, I see by the paper, wuz fiscially declared at 8.45 last evening. that's what's started the weather. Cant remember what else.

Dined at Sayre's on Monday, motored to Genoa yesterday. Joyce is suing Roth, and wants me to alfreddavid something or other. Carnevali evidently wants to rise and assassinate Roth. etc.

six vols. of one kind or another are suspended in various parts of the planet. Rodker struggling with Brit. printers. etc.

As Nero remarked: he wished that the Roman people had only one neck.

If I had brains enough to write another canto I might be less annoyed by the god damned imbecility of nearly all the rest of humanity.

Amiable letter from young Zukofsky. also from Sem Benelli's onforchoonate sekertary who hopes to import the Celtic Drammer into Italy. deeply grateful for my assistance.

W. B. preparing some sort of misconception of Guido for Cuala Press, to be accompanied by some fragment of my projected edtn.

Re Becker: enforchoonately Walter did set the verses to music, but fortunately they are not easy to get. I trust no one will endeavour to do so. All except THE RETURN, which is nice moozik, but such that no one has ever endeavoured to sing it.

Love to you and mother

E

In the event Pound did not sign a protest against **Roth**'s *pirating Joyce's* Ulysses, *on the ground, as he told Joyce, that that the protest should be directed against the copyright and* *indecency laws which the unscrupulous publisher was exploiting. The Yeats/Pound book on **Guido Cavalcanti** from the Cuala Press did not in the end materialise. But Yeats did write* A Packet for Ezra Pound, *which was published by the Cuala Press in August 1929, and of which the first part, headed 'Rapallo' and dated 'March and October 1928', includes an account of his conversations with and observations of Pound. **John J. Becker** would compose a musical setting for Pound's 'Dance Figure' in 1932. **Walter Rummel** had published* Three Songs of Ezra Pound with Instrumental Accompaniment *in 1911, the three being 'Madrigale', 'Au bal masqué' and 'Aria'; and in 1913 he had published a setting of 'The Return'.*

+≻⋅≺+

818. TLS

[28 March 1928]

[Rapallo]

Respected progenitor:

You needn't have worried so about the female idiot. When guaranteeing not to injure the feelings of idiots, one take[s] count of intention. The enc. review. prob. proceeds from similar sort of Canadian idiot. etc.

You may forward the other enc. to Irwin, if you like.

I see by Hughes last pamphlet that my Kung fu tseu is next on list. You will receive 20 copies. Ten to distribute on such evangelical basis as you see fit.

Ten to 'hold at my disposition'.

Yeats seems to be trying to do some sort of note on the Guido, for a Cuala booklet.

Another note of Middle Ages, has been corrected. Due to appear in March Dial.

Exile reported due in April.

Eliot reported to be producing annotations for my English edtn. of poems. Wot ells.

No nooz of 'Machine Art', but Cov. has got round to signing Rodker's contract, so mebbe he'll git on to other work IN TIME.

Fine cine with Tigers and Elephants last evening. labled Gods, Beats and Men. Yeats somewhat indignant that connection with Ossendowsky was not apparent to naked eye.

Did I say that Ole Bill Taft, at my instigation has kicked that swine Kellogg in the posterior parts with net result of five pages from Genoa consulate trying to justify incompetence of State Dept.

yes, I doubtless ought to be edited, with letters of gold on an ivory background, but 67½% of the murkn peepul, and 98¼% of the <u>prominent</u> or protuberant americans ought to be effaced and eliminated from the kawsmoss at large. (perhaps this estimate is a bit high)

I am glad to see the TeaPot is still bubbling. Even the Dean of Windsor is deprecating the 18th abomination.

Undsoweiter. Believe most of the packages, in fact all listed in yr. letter to D. have arrived.

Love to you & dad

E

The *'female idiot'* was presumably Mary Dixon Thayer, who had published in the Philadelphia Evening Bulletin *of 20 February 1928 a piece entitled, 'Ezra Pound's Father Tells How Son Went to London With a Shilling and Found Fame'.* **William B. Taft** *was a past President of the United States, and* **Frank B. Kellogg** *was the current US Secretary of State. The* **Dean of Windsor**, *Reverend Albert Victor Baillie (1864–1955), had entered the controversy over the publication of Radclyffe Hall's lesbian novel,* The Well of Loneliness—*but the 18ᵗʰ* **Amendment** *to the US Constitution was to do with the prohibition of alcoholic liquor.*

Homer had written that he was expecting to retire 1ˢᵗ July and that his pension should be $1200 per year. He was 'wondering what you want us to ship over, when we get ready to depart?' He also remarked, 'Am told that you have to buy <u>Automobile</u> *made there as Muscillini will not allow any foreign machine sent there, &&&, but as I never expect to own or to run a* <u>Motor</u> *that does not scare me.'*

+≻━≺+

819. TLS

5 April [1928]

[Rapallo]

Dear Dad:

Yaas, as I have remarked, I think you can live here vurry comfortable on $100 a month, if you act with a little care n foresight.

In the main: DON'T bring furniture. In a climate like this the inside of a home is less used. The necessary furniture can be got on the spot, consisting in beds, table, and a couple of canvass deck chairs.

ON the other hand, I suggest that you bring bedding, blankets, any sort of hangings, draperies etc.

Both in Paris and here I have built the more ambitious bits of furniture. Arm chairs etc.

For books, I dunno how many you still have. On leaving Paris I had a book box made that now serves as book case. You shd. carefully <u>MEASURE the size</u> of the books you want to bring. You prob. wont need such a DEEP case as mine, as I had folios.

[diagrams]

Note that the DOORS fold in flush with the top and bottom, as noted at

654

'flange'. there are clamps top and bottom, pad locked. For your books, a shallower case, wd. prob. serve, with three straight shelves.

When we came down from Paris, didn't know where we wd. settle, so were prepared for shifts. Case in plain pine, not too heavy, but still heavy enough to stand chucking about.

I think the big portrait shd. have a case on same pattern, and one cd. PUT shelves into it after its arrival here. Leave enough space for shelf-ridges between frame and edge of box. <books accumulate have enough here now to fill extra case for you> and have case 6 1/2 inches deep, which is deep enough to take most books.

I don't imagine you will want to bring more books than will go into ONE smallish case. The one I brought from Paris is; 18 by 24 by 12 <inches>. Cant think you will want anything deeper than 9 inches, if that. Books shd fit quite snugly, not jammed, but snug, better for travel, and take less dust when set.

In the way of what I want brought. I want the portrait, and the Howe arms, don't recollect anything much else.

As a small item, it is hard to get good simple picture frames here. Have in mind the broad rosewood frame around one Van Dyke photo, etc. IF you bring any, not more than half a trunk full, and REMOVE THE GLASS. <u>MAKE SURE THAT YOU REMOVE THE GLASS</u>, put a bit of card board in place of it.<for travel.>

Bring silver, knives, forks etc. but not china, at least not without very careful computation of what it will cost.

I SED, bring nothing that cant go with you on steamer, as luggage. The padlocked cases CAN go as luggage, much less fuss at customs <(than nailed cases.)> etc, AND they serve as furniture AT once on arrival. Also if you don't get the flat you want at once, easier to shift again.

A pillow or two as pack padding, possibly. Cant believe that kitchen utensils are worth packing.

I shd. say, any bedding, stuffs, etc. pillows only where useful as wadding. <cost a certain amount & don't weigh very heavy>

Very few pictures. and still fewer frames. after all one can get frames from Genoa. that is merely small detail, that there aren't good plain picture mouldings in local shop. Besides one wants FEWER wall ornaments in this climate.

I doubt if the HEAVY gold frames on Portrait and arms are worth transport. or if the portrait frame wd. stand trip. That's as may be. I have an idea for simpler big frame that I shd. have made here.

with which above exceptions, shd. say, when in doubt about any object, sell it or give it away. (I take it the three Feet menages can absorb what you cant sell.)

Shdn't. think china worth bringing, save mothers four hand painted plates. Certainly NO bricabrac. Original woiks of aht? apart from the brass 'rabbit' i.e. faun. NO picture glass on any account. I know it is a bore to take glass out of frames, but it WEIGHS and it busts.

Don't bring a hell uv a lot of old clothes. At same time there is a fortnight every year when you want the heavy stuff, don't throw away you heaviest overcoat just cause you think you are heading for the tropics. DON'T buy anything new to come in. Believe everything is cheaper here save wool sox. which you wont much need.

I don't know what sweaters cost now in America. they are expensive in europe, and hard to find THICK ones. That is about the only item I shd. think you might invest in as preparative. at any rate look at a good heavy button down front sweater (with sleeves) <good vests are cheap here> and also at a somewhat lighter sleeveless wool vest and let me know what the local price is. Might be useful on steamer also. Prob. the vest can be got here, and prob. the heavy worth getting in Phila. but lemme know local 'quotations'.

A good one lasts forever, so don't skimp. Might even have you get one for me, IF the saving amounts to anything. DON'T do so without my ordah, s.v.p. I may see something in Vienna if I get there.

WHEN IN DOUBT about particular items write to me for inflamation. Take it simplest route is straight to Genova. Any travelling you want to do can be done with greater return per dollar in Italy than elsewhere. There is a lot of it you haven't seen. Otherwise I might suggest meeting you in Paris, but you have seen Paris, and there's a lot of Italy you haven't seen.

You cd. have a week in Perugia for price of French visa.

Some boats come via Naples, think fare is the same, dunno if you get a day on shore there. It wd. be worth considering, for sake of the aquarium. and only a day or so longer, one day sailing, and Mediterranean easy for big boat.

Ask for my friend Yusuf Benamore in Gib. I dunno if Althouse still exists, he might have Benamores address. Shd like Yusuf to see himself in de luxe Cantos. If not ask for him on the dock. He may be a millionaire by now. on the other hand he may not. Anyhow, you've seen all Gib. except the old synagogue, and may as well spend yr. time hunting for Yusuf and doing anything else.

If that <isn't> an answer to what you want, lemme have deetails.

Nooz here is that the kid I play tennis with has at age of 15 gone up to Genova and licked the champion of Italy in tournament, day before yesterday. Possibly due to champion's age, hasn't got to end of tournament, and had Bocciardo still to deal with. However we are all feeling several years younger.

Have had proofs of another article from 'Nation', dare say you'll have seen it by time you get this. wot ells?

love to you & mother

E

yes. I get Dial when there is anything of mine in it. Re Italy – rot. plenty of autos imported---naturally favour home products.

╫══╫

820. ALS

15 May. [1928]

Wien (mail address Rapallo)

Dear Dad.

Yrs. to hand. hope you have jjoyous birthday.

Will report on Wien later. am feeling much better.- change to ½ mountain air, I spose.

If you see E.K. say I have recd. his letters. – can't carry on correspondence - in ink, & cdn't even if I had typewriter - no harm in his writing - you can assure him letters are recd. & read. - only thing needing answer in 'em is that I do <u>not</u> think of A. Lowell. - & think it wd. be waste of time to do so.

- No - I don't want the bronze mask sent to Idaho. after all. These things have a potential value. I shall prob. not leave a vast fortune. & ones gt. gnd. children shd. have something to hock.

Pity some of these g.d. collectors dont buy <u>mss</u> etc. at a time when it wd. be some use to the so admired author instead of supporting the old clothes men.

The only collectors who ever approach an author direct are those wanting autographd hand outs.

Dial sez it is running more Guido in June issue.

Love to you & mother

E

*Homer had reported being visited by 'E. K. = your young <u>Polish</u> poet', and by 'a Mr. Morris S. Savett', a **book collector** and an 'Ezra P. collector', who 'said he had been tempted to write you'. E. K.'s full name was Edward Kowalewski. Pound did not after all want the bronze of his life **mask** sent to Mrs Trego's Collection in Idaho.*

821. ALS

21 May [1928]

Osterreichischer Hof. | Wien

Dear Dad:

Horses sill doing these stunts in same building - supposedly as in 1570. etc.

Think I may have found a contralto. at any rate am providing copies of 'Heaulmiere' from Villon opera. with chance of its being sung possibly with orchestra here in autumn.

Have asked a number of questions during last 3 weeks – don't know that shall print anything as the result - etc.

good climate. - suppose I shall start going to the opera now that the Vienna company has come back.

Love to you & mother

E.

Horses, a reference to the show put on by the Lippizaner stallions of the Spanish Riding School in Vienna.

⊹⊱⋯⊰⊹

822. ALS

30 May [1928]

Wien

Dear Dad:

Cant remember what I have answered.

1. Did not receive medal or letter from <u>asst</u>. Engraver. - at least no recollection of doing so.
2. Translation of chinese poems in picture book is at Rapallo.

They are poems on a set of scenes in Miss Thseng's part of the country. - sort of habit of people to make pictures & poems, on that set of scenes.

NO. Mask is not to go to Idaho. - guess you'd better bring it along with you.

Of course the chess men wd. be pleasant to have. - not worth while to sell them at a sacrifice.

Ta Hio is pronounced I suppose Tāā [Tah. Hee oh.]

No. I did not have copy Exile 3 'long ago'. I have <u>at last</u> one that D. bought in London, or got from Neumayer there. –

I suppose a copy will arrive in Rapallo IN TIME. [this is 30<u>th</u> May. & nothing from Cov. yet recd.]

Recd. Nations etc. mentioned in yrs. 5<u>th</u> or 6<u>th</u> inst. - <u>why</u> call my attention to <u>Broun</u>. Thought he had had more'n enuff.

Make Jake buy the house. aint he allus takin' on real estate? Probably has moral urge against yr. leaving amerika?? no hardly.

Yrs

E

⊹⊱⋯⊰⊹

823. ALS

8 June [1928]

Osterricher Hof | Wien

Dear Dad

Congratulations. & hope you enjoy your vacation & leezhure.
You can spend part of it translating the enclosed.
which reveals new talent on my part of talking like a trained seal.
also one or two innovations on part of interviewer. or printer

Yrs

E

*Homer had written. 'Dad expects to leave the Mint on the 21ˢᵗ [May] first for 30 days leave, and on June 27ᵗʰ will be retired.' **Enclosed** was a cutting from the* Neues Wiener Journal *of 5 June 1928, 'Ezra Pound und seine Wiener Pläne', an interview by Julius Sachs.*

+>==+

824. TLS [on 'Ezra Pound | *res publica, the public convenience*' letterhead]

28 June [1928]

Rapallo | via Marsala, 12 int. 5

Dear Dad:

Am swatting away at typewriter.
Tell yr. fiend E.K. that I hope to print him some time. Dont know his name as he never signs it.

He is still in state of subjection to pre-extant literature and gives (so far as verbal manifestation goes) no sign of direct contact with outer world, by which alone contact with inner world becomes articulate.

His rhoosian friend better communicate with Bob McAlmon 1.rue d'Antin, Paris. Bob restarting some sort of publication house.

more anon

E

+>==+

825. TLS

1 July. 1928

[Rapallo]

Dear Dad:

Trust you enjoyed yr. birth day.
Have shoved off ms. of Xile 4. Hope Cov's new partnership dont mean

atrophy or entry into strictly commercial life. Wish he wd. git on with the work Rodker, Mc Almon, Machine Art, etc.

Have been trying to get thru mass of truck lying about desk, floor, etc, Re/ LIB MAN No. 4. Only thing of interest yet found in said sheet is a translation of De Musset, signed with an unintelligible squiggle, possibly an R.S. monogram (Remington Stone??)

At any rate you can tell the edtr. that I have noticed the poem, and wd. be glad to look thru mss. by the author (translator) if he cared to submit same for Xile.

The verse shows serious intentions. E.K. still too immature. He has got to work thru a lot of derivative language, attitudes etc. before there wd. be any use in 'presenting' him. False start, start made too soon, merely retards.

I am afraid it is closed season for Fauns. The mould didn't work well on the last one, and I cant have the original subjected again to mould-taking, the powder gets into stone, etc. sorry. Better hang onto the one you have.

No, there are several misprints in Wien interview, including the 'Grosse Irische' Poet Beerbohm Yeats. Sachs blamed it on printer. The 'dichter' is HENRY JAMES, not the much less important Frances Jammes.

I have no Indiscretions. May be possible to get 'em from Three Mts. Press, but the Printer has his right to get paid. Near as I remember it was three bucks. Not my affair. sorry not to oblige.

Damn it, you dont indicate what paper Mr Yust writes in. Please forward him the enclosed if you can trace him.

You look into your morning paper, and wait till you find which one he writes in. Walter Yust.

Yust so.

Love to mother.

Yrs.

E.

[Enclosed letter:]

TLS [on 'Ezra Pound *res publica, the public convenience*' letterhead]

8 July 1928

Rapallo

Dear Sir, and Brilliant Spark:

For some unknown reason my august progenitor has sent me yr. blurb re E. K. Kane.

Naow ef yew wanter know, you can find the diagnosis of the later poesy as 'neo-gongorism' in a note of mine pubd. several years ago. I have forgotten where, but I think apropros of Mr Cummings.

so that's that, and you can now procede to tell papa how to suck eggs.

Only of course you shd. distinguish between one kind of egg and another, and observe where and when the Gongorism, which sis not my leetle movemeng sets in.

To Mons. Walter Yust.

———

YES. MY BEAMISH BUCKO, I happen to have found it. 'Poetry' for Sept. 1925. P. 342. lines 3 and 4 you will find the name (prae- and cog- nomens) of Don Luis de Gongora.

In fact those lines might seem to furnish a text to Mr Elisha K. K.

E P

*Pascal **Covici** had moved from Chicago to New York and formed a new partnership with Donald Friede. 'R. S.' was Gordon Keith Stover. Homer, having had the Vienna **interview** 'done into the American Language', had queried whether by 'The only poet who created something that did not already exist in French Lit' Pound had meant, not 'Henry James', but Francis Jammes. Walter **Yust** (1894–1960), US journalist and writer, began his career on the Philadelphia Evening Ledger in 1926. He was editor-in-chief of Encyclopaedia Britannica 1938–60.*

⊦⊱⊶⊰⊦

826. TLS [on 'Ezra Pound | *res publica, the public convenience'* letterhead]
22 July [1928]

Rapallo | via Marsala, 12 int. 5

Dear Dad:

Can not recall having recommended Mr Norman Douglas to anyone. As fer being talked about, it all depends on the 'by whom'.

Re the Gaudier, it is the end of the edtn. a couple of hundred copies that weren't bound when the first lot were, and now it costs too much to set up the die, or something of that sort. yr. friend lucky to get the book at all, as it presumably wont be reissued.

No particular news.

All foreign books very expensive in U.S., I believe as long as the worst filth of country makes its laws, etc. . . .

ALL these kids ought to turn onto writing prose analyses (novels, stories etc) presenting actual quality of sons of bitches who are IN the working organism of the place. The types that make and administer the travesty of law and disorder and general swindle. 'Revelry' was a start, but the place needs more of it, not merely of Harding, but of the blighters all the way down the line.

Portrait of city councilor presented with an idea, etc.

Undsoweiter.

E

Will try to copy out those Chinese poems for you sometime, when therm-
ometer is lower.

Again re/ getting books etc. There has to be continual work of organization.
Heaven knows I have done enough of it from time of Egoist on. Lot of people
with no more gift than I have, think themseleves too dd important or artistic to
work at organization.

The Lib. typescript show proper tendency to form active group, but that
appears to be a lone manifestation, once in 20 years.

> *Homer had written: 'Mama is reading South Wind by* **Norman Douglas**. *I have an idea
> she is not over pleased with it. Have you read it? It is one of the books talked about.' He
> had also mentioned that their new young friend Frank Ankenbrand, Jr., a poet and Pound
> devotee, had acquired a copy of Pound's memoir of* **Gaudier-Brzeska**, *but it lacked the
> design stamped on the cover of the 1ˢᵗ edition. Ankenbrand and his wife were renting the
> third storey of the Pound residence.*

─────

827. TL [on 'Ezra Pound | *res publica, the public convenience*' letterhead]

30 July [1928]

Rapallo | via Marsala, 12 int. 5

Dear Dad:

Portrait by Stowitz, done Venice last year, quite good and very bad. Photos,
recd. from Dutch East Indes, a few days ago. He is out there painting rajas and
doi[n]g a book on Bali art.

1. RAIN   / / /

Chinese book reads as follows, rough trans.

Rain, empty river,
Place for soul to travel
     (or room to travel)
Frozen cloud, fire, rain damp twilight.
One lantern inside boat cover (i.e. sort of
     shelter, not awning on small boat)
Throws reflection on bamboo branch,
     causes tears.

          / / / / / / /

AUTUMN MOON ON TON-Ting Lake

West side hills
screen off evening clouds

Ten thousand ripples send mist over cinnamon flowers.

Fisherman's flute disregards nostalgia
Blows cold music over cottony bullrush.

Monastery evening bell
/ / / / /
Cloud shuts off the hill, hiding the temple
Bell audible only when wind moves toward one,
One can ~~see nothing higher in the hills~~
   -not tell whether the summit, is near or far,
Sure only that one is in hollow of mountains.
   / / / / / / / / / / / / /
Autumn tide,
AUTUMN TIDE, RETURNING SAIIS

Touching green sky at horizon, mists in suggestion of autumn
Sheet of silver reflecting all that one sees
Boats gradually fade, or are lost in turn of the hills,
Only evening sun, and its glory on the water remain.
   / / / / / / / / / / /

Spring in hill valley

Small wine flag waves in the evening sun
Few clustered houses sending up smoke
A few country people enjoying their evening drink
In time of peace, every day is like spring

SNOW ON RIVER

Cloud light, world covered with milky jade
Small boat floats like a leaf

Tranquil water congeals it to stillness
~~In Sai Yin there dwell people of leisure~~
The people of Sai Yin are unhurried

/ / / / / / / /

Wild geese stopping on sand

Just outside window, light against clouds
~~Light clouds show in sky just beyond window ledge~~
A few lines of autumn geese on the marsh
Bullrushes have burst into snow-tops / at their [tops]
The birds stop to preen their feathers.

EVENING IN SMALL FISHING VILLAGE.

Fisherman's light blinks
Dawn begins, with light to the south and north
Noise of children hawking their fish and crawfish
Fisherman calls his boy, and takes up his wine bottle,
They drink, they lie on the sand
    and point to marsh-grass, talking.

---

828. TLS

1 Aug. [1928]

[Rapallo]

Dear dad:
    I copied out the Chinese poems two days ago but don't know whether I can trust you to return copy, you have horrible habit of taking copies etc.
    IF I fix up a printable version later I DON'T want rough draft left lying about. When enlightened on this pt. will consider remitting the draft. copy.
    Enc. photo Stowitz portrait done last year Venice, quite good AND VERY bad. Just recd. photos from Dutch E. Indies <Java>, where he is studying Bali art, and probably painting rajas.
    He never got here last year as had hurry call to do Muss.
    Re/ your Bosche bonds, I dare say they are all right but am not frightfully keen on 'em. Mr Parker or whatever his name is probably right about 'em.
    Equitable recommended some French stuff years ago. It is NOW O.K. but one wd. have had a lot of anxiety if one had taken it when first put on market.
    If you are investing say 5000, put it in five different places. Just as easy, and leaves one less disturbable by winds of political hogwash, wars pestilences etc.
    Re/ E.K.; all right his 'taking me for model', but he'd better consider how things are done. I mean I did a lot of spade work, some years of it, as you may remember, and I still continue.
    He can't merely come along and take my surface results and think he going to get anywhere with 'em. He can USE 'em as an ingredient. and they may save

him a lot of errors, or inefficiencies that used to be in nearly everyone's poetry in 1900, but that <alone> wont get him anywhere.

U.S.A. probably WORSE now than it was 25 years ago. Will take a lot of fibre to stand it, or even to get out out of it and free of it.

Training for priesthood, or a dab of it, excellent asset for writer.

Bookman a HORRIBLE paper. More corpse.

If you see Stover you might discuss cellularizing Exile. I don't want to join class of magazines who print poems on condition authors subscribe; but question of representing various local groups MIGHT be kept free of that taint. There is a danger of local sewing society atmosphere in the procedure . . .

Shd. like to see something of Stover's own (orig. or trans.), also a group of stuff selected by HIM without advice of other Lib Man. contributors.

Might do it once in Xile, or might have, instead of foreign letters, group of stuff from various sections in U.S.A.

am dubious about the whole matter.

Take it he is a few years older than the others, who aren't yet ripe. Have seen some 15,000 'of promise'. Used to cause more enthusiasm. I know more about why these promises so seldom WORK OUT.

Love to you & mother

E

*To Pound's hesitation over sending the translation of the **Chinese poems** a nettled Homer responded on 14 August, 'advise you to keep rough draft, until you can send me the finished version'. Pound appears to have sent it after all. Re. the '**Bosche bonds**', Homer had written: 'Had long distance call from Parker Monroe this morning. He has returned to New York—with Harris Forbes & Co. Bankers & Brokers. Thinks German Bonds at 6% good investments.'*

+≻=≺+

829. TLS [on 'Ezra Pound | *res publica, the public convenience*' letterhead]
19 Aug. [1928]

Rapallo | via Marsala, 12 int. 5

Dear Dad:

Ellis always was a g.d. fool. Tell him I hope Smith will be elected if only as a slap in the eye to the brand of Xtn. whose only tenet is – Mess into thy neighbours business.

Give him a Ta Hio if you think any of it capable of penetrating his hide.

When sending fool cols. please leave on name of paper.

Re / WIEN, whasser use talking until one sees if they are any RESULTS. Hope I have put a tack on one or two chairs, but remains to be seen if they will cause anything to RISE.

Glad you like Becker. D. sez. she has writ. you since return here in June. (24th.)

As for this damn fool amendment, Hoover can go to hell too. Why the hell they cant distinguish between what govt. is for and what is business of individual . . .

besides the damn thing ect etc. whass the use my saying what even thick witted senators have discovered.

Glad to see one inhabitant out of ever 5 in Wash D.C. has been jailed <during past year>.

If govt. wd. attend to its own biz. i.e. to keep cabinet members from larceny etc.

As for the general hypocracy, Wilson <who Ellis praises,> was drunk at peace conference, Coledge is not teetotal, etc. man with some sense of what govt. is, let us say Muss. don't booze, but refuses to make an ass of the state by having it butt into questions of diet.

Sure win for Hoover if on Nov. 2. he sez he wuz wrong, is ready to efface the damn fool amendment. However Ohio gang will be there.

Suppose Ellis is out for Vare. Are the young Elli making much in the hootch bizniz yet?

Have signed title pages for XVII: XXVII, suppose they will get bound sometime. etc.

Eng. edition of Selected Poems, with Eliot introd. and notes said to be in manufacture. Contract signed.

Nancy Cunard has taken over Bill B's press, also wants to continue printing. Expecting our illustratress or capitalistress in a week or so.

D. spent day drawing large GREEN grasshopper that has arrived on terazza. G.g. loafed and chawed through large chunk of grape. last seen climbing rope of tenda. (awning). remains to be seen if present tomorrow. about size of katydid.

RANDOM house yelling fer Pome.

~~Curwen~~ Currier Press wants to print Guido stuff from July Dial

Already set to be printed by Yeats, Cuala

Twenty Bucks out of C. Boni, for anthology rights on 2 pomes. wot ells.

Sent off long curse to Nation two days ago. more lucid than present epistle. Why don't that fool Ellis fuss about something that is a nuisance, or LEARN to brush his teeth and keep clean.

Has he voted for a law to keep Darwin out of the school books; or was he there in Tennysee??

Aldington has done a good job on that Gourmont translation, don't tell Willie or he'll have the post office onto it.

Oh yes, some son of a bitch in yr. honoured customs has torn out the pages of a 50 dollar cantos 1-16 and delivered the cover. A great pity this type of American cant (about 30 million of him) be burried permanently in one dung heap and left without postherity.

Has Ellis ever read Art. 211, and does he admire its lucidity, and its clarity, and the skill with which things are distinguised one from another?

Poke him up. Birth controll, ought to be a purrfek subjek for him

Und so weiter

CHEERS!!!

love to you and mother.

E

Evidently Pound had been sent a clipping of an article by **William Ellis**, *a Philadelphia journalist writing on religious matters. In the 1928 presidential election the Democrat candidate was Albert E.* **Smith**, *Governor of New York, a Roman Catholic, and an opponent of Prohibition. Herbert* **Hoover** *would win the election by a landslide. William S.* **Vare**, *a Philadelphia political boss, had been elected Senator from Pennsylvania, only to be unseated in 1927 for election fraud.* **Nancy Cunard** *would use Bird's antique printing press for her Hours Press books, among which would be* A Draft of XXX Cantos *(1930). The '**illustratress or capitalistress**' was Gladys Hynes who designed the caption and ornamental initial for each of the cantos in Rodker's de luxe edition of* A Draft of the Cantos 17–27 *(1928).* **Currier Press** *of New York did not 'print Guido stuff from July* Dial'. *(Curwen Press were the printers of* A Draft of the Cantos 17–27.) **Random House** *yelled to no effect. Pound's '**long curse**' did not appear in* Nation—*it may have become 'Bureaucracy the Flail' in* Exile *no. 4.* **Remy de Gourmont**, Selection from All His Works, Chosen and translated by **Richard Aldington**, *had just been published by Covici in Chicago. Pound reviewed it in* The Dial *of January 1929.*

+≡≡+

830. TLS

Sept. 1. [1928]

[Rapallo]

Dear Dad:

Given infinite time I MIGHT be able to read a Chinese poem : thass to say I know how the ideograph works, and <u>can</u> find 'em in the dictionary or vocabulary,

BUT I shd. scarcely attempt it unless there were some urgent reason. Also some of the script in that book was fairly fancy.

For Cathay I had a crib made by Mori and Ariga, not translation or anything shaped into sentences, but word for sign, and explanation with each character.

For your book Miss Thseng, descendent of Kung read out the stuff to me.

Am perfectly able to look up an ideograph and see what shade it can be given etc.

BUT it za matr of time. wd. be no point in it.

No I am not a sinologue. Dont spread the idea that I read it azeasy as a yourapean langwidg.

Stowitz is a feller from Californy, at the age of say 22 he was actink in some college theatricals of something and Pavlova saw him, and took him on as dancing partner. He got bored with being a Nijinsky and started to design costumes, then to paint. Has now done me and Muss. and gone to Java or thereabouts to do book on Bali art, and paint rajas.

Simple-minded, talented cuss. Meant to follow my directions and look at some good painting (Perugia etc.) so'z to see what it wuz like, but got the order to do Muss. and then shipped to the orient. Still young enough to do something.

Believe he was really good as dancer, but had too much intellectual unrest to stop there.

Have had proofs of Brit. Selected Poems.

believe Cuala is about to start on 'Donna Mi Prega'.

Did you ask for some translations of the latin? I fergitt. It IS mostly explained in the english, the latin etc, and french merely to indicate what he might have had in mind first.

By the time Unkl, Wm. Yeats has done his commentary it will have reentered the domain of the wholly incomprehensible and all will be well.

I hear Howard Weeks died in June, one of the livest of the younger prospects.

Bill Wms. new book said to be on the way.

Mass of Joe Gould's History arrived in mss. wot ells.

D. repeats that she has several times communicated, or at least sent off letters to you since her return here in June.

Cantos are sposed to be printed and in the bindery.

love to you and mother
E.

N x time your're in N.Y. drop a line to L. Zukofsy 57 E. iii th. if Stover is going over, might let him do likewise.

Young Jarge is goin' strong

*Homer had written: 'In order to settle a disputed argument, will you kindly inform me if the translated version is your own or someone else's. Dad has made several statements about the matter of your **Chinese** work, and, I have said you were able to translate the poem yourself. I would like to be set right in this matter.' The '**Donna Mi Prega**'—which the Cuala Press would abandon due to Yeats becoming seriously ill—was the long essay published in The Dial in July 1928 as 'DONNA MI PREGA BY GUIDO CAVALCANTI / WITH TRADUCTION AND COMMENTARY / BY EZRA POUND: FOLLOWED BY NOTES / AND A CONSIDERATION OF THE SONNET'. In the commentary there were some quotations in **Latin** and in **French**. William Carlos **Williams' new book,** A Voyage to Pagany, had this Dedication: 'To the first of us all, my old friend Ezra Pound, this book is affectionately dedicated'. Pound printed a part of **Joe Gould's** endless and largely unwritten 'Oral History of Our Time' in Exile.*

831. TLS

13 Sept. [1928]

[Rapallo]

Dear Dad:

Tickets for Perugia, in pocket. Whence to the Abruzzzz.

Grainger Kerr, and the Hynes (G. and sister) departed yesterday in op. directions.

Various small jobs for Dial, will appraise you in time of recent activity.

Uzual rush to git orf.

One copy of vellum cantos reported bound, but shant see it fer a month, as dont want it chasing me all over the Gran Sasso.

D. sent packet or rather envelope to I.W.P. this a.m.

Jarge in Wien. Richard Aldington trying or trying not to make junction, probably in Rome at end of month. He got the Confucius printed, or at least formed the link with Hughes. etc.

Planning to have little more paint on walls when we get back. Glad pension dept. has at last remitted.

love to you and mother. Hope to see Orrick Johns in Firenze tomorrow.

E

832. ALS

4. oct. [1928]

[Rome]

Dear Dad:

Been sweating in Vatican library. etc.

Have now photos of <u>mss</u> for half the G. Cavalcanti.

& pubshrs. not wanting to print 'em

Cantos reported in print.

Have seen Eliots introd. to his edtn of me. (proofs).

Starting fer mts. tomorrow unless deluge continues.

E

833. **TLS** [on 'Ezra Pound | *res publica, the public convenience*' letterhead]

19 Oct. [1928]

Rapallo | via Marsala, 12 int. 5

Dear Mother:

Thanks for invitation; am too busy to think of it.

IF however you think it wd. do dad good to a run about, I wd. cheerfully put up 200 bucks for his ticket to here and back. I can see 200, but onforchunately I cant see 400.

I dont know that it is a particularly good moment. You prob. want him to run the furnace. It wd. be good if he cd. come at a time (weather) suited to have ten days trip across to Venice. I mean that is small rail-way expense, and a lot en route, Pavia, Milan, Brescia, Verona, Vicenza, Padua, Venice, all in a string, half hour or hour apart.

If etc.

Slammed this machine about eight hours yesterday. Schloezer, and G.Cav. notes. etc.

Still hung up over question of fac-similes, or not for the G.C. etc.

love to you & dad

E

Isabel Pound had written her **invitation** *on 22 September 1928: 'My Dear Son—It would seem we are destined to remain in the old home this winter. Here much of our capital is invested and until we can liquidate the estate we must stay with it. Why cannot the three or four of you spend the season with us?' In June, Pound had sent a photograph of a fair-haired child, clearly not Omar, and Homer had written on 10 July 1928, 'You do not tell us who the photograph is, the child shown—is it the same one as you sent a year or so ago?' He added, 'Mama wonders why she is the recipient of strange children without name or habitation or connection.' It was in fact another photograph of Maria—Pound had stopped off to see her on his way to Vienna—but he appears not to have responded to Homer's question, hence Isabel's uncertain 'the three or four of you'. Pound's translation from the French of* **Boris de Schloezer's** *book on Igor Stravinsky was being serialized in seven instalments in* The Dial.

834. **ALS**

[after 20 October 1928]

Venezia, address Rapallo

Dear Mother:

Sent you note on wrought iron, picked up in Milan.

My view on large metal dishes (by whatever name) is that they take up room, & that bonds bearing interest are vastly preferable

I am all for simple life - with no god damned nonsense about weaving & milking cattle & other bucolic or artisan or bourgeois complications.

Audenbrand sounds <u>like</u> typical american candidate for licherary honours. Thanks for warning - Yes Ford is an impious catholic & a good sailor Stovitz paints too quickly I suppose - seems very simple, lots of 'em do.

Bunting is exmusic critic of the no longer extant London 'Outlook', wanted or rejected by the police in several countries -

Boni & L. can only launch books which descend to or refrain from ascending from the level of murkn 'intelligence'. This level is lower each year.

Saw 2 more Guido mss. in Verona on my way here. Still waiting contract. etc

Love to you & dad.

E

Homer Pound had written: 'I have a request to make of you. We have here in town an artist in iron by name of Sabastian. He has a shop next to your friend Chris Myers the Blacksmith (who always asks about you) and still keeps the same old shop. Now Sabastian wants me to ask you to send him a book on **Italian Iron designs** *for gates, signs &&.'*

+≡+

835. LS [on 'Ezra Pound | *res publica, the public convenience*' letterhead]
10 Nov. [1928]

Rapallo | via Marsala, 12 int. 5

Dear Dad and Mother:

Thanks fer the pijamas. Has there been opened a Japanese bordello in Wyncote, or whence have they come? and to what extent am I expected to outrage the meurs of Ytalie, in order to live up to them.

D. was trying to copy some Iron designs. Rapallo has no large book shop. Will look for design book when <next> I am in some larger city.

Remember me to Chris. can he still throw the anvil?

I am still waiting for Cantos, in vellum, and the Eliot edtn. sposed to be out tomorrow (?) I suppose that means monday or some time.

Swamped in mediaeval phylosophy necessary for notes on edtn. of G. Cav.

Yeats and Stokes now here in Rap.: Adrian Kent (pittore) is gone to Firenze and kicking my fotografer into action re more G. Cav. fotos.

Am vainly trying to make one or two of the early G. C. traductions readable, which they never were before. Don't expect it will have much effect.

Bacon is Milan, down with Bronchitis, may come along here if he gets better before he has to sail.

love to you and mother

E

The **pyjamas** *were made by his mother.*

+≥—≈+

836. TLS [on 'Ezra Pound | *res publica, the public convenience*' letterhead]

23 Nov. [1928]

Rapallo | via Marsala, 12 int. 5

Dear Dad:

Since the gorillas in the St. Louis Post Office destroyed copy of vol. 1. of Cantos, Rodker is holding your copy of Cantos 17-27 till he can get it carried to you by hand.

Yaas, we have no Arkansas!!

Still plugging on Guido. no end to job. Stravinsky stuff continues in Dial.

Bacon been here with his new spouse, and left few days ago.

W.B.Y. fighiting irish imitation of our louse law, 211.

Wot ells.

You might drop a line to E. G. Rich, Curtis Brown Ltd. 116 W. 39th. and ask what it wd. cost to sue the Herald supplement. (I dont mean to commit yourself to anything . . . just a touch from nearer at hand.)

Dial fairly stocked up with stuff. Seem to have been pounding this machine fairly continuous.

17-27 looks very handsome.

The Faber and Gwyer edn. costs 7/6 shillings seven shillings six pence. Their addrress is 24 Russel Sq. W.C.1., last I heard it was to be out on monday.

Also they have had hundred title pages signed, first I heard of it was arrival of the packet of pages. That's fer some sort of more luxsome edtn. I dunno yet what it is going to cost.

An norther's copy will be sent you, with no outlay on yr. part.

Bill seems content with my remarks in last Dial.

etc.

Yrs

E

One hundred numbered and signed copies of Selected Poems, *Eliot's selection of Pound's shorter poems, were printed on hand-made paper and issued on 10 December 1928. Pound's article, 'Dr. Williams' Position', ostensibly a review of* Voyage to Pagany, *was in the November* Dial. *Williams had sent Pound a grateful letter beginning, 'Nothing will ever be said of better understanding regarding my work than your article in The Dial.'*

+≥—≈+

EZRA POUND

res publica, the public convenience

RAPALLO
VIA MARSALA, 12 INT. 5

23 Nov.

Dear Dad :

Since the gorillas in the St. Louis Post
Office destroyed copy of vol.1. of Cantos , Rodker is
holding your copy of Cantos 17-27 till he can get it
carried to you by hand.

Yaas, we have no Arkansas !!

Still plugging on Guido. no end to job. Stravinsky
stuff continues in Dial.
Bacon been here with his new spouse, and left few days
ago.
W.B.Y. fighting irish imitation of our louse law , 211.
Wot ells.

You might drop a line to E.G.Rich , Curtis Brown Ltd.
116 W. 39th. and ask what it wd. cost to sue the
Herald supplement. (I dont mean to commit yourself
to anything... just a touch from nearer at hand.)

Dial fairly stocked up with stuff . Seem to have been
pounding this machine fairly continuous.
17-27 looks very handsome.
The Faber and Gwyer edtn. costs 7/6 shillings
seven shillings six pence. Their address is
24 Russel Sq. W.C.1. , last I heard it was to be
out on monday.
Also they have had hundred title pages signed , first
I heard of it was arrival of the packet of pages.

836. EP to HLP, from Rapallo, 23 November [1928], *first page.*

837. TLS [on 'Ezra Pound | *res publica, the public convenience*' letterhead]
2 Dec. [1928]

Rapallo | via Marsala, 12 int. 5

Dear Dad:

   The Guido is out of the house all except the photos, some ov which are still
to arrive.

I hear Eliot's edition has reached Paris and Dublin; no copy here yet.

Cov. sez another Exile is about to be out.

Any suggestions as to how most easily to assassinate 2½ million murkns. gladly recd.

Haven't yet recovered from the Guido. Covici has died on the machine book. I don't know how culpable he is.

The cheerful nooz that Mr Roth is in jail arrived a few days ago. I suppose he has had a glass of cognac or something. Inconceivable that he shd. have been jailed merely for theft and robbery.

The Chi. Trib. reports a child with seven inch tail born in Kentucky. Arkansas next.

No nooz from outer world. At least I've forgotten it. Yeats in residence. Hauptmann ditto. very affable. Stokes and Kent departed to Paris.

Profit due on Cantos, if last American agent pays up. He has been known to pay.

Grabbit started yesterday.

Have still got some Schloezer to do. Yeats disgusted with his damn country for copying our putrid postal laws. Hungary another backward and foetid state trying to do the same.

High time some sort of serum was invented to prevent the general pollution of the planet.

French witz seems to be recovering a bit.

Man murdered a consul in paris, jury refused to convict him; finally consented to give him two years; as he has been waiting trial fourteen months, and get six months off, he has about two to go. Man was irritated over passport bother. Unfortunately it was not the american consul. Also, of course, it is no use eliminating minor officials.

I am not offering it as a model of conduct, but as indication that the passport imbecility is causing annoyance.

love to you and mother

E

'**witz**', *German for 'wit', spoken aloud as English gives 'wits'.*

⊹⟞⟝⊹

838. TLS

8 Dec [1928]

[Rapallo]

Dear Dad:

All right: ONE copy of Eliot's edition is on the way to you. Send ME 15 shillings, alias 3.75 dollars and you will receive two more copies. In fact I will order them sent NOW.

No bibliography has reached me. And nobody has applied to me for information re/ what ought to be in it.

If whoever it is, wants me to see a bibliography, send it by registered post, and I will respond.

Congrats, somewhat delayed, on yr. 44 th.

Incidentally the price of Selected Poems is 7/6, seven shillings, six pence. say TWO dollars. I enc. Faber and Gwyer card.

Have had sample page of the Guido.

Put Centaur Book shop, or as many as you know onto the HOURS PRESS.

I did the first draft of Beowulf essay this a.m.

Sorry you can't get over. Hope something can be fixed, sometime before long. Don't know my own dates, and can't fix appointments.

also travel expensive and incalculable. I can see cost of boat fare, from N.Y. to Genova, and feed you here, but trips about Europe, etc . . . cant calculate. etc . . .

W.B.Y. fighting the Irish censor bill, modeled on our own god damnd imbecility.

love to you and mother
E

Three dollars O.K. for Centaur, as they have to pay the customs thieves.

If Centaur is trustworthy, tell him to apply for agency of HOURS PRESS, saying you told him to.

---

*Frank Ankenbrand was working on a **bibliography** of Pound's published writings. The 'Beowulf essay'—full title 'The Probable Music of Beowulf, A Conjecture. With reproduction of the music'—was intended to work out Pound's conjecture that a particular Hebridean song he had heard sung by the Kennedy-Frasers in 1918 fitted some lines of Beowulf and thus gave an indication of how the Anglo-Saxon bards might have performed the poem. Nancy Cunard was eager to print the essay at her Hours Press and announced an edition of 120 signed copies to appear in May 1929, but there was a problem matching text and music for reproduction and the essay would remain unfinished and unpublished.*

+===+

839. **TLS** [on 'Ezra Pound | *res publica, the public convenience*' letterhead]
16 Dec. [1928]

Rapallo | via Marsala, 12 int. 5

Dear Dad:

Thanks for handsom sweater jacket reçove yesterday.

And very timely. Have been down with some sort of bronchite.

Am now Up as far as this, and the terrazza. Certainly shall not attempt America in winter. If your natal country werent so full of thieves and scounrels I might be able to pay both of yr. boat fares. Season unsettled. I dont yet know where I shall have to be when.

I think.I sent you one of the enc. circs.?

Had a most enormous and magnificent dinner with old Hauptmann the other evening. Minus his plus-fours and in a proper german afternoon coat or whatever the name is, he is more Goethe-Ibsen than ever.

As far as I can make out, he has staged a come back and done good job in his last : Eulenspiegel.

etc.

love to you & mother

E

Have ordered the Poems to be sent you from London

+⊨═━⊣+

840. TLS

20 Dec. [1928]

[Rapallo]

Dear Dad:

Its not what the bloody scoundrels print, it's what they dont print. Having ordered it, and kept it a year.

The London edtn. is NOT for sale in America. Liv. has americ. edtn. (better edtn.).

I dont know anything about Exile. Why shd. I? Cov. <u>says</u> he is printing the 4th. number, and that it is actually in the press. (WAS in the press, according to him, some time ago.

NO, I certainly dont you bothered with publishing it.

Am more or less indifferent about receiving the Nation. Send it if there is anything special, but dont buy it on purpose.

Glad to hear Saint is employed. IS the stuff any good?

Painter been in to see about beautifying the boidoir and bringing it up to palatial level of the rest of aptmt.

Long letter from Fitz. trying (uselessly) to justify existence of Oireland.

Few more Guido fotos. recd. from Dazzi this a.m.

Oh well, Merry Xmas.

Hope I'll be back on tennis court by then.

love to you and mother

EP

Agreement with Covici ends after No.4.

Know anybody who wants to BUY the paper ?

*Lawrence Bradford **Saint** was designing and making stained glass windows for the new Washington National Cathedral, and also for Bryn Athyn Cathedral of the Swedenborgian church in Pennsylvania.*

+>=<+

841. TLS

23 Dec. [1928]

[Rapallo]

Dear Dad:

Recd. notice from Covici this a.m. that 'fourth and last' edtn. of Exile wd. be out this month.

I dont know whether this is a piece of malice on the part of that lousy little kike Friede, but you prob. have more time than I have, and you can spend some of it, saying that the statement is wholly unauthorized.

My agreement with Covici terminates, but I have never yet waited for anybody's permission to print anything, and shall not start such waiting now.

Exile will appear when and where I see fit, without Mr. Covici's or Friede's permission, at such time, probably, as the amount of material 'unprintable' for American and sordid reasons, i.e. because it is thought to be unsaleable to the anti-evolutionists of Arkansas and the lower states, shall seems to me of sufficient importance to demand a new issue.

etc. Merry Xmas.

E

+>=<+

842. TLS

28 Dec. [1928]

[Rapallo]

Dear Mother:

Nice bloody wet, warmy-cold day. Hope the winter is bust. The Gov. Generl due to tea, but reckon he wont arrive as it'z too wet. Did I say that old Hauptmann fell for the Gaudier's, slam-bang?

Young McGreevy, last celtic bard, in yesterday. Is visiting W.B.Y.; renowned for his discovery that Card. Newman was a jew; which xplains quite a lot.

What else. Oh yes, packet with, Rich. Wilhelm book in it. Book very good, as much as I have yet read.

Few squibs about Irish Censorship, appearing here [&] there. More crafty than our baboon bill, but still disthressful.

Richard (Aldington) seems to have renewed his youth and vigour by emergences from England. trust his early promise may be about to fullfill etc.

Both he and Yeats filled with horror by Eliot's last pious essays.

McGreevy says great era in carpet making, due to some bloomin french senators wife having asked permission for morocco cheap labour to copy Leger's pictures in carpet.

D. sends thanks for silk scarf.

Love to you & dad,

E

The '**Richard Wilhelm book**' *was* The Soul of China *(1928)*. '***Eliot's last pious essays***' *were* For Lancelot Andrewes. Essays on Style and Order *(1928)*. *In his Preface Eliot had declared, 'The general point of view may be described as classicist in literature, royalist in politics, and anglo-catholic in religion'*.

⊹═─═⊹

843. TLS [on 'Ezra Pound | *res publica, the public convenience*' letterhead]

9 Jan. [1929]

Rapallo | via Marsala, 12 int. 5

Dear Dad:

Thanks fer the saltz-zellers. arrived this a.m.

Re/ Audenbrand; good gord, the thinks peepul think-uv. I dunno wot I can do to assist him. Shd. think a good deal of it. . . . etc.

Quinzaine was printed. 100 copies by Pollock, I think in Dec. 1908.

Second printing, 100 copies, printed by Pollock, pub. by Elkin Mathews, a few weeks later, possibly Jan. 1909, or possibly Dec. 1908.

No, you are certainly NOT to reprint it.

Any exuberence of that sort can be directed to printing something that isn't in print and can't get printed.

DONT send chq. for anything.

Machine bk. mss. now here, so you needn't worry about that.

Sorry mother has had cold, have had rotten one myself. Cured, and now got the start of a soARR thROATT, which hope to head off.

Whatter baht Payne of texas? I cant remember anything.

I wish George cd. see the foto of himself on the 2 cent stamp, and express his opinion of the sons of bitches now running the country. For purely ploppy blah and hypocracy it is about THE limit.

Bee yew teeful weather for several days. Painters raising enormous stink in bed room. etc.

Love to you and mother.

EP

Ankenbrand's enquiries for his bibliography of Pound had set Homer wishing for a **reprint** *of* A Quinzaine for This Yule. *About* **'Payne of Texas'** *Homer had written:* *'Just been loaned a new book. Wonder if you have seen it. Later American Writers, Part two of selections from American Literature by Leonidas Warren Payne Jr. and published by Rand McNally of Chicago. Payne includes one Ezra Pound and I think a very fine write up of him. Payne seems is Prof. of English, University of Texas.' It was* **George Washington** *on the 2 cent stamp.*

+≻═━≺+

844. TLS [on 'Ezra Pound | *res publica, the public convenience*' letterhead]
16 Jan. [1929]

Rapallo | via Marsala, 12 int. 5

Dear Mother:

Yeats back from Rome. Hauptmann has invited us to lunch on Sunday to meet Emil Ludwig, the new local 'ploot' who is renting the castello at porto fino. (As old H. says: He's got *your* (i.e. my) dollars to do it with.

Haup. also very much diverted at having just received violent denunciation from burgomasters wife in small village, reproving him for his last book.

Hem. and Dos Pasos both going strong in french translation.

Benelli's secretary has just been sent on to interview W. B. Y. for La Prensa de Buenos Ayres. etc.

Aldington here, doing new (unnecessary) translation of Decameron for that ass Covici.

Cheerful note from old McDaniel this a.m. recommending 7 minutes under water for all men void of a sense of humor.

Etc.

love to you and dad
E

+≻═━≺+

845. TLS [on 'Ezra Pound | *res publica, the public convenience*' letterhead]
20 Jan. [1929]

Rapallo | via Marsala, 12 int. 5

Dear Dad:

Fortunately Hauptmann dont care a damn about my not knowing "exactly what he has produced"; I have had a look at his Eulenspiegel, new poem, which I believe to be animated (tho dont believe anyone can do 400 pages of poem in two or three years that I much want to read.)

Joyce is sposed to have translated a couple of his plays before the Oirish or

679

Abbey teeayter was constituted to act foreign plays, and Yeats says one or two Haupt. plays have done well later at the Abbey.

The old man says: Man muss essen, and waves an arm toward the bay, saying it is much better to look at it than to jaw about literature. He still bathes in same daily at all temperatures, whether it has fruz the night before. Also expressed approbation when I said a day or two ago that my cold was better and my stupidity undiminished. plus a few derogations of people who try to be intelligent all the time.

(H's) Secretary just in to say will we meet Ludwig on Wednesday. Dare say that means eating from two till 5.30.

The enc. is about as far as the gordam english can get.

There is no reason for keeping the Eng. vol. save for curiosity of Eliots preface (not so noble as his Dial article). the book is poor substitute for Liv's collected vol. Good enough for the bleating islanders.

The french reviews of Hemingway are a fair treat. (reviews of french translation). very enthusiastic but hope Hem's sense of Humour is surviving Arkansas, otherwise he'll come back and assassinate me, for having shipped him the french comments. He and Dos Passos are now leading french authors.

Jan. Asia has arrived, and a couple of as usual Nations. Praps an Am. Murk-ury wd. be a change.

Yesterday mostly spent on supervising turning coal hole into cupboard for papers. also convarsation with W.B.Y. and R.A. or vice-versa.

Love to you and mother.

what is the 1919 census of FEET?

E

+⸺⸺=+

846. TL [on 'Ezra Pound | *res publica, the public convenience*' letterhead]

22 Jan. [1929]

Rapallo | via Marsala, 12 int. 5

Dear Dad:

Glad you are pleezd with the Cantos (at last, I mean arrived at last.) also XILE. 4. (which I have not yet seen)

<u>NO</u>

I do not think it wise for you to monkey with publishing, the fambly has done enough impractical things. and enough boosting. IF there isn't now enough energy to print it in America without you're investing your hard earned, then it had better take a wakation.

There are also other reasons for suspending it, indefinitely.

1. Dial, fairly open.

2. C. H. Ford is starting a local show, with Spector, Bill Wms. and Vogel, and printing Zuk.

let's see what they can do.

3. Nancy's press can take care of some of the items.

Also having blown the bloomink horn, a few months silence may be as effective as yawp.

The Bellyachic isles are over by Spain. Ole Freddy Chamberlain lives there. They are cheap, I hear, and as far as I am concerned, inaccessible.

Will answer Blackmoor's letter, direct to him.

Pound was at this time corresponding with many young American writers, giving them advice and encouragement, and urging them to form themselves into active groups. **Charles Henri Ford** *(b. 1913), poet, novelist, editor, and painter, was starting* Blues: A Magazine of New Rhythms *in Mississippi, and Pound was suggesting he involve Herman Spector and Joseph Vogel as contributing editors.* **Spector** *(b. 1905), a radical poet and prose writer, would be much associated with* New Masses. **Vogel** *(b. 1904) was also then a proletarian poet and critic. 'The* **Bellyachic** *isles' = the Balearics.*

847. TL [on 'Ezra Pound | *res publica, the public convenience*' letterhead]
2 Feb. [1929]

Rapallo | via Marsala, 12 int. 5

Dear Mother

Apropos of that Hauptmann caricature in the 'Living' Age (and a bloody dead paper it is too) Mrs Hauptmann has for three weeks been going to bring me a caricature of Antheil, which she had spotted in the Berlin Tageblatt; today at last she remembered it.

I go on record that I have never until today seen a camera anywhere near the noble Gerhart UNTIL this morning; or rather until 2 P.M. but having offered yesterday to swap the L.A. caricature for the one of Jawg; what arrives this day but two danes; one with cine and one with ordinary; and they procede to snap G.H.

so thass thaat.

Hope to finish the Schloezer before end of next week.

Hughes been here and gone. wot ells. George hopes to get here. etc.

6. Feb.

Dear Dad:

Saw better poem by Aukenbrand in Palo Verde. Yes naturally I saw Bill's book as I reviewed it in DIAL. Dont know how many Cantos rodker sent to U.S. I take it he sent you ONE copy.

Homer had sent Ezra Frank Ankenbrand's 'Mad Smoker', a poem 'in free verse':

God strikes his
matches
across the angry
blue of the sky
and blows
racing winds
and
dark clouds
thru
his nostrils.

Palo Verde, *a little magazine edited by Norman Macleod.*

⊹⊱—⊰⊹

848. TL [on 'Ezra Pound | *res publica, the public convenience*' letterhead]

12 Feb. [1929]

Rapallo | via Marsala, 12 int. 5

Dear Dad

Up to neck in too g.d. much correspondence. Various notes recd.

1. Zukofsky is coming to Phila. re/ a new quarterly mag.

I shd. be glad if you cd. put him up for night or two; and interjuce him to Aukenbrand etc. etc.

address 57 E. One hundred and eleventh st. N/Y/ (you might invite him at once, unless race prejudice intervenes. Bill Wms. likes him.

2. No copy of Payne's book recd. from him or Univ. of Texas.

Yes; I get the Dial. and Rich shd. send me the xtra copies of Herald "Books".

hastily

Pound's 'How to Read' was appearing in three instalments in New York Herald Tribune Books.

⊹⊱—⊰⊹

849. TLS [on 'Ezra Pound | *res publica, the public convenience*' letterhead]

3 March [1929]

Rapallo | via Marsala, 12 int. 5

Dear Mother:

Ceremony of introducing Yeatsz and Hauptmanns passed off calmly last evening with sacrifice of two pheasants. No other bloodshed.

Richard gone to Paris. Bunting now present and entertaining the Antheils. various delays and blockages in everyone's affairs. Sill cold. Able to smack a tennis ball now and then. Had snow on edge of court last week.

Dunno that ther'z much else to report.

love to you & Dad

E

Homer wrote on 10 April 1929: 'Have reservation for June 1. Plan for 3 mo. stay'. Ezra and Dorothy met Isabel and Homer in England, and they had sight of Omar at last. They went on to Rapallo, and before their three months were up decided to take up permanent residence there. From that time on Pound of course wrote to them only when he was away from Rapallo, and usually on post cards or in brief notes. Their letters were no longer the vital means of communication that they had been since Ezra's college days.

★★★★★★★★★★★★★★

Some Abbreviations Used in the Letters

AF	Aunt Frank	HSM	*Hugh Selwyn Mauberley*
BE	Bel Esprit	IWP	Isabel Weston Pound
Bib	Ibbotson, Prof. Joseph Darling	JH	Jane Heap (of *The Little Review*)
Bill	Prof. William Pierce Shephard,	JJ	James Joyce
	also William Carlos Williams	JQ	John Quinn
BVM	Beata Virgo Maria	LR	*Little Review*
C	Guido Cavalcanti	NA	*New Age*
CMA	Cheltenham Military Academy	NC	Nancy Cox McCormack
CoA	College of Arts	NF	*New Freewoman*
CTC	Carlos Tracy Chester	OR	Olga Rudge
D	Dorothy Pound	OS	Olivia Shakespear
EP	Ezra Loomis Pound	Prex	Hamilton College President
FFV.	First Family of Virginia		Melancthon Woolsey Stryker
FICP.	First Italian Presbyterian Church	QPA	*Quia Pauper Amavi*
FMH	Ford Madox Hueffer	SofR	*Spirit of Romance*
GA	George Antheil	SS	*Smart Set*
GC	Guido Cavalcanti	TCP	Thaddeus Coleman Pound
GCW	Graham Cox Woodward	TP	*T. P.'s Weekly*
HHS	Henry Hope Shakespear	TQ	*This Quarter*
Hilda	Hilda Doolittle	UP	University of Pennsylvania
HJ	Henry James	WBY	William Butler Yeats
HLP	Homer Loomis Pound	WL	Wyndham Lewis
HM	Harriet Monroe	WR	Walter Rummel
HPC	Holland Place Chambers	WW	Woodrow Wilson

Glossary of Names

Ackers, Philadelphia confectioners, provider of chocolates
Adcock, St. John (1864–1930), English novelist and poet
Adkins, Marius David, EP's pseudonym as drama critic, briefly, in 1919
Aeschylus (c.525–c.456 BC), Greek tragic dramatist
Agricola, Rodolphus (1443–85), humanist scholar and poet
Aiken, Conrad (1889–1973), US poet, novelist, critic, and editor
Aldington, Richard (1892–1962), English poet, novelist, editor, and biographer
Althouse, Philadelphia travel agent, organised Select Foreign Tours
Ames, Herman Vandenberg (1865–1935), Professor of US Constitutional History,
   University of Pennsylvania
Anderson, Sherwood (1876–1941), US fiction writer
Ankenbrand, Frank, Jr., co-author with Isaac Benjamin of *The House of Vanity* (1928), a
   small book of poems from a vanity press, with introduction by Countee Cullen
Antheil, George ['Jawg/Jarg'], (1900–59), US avant-garde composer and pianist
Antonini, A., Venice printer
Appleton, New York publishing house
Apuleius, Lucius (2C. AD), Roman writer, satirist, and rhetorician
Aquinas, St. Thomas (1225–74), Italian scholastic philosopher and theologian
Aristotle (384–322 BC), Greek philosopher
Arnold, Matthew (1822–88), English poet, critic, educationist
Asquith, Herbert Henry, Earl of Oxford (1852–1928), English statesman, Prime
   Minister 1908–16
Atheling, William, EP's pseudonym as music critic of the *New Age*
Augener Ltd., London music publishers
Augurellus, Johannes Aurelius (?1454–1537), Renaissance humanist, alchemist, and Latin
   poet

Backus, Oswald Prentiss, Jr. (1883–1956), Hamilton class of '08
Bacon, Francis S. ['Baldy'] (1877–1941), New York businessman
Bacon, Robert (1860–1919), US Ambassador to France 1910–12
Baerlein, Henry (1875–1960), prolific English writer
Baker, Captain Lionel Guy (?1874–1918), London friend of EP (see Canto 16)
Baldwin, Stanley (1867–1947), English Conservative politician and Prime Minister
Balfour, Arthur James (1848–1930), English Prime Minister 1902–5, Foreign Secretary
   1916–19
Bard, Joseph (1882–1975), expatriate Hungarian writer
Barker, Wharton (1846–1921), Philadelphia banker, international financier, US agent of
   the Czar, Trustee of University of Pennsylvania; friend of Thaddeus C. Pound and
   of Homer Pound

Barnes, Djuna (1892–1982) US novelist, poet, and illustrator

Barney, Natalie Clifford (1876–1972), writer and wealthy expatriate American in Paris presiding over a famous literary salon

Barnum, Phineas Taylor (1810–91), US impresario, co-founder Barnum & Bailey Circus

Barrie, J. M. (1860–1937), dramatist, best known for *Peter Pan* (1904)

Barry, Iris (1895–1969), poet, novelist, and film historian

Bartram, John (1699–1777), US botanist, established botanical garden near Philadelphia

Bassiano, Princess of, an American, married to an Italian, living in Paris

Baxter, Gwendolen (d.1935), US sculptor, sister of Viola Baxter

Baxter, Viola Scott [later Jordan] (1887–1973), a lifelong friend of EP

Baynes, Harold Ernest (1868–1925), naturalist and writer

Beck, Jean (1881–1943), Alsatian, later American, authority on Provençal music

Becker, John J. (1886–1961), American composer, advocate of contemporary music

Bedford, Agnes (1892–1969), English musician

Beecham, Sir Thomas (1879–1961), English conductor and impresario

Beerbohm, Sir Henry Maximilian [Max] (1872–1956), English writer and caricaturist

Belasco, David (1853–1931), Broadway impresario, producer, director, and playwright

Bell, (Arthur) Clive Heward (1881–1964), English art and literary critic

Bell, Gertrude M. L. B. (1868–1926), British authority on the Near East, where she served as military intelligence agent and political secretary

Belloc, Hilaire Pierre (1870–1953), British writer and poet

Bellotti, owner of Bellotti's Ristorante Italiano, 12 Old Compton Street, London

Benamore, Yusuf, a Gibraltar tour guide

Bennett, [Enoch] Arnold (1867–1931), English novelist

Benson, A. C. (1862–1925), writer, biographer, EP's archetypal 'man of letters'

Berenson, Bernard (1865–1959), expatriate American art critic and connoisseur

Berman, Louis (1893–1946), US physician, endocrinologist, and writer

Beyea, Dr James Louis, married Frances Weston in 1906

Bierce, Ambrose Gwinnett (1842–1914), US short-story writer and journalist

Binyon, Laurence (1869–1943), poet; Keeper of Oriental Prints and Drawings, British Museum; later translator of Dante's *Divine Comedy*

Bird, William/Bill ['S'Oiseau'] (1889–1963), Paris manager of Consolidated Press Association, founded Three Mountains Press there (1921–5)

Birrell, Augustine (1850–1933), English civil servant and essayist

Blaine, James Gillespie (1830–1893), US politician, diplomat, orator, and journalist

Blériot, Louis (1872–1936), French aviator

Blunt, Wilfred Scawen (1840–1922), English diplomat, poet, supporter of Egyptian and Irish nationalism

Bodenheim, Maxwell (1893–1954), US poet and novelist

Boissier, Gaston (1823–1908), French historian and philologist

Bok, Mrs E K, wealthy Philadelphian, married to Edward William Bok, conductor of Philadelphia Orchestra, patron of Antheil

Boni, Albert and Charles, New York publishers

Boni, Charles, and [Horace] Liveright, New York publishers

Boni, Giacomo (1859–1925) Italian Senator, classicist, and archaeologist

Borah, William Edgar (1865–1940), Idaho Senator (Republican) 1907–40

Born, Bertrans de (c.1140–c.1212–15), Provençal soldier and poet

Borrow, George Henry (1803–81), English writer and traveller

Bosis, Lauro de (1901–31), Italian poet, dramatist, translator, and anti-Fascist

Bosschère, Jean de (1878–1953), Flemish poet, book illustrator, artist

Bowen, Stella (1893–1947), expatriate Australian artist, partner of Ford Madox Ford 1917–27

Brancusi, Constantin (1876–1957), Romanian-born, Paris-based sculptor

Brandt, Herman Carl George (1850–1920), Professor of German, Hamilton College

Brass, Italico (1879–1943), Venetian painter and sculptor

Bridges, Robert (1844–1930), English poet, made poet laureate in 1913

Brinkley, Frank (1841–1912), Anglo-Irish journalist and scholar resident in Japan, author of a 12-volume study of Japan and China (1901)

Bronner, Milton, US journalist, editor, and critic, early friend of EP

Brooks, Romaine (1870–1970) expatriate American portrait painter, companion of Natalie Barney

Brooks, Van Wyck (1886–1963), US critic, biographer, and literary historian

Brownell, William Cary (1851–1928), US critic and author

Browning, Robert (1812–89), English poet

Brunton, Winnifred Mabel (née Newberry) (1880–1959), English painter

Brussof/Bryussov, Valeri Yakovlevitch (1873–1924), Russian poet, critic, editor, and translator

Bryan, William Jennings (1860–1925), US politician, Democratic presidential candidate, Secretary of State under Woodrow Wilson

Brzeska, *see* Gaudier-Brzeska

Bubb, Reverend C. Clinch, publisher, ran the Clerk's Press in Cleveland, Oh.

Bunting, Basil (1900–85), English poet

Burne-Jones, Sir Edward Coley (1833–98), English painter

Burns, Robert (1759–96), Scottish poet and songwriter

Burton, Sir Richard (1821–90), English explorer, linguist, and diplomat

Busha, Charles Thomas, Sr. (1858–1930), married a cousin of Homer Pound in 1885

Busha, Charles Thomas, Jr. (1890–1956), US army captain in World War One

Buss, Kate (1884–?), US critic, reviewed and corresponded with EP

Butler, Samuel (1835–1902), English author and translator

Byington, Homer, US Consul in Naples

Bynner, Witter (1881–1968), US poet, translator, editor, and critic

Calvin, John (1509–64), French Protestant theologian and reformer

Campbell, Joseph (1879–1944), Irish poet

Cannell, Skipwith (1887–1957), US poet, played a role in London Imagist movement

Carman, Bliss (1861–1929), poet, author (with Richard Hovey) of 3 collections of *Songs from Vagabondia* (1894, 1896, 1901)

Carnegie, Andrew (1835–1919), US steel magnate and philanthropist

Carnevali, Emanuel (1897–1940?), Italian poet, translator, and editor

Carus, Paul (1852–1919), editor of the *Monist*, ran Open Court Publishing Co.

Casella Alfredo (1883–1947), Italian conductor and pianist

Catullus, Gaius Valerius (c.84–c.54 BC), Roman lyric poet

Cavalcanti, Guido (c.1240–1300), Italian poet

Cézanne, Paul (1839–1906), French painter

Chamberlain, (Arthur) Neville (1869–1940), Conservative politician, Prime Minister 1937–40

Chamberlain, Frederic, English author, *The Private Character of Elizabeth* (1922)

Chambers, Robert W. (1865–1933), prolific and popular US author

Chester, the Reverend Carlos Tracy (1851–1927), pastor, Calvary Presbyterian Church, Wyncote (1892–1901); co-editor, *Philadelphia News Monthly*, *Book Monthly*, and *Booklovers' Magazine*

Chester, Hawley, son of Carlos Chester

Chesterton, Gilbert Keith (1874–1936), English critic, novelist, and poet

Child, Dr Clarence G., Professor of English, University of Pennsylvania

Christian, pseudonym of **Herbiet, Georges** (1895–1969), French artist

Churchill, Sir Winston Leonard Spencer (1874–1965), English statesman

Chute, Father Desmond Macready (1895–1962), follower of Eric Gill, Rapallo resident

Ciolkowska, Mme Muriel, Paris correspondent of *The Egoist*

Coburn, Alvin Langdon (1882–1966), US photographer

Cochran family: **Tommy** (childhood friend of EP), **Joe**, and **Catherine**,

Cocteau, Jean (1889–1963), French poet, playwright, and film director

Collier, William [Bill] Miller, US Ambassador to Spain

Collignon, Raymonde (1894–?), French soprano and 'diseuse', especially of troubadour and folk song

Collins, John Churton (1848–1908), university extension lecturer and critic

Colum, Pádraic (1881–1972), Irish poet and playwright

Colvin, Professor Sir Sidney (1845–1927), literary critic and art historian

Comparette, T. Louis (1868–1922), Curator of the Museum of the Philadelphia Mint

Comstock, Anthony (1844–1915), in 1873 founded New York Society for the Suppression of Vice; the same year Congress passed the 'Comstock Act'

Conder, Charles (1868–1909), English-born Australian artist

Confucius (551–479 BC), Chinese philosopher

Conrad, Joseph (1857–1924), Polish-born British novelist

Coolidge, John Calvin (1872–1933), 30th President of the USA (1923–9)

Coomaraswamy, Ananda Kentish (1877–1947), Ceylonese art historian, writer, and critic

Corbin, Alice, *see* Henderson, Alice Corbin

Corelli, Marie [Mary Mackay] (1855–1924), English novelist

Cosgrave, William Thomas [also Cosgrove] (1880–1965), Irish statesman

Cournos, John (1881–1966), Russian-born US poet, novelist, journalist, and translator

Courtney, W. L., editor, *Fortnightly Review*

Covici, Pascal (1888–1964), US publisher and editor

Cowdray, Weetman Dickinson Pearson, 1st Viscount Cowdray (1856–1927), engineering and oil tycoon, philanthropist

Cowley, Malcolm (1898–1989), US literary critic

Cox, Nancy, *see* McCormack

Craig, [Edward] Gordon (1872–1966), English scene designer, producer, actor; also woodcut engraver and book illustrator

Cran, Marion (1879–1942), English poet

Craven, Thomas Jewell (1889–1969), US art critic

Cravens, Margaret Lanier (1881–1912), US student of the piano, EP's Paris patron

Cromwell, Oliver (1599–1658), soldier, regicide, and Lord Protector of England

Cros, Guy-Charles (1879–1956), French poet

Cross, Mrs James Frederick (Mary Moore of Trenton, m.1912)

Cummings, Edward Estlin (1894–1962), US writer and artist

Cunard, Lady Maud [Emerald] (1872–1948), patron of the arts, mother of Nancy Cunard

Cunard, Nancy (1896–1965), English poet, publisher, and patron of the arts, resident in France, founded the Hours Press in Paris (1928)

Cunningham/e Graham, Robert Bontine (1852–1936), Scottish author and politician

Curtis, Cyrus H. K. (1850–1933), editor *Ladies Home Journal*, friend of the Pounds

Dale, Alan [b. Alfred J. Cohen] (1861–1928), New York journalist

Damrosch, Frank Heino (1859–1937), German-born American music director, chorus master Metropolitan Opera (1891–5)

Damrosch, Walter Johannes (1862–1950), German-born, US composer and conductor

Daniel, Arnaut (fl. late 12c.), Provençal poet

D'Annunzio, Gabriele (1863–1938), Italian poet and dramatist, adventurer, and political leader

Dante Alighieri (1265–1321), Italian poet

Darantière, Maurice, French printer in Dijon

Davies, W. H. (1871–1940), Welsh poet, best known for *Autobiography of a Super Tramp* (1908)

Davis, Joseph Jones (1885–1961), class of '08, Hamilton College

Davray, Henry D. (1873–1944), literary editor English language section of *Mercure de France*, translator of Yeats, and of other major writers

Day, George Martin (1882–1958), class of '05, Hamilton College

Dazzi, Manlio Torquato (1891–1968), librarian, scholar, translator, Director of the Biblioteca Malatestina in Cesena and later of the Querini-Stampalia in Venice

Debussy, [Achille-] Claude (1862–1918), French composer

Dcfoe, Daniel (1660–1731), English writer and adventurer

DeKruif, Paul (1890–1971), US microbiologist, author of *Hunger Fighters* (1928)

DeMorgan, William Frend (1839–1917), English artist and novelist

Demuth, Charles (1883–1935), US painter and book illustrator

Dent, J. M. (1849–1926), London publisher

Depew, Chauncey Mitchell (1834–1928), president of the Vanderbilts' New York Central Railroad (1895–8); also active in politics, US Senator from New York 1899–1911

Descartes, René (1596–1650), French philosopher and mathematician

DeThou, Jacques August (1553–1617), French magistrate and historian

DeVoto, Bernard (1897–1955), US historian and writer

Dezire, Henri (1878–1965), French artist

Dias, B H, EP's pseudonym as the *New Age* art critic

Disraeli, Benjamin (1804–81), English statesman and novelist

Divus, Andreas, Renaissance Latin scholar; his translation of Homer's *Odyssey* published in Paris in 1538

Dolmetsch, Eugene Arnold (1858–1940), born in France, in England developed interest in early music and made early music instruments

Dondo, Mathurin (1884–1968), French poet and playwright, studied at University of Pennsylvania

Doolittle, Frederick, taught Latin and Greek at Cheltenham Military Academy

Doolittle, Gilbert, brother of Hilda; student of Civil Engineering, Class of '05 at University of Pennsylvania

Doolittle, Hilda [HD] (1886–1961), expatriate US Imagist poet and novelist

Dos Passos, John Roderigo (1896–1970), US novelist, playwright, and journalist

Doughty, Charles M (1843–1926), author, *Travels in Arabia Deserta* (1888)

Douglas, Clifford Hugh (1879–1952), English engineer, economist, founder of Social Credit movement

Douglas, Norman (1868–1953), English novelist and essayist

Dowden, Edward (1843–1913), university professor and Shakespeare critic

Dowson, Ernest Christopher (1867–1900), English poet

Doyle, Sir Arthur Conan (1859–1930), Scottish writer of detective stories and historical romances

Draper, Ruth (1889–1956), US monologuist

Dreiser, Theodore Herman Albert (1871–1945), US novelist

Duchamp, Marcel (1887–1968), French-born US artist

Duhamel, Georges (1884–1966), French novelist and poet

Dulac, Edmond (1882–1953), French-born British artist and book illustrator

Dunning, Ralph Cheever (1878–1930), American poet resident in Paris

Durer, Albrecht (1471–1528), German painter and engraver

Echegaray, José (1832–1916), Spanish dramatist

Eckfeldt, J. B. (1846–1938), Chief Assayer at the US Mint in Philadelphia

Eden, Rev. Frederick and **Mrs Eden**, friends in Venice of Olivia Shakespear

Eliot, Thomas Stearns (1888–1965), US-born expatriate poet, literary and social critic, publisher, dramatist

Elizondo, Padre José Maria de, Spanish Franciscan scholar met in Madrid 1908

Ellis, William [Willie] Thomas (1873–1950), US journalist of religious matters, let his house in Swarthmore to the Pounds in 1910

Elsea, [Elsey] Richard [Dick] Matthews (1884–1962), class of '07 at Hamilton

Elson, H. P., missionary at Raymond Lull Home, an orphanage in Tangiers, Morocco

Emerson, Ralph Waldo (1803–82), US transcendentalist philosopher, essayist, and poet

Epstein, Jacob (1880–1959), American-born British sculptor

Estaunié , Édouard (1862–1942), French novelist, elected to Académie Française 1923

Etchells, Frederick (1886–1973), English Vorticist painter

Faber and Gwyer, London publishers, later Faber and Faber

Fairfax, James Griffyth (1886–1976), Australian-born poet, English barrister, and politician

Fanelli, Ernest (1860–1917), French composer

Farr, Florence (1860–1917), English actress and theatre director, particularly in and of plays by Shaw, Ibsen and Yeats; feminist; occultist; performer of Yeats' poetry to the psaltery harp; teacher in Ceylon

Faust, Horace, childhood friend of EP

Fenollosa, Ernest (1853–1908), scholar and teacher of traditional arts of Japan in both Japan and America; Commissioner of Fine Arts in Japan, 1886–90; Curator of Oriental Art, Boston Museum of Fine Arts, 1890–6

Fenollosa, Mrs Mary McNeil, edited and published her husband's work

Field, Michael, pseudonym under which Katharine Harris Bradley (1846–1914) and her niece Edith Emma Cooper (1862–1913) published poetry and verse drama

Finger, Charles Joseph (1869–1941), US founder, editor and publisher of *All's Well, or The Mirror Repolished*, a literary journal

Fitch, Edward ['Little Greek'], Edward North Professor of Greek, Hamilton College

Fitzgerald, Desmond (1889–1947), Irish revolutionary and statesman

Flaminius, Marcus Antonius (1498–1550), Renaissance Latinist and historian

Flaubert, Gustave (1821–80), French novelist

Fletcher, John Gould (1886–1950), US poet and essayist

Flint, Frank Stewart (1885–1960), English civil servant, poet, critic, and translator

Florence, Aunt, *see* Foote family

Foch, Ferdinand, Marshal of France (1851–1929), French commander in World War One

Foote family: EP's aunt **Florence**, and cousins **David** (1893–1976) and **Homer**

Forbes-Robertson, Sir Johnston (1853–1937), British actor

Ford, Charles Henri (1913–2002), US poet, novelist, visual artist; editor, *Blues: A Bisexual Bimonthly*

Ford/Hueffer, Ford Madox (1873–1939), English novelist, poet, founding editor of *English Review* and *Transatlantic Review*

Ford, Henry (1863–1947), founder of the Ford Motor Company in Detroit

Ford, Henry, Proprietor of Wayside Inn, Sudbury, Mass., c.1925–6

Foster, Mrs Jeanne Robert (1879–1970), model, journalist, poet; John Quinn's companion 1916–24; literary editor, social worker

Fowler, Eva (1871–1921), American, married to Alfred ('Taffy') Fowler (1860–1933), ran a literary salon at her home in Knightsbridge, London, and went in for psychic experiments at her cottage, Daisy Meadow, The Chart, Brasted, Kent

Frank, Aunt, *see* Weston and Beyea

Frank, Waldo David (1889–1967), US novelist and journalist

Fraser, *see* Kennedy-Fraser, Marjorie

Frost, Robert Lee (1874–1963), US poet

Galdós, *see* Pérez Galdós, Benito

Galton, Reverend Arthur (1852–1921), classical scholar, vicar of Edenham in Lincolnshire, where he gave Frederic Manning a home

Garfield, James Abram (1831–81), 20th President of the USA (1881)

Garnett, Constance (1861–1946), English translator of Russian literature

Garvey, Marcus Moziah Aurelius (1887–1940), African-American leader in US

Gaudier-Brzeska, Henri (1891–1915), French sculptor

Gautier, Judith (1845–1917), French poet, translator of Chinese and Japanese poetry, historical novelist, and woman of letters

George, W[alter] L[ionel] (1882–1926), English writer

Ghose, Koli Mohan, pupil of Tagore, worked with EP on translations of Kabir

Gilder, Richard Watson (1844–1909), US poet

Glenconner, Edward Priaulx Tennant, 1ˢᵗ Baron Glenconner (1859–1920), and **Lady Glenconnor** (*née* Pamela Wyndham) (1871–1920)

Goldman, Emma (1869–1940), Russian-born US anarchist, activist, lecturer, writer

Goldring, Douglas (1887–1960), English writer and journalist

Gonne, Iseult (1895–1954), daughter of Maud Gonne the agitator for Irish Independence

Gosse, Edmund William (1849–1928), English literary critic, autobiographer, Librarian to the House of Lords (1904–14)

Gould, Dr George Milbry (1848–1922), Philadelphia ophthalmologist, author of medical textbooks

Gould, Joe [Joseph Ferdinand] (1889–1957), New York bohemian and 'oral historian'

Gourmont, Remy de (1858–1915), French poet, essayist, novelist, and critic

Goya, Francisco de (1746–1828), Spanish artist

Graham, R. B. Cunningham, *see* Cuningham Graham

Graham/e, Kenneth (1859–1932), Scottish children's writer

Grainger-Kerr, Mary Elizabeth (1864–c.1950), Scottish concert singer, with special interest in modern British music and Hebridean folk songs

Grant, Ulysses Simpson (1822–85), 18ᵗʰ President of the USA (1869–77)

Granville, Charles [alias Charles Hosken] (1867–?), colourful English author and publisher, proprietor of the *Freewoman* and *Future*, manager of Stephen Swift & Co., publishers

Green/e, Reverend Richard [Dicky], of Grace Presbyterian Church, Jenkintown, PA, 1886–94. EP's parents joined the church in 1891

Gregg, Frances Josepha (1884–1941), poet and short story writer, later Mrs Wilkinson, close friend of Hilda Doolittle

Gregory, Lady Isabella Augusta (1852–1932), leading figure with W. B. Yeats in the Irish literary revival; collector of Irish mythology and folklore; co-founder of Dublin's Abbey Theatre for which she wrote plays about the Irish peasantry

Grinnell, Charles Edward (1841–1916), US lawyer and writer on legal matters

Guerbel, Jenny Ward, Countess of, *see* Ward, Genevieve

Guiney, Louise Imogen (1861–1920), US poet and essayist

Gurdjieff, Georgei Ivanovich [EP's Godjeff/Gotchoff/Gotcheff] (c.1865–1949), Armenian-born charismatic Christian gnostic; in 1922 set up his Institute for the Harmonious Development of Man at Fontainebleau in France

Hagedorn, Hermann (1882–1964), US poet

Harding, Warren Gamaliel (1865–1923), 29ᵗʰ President of the USA (1921–3)

Hardy, Thomas (1840–1928), English novelist and poet

Harris, Frank (1856–1931), Irish writer and journalist

Harte, [Francis] Bret[t] (1836–1902), US poet and short story writer

Hartmann, Sadakichi (1867–1944), US poet and critic, born in Japan, raised in Germany

Hastings, Beatrice, a pseudonym of Emily Alice Haigh (1879–1943), English critic and writer, associated with Orage's *New Age*

Hauptmann, Gerhart Johann Robert (1862–1946), German dramatist and novelist; Nobel Prize winner (1912)

Hayes, Roland (1887–1977), US black tenor, noted for his interpretation of both *lieder* and spirituals

Heacock, Annie, ran Chelten Hills School, Wyncote, attended by EP 1893

Heap, Jane (1883–1964), co-editor of the *Little Review* (1916–29)

Hearst, William Randolph (1863–1951), newspaper magnate and politician

Hecht, Ben (1894–1964), US journalist, novelist, short-story writer, poet, playwright and Hollywood screenwriter

Heinemann, William (1863–1920), English publisher

Helston, John (1877–1928?), poet, turner, and fitter

Hemingway, Ernest Millar ['Hem'] (1899–1961), US writer of novels and short stories; Nobel Prize winner (1954)

Henderson, Alice Corbin (1881–1949), poet, assistant editor of *Poetry*

Henley, William Ernest (1849–1903), poet, critic, and editor

Hennessy, Dr Margaret E (1857–1915), practised medicine in Utica

Herbert [of Cherbury], Edward Herbert, 1ˢᵗ Baron (1583–1648), English soldier, politician, and philosopher

Herodotus (c.485–425 BC), Greek historian

Hessler, Lewis Burtron [Burt] (1884–1958), US teacher and scholar; contemporary of EP at University of Pennsylvania

Hewlett, Maurice (1861–1923), writer of historical novels and poems, and a power in Edwardian literary society

Heyman, Katherine Ruth (1877–1944), US concert pianist, renowned performer of Scriabin

Hickock, Guy Carleton (1888–1951), US journalist, manager *Brooklyn Eagle* Paris Bureau 1918–33

Hilda [HD], *see* Doolittle

Hinckley, Theodore Ballou, editor of *Drama*, Chicago

Hindenburg, Paul Ludwig Hans Anton von Beneckendorff und von (1847–1934), German general, President of German Republic 1925–34

Hokusai, Katsushika (1760–1849), Japanese artist and wood-engraver

Hoover, Herbert Clark (1874–1964), 31ˢᵗ president of the USA (1929–33)

Hornung, Ernest William (1866–1921), English novelist, creator of 'Raffles' the gentleman burglar

Howells, William Dean (1837–1920), US editor, critic, novelist

Howland, Louise (1857–1934), editor of *Indianapolis News*, 1911–1934

Hubbard, Elbert (1856–1915), US writer, editor, publisher, promoter of Arts and Crafts movement

Hudson, William Henry (1841–1922), British writer and naturalist

Hueffer, *see* Ford/Hueffer

Hughes, Charles Evans (1862–1948), US jurist and politician, presidential candidate in 1916

Hughes, Glenn (1894–1964), US professor at the University of Washington in Seattle, edited series of Chapbooks, wrote on Imagism, directed the drama program

Hugo, Victor Marie (1802–85), French poet and novelist

Hulme, Thomas Ernest (1883–1917), English critic, poet, and philosopher

Hunt, Violet (1862–1942), English artist, journalist, and novelist; London literary hostess; companion of Ford Madox Hueffer 1909–19

Hurlbut, William (1878–1957), US dramatist and Hollywood screenwriter

Hyde-Lees, Bertha Georgie (1892–1968), married W. B. Yeats 1917

Hynes, Gladys (1888–1958), English artist

Ibbotson, Joseph Darlington ['Bib'] (1869–1952), Professor of English Literature, Anglo-Saxon and Hebrew at Hamilton College

Image, Selwyn (1849–1930), artist in stained glass and religious versifier; a founder of Century Guild; Slade Professor of Fine Art at Oxford 1910–16.

Ingersoll, Robert Green (1833–99), US lawyer, politician, and orator

Ingle, Henry Bass, the Pounds' family doctor in Philadelphia

Ionides, Luke (1837–1924), Greek-born English stockbroker, merchant, and patron of the arts; friend of Olivia Shakespear; his *Memories* published in Paris, 1925

Irving, Sir Henry (1838–1905), English actor

Itow, Michio (1893–1961), Japanese artist and dancer

James, Henry (1843–1916), US-born, expatriate novelist, and writer of short stories

James, William (1842–1910), US philosopher and psychologist, elder brother to Henry James

Jefferson, Thomas (1743–1862), 3rd President of the USA

Jenks, Leon (1876–1940), class of '05, Hamilton College

Jepson, Edgar Alfred (1863–1938), English novelist

John, Mrs Dalliba, patron of the arts, friend of Olga Rudge

Johns, Orrick (1887–1946), US poet

Johnson, Lionel Pigot (1867–1902), English poet and critic

Jones, Walter Falke (1886–1947), class of '05, Hamilton College

Jordan, *see* Baxter, Viola Scott

Joyce, James (1882–1941), Irish novelist, short-story writer, poet, and playwright, author of *Ulysses* (1922)

Kahn, Otto Hermann (1867–1934), German-born American investment banker and patron of the arts, supported *Little Review*

Keith, W. E., Philadelphia optometrist

Kennedy-Fraser, Marjorie (1857–1930), collector and arranger of Gaelic folk-song

Kennerly, Mitchell (1878–1932), US editor *Forum* 1910–16

Kent, Adrian, English painter

Kerr, *see* Grainger-Kerr, Mary Elizabeth

Keynes [of Tilton], John Maynard Keynes, 1st Baron (1883–1946), economist

Kildare, Owen (1864–1911), editor, *Pearson's Magazine*

King, Dr Robert Augustus, Professor of German at Wabash 1891–1918

Glossary of Names

Kingston, Gertrude [Gertrude Angela Kohnstamm] (1862–1937), English actress and producer

Kipling, Joseph Rudyard (1865–1963), English writer, Nobel Prize winner (1907)

Knopf, Alfred A. (1892–1984), New York publisher

Konody, Paul George (1872–1933), Hungarian-born, British journalist, and art critic

Koumé, Tamijuro (1893–1923), Japanese painter, also schooled in *Noh*

Kreymborg, Alfred (1883–1966), US poet, editor *The Glebe* (1913–14) and *Others* (1915–19)

K'ung, *see* Confucius

La Follette, Robert Marion (1855–1925), US politician

LaForgue, Jules (1860–87), French poet

Lamberton, Robert [Bob], class of '06, University of Pennsylvania

Landor, Walter Savage (1775–1864), English writer

Lane, John (1854–1925), publisher, sometime partner of Elkin Mathews, founder of the Bodley Head

Langley, Mrs, EP's landlady at 5 Holland Place Chambers, London

Larbaud, Valéry (1881–1957), French poet and novelist

Larzelere, Dayton ('Skinny'), childhood friend of EP in Wyncote

Lauder, Sir Harry [Henry] (1870–1950), Scottish actor, singer, and comedian

Lawrence, D[avid] H[erbert] (1885–1930), English novelist, poet, and essayist

Lawrence, Col T[homas] E[dward] (1888–1935), Anglo-Irish soldier and writer, known as 'Lawrence of Arabia'

Lawrence, William George (1889–1915), brother of T. E. Lawrence

Léger , Fernand (1881–1955), French artist

Legouis, Émile (1861–1937), Professor of English at the Sorbonne in Paris

Leonardo da Vinci (1452–1519), Italian painter, sculptor, architect, and engineer

Leslie, Sir (John Randolph) Shane (1885–1971), Anglo-Irish diplomat and author

Levy, Professor Emil (1855–1918), German scholar of Provençal language and literature

Lewis, Percy Wyndham (1882–1957), English artist and writer

Lhote, André (1885–1962), French artist, teacher, and writer on art

Linati, Carlo (1878–1949), Italian writer and translator

Lincoln, Abraham (1809–65), 16th President of the USA

Lindsay, Vachel (1879–1931), US poet

Little Greek, *see* Fitch

Liveright, Horace B (1884–1933), New York publisher

Llone/Llona, Victor (1886–1953), Peruvian-born multilinguist, resident in Paris, writer, and translator

Lloyd-George, David, 1st Earl of Dwyfor (1863–1945), Welsh statesman, Prime Minister 1916–22

Loeb, Harold A. (1891–1974), US novelist, editor of *Broom* (1921–4)

Longfellow, Henry Wadsworth (1807–82), US poet

Lorimer, George Horace (1868–1937), Wyncote neighbour and editor-in-chief of the *Saturday Evening Post* (1899–1937)

Lovell, Mrs Mary, a family friend in Wyncote who became a paying guest

Low, Lady Anne Penelope, close friend of Olivia Shakespear; held an important literary salon at her home in London

Lowell, Amy (1874–1925), US poet and critic

Lower, Reverend William Barnes (b. 1868), Presbyterian minister in Wyncote, lived with Pounds 1901–2

Loy, Mina (1882–1966), English-born US poet and artist

Ludwig, Emil (1881–1948), German, later Swiss, journalist, romantic biographer

Luther, Martin (1483–1546), German religious reformer

McAlmon, Robert (1895–1956), US short-story writer, editor, and publisher

McClure, Rev., A. J. P., minister of the Protestant Episcopal Church in the Diocese of Pennsylvania

McCormack, Nancy Cox (1885–1967), US sculptress

McDaniel, Walton Brooks (1871–1978) Professor of Latin, University of Pennsylvania

McGreevy, Thomas (1893–1967), Irish poet, literary critic, and art critic.

McKay, Claude (1890–1948), Jamaican-born US poet and novelist

Macaulay Company, New York publishers

Macaulay [of Rothay], Thomas Babington, 1ˢᵗ Baron (1800–59), English historian and poet

Macchiavelli, Nicolò (1469–1527), Italian diplomat, political philosopher, and historian

Mackail, John William O. M. (1859–1945), Scottish classical scholar, literary historian, and biographer; Professor of Poetry at Oxford (1906–11)

Mackaye, Percy (1875–1956), US poet and playwright

MacKintosh, Dr George Lewes, President, Wabash College, Indiana 1907–26

Macleod, Fiona, pseudonym of William Sharp as author of Celtic tales and romances

Macmillan Co., publishers in London and New York

Maitland, Robert (b. 1875) English bass-baritone

Mallarmé, Stéphane (1842–98), French Symbolist poet

Manning, Frederic (1882–1935), Australian-born British novelist and poet

Mapel, Misses Ida (d. 1960) and **Adah Lee** (d. c.1955), sisters who met EP in Spain in 1906, and later lived in Washington, DC, and visited him in St Elizabeths

Marchetti, Averardo, proprietor of Palace Hotel and Commandante della Piazza in Rimini, 1923–

Marconi, Guglielmo (1874–1937), Italian inventor, famous for radio-telegraphic communications

Marks, Mrs Josephine Preston Peabody (1874–1922), poet and dramatist

Marquesita, Violet [Violet Hume] (b. 1896), contralto, famous as Lucy Lockit in *The Beggars' Opera*

Marsden, Dora B. A. (1882–1960), militant suffragette; founded and edited *The Freewoman* (1911–12), a feminist review, then *The New Freewoman: An Individualist Review* (1913), which became *The Egoist* in 1914; developed in articles and books her own Individualist philosophy

Marshall, John, New York publisher

Masaryk, Tomáš Garrigue (1850–1937), Austro-Hungarian and Czechoslovak statesman, first President of Czechoslovakia 1918–35

Mascagni, Pietro (1863–1945), Italian opera composer

Masefield, John Edward (1878–1967), English poet and novelist

Masterman, Charles Frederick Gurney (1873–1927), English journalist, author, politician; head of British propaganda in World War One

Masters, Edgar Lee (1869–1950), US writer and poet

Mathers, E[dward] Powys (1892–1939), poet and translator of Asiatic poetry

Mathews, [Charles] Elkin (1851–1921), London bookseller, editor, publisher

Maynard, S., *see* Small Maynard & Co.

Mead, George Robert Shaw (1863–1933), writer on religion and philosophy, founded the Quest Society; editor, *The Quest* 1909–30

Medbury, Dr, pastor of Baptist church, Jenkintown, Philadelphia

Medici, Lorenzo de, called 'The Magnificent' (1449–92), Florentine ruler

Melzer, Charles Henry (b. 1853), US international journalist and critic

Mempes, Mortimer (1855–1938), Australian-born British painter, engraver, book illustrator and fruit farmer

Mencius (c.372–c.289 BC), Chinese philosopher and sage

Mencken, Henry Louis (1880–1956), US journalist, editor, critic, polemicist, and historian of language

Menegatti, E., proprietor, Hotel Eden, Sirmione

Mérimée , Prosper (1803–70), French novelist

Merrill, Stuart Fitzrandolph (1863–1915), US-born French Symbolist poet

Methuen, Sir Algernon Methuen Marshall (1856–1924), English publisher

Meynell, Alice Christiana (1847–1922), English poet, essayist, and critic

Meynell Wilfred (1852–1948), editor, author, and journalist

Michaud, Joseph (1767–1839), French historian, author of *History of the Crusades*, 3 vols. (1812–17)

Michelet, Jules (1798–1874), French historian; author of *Le Peuple* (1846), a treatise on economic and political transformations in 19th C. France

Michelson, Max (1880–1953), US poet associated with *Poetry* (Chicago)

Milford, Arthur B., Professor of English Literature, Wabash College

Milton, John (1608–74), English poet

Mirandola, *see* Pico Della Mirandola

Miraval, Raimon de (c.1135/1160–c.1220), French troubadour poet

Miró, Joán (1893–1983), Spanish artist

Mitchell, [Robert] Stewart (1892–1957), managing editor of *The Dial* (1920)

Mockel, Albert Henri Louis (1866–1945), Belgian-French poet and critic

Molière, pseudonym of Jean Baptiste Poquelin (1622–73), French playwright

Monck, Nugent (1877–1958), London theatre director

Monro, Harold [Edward] (1879–1932), English poet, publisher, bookseller, editor

Monroe, Harriet (1860–1936), US poet, founding editor (1912–36) of *Poetry: A Magazine of Verse*

Montaigne, Michel Eyquem de (1533–92), French essayist

Montesquieu, Charles-Louis de Secondat, Baron de la Brède et de (1689–1755), French philosopher and jurist

Moore, George Augustus (1852–1933), Irish writer

Moore, Marianne Craig (1887–1972), US poet; edited *The Dial* (1926–9)

Moore, Mary S. (Mrs Mary Cross) (1885–1976), 'Mary Moore of Trenton' to whom EP dedicated *Personae* (1909) 'if she wants it'

Moore, Thomas Sturge (1870–1944), English poet, critic, wood-engraver

Moorhead, Ethel (1869–1955), Scottish painter and suffragette; edited *This Quarter* (Paris) with Ernest Walsh, 1925–7

Morand, Paul (1888–1976), Russian-born French novelist, poet, and diplomat

Mordell, Albert (1885–), literary critic and editor

Morgan, George Campbell (1863–1945), minister at Westminster Congregationalist Chapel, London, preacher, and Bible teacher

Morgan, J[ohn] P[ierpoint] (1837–1913), US banker, financier, and art collector

Moring, Alexander, London printer and publisher at the De La More Press

Morley, Christopher Darlington (1890–1957), US novelist and essayist; columnist in *New York Evening Post*

Morrill, Albro David, Professor of Biology, Hamilton College

Morris, William (1834–96), English craftsman, poet, and socialist

Mosher, Thomas Bird (1852–1923), private press publisher in Portland, Maine

Mozart, Wolfgang Amadeus (1756–91), Austrian composer

Munson, Gorham Bert (1896–1969), US critic and editor

Murillo, Bartolomé Esteban (1618–82), Spanish Baroque religious artist

Murphy, Dudley (1897–1968), US film-maker

Murry, John Middleton (1889–1957), British writer and critic; editor London *Athenaeum* 1919–21

Mussolini, Benito Amilcare Andrea (1883–1945), Italian political leader, head of the Italian Fascist government 1922–43

Naidu, Sarojini (1879–1949), Bengali poet and social reformer

Neumayer, F. B., London bookseller on Charing Cross Road

Nevinson, Christopher Richard Wynne (1889–1946), English artist, associated with Futurism and Vorticism, World War One artist

Newbolt, Sir Henry John (1862–1938), English barrister and poet, known for 'Drake's Drum' and other songs of sea and Empire

Nijinsky, Vaslav (1890–1950), Russian dancer and choreographer

Noguchi, Yone (1875–1947), Japanese poet, popularizer of Japanese literature, and culture

Norton, Charles Eliot (1827–1908), US Dante scholar and translator, editor *North American Review*, Harvard Professor of the History of Art, social reformer

Orage, Alfred Richard (1873–1934), English social and economic reformer; founder and editor of *New Age: A weekly review of politics, literature, and art* (1907–22); follower of Gurdjieff 1923–31; founded *New English Weekly* 1932 to promote Social Credit

Ouspensky, Peter (1878–1947), Russian philosopher

Padre José, *see* Elizondo

Pansaers, Clement (1885–1922), Belgian poet and artist

Paracelsus (1493–1541), German alchemist and physician

Paris, Gaston (1839–1903), French scholar of Romance literature, Professor at Collège de France, member Académie Française

Parkhurst, Charles (1842–1933), Minister Madison Square Presbyterian Church, New York, crusading preacher and civic reformer

Pascal, Blaise (1623–62), French mathematician, inventor, Jansenist writer and thinker

Pater, Walter Horatio (1839–94), English aesthete and essayist

Patmore, [Ethel Elizabeth Morrison-Scott] **Brigit** (1882–1965), Ulster-born, member of EP's London literary circle

Paul, Sir Aubrey Edward Henry Dean, 5ᵗʰ Baronet, (1869–1961)

Pavlova, Anna (1881–1931), Russian ballerina

Peabody, *see* Marks

Peacock, Thomas Love (1785–1866), English novelist and poet

Pearse, Patrick (1879–1916), Irish writer; a leader of the Gaelic revival; Commander-in-Chief of the nationalist insurgents in the 1916 Dublin Uprising, shot by the English when it was put down

Peary, Robert Edwin (1856–1920), US naval commander and Arctic explorer

Penniman, Josiah (1868–1941), Professor of English and Dean, University of Pennsylvania

Pérez Galdós , Benito (1843–1920), Spanish novelist and dramatist

Picabia, Francis (1879–1953), French artist, associated with the Dadaists in Paris

Picasso, Pablo (1881–1973), expatriate Spanish painter resident in France

Pigott, Montague Horatio Mostyn Turtle (1865–1927), writer and anthologist of humourous verse, songs, and parodies

Pigou, Arthur Cecil (1877–1959), Cambridge Professor of Economics

Plarr, Victor (1863–1929), English poet

Plato (c.428–c.348 BC), Greek philosopher

Poe, Edgar Allan (1809–49), US poet and short-story writer

Polk, James Knox (1805–49), 11ᵗʰ President of the USA (1845–9)

Pope, Alexander (1688–1744), English poet

Pound, Albert E., EP's great-uncle

Pound, Dorothy, *see* Shakespear

Pound, Ezra Loomis [EP] (1885–1972), son to Homer and Isabel

Pound, Isabel Weston (1860–1948), EP's mother

Pound, Homer Loomis (1858–1942), EP's father

Pound, Susan Angevine Loomis (1835–1924), EP's paternal grandmother

Pound, Thaddeus Coleman (1832–1914), EP's grandfather: made and lost a fortune in the lumber business; Wisconsin State Assemblyman and Speaker 1864–9, Lieutenant-Governor 1870–1, US Congressman 1876–84; farmer

Powys, John Cooper (1872–1963), English novelist, poet, essayist, and lecturer

Pratz, Mlle Claire de, French journalist, author, and translator

Prex, *see* Stryker

Proctor, Katharine Wright, tutored by EP in Wyncote; married Laurence Saint

Propertius, Sextus (c.48–c.15 BC), Roman elegiac poet

Prothero, Sir George Walter (1848–1922), historian, editor *Quarterly Review* 1895–1921

Proust, Marcel (1871–1922), French novelist

Putnam, Samuel (1892–1950), US essayist, translator, editor, publisher

Quay, Matthew Stanley (1833–1904), US senator from Pennsylvania (1899–1904)

Quiller-Couch, Sir Arthur (1863–1944), English anthologist, novelist, critic, and, professor

Quinn, John (1870–1924), Irish-American financial lawyer, collector and patron of the arts

Ray, Man (1890–1976), US painter, sculptor, photographer, and filmmaker

Reid, Whitelaw (1837–1912), US diplomat, author, editor *New York Tribune* (1869–1905), Ambassador to Great Britain 1905–12

Régnier, Henri Francois Joseph de (1864–1936), French Symbolist poet, novelist, and critic

Rennert, Hugo Albert (1858–1927), Professor of Romance Languages at University of Pennsylvania; wrote a biography of Lope de Vega (1904)

Respighi, Ottorino (1879–1936), Italian composer

Rhys, Ernest (1859–1946), Welsh mining engineer; poet, essayist, critic; founding editor of Dent's Everyman's Library

Richard of Saint-Victor (d. 1173), mystical theologian

Ricketts, Charles (1866–1931), London artist, illustrator, book designer, and theatre designer

Roberts, William (1895–1980), English painter, Vorticist, war artist

Robertson, Dr Alex, Scottish minister of Presbyterian Church, Venice

Rockefeller, John D. (1839–1937), US industrialist and philanthropist

Rodin, Auguste (1840–1917), French sculptor

Rodker, John (1894–1955), English poet, dramatist, novelist, translator, critic, editor, and publisher

Rodeheaver [Rodyheaver], Dr Joseph N., Instructor in Psychology & Public Speaking, Wabash College

Romains, Jules [Louis Farigoule] (1885–1972), French poet, playwright, and essayist

Roosevelt, Theodore (1858–1919), 26th President of the USA (1901–9)

Root, Edward Wales (1884–1956), son of Elihu Root; class of '05, Hamilton College; collector of abstract painting; lecturer in Art at Hamilton 1920–40

Root, Elihu (1845–1937), lawyer, statesman, US Senator; recipient of 1912 Nobel Peace Prize

Root, Reverend Oren (1838–1907), brother of Elihu Root; became Professor of Mathematics and Registrar, Hamilton College

Rosing, Vladimir (1890–1963), Russian-born tenor and US opera director

Rossetti, Dante Gabriel (1828–82), English pre-Raphaelite painter and poet

Rossini, Gioacchino Antonio (1792–1868), Italian operatic composer

Roth, Samuel (1893–1974), born Ukraine; US Jewish poet; publisher in New York, editor, *Two Worlds*

Rousseau, Henri ('Le Douanier') (1844–1910), French painter

Rousseau, Jean Jacques (1712–78), French political philosopher, educationist and author

Rubinstein, Artur (1887–1942), Polish-American pianist

Rudge, Olga (1885–1996), violinist; born Youngstown, Ohio; studied in Paris; performed throughout Europe; EP's intimate friend and partner from 1923, and mother of his daughter Mary (b. 1925); resided Venice and Rapallo

Rummel, Walter Morse (1887–1953), concert pianist and composer; born Berlin, studied and lived in Paris; collaborated with EP on troubadour lyrics

Sady, *see* Wessells, Sarah

Saint, Laurence Bradford (1885–1961), US artist in stained glass

Sandburg, Carl (1878–1967), US poet, folklorist, and biographer

Santayana, George (1863–1952), Spanish-born Harvard philosopher, poet, and writer

Sargent, John Singer (1865–1925), US painter and portraitist

Satie, Eric Alfred Leslie (1866–1925), French composer

Saunders, Arthur Percy ['Stink'], Professor of Chemistry, Hamilton College

Saunders, Samuel J. ['Pill'], Professor of Physics, Instructor in Astronomy and Registrar, Hamilton College

Savitzky, Ludmila [Bloch-Savitzky] (1881–1957), Paris author and translator

Schelling, Felix Emmanuel (1858–1945), Professor of English, University of Pennsylvania

Schloezer, Boris de (1881–1969), Russian-born French-educated critic

Scollard, Clinton, contemporary of EP at Hamilton College

Scott, Sir Walter (1771–1832), Scottish novelist and poet

Scott-James, R A (1878–1959), English literary critic and editor

Scriabin, Aleksandr Nikolayevich (1872–1915), Russia composer and pianist

Scudder, John, of Scudders Falls near Trenton, New Jersey, tutored by EP in 1907

Seaver, Edwin (1900–87), author, critic, editor; literary editor *Daily Worker*; helped found *New Masses*

Seldes, Gilbert Vivian (1893–1970), associate and managing editor of *The Dial* (1920–3)

Server, John William (b. 1882), Philadelphia artist

Seurat, Georges Pierre (1859–91), French artist

Seymour, Ralph Fletcher (1876–1960), Chicago artist, designer, and publisher

Shackleton, Sir Ernest Henry (1874–1922), Irish Antarctic explorer

Shakespear, Dorothy (1886–1973), married EP in 1914; artist; illustrator of some of his and of others' publications

Shakespear, Henry Hope (1849–1923), London solicitor, father to Dorothy Pound

Shakespear, Olivia (1863–1938), married Henry Hope Shakespear (1885), mother to Dorothy Pound; novelist and a significant figure in London literary society

Shakespeare, William (1564–1616), English playwright, poet, and actor

Sharp, Evelyn Jane (1869–1955), journalist, Suffragette, writer of children's stories

Sharp, William [pseudonym, Fiona Macleod] (1855–1905), Scottish writer

Shaw, George Bernard (1856–1950), Irish dramatist and critic; Nobel Prize winner (1925)

Shepard, William ['Bill'] **Pierce** PhD (1873–1948), Professor of Romance Languages and Literature, Hamilton College

Sickert, Walter Richard (1860–1942), British artist

Siki (1897–1925), Senegalese-born light-heavyweight boxer

Sinclair, May (1863–1946), novelist, feminist, and writer on philosophical idealism

Skidmore, Dr Sidney Tuthill (b. 1844), Professor of Physics at Philadelphia Normal School, author of *The New Pilgrim's Progress: A Modern Aspect* (1925)

Small Maynard & Co, Boston publishers

Smith, William Brooke (1884–1908), Philadelphia artist to whom EP dedicated his first book of poems, *A Lume Spento* (1908)

Smith, William T., Philadelphia travel agent

Snively family of Jenkintown, Philadelphia: Alfred de Forest, friend of EP at University of Pennsylvania, and sisters Margaret [later Pratt], Ethelwyn, and Muriel

Sordello (c.1200–69), Italian troubadour poet

Speiser, Maurice J. (1880–1948), Philadelphia attorney, collector of Hemingway

Spengler, Oswald (1880–1936), German philosopher of history, author of *Decline of the West* (1918–22, translated 1926–9)

Stanton, Theodore (1851–1925), editor department of American literature for *Mercure de France*

Steed, Wickham (1871–1956), English journalist and writer; editor of *The Times* 1919–22

Steffens, [Joseph] Lincoln (1866–1936), US investigative journalist and author

Stendhal [Henri Marie Beyle] (1783–1842), French novelist

Stevenson, Robert Louis Balfour (1850–94), Scottish writer

Stokes, Adrian (1902–72), English art critic and painter

Stokowski, Leopold (1882–1977), US conductor

Storer, Edward (1880–1944), English poet and translator

Stork, Charles Wharton (1881–1971), US poet and playwright; editor of the poetry journal *Contemporary Verse* (Philadelphia); sometime Instructor in University of Pennsylvania English Department

Strachey, [Giles] Lytton (1880–1932), English writer, critic, and biographer

Strachey, John St. Loe (1860–1927), editor of *The Spectator* 1898–1925

Strater, Henry Hyacinth (1896–1987), US artist

Straus, Henrietta, US music critic

Stravinsky, Igor Fyodorovitch (1882–1971), Russian-born composer

Strindberg, Mme Frida (1872–1943), Austrian, divorced second wife of the playwright August Strindberg; in London in 1912 opened the Cave of the Golden Calf, a cabaret theatre club; in 1914 moved on to America and Fox Film

Stryker, Professor Melancthon Woolsey ('Prex'), President of Hamilton College 1892–1917

Sullivan, Sir Edward 2ⁿᵈ Baronet (1852–1928), Irish barrister, author, and editor

Sumner, John S. (1876–1971), headed New York Society for the Suppression of Vice

Swinburne, Algernon Charles (1837–1909), English poet and critic

Symons, Arthur (1865–1945), English poet, translator, and critic

Taft, William Howard (1857–1930), 27th President of the USA (1909–13)

Tagore, Rabindranath (1861–1941), Indian poet and philosopher, Nobel Prize winner (1913)

Tailhade, Laurent (1854–1919), French poet and man of letters

Taine, Hippolyte Adolphe (1828–93), French critic, historian, and philosopher

Tanner, Henry Ossawa (1859–1937), African-American painter; a victim of racial prejudice in US settled in France 1891

Tauchnitz, German publisher of books in the English language

Tennyson, Alfred, 1ˢᵗ Baron Tennyson (1809–92), English poet

Terrone, Leonardo, fencing master at University of Pennsylvania

Terry, Dame [Alice] Ellen (1848–1928), English actress

Tertullian (c.160–c.220 AD), North African Christian theologian

Téry, Simone (1897–1967), French writer, especially on Irish literature

Thayer, Scofield (1890–1982), co-owner and editor *The Dial* 1920–5

Theocritus (c.310–250 BC), Greek pastoral poet

Thomas, [Philip] Edward (1878–1917), British poet and nature writer

Thompson, Francis (1859–1907), English poet and critic

T(h)seng, Pao Swen (1893–1978), Chinese poet, founding president of a girls' college in Hunan

Tinayre, Yves (1891–1972) French lyric tenor specialising in early music

Titherington, Richard H. (1861–1935), US writer, editor *Munsey's Magazine*

Todhunter, John (1839–1916), Irish poet and playwright

Tolstoy, Count Leo Nikolayevich (1828–1910), Russian writer, aesthetic philosopher, moralist, and mystic

Tree, Sir Herbert [Draper] Beerbohm (1853–1917), English actor-manager

Trego, Mrs Byrd, wife of editor-proprietor, *The Idaho Republican*

Trench, Herbert (1865–1923), Irish poet

Tucker, Henry Tudor (1866–1943), collector and patron of the arts, Olivia Shakespear's brother

Turgenev, Ivan Sergeyevich (1818–83), expatriate Russian novelist in Paris

Turner, Joseph Mallord William (1775–1851), English painter

Twain, Mark [Samuel Langhorne Clemens] (1835–1910), US writer and journalist

Tyler, John (1790–1862), 10th President of the US (1841–5)

Ullman, Eugene Paul (1877–1953), US artist, painted EP's portrait in Paris (1911)

Ullman, Mrs Alice, *see* Woods, Alice

Uncle James, *see* Beyea, Dr James

Underhill, Evelyn (1875–1941), English poet, novelist, and mystic

Upward, Allen (1863–1926), English barrister; writer of poems, plays, novels; political activist; British Resident Administrator in Nigeria 1901–5; philosopher of religion and culture

Valette, Alfred Louis Edmond (1858–1935), founder, with other Symbolists, of the *Mercure de France*

Vance, Frederick Nelson (1880–1926), painter and owner of Vance Studios, Crawfordsville

Van Cleve, Morrison Rob [Van], class of '05, University of Pennsylvania

Vanderpyl, Fritz-René (b. 1876), Flemish poet, novelist, and art critic

Van Dine, S. S., pseudonym of US editor and novelist Willard Huntingdon Wright (1888–1939)

Van Dyke, Henry (1852–1933), US clergyman, literature professor, writer; US Minister to Holland, and Luxembourg in 1914

Vandyke, Sir Anthony (1599–1641), Flemish painter

Van Vorst, Marie (1867–1936), US author, painter, and poet

Vega, Lope de, Felix de Vega Carpio de (1562–1635), Spanish dramatist and poet

Velásquez, Diego de Silvay (1599–1660), Spanish painter

Verlaine, Paul (1844–96), French poet

Vildrac, Charles [Charles Messager] (1882–1971), French poet and dramatist

Villon, Francois (1431–after 1463), French poet

Vogel, Joseph (b. 1904), US poet, novelist, critic, and editor

Volstead, Andrew Joseph (1860–1947), US Republican politician; the Volstead Act of 1919 enforced Prohibition in the United States

Voltaire, François Marie Arouet (1694–1778) French writer and historian

Wack, Henry Wellington (1869–1954), US painter, author, editor of the *Newarker*

Wadsworth, Dr Augustus Baldwin (1873–1954), son of Charles David Wadsworth, New York physician, bacteriologist, Director of Laboratories New York State Department of Health; distant cousin of EP

Wadsworth, Charles David (1847–1942), member New York Stock Exchange; distant cousin of EP

Wadsworth, Edward Alexander (1889–1949), English artist and member of the Vorticist group

Wadsworth, William Baldwin (1849–1934), brother of Charles David Wadsworth, member New York Stock Exchange; distant cousin of EP

Wadsworth, William (1882–1934), son of Charles David Wadsworth; New York lawyer and banker; retired gentleman farmer; distant cousin of EP

Waley, Arthur David (1889–1966), English Orientalist and Sinologist, translator

Wallace, Hugh C. (1863–1931), financier; US Ambassador to France 1919–21; was selling land in Hailey Idaho when HLP was in charge of the US Land Office there

Waller, Henry (1870–1952), US composer

Walsh, Ernest (1895–1926), US expatriate poet, editor of *This Quarter* (Paris)

Ward, Genevieve [Jenny], Countess de Guerbel (1837–1922), actress and singer

Washington, George (1732–99), 1ˢᵗ President of the USA (1789–97)

Watson, James Sibley, Jr. (1894–1982), co-owner and editor *The Dial* 1920–9

Watson, William (1885–1935), English poet

Watt, A. P., London literary agency

Weaver, Harriet Shaw (1876–1961), voluntary social worker; financial supporter *New Freewoman* and *Egoist*, edited the latter 1914–19; set up Egoist Press; published and gave financial support to James Joyce

Weber, Joseph John ['Pop'] (1877–1946), class of '05, Hamilton College

Wedmore, Sir Frederick (1844–1921), English writer and art critic

Wells, Herbert George (1866–1946), prolific English writer of novels, science-fiction, social commentary, and popular history

Welsh, Robert Gilbert (1869–1924), US poet, playwright, and journalist; drama editor of the *New York Herald*

Wescott, Glenway (1901–87), US novelist

Wessells, Sarah ('Sadie'), cousin of EP, niece of Aunt Frank (Weston)

Weston, Ezra Brown (1824–94), Isabel Pound's uncle and adoptive father

Weston, Frances Wessells (?1832–1913), EP's much loved Aunt Frank, wife of Ezra B. Weston, later of Dr James L Beyea

Weston, Harding (d. 1927), father of IWP

Whistler, James Abbott McNeill (1834–1903), US artist

Whitechurch, Miss, a family friend, became paying guest of EP's parents

Whiteside, Frank Reed (1866–1929), landscape painter, instructor at Philadelphia Academy of Fine Arts

Whitman, Walt (1819–92), US poet

Whittam, William, Professor of Physics (1906–10), Wabash College

Wiggin, Kate Douglas (1856–1923), US pioneer of kindergartens; writer of children's books, including *Rebecca of Sunnybrook Farm* (1903)

Wilcox, Mrs Ella Wheeler (1855–1919), US writer of popular verse; school friend of Homer Pound

Wilde, Oscar [Fingal O'Flahertie Wills] (1854–1900), Irish playwright, novelist, essayist, poet, and wit

Wilenski, Reginald Howard (1887–1975), English painter, critic, and art historian

Wilkinson, Mrs Frances, *see* Gregg, Frances

Williams, William Carlos (1883–1963), US physician, poet, playwright, novelist

Wilson, [Thomas] Woodrow (1856–1924), 28th President of the USA (1913-21)

Windeler, B Cyril, English wool broker and writer

Wood, Mrs Derwent (Florence Schmidt) (1873–1969), Australian-born English soprano

Wood, Francis Derwent RA (1871–1926, eminent English sculptor

Wood, Dr Frank Hoyt (1864–1930), Professor of Political Science and American History, Hamilton College

Wood, Leonard (1860–1927), US soldier and administrator, leader of Theodore Roosevelt's 'Rough Riders'

Woods, Mrs Margaret Louisa (1856–1945), poet and novelist; wife of Rev. Henry George Woods (1842–1915), Master of the Temple Church of the two Inns of Court, the Inner Temple and the Middle Temple

Woods, Alice, (Mrs Eugene Ullman) (1871–1959), US writer, friend of Margaret Cravens

Woodward, Graham Cox (1880–1946), Philadelphia attorney-at-law, graduated University of Pennsylvania Law School 1904

Wordsworth, William (1770–1850), English poet

Wright, Wilbur (1867–1912), US inventor with his brother Orville (1871–1948) of first practical flying machine; their first public exhibition flight 1908 in France

Wright, Willard Huntingdon (1888–1939), novelist, editor *Smart Set* 1912–14

Wyndham, George (1863–1913), British politician and man of letters

Xenophon (c.444–357 BC), Greek military commander and historian

Yeats, William Butler (1865–1939), Irish poet, playwright, and prose writer; Nobel Prizewinner 1923

Zukovsky, Louis (1904–78), US poet and prose writer

Zurbarán, Francisco (1598–1662), Spanish religious painter

General Index

Entries in *italic* refer to notes and commentary; entries in **bold** refer to the Glossary of Names.

General Index

Butler, Samuel (*cont.*)
  Diary 303
  Way of all Flesh, The 303, 368
Butts, Mary 475, 570
Byington, Homer 118, 550, 560, **687**
Bynner, Witter 237, **687**

C.E. (Christian Endeavour) 12, 13
Cabaret Theatre Club (The Cave of the Golden
  Calf) 310, *311*, 312
Cadiz (Spain) 107
Cadmon, Dr 47
Calcutta (India) 300, 314, 324
Calvary Presbyterian Church *xi*, 528, 529, 532–3
Calvin, John 403, **687**
Camas Prairie *xvi*
Cambridge University 271, 277, 305, *554*
Camoens, Luís Vaz de 174
  Obras 555 n.
Campbell, Joseph 84, 207, 208, 211, 338, 339, **687**
  Judgment 339
  Mearing Stones 339
Can Grande de la Scala 229
Canada 77, 175, 368, 409, 410, 411, 518, 523, 623,
  650
Cannell, Skipwith 304, 306, 307, 308, **687**
Cardenal, Peire 48
Carducci, Giosuè 555 n.
Carman, Bliss 217, 253, **687**
Carmona, Señora 75, 77, 81
Carnegie, Andrew 87, **687**
Carnegie Foundation 87, 500
Carnegie Libraries 650
Carnevali, Emanuel 566, 577, 604, 635, 652, **687**
Carranza, Venustiano 591, *592*
Carson, George Campbell 558
Carson, Mrs. 121
Carus, Paul 408, 419, **687**
Casella, Alfredo 598, 599, **687**
Casella, Stefano Maria *xxv*
Cashmere 339
Castelani (Italian painter) 632
Castellanos Poesias Selectos (1817) 228
Castellucho, Claudio 250
Catholic Church 46
Catholicism 215, 404
Cato 436
Catullus, Gaius Valerius 71, 228, **687**
Cavalcanti, Guido *xviii*, 216, 229, 237, 238, 239, 269,
  291, 296, 413, 428, 449, 477, 639, 640, 642, 652,
  653, 666, 672, **688**
  'Critical Text, with Translation and
    Commentary and Notes by Ezra Pound' 640,
    642, 643, 644, 646, 649, 650, 657, 669, 670, 671,
    673, 674, 675, 676
  'Donna Mi Prega' 668
Cawein, Madison 285
censorship 363, 409, 485, 498, 535, 594, 609, 675, 677

Central High School (Philadelphia) 59
Century Magazine 193, 255, 326, 342, 351, 403, 460,
  501, 629
Cervantes, Miguel de:
  Don Quixote 175
Cézanne, Paul 250, 340, **688**
Chamber, Miss 19
Chamberlain, Arthur Neville 584, **688**
Chamberlain, Dr 183
Chamberlain, Frederic 384, 681, **688**
Chamberlin, Miss (or Mrs) 127
Chamberlin, Mr 146
Chambers, Robert W. 403, **688**
Champs Elysées theatre (Paris) 600
Chanson de Roland, La 52
Chansons de Geste 55
Charlemagne 43
Charles V, King 436
Chaucer, Daniel 257; *see also* Ford/Hueffer, Ford
  Madox
Chaucer, Geoffrey 55, 260, 360, 462, 469
Chauve Souris 512, *513*
Chaytor, Henry John:
  Troubadours of Dante, The 53, 55
Chelsea Arts Club 218
Cheltenham Military Academy (C.M.A.) 4–8, 62,
  64, 65, 95, 348
chemistry 43, 218
Cherchi, Marianna *xxv*
Chester, Carlos Tracy (Rev. and Mr) 76, 79, 81, 82,
  86, 92, 98, 119, 183, 326, 355, 361, 528, **688**
Chester, Clarence 532
Chester, Hawley 503, 504, **688**
Chesterton, Gilbert Keith 234, 393, **688**
Chicago Tribune (Paris) 497, 514, 525, 583, 587, 599,
  634, 641, 647, 650, 674
Chicago University 240
Child, Dr Clarence G. 52, 183, 353
Children's Crusade, The (Marcel Schwob) 135
Chile 72
China 220, 221, 316, 317, 438, 625, 629
Chippewa Falls (US) *xxiv*, 56, 118, 121, 141, 155, 181,
  182, 317, 605
Christian (pseudonym of Georges Herbiet) 482,
  486, 488, **688**
Christianity 184, 215, 327, 336, 380, 404, 485, 514, 589,
  590, 638, 665
Chubb, Elmer 480; *see also* Masters, Edgar Lee
Church of England 404
Churchill, Sir Winston Leonard Spencer 503, 504,
  688
Chute, Father Desmond Macready *xix*, 610, **688**
Cicero:
  De Senectute 555 n.
Cid, Poema del 55, 59, 178, 212, 220, 555 n.
Ciolkowska, Mme Muriel 461, **688**
Cincinnati (US) 317
cinema 449, 497, 520

General Index

Yeats, G. 621

Yeats, William Butler *xi*, *xiii*, 118, 120, 147, 159, 160, 162, 166, 170, 171, 172, 175, 182, 186, 203, 204, 209, 215, 222, 223, 224, 231, 233, 239, 245, 248, 249, 258, 265, 269, 273, 276, 277, 284, 285, 287, 289, 290, 294, 295, 296, 297, 298, 299, 301, 306, 307, 308, 309, 312, *313*, 314, 315, 316, 317, 318, 321, 325, 326, 334, *335*, 336, 337, 341, 342, *343*, 344, *349*, 352, 355, 356, 358, 361, 362, 363, 364, 366, 368, 369, 376, *377*, 383, 395, 396, 404, 405, 410, 412, 416, 417, 419, 420, 421, 433, 440, 451, 455, 470, 475, 489, 503, 505, 542, 549, 551, 552, 553, 568, 621, 624, 650, 651, 652, *653*, 660, 666, 668, 671, 672, 674, 675, 677, 678, 679, 680, 682, **705**
 At the Hawk's Well (1917) *346*, *363*, 367
 autobiography 341, 468
 Deirdre 147
 on Ezra Pound 233
 marries Georgie Hyde-Lees (1917) 407
 Only Jealousy of Emer, The (1919) *652*
 Packet for Ezra Pound, A (1929) *653*
 Player Queen, The (1922) 355, *356*
 'Red Hanrahan's Song about Ireland' 186
 Responsibilities (1914) *325*
 'Speaking to the Psaltery' 179
 The Wild Swans at Coole (1917) *504*
 The Wind Among the Reeds (1899) 186

Young, Edward:
 Night Thoughts 555 n.

Young, Mary S. 97, 100

Youth 493

Yust, Walter 660, 661

Zaharoff, Sir Basil *592*

Zampieri, Massimiliano *xxvi*

Zarlatti 561, 562

Zeublin, Charles 239, *240*

Zimmerman 138

Zion 639

Zukovsky, Louis *635*, 652, 668, 682, **705**

Zurbarán, Francisco 310, **705**

Zurich (Switzerland) 369, 371